An Economic History
of the United States

An Economic History of the United States

From 1607 to the Present

Ronald E. Seavoy

Routledge
Taylor & Francis Group
New York   London

Routledge is an imprint of the
Taylor & Francis Group, an informa business

Routledge
Taylor & Francis Group
270 Madison Avenue
New York, NY 10016

QM LIBRARY
(MILE END)

Routledge
Taylor & Francis Group
2 Park Square
Milton Park, Abingdon
Oxon OX14 4RN

© 2006 by Taylor & Francis Group, LLC
Routledge is an imprint of Taylor & Francis Group, an Informa business

Printed in the United States of America on acid-free paper
10 9 8 7 6 5 4 3

International Standard Book Number-10: 0-415-97981-1 (Softcover) 0-415-97980-3 (Hardcover)
International Standard Book Number-13: 978-0-415-97981-8 (Softcover) 978-0-415-97980-1 (Hardcover)

Library of Congress Cataloging-in-Publication Data

Seavoy, Ronald E.
  An economic history of the United States : from 1607 to the present / by Ronald E. Seavoy.
     p. cm.
  Includes bibliographical references and index.
  ISBN 0-415-97980-3 (cloth : alk. paper) -- ISBN 0-415-97981-1 (pbk. : alk. paper)
  1. United States--Economic conditions. I. Title.

HC103.S42 2006
330.973--dc22   2006006878

Visit the Taylor & Francis Web site at
http://www.taylorandfrancis.com

and the Routledge Web site at
http://www.routledge-ny.com

Contents

Introduction

I wrote this book because I wanted to know how the United States became the world's leading industrial producer one hundred years after independence (1890) and, at the same time, settled a continent. These events did not happen accidentally.

My first book, *The Origins of the American Business Corporation, 1784–1855*, helped answer these two questions. It indicated that there was a very close relationship between politics and the creation of new wealth. The rapid creation of new wealth required a means of mobilizing capital from many sources and allocating it to investments in new technologies. The business corporation made this possible.

The modern business corporation was created in the United States immediately after the war for independence and came into general use in the 1830s. It was accepted as socially useful because it democratized business opportunities. Entrepreneurs were encouraged to incorporate by a cheap and simple legal procedure. Its democratic use was a key policy of political economy that helped propel the rapid economic development of the United States.

The term *political economy* comprehends the statute laws and court decisions that encouraged investments in new and old technologies. Politics comes first. After independence, the principal policy of the national and state governments was encouraging the production of new wealth in the shortest time because it was obvious that there was a huge potential for wealth creation. Both Congress and state legislatures enacted statutes that democratized opportunities to create new wealth by encouraging the maximum number of people to contribute their labor to bring new land under cultivation and establish new industries in new cities.

After independence, all states required banking to be conducted by corporations in an attempt to regulate their credit practices. Economic development requires huge amounts of credit; therefore, there had to be many banks to provide credit to local businessmen. The demand for abundant credit created continual inflationary pressures that were not adequately controlled by state regulation. At the same time, state governments used their credit resources by pledging future tax revenues to underwrite bonds. The funds obtained were used to build transportation arteries (canals, railroads, turnpikes) that could carry commodities to domestic or export markets. Credit was the principal fuel for rapid economic development.

This is the conventional analysis of the economic development of the United States before the Civil War. This book agrees with this analysis, but emphasizes the preeminence of state policies of political economy before the Civil War (1861) and the preeminence of national policies of political economy after the Civil War (1865).

National policies of political economy after 1865 meant accelerated industrialization. Accelerated industrialization required huge amounts of capital and credit. Seven policies supplied the requisite funds:

1. no national taxation of corporate earnings
2. high railroad rates for agricultural commodities

3. a banking system that concentrated credit in city banks
4. deflation, where the dollar gradually appreciated in purchasing power
5. protective tariffs
6. borrowing from Europe
7. a small national government with an equally small operating budget

The three most controversial policies were (1) high railroad rates for agricultural commodities. Railroads charged high rates because rural communities had no competitive transportation. The capital obtained from the agricultural sector was invested in technologies that improved intercity transportation that served industry. (2) Deflation. Farmers who purchased land on credit had to repay mortgages with dollars that were appreciating in purchasing power. At the same time, there was a prolonged price decline for the commodities they produced. (3) The national banking system concentrated credit in cities where it was lent to business corporations instead of being available for rural loans. These policies squeezed capital from the agricultural sector for the benefit of the industrial sector located in cities and were enormously successful in mobilizing capital for investment in urban industries.

During the 1920s the productive capacity of manufacturing corporations produced the first consumer culture in the world. U.S. political leaders believed that the policies of political economy that achieved rapid industrialization and produced a huge variety of consumer products were models for the rest of the world to copy. They were half correct. Policies that created the industrial base of a consumer culture were a worthy model, but the model was inadequate for sustaining it.

The wake-up call was the Great Depression. It began in 1930 and lasted until 1941. It was a traumatic national experience. The production of new wealth stopped and then reversed because the policies of political economy that created the consumer culture no longer worked. Sustaining the operation of a consumer culture required different policies than the policies that made the United States into the leading industrial nation.

The two policies essential for sustaining a consumer culture are free trade in manufactured products among industrialized nations, and massive spending by the national government during downturns in business activity. Competitive free trade translates into cheap consumer products. Massive government spending translates into sustaining employment. If people know that employment opportunities are available to replace lost jobs, they will not reduce their level of welfare by excessive savings. The Great Depression ended when it was necessary for the United States to prepare for entry into World War II. Preparedness required a rapid build-up of military and naval weaponry financed by a huge increase in spending. This spending ended the Great Depression.

Since the mid-1960s the United States has increasingly participated in the modern global market that came into being after 1945 under the protective umbrella of NATO. The creation of the post-World War II global market has been the dual accomplishment of political leaders in Western European nations and the United States, but especially European leaders. They envisioned consumer cultures for all industrial nations, and that consumer cultures could be rapidly achieved by increased global trade.

Success was achieved by an extraordinary amount of cooperation among advanced industrial nations. They delegated management of the global market to the International Monetary Fund (IMF), World Trade Organization (WTO), World Bank, North American Free Trade Agreement (NAFTA), European Union, and other regional trade organizations. Management of trade was essential in order to resolve trade disputes before they generated hostilities. This is the new world order of the global market where national markets for most products are no longer clearly recognizable.

The goal of the post-World War II political leaders in Western Europe and the United States was achieved by 2005. The economies of advanced industrial nations are so tightly integrated that a third global war is unthinkable. At the same time, participation in the global market is open ended. Industrial nations participate on more or less even terms in direct ratio to their ability to produce export products at competitive prices.

Chapter 1

English Commercial Revolution of the Seventeenth Century

Examined from the perspective of the twentieth century, colonial societies in English-speaking North America had to be pervasively commercialized during the colonial era; otherwise, the industrialization that accelerated after the War for Independence could not have been sustained. During the colonial era over 90 percent of the population cultivated the land; therefore, analysis of the commercializing policies of colonial governments in North America must begin with the extent of commercial agriculture.

This chapter examines how commercial agriculture was being enforced in England in the seventeenth and eighteenth centuries, and how some English peasants sought to escape the performance of commercial labor norms by immigrating to America. Chapters two and three describe the extent of commercial agriculture in southern and northern colonies during the colonial era, and how it operated. Chapter four describes the scope and size of colonial commerce and manufacturing, and how Americans participated in the British commercial empire. Analysis also comprehends the similarities and differences of those who preferentially immigrated to southern and northern colonies and how the social values that accompanied them evolved into differing institutions of governance, taxation, and commerce.

The key questions are:

1. Who emigrated from Britain to North America?
2. Why did they emigrate?
3. Where did they go?
4. What kind of governments were established by the colonists?
5. Who participated in governance?

Before we can answer these questions in chapters two, three, and four, it is necessary to understand what was happening to English agriculture in the seventeenth and eighteenth centuries, and how commercializing policies in England propelled continuous immigration. Understanding the impact of English commercializing policies on the colonization of North America requires that readers understand the revolutionary difference between subsistence and commercial labor norms.

Subsistence Social Values

Peasants perform subsistence labor norms in agriculture and measure their social security by control of land use, not monetary incomes. Control of land use allows them to perform subsistence labor norms. They produce marginal food and commodity surpluses for market sale in normal crop years. Peasants know that every crop year is not normal but they willingly endure seasons of hunger in years of hardship in order to minimize agricultural labor. Furthermore, they willingly risk famine conditions in consecutive years of poor crops in order to preserve subsistence labor norms.

They believe that a fixed amount of labor in years of normal crop production produces adequate harvests to feed all village households at a subsistence level of nutrition, plus a small surplus that is a tribute to feudal landowners who allow peasant communities to control land use, in addition to a small surplus to feed a clergy. After subsistence food needs have been satisfied, indolence is the proper way to enjoy life.

> The peasant concept of the good life is the minimum expenditure of physical labor. When applied to food production, peasants attempt to grow enough food to last until the next harvest with the minimum expenditure of labor, on the assumption that every year will be a normal crop year. This defines the subsistence compromise.[1]

In order to maximize indolence, adults in peasant households seek to transfer as much labor as possible to others. The principal means of doing this is having many children. Sharecropping and slavery are other means of transferring labor. Peasants also seek to minimize the risks of seasonal hunger and famine conditions. When they control land use, communal councils equalize the distribution of cultivation units among village households and equalize the distribution of harvests in years of poor yields. Maintaining equality in the size of cultivation units requires some variety of communal tenure in order to periodically redistribute land on the basis of the subsistence needs of new households.

Subsistence food production means that, in years of normal crop production, minimal amounts of food are available for sale on anonymous markets in order to purchase a limited variety of artisan manufactured products. In contrast, in years of low yields no food is sold. The lack of an assured food surplus means that food to feed city residents and artisan manufacturers (who produce products for sale on anonymous markets) is not available on an annual basis. This imbalance places a huge restraint on increasing commercial wealth because only commercial agriculture can produce assured food surpluses in all crop years that are essential for feeding artisan manufacturers or urban factory workers.

Commercialization of Agriculture

Commercial agriculture requires commercial land tenures and the performance of commercial labor norms. Commercial agriculture means fewer people working longer hours to produce substantially larger harvests compared to the subsistence labor norms of peasants. In the commercialization process,

> central governments must put control of land use into the hands of commercially motivated persons or organizations (yeomen, farmers, plantations, collectives). This cannot be done unless central governments adopt policies that force the replacement of communal tenure with commercial tenure (freehold, leasehold, collective).[2]

Commercial tenure allows commercially motivated landowners to replace peasants with supervised paid laborers who perform commercial labor norms. Unneeded peasant households are evicted (displaced). They are forced to become full-time paid agricultural laborers; or migrate to cities and became full-time wage laborers; or live in hovels on the peripheries of common pastures and graze livestock (until commons are enclosed); or become vagabonds, vagrants, or sturdy beggars (masterless men); or emigrate to North America as indentured servants in search of subsistence opportunities.

Rents are raised on the remaining tenants. Higher rents induce the remaining households to increases per capita labor expenditures. Much of the labor is often performed by full-time paid laborers. Increased per capita labor produces an assured food surplus in all crop years, and this surplus is sold on anonymous markets.

In seventeenth-century England, cultivators who performed commercial labor norms were yeomen, farmers, and servants in husbandry. Servants in husbandry were full-time paid laborers hired by yeomen and farmers. Frequently, they were evicted peasants or the children of evicted peasants. Their labor was rewarded with sufficient money to constitute an income that was used to purchase food, clothing, and housing on an anonymous market.

The social security of paid agricultural laborer is like the social security of city residents. It depends on laboring every day to earn money incomes. This is very different from peasants. Although English society was thoroughly monetized in 1600, monetization is not the same as a money income. As long as peasants control land use they can live, if necessary, with minimal amounts of money—sufficient to pay a poll tax or to annually purchase a few metal tools.

After peasants lose control of land use, they have little choice except to perform continuous commercial labor norms on tasks assigned to them. If they fail to perform this labor, they can be replaced by people who will. All commercial cultivators and paid laborers (agricultural or factory workers) measure their social security by money incomes earned by producing products for sale on anonymous markets. Examined from another perspective, commercial food production meant substituting money incomes for control of land use as the means of obtaining social security.

The commercialization of English society rapidly accelerated during the seventeenth century. Commercialization was driven by agriculture because 70–80 percent of the population subsisted through cultivation of the land. Between 1600 and 1650, a substantial portion of English agriculture was commercialized; although, there were large numbers of peasants, particularly in the North, who continued to cultivate land in copyhold tenure. Copyhold tenure was a variety of communal tenure. It gave peasants a hereditary claim to land use and a legal right to control their labor expenditures. They lived in dwellings that paid no rent, and they harvested enough wool from sheep grazing on common pastures to spin into the thread that was woven into the cloth that clothed them.

During the commercializing process in the reigns of Elizabeth and the first two Stuart kings (1558–1640), there was a continuous outpouring of public concern and parliamentary statutes about the socially destabilizing conduct of evicted peasants because they wandered in rural areas and often engaged in petty thievery. Historians and economists usually call these people unemployed. They were not. They were *displaced* peasants who sought to avoid becoming full-time paid laborers. After 1630, avoidance was possible by immigrating to America where vacant land was known to be available.[3]

In spite of the social destabilization caused by commercializing policies, governance under Elizabeth and the Stuart kings encouraged landowners to commercialize agriculture because an assured food surplus was necessary to feed artisan manufacturers and urban residents who produced new wealth that could be taxed. The two principal ways the English government encouraged the commercialization of society were through (1) decisions by national courts, (2) parliamentary statutes favoring landowners who wanted to convert copyhold tenure (subsistence tenure) into freehold and leasehold tenures (commercial tenures). Parliament was controlled by landowners who were acutely aware that land had little commercial value unless there were laborers to cultivate it; and these laborers had to perform more labor than was required for subsistence. This was the origin of the Statute of Laborers (1349), the Statute of Artificers (1563), the Poor Law of 1601, and acts of parliament that authorized enclosure.

> The Statute of Artificers was a national labor code that authorized justices of the peace to compel displaced peasants, and their children, to labor in either agriculture or handicraft manufacture as a way of banishing idleness....It also authorized justices of the peace to fix wages annually in relation to food prices; to place persons in one year labor contracts where they had to labor for a fixed number of hours per day; and to punish laborers who did not complete their tasks.[4]

The Statute of Artificers was difficult to enforce in rural areas, and in 1572 a more workable statute was passed. The 1572 statute: "allowed local authorities to confine vagabonds to houses of correction (jails) where they had to card wool or spin thread. For repeated attempts to avoid useful labor they could be hung." This statute proved to be unworkable in the famine year of 1597. Parliament revised the statute in 1601 based on the assumption that all people ought to be employed for wages and that those who were physically unable (the poor) ought to be supported in parish poor houses at public expense.[5]

> The 1601 poor law had three purposes: 1) provide temporary relief for indigents; 2) put displaced peasants (who refused to perform paid labor) in workhouses where they had to perform useful labor; 3) punish sturdy beggars. In 1609, parish Overseers of the Poor were authorized to send able-bodied persons who refused to labor to houses of correction. There they would be forced to perform useful labor.....Workhouses supported by poor law taxation were to be schools to teach the virtue of disciplined commercial labor.[6]

The Statute of Artificers and the Poor Law were enforced in England until the nineteenth century. They were part of the intellectual and institutional baggage that royal governors carried across the Atlantic in the seventeenth and eighteenth centuries. The intent of these two statutes exactly coincided with the ambitions of royal governors and the governing elites in all North American colonies. Both agreed with mercantile writers:

> that displaced peasants who were forced to become wage laborers (working poor) had to be kept poor or they would not perform continuous labor. Their admonition to employers to pay only subsistence wages recognized that most displaced peasants would labor only when they had no choice and only for as long as was necessary to supply their subsistence needs....In the language of the time, mercantile writers said that the wealth of a nation depended on keeping its laborers poor. This is another way of saying that displaced peasants would not engage in paid labor or artisan manufacture unless hunger forced them.[7]

Converting subsistence tenure into commercial tenure by statute or judicial law was usually a prelude to enclosure (fencing fields) that allowed landowners to intensify cultivation by using supervised paid laborers to perform the commercial labor norms necessary to produce assured food surpluses. Enclosure also allowed landowners to change land use from the subsistence cultivation of food grains to grazing sheep or cattle in order to produce wool, butter, cheese, or meat for sale on anonymous markets. The sale of these commodities on anonymous markets increased the incomes of commercially motivated landowners.

Christopher Hill quotes an anonymous writer of 1677 to the effect: "Their masters allow wages so mean that they are only preserved from starving whilst they can work…In such circumstances men fought desperately to avoid the abyss of wage-labourer." Immigration to America was a subsistence refuge.[8]

Servants in Husbandry

Servants in husbandry were full-time, supervised, paid agricultural laborers. Most were young male and female children of peasants, and a high percentage were illiterate. They usually began their journey to adulthood by becoming servants at about age fifteen. Their first experience as paid laborers often began when their parents took them to a hiring fair where they made an oral contract that placed a son or daughter in service for one year with a yeoman or farmer.

Yeomen were cultivators who owned or leased units of agricultural land (seventy-five to two hundred acres) and owned a full complement of agricultural implements and draft animals. They required one to four servants in husbandry every year. The servants they hired lived in the yeoman's house, ate from his table, and worked side by side with him in the fields or at any other task that was required to optimize production of crops or agricultural commodities for sale on anonymous markets.

Farmers were leaseholders of larger units of agricultural land and, like yeomen, they had long leases on the land they cultivated (usually twenty-one years); and like yeomen they owned a full complement of cultivation implements and draft animals. Farmers differed from yeomen because they sought to maximize the production of crops and livestock for market sale by maximizing labor inputs into cultivation. The servants they hired may or may not have lived with them. They might live in dormitories or in a wing of the farmer's home. The number of servants and their living arrangements would depend on how much land was managed by the farmer.

Both yeomen and farmers measured their social security by money incomes earned by their own labor or managing the labor of servants in husbandry in order to produce and sell food and commodities on anonymous markets. The anonymous market was usually the nearest city but it could also be clusters of artisans engaged in weaving, making metal implements, pottery products, or coal miners. In both instances, servants in husbandry were forbidden to marry because yeomen and farmers wanted no diversion from their labor.

Under terms of the contract, yeomen and farmers had to provide servants with a suit of clothing and a pair of shoes at the end of a year's work. In addition, they were paid a sum of money that could be given quarterly or as a lump sum at the end of the contract. In the seventeenth and eighteenth centuries, the several years spent as servants in husbandry was a rite of passage for young people on their way to becoming adults in their community. This status was usually achieved by about the age of twenty-six when they became full-time paid agricultural laborers who were hired by the day, week, month, or to complete a specific task. They earned large enough incomes to marry and establish a household in their community, but they would be paid laborers for the rest of their lives, even if they migrated to cities.

One of the most effective policies to force rural youths to become servants in husbandry were acts of Parliament that steadily decreased the number and size of communal pastures (commons) in village communities. There were two reasons for extinguishing communal pastures:

1. Cottagers living on their perimeters subsisted in relative idleness. They would labor for money only when necessary; otherwise, they gained the principal part of their subsistence by grazing a few head of livestock on the commons and occasionally selling one, or selling small amounts of wool or milk. This source of subsistence was often supplemented by leasing one or two acres in order to plant a garden. Access to communal pastures allowed

displaced peasants to continue to perform subsistence labor norms without having a claim to a specific parcel of land.

2.   No person was responsible for the care of communal pastures. They produced marginal amounts of food (mostly livestock) for market sale. Their subsistence function was described in 1639:

> the more large the waste grounds of a manor are, the poorer are the inhabitants; such common grounds, commons, or waste grounds, used commonly as they are…draw many poor people from other places, burden the township with beggarly cottages, inmates, and alehouses, and idle people; where the greater part spend most of their days in a lazy idleness and petty thieveries, and few or none in profitable labor.[9]

More succinctly, in 1653 an agricultural writer described communal pastures "as the excuse for the poor to develop stratagems to avoid work." When communal pastures were converted to freehold tenure and fenced, owners could apply the labor of servants in husbandry. Agricultural production quadrupled or quintupled with the surplus available for sale to artisans, city residents, or other persons performing paid labor.[10]

Arthur Young, an eighteenth-century writer on agricultural practices in England, accurately observed the peasantry's preference for indolence.

> Higher wages for agricultural laborers did not stimulate greater production. In fact, the opposite occurred. Higher wages decreased the supply of labor because displaced peasants valued indolence more than higher money incomes that continuous labor could earn….'If you talk of interests of trade and manufactures, everyone but an idiot knows that the lower classes must be kept poor or they will never be industrious.' More indolence (independence, natural freedom) was their social preference, rather than enjoying a higher standard of welfare.[11]

The best measures of the agricultural revolution that was proceeding in England in the seventeenth century can be seen in three parliamentary statutes. The first, in 1663, authorized merchants to store food grain for an indefinite period in order to sell for the highest price on the domestic or overseas market. "In political terms, the 1663 statute meant that the central government no longer had to concern itself with local food shortages in poor crop years because merchants always had sufficient stores available for transportation to places where prices were high, but not at starvation levels."[12]

The second statute, passed in 1673 and in effect for five years, paid a bounty on food grain exports if domestic prices declined below a minimum level. The third statute, passed in 1689, made the bounty on grain exports permanent. The 1689 statute:

> reflected three highly beneficial developments in the previous 50 years: 1) England produced an assured food surplus to feed an increasing population that was employed in artisan manufacturing or as paid laborers; 2) the production of wheat (the best breadstuff) steadily increased; 3) grain exports steadily increased to 1750 and averaged about ten percent of domestic production.[13]

Ian C. Graham documents how commercializing agriculture in Scotland in the second half of the eighteenth century impacted peasants, especially highland peasants where landowners changed land use from subsistence cultivation of oats, barley, and potatoes to sheep and cattle grazing. In every way this commercializing process was similar to what happened in the first half of the seventeenth century in large parts of England. In the ten years before the War for

Independence, evictions forced many highland peasants to emigrate. Their preferred destinations were frontier settlements in North Carolina, New York, and Nova Scotia where land grants for military service were available and where subsistence cultivation was most easily replicated.

An accurate measure of the amount of subsistence indolence practiced by highland peasants is the number of men of prime laboring age that could be absent without affecting the size of harvests. In order to eject French troops that had fortified the headwaters of the Ohio River Valley (Fort Duquesne) in 1753, the British army recruited soldiers in the highlands. "Two highland parishes were able to furnish four hundred recruits for regiments in America without interfering with the working of their farms."[14]

It was the assured food surplus, produced by supervised paid laborers performing commercial labor norms that made possible a rapid increase in artisan manufacturing in England in the seventeenth century and propelled the industrial revolution that began in the last half of the eighteenth century. Beginning in the nineteenth century, the ability of commercially motivated cultivators in Scotland to produce an assured food surplus propelled Scottish industrialization.

Transfer of Commercial Agriculture to America

The successful colonization of North America required (1) protection by the Royal Navy from Spanish and French incursions, (2) production of an assured food surplus, (3) production of commodities that could be sold in England and Europe to purchase essential manufactured products, (4) markets in the Caribbean islands where mainland commodities could be exchanged for tropical commodities.

English colonization of North America began at the same time the central government of England was actively encouraging the commercialization of English society. The charters of all colonial governments contained clauses of political economy that were intended to establish commercial cultures; however, the production of an assured food surplus in the North American colonies was not assured. Royal governors, proprietary governors, and elected governors had to establish and mold institutions similar to those in England; otherwise, a high percentage of cultivators would not produce sufficient food and commodity surpluses to make the colonies self-supporting and self-defensible. Coercion was required. In the southern colonies, the two principal coercions were indentured laborers and slavery.

Governors, with the assistance of resident elites, were delegated the task of creating commercial cultures in America by establishing the requisite institutions. These institutions were (1) all agricultural land was held in freehold tenure; (2) land had surveyed boundaries; (3) registration was necessary for all land titles; (4) a free market existed for land sales; (5) governance was by commercially motivated elites; (6) written laws operated by consent; (7) legal protection existed for persons who produced and marketed products for sale on anonymous markets, especially export markets. Other policies that induced commercialization were (1) monetization, (2) monetized taxation, (3) money rewards for persons performing commercial labor norms, (4) high social value of literacy. These were the same policies that were commercializing English society.

Most economic historians of the United States assume all of these policies were operational when they analyze the colonial origins of U. S. economic development. This assumption is correct, but their analysis usually begins with governance by commercially motivated elites and ignores how colonial governments did everything possible to neutralize the resistance of peasants to commercializing policies while, at the same time, creating institutions that served the needs of commercially motivated cultivators, artisan manufacturers, and merchants.

Policies to commercialize agriculture were not the legacy of the colonial governing elites of Spain, Portugal, and France. During the sixteenth, seventeenth, and eighteenth centuries, the central governments of these nations did not vigorously enforce policies to pervasively commercialize culture in Europe. Instead, feudal institutions, most notably communal land tenure, were transferred to the colonies because they helped guarantee hierarchical governance. Commercial labor norms in their colonies were performed only in commercial sectors that were embedded in much larger subsistence sectors. Subsistence labor norms dominated food production in their colonies. This was a major constraint on establishing self-sufficiency in artisan manufactured products, especially compared to England's North American colonies.

The successful transfer of English institutions that induced commercial agriculture was one of the principal legacies of colonial governance that contributed to the rapid industrialization of the United States in the nineteenth century. Two major questions are asked and answered in the next two chapters: (1) *How prevalent was commercial motivation during the colonial era?* (2) *How prevalent was commercial agriculture during the colonial era?* This discussion lays the foundation for analyzing how sectional differences after independence dictated the speed and scope of industrialization in the United States.

Chapter 2

Agriculture in the Southern Colonies

Colonial Political Economy

All colonial governments institutionalized freehold tenure, and all freehold land had measured boundaries. Freehold tenure prevented freemen from escaping taxation by moving to the frontier, squatting on public land, and then claiming a prescriptive right to establish communities with communal tenure. Taxation of freehold land was always money taxation or an amount of a commodity with an official money value. Its payment required landowners to produce a marketable surplus of food or other commodities in order to pay it.

This chapter describes (1) how commercial institutions were established in Virginia and Maryland, (2) how they operated in agriculture, (3) how much commercial agriculture was practiced between settlement and independence.

The first necessity was the production of an assured food surplus. This required a high percentage of the earliest immigrants to be cultivators because the agricultural technology of the seventeenth and eighteenth centuries was labor intensive. Sufficient labor had to be expended to produce a large enough food surplus to feed (1) newly arrived immigrants until they became productive; (2) sailors making return voyages; (3) men who were mobilized to repel Indian attacks or undertake retaliatory warfare; (4) the 5 or 6 percent of the population who were engaged in governance, commerce, or clergy; (5) artisans who manufactured products for local consumption.

Five principal groups of cultivators emigrated to the southern colonies: (1) adult children of displaced British peasants who came as indentured servants, (2) petty criminals who were forcibly emigrated as indentured servants, (3) African peasants who were forcibly emigrated as slaves, (4) planter adventurers who invested in land in order to produce agricultural commodities for export, (5) commercially motivated yeomen who were often religious dissenters. Until the beginning of the War for Independence, displaced peasants (European and African) were a large majority of all cultivators who settled in the southern colonies. The middle and northern colonies attracted a much higher percentage of commercially motivated yeomen. In northern colonies they were probably a majority of cultivators, and they were certainly a majority of New England immigrants.

The seven principal components of analysis in this chapter are (1) who immigrated to the southern colonies, (2) amount of per capita labor performed by cultivators, (3) land tenure, (4) governance, (5) suffrage, (6) taxation, (7) literacy.

Indentured Servants

Who were the indentured servants that immigrated to America? What type of labor did they perform? How many years were they obligated to serve upon arrival? What was their status after completing their contracts? David W. Galenson defines the status of indentured servants as "the voluntary exchange by an English man or woman of labor servitude to a designated master during a fixed period of time for passage to the New World and maintenance there during the term of the contract." Indentures were labor contracts that could be sold. As with servants in husbandry in England, indentured servants were prohibited from marriage because purchasers did not want any diversions from their labor.[1]

A high percentage of indentured servants were young, illiterate males without a claim to land use in England, or they were young females who would probably marry landless agricultural laborers or remain unmarried. The highest percentage of indentured servants immigrating to America were males who had been servants in husbandry in England, but when they signed indentures in England they often listed their residence as the nearest town or the port city from where they embarked. Before 1660, a large majority came from the southern and western counties where commercializing policies were intense (ending copyhold tenure, changing land use to grazing, enclosing open fields and common pastures, increasing money rents). Many skills (weaving, carpentry, shoemaking) were claimed by male servants when clerks in port cities recorded their departure, but the youth and illiteracy of most indentured males meant that they were not craftsmen or journeymen. At most, they had a young apprentice's knowledge of the skills they claimed to possess.

It is safe to assume that most people without skills who voluntarily signed indentures in England sought opportunity in America. *What sort of opportunity did these unskilled laborers seek?* This is crucial for understanding the reason for the emigration for a high percentage of indentured servants. Most historians and economists assume they sought opportunities to improve their status. *What social status did they seek to improve?* This question is seldom asked because historians and economists assume that all or almost all indentured servants were commercially motivated. This interpretation tends to project the present into the past and is, therefore, a false assumption.

After English landowners extinguished communal tenure (copyhold tenure), it was impossible for the sons of displaced peasants to acquire the use of land. It was equally impossible for them to practice subsistence labor norms. They were forced to perform full-time paid labor. A high percentage of indentured servants who immigrated to America sought to gain control of land use because control of land use allowed them to control labor expenditures. Control of labor expenditures meant they could practice subsistence labor norms and retain their status as peasants.

This was the opportunity that most young males sought when they voluntarily indentured themselves to come to America. For them, the cost of trans-Atlantic transportation was a form of subsistence credit that would enable them to transfer their peasant status from England to America.

Indentures allowed people in England with neither money nor credit to make the voyage to America. The security of the lender was a signed contract to labor for a fixed number of years for the person who purchased the indenture. Ship captains provided the transportation and food during a voyage that could last sixty to ninety days. On arrival, captains sold indentures to prospective purchasers. The number of years of labor in an indenture depended on the cost of transportation and the number of years of labor that were required for the purchaser to get his money back. This, in turn, depended on the quantity and price of export commodities produced by the supervised labor of indentured servants. The earliest indentures in Virginia were for seven years but thereafter in Virginia and in other colonies they were usually four years, if persons were seventeen years of age or older. If they were younger, they served until they were twenty-one.

A very high percentage of indentured servants were between the ages of fifteen and twenty-four, with ages of eighteen to twenty-two predominating. In the earliest years of settlement, females constituted only about 15 percent of indentured servants. After 1660, they were between 25 and 35 percent of immigrants. About three-quarters of male servants were two-stage immigrants. Their first experience as full-time paid laborers was as servants in husbandry that begin at about age fifteen. They probably served three or four annual contracts before migrating to a provincial town and performing wage or piecework labor (weavers) for one or two years. If they moved to London or Bristol, they found labor discipline more demanding and living conditions cramped and unsanitary. These young men were candidates for immigration to Virginia and other southern colonies where they had the opportunity to resume the less laborious life of peasants after they gained control of land use.

In America, after the end of their indenture, they could become owners of substantial land units if they acquired sufficient money by continuing to perform commercial labor norms. Alternatively, they could lease land or become sharecroppers in a pioneer society that was desperately short of labor. A high percentage of displaced peasants who completed their indentures became leaseholders and sharecroppers. They achieved their goal. They gained control of land use and this allowed them to perform subsistence labor norms.

Most indentured servants came from the lowest social order. They implicitly understood that their illiteracy handicapped them in learning commercial skills. Illiteracy, however, was not a handicap if they wanted to become weavers, enlist as soldiers or seamen, or sign indentures that gave them an opportunity to become landowners or landholders in America. Stated in general terms, the intensity of commercializing policies (demanding full-time paid labor) by English landowners and artisan manufacturers propelled a continuous migration of displaced peasants.

Immigration, however, was not always voluntary. Many were forcibly indentured. Local authorities made no clear distinction between petty thieves and vagabonds; both were jailed with equal vigor. They were deported to North American and Caribbean colonies, which became dumping grounds for undesirables who populated the jails of British seaports. Kenneth Morgan estimates that fifty thousand convicts were shipped to North America between 1718 and 1775.[2]

There were two other groups of involuntary of indentured servants: orphan children and residents of parish poorhouses. Poorhouse overseers were the legal guardians of orphans and they signed indentures for them. They also induced other poorhouse residents (e.g., wives and children of displaced peasants whose husbands had deserted them after moving to a city) to consent to indentures. Parish authorities wanted to exile these people in order to reduce tax rates that supported the poor. For these people, signing indentures was often an act of last resort. On the other hand, for petty criminals, emigration to America was an attractive alternative to incarceration in a house of correction.

Almost all of these groups went to Virginia and Maryland. The regularized trade of tobacco made it possible for the port cities of Britain to continually empty their poorhouses and jails. English mercantile writers were accurate when they described a high percentage of indentured servants as "idle, lazy, simple people…such as have professed idleness, and will rather beg than work."[3]

The largest market for indentured servants in the seventeenth century was the Chesapeake Bay region where tobacco cultivation was firmly established. Male servants were employed to clear land in order to plant tobacco and food crops, manage livestock, and help build residences and barns. In other words, they performed large amounts of pioneer labor as well as cultivating crops. Female servants tended poultry, milked cows, made butter and cheese, weeded gardens, cooked, spun thread, washed clothing, and did other agricultural chores. They were also purchased to be wives. Indentured servants were in strong demand because the cultivation of tobacco was very profitable until about 1660.

Many servants were in poor health when they embarked (often due to malnutrition) and they often received inadequate food during the Atlantic crossing. After arrival, they were put to work as soon as possible. They were expected to perform commercial labor norms in agriculture for those who purchased their indentures. High mortalities were the norm. The highest mortalities were during the crossing and within a year of arrival, with the highest mortalities among orphan children. After one year, mortalities decreased, but one estimate is that 40 percent of servants died before completing their indenture. There are, however, no public records and few private records because of the illiteracy of most servants.

Unlike England, most indentured servants in America were not considered temporary members of a family. They were laborers under long-term contract. Indentures made servants into a labor commodity during the length of their contract. They did, however, have redress for poor treatment. They could appeal to county justices and their complaints would be heard and, if judged to be genuine, they were remedied.

It is, however, known with certainty that mortalities were high in the initial years of settlement at Jamestown. The causes were mismanagement by the London directors of the Virginia Company, the refusal of indentured servants to cultivate adequate amounts of food crops, and locating Jamestown in the brackish water zone of the James River, thereby exposing the inhabitants to water transmitted diseases. Edmund Morgan has conclusively shown that malnutrition created conditions for high mortalities, and Wesley F. Craven documents in great detail the high mortalities from 1607 to 1624.[4]

The first priority of settlers, from the moment of landing, should have been producing sufficient food to feed themselves and those who would follow. This was not done at Jamestown. The London managers of the Virginia Company attempted to establish a colony with a full range of artisan skills because Jamestown was to be a base for expeditions into the interior to loot precious metals from Indians. Cultivating food crops was a secondary concern. After no precious metals were found, other projects were undertaken to produce export commodities (salt by evaporation, smelting iron ore, naval stores, hemp, cordage, wine, and silk). All of these projects diverted labor from the cultivation of food crops. Inadequate food production was aggravated by London managers sending indentured servants faster than food was produced to feed them. In addition, many of them were unfitted to be pioneers. Pioneering required laboring men. Laboring men meant experienced cultivators, and they were a small proportion of the initial immigrants.

Low per capita food crop cultivation was further exacerbated because all settlers were employees of the company and many were from London—with considerable numbers of vagrants, paupers, and petty criminals among them. Those who were assigned to agricultural labor cultivated land owned by the company. They had no direct interest in maximizing food production. Only after the nonagricultural projects failed, did managers in London change priorities. Only then did they encourage the cultivation of food crops and tobacco because tobacco had a highly profitable market in England.

Another contributing factor to deficient food production was the settlers' attempt to cultivate European food grains among the stumps of felled trees. Tobacco and maize are tall plants that grew well among stumps, but European food grains did not, nor did root crops. Not until Virginia settlers learned to cultivate maize among the stumps, like the Indians, was the food crisis alleviated. Maryland settlers learned from Virginia's mistakes. From the first probate inventories in Maryland in the 1630s, maize was the principal food grain. Wheat did not appear in probate inventories until the 1660s when the first stump-free fields could be plowed; and it was not commonly planted until the 1680s.

Tobacco production dramatically increased in Virginia after 1616 when servants who had completed their service became sharecrop tenants on company land. They concentrated their labor on tobacco cultivation and neglected the cultivation of food crops because of tobacco's profitability. They grew only enough food to feed themselves for three months because they thought that sufficient food would arrive from England in ships bringing new settlers. This did not happen in sufficient amounts to avoid serious hunger and, as a result, mortalities were excessively high.

In 1616 Virginia's population was about 400, with only about 200 persons capable of agricultural labor. Virginia barely survived the first decade of settlement. By 1622 Virginia's population was 3,500, but there were severe food shortages because of a flood of new arrivals and inadequate food production. The Indian attack of March 1622 killed about one-quarter of the population and intensified existing hunger. Many settlers survived by eating livestock that was to be the breeding stock for future needs. By 1623, starvation and disease reduced Virginia's population to 1,275.

In the census of 1624–1625, there were 309 households, 483 indentured servants, 1 Indian, and 23 African slaves. Seventy-six percent of the population were males, 73 percent were between the ages of 15 and 34 (49% between 20 and 29), and 71 percent were unmarried. As one would expect in a population with a high percentage of servants (and ex-servants), Virginia society was highly stratified. The highest strata was the sixteen households of planter adventurers. They had the services of 289 servants (57% of the 507 servants and slaves in the census). There was a middling group of thirty-two households that had the services of three to seven servants. These households had a total 149 servants (29%). This group of cultivators was a reasonably close approximation of English yeomen cultivators. Peasants occupied the lowest strata. These were the 213 households that had no servants; and if 46 households with one to two servants are added, 259 of the colony's households (84%) produced food and commodities at a subsistence level of production and consumption.

By 1700 there was a stratified peasantry in Virginia and Maryland that would be duplicated in other southern colonies after they passed the pioneering stage of settlement. There were four strata of peasants. The highest was landowners, often with substantial holdings that were largely uncultivated. This was followed by lifetime leaseholders and sharecroppers who controlled land use that enabled them to practice the subsistence compromise. The third was unmarried male freemen who were permanent servants in husbandry. They usually lived with a peasant household that controlled land use and both the landholder and freeman performed subsistence labor norms. The lowest strata was enslaved African peasants who were permanent agricultural laborers without an opportunity to accumulate money or migrate.

The ultimate solution to endemic food shortages and a demographic profile bulging with young unmarried males (who could not sustain the colony), was conveying land in freehold tenure to attract settlers. Beginning in 1618, land was conveyed in freehold tenure to several classes of settlers:

1. One hundred acres were granted to those who emigrated at their own expense before 1616.
2. Servants who completed their time by 1616 were granted one hundred acres. Presumably, these were ex-servants who were sharecrop tenants on company land.
3. All future immigrants who came at their own expense were granted fifty acres. If a man and wife immigrated, they could qualify for fifty acres each.

4. All servants who came at company expense after 1616 and who completed their service were also granted fifty acres.
5. Artisan manufacturers who established a business were granted a town lot of four acres on which to build a house and conduct business.
6. Stockholders who were planter adventurers (plantation entrepreneurs) were granted land dividends at the rate of one hundred acres per share. An additional fifty acres was granted for every indentured servant they brought with them, or whose contracts they purchased. This was the headright system. Its purpose was to extend settlement inland in order to create a buffer zone that protected the core settlement around Jamestown from Indian attacks.

The new land and tenure policy and the impending bankruptcy of the company after Indian warfare in 1622, greatly reduced the number of servants who immigrated at company expense. Most new settlers were indentured servants recruited by planter adventurers who immigrated to Virginia to cultivate tobacco or produce other commodities for export. In order to sustain production, planter adventurers needed a continuous supply of labor to replace servants whose indentures expired. It was a common practice for planter adventurers to arrange for relatives in England to recruit indentured servants.

Planter adventurers were attracted to Virginia (and Maryland) because they did not have to pay high legal expenses, as they did in England, to extinguish communal tenure (copyhold tenure); nor did they have the expense of consolidating scattered cultivation strips into enclosed fields that were necessary for efficient cultivation. From the first day of settlement, freehold land in America could be enclosed as soon as it was reclaimed from the forest. Thereafter, maximum amounts of labor could be applied because all harvests were the property of landowners.

Land grants in freehold tenure to planter adventurers and ex-indentured servants made the risks of pioneering attractive—but for radically different reasons. Commercially motivated planter adventurers wanted to increase the area of land under cultivation in order to increase harvests for export. They wanted to become wealthy. Subsistence motivated freemen (the status of servants after completing their indentures) wanted to own or control enough land to reduce agricultural labor expenditures. This meant performing only enough labor to achieve an acceptable level of subsistence welfare.

Russell R. Menard estimates that "during the seventeenth century…the vast majority of immigrants—at least 70 percent and the proportion may have reached 85 percent—arrived as servants." Most became agricultural laborers after arrival. Immigration of servants to Virginia and Maryland peaked about 1660, then stabilized until about 1680. After 1680, indentured immigration slowly declined because planters preferred to purchase African slaves as agricultural laborers, and because indentured servants preferred to immigrate to the Carolinas where land was more easily obtainable.[5]

Menard's data on immigration to Maryland (and Virginia) is in very good agreement with the commercializing policies being enforced by English landowners in the first half of the seventeenth century. By about 1650, a large part of English agriculture was commercialized, but at a low level of efficiency. The fundamental component in the commercializing process was inducing fewer people to labor every day for more hours than peasants labored. Landowners evicted unneeded peasant households. Scattered cultivation strips were consolidated. In time, the aggregated strips were converted into fenced fields. After 1650, the intensity of commercialization accelerated and eviction rates increased until about 1680. By that date, communal tenure had been extinguished in most districts in England but much enclosure remained to be done. Many displaced peasants opted to migrate to London, which grew from 200,000 people in 1600 to 575,000 in 1700, thereby resulting in diminishing numbers of peasants who were candidates for emigration to North America.

During the eighteenth century, there was a change in the geographic source of emigrants from Britain. A high percentage of indentured servants came from Yorkshire because northern landowners had been slow to adopt commercializing policies during the seventeenth century. Two other sources of emigrants were Scotland and the Scots-Irish from Ulster. Two strong impulses to leave Scotland were the Jacobite Rebellions in 1715 and 1745. Highland peasants supported the Stuart pretender to the British throne because the commercializing policies of highland landowners were ending peasant control of land use.

Scottish landowners took advantage of the rebellion to replace subsistence agriculture with cattle and sheep grazing to produce meat and wool for market sale. Commercializing landowners evicted peasants and had them transported to America in chartered ships that were packed with one hundred to three hundred persons in family groups. Upon arrival, most of them became indentured servants. The highland clearances ended endemic seasonal hunger that was inherent in the subsistence agriculture practiced in the marginal climate of the highlands. A high percentage of highland Scots immigrated to Virginia, Maryland, and the Carolinas. They were in great demand in the Carolinas and Georgia to settle the frontier in order to protect the small and vulnerable coastal villages.

Likewise, there was a steady stream of immigrants from Ulster because the export market for linen cloth, a staple of the Ulster economy, underwent fluctuations in demand (and price) due to almost continuous warfare in Europe during the first sixty years of the eighteenth century. Ulster immigrants concentrated in Pennsylvania, New York, and North Carolina; and immigrants from London with artisan or commercial skills concentrated in Pennsylvania. During the eighteenth century only a trickle of British immigrants went to New England.

In more general terms, displaced English and Scots peasants preferred to immigrate to southern colonies where land was available on easy terms. This was particularly true for highland Scots who immigrated to North Carolina.

Freeman and Freeholders

What happened to freemen who failed to become landowners? What percentage of freemen became landowners in the seventeenth century, and what percentage became tenants? What was the political and social status of freemen and freeholders in Chesapeake society? Posed as a more general question: what percentage of initial settlers were commercially motivated? What role did freemen and freeholders play in county and colonial governance? Freemen were indentured servants who had served their time, and freeholders were those who owned land in freehold tenure. Russell R. Menard answers these questions for Maryland, and Thomas J. Wertenbacker answers them for Virginia.[6]

Menard bases his analysis on a sample of indentured men who arrived in Maryland during the first eight years of colonization (1634–1642). In his sample, 40 percent did not appear in the record as freemen. Of the 60 percent who became freemen, about half became landowners in Maryland, and others are known to have moved to Virginia and acquired land.

Freemen had four options after their indentures expired. They could become (1) landowners, (2) leaseholders or sharecroppers, (3) permanent servants in husbandry (as single men), or (4) migrate to other southern colonies where frontier land could be obtained with less effort.

If they became leaseholders or sharecroppers, they had three options: (1) perform subsistence labor norms, (2) continue to perform the same commercial labor norms they had performed as indentured servants in order to accumulate money to acquire land, or (3) after acquiring land they could continue to perform commercial labor norms and become yeomen cultivators or they could perform subsistence labor norms and become upper-strata peasants.

Although, freemen were entitled to a grant of land from the public domain after their indentures expired, land acquisition required sufficient money to pay for surveying boundaries and registering titles. Similarly, retaining ownership required earning sufficient amounts of money to pay taxes. For a high percentage of freemen, the labor needed to grow the crops needed to acquire the money to acquire land was more labor than was required for an acceptable level of subsistence welfare. They were unwilling to perform sufficient labor to become landowners. They preferred becoming lifetime leaseholders or sharecroppers, often on the same land they had cultivated when they were indentured servants. Single males who never married because of a shortage of women lived alone or became lifetime agricultural laborers in married households of landholding peasants.

In Maryland, the right of freemen to acquire fifty acres of land was approved by the proprietor in 1648 in order to keep them from migrating to Virginia where fifty acres was available under the headright system. Freemen who acquired land in Maryland usually did so within eight years after becoming freemen. Most holdings were small. A similar pattern operated in Virginia. Probate inventories indicate that all ex-servant who became freeholders had meager household possessions. Livestock accounted for half of their assets. Few had the services of indentured servants and fewer owned slaves. Almost all were probably illiterate.

Freemen who became lifetime leaseholders or sharecroppers were probably allocated twenty to fifty acres of land, of which ten to fifteen acres were cultivated. Cultivated fields were full of stumps and half-burned tree trunks, and were overgrown with weeds. In the spring, the weeds were chopped with hoes and subsistence amounts of maize (the principal food crop) were planted. The annual tobacco crop (necessary to acquire money) was planted on three to five acres of newly cleared ground that was free of weeds. Leaseholders and sharecroppers paid the rent on their land with the proceeds from the sale of tobacco.

Most freemen were not motivated to improve their social status after they gained control of land use by ownership, lease, sharecropping, or as bachelors living in peasant households. Lois G. Carr and Russell R. Menard summarize their social goal as follows: "Apparently, most men who did not form households and establish their own farms were unable to improve their positions even after years of labor...Longevity made little difference to prosperity." This is an accurate summary of their behavior. Material prosperity was not their goal. When most freemen gained control of land use, they achieved their goal for immigrating to America—the performance of subsistence labor norms. They became the white American peasantry.[7]

Until about 1680, shifting cultivation was the principal cultivation technique used by all cultivators in Virginia and Maryland. It was also the technique used by Indians. Trees were felled and burned and crops planted on mounds of earth (scraped up with hoes) among the half burned tree trunks and stumps. The usual practice in Virginia and Maryland was to plant three consecutive crops of tobacco followed by three consecutive maize crops. When fields became overrun with grass, weeds, and tree saplings, they were allowed to revert to secondary forest. Cultivators then made a new field by felling and burning trees.

In about twenty-five years, the secondary forest that grew on abandoned fields was tall enough to shade grasses and weeds to death. Trees were again felled and burned, and for five or six years tobacco and food crops were planted among the stumps. For every acre of secondary forest that was cut and burned, an equal number of acres of rough pasture were allowed to revert to secondary forest. This was the technique of nibbling shifting cultivation. "The great virtue of shifting cultivation is that it minimizes the labor of ground preparation. Trees shade grass and weeds to death so that turning the soil to destroy them is unnecessary. Seeds can be directly planted in the soil."[8]

We know that shifting cultivation was the normal cultivation practice of pioneers in Maryland and Virginia because hoes and axes were present in all probate inventories of cultivating households. This is confirmed by a law passed by the Maryland assembly in 1638 that required four years of labor from all indentured servants who were eighteen years or older if they arrived in Maryland without a signed indenture. When they became freemen their master had to provide them with a suit of clothing, three barrels of grain, a hilling hoe, a weeding hoe, and an ax. It is safe to infer that for the first fifty years of settlement, most crops of most cultivators in Virginia and Maryland were planted among stumps; however, most households also had an intensively cultivated garden located near their residences. Plows and carts do not appear in probate inventories in Maryland households until the 1680s and then only occasionally.

During the summer, cattle grazed on rough pastures (land in process of reverting to secondary forest). After the harvest, cattle ate standing maize stalks with bean vines growing on them. During the winter, they browsed on under-story plants in the forest. Custom recognized that forest land owned in freehold tenure was a communal resource where livestock could browse and root. The only cultivated forage crop for feeding cattle during the winter were maize husks and cobs. The reciprocal of the commonage of forests was that all fields of planted crops had to be fenced, particularly against rooting hogs. In 1632, the Virginia assembly passed a statute requiring all cultivated fields to be fenced. This was the law until early in the twentieth century.

After 1660, it was more difficult for freeman households in tidewater counties to accumulate enough money to become landowners due to a steep decline in the price of tobacco. At the same time, the price of unimproved land doubled because it had easy access to water transportation. Sharecropping and leaseholding households were content to remain tenants. They were content because these tenures gave them what they wanted—control of land use.

As long as a household controlled land use, it could practice the subsistence compromise and, as long as land was available for sharecropping or lease, they would not expend the additional labor required to grow enlarged harvests necessary to accumulate money needed to become landowners. The system of sharecrop cultivation that evolved in tidewater Virginia and Maryland in the seventeenth century was extended onto the piedmont in the eighteenth century and into the trans-Appalachian west in the nineteenth century.[9]

The normal interpretation of the social structure that emerged after the frontier stage of settlement is that the governing elites of tidewater plantation owners in Virginia and Maryland prevented upward mobility by engrossing the purchase of frontier land. I do not think this is an accurate interpretation. A study of probate inventories in the second half of the seventeenth century in Maryland by Lois G. Carr and Russell R. Menard documents that a high percentage of freemen failed to improve their status after their indentures expired, in spite of the easy opportunities to become owners of frontier land.

Kevin P. Kelly documents the average price of land in Surry county Virginia from 1670 to 1700. Surry country was frontier land that was vulnerable to Indian attacks until about 1685, even though it was only twenty to twenty-five kilometers from tidewater and not much further south of Jamestown. From 1670 to 1680 the price of land averaged ten pounds of tobacco per acre; sixteen pounds per acre from 1680 to 1690, and seventeen pounds per acre from 1690 to 1700. Prices in Maryland were similar. From 1670 to 1680 unimproved land could be purchased for an average of twenty pounds of tobacco per acre; from 1680 to 1690 the average price was twenty-seven pounds per acre; and from 1690 to 1700 the average price was thirty-two pounds per acre.

If freeman households worked hard, they could harvest in excess of three thousand pounds of tobacco per year on newly cleared ground that was free of grass and weeds and had a store of mineral nutrients in the upper layer of the soil profile. Money to purchase land was within easy reach of households that maximized tobacco cultivation on leased or sharecropped land and labored during winter months to produce wood products such as barrel staves, shingles, potash, or grew maize for market sale. Instead, tobacco yields of sharecrop households averaged about six hundred pounds per acre and few households produced additional products for market sale.[10]

If freemen "managed to become small landowning planters, their children maintained that position but seldom moved beyond it. If [some] small freeholders were more successful and obtained offices of power, their children sometimes were able to maintain the family station but often experienced downward mobility into small planter status." On their own terms, ex-servants who became "small land owning planters" were successful immigrants because landownership allowed them to perform subsistence labor norms that would have been impossible had they remained in England. By emigrating they escaped having to perform commercial labor norms (continuous paid labor); and avoidance of this labor was a principal cause for emigrating.[11]

Governance

The London directors of the Virginia Company instituted two governing policies in 1618: (1) The governor was authorized to enact laws after consultation with an assembly of resident landowners who were stockholders. Landowners who were stockholders demanded it and the London managers of the company agreed because it was a prerogative of English landowners to participate in governance. (2) Warehouse receipts of tobacco awaiting export were given a fixed money value and authorized to circulate as legal currency for paying taxes and private debts contracted in Virginia.

The first meeting of the Virginia Assembly was in July 1619. The first order of business was attracting more planter adventurers who would risk their capital by investing in land, and who had the ability to recruit indentured servants to cultivate it. Immigration had to be made more attractive because an increased population was essential for repelling Indian attacks. Virginia's first assembly clearly understood that the abundance of uncultivated land was a major incentive for men with capital to immigrate to Virginia. They equally understood that planter adventurers needed more laborers. An unplanned event in 1619 offered a long-term solution to the labor problem—a Dutch ship brought a cargo of African slaves into Jamestown harbor. Suddenly, agricultural laborers were available to planter adventurers without the difficulties of having to recruit indentured servants in England.

The first assembly stated that it was their intent to establish the same offices of local government that operated in England, and that they intended to follow English legal procedures. Counties would be the framework of local government, but in 1619 there were too few people and they were highly dispersed. County governments were not established until 1628 the first assembly under royal governance.

The four most important functions of county governments were (1) recording land titles, land transfers, leases, and probate inventories in order to insure the orderly transfer of land and other forms of wealth; (2) collecting taxes for both county and colonial uses; (3) conducting elections to the assembly, which usually meant that local officeholders managed the election by nominating preferred candidates; and (4) settling local disputes. The three most frequent disputes centered on collecting subsistence debts owed to landowners by leaseholder and share-crop households, collecting debts owed to storekeepers who were usually export merchants, and settling boundary disputes between adjacent landowners because of the inaccuracies of initial surveys.

At the first layout of county boundaries, the governor appointed all the men who filled offices of the county court. Almost immediately county courts became self-perpetuating institutions that were always staffed by commercially motivated cultivators or their nominees. County courts institutionalized freehold tenure, validated the operation of subsistence credit that landowners and storekeepers extended to peasants, and enforced the collection of all taxes. In 1634, the crown granted a petition of Virginia landowners that confirmed freehold titles to the land acquired under company governance.

Like in England, the power of governance was concentrated in the hands of landowners, and leadership in county courts was concentrated in the hands of the principal landowners. County courts were the guardians of commercial social values. To a remarkable degree, the powers of county governments in England were transferred to Virginia and Maryland.

The first royal governor conducted public affairs with the help of the same council that had assisted the last governor of the Virginia Company. The instructions of the royal governor did not explicitly authorize him to govern with the consent of an assembly. In 1627, the council petitioned the crown to have the company's council restored. Their petition was granted, and an election was held in 1628 with the same electorate under company governance. One of the first orders of business was levying a poll tax on all males sixteen years of age or older. Thereafter, the assembly controlled all taxation and fees collected by the governor, sheriffs, and other officials. The assembly, however, was not authorized to hold annual sessions until 1638.

Royal governors also retained the company's headright policy of granting fifty acres to all persons who immigrated at their own expense and granting fifty acres to indentured servants who served their time. All persons receiving grants of frontier land could choose locations, but the boundaries had to be surveyed and the location and size of the grant had to be registered at the county courthouse. New landowners had to pay the cost of surveying and a fee for registering titles. Surveyed boundaries and registration made ownership a matter of public record for purposes of taxation and voting. Clear titles and defined boundaries also made land an item of commerce.

Seven years after a settler acquired ownership of frontier land, it became taxable. If improvements were not made (a cleared field and a residence) and taxes were not paid, the land escheated to the colonial government and was sold for small amounts of money to cultivators who were actual settlers.

The success of the headright system of land grants accelerated the cultivation of tobacco. The governing elite in Virginia lobbied Parliament to exclude tobacco grown in Spanish colonies from the English market. Both Parliament and the crown obliged and went one step further: cultivation of tobacco was forbidden in England. Tobacco grown in Virginia, Maryland, and Bermuda was granted a monopoly market in England. Tobacco imported into England was highly taxed and made a substantial contribution to crown revenues. It also assured the survival of Virginia.

From the earliest years of royal governance, the assembly began to accrete power. This was facilitated by the increasing difficulties that king Charles I had in governing England. During these years of crisis in England, Virginians were left alone to govern themselves, which they did by establishing civil and ecclesiastical institutions in forms that met their needs.

The transition from indentured servant to freeman is better documented in Maryland than Virginia; and this transition documents how indentured servants who served their time fitted into the colonial political and social structure. The operation of governing institutions in Maryland and the headright system in Maryland were:

> not greatly different from what it had been in Virginia. Through the years that followed (settlement), governor and council in each colony sat in consultation on questions of policy, acted as the highest provincial court, undertook to assume the leadership of the general assembly, and exercised such administrative functions as the occasion required.[12]

Maryland was established in 1632 by a proprietary grant by the crown to Sir George Calvert. The first settlers arrived in 1634. The land policy of the proprietor was based on Virginia's experience because it was clear by 1632 that cheap land in freehold tenure was a powerful attraction for planter adventurers as well as indentured servants who sought to become landowners after serving their time.

Initial planter adventurers received generous grants in freehold tenure. If they brought five servants with them between the ages of sixteen and fifty, they received two thousand acres, plus an additional one hundred acres for each additional servant. Families that immigrated at their own expense were granted one hundred acres per adult, an additional one hundred acres per servant; and fifty additional acres for children under sixteen years of age. The second wave of pioneering planters had to bring ten servants to qualify for a grant of two thousand acres. After 1642, planter adventurers had to bring twenty servants with them to qualify for a land grant of two thousand acres; and families that immigrated at their own expense were granted only fifty acres for each member of their households. Most servants who accompanied planter adventurers to Maryland were servants in husbandry.

Not until 1648 did the proprietor grant fifty acres of land to servants who had served their time. Otherwise, they would migrate to Virginia and claim land under Virginia's headright system. Opportunities to own land were essential for keeping freemen in Maryland after they had served their time.

A partnership between planter adventurers and governors (royal or proprietary) had the task of managing the votes of freemen after the end of pioneering in order to govern in the interests of economic development. This task required unrelenting effort. In Maryland the effort began with the first meeting of the assembly in 1638, four years after the first settlement. Its principal purpose was to enact into statute laws policies recommended by the proprietor. There were four principal considerations: (1) establish a central government based on consent (2) establish a means of mobilizing manpower to counter the constant danger of Indian warfare, (3) settle disputes over poorly surveyed property boundaries, and (4) enact statutes to encourage the production of export commodities so that landowners could acquire sufficient money to pay taxes to the colonial government and quitrents to the proprietor.

During the first fifty years of settlement in Maryland, when governing institutions were being established, many offices had to be filled with illiterates because there was no one else available. The service of illiterates was necessary for governing a dispersed population because local hierarchies were weak due to small numbers of qualified persons, high mortalities, and frequent migration. Illiterates were appointed militia officers, constables, deputy sheriffs, jurors, overseers of highways, and county justices. They were usually landowners and usually served for short periods of time. A small minority (about 4%) of the earliest indentured servants joined the governing elite after becoming freeholders. A good indication of the low social origins of many pioneering landowners was that some illiterates are known to have held major county offices in Maryland until 1690.

After 1660, literate landowners steadily replaced illiterate freeholders as county justices. Indicative of the availability of better qualified men for local governance was the proprietor's proclamation of 1670 that disenfranchised all freemen who did not own fifty acres of land or a visible estate worth at least forty pounds sterling. Landless freemen were excluded from governance because "the freeholders are the strength and only strength of this province, not the freemen. It is their persons, purses, and stocks must bear the burden of government both in peace and war, and not freemen who can easily abandon us." The Maryland assembly enacted the proclamation into law in 1692.[13]

This settled the question of who would govern. Freemen would not govern because most of them refused to make sufficient labor inputs into cultivation in order produce adequate amounts of crops or other commodities for market sale. They had achieved their purpose: the practice of subsistence labor norms in America. They would produce only enough tobacco or other exchange commodities to acquire the money needed to purchase essential metal tools and textiles. After this sum was acquired, they ceased laboring. Maryland would be governed in the interests of landowners, especially plantation owners who managed the labor of indentured servants and African slaves who could be coerced to perform commercial labor norms.

In the same year (1670) that the Maryland proprietor disfranchised landless freemen, the Virginia legislature enacted a statute that only "freeholders and house keepers who are answerable to the public for the levies, shall hereafter have a voice in the election of any burgess in this country" because "the laws of England grant a voice in such elections only to such as by their estates, real or personal have interest enough to tie them to the endeavors of the public good." The immediate causes of the disfranchisement of freemen were disturbances at polling places by landless freemen. They created disorder when men arrived to orally cast their votes. The 1670 law did not operate as intended. Candidates for the assembly often created fraudulent landowners by giving them an acre of land to qualify for voting.[14]

The assembly that met during Bacon's Rebellion in 1676 re-enfranchised landless freemen. That ruling, however, was soon reversed and freemen were disfranchised by a direct order from the crown: "you shall take care that the members of the assembly be elected only by freeholders." This was modified in 1684 by a statute that extended the privilege of voting to men who held lifetime leases on the land they cultivated. In every American colony in the late seventeenth century, statutes were enacted that required "some sort of property qualification, and the tendency during the middle of the eighteenth century, was toward a certain amount of uniformity throughout the colonies."[15]

In 1736 qualifications for electing delegates to the Virginia assembly were defined in greater detail. Voters had to own at least one hundred acres of uncultivated land or twenty-five acres of cultivated land with a house on it, or a town lot with a house on it, or have a lifetime lease to one hundred acres that was recorded at the country courthouse, or possess a leasehold that was registered at least one year before an election. Revisions in 1762 and 1769 allowed plural voting by removing the requirement that landowners had to be county residents. Men owning land in two or more counties could vote in each county because elections were often held on different days.

In the eighteenth century, leaseholders for life probably constituted about 20 percent of the Virginia electorate. They were concentrated in frontier counties where large landowners gave lifetime leases on easy terms because their objective was not immediate profits. These leases required leaseholders to annually clear a fixed area of land. When the leasehold reverted to the owners there were substantial areas of cleared land or secondary forest that could be quickly brought under cultivation by slaves.

What percentage of white males over twenty-one years of age constituted the electorate? It varied in Virginia between tidewater counties and frontier counties. Limited data suggests that about 50 percent of the white males who paid poll taxes were landowners and another 20 percent were lifetime leaseholders. Sharecrop tenants could not vote. A substantial majority of landowners and most leaseholders were upper-strata peasants. In elections to the Virginia assembly between 1752 and 1773, voter turnout averaged about 60 percent of eligible males. In the surviving records of elections, the highest number of voters in a county was 1,201 and the lowest number was 109, with an average somewhere near 350. Enfranchised males were about 15 percent of the white population. This was a manageable electorate.

Managing elections to the assembly (House of Burgesses) was a principal function of county courts. County courts acted as nominating committees for candidates. Nominees always had experience in country governance, and during the electoral process the justices of the courts always made their preferred choices known to the electorate. Once elected to the assembly, most burgesses continued to retain their seats on country courts. County courts were self-perpetuating oligarchies because the governor always appointed the candidates nominated by the sitting court. In almost all instances, the men who were nominated were large landowners and slave owners, who often had extensive business interests.

Once a landowner was appointed, he could remain on the court for life if that was his wish. This institutional arrangement strongly contributed to preserving governance in the hands of elite plantation owners. The Virginia assembly "was, in effect, a league of local magnates secure in their control of county institutions." This arrangement effectively neutralized the political aspirations of white peasants.[16]

The governing elites of Virginia and Maryland in the seventeenth and eighteenth centuries had to govern with restraint because they could not enforce a full range of commercializing policies on white peasants. There was too much frontier land available and there were no barriers to intercolonial migration. The governing elite needed the white peasantry's acquiescence to their governance in order to retain their favored position for business opportunities, especially in the disposition of frontier land; and white peasants living in tidewater counties needed access to frontier land where their sons could settle. The governing elite also needed peasant militiamen to expand the frontier. Political stability required that the governing elite had to share access to frontier land with the sons of peasant cultivators and ex-servants.

The necessity for sharing the subsistence opportunities of frontier land with peasants insured that governing elites could not monopolize the ownership of frontier land; although, they usually had first choice in acquiring it. Sharing the disposition of frontier land was a principal way governing elites secured the acquiescence of freeholders to their governance. The compromise over the disposition of frontier land committed the governing elites of Virginia and Maryland to protecting the subsistence labor norms of peasants, whether they were landowners, leaseholders, or sharecroppers.

This protection had two long-term consequences. First, after about 1700, slave labor became essential for maintaining the political power of governing elites because fewer indentured servants emigrated from Britain. Second, servants who became freemen were increasingly likely to move to the frontier.

The political power of planters depended on agricultural laborers who performed commercial labor norms. Most sharecrop tenants rejected commercial labor norms, but commercial labor norms could be coerced from slaves; therefore, in the course of the eighteenth century the number of slaves increased in tidewater counties. After 1703, indentured laborers and lifetime leaseholders were increasingly replaced with slave labor. The number of white peasants living in tidewater counties decreased and this helped entrench in power the governing elites of Virginia and Maryland. Furthermore, the indifference of most white peasants to literacy was endorsed by the governing elites of southern colonies because illiteracy helped preserve the acquiescence of white peasant landowners to their governance.

Slaves had two different functions in southern culture. Plantation owners could coerce commercial labor norms from slaves and thereby increase their own wealth. Peasant slave owners could transfer subsistence labor to them and obtain an acceptable level of subsistence welfare with minimal agricultural labor. Governing elites were forced to protect the subsistence labor norms of most white peasant landowners rather than advocate higher taxes to teach literacy in common schools—as an essential policy of economic development. The principal economic consequence of slavery was that slaves performed most of the commercial labor norms in agriculture; therefore, commercial labor norms in agriculture had a low social value because only slaves performed them.

In the long run, the production of commercial wealth was hugely retarded by governing elites that protected the subsistence labor norms of white peasants, were indifferent to mass literacy, and were committed to the inefficient agricultural labor performed by slaves. Literacy was necessary to acquire advanced artisan and commercial skills and a shortage of these skills made southern colonies excessively dependent on merchants from northern colonies or from Britain, as well as being excessively dependent on imported manufactured products.

Bacon's Rebellion

The two most violent contests over land policy and governance in colonial America were Bacon's Rebellion in Virginia between March 1676 and May 1677 and the Regulator Rebellion in North Carolina in 1770–1771. The participants in Bacon's Rebellion were indentured servants, freemen who were tenants, and slaves. All were living at a subsistence level of welfare on dispersed plantations and homesteads on the piedmont frontier, a region vulnerable to Indian attacks. The leader was Nathaniel Bacon, an owner of a large block of recently purchased frontier land.

In 1676 Virginia's population was about forty thousand, with six thousand indentured servants and twice that number of freemen. About one-third of the freemen were unmarried males because of a shortage of women. They were rootless young males cultivating leased or sharecropped land. There were also about two thousand African slaves. Frontier cultivators had two grievances that affected them directly: the frequency of Indian massacres and the failure of Governor William Berkeley to authorize retaliatory warfare. They also shared two additional grievances with a high percentage of freemen and freeholders in tidewater counties: high poll taxes and misappropriated public funds.

Governor Berkeley, aged seventy, did not adequately respond to frontier warfare. Many people accused him of protecting Indians because of the considerable income he derived from licensing Indian traders. Added to this was the colonists' endemic hunger due to deficient harvests. Famine conditions were averted in 1674 only by importing food from New England. Harvests were also deficient in 1675 and endemic hunger persisted. King Philips War in New England ended food imports from there. Indian depredations, high taxation, corrupt governance, and hunger created a volatile political mixture.

The most important grievance was the failure to protect the frontier from Indian attacks. Planter adventurers, peasant landowners, sharecroppers, unmarried freemen, and indentured servants agreed that the first order of governance was frontier protection. They also agreed that high taxes had been largely misappropriated into the hands of Governor Berkeley's favorites—to the neglect of frontier defense. High poll taxes (paid in pounds of tobacco) were especially resented because they were disproportionately paid by freemen, especially those living on the frontier where pioneering subsistence was the norm. In poor crop years, the subsistence labor of white peasants did not produce enough tobacco to pay the poll tax and have enough to purchase their annual needs of manufactured products.

Nathaniel Bacon confirmed the subsistence stress of frontier cultivators when he sent Governor Berkeley a description of his victory over the Indians. Bacon's campaign against the Indians had to be truncated becausee his small force did not have enough food to remain in the field: "That when we came to action we had not to half the company one day's provision, and very many none at all, so that upon equal sharing which was prepared, we found ourselves not able to subsist three days."[17]

Nathaniel Bacon had arrived in Virginia two years earlier as a planter adventurer and had purchased a large estate on the frontier. After Indians killed several of his servants, along with servants and tenants of other frontier landowners, he mobilized a volunteer company of frontiersmen and led an unauthorized attack that massacred Indians in their villages. Berkeley's response was to brand him an outlaw because the volunteers were not mobilized and led by militia officers that he appointed. Berkeley's failure to endorse retaliatory warfare completely misread the opinions of almost all landowners on the western shore of Chesapeake Bay. They wanted a concerted effort to exterminate the Indian population and permanently end their competition for land use.

When frontiersmen heard that Bacon had been outlawed, they marched to Jamestown where the newly elected Virginia assembly was in session. Eight policies constituted their agenda:

1. a general war against Indians conducted by volunteers led by Bacon instead of militia levies led by officers appointed by the governor;
2. lower taxes, particularly poll taxes; and ending exemptions from poll taxation by the principal officeholders of the Virginia government;
3. enfranchise all freemen;
4. election of representatives to county courts in equal number to the justices appointed by the governor. The elected representatives would have equal votes with appointed justices in levying county taxes;
5. elected vestries of parish churches;
6. reduced fees charged for government services (probate, land transfer, registration of land titles);
7. end plural office holding, particularly the practice of allowing members of the governor's council to retain a place on county courts;
8. forbid the export of food grains.

Prohibiting the export of food grains would retain sufficient amounts of food in Virginia in poor crop years so that the assembly, dominated by freemen, could regulate the fair distribution of the available food. This is a peasant response to subsistence privation, and is diametrically opposed to the commercial solution for ending food shortages—expending more per capita labor in the cultivation of food crops.

The arrival of Bacon's frontiersmen in Jamestown induced the assembly to commission him a frontier general. He then marched his troops westward to fight Indians. As soon as they left, Governor Berkeley rescinded his commission and tried to rally tidewater landowners on the eastern shore. He called Bacon a rebel and organized troops to restore governance on his terms. Berkeley had little support. Tidewater landowners wanted the Indians exterminated as much as frontiersmen, not only because of the threat they posed to the dispersed population of the colony but because their removal would open the piedmont to land speculation and settlement.

Bacon's troops, now much increased, marched back to Jamestown, expelled Berkeley and his troops and held a convention composed of a majority of Berkeley's council and the officers of Bacon's troops. Thereafter, they engaged in open rebellion. They declared Berkeley a traitor, burned both public and private buildings in Jamestown, and authorized looting the estates of landowners who supported Berkeley. Berkeley's intransigence regarding frontier protection and taxation policies converted legitimate grievances into armed rebellion that threatened social upheaval.

Order was restored after the arrival of six warships from England and eight other ships carrying 1,100 troops. They came because King Charles had to have the 100,000 pounds sterling of annual revenue produced by import taxes on tobacco. The king's commissioners did what Berkeley refused to do. King Charles had ordered Berkeley to pursue healing policies. He did not. He pursued a policy of retribution. Only loyalists to Governor Berkeley could participate in the governance of Virginia. The king's commissioners, who accompanied the troops, revoked these laws, removed Berkeley from office, and sent him to England.

Thereafter Virginia's governing elite pursued a policy of reconciliation and accommodation—this was the only policy that could effectively govern Virginia in the future. To this end,

King Charles drafted a proclamation of amnesty for all participants in the rebellion and a subsequent assembly enacted it into law. All assemblies after Bacon's Rebellion were elected under the pre-rebellion suffrage rule. Only landowners voted.

When it was apparent that 1682 would be a good crop year for tobacco, the governor convened the assembly to legally restrict the planting of tobacco. It was hoped that a reduced harvest would raise prices by bringing production into balance with consumption in Europe. A direct order from London forbade the Virginia assembly to consider this option because it would reduce the King's revenue from the tobacco tax. The peasant response was a mini-rebellion.

Gangs of freemen and peasant landholders invaded the fields of larger landowners (at night) and cut the stalks of half the tobacco crop. Larger planters were targets because, by about 1680, they were using economies of scale in allocating slave labor to cultivate and cure tobacco. Even with low tobacco prices, cultivation was profitable. The peasantry would disproportionately benefit from higher prices because they would not have to resort to other forms of labor to produce export commodities needed to acquire money. Armed horse patrols were organized to capture the rebels. No sooner was one group caught in one county than similar outbreaks occurred in other counties. A few hangings of rebel leaders restored order.

During the first sixty-eight years of settlement, the divergence of interests between peasant landholders and commercially motivated landowners was postponed. The colony was governed on the assumption that land policies and representative institutions should operate in the interests of commercially motivated landowners. Most former servants who became free-man thought that the abundance of vacant frontier land should be used to provide subsistence opportunities for them rather than to create fortunes for land speculators who were clients of the governor. In the aftermath of Bacon's Rebellion, Virginia's colonial and county governing elites evolved into more responsive oligarchies that actively sought the acquiescence of peasant landowners to their rule.

Participants in the Regulator Rebellion were largely squatters on frontier land owned by speculators. They resisted paying surveying costs and the sale price for the land they were cultivating. Much of Regulator rhetoric had egalitarian overtones. Many peasants wanted to convert land owned by speculators into some variety of communal tenure—like copyhold in England, rundale in Ireland, and runrig in Scotland—that gave peasants control of land use. A high percentage of Regulators were Ulster Presbyterians and former indentured servants. They claimed that occupancy of unsurveyed land conveyed permanent cultivation rights.

In North Carolina in the 1770s, land was not taxed. Poll taxes supplied more than 80 percent of the revenues of colonial and county governments; and poll taxation meant that land-less peasants paid a disproportionately high percentage of the cost of governance. Somewhere between 20 and 30 percent of cultivating households were landless. Landless peasants were probably a majority of the population in frontier counties. A high percentage of frontier residents were squatters. Squatting was a way of escaping the poll tax. Resistance to poll taxation was supported by many dissenting clergymen who objected to tax revenues being used to support the Anglican clergy. The rebellion was suppressed by armed force.

Warped Commercialization

In the twenty years following 1680, annual tobacco production doubled from fourteen million pounds to about thirty million pounds; and from 1700 to 1750 production steadily increased from thirty million pounds to eighty-five million pounds. During these years, the most energetic landowners in tidewater counties began assembling large land units. American usage calls them plantations. They were, in fact, agricultural factories using indentured and slave labor. After 1680, plantation owners increased their purchase of slaves because slaves were a permanent labor force from whom they could coerce commercial labor norms. At the same time, they began dispensing with indentured servants, lifetime leaseholders, and sharecroppers because it was difficult to induce them to perform commercial labor norms.

Plantation overseers and drivers supervised gangs of slave laborers who cultivated tobacco crops much more carefully and in larger per capita amounts than white peasants. Supervised slave labor performed about 40 percent more per capita agricultural labor than white peasants (sharecroppers, leaseholders, and landowners). Even with average low prices after 1680, efficiently managed slave labor made plantation owners rich.

In 1705 Virginia's population was about 64,000, including 4,000 servants and about 6,000 slaves (9% of the population). The census of 1705 counted about 6,500 landowners. This is a small number of landowners for the number of white males who paid the poll tax. By 1710 slaves accounted for about 25 percent of the population of Virginia and Maryland, and by 1775 they were about 35 percent of the population.[18]

In Chesapeake society, there were thus two opposite reasons for owning land and two opposite motivations for owning slaves. First, plantation owners used slave labor to increase their incomes because their management skills coerced commercial labor norms from them. Profit margins were further increased because slaves were forcibly kept at a subsistence level of welfare. Second, upper strata peasants, who were usually landowners, purchased slaves to transfer subsistence labor to them. Slaves performed disproportionately large amounts of agricultural labor that allowed them to live a life of subsistence indolence. This is the *warped commercialization* of the Chesapeake Bay society.

After 1700, the large investments in slaves by commercially motivated landowners had four results:

1. Fewer lifetime and sharecrop leases were made to white peasants because land was more efficiently cultivated by slaves.
2. The greater efficiency of supervised slave labor was the opportunity for plantation owners to achieve economies of scale.
3. In tidewater counties the number of peasant landowners declined because plantation owners bought their land when it became available and added it to their holdings.
4. Reduced electorates in tidewater counties made governance more manageable by the governing elite.

In 1730 plantation owners finally got the Virginia assembly to pass a warehouse law. It required the construction of public warehouses throughout Virginia. Under its provisions, all tobacco used in payment of taxes or debts had to be delivered for inspection. If the tobacco was found acceptable, it was graded into several qualities and receipts issued. If it was found inferior, the law authorized inspectors to seize and burn it; and this was done in substantial amounts. Peasant cultivators strongly disliked the law because inspectors issued receipts based on quality, not weight, and because there were inspection fees. The Maryland assembly passed a similar law in 1747. Tobacco warehouse receipts circulated as money until storekeepers, who were often tobacco exporters, accumulated them and exchanged them for manufactured products arriving from England.

Plantation owners also made concerted efforts to load ships as soon as possible after arrival because shortened turn-around times lessened the cost of transportation and increased profits. By 1750, plantation grown tobacco was recognized as a superior product that sold for premium prices compared with tobacco grown by peasant landowners and tenants. Commercial labor norms coerced from slaves, economies of scale, and quality control in harvesting, preparation, and shipping allowed Virginia and Maryland tobacco to capture the bulk of the European market when it was re-exported from Britain.

Between 1771 and 1775, the American colonies annually exported an average of fifty-five million pounds of tobacco to England and Scotland. An average of forty-six million pounds was re-exported to Europe. Until about 1765, tobacco was the second most valuable agricultural commodity imported into England. Sugar was first. Tea surpassed tobacco after 1765. The reciprocal of the tobacco trade was a visible increase in the wealth of plantation owners in Virginia and Maryland—an increase that was directly attributable to the use of supervised slave laborers who performed commercial labor norms.[19]

By 1775, large plantations were the norm for tobacco cultivation in tidewater and piedmont counties. The author of *American Husbandry*, published in 1775, described the revolution in tobacco cultivation that evolved after 1700. He also described the diversified agriculture being practiced by plantation owners. Wheat began to appear in probate inventories about 1700, but this wheat was for household consumption. After 1740, wheat, like tobacco, was grown for sale on export markets. Almost all of it was grown on plantations where it was a complementary crop to tobacco because the labor demands for winter wheat and tobacco did not overlap.

Wheat was planted in autumn after the tobacco harvest, and harvested the following July before the tobacco harvest began. It was a crop that used slave labor in an otherwise slack interval in the crop year. Hemp was a similar crop. In 1770, wheat was the third most valuable export from Virginia and Maryland; exceeded only by tobacco and naval stores (turpentine, pitch, tar). Other export commodities were flax seed, maize, and beans. This was a radically different labor regime than performed by white peasants. For them the slack season began immediately after the tobacco harvest. Thereafter, minimal amounts of any labor were performed.[20]

Darrett and Anita Rutman describe how, by 1750, the development of plantation agriculture in Virginia and Maryland had stabilized into a highly stratified social structure. Plantation owners visibly increased their wealth in the first half of the eighteenth century, but the peasantry's material welfare was approximately what it had been fifty years previously.

> In the first decade of the eighteenth century, those whose personal estates were such as to place them in the bottom levels of society—roughly two-thirds of the male heads-of-households—owned on average goods valued at no more than the average goods of their compeers of the seventeenth century…In the first decades of the eighteenth century, the distance between the poorest sort and the uppermost economic levels almost doubled. By mid-century, the county-oriented families were on average thirty times as wealthy as the poorest, and the great cosmopolitan families well over a hundred times.[21]

By 1750 the social structure of Virginia and Maryland was clear. There was a governing elite consisting of larger plantation owners or their nominees who conducted colonial governance. County governing elites were composed of plantation owners and yeomen cultivators. Yeomen cultivators labored at about the same efficiency as slaves and produced tobacco in about the same per capita amounts. They also produced some maize, hemp, flaxseed, or wood products for market sale.

Peasants were at the bottom of the social order, and they were highly stratified. Landowners who often owned one or two slaves occupied the first tier. Below them were life leaseholders and sharecroppers, and below them were indentured servants. Negro slaves were the lowermost members of the stratified peasantry. Richard R. Beeman's study of Lunenburg County, Virginia, *The Evolution of the Southern Backcountry*, clearly describes a stratified peasantry that persisted with no great changes from 1760 to 1830.

> We wonder what qualitative benefits ordinary planters were receiving from their larger slave forces and tobacco crops (because) the quality of material life seems to have changed hardly at all….Their ownership of slaves allowed them to generate the profits that

promoted investment in still more slaves and a few additional consumer goods…but in general we are struck by the continuities of material life (that created) a life of self-sufficiency.[22]

Between 1760 and 1830, about 25 percent of white households in Lunenburg County owned no land and about 40 percent of white households owned no slaves. During these same years, the average size of peasant landholdings steadily decreased because land units were divided among sons. Smaller landholdings had to be more intensively cultivated, which usually meant more land had to be plowed, but the social purpose of land use and labor was unchanged. Only as much labor was performed as was necessary to achieve an acceptable level of subsistence welfare.

Literacy

What was the social value of literacy in the stratified peasantry of Virginia and Maryland? The best judges of its value were the justices sitting on county courts. They performed numerous functions that affected the entire community. The most common were adjudicating contested debts, fixing disputed land boundaries, appointing juries to render a verdict for misdemeanors (civil and criminal), assessing local taxes, and supervising the collection of taxes, especially the poll tax.

Other functions were registering land titles and leases, probating wills, recommending tobacco inspectors for appointment by the governor, maintaining roads, choosing contractors to build bridges and other public works, licensing taverns, licensing water powered mills (grist saw), registering apprentice indentures, providing assistance to resident indigents (widows, old men, orphans), and conducting elections to the assembly. Levying taxes to support primary education was not one of their duties.

The surviving records of county courts indicate that the white peasant electorate had little interest in paying taxes to establish common schools to teach functional literacy. These records indicate that justices concerned themselves with literacy only when they (1) investigated the conduct of trustees of estates left to small children to ascertain if they had been taught literacy as part of their duties as trustees; or (2) investigated the conduct of artisans and tradesmen to ascertain if literacy had been taught to apprentices as required by indentures. Otherwise, acquisition of literacy was almost exclusively a private affair.

A statement made by Governor William Berkeley in 1671 summarizes the indifference of Virginia's governing elite to actively exerting their authority to levy sufficient taxes to establish common schools in parishes that could teach functional literacy to the children of freemen (white peasants).

I thank God there are no free schools nor printing, and I hope we shall not have these (for a) hundred years; for learning has brought disobedience, and heresy, and sects into the world, and printing has divulged them, and libels against the best government.

During the entire colonial period: "It was clear that with negligible exceptions the parishes in colonial Virginia did not aid in the education of their children by establishing schools, by paying for instruction in private schools, or by furnishing community school buildings." Only two free elementary schools and six grammar schools (charging tuition) were established in Virginia before 1789, with another in Maryland. This compares to New York (with its much smaller population) that had eleven grammar schools and Massachusetts with twenty-three.[23]

The lowermost and uppermost strata of Virginia's and Maryland's social structure are easily identified. The lowermost strata was occupied by negro slaves. They were forcibly deprived of opportunities to acquire literacy because illiteracy made them easier to manage. The uppermost strata belonged to the governing elite. They placed a high value on literacy because they could not govern without it. Their children and their neighbor's children were often taught by a resident tutor or by the clergymen of the Anglican parish, if he resided nearby. Only the children of the governing elite attended grammar schools (academies).

The rest of the white population was somewhere in between. It was essential for commerce that yeomen landowners, skilled artisans, storekeepers, and tobacco inspectors be functionally literate. Functional literacy is the ability to "perform all activities for which literacy is required. (It) enables persons to use reading, writing, and arithmetic calculations to perform labor that is for their benefit and that also contributes to their community's welfare."[24]

Yeomen landowners and plantation owners measured their social security by money incomes from the sale of tobacco, livestock, other agricultural and forest products. Most of the labor on their land was performed by the five to one hundred slaves they owned. They had to be literate to continually market surplus products. Skilled artisans and storekeepers living in villages and towns had to be functionally literate to keep accounts. Skilled artisans were blacksmiths, wheelwrights, ships carpenters, tanners, brick makers, operators of water powered mills (grist and saw), and printers.

Functional literacy was often taught by resident or itinerant schoolmasters licensed by the governor's council. Parents often paid skilled artisans to accept their sons as apprentices but specified that they must be instructed "in the art of writing and to teach him the science of arithmetic." Other apprenticeship indentures required two or three years of instruction sufficient to read a chapter in the Bible and the Lord's Prayer, but this was often qualified, "if a school master was to be found in the parish."[25]

Artisans with lesser skills may or may not have been literate. These skills were house carpenters, bricklayers, weavers, tailors, shoemakers, and coopers. They learned their skills by being apprenticed at the age of seven or eight. In the eighteenth century, lesser skilled artisans were increasingly dispersed to slaveholding plantations because the largest plantation owners tried to make their plantations into self-sufficient agricultural factories. When lesser artisans resided on plantations they were often paid to teach their skills to slaves. Literacy was not essential for slave artisans because they did not sell their products on an anonymous market.

Between 1640 and 1700, about 45 percent of freemen were literate enough to sign their names to deeds and other legal documents. Between 1700 and 1745, the percentage of signature literacy among cultivating males increased to about 65 percent. *Did the ability to sign your name equal the ability to read, write, and calculate in situations where literacy was required?* The lack of books in probate inventories of freemen cultivators (ex-indentured servants), compared to probate inventories in the New England colonies, indicates that many males who signed their names were illiterate.

Literacy was not essential for most peasant landowners, lifetime leaseholders, and sharecrop tenants because storekeepers, neighboring plantation owners, export merchants, or inspectors at district tobacco warehouses could conduct business transactions for them using money of account. Money of account had many names during the seventeenth and eighteenth centuries. Among them were commodity money, bookkeeping barter, bills of exchange payable in kind, contracts partly in cash and partly in credit, contracts in a stable currency, and warehouse receipts.[26]

Richard R. Beeman summarizes the peasantry's indifference to literacy and their minimal commitment to commerce.

> In common with the rest of the commonwealth, tidewater and backcountry alike, Lunenburg's citizens continued to display a nearly complete unconcern for public education. In spite of the high-sounding proposals of such luminaries as Thomas Jefferson,...Virginia's

political leaders did almost nothing to…educate the youth of the state. Belatedly, in 1796, the General Assembly passed legislation that would have enabled each county to establish its own public school system, but it left the funding of that plan up to the counties themselves, a provision which doomed public education in virtually every county in the commonwealth.[27]

Lee Soltow and Edward Stevens confirm Beeman's evidence. They found little interest in southern colonies to teach universal functional literacy. They estimate that the illiteracy rate of whites was 40 to 50 percent in 1800. For both governors and the governed, teaching of functional literacy had a low political and social priority. The physical evidence for southern indifference is the absence of schoolhouses in the rural landscape. Southern indifference to teaching literacy compares with the strenuous efforts made by the governing elites of northern colonies to teach functional literacy to rural residents, even during the hardships and isolation of frontier settlement.

Summary

In the seventeenth century, the productive capacity of Virginia and Maryland was largely dependent on the labor of indentured servants. They were peasants who were escaping from districts in Britain where landowners were in the process of commercializing agriculture. The principal motive for immigration was avoiding the necessity of performing full-time paid labor for the rest of their lives. They sought opportunities to practice subsistence cultivation in America because commercial agriculture in England deprived them of land use. Put another way, the abundance of land in America was an opportunity for displaced peasants to own or control land use that would allow them to practice subsistence labor norms. Immigration was an opportunity to transfer their peasant status to America.

Displaced English peasants had two problems: *How to arrive in America?* and *How to acquire land after arrival?* They could get to America by becoming indentured servants. The incentive to sign indentures and risk crossing the Atlantic was the knowledge that they could acquire ownership of land from the public domain after they became freemen. During their indentures, they performed commercial labor norms as they did in England when they were servants in husbandry. It was done with reluctance because it was necessary if they were to become landowners or landholders in America.

A high percentage of freemen, however, never became landowners because they could gain control of land use without ownership. Lifetime leases and annual sharecrop contracts were available from large landowners because they wanted land cleared preparatory to planting larger tobacco crops. Leasehold and sharecrop tenures made it possible for freemen to bargain to make minimal improvements because land was abundant and labor scarce. With these options, freemen did not have to accumulate money in order to gain control of land use.

Indentured servants, however, were an unpredictable and unstable supply of agricultural labor. The prosperity of Maryland and Virginia in the eighteenth century required many more commercially motivated cultivators. This did not happen because Virginia and Maryland did not attract enough yeomen cultivators to perform commercial labor norms; and most freemen rejected performing commercial labor norms after they completed their indentures. As long as most freemen could perform subsistence labor norms on land they owned, leased, or sharecropped, Virginia and Maryland could not produce commercial wealth to the potential of its soil.

The rapid increase in the number of negro slaves in the eighteenth century America helped solve the labor problem for commercially motivated cultivators because slaves were permanent agricultural laborers. No longer were plantation owners dependent on an unstable supply of indentured servants. Furthermore, slaves could be physically coerced to perform commercial labor norms, which could not be done with freemen who were landowners, leaseholders, and sharecroppers.

Plantation owners and yeomen owned a high percentage of slaves and their prosperity was a direct result of the development of management skills that coerced commercial labor norms from slaves. The commercial labor norms of slaves formed the basis for the highly visible prosperity of plantation agriculture in Virginia and Maryland during the eighteenth century. Their labor produced a disproportionately high percentage of tobacco and other export commodities. Although white peasants were a majority of the population of Virginia and Maryland during the eighteenth century, their per capita production of marketable commodities was far less than per capita production by slaves living on plantations, and it was far less than per capita production by yeomen in northern colonies.

In order to retain power, the governing elites of southern colonies had to govern by the consent of all landowners and leaseholders. This meant that governing elites had to accede to peasant interests in matters of taxation. Peasants wanted low taxation because it minimized the labor needed to acquire the requisite money (tobacco warehouse receipts or money of account with storekeepers). The governing elites of southern colonies acceded to this policy because the consent of white peasants was necessary to retain the power of governance.

The desires for low taxation extended to the acquisition of literacy because tax funded common schools are expensive. Low taxation directly translated into high rates of illiteracy in Virginia and Maryland. It equally applied to other southern colonies that attracted the overwhelming majority of indentured servants. As long as peasant households had the services of literate storekeepers who could conduct their business transactions, they were indifferent to acquiring functional literacy. Two other results of low taxation were inadequate investments in infrastructure projects and a small number of villages and cities.

The low per capita amounts of marketable commodities produced by white peasants in southern colonies, and the high per capita amounts of marketable commodities produced by yeomen in northern colonies has remained almost invisible to historians and economists. The lack of comparative analysis of per capita marketable commodities is based on a wrong assumption. A high percentage of contemporary U. S. historians and almost all economists assume that emigration from Britain during the colonial era was motivated by a search for commercial opportunities.

This assumption disregards huge amounts of evidence that a high percentage of emigration from Britain during the colonial era was a search for subsistence opportunities; and that the legacy of this immigration was the persistence of huge numbers of peasants (cotton and tobacco sharecroppers) into the mid-twentieth century. The assumption that all European immigrant cultivators practiced commercial labor norms from the day of their arrival in American seriously distorts U.S. history. When this is pointed out to historians and economists, the response is extreme silence.

Chapter 3

Agriculture in the Northern Colonies

Most of the initial immigrants to New England, New York, and Pennsylvania shared ten characteristics:

1. They were commercially motivated.
2. A high percentage had not worked in agriculture in England (probably less than one-third in New England). Most, however, had been born in rural villages and had participated in cultivation during their youth.
3. They emigrated to larger villages and cities where they practiced artisan and commercial skills with varying degrees of competency and they had achieved varying degrees of prosperity.
4. They were motivated by a strong religious commitment that generated an equally strong commitment to perform the labor that was necessary for their American communities to survive.
5. Probably more than three-quarters of male immigrants were functionally literate, with a smaller percentage able to keep accounts.
6. Somewhere between two-thirds and three-quarters were members of the English middle class.
7. Somewhere between one-half and three-quarters paid their passage and brought with them agricultural implements and sufficient food to insure survival for one year or longer after arrival.
8. Most came as family groups.
9. Indentured servants were a small percentage of immigrants and they were usually in the service of a family they knew in England.
10. They immediately founded cities because cities were essential for duplicating the commercial culture they left in England.

In other words, a high percentage of initial immigrants had accumulated sufficient possessions in England that could be sold to pay their passage to America with enough additional money to purchase the agricultural implements necessary to establish homesteads. Almost certainly these households were literate and commercially motivated. The high literacy rate of immigrating families was a coproduct of the educational revolution that was concurrent with the commercialization of English agriculture.

These immigrants knew they had to feed themselves immediately after arrival, as well as produce export commodities. This meant that they had to make wood products, preserve fish and meat, and produce flour or other food grains for export markets because they had no staple crop like tobacco. Alternatively, they had to build furnaces to produce bar iron (using charcoal fuel that was scarce in England) or build ships for sale to English merchants in England, or to carry American commodities to England, Caribbean colonies, and southern Europe.

The response of most immigrants to New England and Pennsylvania was very different from most immigrants to Virginia, Maryland, and other southern colonies. Most initial immigrants to New England and Pennsylvania embraced the commercialization of culture in England, including agriculture. A high percentage had obtained social security in England by earning money incomes. They had no argument with the commercializing policies of the English government. Their grievance was the attempt by the English government to enforce religious uniformity. In all other respects, a high percentage of them, and especially their leaders, had been at the cutting edge of commercializing policies in England, especially at the local level, where it was enforced.

David H. Fischer uses five indices to measure the middle class origins of a high percentage of immigrants to New England: (1) a high percentage came as families, (2) a low percentage came as indentured servants, (3) a high percentage had been city and village residents, (4) a high percentage paid their way and brought agricultural implements and other possessions with them, and (5) a high percentage were literate. Literacy was especially prominent in the Plymouth colony where at least two printers were among the initial settlers.

Pioneer Agriculture

Darrett B. Rutman's study of the pioneering agriculture of Pilgrim settlers at Plymouth indicates that most households had been city residents in Europe. During the first ten years in America, the welfare of most cultivating households was near subsistence, but their subsistence was due to the rigors of pioneering, not a commitment to subsistence labor norms. During these years, cultivating households had to clear sufficient land for food crops, learn new techniques of cultivation, and accumulate livestock and plows. The initial settlers brought neither livestock nor plows with them. Plymouth settlers did not possess plows until twelve years after settlement. In addition to performing agricultural labor during pioneering years, they had to produce sufficient amounts of marketable commodities for the colony to survive.

Plymouth settlers soon discovered that rye was the only European grain that produced consistent yields; and it had to be planted in plowed fields. There were few stump-free fields that could be plowed. The alternative was cultivating maize as their principal food grain. They learned the technique of maize cultivation from Indians. Like cultivators in Virginia and Maryland, shifting cultivation was the principal technique used during the pioneering years. Maize was planted among tree stumps on widely spaced mounds made with hoes. After its stalks were knee high, a vine habit bean was planted on the mounds. They climbed the maize stalks and stumps and produced easily harvestable pods, as well as producing vines that were excellent winter forage for livestock.

At the same time that vine habit beans were planted, ground creeping squash vines were planted. They were usually varieties that preserved well during the winter (pumpkins). They grew among the mounds. Maize yields were low, but the bean and squash intercrops produced substantial additional harvests.

What is the evidence for Pilgrim households transforming themselves into yeomen cultivators? As soon as the permanence of Plymouth was secure, each household was allocated twenty acres of land in freehold tenure, with additional allocations at later dates; and tidewater meadows were also allocated to households. Thereafter, Plymouth cultivators produced an assured food surplus for sale on an anonymous market in Boston (or for export). In 1627 a bushel of grain (mostly maize) was given a fixed money value. Thereafter, a bushel of grain was legal tender for all debts because there were insufficient coins for a circulating medium. Massachusetts Bay followed this precedent in 1631. Nonetheless, all accounts were denominated in money. Although the grain surplus produced by the two hundred residents of Plymouth was small, it was a valuable contribution to the food needs of the initial settlers of Massachusetts Bay in 1630. It also alleviated seasonal hunger in Virginia in 1631 and 1634.

Massachusetts was settled by Puritans in a meticulously planned operation. It began in 1630 with the departure of seventeen ships from England carrying about one hundred passengers each. Each ship was self-contained with food for one year, seeds for the first crops, and livestock to form the nucleus of breeding herds. Between 1630 and 1641, about two hundred ships sailed to Massachusetts carrying immigrants. In these eleven years, about twenty-one thousand persons made the voyage. After 1641, immigration slowed to a trickle because most Puritans remained in England where they supported Parliament's army in the civil war that they believed was a heaven sent opportunity to remodel the Anglican church root and branch.

During the first ten years of settlement, most households lived a little above subsistence welfare, but after the pioneering period New England towns did not experience seasonal hunger. In fact, they exported large amounts of foodstuffs. Twenty thousand bushels of grain were exported in 1654, but the main exports were preserved fish, preserved meat, and wood products. Preserved fish, especially cod, was an export commodity that compared favorably to tobacco exports from Virginia as a source of prosperity.

Not only was the Puritan migration well organized, but it was a highly selective slice of English society. There were a very high percentage of literate males and few indentured servants. Most immigrants were willing agricultural laborers. David H. Fisher summarizes: the founders of Massachusetts "deliberately eliminated both the top and bottom strata of the East Anglican social order, and at the same time carefully preserved its middling distinctions." The three ranks in English culture that provided most of the immigrants were the lesser gentry, yeomen, and cottagers. These people worked with their hands to perform commercial labor norms. They willingly accepted the risks of colonization because it was an opportunity to improve their status, relative to their status in England. They expected to be rewarded for their labor with ownership of land but they did not expect to become rich.[1]

Stephen Innes accurately describes the commitment to manual labor that motivated most immigrants to New England—a commitment that was essential for creating a social structure where households would share opportunities to own land in proportion to their labor and skills. "Virginia's mistakes in labor recruitment were precisely the ones the Puritans were eager to avoid." The Virginians "used unfit instruments, a multitude of rude and misgoverned persons, the very scum of the land…instead of relying on godly, sober, and disciplined laborers." The commitment to manual labor in New England established a stable social order within a decade.[2]

Allocation of Land

Like Virginia and Maryland, there was an intimate connection between land acquisition and governance, but the method of conveying land to cultivators was radically different. The earliest grants in New England were to voluntary groups that petitioned the colonial government to settle a specific tract of wilderness. To insure clear title, colonial governments purchased it from Indians or authorized a group of settlers to purchase it from them. Land was allocated to these groups as large blocks and called a town. Members of the group were the town's proprietors. Proprietors were the sole owners of the undivided land and had the power to allocate it among themselves or to other households that were acceptable to them. All allocated land was in freehold tenure.

Town proprietors always had leaders who were instrumental in securing land grants, organizing nuclear villages, recruiting the services of a blacksmith, grist/saw miller, wheelwright, minister, and teacher, as well as recruiting people who were capable of organizing the construction of a meetinghouse, organizing defense, and laying out roads. Town leaders were also authorized to organize town governments.

Land grants were conditional on occupancy. The initial allocations were subsistence sized and were in a compact group. After allocations were made, they were surveyed and titles recorded in the town registry. Initial allocations were always centered on a meetinghouse that served as a place of worship and a place of governance by town meetings.

Nucleated villages had three purposes: (1) defend against possible Indian attacks, (2) facilitate the exchange of labor among households during the pioneering period, and (3) induce households to practice intensive cultivation by creating plow lands as soon as possible. Plowed ground produced higher sustainable yields and more predictable harvests.

Initial land allocations were in two parcels: (1) a house lot of two to five acres that was large enough to plant an orchard and cultivate a garden, and (2) cultivation units that varied between ten and twenty acres. Cultivation units were usually in a common field that was fenced as soon as possible. Fence viewers were responsible for mobilizing the labor to build and maintain fences so that they were sufficiently high and strong to exclude livestock that grazed, browsed, or rooted on unallocated land. Ground within fenced fields was planted in food grains or root crop; or were meadows from which hay was harvested to feed plow oxen and milch cows during the winter. Within common fields, households had to coordinate ground preparation (hoeing around stumps, plowing), planting, and harvesting.

In the earliest towns during pioneering years, land allocations were usually made by elected selectmen and ratified by town meetings. Allocations were made to men "according to their estates and persons." They were never equal. Variable sized allocations were based on political and economic rank among the proprietors.

Second and later land allocations were larger and at distant locations from nuclear villages. Like the initial allocations, they were of variable size. They were made on the basis of need (size of families) and on the services that families provided the town. If an original proprietor lived long enough, he would be allocated seven or eight scattered parcels that totaled between fifty and one hundred hectares (one hundred twenty-five and two hundred-fifty acres). These scattered parcels were converted into rough pastures after the timber on it was cut and made into semi-finished wood products or chopped into firewood. The more distant pastures were then allocated to sons upon marriage who converted them into plow land. The largest allocations were never disproportionately large relative to allocations to other households. Put in another perspective, there were few rich cultivators in New England towns.

During the first and second generations of settlement, new immigrants or outside households could petition selectmen to become town residents and be allocated land. These households had to be acceptable to selectmen and own sufficient cultivation implements and livestock to establish a household or possess artisan skills needed by the community. Alternatively, households that were acceptable to town residents were allowed to purchase land. By the third generation, however, town meetings generally stopped allocating land to outside households because the grandchildren of the original proprietors needed unallocated land for their children.

By 1660 some men began specializing in organizing frontier towns and by 1700 it was a business. A partnership developed between active partners and passive investors. Active partners were usually Indian traders who were familiar with the agricultural potential of frontier land or men with military experience who could organize defense. Indian traders spoke the languages of the tribes and could negotiate purchases. Passive partners were often members of the governing elite. They supplied money to purchase the land from the Indians, survey town boundaries and the internal boundaries of land allocated to the active and passive partners, or the boundaries of homestead sold to actual settlers.

After 1700 New England governments began using the public domain as a source of revenue. Syndicates of speculators petitioned the assembly to open frontier lands for settlement by auctioning land in town-sized units (approximately thirty-six square miles: ninety square kilometers). Purchase was on three years credit. Immediately after a syndicate gained title, the land was surveyed and divided among the proprietors on the basis of the amount of money each pledged toward the purchase price.

Each proprietor received a share of fertile land, meadows (if any), and uplands. The rest of the land was surveyed into twenty hectare (fifty acre) units for sale (often on credit) to the sons of families from established towns. Many, but not all of the proprietors, moved onto the most fertile land and began pioneering cultivation. Not only did pioneering households have money (or credit), they also had cultivating implements and livestock. The money (or credit) to become frontier landowners came from parents who had saved it from the sale of commodities or by performing artisan or craft skills. The demand for land was continuous because of high birthrates. Several demographic studies of the earliest towns to 1750, indicate that the average number of children born to married couples was between 4.7 and 7.0; and child mortalities were exceptionally low.[3]

After 1720 speculators in frontier land were usually merchants. They seldom settled in the frontier towns they helped establish. Their reward was a share of undivided land that could be sold to actual settlers. To retain ownership they had to recruit enough settlers to form a town government. Land would not appreciate in value until the town was settled. If a town was not settled to the satisfaction of the governor, the land would revert to the government. It was often in the interests of speculators to pay households to be initial settlers as a means of confirming their titles to their share of undivided land.

Colonial governors recognized the public service performed by land speculators who were able to recruit actual settlers on frontier land, lay out roads, plat villages, and convey compact land units to settlers with freehold titles. They were also careful to prevent the accumulation of large tracts of wilderness land by a few individuals. As long as the public domain existed, it was used to perpetuate a stable social order by equalizing land owning opportunities among the sons of New England yeomen.

Commercial Motivation in New England

Survival of all American colonies depended on maritime commerce. Almost from the beginning of settlement, but especially after 1640, New England merchants traded in ships built in New England. Maritime commerce flourished because New England settlers produced a large volume and variety of forest, marine, and livestock products for export, as well as an assured food surplus to feed village craftsmen and artisan manufacturers who produced products for export and local consumption.

Merchants established markets for preserved fish, meat, and wood products in sugar colonies in the Caribbean, southern Europe, and England. Other exports to the Caribbean were oxen, horses, and small amounts of beans, butter, and cheese. On return voyages from the Caribbean, the ships brought molasses and cotton. Alternatively, they carried Caribbean sugar to England and used the profits of the carrying trade to purchase manufactured products for sale in New England. Principal among products exported to England were ships, ship timbers, masts, spars, boards, barrel staves and headings, shingles, tar, and potash. On return voyages from southern Europe they brought salt, wine, and specie.

Probate inventories are one means of confirming the commercial motivation of most New England cultivators because, after 1660, most cultivating households had (1) a full complement of agricultural implements, including plows and harrows; and many households owned carts and a few owned wagons (*wains*); (2) artisan tools and looms to make products for market sale; (3) large amounts of semi-finished products produced during the winter when agricultural labor was minimal; and (4) books (indicating a high rate of literacy).

Possession of carts and wagons is especially indicative of commercial motivation because they were the means of carrying agricultural surpluses and other products to market. The possession of carts and wagons in probate inventories, plus a full array of agricultural implements, is radically different from the probate inventories of most freemen cultivators in seventeenth century Virginia and Maryland. Wagons were nonexistent, carts and plows were rare, as were tools for artisan manufacture.

Jackson T. Main estimates that 20 percent of cultivators among initial immigrants had artisan or craft skills that they practiced on a part-time basis. This is radically different behavior compared to households of illiterate white peasants in Virginia, Maryland, and other southern colonies where only slaves were full-time laborers for twelve month of the year, and where there were relative few yeomen who practiced artisan and craft skills.[4]

Philip J. Greven's *Four Generations* clearly documents that over four generations a high percentage of New England landowners taught their sons artisan and craft skills, and that money transactions were frequent events in the lives of second, third, and fourth generations of yeomen cultivators. Some of the artisan skills yeomen practiced on a part-time basis were weaving, harvesting tanning bark, tanning hides, shoemaking, making barrel staves and headings, making charcoal, or preserving fish and meat for export. Other yeomen cultivators were carpenters, wheelwrights, housewrights (joiners), coopers, brewers, innkeepers, or kept a store of manufactured items to sell to neighbors with payments being made in grain, semi-finished wood products, or cloth.

A successful New England storekeeper might expand his activities into land speculation by purchasing the small land units allocated to town proprietors during the initial years of settlement when defense required settlement in nucleated villages. These small parcels were sold to households that wanted to consolidate land into compact farms. By all accounts, during the first fifty or sixty years of settlement, there was an immense amount of commerce in land because most of the sons and grandsons of original town proprietors wanted compact farms on which to build new houses.

Another indication of the commercial motivation that pervaded New England in the seventeenth century was the increasing percentage of its population who were employed as full-time laborers in the production of marine and forest products, shipbuilding, and iron smelting. The ability of cultivators to feed these people so soon after settlement in all crop years is very good evidence for commercial labor norms applied to agriculture.

An additional indication of commercial motivation was the frequency of fences. During the initial years of settlement, boy herdsmen prevented livestock from foraging in planted fields. Livestock foraged, browsed, and rooted in woodlands because custom made woodlands a communal resource to feed a community's livestock (as in Virginia and Maryland). The next step in pioneering was building a common fence to enclose the cultivated fields of nuclear villages.

This practice reduced the amount of labor required for fencing and allowed more labor to be applied to clearing land and producing marketed commodities. Within fenced fields households had to coordinate planting and harvests, so that after the harvest livestock could graze on the stubble and gain some fat before the onset of winter.

Common fences were also erected around meadows where hay was cut to feed plow oxen during the winter so they were strong enough for spring plowing. Milch cows were also fed during the winter so that families would have a continuous supply of milk and butter. In order to produce milk during the winter, milch cows had to be fed with harvested hay and forage crops. This was labor that most freemen cultivators in Virginia and Maryland did not do.

Commonly fenced fields did not usually persist into the third generation because yeomen households wanted individually fenced fields, even though fences were labor intensive to build. Fences gave them full control over land use so that they could cultivate forage crops. Cultivated forage crops were necessary to feed penned hogs during the year and cattle and oxen during the winter.

New England households had more per capita livestock than freemen in Virginia and Maryland. Livestock were a significant source of income for yeomen households in interior towns because animals could be walked to market. In the late autumn they were slaughtered and their meat barreled in brine or smoked for export; in addition large amounts of fish were brined, dried, or dry salted for export. During the seventeenth and eighteenth centuries, preserved meat and fish were minor export products from Virginia and Maryland; although, the larger populations of the Chesapeake colonies could have produced very large amounts from the fertile waters of Chesapeake Bay, if sufficient labor had been expended.

The structure of household debts is also strong additional evidence for the commercial motivation of most cultivating households. There were two tiers of debts in New England towns. A high percentage of households made loans to neighbors. These debts were for the exchange of products and labor with the expectation that most of these debts would cancel. The second tier of debts was to storekeepers and skilled craftsmen like blacksmiths. Yeomen, who were continuous producers and sellers of food grains, livestock, marine, forest, and artisan products, continually paid their debts to storekeepers. Storekeepers, millers, and craftsmen accumulated commodities and sold them for money on anonymous markets.

The continuous production and sale of these products by New England households produced sufficient income to sustain a network of credit among town residents. This was commercial credit. Put another way, as long as a household had a money income (denominated in commodity prices), it could choose the neighbors and storekeepers with whom it did business. A choice of where to do business is a sure indication of commercial motivation.

Peasant households in Virginia and Maryland did not have this choice. They were clients of storekeepers, plantation owners, or export merchants who supplied them with manufactured products during the year. In return for subsistence credit, client household had to market all of their exchange commodity crops (tobacco) with that storekeeper, plantation owner, or export merchant. Marketing tobacco was a one-time annual event because white peasants produced few other saleable products during the rest of the year and refused to perform paid labor except by necessity.

Literacy was essential for New England yeomen because they: (1) marketed over half of their crops, (2) produced substantial amounts of household manufactured products for sale on anonymous markets, (3) performed large amounts of part-time paid labor as craftsmen. The money earned from these activities was used to purchase cultivation implements for their sons, if they moved onto some of their father's land, or to purchase frontier land after marriage. Money was also the means of purchasing manufactured products (imported or made by local artisans) and paying for the services of local craftsmen.

Greven's study of Andover, Massachusetts indicates that the average age of marriage is congruent with commercial motivation. In the second generation, he found that the average age of marriage for males was 27.1 years and for females 22.8 years. Marriage was delayed because parents wanted the labor of their sons during the rigors of pioneering. Only after parental land was in full production could sons marry with the expectation of receiving land and implements to cultivate it. Upon marriage, a male received cultivation rights to a parcel of his father's pasture land that could be converted to cultivation; and the bride's family contributed livestock and cultivation implements. Marriages were often arranged.

The youngest son would inherit the home farm. After a son received parental land, he had full use of harvests in order to raise a family but he did not usually get legal title to it until his father died and he inherited it. During these years he was a landholder rather than landowner, but he was no longer a dependent and was, therefore, entitled to participate in town governance.

The land needs of other sons were satisfied by migration. They went to new towns on the western and northern frontiers. Migrant households had to have enough money (or credit) to purchase land. Sometimes the frontier was only one town away, if a new town was organized by the proprietors of an adjacent town. All settlers in new towns had to bring one year's food supply and enough agricultural implements and livestock to establish homesteads. The possession of money (or credit), agricultural implements, and livestock by pioneering households is solid evidence for commercial motivation.

Finally, the absence of seasonal hunger and longevity of pioneer families strongly indicates the commercial motivation of most households. John Demos's and Philip J. Greven's studies of demography, family structure, and commercial activity of households in Plymouth and Andover from initial settlement to the mid-eighteenth century indicate low rates of infant and child mortality and that persons who lived to the age of twenty-one could expect to live into their mid-sixties or longer. This longevity is comparable to contemporary commercial cultures. A principal cause of longevity was good nutrition that was the result of commercial labor norms in cultivation that produced assured food surpluses in all crop years.[5]

Governance

A common phrase used in the earliest town records was "ordered and agreed by the inhabitants of the town." During the first decades of pioneering, the usual practice was to delegate governance to elected selectmen so that households could concentrate their labor on the necessities of subsistence. Selectmen were a Massachusetts version of the select vestrymen that governed Anglican parishes in East Anglia in England. During the pioneer decades, selectman in Massachusetts usually had long tenures in office. This was acceptable because selectmen of the first and second generations administered consensus government.

In the pioneer years, there was no clear distinction between governance and land ownership because almost all households were landowners. The freehold tenure of all allocations made all recipients "at once a landlord and a tax payer." Town meetings were proprietor meetings. In the town of Sudbury, Massachusetts between 1639 and 1656, 132 town meetings issued more than 650 orders that were "agreed by the town." Forty-five percent were about allocation of land or how undivided land should be used, 35 percent dealt with town governance, and 9 percent involved taxation, especially corvée labor (unpaid labor) to build and maintain roads, build a meetinghouse, and construct a bridge.[6]

Landownership was the basis for taxation in New England towns. The bulk of a town's revenue came from a general property tax on improved land. Livestock, personal property, and inventories of storekeepers and artisan craftsmen were also taxed. Undivided land or land reverting to secondary forest (brush pasture) was not taxed. Landowners paid five tax rates: one for the town, one for the county (after counties were established), one for the colonial government, one to support the minister, and one to support primary education.

Poll taxes were levied in Massachusetts and Connecticut on males sixteen years and older; and after 1640 excise taxes were levied on retailers of liquor and beer and on imported wines and liquor. Excise taxes supplied about one-third of the revenues for colonial governance. Revenue from poll and excise taxes was not shared with towns. In addition, in time of Indian threats or war there was a military tax. Compared to Virginia and Maryland, the inhabitants of New England towns were highly taxed, and taxation was by consent.

New England governments delegated the assessment and collection of all taxes to the towns. All towns elected someone who listed all of the landowners who were eligible for taxation and a constable who helped collect taxes. Frequently, this person was also the rate maker (assessor). New England settlers could not have paid the taxes levied on them by their elected officials unless they were commercially motivated, had a strong sense of community purpose, and a willingness to share the labor needed to build commercial infrastructure projects.

The largest tax source in New England—property tax—was radically different from that of Virginia and Maryland because most New England households were landowners. In Virginia and Maryland, the poll tax was the principal source of revenue for county and colonial governance because there was a high percentage of indentured servants, landless freemen (sharecroppers, leaseholders), and slaves who would otherwise escape taxation if a land tax was the principal source of revenue.

Like Virginia and Maryland, landownership was the basis for voting. During the initial years of settlement in the earliest towns, there was no distinction between landownership and voting because most households were landowning proprietors. About 1680, voting in town meetings was restricted to inhabitants. Inhabitants were landowners or skilled artisans who were heads of households that had a permanent interest in a town's welfare. Transients without property or artisan skills were excluded.

As soon as a town was firmly established, which meant building a meetinghouse and supporting a clergyman, it could petition for representation in the colonial assembly. The franchise for electing delegates to colonial assemblies was different than for electing town selectmen. Voters had to be freemen. The original freemen were stockholders in the Massachusetts Bay Company who immigrated to Massachusetts. Only freemen could vote to annually elect a governor, assistant governor, delegates to the assembly, and other colonial officeholders. One year after settlement (1631) the general court (company government) restricted freemen to church members (visible saints). Creating an electorate of saints was the means of creating a governing elite that represented consensus. A similar consensus government evolved in Connecticut.

Three years later (1634) the general court assumed the authority to admit new freemen, and in 1642 the assembly delegated the authority to county courts in order to enlarge the electorate. This was essential in order to convert the corporate government of the Massachusetts Bay Company into the civil government of colonial Massachusetts.[7]

Besides being church members and permanent town residents, freemen had to be landowners and substantial taxpayers. They could not be dependent on others for their welfare. Persons disqualified from taking the freeman oath were transients, tenants, and bachelor sons of landowners who were not yet settled on their own land. During the first sixty years of settlement, somewhere between 60 and 75 percent of landowners could qualify as freemen but only about half bothered to qualify, and only about 50 percent of qualified freemen usually voted for governor and other colonial officeholders. That only half of landowners made the effort to qualify as freemen and that a low percentage of them actually voted indicates they were satisfied with consensus governance.

Katherine Brown interprets the explicit policy of creating towns of landowners as political democracy. In a sense, this is accurate because most households were landowners that carried the right to vote in town governance. All landowners were also committed to the success of their church because it was the glue that held their community together. They were equally committed to landownership for their sons. These commitments were the basis for town governance by consensus; however, consensus governance was not exactly the same as political democracy. It was, however, the closest approximation to it in the seventeenth century.

The New Priority

The new priority was maximizing the production of commercial wealth. This social goal was present from the first settlements in New England but it assumed increasing importance after the rigors of pioneering were past. Coastal towns were the first to evolve a social structure based on increased commercial wealth. The source of that wealth was trans-Atlantic and Caribbean trade.

During the third and fourth generations, the practice of allowing selectmen to manage town affairs underwent gradual and subtle changes. The basis of these changes was the commercial differentiation that evolved in the oldest towns on the coast. When there were disputes, the votes of all men who attended town meetings were counted. Counting the votes of all men who were present was governance by consent.

Governance by consent evolved as the norm when there were choices of political and commercial policies that affected town welfare. Selectmen became managers of policies agreed to by consent instead of being elected to conserve governance by consensus. In effect, an enlarged electorate wanted to use the power of town and colonial governments to promote the production of new commercial wealth instead of preserving religious orthodoxy. In the forty years after 1680, consensus governance imperceptibly replaced governance by consent.

Bernard Bailyn observed this change of social priorities in seaport towns after 1680 where there was declining interest in religious orthodoxy and a strong desire to expand commercial opportunities. New commercial wealth propelled the transition from governance by consensus to governance by consent.

> In the larger port towns of provincial New England, particularly those in continuous touch with Europe, the business community represented the spirit of a new age. Its guiding principles were not social stability, order, and the discipline of the senses, but mobility, growth, and the enjoyment of life.

Commercially energetic men in the third and fourth generations in coastal towns wanted the first priority of governance to be opportunities to earn commercial wealth. What Bailyn observed in coastal towns after 1680 progressively took place in inland towns after the rigors of pioneering were past.[8]

In 1691, when the crown imposed royal governance on Massachusetts, commercially energetic men favored royal governance because it clearly defined an imperial commercial policy that was profitable to Massachusetts merchants. In other words, royal governance of Massachusetts was guided by commercial policies that took precedence over religious orthodoxy. Merchants "considered the advent of a second royal governor less an abridgment than a guarantee of their liberties." The best study of the transition from consensus governance to governance by consent, (for the purpose of promoting economic development) is Richard S. Dunn's *Puritans and Yankees*.[9]

During pioneering years, selectmen bulwarked the social discipline preached by the clergy that helped produce the political stability that strongly contributed to the rapid production of new wealth. After 1680, "The locus of effective political power…shifted from one body—the board of selectmen—to another—the town meeting—and the locus of power remained firmly with the meeting thereafter." In consensus governance, selectmen were mandated to guard the religious orthodoxy of the original town proprietors. In the order that evolved after 1680, town meetings were increasingly devoted to commercial problems that were decided by majority votes. This was governance by consent.[10]

At the same time that town selectmen were gradually losing control of town governance, they were also losing control of school policies. Town meetings made school policies by majority votes and selectmen administered these policies. The transition to control of school funding by town meetings began in coastal towns about 1662 when the Puritan church split after it adopted the Half Way Covenant. The Half Way Covenant weakened governance by consensus in coastal towns and was the opportunity for maritime merchants to gain control of town meetings and govern in their interests.[11]

The cumulative effect of four generations of commercial labor norms was that nuclear villages of pioneer cultivators evolved into market villages that resembled English villages that served the needs of yeomen and farmers. They had resident storekeepers, physicians, lawyers, artisan manufacturers, and artisan craftsmen. Many men wanted a new priority that served the interests of this social change. Chief among them was selling land for the highest price to whoever had enough money. Religious orthodoxy, a narrow community identity, and consensus governance no long served the needs of towns that were integrated into intercolonial and trans-Atlantic commerce.

Commerce in Land

As the founding proprietors of the earliest New England towns died, disputes over the disposition of unallocated town land increased. In 1682 the assemblies of Plymouth and Rhode Island granted town proprietors and their descendents full control over unallocated land; and in a series of statutes, the Massachusetts assembly did the same in 1692, 1694, 1698, and 1703. The descendents of the original town proprietors were made into landowning corporations. Owners of unallocated town land formed a separate organization from town governance.

After owners gained legal title to all unallocated land, they no longer had to restrict voting rights in town meetings in order to protect their land interest. Separate meetings of town inhabitants opened town meeting to consideration of a wider range of issues. Town meetings became forums where all residents could voice concerns about other economic issues than land, and vote accordingly. The transition to an inclusive franchise in town meetings in Massachusetts was linked to the 1692 statute (under the new royal charter) that set a property qualification for voting. Its effect was to accelerate the end of consensus governance by removing religious orthodoxy as a qualification for voting in town elections. Property holding became the only qualification for voting.

A majority of shareholders in town land corporations wanted to sell unallocated land to the highest bidder and divide the money among themselves. They wanted a free market in land. As long as there was consensus governance the free alienation of land was not a commercial right. Undesirable persons, even if they had sufficient money to purchase land, could be prevented from settling in towns governed by consensus.

The primacy of town meetings as instruments of governance did not necessarily repudiate consensus governance but the third and fourth generations wanted a community with more social and economic mobility based on commercial skills, and especially on the free sale of land. "In the eighteenth century, after the proprietors took charge of their common and undivided lands, and their exclusive power over land was legally recognized, the freedom of alienation of…land was universally recognized." This development accelerated the end of consensus government.[12]

Confusion over how meetings of land corporations could be called prompted the Massachusetts assembly to define a procedure in 1713. This statute also validated titles to town lands that were sold or otherwise alienated by land corporations. New Hampshire followed Massachusetts's lead in 1718 and 1719 and Connecticut followed in 1724, 1727, and 1732. The last unallocated land in most towns was unsuitable for cultivation and was usually sold and the money divided among shareholders. Selling the last parcels of unallocated land prevented disputes over what household had the best claim to the remaining land. When all unallocated land was sold, the land corporation dissolved.

The legal separation of town governance from unallocated land meant that money became the means of land transfer (except for inheritance). After all town lands were disposed of, the sons of yeomen cultivators had to purchase land in frontier towns as individual households or in groups of three or four households. Consensus governance dissolved on the frontier because it did not serve the needs of a commercial culture. Money became the principal measure of social priorities, a development that had occurred in seaport towns at the end of the seventeenth century.

It is accurate to conclude that after one hundred years of settlement the social structure of established New England towns was a middle-class yeomanry that wanted to use their labor more efficiently. They moved out of nuclear villages to live on the land they cultivated without the necessity of walking or riding to it. If a household inherited several parcels that were distant from their main farm, they wanted to sell these parcels and use the money to purchase land adjacent to their homestead. Third generation families had a strong interest in the free alienation of land in order to assemble scattered parcels into compact farms or to purchase homesteads in compact units in frontier towns.

New Wealth

The transition to governance by majority consent accelerated during the administration of Edmund Andros, governor of the Dominion of New England (1686–1689), and was further propelled by the turmoil in New England that followed the Glorious Revolution (1688), followed by the imposition of a royal charter on Massachusetts in 1691. Events during the forty years between 1660 and 1700 created conditions in New England where the church ceased being the dominant unifying force in society. The imperceptible transition of consensus government to government by consent had the effect of subordinating the church to the state. The establishment of royal governance in 1691 made this effect visible. Concurrent with the establishment of royal governance, and the recognition that good imperial relations were necessary for commercial prosperity, was the entry of Anglicans, Baptists, and Quakers into the mainstream fabric of New England society.

Lockridge's study of probate inventories in the towns of eastern Massachusetts in 1660 and 1765 indicates that during this century an average household increased its wealth by about two-thirds. In his 1660 sample, about 4 percent of the estates (13 of 300) were relatively affluent. In his 1765 sample, about 17 percent of estates (53 of 310) were relatively affluent. All land appreciated in value in one hundred years, but due to inheritance practices most households cultivated smaller farms more intensively. Yet, average household wealth remained more or less equal, but at a higher level of welfare than one hundred years previously. The new wealth came from using household labor to weave woolen cloth or sailcloth, make barrel staves and other wood products, make shoes, work as house and ship carpenters, or as seasonal labor to preserve meat and fish.[13]

Greater market participation was possible because markets were larger and better developed. Households that increased market participation derived less income from cultivation and more income from nonagricultural labor. The reciprocal of performing more nonagricultural labor was that New England became an importer of food grains to feed its coastal towns and cities. The rapid increase in the value of commerce was the opportunity for a few men who assembled products for export and who specialized in maritime commerce to dramatically increase their wealth.[14]

After about 1700, governance of towns was by an inclusive franchise where majority votes accommodated the interests of new, nonagricultural wealth. "Everyone was admitted to vote, qualified or not. The principle which governed such universalism was not deliberate democracy; it was merely a recognition that the community could not be governed solely by qualified voters if they were too few in number."[15]

Destitution

Commercial cultures assume that all people should perform commercial labor norms, and that the value of their labor is measured by money incomes. Money incomes are earned by producing products and services for sale on anonymous markets. Money becomes necessary to purchase food, clothing, and housing, or a substantial part of them. The process of commercial growth is also a process of social differentiation. In the process of commercial growth, there are always people who fail to compete and become destitute. There are also some who become destitute through no fault of their own.

Compared to Virginia and Maryland, New England had a small percentage of indentured servants. They were concentrated in coastal towns and most of them arrived during the first twenty years of settlement. Small cultivation units were often allocated to them after they completed their indentures. More often, however, ex-servants became leaseholders for seven or eight years until they accumulated sufficient money to purchase land or they continually renewed leases until they died. Freemen who failed to become landowners or leaseholders were often allowed to build a cottage on a small plot of town land. They became wage laborers working to produce products for local sale or for export. These persons were similar to upper strata peasants in Virginia and Maryland. They were often destitute in old age.

The assemblies of all New England colonies required towns to support their destitute inhabitants (resident poor). These same laws authorized town selectmen to send destitute transients to towns where they were legal residents. This was usually the town where they were born. Transients were those who lived and worked in towns but did not own property. Legally, they could be transients for many years unless admitted as inhabitants. The process of returning destitute transients to their towns of legal residence was called warning-out. Warning-out prevented destitute transients from becoming charges on town revenues. Many of these people rejected performing full-time commercial labor norms and were candidates to become wandering vagabonds. Selectmen were very hostile to able-bodied people who refused to labor because there was an insatiable demand for labor to create a civilization out of the wilderness.[16]

In eighteenth century Rhode Island, Ruth W. Herndon examined warning-out notices in town records in order to document who were the destitute. She found that 96 percent were native born, over half were illiterate, and about half were manumitted slaves, ex-indentured servants, and partially assimilated Indians. Sixty-four percent were legal residents of towns within fifteen kilometers (ten miles) of the towns that expelled them.

About two-thirds of white transients were women. Family groups were 42 percent of people warned-out, and over half of them had minor children. Other destitute women were wives with husbands, widows with no immediate relatives, wives whose husbands deserted them, and girls between sixteen and twenty-one, who often had illegitimate children. Among destitute women, over 20 percent had husbands who were seamen or were wives of long-absent seamen.[17]

When destitute families with small children were returned to their legal residence, their children were often treated as orphans. If the children were too young to perform useful labor, the town paid households to care for them until they could. At the age of seven, they were indentured as servants of husbandry or apprentices. At the same time, indigent parents were put in the care of guardians who could induce them to perform useful labor. This policy had three purposes: (1) towns minimized the costs of child support, (2) children learned the value of steady labor, and (3) they had an opportunity to acquire literacy.

There were also resident poor. They were infirm town residents. Among these were those who had serious accidents or prolonged illnesses, old people without relatives, deserted wives with small children, or women with illegitimate children under the age of seven. In addition, there were people who engaged in noncriminal destructive behavior. Most were alcoholics, but there were also mentally ill and mentally retarded individuals without guardians. The usual way to care for them was to provide room and board with town families, paid for with town tax revenues.

Boston was a special case after 1680 because it attracted large numbers of wage laborers who were not legal residents (property owners), although they performed essential wage labor. During downturns in business they were unemployed. In 1682 the Boston government provided relief by building an almshouse to accommodate them. At the same time it established two free elementary schools for the children of city residents who owned no property. After 1700, there was persistent numbers of unemployed laborers who sought full-time employment in their skills, but could not find it. In 1735 Boston built a workhouse to employ these people. After 1750, temporary indigents were also found in interior towns, but in smaller numbers. In both places unemployment was the byproduct of accelerating commercial activity. When there were temporary periods of reduced demand for export commodities, many laborers and artisans became unemployed. Many had no safety net such as returning to family farms.

Literacy in New England

Literacy is the fundamental commercial skill. From the moment of settlement, the government of Massachusetts did everything in its power to ensure the teaching of functional literacy to the children of settlers. Functional literacy is best defined as being able to read, write, and do arithmetic calculations in productive and trading activities. Functional literacy enables persons to receive full value for the labor they perform. This benefits the welfare of households and contributes to community prosperity.

The governing elite of Massachusetts clearly recognized that there was a very close linkage between functional literacy and commercial prosperity. By 1635 there were several primary schools in Massachusetts, but it was clear to the governing elite that the rigors of pioneering were endangering the perpetuation of functional literacy by home schooling. An attempt was made to enforce home schooling in 1636 by a statute that required:

> the chosen men of the towns to see that parents train up their children in learning, labor, and employment...If not...they may impose fines upon such parents as refuse to give the account of their children's education...(and)....With the consent of two magistrates they have the power to put for apprentice such children whose parents are not able and fit to bring them up.[18]

Perpetuating functional literacy required primary schools in nuclear villages. Some towns began collecting an annual contribution from residents (according to means) as an involuntary subscription to supplement tuitions. This proved inadequate to support a schoolmaster. Towns had to be obligated to levy taxes to supplement tuition in order to pay a schoolmaster. In 1642 the Massachusetts assembly acted to ensure that apprentices received primary education.

> In consideration of the great neglect in many parents and masters in training up their children in labor and learning and other employments which may be profitable to the Commonwealth,... in every town the chosen men appointed for managing the prudential affairs shall henceforth stand charged with the care and redress of this evil. They shall ... have power to take account from time to time of their parents and masters of their children,... especially their ability to read and understand the principles of religion and the capital laws of the country.

After 1644, town selectmen assumed the authority to organize schools and levy taxes necessary for their support to ensure that children whose parents could not pay tuition were taught functional literacy.[19]

Most classes in the seventeenth century were held in a room in the teacher's home. Town teachers were often the minister, the assistant minister, a physician, or a literate woman who conducted a dame school in her home. When towns hired a full-time schoolmaster, he often had to perform additional duties: ringing the church bell, leading the Sunday choir, or digging graves. Schoolmaster salaries were paid by tuition, plus money from a tax levy, plus a contribution of firewood during winter sessions; however, this did not always yield enough money to attract competent teachers. If a teacher was competent and was accepted as a town inhabitant, he was often allocated land on which to build a house.

The Massachusetts statute of 1642 (that applied to apprentices) was made general in 1647. Both the 1642 and 1647 statutes were secular laws, although, all of the teaching material had a very strong religious content. Using the English translation of the bible in primary instruction meant that the language of religion and commerce were identical. There was a symbiotic relationship between functional literacy necessary to read the bible and functional literacy needed to conduct commercial transactions.

> It being one chief project of that old deluder, Satan, to keep men from the knowledge of the Scriptures,... it is therefore ordered that every township in this jurisdiction, after the Lord hath increased them to the number of fifty householders, shall then forthwith appoint one within their town to teach all such children as shall resort to him to write and read, whose wages shall be paid either by the parents or masters of such children, or by the inhabitants in general.[20]

The Connecticut assembly combined both Massachusetts statutes into one law in 1650 to achieve the same purposes. Children and apprentices had to be catechized and prepared "in some honest Lawful labor or employment, either in husbandry, or in some other trade profitable to themselves and the commonwealth." If parents refused to cooperate, selectmen, with the approval of two magistrates, could place children with artisans, craftsmen, or cultivators who would ensure that they acquired functional literacy. In 1677, two years after the end of King Philips War, the Connecticut assembly authorized towns to levy a rate sufficient to fund primary instruction for the children of town residents who could not afford tuition.

Although the governing elites of the New England colonies made strenuous efforts to ensure that children acquired functional literacy, there was no provision for compulsory attendance. Enforcing attendance was the responsibility of selectmen. It was a continual struggle.

In many towns, selectmen authorized committees of inspection to report families that had illiterate children, because the parents were illiterate or semi-literate, were too poor to pay tuition, or were located a long distance from a school. Frequently, the children of these parents were apprenticed at the age of seven or eight to people who would ensure they were catechized, learned steady work habits, and acquired functional literacy.

Selectmen were also enjoined to organize grammar schools (academies) whenever a town's population increased to one hundred households in order to prepare some children for entry into Harvard College. Establishing grammar schools in interior towns was usually ignored and if one was established it was a grammar school in name only. It functioned as an elementary school. In frontier towns there was small demand for secondary education based on learning Latin. This demand was concentrated in Boston and other commercial centers. Inland towns preferred to pay fines to the colonial government for noncompliance because it was cheaper than establishing a grammar school.

Neither the New Hampshire assembly (where a majority of initial settlers were not Puritan) nor the New York assembly followed the example of Massachusetts and Connecticut. Ultimately, however, New Hampshire passed statutes in 1719 and 1721 that required towns to fund schools to teach functional literacy. New York followed a different path. After New York came under English rule in 1664, it was impolitic to have tax supported elementary education even though Dutch settlers valued functional literacy as highly as Puritan settlers in Massachusetts and Connecticut. Nonaction avoided a potential conflict between English and Dutch language schooling. Part of the gap was filled by English language elementary schools established by the Society for the Propagation of the Gospel in Foreign Parts.[21]

Artisans and craftsmen who had apprentices living in their households were legally obligated to teach literacy. This obligation was included in almost all of the earliest indentures, and all indentures had to be recorded in the town register. Apprenticeship laws in the New England colonies and New York were transferred intact from old England. Alternatively, artisans and craftsmen had to allocate time for apprentices to attend schools where they could learn to read, write, and cast accounts. Male apprenticeship was for seven years, or until the age of twenty-one, if apprenticeship began before the age of fourteen. Female children who were put into service with cultivating households worked until they were eighteen.

Not all artisans and craftsmen who accepted pauper apprentices were literate. Many indentures were signed with a mark. It was clear that these apprentices could not be home schooled. Two free elementary schools were established in Boston in 1682 to teach literacy to apprentices. In New York City, beginning about 1690, apprentice schools were held for three months during the winter. Attendance was usually for six years or as long as it took to learn to read, write, and cast accounts to the rule of three (addition, subtraction, multiplication). Like indentured servants in the southern colonies, the labor of apprentices could be sold; however, apprentices had to consent to the sale of their indentures. At the end of their apprenticeship, journeymen received two suits of clothing, one for work and the other for attending Sunday worship.

One of the aftermaths of King Philips War (1675) was the end of Indian threats to frontier towns. Peaceful conditions set in motion another event. Nucleated villages rapidly dispersed because cultivating households moved onto their farms in order to more efficiently use their labor. As village residents dispersed, it became increasingly difficult to send children to a centrally located school and equally difficult to get town meetings to fund schools where attendance was difficult or a hardship. Statutes in Massachusetts in 1683, 1692, and 1701 fined towns that did not levy a tax to support free schools. The fines equaled the rates necessary to pay teachers adequate salaries. The statute of 1701 had the desired effect.

In return for voting sufficient taxes to pay adequate salaries to teachers, teachers were required to hold classes at two or three locations within the town. This was the moving school.

Town meetings allocated all of the revenue collected in a neighborhood to pay the teachers who taught the neighborhood children. Sessions at distant locations were of variable length, with the sessions at the central school being the longest. By 1725 moving schools were a common practice for teaching functional literacy to the children of dispersed yeomen households in Massachusetts and Connecticut.[22]

The long-term effect of the 1701 statute was to convert moving school sessions into school districts. The next step was building schoolhouses to serve the needs of neighborhoods. Frequently, the boundaries of school districts were also the boundaries of new parishes that were created to serve the needs of an increasing population or approximated the boundaries of highway districts (where adult males were required to perform ten or more days of corvée labor per year to build or maintain roads). The Connecticut assembly in 1766 was the first New England colony to authorize towns to divide themselves into districts in order to organize primary schools, but town meetings retained the power to make tax rates.

In 1789 the Massachusetts legislature copied the Connecticut statute that authorized towns to establish school districts so that neighborhoods could build schoolhouses and hire teachers. Like Connecticut, the taxing power remained with town meetings but ownership of school property and the expenditure of tax funds were in the hands of district boards of trustees—not selectmen. Not until 1800 were primary school districts in Massachusetts granted the authority to levy taxes if town meetings approved. The purpose of this statute was to allow villages and cities to tax themselves at higher rates than rural towns so that better qualified teachers could be hired, to ensure higher quality instruction. Not until 1817 were school districts granted a separate corporate existence from town governments.

After the War for Independence, the New York legislature copied the Massachusetts statute of 1789 and passed a statute in 1795 requiring primary education in all towns, but not until 1815 were primary school districts made into corporations in order to better manage their affairs. By 1823 New York had 7,300 incorporated primary school districts.[23]

Jackson T. Main's investigation of probate inventories in mid-eighteenth century Connecticut indicates a high level of functional literacy among inhabitants. "Among free laborers, 43 percent had at least one (book)…and…three out of four farmers and artisans had one or more. They clearly read." Kenneth Lockridge's investigation confirms that by 1760 there was near universal male literacy in New England because moving schools had effectively reached thinly populated rural districts.[24]

The quickening of commercial activity in New England after 1700 is accurately measured by increased opportunities for more people to use functional literacy to acquire vocational skills. By 1706 the demand for persons with advanced vocational skills was sufficiently large for private instructors to advertise their schools. The vocational skills they taught were accounting, navigation, surveying (with or without theodolites), shorthand, astronomy, geography, as well as how to draft legal instruments like bonds, mortgages, leases, indentures, and bills of exchange. Other teachers advertised that they held night school to teach reading, writing, and arithmetic, presumably to apprentices. The opportunity to learn these skills is another indication of the emergence of a fully commercial culture in New England by 1760.

Other Northern Colonies

This section concentrates on Pennsylvania because a high percentage of its initial immigrants had similar social origins to the initial immigrants to New England and, in both cases, economic results were similar. Within one hundred years, there was a high degree of commercial prosperity for a high percentage of the population because, like New England, Pennsylvania had a high percentage of yeomen cultivators among its initial immigrants and a much smaller percentage of indentured servants and African slaves than did Virginia, Maryland, and other southern colonies.

Pennsylvania settlers were not the first in the region. Both Sweden and the Dutch established fragile settlements in 1640 on the lower Delaware River. The Dutch also had a scattering of settlers in New Jersey. After England seized the Dutch settlements in 1664, the Duke of York was given jurisdiction over these lands. He immediately promulgated a law code to guide orderly settlement—and generate revenue for his use. Title to all land acquired by grant or sale was in freehold tenure. All land transfers required a written deed bearing an official seal that was recorded in a court of law. Land titles without these safeguards were invalid.

Under the Duke of York's governance, a steady stream of English (and Dutch) settlers moved onto vacant lands in New York and New Jersey, but the Delaware River Valley remained practically vacant. This changed in 1681 when William Penn was granted a royal charter to colonize the west side of the river. He immediately became the largest landowner and land speculator in North America. One of the first acts of his proprietorship was promulgating a legal code requiring freehold tenure, surveyed boundaries, and registration of titles so that land could be bought, sold, and taxed. Among his other policies were active recruitment of settlers and purchasing land from Indians prior to settlement. Private purchases were forbidden unless authorized.

Like New England, most initial settlers were religious dissenters. They migrated in order to practice their version of Christianity without state interference. Most were Quakers from England but there were also substantial numbers of Welsh and Irish Quakers. The first shiploads arrived in December 1681, in order to be housed before planting crops in the spring of 1682. The immigration of Quakers to Philadelphia was as efficiently organized as the emigration of Puritans to New England.

Like most New England settlers, they strongly approved of the policies that were commercializing English agriculture. Their positive response was part of the social baggage they carried to America. Like yeomen in New England, they wanted to improve their social status by becoming landowners in freehold tenure, and, like a high percentage of the initial immigrants to New England, they practiced artisan and craft skills to augment their incomes from the sale of agricultural commodities. They did not expect to become rich but they did expect to accumulate enough material wealth to lead more comfortable lives than they could enjoy in England.[25]

In order to attract commercially motivated households during the first ten years of settlement, Penn reserved several tracts of land to allocate one hundred-acre homesteads to families who paid their passage. Alternatively, the earliest indentured servants could claim warrants for land (freedom land) after they became freemen. This form of headright was little used because it required money to survey boundaries and register titles. Ex-servants usually sold their warrants and moved to the frontier where they could squat.

Surveying land did not keep pace with the arrival of settlers. After 1700, frontier settlers defined their homesteads by blazes and other marks (indiscriminate location) and then sought warrants for the acreage of land they claimed. Warrants allowed them to delay paying for their land, surveying, and registering titles for many years The hiatus between settlement and paying for land was, in effect, long-term credit to settlers. Between 1701 and 1750, this form of squatting was the norm for a high percentage of immigrants. After 1750, in order to generate income, the proprietors recognized settlement rights (squatting) as the basis for valid titles, provided households paid for the land they were cultivating.

The second principal group of immigrants to Pennsylvania was from the German principalities along the Rhine River (Palatinate). Smaller numbers immigrated from Switzerland, plus a sprinkling of French Reformed (Huguenots). They usually came as families and began arriving within two years of settlement. They came at the invitation of William Penn who sent agents into the Palatinate to inform yeomen cultivators that large units of land were available for purchase and that Pennsylvania practiced religious toleration and had peaceful relations with Indians.

Immigration was an opportunity to escape the continuous warfare in the Palatinate during the late seventeenth and early eighteenth centuries. After 1719, the number of Palatine immigrants continued to increase until 1754. Thereafter, until the War for Independence, they continuously augmented Pennsylvania's population. In the first census of 1790, Germans constituted about 40 percent of Pennsylvania's population.

Most Palatines, like most Quakers, were yeomen cultivators who paid their passage because they sold assets before they left and often brought household items with them. Families that could not pay their passage, or chose not to pay their passage, came as redemptioners. They often agreed to pay passage money on arrival with money they carried with them or with money supplied by relatives already in Pennsylvania. If they chose not to pay their passage upon arrival, they negotiated the length of their indenture with people who would pay ships captains the cost of passage. Palatine yeomen had the privilege of being redemptionists because they arrived as families and were known to perform commercial labor norms sufficient to earn enough money to repay persons who purchased their labor.

Upon arrival, families with money purchased land warrants from Penn's agents and then went to the frontier to locate their acreage. Alternatively, they purchased land in tracts that had been reserved by William Penn or from the agents of other Quaker merchants (in England) who had purchased large tracts on speculation. These reserved lands were the most fertile and were favorably located to supply Philadelphia with food.

The landholding pattern of the initial Palatine settlers of Germantown, Pennsylvania (1689) bears a strong resemblance to the yeomen cultivators that settled many New England towns. There were no large or small holdings. Most males, like most males in Puritan households, had artisan or craft skills that provided them with comfortable livings after the pioneering period.[26]

Six of the best measures of the commercial motivation of Palatine cultivators were:

1. They removed stumps and tree roots from their land as soon as possible so that it could be plowed in order to grow wheat and other small grains.
2. They used horses for plowing instead of oxen because they were stronger and moved faster (if adequately fed during the winter).
3. They grew forage crops to feed horses and milch cows during the winter.
4. They built sturdy barns that kept livestock warm during the winter to minimized weight loss.
5. After pioneering was over, most households purchased wagons or carts or both (peasants owned neither).
6. Like a high percentage of Puritan settlers in New England, a high percentage of households practiced artisan and craftsmen skills. The Dutch cultivators who settled in northern New Jersey and New Netherland were also yeomen whose cultivation practices were similar to those of the Palatines.

Most Quaker and Palatine yeomen sold 40–50 percent of their food grain crops. In addition, they sold variable amounts of wood products that were manufactured with household labor during the winter. They also sold livestock that was exported to sugar colonies in the Caribbean, or consumed in Philadelphia, or converted into preserved meat for export. Quaker and Palatine cultivators used few indentured servants or slaves and produced much higher per capita quantities of food and export commodities than did freemen landowners, leaseholders, and sharecrop cultivators in Virginia and Maryland.[27]

Contemporaneous with German immigration was Scots-Irish (Ulster) immigration. Ulster immigrants were the grandchildren of lowland Scottish peasants who had immigrated to Ireland in the first half of the seventeenth century where they replaced Irish peasants killed in wars of rebellion that were especially severe in Ulster. They settled on land confiscated from rebellious Irish aristocrats and sold to English or Scots aristocrats or merchant speculators who then leased large land units to farmers for twenty-one or thirty-one years. Farmers recruited young peasant households from lowland Scotland and England to cultivate it.

Most farmers did little to control land use. They allowed runrig, a form of communal tenure in Scotland, to be transferred to the depopulated lands of Ulster. The peasantry's food grain was oats, and they paid their rent by cultivating a patch of barley. As the population increased, their cultivation units were divided among their sons (partible inheritance), and successive generations had to practice more labor intensive cultivation in order to produce subsistence amounts of food that was necessary to feed more people from the same area of land. During the eighteenth century, their principal subsistence food crop gradually changed from oats to potatoes because, in cool temperate climates, potatoes are the most productive subsistence crop in terms of labor expenditures.

After 1700 the reluctance of many households to practice more intensive cultivation became an incentive for immigration. At the same time, a few Ulster landowners initiated commercializing policies. The three principal ones were replacing communal tenure with leasehold tenure, increasing rents, and introducing the cultivation of flax. Household labor retted the flax, spun it into thread, and wove it into linen cloth. After 1710, many households began paying their rent with money acquired from weaving.

These households leased six to eight acres of land on which they grew their subsistence food supply, plus a small patch of flax that they converted into unbleached (brown) linen cloth. The cloth was sold to merchants who bleached it and exported it. Many households transformed themselves into yeomen weavers. Their social security became dependent on money earned weaving linen cloth that was supplemented by the cultivation of a food crop. It was similar to the transformation that occurred one hundred years earlier in England when displaced peasants transformed themselves into yeomen weavers of woolen cloth.[28]

In the first decade of the eighteenth century, Ulster landowners could increase rents because: (1) high peasant birthrates restored the population density to 1600 levels, (2) late seventeenth century leases were expiring, and (3) peasants in Ulster competed with yeoman weavers for subsistence opportunities. This was particularly true of Roman Catholic peasants because a high percentage of them had been forcibly settled on marginal lands during the Ulster plantation. They were willing to pay higher rents for better land because they could improve their subsistence welfare (grow more food crops) by performing the same amount of labor that they expended on poor soil.

Coincident with rent increases were consecutive poor crop years that produced prolonged seasons of hunger in 1717–1719 and 1726–1729. Like displaced English peasants in the mid-seventeenth century, Ulster peasants who rejected performing commercial labor norms were candidates for immigration to America. In the terminology of the time, the availability of frontier land made the American colonies into the best poor man's country because they could transfer subsistence labor norms to America.

Presbyterians constituted a high percentage of Ulster immigrants because the governing oligarchy in Dublin excluded them from political office and made their schools illegal by requiring teachers to be licensed by bishops of the Church of Ireland. By 1717 these disability laws were seldom enforced but the fact of their existence labeled Presbyterians, like Roman Catholics, as inferiors in the political and social structure of Ireland.

One disability, however, continued to be enforced. It was a tithe (tax) to support the clergy of the Church of Ireland. Presbyterians bitterly resented it. Although, these disabilities were galling, the principal propellant for immigration was hunger in consecutive poor crop years. The subsistence labor norms of Ulster peasants produced endemic hunger, and it was widely known that indentured transportation was available to Pennsylvania (and New York) on ships that carried flax seed grown in America to Ulster for purchase by yeoman weavers.

Between 1715 and 1775, (with large spurts in 1740–1741 and 1754–1755) at least two-thirds of Ulster immigrants came as indentured servants. They were peasants fleeing endemic hunger in consecutive poor crop years. Their usual term of service was four years. At least a quarter of them worked in Philadelphia—beside slaves—where they provided much of the labor in the middle of the eighteenth century that built Philadelphia into the principal colonial city in North America.

After completing their indentures, a high percentage moved to the Pennsylvania frontier and squatted on unsurveyed land, or became cottagers or agricultural laborers in eastern Pennsylvania or migrated to Virginia or the Carolinas where frontier land was more easily obtainable; or they subsisted on relief in Philadelphia, if they rejected performing full-time paid agricultural labor, or performed it only during the summer. The destitution of unemployed unskilled laborers (mostly illiterate and mostly Irish) became a serious problem after 1760 whenever there were declines in prices of export commodities.

The spurt of immigration in the 1770s, just before the War for Independence, had a different cause. It was the collapse of the export market for linen cloth aggravated by increased rents. The best estimate is that about 40 percent of these Ulster immigrants came as paying passengers in family groups. They had money to pay their passage because their commercial labor norms as weavers had enabled them to accumulate salable assets. Nearly 90 percent of voyages from Ulster during the 1770s were to Philadelphia and New York City. These immigrants sought commercial opportunities. In the 1790 census Ulster Irish were about one-quarter of Pennsylvania's population.[29]

Surviving tax records from the eighteenth century indicate that land owned by yeomen cultivators was the source of most of Pennsylvania's revenue. Yeoman cultivators comprised about 60 percent of the population and, during the eighteenth century, they paid about 65 percent of colonial revenues. About 30 percent of the colony's annual revenue was paid by 10 percent of the population who were concentrated in Philadelphia and other towns. They were usually engaged in domestic and export commerce. Only five percent of Pennsylvania's annual tax revenues came from freemen who were about 30 percent of the population. Most of it was a poll tax levied on males over sixteen years of age who had minimal personal property. These men were wage laborers in Philadelphia, leaseholders, sharecroppers, cottagers, or agricultural laborers.[30]

Wheat and wheat flour were Pennsylvania's principal export commodities, and, after 1715, flax seed was continuously exported. Wheat and flax cultivation required fields free of stumps. By mid-century, substantial amounts of wheat flour was baked into ships biscuits and exported. Like New England, Pennsylvania exported large amounts of tanned hides, preserved meat, and wood products. Pennsylvania was also a major shipbuilding center for Philadelphia and British merchants. Enough hemp was grown to weave into sailcloth for ships built in Pennsylvania, but neither hemp fiber nor hemp sailcloth became export commodities.

Literacy in Pennsylvania

William Penn's writings defined educational policies for Quakers in England and, by extension, the educational policies of Pennsylvania. Like New England, a high percentage of the initial

Quaker immigrants were yeomen cultivators who were actively engaged in commerce. They were literate, but it was literacy directly related to useful knowledge. William Penn recommended a curriculum borrowed from dissenting academies in England, rather than from grammar schools that trained the governing elite.

> I recommend the useful parts of mathematics, as building houses, or ships, measuring, surveying, dialing, navigation, but agriculture especially is my eye …(because)…the prosperity and welfare of any people depends in great measure upon the good education of youth and their early instruction in the principles of true religion and virtue…by breeding them in writing and reading and learning of languages, and useful arts and sciences…which cannot be effected in any manner or so well as by erecting public schools.[31]

Like primary schools in New England, the curriculum of Quaker schools had a strong moral content, and like New England they taught functional literacy and casting accounts. Instruction came from the bible, William Penn's *Advice to His Children,* and George Fox's *Right Spelling* (reprinted in Philadelphia in 1702). Primary schools for Quakers, like primary schools in New England, were established in Philadelphia within a few years of settlement and were especially designed to teach functional literacy to apprentices. The earliest schools were held in the homes of teachers or in a room in a meetinghouse, or in a church building as soon as one was completed.

Immediately after settlement, Quaker leaders contemplated taxation to support a public school system. It was not, however, institutionalized by statute law because Pennsylvania's policy of religious toleration fragmented support for a public school system. The several denominations of Christianity that immigrated to Pennsylvania wanted their version of Christianity taught in schools they controlled; therefore, public schools could not be funded. Put another way, there was no consensus government that would approve taxation to support a public school system.

In 1697 the Philadelphia yearly meeting established a free public school in Philadelphia. Its operation was funded by subscription from wealthy Quaker merchants. William Penn confirmed its charter in 1701. At the same time, he presented the assembly with a new charter that transferred the bulk of policy making powers to the assembly. The new charter had no provision for primary education so that teaching functional literacy devolved on the several Christian denominations according to their numbers, the value that congregations placed on literacy, and the money that congregations were willing to contribute to teaching literacy. The Pennsylvania assembly institutionalized this policy in 1715 by authorizing all Protestant Christian congregations to purchase land in order to erect schools and receive funds to operate them.

For Quaker communicants, monthly meetings were responsible for establishing primary schools; however, if a meeting was slow in doing so, the leaders of quarterly meetings, prodded them. Prodding was done with strong support from the yearly meeting in Philadelphia. This was the only form of centralized control exercised by the Quaker governing elite during the initial years of settlement when there was a very close correlation between business and religious leaders.

Quaker schools had four sources of funding: tuition, subscription, legacies, and selling interest bearing bonds. Subscriptions (voluntary donations) from members of monthly meetings were used to pay the tuition of poor children from Quaker and non-Quaker families, but the children of more affluent families paid tuition. Money raised from selling bonds was invested in real estate in Philadelphia that would yield sufficient income to pay the salaries of teachers. By 1778 there were five Quaker funded public schools in Philadelphia housed in schoolhouses with multiple teachers. Under the leadership of the Philadelphia yearly meeting, free public schools were established in all of the counties surrounding Philadelphia.

A high percentage of Scots-Irish peasants who emigrated before 1760 were indifferent to teaching functional literacy to their children. A high percentage lived in dispersed frontier settlements where the acquisition of literacy required a commitment. Many households lacked this commitment. As long as Pennsylvania had no legislation that required local governments to tax themselves to establish primary schools, a high percentage of households living on the frontier were content to replicate the illiteracy they carried from Ulster. On the other hand, Scots-Irish clergy and merchants made a strenuous effort fund academies that could train educated clergymen who would serve frontier congregations and use their influence to establish primary schools.

German yeomen had a strong commitment to literacy, but it is not well documented. Among the initial immigrants, schoolmasters far outnumbered clergymen. Often, schoolhouses were built before churches and before the availability of clergymen. In strong contrast to Quakers and Ulster Presbyterians, Palatine yeomen came in search of commercial opportunities, rather than fleeing religious persecution. They explicitly knew that functional literacy was required if they and their children were to achieve the commercial prosperity they sought.

Like Quakers and Presbyterians, the organization of elementary schools in German communities was very closely associated with teaching their children to read the bible. In these communities functional literacy was taught in German and this continued as long as the community was cohesive. Having said this, there were very strong pressures to use English—the language of commerce and government. It was also the language that the children of initial settlers used when they purchased land on the frontier where communities were ethnically mixed.

Summary

One of the long-term aftermaths of the Reformation was a close association of religious dissent and political discontent. Political discontent was often concentrated in religious groups that were actively implementing policies to commercialize agriculture. These religious dissenters believed they should be better represented in the councils of governing elites. In practical terms, this meant that the principal weight in governance ought to be exercised by households that measured their social security by earning money incomes that were taxed. In other words, all people who performed commercial labor norms by producing optimum amounts of commodities or services for sale on anonymous markets should have a larger share of political power. European governments usually rejected sharing governance with them. Englishmen who earned money incomes that were taxed but were excluded from governance were candidates for immigration to America.

The economic development of England's North American colonies depended on: (1) the performance of commercial labor norms, especially in agriculture; (2) freehold tenure; (3) institutions that guaranteed legal titles for agricultural land; (4) laws that encouraged and protected persons who produced commercial wealth; (5) protection of maritime commerce during wars; (6) replication of the functional literacy that immigrants brought with them from Europe; (7) because literacy is the fundamental commercial skill.

A high proportion of initial immigrants to northern colonies were yeomen cultivators. Even when the immediate propellant for immigration was escape from religious persecution, the search for commercial opportunities was always a clearly understood co-incentive for immigration.

Yeomen performed commercial labor norms to produce assured food surpluses. After harvests were completed, they continued to labor to produce artisan manufactured products for sale on anonymous markets or they practiced craft skills. Most of their incomes were in the form of money of account because of the lack of an adequate currency. The use of money of account was expedient as long as debts were paid at regular intervals (monthly or quarterly). Interest was not charged on these debts unless it was by mutual agreement.

By 1775 the literacy rate in New England was near 90 percent and in other northern colonies it was probably 80 percent among males. They received full value for their labor because they were literate and knew the market value of the products they produced and the items they purchased. Yeomen in northern colonies could say of their neighbors, as English yeomen said of theirs, that he was worth (had a money income of) 20 to 30 pounds (sterling) per year—an amount of money beyond subsistence necessities.

At the close of the colonial era, the northern colonies had a pervasive commercial culture even though it was overwhelmingly rural. Independence was the opportunity for the commercial agriculture in northern states to evolve into diversified commercial activity by creating new business organizations and borrowing new technologies from Europe in order to create new forms of wealth that did not exist in the colonial economy.

Chapter 4

North Atlantic Commercial Empire

During the first thirty or forty years of settlement, all North American colonies depended on trans-Atlantic commerce for their survival. From the moment of settlement, a large part of the labor of settlers was devoted to producing products for export to Europe. A variant of this trade was exporting food and commodities to the Caribbean islands that produced sugar that was exported to Europe. Almost all American exports were agricultural, forestry, or fishery commodities. In the northern colonies, almost all of these commodities were produced by yeomen cultivators, and in southern colonies a high percentage of export commodities were produced on plantations using indentured and slave labor. In all cases, however, household survival depended on acquiring sufficient money from producing export commodities to purchase essential manufactured products.

Navigation Laws

By 1650 commerce originating in North American and Caribbean colonies was large enough for Parliament to direct its flow in order to maximize revenue from it. This was done by enacting navigation laws in 1651 and 1660. These laws reserved the trade between England and the North American and Caribbean colonies to English and colonial merchants, in ships that were built in England or the colonies, were manned by English or colonial crews, and were owned by English or colonial merchants. Colonial merchants competed on even terms with English merchants in the trans-Atlantic trade, and there were no restrictions on intercolonial trade, but colonial merchants were excluded from the coastal trade of Britain.

Products produced in Europe but destined for colonial consumption had to be landed in England before being transported across the Atlantic in English or colonial owned and colonial manned ships. There were two exceptions. Salt produced in southern Europe (destined for New England fisheries) and wine produced in the Portuguese colonies of Madeira and the Azores (wine islands). They could arrive directly from their places of origin, usually in colonial owned ships that delivered rice, salted fish, and wood products to southern Europe and the wine islands.

The law of 1660 listed seven colonial products that could only be exported to England. The most important were sugar, tobacco, cotton, and indigo. During the first twenty years of the eighteenth century, rice, naval stores, hemp, copper, beaver pelts, and tanned hides were added to the list. Further additions (by 1764) included pot and pearl ashes (for making soap and glass), bar iron, lumber, ships timber, and masts. Great quantities of naval stores and indigo were needed in England. Rice was soon removed because one-third of the crop was marketed in southern Europe and the wine islands.

The purpose of navigation laws was to exclude Dutch merchants from the colonial trade, reduce the Dutch carrying trade among European nations (in order to give English merchants a competitive advantage), and direct the flow of colonial raw materials to England. The raw materials produced in the North American and Caribbean colonies would (1) contribute to national revenue because most colonial products were taxed upon entering England, (2) provide abundant raw materials for artisan manufacturers, (3) provide employment for displaced peasants who were forced to become full-time paid laborers in commerce and artisan manufacturing, and (4) monopolize colonial markets for products manufactured in England.

For the most part, navigation laws specified products that could only be exported to Britain. The laws operated without objection from colonial merchants or from producers of export commodities because they appreciated the monopoly of tobacco in the English market and the assured market for the other products that colonists produced for export. The assured market for colonial raw materials helped maintain profit margins so that colonial merchants could accumulate capital. Furthermore, American merchants had the same benefit as British merchants: protection by the Royal Navy.

There were occasional irritants but they were usually of short duration. The first irritant was the passage of the Molasses Act in 1733. It imposed a prohibitive tariff on molasses imported from the more efficient sugar plantations on the French and Spanish islands in the Caribbean. The Molasses Act was actually domestic legislation. Parliament passed it to create a monopoly market in the North American colonies for molasses produced by English planters on Barbados, Jamaica, and other Caribbean islands. Many of these planters were absentee owners who were members of Parliament.

Molasses was the raw material for distilling rum. Enforcement of the act would have raised the cost of rum and seriously harmed a substantial industry in New England where it was consumed in large quantities by seamen and yeomen, as well as being an important commodity in the African slave trade conducted by New England merchants. Imperial authorities acquiesced to the noncollection of the tax and it did not bankrupt rum distillers. The Sugar Act passed in 1764 lowered the tax and a strenuous effort was made to collect it. Attempts to collect it became a source of contention because colonial assemblies did not control the revenue. Its political impact is discussed at the end of this chapter.

Other minor irritants were prohibitions on the sale of woolen yarn and cloth outside the colonies where they were produced, and on hats made of felted beaver fur. In both cases, the colonial manufacture of these products satisfied local needs. Something of the same situation applied to the fabrication of iron. By the 1750s the North American colonies had many furnaces that smelted ore from many small deposits. Almost all iron was cast into shapes or forged into products for local consumption: pots, nails, hinges, horseshoes, ship and wagon fittings, and wagon tires. After 1730, small amounts of pig and bar iron were exported to England in ballast.

Iron forges in England wanted cheap pig and bar iron from the colonies but did not want competition from colonial forges for the colonial market for fabricated products. Tariffs on pig and bar iron were ended in 1750 in order to encourage colonial production for export, but the same statute prohibited the building of new forges, slitting mills, hammer mills, and steel furnaces. This legislation had little effect. Both colonial ironmasters and imperial authorities ignored it. Exports of pig and bar iron were not greatly stimulated because most iron produced in America was fabricated into products for consumption in America.

These irritants were more than compensated by bounties paid for the production of naval stores, masts, and indigo and the monopoly market in England for tobacco. There was, however, one serious grievance and it grew more acute with the increasing volume of imperial commerce. It was an inadequate currency. While not intrinsic for the operation of navigation laws, it was a serious impediment to the smooth flow of imperial commerce. More important, from the perspective of colonial governing elites, it was a serious impediment to the orderly and timely collection of taxes and for maximizing the production of new commercial wealth in the colonies.

> The various acts of parliament regulating the value of foreign coins and limiting the issue of paper money were more important, effected more people, and were probably productive of more friction and irritation than all of the other regulations combined.... The rapidly expanding trade of the colonies with each other and with other parts of the empire, along with the extensive credit system upon which nearly all trade was conducted, made any local solution of such an issue impossible....A common monetary system for the entire British colonial empire was an unsolved problem at the time of the Revolution.[1]

In spite of their deficiencies, navigation laws served the needs of both English and colonial governing elites. Their great strength was that they created grooves of commerce that rapidly increased tax revenue in England and commercial wealth in the North American colonies.

The policy that guided the growth of the North Atlantic commercial empire between 1715 and the beginning of the Seven Years War in 1754 was called salutary neglect. Salutary neglect accommodated a growing awareness by colonial governing elites that the political and commercial interests of the North American colonies were not identical with English interests. The most important accommodation during these years was the gradual assumption by colonial assemblies of more power to conduct their internal affairs, especially in matters of taxation.

The authors of the policy of salutary neglect were Robert Walpole who was prime minister (First Lord of the Treasury) from 1721 to 1742 and the Duke of Newcastle who was secretary of state for the southern department from 1724 to1748. Walpole was principally concerned with increasing the taxable wealth of England in order to fund debts that had been incurred in past and contemporary wars with France and Spain.

Newcastle was responsible for managing commercial relations between England and the North American and Caribbean colonies. Walpole and Newcastle had three principal interests in colonial governance: (1) a source of patronage to help maintain a majority of supporters in Parliament, (2) increased revenue by taxing increasing amounts of colonial products entering England, and (3) increasing exports of manufactured products to the colonies in order to increase employment in Britain. As long as this flow of trade continued without colonial opposition, Walpole and Newcastle could focus their energies on the governance of Britain and advancing British interests in the power politics of western Europe.[2]

Salutary neglect ended in 1763, after the end of the Seven Years War (1754–1763). Parliamentary leaders were determined that some of the expenses required to expel the French from Canada and from the trans-Appalachian west should be paid by Americans. Furthermore, continuing revenue would be needed to fund enlarged military and naval establishments in America to protect the enlarged empire. The conduct of the war strongly impressed colonial governing elites that there was a strong community of interest between Britain and the colonies in military and naval affairs. This mutual interest was essential for protecting the volume of American commerce that had evolved during the eighteenth century. The great unanswered question at the restoration of peace in 1763 was *Who was going to pay the cost of protection?*

American Merchants

In both 1700 and 1770, Britain was the principal destination of exports from America. The best estimates are that Britain imported commodities worth 395,000 pounds sterling in 1700, but 1.4 million pounds in 1770, an increase of 350 percent. By the best estimates, Britain received 52 percent of American exports in 1770, the Caribbean islands 27 percent, and southern Europe 19 percent. Tobacco from Virginia and Maryland, indigo from the Carolinas, and wood products from most colonies were the principal exports to Britain.

During these same seventy years, the North American colonies increased their imports from Britain from 344,000 pounds sterling to 1.87 million, an increase of about 540 percent. In 1770, Britain supplied approximately 60 percent of all imports of the North American colonies, which were about 30 percent of all British exports and about 40 percent of the exports of all manufactured products from Britain. The principal manufactured products were woolen textiles and metal products. The 40 percent of non-British imports were molasses, salt, and wine, plus slaves from Africa. The large gap between imports and exports was paid for by profits earned carrying sugar and other Caribbean products to England, by bills of exchange from American merchants trading in southern Europe, and by purchases of American-built ships for use by British merchants in coastal and European trade.[3]

Until about 1750, British merchants preempted the export of tobacco, indigo and about two-thirds of the rice crop because these commodities went directly to England. American businessmen assembled them for export. Likewise, until about 1750, most of the direct trade with Britain from the middle colonies and New England was in the hands of British merchants. On the other hand, from the beginning of settlement, most of the commerce to the Caribbean islands and southern Europe was conducted by American merchants in American owned and American built ships. With the exception of rice, New England and the middle colonies produced most of the commodities exported to the Caribbean and southern Europe.

Marketing colonial commodities by American merchants, whether they traded to Britain, the Caribbean, or southern Europe, depended on agency relationships with English merchants. English merchants were frequently family members or religious brethren. They supplied credit to purchase manufactured products in England, transferred funds by bills of exchange, and managed the re-export of colonial products into northern European markets. The usual credit was twelve month and, in order to make timely repayments, American merchants frequently purchased bills of exchange from other American merchants or from English merchants in ports where they sold American export products. If full repayments of credit were postponed, American merchants paid five to eight percent interest on unpaid balances. Credit dependency guaranteed that a high percentage of colonial commerce would be conducted within the empire.

American merchants steadily accumulated capital between 1750 and the beginning of hostilities in 1775. During these years, merchants in the northern colonies increased their share of marketing colonial commodities destined for Britain. In 1770, 75 percent of New England's direct trade with Britain was carried in ships owned by American merchants, but this trade represented only 17 percent of New England's commerce. New England merchants dominated the coastal trade and shared the Caribbean and southern European trade with merchants from New York, Philadelphia, and the Chesapeake.

Philadelphia and New York merchants were also competitive in direct trade with Britain. Philadelphia merchants owned 37 percent of the ships engaged in this trade and New York merchants controlled 25 percent, but like New England, only 22 percent of their commerce was direct trade with Britain. In the Chesapeake and lower South, however, American merchants were a negligible factor in direct trade with Britain. Although, 81 percent of Chesapeake commerce and 71 percent of commerce in the lower South was direct trade with Britain, American merchants conducted only 12 percent of this trade.[4]

Twenty years after settlement (1650), Boston merchants were exporting wood products, dried and salted cod, and other provisions to English colonies in the Caribbean, the Azores, Madeira, and southern Europe. By 1680 New England merchants controlled most of the export of these commodities. In 1755 Boston was the leading commercial city in North America. It achieved this eminence in spite of the serious disadvantages of having no river entry into the interior and a small, infertile agricultural hinterland. Its natural advantages were a deep, sheltered harbor with minimal tides, abundant timber resources that were accessible at tidewater locations along the deeply indented coast of New England, and proximity to the super-abundant fisheries of the continental shelf.

Boston prospered for reasons other than its natural advantages. The most important cause of its success was yeomen cultivators who composed the bulk of New England's population. They produced substantial quantities artisan manufactured products that were marketed by an energetic community of merchants who found markets in the coastal villages of the southern colonies and the Caribbean islands. Boston was the entrepot for New England merchants from smaller New England ports who produced preserved fish and wood products for this trade. In addition, Boston and its environs became the principal shipbuilding center in North America, not only for its own merchants but also for sale to British merchants. None of this commerce was inevitable, nor was it like the simple bilateral trade that operated in the southern colonies. The development of complex commerce by New England merchants was directly related to the commercial social values that pervaded rural New England.

In contrast, Philadelphia had a large and fertile agricultural hinterland that was made highly productive by the labor of Quaker and German (Palatine) yeomen cultivators. Immediately after the end of pioneering years, wheat and wheat flour became the principal export commodities. Wheat production in Pennsylvania coincided with an abundant market for flour in southern Europe, the Caribbean, and in Britain after 1755. Complementing wheat cultivation was the export of preserved beef and pork, co-products of the diversified agriculture of Quaker and German yeomen.

Prior to 1750, much of Philadelphia's commerce was the multilateral exchange of flour and preserved meat for Caribbean molasses and sugar and salt and wine from southern Europe. Much of the substantial profits from this trade were sent as bills of exchange to the London agents of Philadelphia merchants. This was accumulated capital that was available after 1750 to finance the export of breadstuffs to supply Britain's increasing urban population. Profits from the export of breadstuffs, preserved meat, hides, and wood products strongly stimulated urban growth. Sometime about 1755, Philadelphia surpassed Boston as the largest and wealthiest city in North America.

In 1770 New York was the smallest of the three northern cities in terms of both population and exports. New York exports were about one-third of those of Philadelphia and about one-half of Boston's because of its limited agricultural hinterland (Long Island, eastern Connecticut, northern New Jersey, and a ribbon of cultivated land along the Hudson River). New York merchants, like Boston merchants, were forced to develop a complex pattern of trade, and like Boston merchants their prosperity was directly attributable to the commercial labor norms performed by yeomen cultivators who produced high per capita amounts of diversified products for export.

Different conditions operated in Chesapeake Bay and the southern colonies. Jacob M. Price's analysis of the business of Buchanan and Simpson, a Scottish company trading into Chesapeake Bay, clearly shows how British merchants dominated direct commerce between the southern colonies and Britain. The key to their success was long-term credit. Long-tem credit made it possible to purchase tobacco and market it in Britain for resale to the French tobacco monopoly, to merchants in Amsterdam, and to the north German principalities.

Tobacco for export was assembled two ways: (1) resident agents (factors) of British merchants in Virginia and Maryland managed small tidewater warehouses containing a store of manufactured products that were exchanged for hogsheads of tobacco, and (2) warehouses with stores of manufactured products for consignment to inland storekeepers who would pay for them with hogsheads of tobacco after the annual harvest. Jacob Price asks the basic question: *Why were there not more indigenous merchants, traders, and artisans in cities in the Chesapeake Bay?* The same question was asked by the governing elites of eighteenth century Virginia and Maryland.

The usual answer by historians and geographers is the ease of water transportation on the many estuaries of Chesapeake Bay. Geography certainly contributed to the lack of cities in Virginia and Maryland. Geography, however, was only a contributing cause. The principal cause for lack of cities was a landholding pattern that reflected the social values of three categories of cultivators: (1) peasants who performed subsistence labor norms, (2) yeomen cultivators who performed commercial labor norms and produced substantial amounts of export commodities, and (3) planters who used slave and indentured labor to maximize production of export commodities.

Peasant cultivators were an overwhelming majority of the white population, and they had minimal interest in increasing the acquisition of money by increasing the production of export commodities. The few manufactured products they needed were purchased using money of account (subsistence credit) provided by storekeepers or factors. A high percentage of manufactured products they purchased came from England by direct trade conducted by British merchants.

For an entirely different reason, planters minimized participation in the local economy. They tried to make their plantations as self-sufficient as possible in craft skills and artisan manufactured commodities by training slaves to perform this labor. At the same time, they kept slaves at a subsistence level of welfare so that the profits of slave labor were used exclusively for their benefit. Planters who produced 50 or 60 hogsheads of tobacco per year had better uses for their profits than investing in maritime commerce. The capital they accumulated was used to purchase more land and slaves, build majestic homes, speculate in land on the frontier, and influence elections in order to conserve their status as the governing elite.

Finally, the small number of yeomen cultivators, did not generate enough internal commerce to sustain vigorous urban growth.

Dispersed peasant households along the estuaries and planters who needed manufactured products (or luxury products), purchased them from numerous tidewater stores that were adjunct to tidewater warehouses operated by factors of Scottish and English merchants. The principal function of American merchants in southern colonies was to assemble export commodities from inland cultivators and transport those commodities to tidewater warehouses where factors of British merchants shipped them to Europe. Alternatively, many plantation owners shipped their tobacco directly to commission merchants in England who sold it at market prices. Indigenous merchants had difficulty accumulating capital to compete with these established export channels.

The commerce of Charleston closely resembled the commerce of Chesapeake Bay, except that Charleston had three principal export commodities: rice, indigo, and forest products. About one-third of the rice went to Britain. Northern merchants carried the rest to southern Europe and the wine islands. All of the indigo went to England, as did a high percentage of forest products used in shipbuilding and ship maintenance. Charleston was more of a warehouse center where export commodities were assembled and imported manufactured products were distributed. Like the tobacco planters of the Chesapeake, the rice and indigo planters of South Carolina used their considerable profits to build mansions (in Charleston), speculate in frontier land, and manage the votes of peasant landowners to conserve their status as the governing elite.[5]

Although direct trade with England was an important part of the commerce of northern colonies, it was only one part of their trade. A high percentage of artisan and food products made in northern colonies were marketed outside the British commercial empire. In 1770, on the eve of the War for Independence, four categories of products provided 85 percent of American exports. In order of importance they were (1) grain products and vegetables; (2) tobacco and indigo; (3) fish, meat, and livestock; and (4) wood products.

Grain and vegetable exports in 1770 were rice, maize, oats, wheat, peas and beans, flour, maize meal, ships biscuits, potatoes, and onions. They were worth 1,084,000 pounds sterling. Tobacco and indigo was worth 1,038 000 pounds sterling. Animal products were salted and pickled fish, beef and pork in brine, butter and cheese, tallow and lard, and livestock. They were worth 552,000 pounds sterling. Wood products were masts and spars, lumber, planks, barrel staves and headings, barrel hoops, hogshead staves, naval stores, pot and pearl ashes. They were worth 265,000 pounds sterling.[6]

Colonial Manufacturing

Only two manufactured products were exported in significant amounts—rum and ships. Nonetheless, by 1770, there was a substantial and rapidly increasing amount of manufacturing in the colonies. A high percentage of it was by yeomen cultivators practicing artisan skills, and almost all of their production was consumed in the colonies where it was produced. Almost all colonial manufacturing was done within households. The principal exceptions were small iron smelters, shipyards, rope walks, sail lofts, wagon and cart makers, gunsmiths, rum distilling; tanning hides, and grist and sawmills. These products were manufactured using full-time laborers, either paid, indentured, or slaves, and their productions were sold on anonymous markets.

This section concentrates on iron smelting and shipbuilding because these two industries required considerable technical skills and large amounts of capital. During the colonial period, both of these industries were solidly established and competed on even terms with similar products made in Britain. When the War for Independence began, the North American colonies were probably the seventh largest producer of iron in the world. Annual production, however, was only about 30,000 tons.

In 1700 the population of English-speaking North America was between 250,000 and 300,000. By 1770 it was probably 2.1 million, an increase of about 800 percent. High domestic demand for iron implements, particularly agricultural implements, meant that bar and pig iron were minor exports even though after 1750, Parliament paid a bounty on imports from the colonies. The statute that ended tariffs on bar and pig iron imports into Britain also prohibited Americans from constructing new rolling, slitting, and hammer mills, and furnaces to make steel. These prohibitions were designed to increase the American market for iron implements made in England. Royal governors did not enforce these prohibitions.

There are many small iron ore deposits east of the Appalachian Mountains and the furnaces built to exploit them had limited capacities. Furnace locations were dictated by proximity to ore. A second constraint on location was the availability of fuel, and a third constraint was the availability of water power to drive the blast. Charcoal was the fuel used to smelt iron ore; therefore, most furnaces were located in frontier or upland forests. Large numbers of unskilled laborers were required to fell trees for conversion into charcoal. A third consideration was availability of food to feed workers because iron smelting was labor intensive.

Generally, the capital to build smelting furnaces came from successful merchants who wanted to diversify their investments, or semi-retire from active trading, or produce a commodity that could be carried in ballast to Britain in ships they owned. By 1770 furnaces were concentrated in Pennsylvania and adjacent portions of New Jersey and Maryland. If a forge was attached to a furnace, a very considerable flow of water was needed to drive the hammer that refined pig iron into bar iron and then converted some or all of the bar iron into consumer products (nails, hinges, ship fittings, agricultural implements). The location of forges was more dependent on water power to drive the hammer than nearness to furnaces.

Shipbuilding was a more visible industry than iron smelting because it was along the coast, rather than at remote interior locations. Between 1770 and 1775, an average of about four hundred ocean-going ships per year were built in North America. Somewhere between one-quarter and one-half were sold to British merchants. The cumulative effects of annual ship sales in Britain were that about one-third of the ships used by British merchants in the coastal trade of Britain, and in European and trans-Atlantic commerce were built in America. American shipwrights built all classes of ships except large warships and large merchant ships designed for East Indian voyages.[7]

Many places along the East Coast of North America were well located for building ships. All colonies built ships for their merchants and to sell abroad. The preferred places were protected harbors, estuaries, or inlets where sawn timbers could be floated down river from saw mills. The wood was seasoned for a year before being used. Ship fittings (made of iron), sails, and rigging could arrive from distant localities, as well as food for the workers..

By 1775, however, shipbuilding was concentrated in the northern colonies, especially in New England. Several factors contributed to this. The two most important were domination of the Caribbean and coastal trade by New England based merchants, and the availability of skilled labor. Other advantages were ease of transporting timbers from logging operations and sawmills along the highly indented coast, proximity of local forges that supplied blacksmiths with rough shapes that would be made into ship fittings; and the abundance of ropewalks and sail lofts in Boston, New York, and Philadelphia.

The least visible form of manufacturing was done in dispersed rural households. In northern colonies households of yeomen cultivators manufactured woolen and linen cloth, hemp sailcloth, hemp fiber for cordage, shoes, and wood products like barrel staves. Sailcloth and linen cloth were woven from the hemp and flax grown and retted by yeomen, and the woolen cloth was from wool clipped from their sheep that children spun into thread.

Paper Currency and Credit

A fundamental weakness of the North Atlantic commercial empire was the lack of a central bank to issue sufficient amounts of paper currency to conduct trade. The smallest part of colonial currency was gold and silver coins. Most were of Spanish origin and there were never enough of them. They were poorly distributed, had variable value, and colonial merchants tended to send them to England in order to pay for manufactured products.

Beginning about 1720, the lack of a reliable currency of uniform value was an increasing source of irritation for both British and American merchants. All colonial legislatures in North America issued paper currency in the form of bills of credit, loan office certificates, and tobacco warehouse receipts. Paper currency was the usual means used by colonial governments to pay for labor and materials used to build infrastructure projects and finance warfare. It was also the usual means for paying taxes. The value of these currencies was highly variable and their circulation was usually limited to a single colony or adjoining colonies. Most local commerce was conducted with money of account supplemented by paper currency.

There was an intimate relationship between emissions of paper currency and taxation. In all colonies, low tax rates supported weak central governments, especially in royal colonies where the salaries of governors and other officials who formed his council were a continual source of contention. Local taxation was another matter. It was relatively high in the New England colonies, moderate in the central colonies, and low in the southern colonies. The principal difference in local taxation was the amount of money raised to build infrastructure projects and support schools that taught functional literacy.[8]

Tax collection depended on local authorities because all colonies lacked bureaucracies capable of quickly collecting revenues during emergencies. The most common emergency was war, either on the frontier or providing manpower and materials to support British military and naval operations in America. An inadequate currency also made taxes difficult to collect when the only means of paying them were pounds of tobacco, bushels of maize or wheat, or monetized amounts of other authorized commodities. Colonial governments had a strong interest in creating acceptable currencies without reference to the periodic necessities of emergency finance.

The most common form of paper currency was bills of credit issued in anticipation of tax revenues. Colonial assemblies emitted them in specific amounts with a specific life, usually five to eight years. At the same time, taxes (poll, excise, property) were increased to redeem bills of credit at their due date. The bills were also issued in small denominations to pay people who performed public services. In effect, they were a floating debt that usually did not carry interest. They were first used in Massachusetts in 1690 to pay soldiers who participated in a failed expedition to capture Quebec. They had value because they could be used to pay taxes that supported colonial governments, and were usually given additional value by being made legal tender to pay all private debts within the colony. Some emissions, however, were not made legal tender because merchants and other creditors feared that the amount being issued would be inflationary. Most people accepted paper currency because of its convenience as a medium of exchange and because depreciation was usually gradual.

If bills of credit were to retain their value, taxes had to be increased to retire them, but since retirement was a gradual process tax increases could be minimal if new taxable wealth increased fast enough to produce the revenue to retire them. Frequently, however, they were not retired because of the persistent demand for a currency to facilitate trade or to fund military expenditures. They were renewed but without increasing taxes to redeem them. Most people accepted depreciation as a hidden form of taxation because it was relatively painless.

Several colonies attempted to use land banks to supply an adequate currency: South Carolina in 1712, Massachusetts in 1714, Rhode Island in 1715, and New Hampshire in 1717. All were varying degrees of failure. The Pennsylvania assembly established a land bank system in 1723 that was successful, but the New Jersey statute of 1723 was even more so. The statute was designed to assist yeomen cultivators who wanted to use credit to improve the productivity of their land. Each county had a loan office and the amount of credit it could create was based on its population. Loan office certificates (mortgages) were issued on improved agricultural land up to 50 percent of its assessed value.

The smallest mortgage allowed was 12 pounds 10 shillings (sterling), and the largest was 100 pounds sterling. Loans were for twelve years and required annual repayments of one-twelfth of the principal and interest. The small size of loans, their geographic distribution, and the subsidized interest rate of 5 percent (merchants paid 8%) were clearly designed to put credit in the hands of yeomen cultivators. This procedure ensured that the credit created by land banks was used to increase the production of marketable commodities and was not for speculation.

After a mortgage was approved, yeomen received a stack of certificates of various denominations, from one shilling to three pounds sterling. The certificates were legal tender and could be used to purchase additional land, livestock, or boards to build a house or barn, or hire people to cultivate more land. The increased harvests were sold and the money used to repay the loan. Persons who accepted loan office certificates as payment for products or services then spent them for similar products and services. If annual payments were not on time, the loan office foreclosed and sold the mortgaged land to satisfy the debt.

As the initial loans were repaid, the New Jersey legislature renewed them and created more credit on the same basis. There were only minor fluctuations in the value of these certificates. For the next thirty years the New Jersey legislature levied very low taxes because the interest on land bank loans supplied a large part of the revenue needed to pay current government expenses. New Jersey's experience in creating credit for the use of yeomen cultivators, and the revenue it generated, made land banks an attractive way to create a paper currency. The New Jersey statute was widely copied but with variant results in other colonies because of the reluctance of loan office managers to foreclose defaulted loans.[9]

A Virginia statute of 1713 legalized the circulation of tobacco warehouse receipts but they had no standard quality attached to them. Cultivators brought their harvests to private warehouses where it was weighed, graded, and stored until exported. Warehouse receipts had variable value because the tobacco they represented was of unknown quality. Cultivators received receipts in various denominations for the value of their tobacco these receipts circulated as currency until the last holder claimed the tobacco. The last holder was usually an English exporter or the factor of a Scots merchant.

In Virginia in 1730 and Maryland in 1747, planters (over peasant resistance) finally persuaded assemblies to pass statutes that required all tobacco grown in the colonies to be inspected and stored in public warehouses until exported. These statutes had the dual purposes of ensuring that warehouse receipts represented tobacco of uniform quality so they could circulate as a currency with a uniform value.

Neither land bank certificates nor tobacco warehouse receipts were sources of contention within the system of imperial commerce, but bills of credit were a continual source of contention because some colonies issued them in inflationary amounts. The earliest offender was South Carolina that emitted its first paper money in 1703. After it became a royal colony in 1721 the change in governance did not end inflationary emissions. The assembly continued to emit them in inflationary amounts, partly for defense, but also for land speculation.

British merchants continually petitioned Parliament and the Board of Trade to stop inflationary emissions of legal tender currency, not only in South Carolina but in other mainland colonies. Neither Parliament nor the Board of Trade intervened because well-managed paper currencies contributed to increasing the volume of imperial commerce. They were equally essential for mobilizing American resources to fund warfare in North America, whether against the French in Quebec or Indians on the frontier.

The emission of 50,000 pounds sterling of legal tender loan office certificates by Rhode Island in 1750 was immediately recognized as a source of monetary instability in New England because a high percentage of this currency would circulate outside of Rhode Island. Even when highly discounted, its steady depreciation would seriously lower the profit margins of both Massachusetts and British merchants. Both British and American merchants petitioned the Board of Trade to disallow the law.

Instead, Parliament passed the Currency Act of 1751. It applied only to New England and to bills of credit that were made legal tender currency. Additional sections of the law limited future emissions of bills of credit to wartime emergencies or for the current expenses of governance. These emissions could not be legal tender for private debts, and there had to be sufficient new taxation to retire them in five years. Furthermore, paper currency in circulation was prohibited from being extended beyond redemption dates. The purpose of the statute was clear. British merchants trading into New England wanted to have sterling loans repaid in sterling funds rather than being forced to accept depreciated legal tender currency that colonial legislatures issued in inflationary amounts.

By 1755 a shortage of paper money in Massachusetts forced the assembly to authorize the acceptance of commodities to pay taxes. Taxes could be paid with bar iron, bloomery iron, hollow ironware, hemp, cordage, canvas cloth, wool, tanned sole leather, long whalebones, tallow, beeswax, bayberry wax, maize, winter wheat, rye, barley, peas, merchantable codfish, and barreled pork and beef. The reversion to commodity taxation in 1755 duplicates a similar crisis in government finance from 1720 to 1723 when a similar group of commodities were authorized as tax payments. William T. Baxter's *The House of Hancock* explains how barter operated in the 1750s and how an inadequate currency needlessly complicated the flow of domestic and imperial commerce.[10]

The end of the Seven Years War (February 1763) coincided with George Grenville becoming prime minister (April 1763). He had a mandate to increase national revenue and restructure imperial governance in order to shift some of the costs of that war to the American colonies. This seemed eminently reasonable to Grenville and his ministerial advisors because the Americans had secured the great benefit of the annexation of Quebec and Cape Breton Island. Annexation removed a long-standing threat to colonial commerce and a barrier to trans-Appalachian expansion. Protecting these additions to the empire required increased revenues to support a larger standing army, with some of that army stationed in America. Grenville and his ministers thought that the search for additional revenue should include America and, in the process of acquiring an American revenue, imperial governance would be centralized. The era of salutary neglect ended.

The attempts by Grenville and his successors to centralize governance of the American colonies generated continual confrontations on three issues: (1) the interests of American merchants were subordinated to the interests of British merchants, (2) the taxation policies of Parliament subordinated the interests of colonial governing elites to the interests of British imperial governance, and (3) the rejection of greater use of paper currency.

This was the occasion for the Board of Trade to propose the creation of a uniform paper currency as part of the Grenville policy of restructuring imperial governance. Creating a uniform paper currency would recognize the reality that there were insufficient gold and silver coins in the American colonies to efficiently conduct commerce, or to pay taxes when due, or to fund colonial contributions to imperial wars. A person outside of Grenville's ministry proposed the creation of a uniform paper currency in 1763. Although it would have levied a stamp tax on colonial legal and commercial documents, the revenue it generated would remain in America. The revenue from the stamp tax would be used:

> to rise a Fund from the Colonies to obtain a Credit for Securing the Issuing of Exchequer Bills...in order to preserve One Uniform Course of Trade and the Colonies bearing the Expence of preserving the Crown's acquisitions in keeping up the Militias.[11]

Benjamin Franklin proposed a similar plan to create large amounts of credit during emergencies and raise imperial revenue without a stamp tax. He proposed the establishment of a system of American loan offices. Parliament would authorize the offices to issue one million pounds sterling of paper currency. Borrowers would qualify for loans by mortgaging real estate up to 50 percent of its assessed value, similar to the New Jersey system. Borrowers would pay 6 percent interest on their loans.

The revenue generated by interest payments would be a tax that would be used to pay some of the expenses of imperial governance in America, but Americans would accept it because it would help create reliable credit. To facilitate acceptance of this legal tender currency, it would be necessary for Parliament to repeal the Currency Act of 1751. Thereafter, all colonial paper currencies would be destroyed after their redemption dates.

Franklin believed that loan offices on a continental scale would provide the colonies with sufficient legal tender currency for the growing volume of colonial commerce, and especially that the plan would create credit that could be used by American merchants. The emphasis of both proposals was to provide a solution to the currency problem rather than generate revenue to pay for stationing British troops in America. Franklin's plan was ignored.

Creating an imperial currency would have been a big undertaking, but the situation warranted it. The Grenville ministry, however, shelved the proposal because it would have required real consultation with colonial merchants and political leaders. Instead of consultation, Parliament passed the Currency Act of 1764 that extended the 1751 Currency Act to colonies south of New England. Instead of prohibiting repayment of sterling debts with legal tender currency, Parliament followed a recommendation of the Board of Trade and in 1764 prohibited all legal tender currency.

Like the Currency Act of 1751 aimed at Rhode Island, the Currency Act of 1764 was aimed at Virginia because it had issued 250,000 pounds of bills of credit during the Seven Years War. Much of this credit was used to support Braddock's army and to mobilize frontier defense after the French defeated his army of regular troops. It was, however inflationary. Furthermore, competition by American merchants in the northern colonies for the direct trade with Britain contributed to a desire by English merchants to reduce inflation. English merchants perceived that inflation gave a competitive advantage to American merchants who used much less long term credit than they did.

The effect of the two currency acts was to prohibit all emissions of legal tender currency to pay private debts and to prohibit the reissue and extension of redemption dates for outstanding issues. Ambiguous wording of the statute seemed to allow colonial governments to emit nonlegal tender paper currency to pay public debts but, in a series of opinions, the Board of Trade interpreted the statute as prohibiting all emissions of paper currency.

After 1750, however, the increased availability of long term credit from increasing numbers of British commercial banks gradually increased the competitive advantage of British merchants in trans-Atlantic trade. Between 1754 and 1774, the number of commercial banks in London increased from eighteen to fifty-two. Institutional credit was unavailable to American merchants because there were no commercial banks (banks of deposit, money banks) in America. During the twenty-five years before the War for Independence, however, American merchants gained experience in using bank credit from their British agents.

The deflationary pressures that followed the 1764 Currency Act generated strong protests throughout the colonies. Colonists petitioned for repeal because there was not enough specie to efficiently conduct commerce. At the same time, colonial assemblies used many subterfuges to evade the law. A New York merchant described the response of a high percentage of American political and business leaders:

> We have no resources upon an Emergency but in Paper Money and if it be duely sunk we don't see the great Mischief of it to the Public...The Colony is chagrined at the Treatment of the Paper Money, considering how dutifully they have obeyed the requisitions of the Crown.

He added that the Currency Act would, in the long run, create a "mighty disturbance, as to shake all the Northern Colonys."[12]

Colonial protests against the Currency Act of 1764 were submerged by the concerted effort by all colonies to force repeal of the Molasses Act of 1764 and the Stamp Act of 1765, both of which had been passed at the insistence of Grenville. In the acrimonious contention preceding the repeal of the Stamp Act in 1766, Franklin quietly repudiated his plan to establish an American loan office. He correctly read political sentiment in America. American political and business leaders rejected all parliamentary taxation on the American side of the Atlantic. He changed the focus of his political activity to repealing the currency acts of 1751 and 1764 so that colonies could supply themselves with adequate amounts of legal tender currency. Due to parliamentary maneuvering and the political turmoil after the passage of the Townshend Revenue Act of 1767, the movement to repeal the currency acts lost momentum.

The need for an adequate currency, however, did not go away. Colonial legislatures changed tactics in order to supply local needs. Paper currency was issued to pay taxes, and tax rates were increased to fund them. This was the same paper currency that had been used for the previous fifty years but without a legal tender clause. Parliament finally acceded to these emissions in 1773. Paper currency could be issued for the limited purposes of paying taxes and building infrastructure like bridges. The statute of 1773 was only a relaxation of imperial distrust of paper currency. This half-way measure, however, did not satisfy American grievances.

At the beginning of hostilities in 1775, various issues and denominations of paper currency were about three-quarters of the money in circulation. Bills of credit formed a high percentage because they could be issued quickly and in large amounts. Loan office certificates and tobacco warehouse receipts were the smallest portion of paper currency because they required collateral that had market value. Although bills of credit were not legal tender, most people accepted them because of their convenience. In the larger picture, the use of paper money was never institutionalized because most emissions were for emergency financing. Fragmentation of emissions over time and place made it difficult to prevent inflation, which was exacerbated by the Board of Trade's suspicion that paper currency was a means of defrauding British merchants. These suspicious, and the lack of imperial concern, made it impossible for colonial legislatures to create an adequate money supply for the needs of domestic commerce.

By 1775 the American merchant community had the skills needed to organize and manage commercial banks. During the previous twenty-five years they had made increasing use of bills of exchange supplied by English banks, through their English agents. They also gained greater experience in using bills of credit, loan office certificates, and warehouse receipts in the conduct local and intercolonial trade. The passage of the Currency Act of 1764 was a stonewall barrier for colonial legislatures to incorporate banks of deposits that could issue banknote currency. Instead, Americans had to be satisfied with restricted emissions of several varieties of nonlegal tender currency. Incorporations of commercial banks to supply banknote currency and commercial credit had to await the success of the War for Independence.

Taxation and War

The purpose of the navigation laws, as they operated under salutary neglect, was to regulate trade. In the aftermath of the Seven Years War, Parliament changed their purpose. Colonial commerce would continue to be regulated but it would also be taxed on the American side of the Atlantic. Colonial products had always been taxed when they entered Britain, but Parliament's new policy was a dangerous innovation because it asked a question that Americans claimed was already settled by custom and usage. That question was the nature of the empire. Americans claimed the empire was federal. Parliament claimed it was unitary.

There were good reasons for taxing Americans on the American side of the Atlantic. The Seven Years War had been expensive and many American merchants had engaged in traitorous conduct by wartime trading with the French. Americans also gained great benefits from the outcome of the war. France was removed as a threat on the northern and western frontiers. American and parliamentary political leaders recognized that the enlarged empire required greater revenue to maintain a larger military establishment to protect it. *The unanswered question in 1763 was who would pay for this protection?* For Americans, it was a matter of negotiations with imperial authorities because, during the Seven Years War, the North American colonies had raised substantial revenues that were used to support British armed forces in America.

Parliamentary leaders had a different opinion. Raising tax revenues to defend the empire was not a matter of negotiation. From its position at the center, Parliament was responsible for raising the revenue necessary to put imperial defense on a sustaining basis; and it was a fact that North American colonies were lightly taxed by their legislatures. The Molasses Tax of 1764 was the first step in raising sufficient revenue to fund an enlarged military establishment stationed in America. It was a revision of the 1733 Molasses Tax that regulated trade rather than raised revenue. The molasses tax, plus taxes on wine and other Caribbean commodities were meant to be collected. To ensure collection, revenues from these taxes were used to pay the salaries of imperial customs commissioners and imperial admiralty judges who were based in Boston.

The molasses tax had ramifications not anticipated by Parliament. It threatened the profitability of rum distilling and the New England fishery because the exchange of preserved fish for molasses was a principal part of New England's trade; and the tax on wine threatened the established markets for provisions and wood products in Portugal and Madeira. American merchants called the tax counterproductive because the money earned from this trade was vital for purchasing manufactured products from Britain. American political leaders also called the tax unconstitutional because the foundation of English liberty was taxation by the consent of the governed. From the moment of settlement, taxation by consent had operated in all colonies. American political leaders claimed that the power to levy taxes in America belonged solely to colonial legislatures.

While opposition to the molasses tax was gaining momentum, Parliament passed the stamp tax. It was similar to the English stamp tax passed in 1694 that was a proven source of revenue because it was difficult to avoid. The stamp tax was a tax on most legal documents at the time of their signing. Confirmation of payment was an embossed stamp attached to the document. Without a stamp, documents could not be admitted as evidence in courts of law. Taxes were levied on licenses of lawyers, innkeepers, ship manifests, performance bonds, written contracts, real estate conveyances (including land grants), mortgages, land titles, leases, indentures, articles of apprenticeship, college diplomas, appointments to public office, newspaper advertisements, and almanacs. Like the molasses tax, all revenues would be expended in America to support troops stationed there.

The passage of the stamp tax transformed simmering opposition to the molasses tax and currency acts into overt resistance. Resistance was led by the best educated and wealthiest men in all colonies because they were the people most affected. They were also the persons most capable of mobilizing resistance. The Stamp Act Congress met in New York in October 1765 and converted colonial resistance into concentrated political action. Governing elites in nine colonies sent delegates. Delegates from the seven royal colonies were chosen at informal sessions of the assemblies that ignored the governors. The declaration issued by the Congress was a clear statement that Americans had exclusive power to tax themselves, and the recent taxes passed by Parliament were both unconstitutional and counterproductive for increasing wealth and tax revenues.

Resistance to collection was sometimes violent, but whatever form it took it effectively prevented collection. Although violence was a useful lever, commercial pressure was more effective. Merchants in Boston, New York, and Philadelphia agreed to suspend purchasing British products rather than use stamped contracts and stamped ship manifests. Imports substantially declined, which forced British merchants to petition for its repeal. Parliament complied in March 1766. At the same time Parliament passed the Declaratory Act.

The Declaratory Act claimed that Parliament had the power to enact laws that applied to all American colonies "in all cases whatsoever."[13] The stamp tax was an extraordinary blunder but the Declaratory Act was a greater blunder. It was a policy statement that told Americans that Parliament was still intent on taxing commerce on the American side of the Atlantic.

Parliament retained the tax on molasses, but lowered it and, taxes were levied on several other commodities in intercolonial trade. In 1767 the Townshend Revenue Act levied taxes on several kinds of paper, glassware, lead ingots, paint pigments, and tea that were imported from England. Nonimportation agreements were immediately revived in the principal cities, but this time political leaders appropriated the power of enforcement. Opposition to parliamentary taxation was fully politicized and most merchants became bystanders.

Politicization forced repeal of the Townshend taxes in 1770, except on tea. The taxes on tea and molasses continued to be collected, and their collection intensified alienation. Another blunder would re-ignite confrontation. The Tea Act of 1773 was that blunder. The act allowed the East India Company to export tea directly to America and undersell tea that was already in the warehouses of American merchants. The Tea Act was proof to American merchants that their interests would always be second to the interests of British merchants. Political leaders, with the full cooperation of merchants, mobilized waterfront workers to forcibly prevent tea from being distributed. In Boston and Annapolis the tea was destroyed.

In retaliation for the destruction of tea in Boston, Parliament passed the Coercive Acts in 1774 that closed the port of Boston to all overseas commerce until the Massachusetts legislature reimbursed the East India Company for its losses. From the perspective of American merchants, closing the port of Boston was the equivalent of cutting the jugular vein of north Atlantic commerce. Colonial governing elites realized that if they did not take united action both self-governance and commercial prosperity would be continuously threatened by legislation passed by Parliament. In September 1774 a Continental Congress met in Philadelphia. Its delegates were elected outside the normal channels of governance.

Congress authorized the people of Massachusetts to form a new government that would continue to collect taxes and conduct the normal affairs of governance. In addition, the Massachusetts legislature was authorized to mobilize the militia in order to isolate the royal governor, and this isolation was to continue until the Coercive Acts were repealed. If he tried to exercise his authority, he would have to use British regular army troops stationed in Boston. Parliament's response to confrontation was intransigence. Regular army troops were deployed to try and reassert the authority of the royal governor. The Massachusetts legislature considered this an act of war and hostilities began at Lexington and Concord in April 1775.

Summary

The attempt by parliamentary leaders to centralize imperial governance without consulting Americans forced American political and business leaders to seek other means for redressing their grievances. Riots, nonimportation agreements, and congresses were tried but failed to solve the fundamental issue of where the powers of imperial governance, taxation, and commercial regulation resided. Parliamentary leaders said the power of governance resided exclusively with Parliament because Parliament was the constitutional arbitrator of empire. Americans claimed that mutual accommodation was the only workable basis for imperial governance, and that a means of accommodation already existed. It was the federal structure of the empire that had evolved during the eighteenth century. Parliament's persistent claim after 1763 that it was the final arbitrator of imperial governance blocked further evolution of the federal empire.

This intransigence convinced a high percentage of Americans that they would be more prosperous if they governed themselves. This was the most important result of the War for Independence. For a high percentage of Americans, the fundamental purpose of independence was preserving the federal structure of imperial governance by a confederation of states managed by Americans.

Chapter 5

Creating a Nation

The War for Independence was about governance. For most people the principal purpose of the war was to preserve self-government within a federal system, similar to what had operated before the war. In comparative terms, the war had minimal impact on the political, economic, and social institutions of most states. Nonetheless, independence guaranteed that institutions of governance would undergo an accelerated evolution. *In which direction would this growth take place?*

The War for Independence was a popular war, and the men who filled the ranks of military units wanted an enlarged franchise. They wanted to expand the basis of governance by consent. Enlarged electorates were created by provisional state legislatures that assumed governance during the war. Generally, the people wanted lowered property qualifications for voting and the reapportionment of state legislatures to better represent frontier counties. A crucial question facing state political leaders was: *How would enlarged electorates act? Would they contain a sufficiently high percentage of commercially motivated persons to revive the momentum of pre-war commercial growth? Or would they use their power to protect subsistence cultivators?*

In the immediate postwar years, governing elites were fully aware that the problem of taxing agricultural land was intimately related to the enlarged postwar electorates. They were also aware of the great unanswered question in the infant republic—*Were there sufficient numbers of commercially motivated cultivators and merchants to govern in the interests of economic development?*

Frontier counties, especially in southern states, had serious problems. One of the principal deficiencies was the lack of good transportation needed to integrate interior areas with tidewater commerce. An equally serious problem was the high percentage of cultivators who were peasants. For the most part, southern peasants were indifferent to full integration, and their indifference translated into deep political divisions over tax policies. Restructuring taxation was a major political issue in all postwar states, but it was an especially intense in southern states.

Prewar tax structures had levied uniform acreage taxation (usually low) on landowners and high, uniform poll taxes. Poll taxes were highly regressive on peasants. Ending the poll tax was the most important goal for all peasants because it would allow them to escape most taxation. The reciprocal of ending poll taxation was levying an *ad valorem* (value) tax on the productive capacity of land. The productive capacity of land was directly related to labor inputs. Landowning peasants made minimum labor inputs; therefore, their land had minimum value and would be lightly taxed. Landowning peasants favored retention of low uniform acreage taxation because it was beneficial to them. They also favored lowering or ending poll taxes.

In comparison, the land of yeomen and plantation owners was more intensively cultivated and had much higher productivity. It would be highly taxed. Valuation taxation would transfer the principal source of state revenue from the numerous peasantries to a small minority of commercial cultivators. It would penalize landowners who sought to increase production of commodities for market sale. The enlarged electorate justified valuation taxation on the principle of ability to pay. On the surface this seems fair, but valuation taxation, coupled with ending poll taxes, would allow a high percentage of white peasants to escape most taxation. Ending poll taxation was strongly opposed by commercially motivated persons, whether yeomen, plantation owners, or merchants. They correctly interpreted valuation taxation as a threat to economic development and the first step in creating a peasant democracy that would quickly dispense with their governing skills.

After the return of commercial prosperity in 1790, the conflicts over taxation between tidewater and interior counties disappeared in most northern states. The pervasive practice of commercial agriculture in northern states, coupled with large amounts of labor applied to building roads, meant that yeomen could profitably sell their surpluses and acquire money to pay taxes. Because of pervasive commercial labor norms applied to cultivation, there was a substantial degree of fairness in a land tax based on valuation, especially if the assessor was a neighbor who was elected.

Most national political leaders knew that a national government had to be strong enough to expand the scope of the commercial policies inherited from colonial governance because commercial prosperity was essential for consolidating independence. It was equally essential for implementing the vision of national political leaders that the United States was destined to be a continental empire. For them, a strong national government was essential for overcoming the postwar weakness of the United States. It was equally essential for providing a stable political environment for state governments to establish stable political institutions.

Only a strong national government could promote commercial prosperity, and commercial prosperity was the best guarantee of future national greatness. The alternative to a stronger national government was a federal government so weak that the United States would debilitate into an unstable agrarian republic that invited intervention by European nations.

Independence was also the opportunity for Americans to participate in the Industrial Revolution that was rapidly transforming English society. If Americans could retain and expand the commercial and political institutions of their colonial legacy, they had an opportunity to convert the raw materials of a continent into similar quantities of new wealth that were being created in England. Independence, however, was only an opportunity. There was no guarantee that Americans could put their political house in order to take full advantage of the commercial opportunities that were theirs for the taking.

Creating political institutions that were friendly to commerce was essential for participating in the opportunities created by independence and the Industrial Revolution. Creating stable political institutions had to begin at the national level so that state governments had a predictable political environment in which to evolve. In order to take advantage of opportunities for economic development, governance of both the national and state governments had to be by commercially motivated electorates that were willing to delegate a broad spectrum of innovative activities to entrepreneurs so they could mobilize capital and labor resources.

The principal problems of independence were implementing policies that would (1) achieve political stability, (2) restore commercial prosperity, (3) generate sufficient revenue for the national government, (4) blunt the centrifugal forces of federalism (states' rights), (5) expand industrial capacity sufficient to equip military forces, (6) expand settlement into the trans-Appalachian west and beyond.

The National Impulse

In the postwar years, there was great political uncertainty of how much power should be granted to the national government in order to implement policies of economic development. Long before the war was won, it was glaringly apparent to most national political leaders that the commercial opportunities inherent in independence would be in great jeopardy unless a stronger national government was created. Winning the war came first, and enough resources were scraped together and enough French help received to obtain the prize. Not until after the war could national political leaders grapple with the problem of creating a more perfect union. Creating a more perfect union meant replacing the loose federal union of the Articles of Confederation with a strong national (central) government in which states were subordinate units of government in all areas of national concern.

The Articles of Confederation were framed by the Continental Congress in 1777 and submitted to the states for ratification. When the last remaining state (Maryland) ratified it in 1781, the United States had its first Constitution. The articles constitutionalized the wartime power of governance exercised by Congress. Congressional power was very limited. Most political power remained with state governments because they controlled all taxation and regulated almost all commerce between the states and foreign nations.

The greatest weakness of Congress was that it had no independent power of taxation. It could only issue paper money, which it did until hyperinflation made congressional money worthless. State taxation supplied a large proportion of the money that supported the army, and the rest was supplied by barrowing by Congress (war bonds). Military funding was always deficient. The reluctance of state governments to levy sufficient taxes to support the army indicated that, if the United States achieved independence, the federal union would be in danger of dissolution because state governments would probably lower taxes to prewar levels as soon as possible. State legislatures would preferentially repay state war debts instead of adequately funding the operation of the national government. This is what happened.

Washington's army dissolved immediately after signing the Treaty of Paris (1783) that ended the war. National political leaders knew that the United States was very vulnerable to becoming a pawn in European power politics. It was, therefore, essential for the United States to find a place among European nations, and that this place could not be secured by a military establishment. The only way the United States could mitigate its weakness was to establish domestic and foreign commerce on a predictable basis because this was the best way to substantiate the claim that the United States was a viable nation. Interstate trade and commercial treaties had to be uniformly enforceable by a national judicial system.

National political leaders had to deal with the reality that the enumerated powers of the articles were too weak to create national political stability or guarantee national survival in a hostile world. National weakness was due to national bankruptcy. Funds to operate the national government had to be requisitioned from the states. Payments were usually much less than requested, often delayed, and sometimes refused. Attempts to amend the articles to allow the U.S. government to collect tariffs on imports were twice rejected. Nor could Congress enforce treaties of commerce (if negotiated). Under the articles, Congress was forbidden to deprive any state of its right to impose taxes on imports without its consent.

Lack of power to regulate domestic commerce was the second great weakness of the articles. Delegates to the Continental Congress were unwilling to trust an American central government (even a very weak one) to exercise this power because it, like taxation, was a principal cause of the war. Furthermore, the articles conspicuously lacked a judicial power. From the achievement of independence (1783) to 1786, all national political leaders, knew that the power to tax, regulate commerce, and adjudicate commercial disputes had to reside in a stronger central government if the nation was to survive.

A concerted effort to strengthen the central government began as soon as the last British troops departed. It was absolutely essential that national political leaders consolidate national political loyalty before the euphoria of winning independence was past; otherwise, a feeble central government would dissipate the popular impulse for national identity. The difficulty of suppressing Shay's Rebellion in Massachusetts (between August 1786 and February 1787), was the death rattle of federal governance under the articles. It occurred on the eve the Constitutional Convention (held in Philadelphia in May 1787) and induced a powerful urgency to the convention's deliberations. Delegates were acutely aware that national identity and the foundation of future prosperity depended on replacing the tottering government under the articles.

In spite of the death rattle of the articles, there were more doubts than assurances that a convention could frame a constitution acceptable to the enlarged, more democratic, and less commercially motivated electorates of many states. These electorates had come into existence under state constitutions adopted during the war and their peacetime behavior was unpredictable. Nonetheless, the delegates framed a constitution that granted preponderant power to a national government in matters of taxation, regulating commerce, and adjudicating disputes in interstate commerce.

The new government became operational in April 1789 after eleven states had ratified the Constitution. National political leaders had succeeded in sponsoring a national convention, framing a nationalist constitution, and securing its ratification. Elections to the first Congress uniformly favored men who had supported ratification and who strongly supported using the powers of the national government to promote the creation of commercial wealth. In many ways the new government would function like the British North American commercial empire, but the relationship between national power and state power was much more clearly defined than the relationship between the colonies and Britain. National political leaders envisioned the new national government as an umbrella for state governments to undertake programs of economic development to the extent of their human and capital resources.

Nationalist Party Program

There was great latitude in thinking among delegates to the first Congress of how strong the national government should be. The leadership of President George Washington was crucial to this debate. Washington and a majority of delegates strongly favored policies to create an energetic national government that would actively promote the creation of new commercial wealth. The institutions and policies that promoted the production of commercial wealth during the colonial era would continue, but under new management.

Nothing could be done, however, until the government had sufficient revenue to pay the current expenses of governance. The Revenue Act of 1789 was the first major legislation passed by Congress after the Constitution became operational. James Madison authored it, and most of its provisions received overwhelming support.

There was general agreement that most revenue had to come from tariffs because taxation of exports was prohibited by the Constitution. Additional revenue would come from a tax on the tonnage of ships carrying imports. There was also general agreement that the tariff should be 5 percent of the value of imported products. There was, however, disagreement over whether some products should be taxed at a higher rate in order to encourage American manufacturers. *Was it in the national interest to use a protective tariff to implement a policy of import substitution?*

For the most part, the Revenue Act of 1789 was for revenue. The Revenue Act operated as projected. The national government secured sufficient revenue to pay operating expenses and fund the war debt. Two other events contributed to national political stability: (1) ratification of the Bill of Rights in 1791, and (2) passage of the Northwest Ordinance of 1787. Both were highly popular.

The Bill of Rights was the first ten amendments to the Constitution. It was ratified to protect the civil liberties of individuals from infringement by the national government. James Madison initiated the adoption process at the same time he was guiding the Revenue Act of 1789 through Congress. It was the second most important item on the agenda of the first Congress. It was quickly framed, passed, and forwarded to the states for ratification. The effects of ratification were immediate. Opposition to the Constitution dissolved. Thereafter, most controversies centered on how much power resided in the national government to actively encourage economic development and how much resided with states so they could protect interests they considered vital to their welfare.

The Northwest Ordinance made a similar contribution to national political stability. It had its origins in the ratification of the Articles of Confederation. It was passed in 1787 during the last days of Congress under the articles. Maryland refused to ratify the articles until all states with claims to land in the trans-Appalachian west ceded their claims to the federal government. Maryland insisted on cession because it had no claims to western land and it feared that states that had claims would eventually have large enough populations to dominate the federal government. Virginia cleared the way for Maryland to ratify the articles by ceding all claims north of the Ohio River and agreeing that the county of Kentucky could enter the confederacy as a state equal to the original states.

After Virginia's cession, other states followed Virginia's example. These cessions created a national public domain and provided for the orderly settlement of vacant land north of the Ohio River and east of the Mississippi River. After its passage, the federal government under the articles collapsed because it was bankrupt.

The Northwest Ordinance required extinguishing Indian occupancy by purchase or treaty as a necessary prerequisite for establishing civil government. Thereafter: (1) all land was surveyed before sale so that settlers had clear titles and were obligated to pay taxes on it, (2) all land was in freehold tenure, (3) all land was sold except for land granted for military service, (4) one section (one square mile) was reserved in each township of thirty-six square miles to fund common schools to teach functional literacy, (5) three to five states could be formed from the territory, (6) new states would enter the confederacy on equal terms with existing states, and (7) slavery was prohibited.

The acquisition of revenue was intimately tied to the passage of the Northwest Ordinance. Land speculators wrote large sections of the law because they needed a civil government to record titles for land they would sell to actual settlers. The federal government had a parallel interest. It wanted to reduce the war debt. War bonds issued by Congress or quartermaster certificates issued by military commanders in exchange for food and supplies, were exchangeable at face value for land.

Settlement, however, was delayed until the new government under the Constitution had sufficient revenue to pacify hostile Indians and pay surveying costs. After the new government had adequate revenue, the Northwest Ordinance and subsequent legislation based on it, was a hugely successful formula that guided the expansion of the nation into the trans-Appalachian west and beyond.

Establishing Public Credit

The first priority after passage of the Revenue Act of 1789 was establishing the public credit because the new government had to be able to borrow money to pay emergency expenses. It was equally clear that the national government would be unable to borrow money until it funded the war debt. Furthermore, the Constitution made it obligatory for Congress to validate all debts contracted under the articles.

Not until the Revenue Act became operational did Congress confirm the appointment of Alexander Hamilton as secretary of the treasury; although he was secretary of the treasury designate. During the debate over the Revenue Act of 1789, its principal author, James Madison, wanted to levy higher tariffs on products imported from England than products imported from France. Hamilton opposed discriminatory tariffs because he would need maximum revenue to fund the national war debt, and maximum revenue was generated by a low tariff that maximized imports. Maximum revenue would come from levying a 5 percent tariff on most imports. Discriminatory tariffs would not serve the revenue needs of the new government.

A high percentage of imports came from Britain where prewar channels of trade were reopened and British banks provided credit to revive trade. There were, however, some protective features in the 1789 Revenue Act. Taxes up to 50 percent of value were put on steel, cordage, salt, and some varieties of cloth. These products were consumed in large quantities in the United States but the nation was not self-sufficient in their production; although, it was obvious that this was possible. High tariffs were also put on ships and tobacco. U.S. shipbuilders supplied the needs of American merchants, and Americans manufactured most of the tobacco products consumed by Americans. High tariffs on these two products were designed to preserve American control of an existing market.

A second provision was that ships owned and operated by American merchants engaged in international commerce paid lower tonnage taxes when entering a harbor than ships of other nationalities. American merchants were given a competitive advantage in international commerce. This advantage was extended to foreign merchants, if their ships had been built in America. A third provision reserved the coastal trade to American owned and operated ships in the same way British navigation laws required domestic maritime trade to be in British owned and operated ships. The Revenue Act of 1789 was, in effect, an American navigation law.

Congress immediately instructed Hamilton to prepare a plan to fund the national debt. In January 1790 he presented Congress with a report on the ways and means of doing it. His program was strongly supported by Washington and it was enacted into law in July 1790. The war debt consisted of a heterogeneous collection of claims. Among them were bonds and debt certificates denominated in congressional currency, state currencies, and specie. These debts were contracted under congressional authority, the authority of state legislatures, and by army quartermasters in order to obtain food and supplies to keep armies in the field. The value of many claims was disputed because they had been contracted in highly inflated currency. In addition, there were land warrants issued as enlistment incentives, and specie loans made to the United States by the French and Spanish governments and Dutch bankers.

Almost all national leaders agreed that the United States had to maintain a good credit rating among European nations. It was essential for legitimatizing republican governance, and it was equally essential for establishing new commercial relationships. Loans from the French and Spanish governments and from Dutch bankers, plus arrears in interest, had to be fully paid. The value of these debts had to be compiled, given a uniform value, arrears in interest calculated, and new bonds issued. The common denominator of all of these debts was they were contracted for national purposes.

Hamilton's plan for funding generated controversy for two reasons: (1) it rewarded the legal owners of war bonds rather than the patriots who purchased them, (2) the national government assumed responsibility for paying that portion of state debts that had been incurred to win independence.

A large majority of original owners were patriots who had accepted quartermaster certificates of debt for food and supplies needed by army commanders. Supplies were purchased at inflated prices. Alternatively, supplies were requisitioned and paid for with certificates of debt. Most providers assented to these transactions. In the immediate years following independence, a high percentage of original bondholders sold them for 10–25 percent of their face value. They needed money during the postwar depression because domestic and foreign commerce did not immediately revive. Furthermore, most original bondholders had serious doubts that they would ever be paid because of the bankruptcy of the federal government under the articles and doubts about the effectiveness of the new national government.

Records of the original bondholders were nearly complete. Both James Madison and Thomas Jefferson (Washington's secretary of state) approved of funding war debts at their full face value but they opposed rewarding speculators. They believed that justice would be better served if half of the value of bonds and other certificates of debt were paid to the original holders and half to legal owners. Madison and Jefferson thought that patriotism should be rewarded. Furthermore, they believed that a more equalized sharing of the largess of the new government would strongly contribute to increasing popular support. These were very powerful arguments.

Hamilton believed that the national government should pay the full face value of war bonds to legal owners. In other words, speculators would be generously rewarded. Hamilton had five purposes for rewarding legal owners: (1) businessmen who owned the bonds would give their loyalty to the national government, (2) funding state war debts would teach businessmen to look to the national government instead of state governments to protect their interests, (3) businessmen who made speculative profits would increase their commercial activities, (4) smaller denomination bonds would be endorsed among businessmen and circulate as a currency in a nation that was without a national currency or coinage. This would help revive commerce, and (5) businessmen who owned most of the domestic war debts were likely to purchase governments bonds to finance future emergencies because they knew that the national government was committed to full payment to legal owners rather than partial payments or repudiation.

The strength of Hamilton's arguments was that businessmen who owned bonds would strongly support the new national government. In broader terms, Hamilton wanted the most energetic and best educated citizens to support programs of national economic development, as opposed to many of the original bond owners who were strongly oriented to state governments. Many original owners, perhaps a large majority, would put their bonds in cookie jars and use annual interest payments for household expenses. The funding act required interest payments to be made with gold coins. Businessmen could use interest money for investment or sell the bonds to raise capital. In contrast, bonds in cookie jars were frozen capital.

The national government acquired the requisite gold coins because the Revenue Act of 1789 required tariffs to be paid in gold coins. The ability of the national government to make interest payments in gold coins greatly enhanced their value as collateral for commercial loans and paying commercial debts. Hamilton had anticipated that this would happen (based on English experience) when he claimed that the debt would become both a political and economic asset of the national government. It would be a political asset because owners would give preferential loyalty to the national government. It would also be an economic asset because bonds could be used as collateral and as currency. At the same time, loyalty to state governments would be weakened so that time and events could build national consciousness.

Hamilton's funding program had two loads of adverse political baggage. It ignored patriotism, and 80 percent of the owners of bonds were speculating merchants concentrated in northern states. Many southern planters were apprehensive that northern merchants would assume the same function as prewar British merchants. They would provide high cost credit that meant perpetual indebtedness. They were reluctant to create a new monied oligarchy at their expense.

Neither Madison nor Jefferson was enthusiastic about funding state war debts because some states, like Virginia, had retained high wartime taxes in order to substantially reduce their war debts. Funding unpaid state war debts, as they existed in 1790, would reward those states that had not adequately taxed themselves to repay their debt obligations. The effect would be that states that had adequately funded their debts would (indirectly) contribute tax monies to the national government to fund the debts of delinquent states.

To remedy this inequity, Madison proposed that the national government assume state war debts, as they existed in 1783 (the year the war ended). Hamilton agreed to increase the national debt in order to get the needed votes for passage. States that had adequately funded their war debts were rewarded with U.S. bonds that could provide revenue for state legislatures to appropriate for expedient purposes. Foremost among them was Virginia, the home state of Madison and Jefferson.

From the perspective of creating stable finances, Hamilton's arguments for his funding program were very persuasive. Nonetheless, it required a political dollop to obtain passage. Hamilton promised Madison and Jefferson that he would use his influence to pass legislation that would transfer the seat of the national government from Philadelphia to a location on the Potomac River. In August 1790, in a close vote in both houses of Congress, Hamilton's funding and assumption program was enacted into law without substantial alteration. Shortly afterward, Congress voted to move the national capital to a new city on the banks of the Potomac River.

After funding was complete, the national debt was seventy million dollars. Of this amount, 18 million was assumed state debts and twelve million was owed to the French and Spanish governments and Dutch bankers. U.S. citizens were owed twenty-seven million, plus thirteen million in arrears of interest. After Congress passed funding, Hamilton's fiscal policies had no intention of reducing the national debt. The tax policies he recommended to Congress were calculated to raise only sufficient revenue to pay current operating expenses of the national government and the annual interest on the national debt. In 1790, 80 percent of national revenue was used to service the national debt.

Hamilton envisioned a perpetual debt, like the national debt of Britain, because surety of interest payments would sustain the nation's ability to borrow. It would also help create a capital market for existing and future bonds. When Hamilton resigned as secretary of the treasury in 1795, the national debt had increased to eighty-three million dollars, largely due to military expenditures on the frontier.

Funding the national debt fulfilled Hamilton's most optimistic expectations. The reliability of interest payments in gold coins was enhanced by the organization of a market for government bonds in taverns along Wall Street in New York City. The establishment of a public market attracted capital from unstable European nations that feared repercussion from the French Revolution that began in July 1789. In April 1791, France declared war on Austria. Thereafter, Europe was engaged in a general war that lasted until March 1802. By May 1795 foreign businessmen owned over twenty million dollars of the national debt; and by 1801 they owned thirty-three million. By 1803 foreign investors owned fifty-eight million, including stock in state chartered banks. Not only did foreign purchasers sustain the value of U.S. bonds, but the safety of capital in the United States was a magnet for attracting additional investment capital.

The Constitution could not operate as the supreme law of the nation without a court system to enforce legal uniformity in matters of national concern. Freedom of interstate commerce and enforcing the obligations of commercial treaties were two of these concerns. The Constitution explicitly made treaties part of the supreme law of the nation and granted congress the power to regulate interstate commerce. After ratification of the Constitution, all of the barriers to interstate commerce passed by state legislatures under the Articles of Confederation went into abeyance.

Congress, therefore, did not have to pass legislation that defined freedom of interstate trade because the national courts enforced a rough uniformity of commercial law by accepting decisions appealed from state courts. In a largely silent way, the Judiciary Act of 1789 preserved the freedom of interstate commerce in the same way that freedom of intercolonial trade had operated prior to the War for Independence.

Bank of the United States

At the request of Congress, Hamilton wrote a report on the advisability of incorporating a central bank. He submitted his report to Congress in December 1790. It outlined the structure, function, and purpose of a bank that was closely modeled on the Bank of England. Hamilton envisioned it as an engine of economic development. Its purpose was debated in Congress with little controversy because commercial prosperity was rapidly increasing. Congress passed it by a substantial majority in February 1791. The vote, however, was more sectional than funding and assumption because a higher percentage of southern (agrarian) congressmen opposed it.

Hamilton expected Washington to immediately sign it into law. It did not happen. Jefferson, Madison, and Edmund Randolph (Washington's attorney general) considered it unconstitutional because the Constitution did not specifically grant Congress the power to pass charters of incorporation. This was a thunderclap to Hamilton because Congress, under the articles, had incorporated the Bank of North America in 1781 as a means of supplying the federal government with enough credit to keep it operating.

Madison's objection reversed the position he had held at the Constitutional Convention (1787). At the convention he had stated that an effective national government had to exercise implied powers in order to support the enumerated powers that the constitution granted to the national government. Madison and Jefferson professed they were unable to see a clear relationship between the national government's power to incorporate a bank and a need to have an emergency source of credit for national defense. Nor did they see a clear relationship between sustaining the public credit and the day-to-day fiscal operations that the bank would perform for the treasury department. On very short notice, Hamilton was forced to write a defense of the bank. He took the occasion to write a short treatise on interpreting the Constitution. He advocated broad interpretation to achieve national goals. Washington digested Hamilton's argument, compared it with Madison and Jefferson's, and signed the bank bill into law.

What were the reasons for Madison's defection from broad interpretation of the Constitution, and the support he received from Jefferson and Randolph? In the 1790s southern planters did not understand the use of bank credit by city businessmen. They were rural residents who depended on factors to supply credit to purchase the manufactured products they consumed. For the most part, plantation owners lived with minimal use of cash money. Most of their income came from once a year sales of harvests that was supplemented by sales of other products liked lumber or ship timbers made by slaves; or from the sale of surplus slaves. Most planters knew how to manage their debts to factors; nonetheless, they were debtors. As long as they dealt with factors on a personal basis, payments could be postponed. City bankers were not as accommodating. They charged high interest rates for deferred payments.

Planters also knew that cash money commands political influence, and they did not have cash money. In the long run, plantation owners knew that the ability of city businessmen to accumulate money (capital) would diminish their influence in governance, particularly national governance. They distrusted a national government that promoted the interests of urban businessmen who insisted on timely repayments of debts. Jefferson, Madison, and Randolph feared that the national government would be dominated by northern businessmen who had minimal sympathy for large landowners and slave owners like themselves.

The bank was chartered for twenty years and capitalized at ten million dollars. This made it the largest corporation in the United States. Its charter granted it a monopoly as fiscal agent of the Treasury Department. All government revenue was deposited in it or in state chartered banks that acted as its agents. The bank, or its agents, also made all disbursements. In return for its monopoly it was obligated to make loans to the national government. The national government owned one-fifth of the bank's shares and private citizens owned the other four-fifths. Forty percent of the purchase price of shares had to be specie and 60 percent could be U.S. bonds. Accepting bonds as part of the purchase price for shares helped sustain the value of U.S. bonds.

An equally important function of the bank was helping businessmen expand the scope and volume of interstate and international commerce. It served their needs by issuing banknote currency and facilitating the transfer of funds among branch offices in order to make timely payments. Like the Bank of North America, the Bank of the United States was a bank of deposit for business funds.

In the terminology of the time, it was a money bank. Its capital could not be invested in mortgages on real property because this would greatly reduce liquidity. Managers also adopted the policy of not making commodity loans on tobacco warehouse receipts. This business was reserved for state banks, and state banks soon proliferated to supply credit to businessmen in inland villages instead of serving the needs of export-import merchants in coastal cities.

Relative to its capitalization, it issued a small amount of banknotes, and they mostly circulated in cities. Among city merchants, they made a visible contribution to increasing liquidity and thus lowering interest rates on business transactions. They also facilitated the collection of taxes, particularly tariffs. Because their banknotes were redeemable in gold and silver coins on demand, Hamilton, in his capacity as secretary of the treasury, authorized their use to pay tariffs.

The bank's monopoly as fiscal agent of the treasury department guaranteed high profits and predictable dividends for shareholders. When shares went on sale in Philadelphia in July 1791, there was a scramble of investors/speculators to purchase them. Almost all purchasers were urban businessmen living in northern cities. They were the people who owned a high percentage of government bonds that could be used to purchase shares. They were also the most likely people to use banking services because they were patrons of the three existing state chartered banks.

Manufacturing

With strong encouragement from President Washington, in January 1790 the House of Representative requested Hamilton to devise a program that would encourage manufacturing in the United States, particularly of military supplies. Military supplies had a high priority because, during the War for Independence, the U.S. army had been heavily dependent on imported supplies, particularly from France.

In December 1791, Hamilton submitted a Report on Manufactures to Congress. He divided American manufacturing into three categories: self-sufficient, established, and infant. Hamilton had accurate knowledge of how machinery exponentially increased labor productivity in the manufacture of cotton textiles. He was also well informed of how the high pressure steam engine, which was perfected in 1780, had exponentially increased the production of bar iron and iron implements. Pervading the whole report was the assumption that the United States was destined to become a great manufacturing nation if it could mobilize the capital and labor to efficiently apply machinery to manufacturing. Mobilization, however, required a friendly political and economic environment, and it was within the power of the national government to provide it. *How could this be done?*

In 1790 the United States was primarily an exporter of agricultural, forest, and fisheries commodities. The market for these commodities did not consistently produce favorable terms of trade because European nations could obtain these commodities from several sources. In both long and short terms, fluctuating prices and highly variable terms of trade for these commodities would reduce the amount of manufactured products that Americans could purchase from European nations.

This condition, however, was not a reason for complaint because the United States could escape these uncertainties by producing an increasing percentage of manufactured products it consumed. Protective tariffs would stimulate self-sufficiency in manufactured products by encouraging American entrepreneurs to make investments to satisfy the domestic market.

Industries that already supplied most of the American market did not need tariff protection. Initial protection should be for products that were being manufactured in substantial quantities in the United States. Foremost among them were iron and steel implements, leather goods, naval supplies, and paper. Infant industries were those that supplied only a portion of the national market. Among them were textiles made in factories using water powered machinery. Water powered machinery to spin thread supplied most of England's needs. Water powered looms were operational but largely experimental. It was obvious to Hamilton that establishing factories in the United States to make textiles was an event waiting to happen, and good policies of political economy could accelerate the acquisition of this technology.

The initial prices of machine made textiles would equal the prices of textiles manufactured by handicraft methods using household labor. High tariffs would guarantee high profits to manufacturers of machine made textiles by protecting them from foreign competition. High profit margins would allow manufacturers to build more productive (and expensive) machinery and establish factory production on a continuing basis. Thereafter, consumer prices would decline because high profits would attract more entrepreneurs who would create a competitive domestic market. What was true for textiles would apply to manufacturers of other products as soon as machinery was invented to lower the costs of production.

The application of water powered machinery to production would vastly increase labor productivity because, full-time, supervised, paid laborers operating machinery was much more productive than similar amounts of labor applied to agriculture or artisan manufacturing. Increased labor productivity would be highly beneficial to American consumers because the amount of manufactured products Americans could purchase would not be dependent on the fluctuating prices of export commodities.

Where would the capital come from to build factories, and where would laborers come from to work in factories? Capital would come from indigenous entrepreneurs and foreign investors escaping from wartime turmoil in Europe ignited by the French Revolution. Both groups would invest because there was a rapidly growing U.S. market. Two additional factors would attract investments in factory manufacturing: (1) increasing availability of bank credit, and (2) a legal system that enforced contracts.

There would be two principal sources of labor. Much of the labor in textile factories would be performed by women and children, as in Britain. In other factories, immigrants would do much of the labor because they lacked pioneering skills to settle vacant land, and most lacked money to purchase operating farms. Americans would preferentially settle the trans-Appalachian west because they had pioneering skills. Put in its broadest context, favorable policies of political economy adopted by Congress could accelerate the production of new wealth beyond the most optimistic estimate of capital availability in the United States.

Hamilton had to justify a policy of active encouragement of manufacturing in a nation that was 90 percent rural and where a high percentage of manufacturing was done with household labor. A high priority was factory manufacture of military supplies (gunpowder, muskets, cannons, and warships) using full-time paid laborers. There was little argument that these industries should be encouraged by the national government. Almost as soon as the new government had sufficient revenue (1792), Congress authorized building two government owned arsenals. The first was at Springfield, Massachusetts in 1793 and the second at Harpers Ferry, Virginia in 1798.

But what of the generality of consumer products like hinges, nails, pots, shoes, glass, paper, and textiles? Many prominent political leaders were ambivalent about an active policy of encouraging manufacturing because they believed that the new government should use its limited resources to encourage rapid settlement of the trans-Appalachian west. Britain had ceded the United States a vast territory of vacant land west of the Appalachian Mountains and east of the Mississippi River; but it did not really belong to the nation until loyal citizens settled it. Only occupancy could make this land part of the United States. For many political leaders, settlement of the trans-Appalachian west was the nation's first priority.

Many southern political leaders, with Thomas Jefferson as their principal spokesman, went one step further. They believed that a rural landholding electorate was essential for sustaining the political stability of the republic. Fortunately for the United States, the abundance of vacant land could accommodate an increasing agrarian population for the foreseeable future. They further believed that the availability of land would make it possible for "natural aristocrats," like Thomas Jefferson, to lead an evolution into democratic governance.[1]

Thomas Jefferson was the principal spokesman for the vision that the United States would be an agrarian republic. He believed that a protective tariff would subsidize a dangerous alliance between businessmen and government that would undermine the political stability of the republic. The best way for the American experiment to succeed was to prevent the formation of a monied oligarchy that employed large numbers of wage laborers working in factories.

According to agrarian analysis, cities were inherently unstable. The principal reason for instability was that unskilled urban wage laborers did not have a stake in society. They were rootless persons because they owned no property and frequently changed employment, and, when they were employed, they were economically dependent on their employers. They were, therefore, an unsafe electorate for republican and democratic governance.

To him, the abundance of unsettled land in the United States dictated that settlement of this land should be the national priority. He expressed his view in *Notes on the State of Virginia* that he wrote between 1781 and 1784. He began writing it when he was wartime governor of Virginia, and had it published in London in 1785 when he was U.S. ambassador to France. He believed that the abundance of vacant land was a one-time opportunity to establish a stable republican government that would show European political leaders that republican governance was politically viable and morally virtuous. The reciprocal of Jeffersonian agrarianism was purchasing most manufactured products from European nations where autocratic governments controlled rootless populations living in unstable cities.

Chapter 19 of *Notes on the State of Virginia* summarizes his vision of the agrarian future of the United States. It was entitled, "The Present State of Manufactures, Commerce, Interior and Exterior Trade."

> Those who labor in the earth are the chosen people of God, if ever He had a chosen people, whose breasts He has made His peculiar deposit for substantial and genuine virtue....Corruption of morals in the mass of cultivators is a phenomenon of which no age nor nation has furnished an example....Dependence (on wage labor) begets subservience and venality, suffocates the germ of virtue, and prepares fit tools for the designs of ambition....Generally speaking, the proportion which the aggregate of the other classes of citizens bears to any State to that of its husbandmen, is the proportion of its unsound

to its healthy parts, and is a good enough barometer whereby to measure its degree of corruption....Let our workshops remain in Europe (because) the mobs of great cities add just so much to the support of pure government, as sores do to the strength of the human body. [2]

The hidden agenda of the book was justifying the public virtue of southern planters like himself. What he muted was as important as what he made explicit. Two muted topics are especially significant: (1) the extent of slave ownership, and (2) the extent of literacy. He called slavery a "great political and moral evil" but owned many slaves until the day of his death in 1826. He ignored the status of slaves who were much more dependent and subservient to their masters than urban wage laborers were dependent on their employers, and he glossed the subsistence welfare that masters imposed on them. He used the innocuous phrase, "under the mild treatment our slaves experience, and their wholesome, though coarse food" that we feed them, allows planters like myself to live in comfort or opulence and have time to devote our lives to public service. In Jefferson's opinion, white peasant landholders were as virtuous as planters in an agrarian republic, provided they were governed by persons like himself.[3]

Also absent from his description of Virginia society was a discussion of the extent of functional literacy and how it was not taught. In Jefferson analysis, universal functional literacy was not clearly linked to an agrarian republic or to democratic governance that he envisioned as the future of the United States.

International Commerce

The European wars ignited by the French Revolution had an immediate impact on the United States. Commodities produced in the United States sold for higher prices in larger markets. From 1793 onwards, American export commerce flourished after Britain and France resumed warfare in February 1793. France needed American commodities to help keep its armies in the field, feed its coastal cities, and feed its Caribbean colonies. The Royal Navy controlled the approaches to French ports and Britain was determined to prevent American commodities from entering France where they would be used to further French ambitions to dominate Europe. The Royal Navy gave Britain the power to control U.S. maritime commerce and make it an adjunct to their own merchant marine.

National political leaders of all persuasions recognized the danger of the United States being sucked into a war at a time when national political and economic institutions were extremely fragile. All national leaders were committed to maintaining peace. President Washington, however, had a very serious problem because the United States had two treaties with France. The first was of friendship and commerce and the second was an alliance that committed the United States to provide military assistance to France in the event of war with Britain. Both treaties were ratified in 1778 when France decided to intervene in the War for Independence, after the British army surrendered at Saratoga in 1777. French intervention guaranteed that the U.S. army would receive vital war materials, as well as several regiments of regular army troops to serve in America.

What was Washington to do? He decided to let the French invoke the aid clause of the 1778 treaty but, unofficially, he informed the French that the clause would not be honored. In order to make his decision explicit, he issued a Proclamation of Neutrality (April 1793). Its substance was that United States commerce would be equally available to both belligerents. Equality, however, was impossible because the Royal Navy enforced a blockade of French European ports and French Caribbean islands. American ships trying to enter these ports were captured.

In 1794 the Royal Navy seized 250 American ships trading in the Caribbean. These seizures were a partial reprisal for allowing the French ambassador to commission privateers that were American owned, manned, and armed. These privateers captured over eighty English merchants ships as they were entering U.S. harbors. In July 1793 the administration forbid equipping privateers in American ports and forbid captured ships from being brought into American ports. Both orders gave substance to the Proclamation of Neutrality. Thereafter, control of the sea by the Royal Navy meant that American commodity exports would preferentially go to Britain during the war.

A high percentage of Americans objected. They wanted American resources to aid France in order to repay France for aid provided during the War for Independence. Friends of France in the United States claimed that neutral ships made neutral goods. In other words, ships of neutral nations, like the United States, had a right under international law to trade with belligerent nations in all varieties of noncontraband commodities; and agrarians claimed that foodstuffs were noncontraband commodities. Jefferson's response to British naval power was bluster. He proposed that it was the duty of the United States, as a neutral nation, to withhold supplies from Britain until U.S. ships carrying noncontraband commodities were allowed free access to French ports. American merchants wanted none of Jefferson's bluster because reality was otherwise.

Induced trade with Britain was no great hardship because a very large majority of American trade with European nations was with Britain, not France. In 1793 the United States imported products worth fifteen million dollars from Britain and only 2 million from France. Furthermore, American merchants wanted regularized access to Canada, Newfoundland, and the Caribbean. It was very much in American interest to ensure that the primacy of British trade continued because Britain was paying high prices for American commodities. The reciprocal was that revenue generated by taxing imports from Britain was essential for sustaining public credit.

If some American merchants wanted to risk having their ships seized by the Royal Navy in order to get higher prices from the French, that was their decision, but British markets were the primary sources of profits for American export merchants. It was, therefore, strongly in the interest of the United States to have a treaty of commerce with Britain in order to put the mutual benefits of commerce on a sustaining basis. It was also an opportunity to settle past and present grievances and provide a means for settling future disputes.

The lack of a treaty of commerce was a legacy of lingering animosities after the War for Independence. Washington, Hamilton, and the new Secretary of State, Edmund Randolph (replacing Jefferson who resigned), decided that the best way to end uncertainties in commercial policies and settle other postwar problems was to send a special envoy to London to negotiate a treaty of commerce. John Jay, chief justice of the United States, was chosen as Washington's special envoy.

The principal purposes of his mission were to (1) regularize commerce between the United States and Britain, (2) reopen trade with British Caribbean islands, (3) compensate American merchants for ships and cargoes seized since 1793, and (4) obtain entry of neutral ships (American ships) carrying noncontraband commodities to French ports. Other American objectives were to (1) clearly define the boundary between the United States and Canada, (2) end occupation of forts in the Northwest Territory that controlled the fur trade, and (3) compensate owners of slaves that accompanied the British army when it withdrew from the United States after the end of the War for Independence.

Britain also had grievances it wanted settled. Britain wanted the United States government to pay prewar debts owed by American citizens to British merchants, and to compensate exiled loyalists for confiscated property. The forts in the Northwest Territory that were occupied by British troops were hostages to induce the United States government to assume these obligations.

Jay's Treaty arrived in the United States in March 1795. Britain agreed to pay compensation for ships and cargoes seized after England and France resumed war. In return, British ships entering American ports paid the same tonnage taxes as American ships. In other words, British and American ships trading into each nation's ports received a most favored nation status because it was mutually advantageous. Britain, however, did not recognize the principle that neutral ships made neutral goods. Foodstuffs were classed as contraband; however, Britain agreed to purchase foodstuffs from American ships that were captured trying to enter blockaded ports. Jay's Treaty had the effect of making American merchant ships an adjunct to British maritime commerce.

Under the treaty, the boundary problem and the amount of the prewar debts owed to British merchants were to be settled by joint commissions. British troops would withdraw from forts on U.S. soil in 1796. Britain, however, refused to pay compensation for slaves that accompanied the withdrawal of their troops. They were freemen living in the maritime provinces of Canada and they would remain free. The reciprocal was that the treaty was silent about compensating exiled loyalists for confiscated property.

Washington was unhappy with several of its articles and solicited opinions from Hamilton and Randolph. Both had serious reservations about some articles but both recommended ratification on the larger issue that the treaty was essential for maintaining peace and for continuing commercial prosperity. Washington submitted the treaty to the Senate for ratification, but with two qualifications. Britain must allow United States ships to deliver flour and food grains to French ports (in conformity with the 1778 Treaty of Commerce) because these commodities were not contraband of war, and Britain must extend the two year permission for American ships trading into British Caribbean ports. The Senate ratified the treaty in June 1795.

Events made the two year limitation irrelevant. As the French war intensified, limitations on American commerce to British Caribbean islands were not enforced. In fact, the opposite occurred. The Royal Navy protected American merchant ships destined for British Caribbean islands. They needed American commodities because Canadian provinces were unable to supply them in sufficient quantities.

After Britain and France resumed war in February 1793, French warships and privateers were authorized to capture American ships carrying commodities to British ports. At the beginning of hostilities, captured ships were taken to French ports, and the French paid for the cargo and released the ship. This practice was not continuously followed due to recurring changes in the ideology of France's revolutionary leadership. In January 1795, a decree exempted U.S. ships from seizure, an exemption that lasted until July 1796. Thereafter, the French government reverted to its earlier policy of capturing American ships destined to or leaving British ports. They now confiscated ships and cargoes. These depredations were retaliatory for the United States ratifying Jay's Treaty.

Between July 1796 and January 1798, American commerce in the Caribbean experienced serious depredations by French warships. In October 1797, President John Adams sent a three man delegation to France to negotiate a treaty of commerce to replace the 1778 treaty. The delegation was refused official recognition. They were informed that the foreign minister required a gratuity (bribe) to initiate negotiations and a substantial loan to the French government would have to be part of the treaty. Both conditions were refused because the delegation had no authority to expend these funds.

Two delegates returned to the United States, while the third remained as an unofficial hostage because the French foreign minister intimated that if he departed, France would declare war on the United States. In April 1798, Adams sent the Senate copies of the official correspondence of the aborted peace mission (XYZ Affair). A large segment of the American public was outraged by French conduct.

Thereafter, the United States prepared for possible war. In the summer of 1798, Congress suspended American trade with France and abrogated the 1778 Treaty of Trade. Congress also established the navy department and the Marine Corps and authorized the capture of French warships, but not unarmed French merchant ships. The navy consisted of three heavy frigates and twenty-four merchant ships that were converted into smaller warships. For the next two years the United States and France engaged in an undeclared naval war that was mostly fought in the Caribbean.

France could not afford to lose American commodities, nor could it afford losses of warships. The French foreign minister invited reopening negotiations. Adams appointed another three man delegation to conduct negotiations. They arrived in Paris in March 1800, immediately after Napoleon seized power. Negotiations lasted until September when a treaty was signed (Convention of 1800).

The Convention of 1800 abrogated the Treaty of Alliance of 1778 and ended naval warfare. Indemnification for seized American ships and cargoes was left for future negotiations, but captured merchant ships that had not been condemned by admiralty courts were returned to American owners, and the United States returned several captured French warships. Restoration of peace produced a huge but unforeseen dividend. It made possible the purchase of Louisiana in 1803. Part of the purchase price was funds the French government was supposed to pay American merchants for ships seized between 1796 and 1798. The United States government, assumed these costs.

While Jay's Treaty was in process of ratification, Washington commissioned Thomas Pinckney to negotiate a treaty of commerce with Spain. The two principal American objectives were (1) recognition by Spain that the western boundary of the United States was the east bank of the Mississippi River, (2) free navigation of the Mississippi River.

American export commerce originating in the watersheds of the Ohio, Tennessee, and Cumberland rivers fed into the Mississippi. Free navigation of the Mississippi was essential for the expansion of the United States into the trans-Appalachian west. Pinckney's negotiations were highly successful. Both objectives were incorporated in a treaty. He also obtained the right of deposit for three years in New Orleans for American commodities that floated downriver in keelboats. At the end of three years, a place of deposit could remain in New Orleans or moved to another location. The Senate overwhelmingly ratified Pinckney's Treaty in June 1795 and, at the same time, barely ratified Jay's Treaty.

A Continental Nation

While the Convention of 1800 was in process of ratification (September 1800–July 1801), Spain retroceded Louisiana to France in the secret Treaty of San Ildefonso (October 1800). A western boundary with Spain was acceptable to the United States because Spanish colonial policies strangled commercial initiatives. Trade in Spanish Louisiana would fall into the hands of American merchants. Pinckney's Treaty indicated that the Spanish presence at the mouth of the Mississippi River was not a serious impediment to the westward expansion of the United States.

A western boundary with France was another matter because France was energetic and expansionist compared to Spain. President Thomas Jefferson was alarmed by a French presence on the nation's western boundary. Something had to be done to neutralize or eliminate it. Jefferson sent a delegation to France to purchase New Orleans in order to guarantee an outlet for export commodities produced in the trans-Appalachian west. Napoleon was highly receptive and decided to sell all of Louisiana. A treaty of cession was quickly signed and immediately ratified when it was presented to the Senate.

Events in Europe motivated Napoleon to sell Louisiana. In 1802, the English and French military establishments were exhausted and both nations needed respite. The Treaty of Amiens (March 1802) was recognized by both nations as a truce that would be of short duration. Warfare resumed in May 1803. Just before the resumption of war (April 1803), Napoleon sold Louisiana. The sale was based on an accurate appraisal of the future of Louisiana. Napoleon recognized that New Orleans would be immediately captured by a British naval expedition. Furthermore, even if France retained possession of Louisiana after the war, it did not have the resources to prevent Americans from settling on the west bank of the Mississippi River.

The acquisition of Louisiana nearly doubled the size of the United States and moved the western boundary of the nation to the Spanish colony of Mexico. From Jefferson's perspective, the acquisition of Louisiana guaranteed that the United State would be an agrarian republic for the foreseeable future. Not only was Louisiana a huge area of vacant land, but it also provided access to the unknown and unclaimed land west of the headwaters of the Missouri River—from the Rocky Mountains to the Pacific Coast at Puget Sound and the mouth of the Columbia River.

The Louisiana Purchase cleared the way for the United States to become a continental nation during the nineteenth century. The process of expansion began immediately. President Jefferson commissioned Meriwether Lewis and William Clark to explore the headwaters of the Missouri and go from there to the Pacific. They departed St. Louis in 1804 and returned in 1806. They performed a service similar to that performed by Alexander Mackenzie of the Northwest Fur Company when he explored North America to the Arctic Ocean in 1789–1790, and to the Pacific Coast at Bella Coola Inlet in 1792–1793. Both the United States and British Canada had tenuous claims to land along the Pacific Coast based on these expeditions and various sea voyages, but neither nation had any resident population.

Taking advantage of Spanish involvement in the Napoleonic Wars, in 1812 the United States expelled a tenuous Spanish presence in west Florida (the Gulf Coast districts of Alabama and Mississippi). Spain protested annexation but could do nothing. In 1819 a greatly weakened Spain recognized that it could not retain possession of the Florida peninsula because colonial governors were powerless to prevent frequent armed incursions by Americans to reclaim escaped slaves living with Indians and punish Indians who were raiding into Georgia. In 1819 Spain was induced to sell Florida because the alternative was unilateral annexation. The Adams-Onis Treaty ceded Florida to the United States. In the treaty, the United States insisted on defining the northern boundary of California at the 42nd parallel. Treaty recognition of this boundary was international recognition that the United States had a preemptive claim to part or all of Oregon country.

A necessary prelude to rapid settlement of the trans-Appalachian west was disarmament on the Great Lakes. This was essential so that the United States could devote all of its resources to westward expansion without incurring heavy military expenditures to defend its northern border. At the end of the Napoleonic Wars, Britain also needed reduced military expenditures in order to manage its war debts and accelerate industrial development. It was in the interests of both nations to demilitarize the Great Lakes.

The Rush-Bagot Agreement was negotiated between the secretary of state and the British ambassador. It was unanimously approved by the senate in April 1817, and was followed by an agreement in October 1818 to extend the U.S. Canadian boundary along the 49th parallel to the Continental Divide of the Rocky Mountains. In 1846 the 49th parallel boundary was extended to the Pacific Coast. Dividing Oregon country gave the United States clear title to all territory south of the 49th parallel to the northern boundary of California. The first American settlers arrived in Oregon country in 1834, and by 1845 there were five thousand people living in the Willamette and Columbia river valleys.

After 1815, the trans-Appalachian west rapidly acquired population because steamboats on western rivers rapidly moved settlers to frontier districts. Louisiana was the first trans-Mississippi state to enter the union. It joined in 1812 and was followed by Missouri in 1820, Arkansas in 1836, and Iowa in 1846.

Spanish neglect and misrule especially affected the remote and scattered frontier outposts in Texas, upper Mexico, and California. Prolonged discontent in lower Mexico erupted into a war for independence that was achieved in 1821. In the same year, Americans began settling in the Mexican province of Texas, but tumultuous governance of Mexico after independence was cause for Texans to declare independence in 1836. In a series of skirmishes and battles, Texans defeated a small Mexican army and achieved de facto independence.

The Mexican congress refused to recognize independence. This forced the Texas government to petition for annexation to the United States (August 1837). The offer was rejected because of increasing northern opposition for adding another slave state, and fear that annexation would provoke a war with Mexico. The annexation issue simmered for the next eight years while the Texas republic struggled to survive. During these years, increasing numbers of southern planters settled on the most fertile soil in order to cultivate cotton with slave labor.

The unstable borders of the Texas republic and its sparse population made it vulnerable to intervention by European nations, especially Britain, in order to end slavery. Cotton planters strongly desired annexation by the United States because it would ensure a government that would protect land titles and recognize slaves as property. A treaty of annexation was drafted in 1844, but there were enough anti-slavery senators to defeat it. Texas annexation was a major issue in the presidential election of 1844. Electoral results indicated that a joint resolution passed by both houses of Congress would approve annexation. This resolution was forthcoming and the president signed it into law. Texas accepted statehood in June 1845, but with borders that the Mexican government rejected. War ensued.

During the war, California was captured by small army units that marched overland from Texas, assisted by a small contingent of marines and sailors who arrived by sea, and militia units recruited from Americans living in California. In the march overland, the isolated settlements in upper Mexico were also captured.

Peace was restored in May 1848 after a small American army landed at Vera Cruz and marched inland and captured Mexico City. By terms of the treaty, the United States annexed the present states of New Mexico, Arizona, and California, and all of the vacant land to the north. A final territorial adjustment was made in 1853 with the purchase of a small slice of desert (Gadsden Purchase) that was added to Arizona territory in order to acquire an all-American railroad route to the largely vacant land surrounding the village of Los Angles. Later territorial additions were the purchase of Alaska from Russia in 1867 and the annexations of Hawaii and Puerto Rico in 1898.

Chapter 6

Agrarian Commerce

Thomas Jefferson served eight years as president (1801–1809). His successor, James Madison, served eight years as president (1809–1817). Madison's successor, James Monroe, also served eight years as president (1817–1825). All three were from Virginia and all three strongly favored political and commercial policies that promoted the interests of an agrarian republic. There were two principal ways of promoting national agrarian policies: (1) ensuring export markets for agricultural commodities, and (2) actively encouraging the westward expansion of the agricultural frontier. These policies were implemented in very strange ways by Jefferson and Madison.

Ensuring the expansion of export markets was done by (1) nonimportation statutes in 1806 and 1809, (2) an embargo on most American maritime commerce in 1807, and (3) war with Britain (1812–1814). These policies sequentially reduced exports and imports. The results of Jefferson's and Madison's diplomacy were severe domestic discord, a precipitous reduction in the revenue of the national government, and national bankruptcy.

Expansion of the agricultural frontier was also implemented in a strange way. The agrarian presidents rejected a national policy to fully mobilize the fiscal resources of the national government to encourage the commercial development of frontier states. After the national government acquired vacant land, pacified it, and sold it, it performed minimal functions. Frontier settlement largely devolved on settlers and the state governments they organized. Slavery was the cause of this policy of default because the expansion of the agricultural frontier was concomitant with the expansion of slave labor agriculture onto vacant land. This generated increasing political conflict after 1815. The impact of slavery on agrarian economic development is discussed in the last section of this chapter.

Abundance of Entrepreneurs

After independence, opportunities for producing new wealth were limitless: (1) the Constitution provided a stable political environment, (2) Hamilton's fiscal policies created a stable financial structure, (3) national courts ensured the unobstructed flow of interstate commerce, (4) the elective process retained national, state, and local governments that encouraged commerce, and (5) the Louisiana Purchase gave promise that the United States would become a continental nation.

Producing new wealth, however, was not an automatic process. Entrepreneurs had to make it happen. Entrepreneurs are promoters and organizers. Joseph A. Schumpeter has the best definition.

The function of entrepreneurs is to reform or revolutionize the pattern of production by exploiting an invention or more generally, an untried technological possibility for producing a new commodity or an old one in a new way....This function does not essentially consist in either inventing anything or otherwise creating the conditions which the enterprise exploits. It consists in getting things done [1]

Why did the United States have an abundance of entrepreneurs compared to most European nations? More specifically: *Why did northern states have an abundance of entrepreneurs?* There are three principal reasons: (1) from the moment of landing in America, settlement on vacant land required establishing public service institutions, and as settlement moved inland these institutions had to be organized by actual settlers; (2) corporations had to be organized to protect ownership of real property used to build public service infrastructure projects; (3) organizing public service corporations was training for organizing corporations for profit.

As settlements moved inland from tidewater, new religious congregations, school districts, townships, and county governments had to be organized. All of these organization, either immediately or eventually had to have a building (church, courthouse, and schoolhouse). These building and the functions they served had to be managed by residents. Somebody had to organize these institutions, supervise construction of buildings, and manage the services they provided. Incorporation protected the ownership of buildings needed to sustain these services on a continuing basis. During the colonial period, several legislatures passed general incorporation statutes to encourage the organization of the public services because they were noncontroversial.

Robert K. Lamb emphatically emphasizes that entrepreneurial activity is conditioned by the social values of the communities where they live.

The individual entrepreneur...taken out of a given social setting is a mere figment of the theorist's imagination; he becomes a reality only when he is studied as a member of his society...Entrepreneurs, like other decision-makers, depend for their success on the measure of acceptance their values and goals of activity command from that society.[2]

Most citizens in northern states recognized that persons who created wealth performed a public service, and persons who created new forms of wealth performed an even greater public service. If entrepreneurs became wealthy, this was an honest reward for their public service. In broader terms, after independence, the commercial motivation of most cultivators in northern states made them receptive to activities of men who ventured to apply new technologies to profit making possibilities.

Organizing public service corporations was training for persons who saw opportunities to organize profit-seeking corporations like turnpikes, toll bridges, and textile mills. The skills required to organize public service corporations were readily transferable to organizing corporations for profit. It was obvious to local communities that profit-seeking corporations conferred visible public benefits and their organization ought to be encouraged. A very efficient way to encourage them was to grant incorporation on request.

General incorporation statutes equalized (democratized) business opportunities, first in franchise corporations like turnpikes, then in manufacturing corporations that sold products on an anonymous market. In the early national period (1783–1815), several northern states passed general incorporation statutes for profit seeking businesses because they were as noncontroversial as religious congregations and town governments. Organizing church congregations, school districts, and turnpikes trained entrepreneurs for mobilizing capital to use new technologies for profit-making opportunities.

Most organizers of town governments or turnpikes were probably not the people who organized corporations to manufacture products in factories using new technologies, but the social environment in which they lived was very friendly to persons who could organize them. Entrepreneurs who were successful in creating new wealth and providing employment were recognized as valuable citizens in the social structures of northern states. The personal wealth they often accumulated was recognized as earned rewards for their energy and innovation in creating new taxable wealth.

Different social values operated in slave states. In the antebellum South, the highest social status was awarded to entrepreneurs who organized plantations using slave labor. Entrepreneurship in slave states operated in the narrow groove of managing slave labor to produce agricultural commodities. In 1815 planters were using the same management practices and cultivation practices they used during the previous hundred years. Investments in new technologies that required wage labor did not have a high social value in slave-labor states. In many ways, entrepreneurs who did not directly service the needs of agriculture were suspect because they were potential competitors for planter control of governance.[3]

Export Commodities

Both northern and southern producers of export commodities agreed with Jefferson's foreign policy. Both sections favored using the power of the national government to expand and protect export markets. This policy was equally acceptable to export merchants who profited from carrying commodities to Europe and returning with manufactured products.

The resumption of the Napoleonic Wars in 1803 (after the Louisiana Purchase) generated a surge in American shipping and an equally large surge in the production and export of cotton. The surge in shipping lasted until 1807 and had two parts: (1) re-exports of commodities produced in the Caribbean, and (2) commodities produced in the United States. American ships visited the Caribbean colonies of European nations and carried their commodities to American ports where they were unloaded and re-exported to Europe in neutral ships. The neutral ships were American.

Between 1803 and 1805, American ships carrying noncontraband cargoes had unobstructed entry to British and continental ports. Although Britain and France were at war, they relaxed their navigation laws because they needed as much commodities as U.S. ships could deliver. In effect, the neutral ships of the United States carried neutral cargoes to British and French ports—if the cargoes were noncontraband. In 1803, about 19 percent of American exports were re-exported commodities, and by 1807 they were 36 percent.

The value of domestically produced exports increased from approximately 52 million dollars in 1803 to 101 million dollars in 1807. Cotton exports increased from 8,635 metric tons in 1800 to 28,635 metric tons in 1807. U.S. grown cotton supplied 60 percent of Britain's needs in 1807. Exports of food grains and flour also increased, especially to Spain where they were consumed by British troops in the peninsular campaign.

The Royal Navy's victory at Trafalgar in 1805 gave Britain control of trans-Atlantic commerce. Britain ended its tolerance of neutral trade and, thereafter, Britain and France attempted to blockade the other's ports. Britain was more successful. Between 1806 and 1812, the Royal Navy captured 528 American ships and the French 389. Although losses by capture were high, profits were high for commodities that reached their destinations without capture. A leading Boston merchant estimated that if only one out of three ships they sent to Europe escaped capture, they would make higher than average profits. American merchants could absorb wartime losses and prosper.

How was the U.S. government to respond to these depredations? President Thomas Jefferson and his secretary of state James Madison faced the same problem as president John Adams had faced in 1798. The United States could not afford to be sucked into the Napoleonic Wars. Both Jefferson and Madison searched for policies that would preserve peace.

There were four alternatives: (1) let American merchants continue to assume all of the risks of wartime commerce and profit accordingly, (2) pursue a policy of seeking competitive concessions from the belligerent nations to the advantage of American merchants and American producers of export commodities, (3) put American commerce under the protection of the Royal Navy, or (4) unilaterally restrict the flow of American raw materials to the belligerent nations in order to force concessions. If American merchant ships received protection from the Royal Navy, they could journey in convoys and their cargoes would be sold only in Britain. British warships would also search American merchant ships for deserters from the Royal Navy and forcibly return them to service. Deserters constituted a significant percentage of the crews of many American merchant ships.

The fundamental assumption of Jefferson's diplomacy was that ships of neutral nations carrying noncontraband cargoes had unobstructed entry to the ports of belligerent nations. It was an unrealistic assumption for four reasons:

1. As the Napoleonic Wars lengthened and intensified, foodstuffs and cotton lost their noncontraband status. They became raw materials for waging war.
2. Unilateral restrictions on commerce would only be successful if the commodities supplied by Americans were essential for sustaining a nations armed forces; however, neither Britain nor France were as dependent on American commodities and shipping services as Jefferson supposed.
3. The United States did not have a navy that could protect American merchant ships, even along the American coast.
4. Most American merchants were willing to assume the risks of wartime commerce because profits were high.

In an attempt to get Britain to restore neutral rights in commerce, Jefferson sent a personal envoy to Britain in May 1806. He was also to seek an end to the impressments of sailors from American merchant ships. As leverage for negotiations, Jefferson asked Congress to pass a nonimportation act. Congress complied in April 1806. The statute prohibited importation of a long list of products from Britain. Principal among them were hemp, leather goods, glassware, paper, tin, brass, and some types of woolen textiles.

The economic pressure of the Nonimportation Act did not have the desired effect and Britain refused to make concessions. Jefferson's personal envoy returned empty handed. Jefferson refused to consider the obvious: place American commerce to Europe under the protection of the Royal Navy in order to preserve the principal European market for American agricultural commodities. British control of American commerce would mean there was only one safe European market for American commodities. This policy was acceptable to most northern merchants, but was totally unacceptable to agrarians because they considered it national humiliation.

Jefferson opted for a defensive policy. He recommended that Congress suspend all foreign commerce as the only way that the United States could avoid further commercial conflicts that would lead to war. An agrarian dominated Congress obliged and passed the Embargo Act in December 1807. It prohibited American merchant ships from leaving U.S. harbors for any destination. It had two purposes: (1) save American ships from seizure and (2) increase discontent in Britain and France by causing high unemployment among persons manufacturing products for export to the United States. The embargo was primarily aimed at Britain.

The embargo caused a sudden contraction of foreign commerce and an equally sudden collapse of urban credit. Large numbers of export merchants and related businesses became bankrupt. Waterfront streets were nearly deserted and the larger ships engaged in trans-Atlantic commerce were tied to docks with the hatches closed and spars and rigging removed from masts. They slowly rotted. Jefferson's commercial policies had an immediate impact on cities because shipping profits were highly concentrated in Boston, New York, Philadelphia, and Baltimore, but cities had few votes. In the census of 1810 urban residents were only 7.3 percent of the population. Boston had a population of 33,000, New York, 96,000; Philadelphia, 91,000; Baltimore, 35,000; Charleston, 24,000. Urban residents were not Jefferson's constituents.

Products manufactured in European nations could only be purchased if exports were sustained. Instead, exports were prohibited and the decline of tariff revenues threatened national bankruptcy. Self-destruction of trans-Atlantic commerce continued for over a year.

The most charitable evaluation of Jefferson's diplomacy is that he failed to understand the objectives of Britain and France in the Napoleonic Wars. Nor did he adequately understand the extent to which each nation would go to achieve their objectives. France wanted to dominate the resources and markets of western Europe and Britain objected. Jefferson did not fully understand that American commerce was a pawn in the Napoleonic Wars, and that there was little room to maneuver because the United States was militarily and economically weak. The embargo inflicted more punishment on the American economy than it did on the economies of Britain and France.

Cotton exports accurately measure the self-inflicted wounds of the embargo. They declined from 30,000 metric tons in 1807 to 5,470 metric tons in 1808.

> Jefferson, Madison, and the Southern Republicans had no idea of the economical difficulties their system created, and were surprised to find American society so complex, even in their Southern States, that the failure of two successive crops to find a sale threatened beggary to every rich planter.[4]

James Madison was Jefferson's choice to succeed him as president. His election accurately measured the small commercial sectors in southern and trans-Appalachian states. They voted for Madison because: (1) southern peasants and yeomen cultivators were relatively unaffected by the embargo, (2) they believed that export merchants were rich speculators, and (3) they were highly receptive to nationalist rhetoric that accompanied American protestations against British wartime policies. When Madison took office in March 1809, he had the opportunity to repair the damage caused by the embargo. The last act of Congress before Madison took office was repealing the embargo because it had failed to achieve the desired results.

Its replacement was the Non-Intercourse Act in March 1809. It reopened all trade except with Britain and France and their colonies but it had an expiration date in 1810. The statute delegated power to President Madison to suspend its operation at his discretion in order to further negotiations with Britain and France for the purpose of recognizing the policy that neutral ships carried neutral cargoes.

Madison's diplomacy was more inept than Jefferson's. At his suggestion, Congress passed the Macon Bill in May 1810 to replace the non-intercourse statute. It authorized the president to resume American commerce with either Britain or France, if the warships of either nation ceased capturing American ships carrying noncontraband cargoes. The nation that stopped capturing American ships would be rewarded by prohibiting American commerce with the nation that continued to capture American ships. Macon's bill invited Britain to control American commerce to help defeat Napoleon. Britain should have seized the opportunity but did not, and French diplomacy was better than Britain's at misleading president Madison.

The United States blundered into war with Britain in June 1812, a war for which it was totally unprepared. The congressional declaration of war found minimal support in the northern states that conducted most of the nation's maritime commerce. It was clear to urban merchants that the United States could gain no commercial advantages by war because the Royal Navy controlled trans-Atlantic commerce. Pro-war votes came from southern and trans-Appalachian states. These electorates wanted to take advantage of Britain's protracted war in Europe and its presumed weakness in North America in order to annex Canada in the same way that west Florida had been bloodlessly annexed in 1810. Invasions of Canada were ineptly led and repulsed. Peace was concluded in December 1814 on the basis of the status quo that existed before the war.

The most remembered event of the War of 1812 was the composition of the national anthem. It was composed by an American civilian prisoner on the deck of a British warship that was part of a small squadron of the Royal Navy that sailed the length of Chesapeake Bay without opposition. The anthem was written while British warships were bombarding the fort guarding the approaches to Baltimore harbor. Transports in that squadron landed troops that burned the White House and then attempted to capture Baltimore and destroy American ships packed into its harbor.

The most important effect of the embargo, non-intercourse statutes, and the war was an enormous incentive for merchants to invest idle capital in manufacturing because, from December 1807 to December 1814, it could not be employed in maritime commerce. The capital came from the sale of inventories of imported products that were sold for increasing prices after imports ceased. Put in another perspective, the foreign policy blunders of Jefferson and Madison had the effect of a very high protective tariff that encouraged investments in factories to manufacture products that were formerly imported. Alexander Hamilton, in his wildest dreams, could not have imagined that two agrarian presidents would adopt policies that were highly conducive to initiating the industrialization in the United States.

Banks and Credit

This section focuses on the creation and use of bank credit from independence to about 1830, because its volume and use indicated an increasing economic and political divergence between northern and slave states.

Congress, under the articles, incorporated the Bank of North America in 1781. Its headquarters was in Philadelphia. Its principal purpose was to lend money to the bankrupt federal government. Robert Morris, who was superintendent of finances for the federal government, solicited the legislatures of all thirteen states to pass legislation to validate its banknotes as legal tender for the payment of taxes and debts. The legislatures of Massachusetts, Connecticut, Rhode Island, New York, and Pennsylvania passed charters of incorporation for the bank in 1782.

From the beginning, banking in the United States was conducted by corporations. Incorporation conferred a public purpose on banks. In the case of the Bank of North America, this purpose was to help the federal government survive. After independence, banks continued to perform public functions, but in a much larger spectrum of activities. Broadly understood, banks in the nineteenth century provided the currency needed for day-to-day business and much of the credit needed for economic development.

Immediately following independence, Philadelphia businessmen needed a local source of credit to help revive export commerce. The Bank of North America became a commercial bank like all the state chartered banks that followed. Its capital was a deposit of gold and silver coins that were lent to merchants in order to purchase an inventory. Banknotes issued by state chartered banks were the money lent to borrowers. They were redeemable for gold and silver coins on demand, but only at the bank's home office.

Repayments of loans were due in thirty, forty-five, sixty, or ninety days, as inventories were sold. Banks that followed the practice of the Bank of North America were organized by merchants in port cities. In the 1790s port cities with banks had adequate currency because the banknote currency they issued was 50 to 200 percent larger than the gold and silver coins on deposit. Merchants who received loans were given a stack of banknotes that were spent as needed. As soon as loans were repaid, banknotes returned to circulation as loans to new borrowers. Banks incorporated by state legislatures after independence helped revive export commerce because the banknotes they issued made business transaction immediately payable with money. Banknote credit meant that more business could be done with the same amount of assets.

In the port cities where all of the earliest banks were located, this procedure was almost immediately replaced by transferring the amount of loans to personal accounts. Merchant then wrote checks against their accounts. When there was more than one bank issuing paper currency, a bank would accept banknotes from other banks for deposit but discount them on the basis of the known or estimated liquidity of that bank. The notes of well-managed banks were discounted one-quarter to one-half of one percent. Banks that were known or suspected of having excessive issues of paper currency had their banknotes discounted, 3, 5, 10, or 20 percent, or they were not accepted for deposit. This was deposit banking.

Pennsylvania agrarians did not understand the need of city merchants for short-term credit. Instead, they wanted the Pennsylvania government to provide long-term credit in the form of an emission of land bank certificates. Their value was guaranteed by mortgages on agricultural land that was assessed at least twice the amount of the loan. Agrarians believed long-term credit to landowners was the best means of reviving commerce.

Land bank credit was also democratic credit because it was allotted to cultivators who were the majority of the population. Furthermore, land bank certificates were a familiar currency and they were allotted to counties on the basis of population. In response to agrarian pressure, the Pennsylvania legislature in 1785 authorized a large emission of land bank certificates to make loans for eight years to cultivators in amounts between $65 and $265 at 6 percent interest. There were 750 borrowers. Two-thirds were farmers and one-sixth were yeomen/artisan landowners; and the remainder was storekeeper/landowners.

The directors of the Bank of North America opposed the emission of land bank certificates because they feared inflation. In the disordered conditions of export commerce in 1785, inflation would become a means of debt repudiation. Furthermore, merchants had withdrawn a high percentage of the Bank of North America's specie reserve to pay debts in Britain, which made its banknote currency vulnerable to nonredemption. In order to protect the integrity of its banknotes, bank directors refused to exchange land bank certificates for specie, even at high discounts. Agrarians objected. They thought that the directors of the Bank of North America conspired to prevent the circulation of precious metal coins in rural areas while, at the same time, they became rich.

In September 1785 the agrarian majority in the Pennsylvania legislature repealed the charter of the Bank of North America because it: (1) refused to make long-term loans on agricultural land, (2) discriminated against cultivators, (3) practiced favoritism (lent only to urban businessmen), (4) insisted on punctual repayments, (5) opposed the emission of paper money at a time when there was a serious shortage of currency in rural areas, and (6) accumulated specie for export instead of facilitating its circulation.

For cultivators and tradesmen who were the overwhelming majority of the population, the bank's lending policies served only the interests of the monied oligarchy of city merchants. It was, therefore, a dangerous and undemocratic institution.

After repeal, the bank continued to operate using a charter of incorporation granted by the Delaware legislature. Opposition to reincorporation by the Pennsylvania legislature was greatly lessened when the directors agreed to accept land bank certificates for deposit on the condition that land bank certificates were used to repay loans denominated in them. The Bank of North America kept separate accounts for its banknotes and land bank certificates. In the next election a coalition of city merchants and farmers actively worked to overcome agrarian opposition to reincorporating the bank. The agrarians lost their majority and a new charter was passed in March 1787. Its life was limited to fourteen years but it could seek reincorporation. Thereafter, the Pennsylvania legislature, like the legislatures of all other northern states, readily incorporated banks to provide businessmen with local sources of credit.

The experience of the Bank of North America in Pennsylvania was only an episode in Pennsylvania history but it took place on the eve of the Constitutional Convention in Philadelphia in May 1787. All delegates were acutely aware of the need to reduce the risks of inflation and create a uniform circulating medium in the United States. A first step had been taken in 1786 when Congress adopted a plan for decimal coinage, but the treasury owned no gold or silver bullion, nor was there a mint to convert it into coins. Copper coins supplied the need for small daily transactions but they were inadequate for larger transactions.

The obvious remedy was paper money, but delegates to the convention strongly distrusted bills of credit and land bank certificates because they often ignited inflation, and inflation was a means of escaping debts. After independence was secured (1783), seven states resumed the colonial practices of issuing legal tender currency. Most delegates to the convention, and especially Alexander Hamilton, wanted to prevent paper money inflation. Hamilton and other delegates wanted to exclude state governments from any control over monetary policies because of their strong tendency to issue excessive amounts of legal tender currency during periods of financial stringency. Article 1, Section 10, of the Constitution prohibited states from emitting bills of credit or other forms of paper currency.

The home office of the Bank of North America was within sight of where the Constitutional Convention held its deliberations. After forbidding states to issue legal tender currency, the delegates had to leave the banking problem undefined. Nonetheless, the nation needed paper currency because there were not enough gold or silver coins to provide for business needs. Presumably, currency needs would be supplied by more banks incorporated by state legislatures. They would issue banknote currencies like the Bank of North America and the Bank of New York that Hamilton had helped organize in 1784. These banks of deposit provided a non-inflationary currency because they redeemed their banknotes for specie on demand.

In 1787 three state banks were in operation, and by 1801, there were thirty-one plus the Bank of the United States. Twenty-five of the state-chartered banks were in northern states. Slave states chartered only six banks and two of them were in Baltimore. The Baltimore banks derived a high percentage of their business by facilitating the export of commodities produced in southeastern Pennsylvania. The other four banks chartered in slave states were in Charleston, South Carolina, Wilmington, Delaware, Alexandria, and Georgetown in the Virginia portion of the District of Columbia. Eighteen of the state charted banks were in New England, five were in New York, and two were in Pennsylvania. The city of Philadelphia had two state chartered banks, plus the Bank of the United States; Boston had two, and New York City had two. By 1800 banknote currency was the lubricant of commerce in coastal cities but was often distrusted by cultivators in the interior, especially in southern states.

Unlike southern states that voted for Jefferson and his successors, northern states that voted for Jefferson had legislatures that were receptive to the needs of urban businessmen. The legislatures of northern states quickly learned that marketing a broad array of agricultural, forest, and fishery commodities, and artisan products made by yeoman households, required large amounts of short-term credit. This credit was most efficiently created and allocated by banks. They readily incorporated banks because the currency they supplied facilitated timely payments to artisan manufacturers and craftsmen for products and services. Banknote currency also facilitated the payment of taxes.

Banks were incorporated to serve the credit needs of specific types of businesses or to help build infrastructure projects. The New York legislature chartered the Merchants Bank in 1805 and the Chemical Bank in 1812. The Manhattan Company, chartered by the New York legislature in 1799, is the prototype of a bank charter linked to an infrastructure project. The ostensible purpose of the Manhattan Company was to supply New York City with potable water from wells distant from city pollution. Inserted into its charter was a section that authorized "the said company to employ all such surplus capital…in any other monied transactions or operation not inconsistent with the constitution and laws of this state." Banking was the real purpose for incorporating the company. To support its journey through the state legislature, New York City was given 10 percent ownership. The state also acquired shares and made the bank its fiscal agent. The Manhattan Company did supply New York City with potable water but most of its capital of two million dollars was used to conduct a banking business.

The subterfuge of inserting "monied transactions" into its charter without calling it banking was not due to agrarian opposition. It was due to potential opposition from the two banks already in operation in New York City. They did not want competition and would have used their influence to prevent the legislature from incorporating a competing bank. After the Manhattan Company affair, entry into the banking business in New York became highly politicized.

Unlike agrarian opposition to all banks, incorporation of banks in northern states was propelled by pervasive commercial motivation. Village businessmen wanted (1) abundant sources of credit, (2) the profits of banking, and (3) the political influence that accompanies control of money. All businessmen wanted local sources of bank credit, and the Jeffersonians who controlled the state legislature of New York after 1800 used the power to incorporate banks as a means of rewarding its supporters. Bank charters were rationed to businessmen with correct political credentials. They went to Jeffersonian businessmen.

The Massachusetts legislature also rationed bank charters but not for political reasons. It adopted the policy of granting all requests for incorporation, but required that one-half of the bank's capitalization be actually in a vault before it began operations. This policy answered the needs of the business community by promoting competitive sources of credit. To ensure that credit was reliable, an 1806 statute required all banks to submit annual financial statements to the government. By 1807 Massachusetts had twenty-three state-chartered banks. In order to reduce agrarian opposition to banks, in 1812, the legislature taxed banks at an annual rate of one percent of their paid-in capital. The tax was highly successful. By 1831 there were fifty-eight banks in Massachusetts and taxation of their capital provided the state with about three-quarters of its ordinary revenue.

In order to exert some control over the issue of paper currency, the Massachusetts legislature enacted a restraining law in 1799 and New York followed in 1804. Only incorporated banks could issue banknote currency. Similar restraining laws were quickly enacted by other state legislatures in an attempt to insure the value of paper currency. A second attempt to ensure the value of banknotes was forfeiture of charters of banks that refused to redeem their notes for specie on demand. Massachusetts inserted this clause in bank charters after 1816, and other states followed. It was, however, ineffective during panics and depressions when there were general suspensions of specie payments. Its enforcement would have dissolved state banking systems and left too many communities without sources of credit when business conditions improved.

Beginning about 1805, the Bank of the United States began to exercise the power of a central bank by discounting the banknotes of state banks. Discounting took place when these banknotes were presented for deposit in Philadelphia or at one of the bank's eight branch offices. If a bank was known to have issued excessive amounts of banknote currency, its notes were highly discounted. If a bank issued speculative amounts of currency, its banknotes were refused deposit. The discounting practice of the Bank of the United States was a real restraint on the credit practices of state banks. It ended, however, before it was fully institutionalized because in 1811 Congress rejected reincorporation. Its central banking function ceased.

Opposition to reincorporation came from three sources of about equal strength: (1) agrarians who opposed all banks because they issued paper money (they were concentrated in southern and trans-Appalachian states);, (2) state banks because the Bank of the United States restrained credit practices, (3) larger banks in the principal port cities because they would be depositories for tariff revenues after the dissolution of the Bank of the United States. Government deposits would greatly increase their ability to lend and greatly increase their profitability. The dissolution of the Bank of the United States ended national leadership in providing sound credit. After its dissolution, state legislatures could create as much banknote credit (by incorporating banks) as they thought necessary for accelerating economic development.

The end of the first Bank of the United States (1811) came at the worst possible time—on the eve of the War of 1812—when the national government required huge amounts of credit. Inflation had to be used to finance the war. The national government sold eighty million dollars in bonds but received only thirty-four million in cash. "The national government was bankrupt and the state banking systems were shaken to their foundations. On the return of peace in 1815, the need for a new central bank was obvious, President Madison's constitutional scruples notwithstanding."[5]

The end of the Bank of the United States in 1811 was a clear signal for all state legislatures to incorporate more banks; and all of them did. In 1811 there were 115 state-chartered banks; in 1815 there were 210, and by 1820 there were over 300. Most new banks incorporated in northern states after 1814 were in interior villages. Their purpose was to create banknote credit to aid local entrepreneurs accelerate economic development, as well as supplying a local currency. Given the enormity of the task of economic development, there was an obvious need for abundant local credit.

The end of credit restraints was also an opportunity for some states to practice business democracy. In 1813 the Pennsylvania legislature incorporated twenty-five new banks in one statute. The governor vetoed it. A similar statute was passed in 1814 that incorporated forty-one new banks. It was passed over the governor's veto. The frontier state of Kentucky followed Pennsylvania's example. In January 1818, the legislature incorporated forty new banks in a single statute. Both Pennsylvania and Kentucky experienced an orgy of inflation followed by large numbers of bankruptcies in the panic of 1819. In contrast, the legislatures of New York and Massachusetts were highly restrained in incorporating additional banks. The New York legislature incorporated only six new banks in 1811 and four more in 1812.

The second Bank of the United States was incorporated by Congress in 1816 in order to rescue the national government from bankruptcy and bring order to the nation's money supply. It opened for business in January 1817 and within a year had eighteen branches. Prices of export commodities were high, especially cotton, as European nations recovered from the dislocations and depredations of the Napoleonic Wars. The Bank of the United States did not perform the function for which it was chartered. It did not restrain the credit practices of state banks, especially southern and western banks. It abetted speculation by accepting for deposit excessive amounts of banknotes issued by these banks. In 1818, there was a steep decline in commodity prices, especially cotton, and the decline continued during 1819.

In order to survive, the Bank of the United States had to quickly and excessively contract credit. Low commodity prices and credit contraction between 1818 and 1821 forced many state banks into bankruptcy. The large numbers of bankruptcies increased agrarian distrust of banknote currency and contributed to a depression that lasted until 1821. After 1821, the Bank of the United States operated as a central bank that restrained the credit practices of state-chartered banks. It effectively performed this function until the Bank War in 1834 that was followed by the bank's dissolution in 1836. The reasons for its dissolution and the effect it had on the economy are discussed in the next chapter.

At the end of the War of 1812 (1815), northern businessmen decisively changed the direction of their interests. Increasing the volume of export commodities lost its primacy. Northern businessmen were motivated by a vision of riches that could be created by using local credit to enlarge domestic commerce. Interior banks with smaller capitalization were highly successful in accelerating economic development, as long a central bank restrained their credit practices.

The rapid increase in the number of interior banks in New England after 1814 required a central bank to restrain credit practices. In 1818, the banks of Boston designated the Suffolk Bank as the central bank of New England. Its principal function was to ensure the value of paper currency. Small interior banks were strongly tempted to issue banknotes in greater amounts than their specie deposits could support because: (1) there was an insatiable demand for credit, (2) banknote circulation was highly profitable, especially in smaller denominations, and (3) bankers in interior villages were partially protected from redemption of excessive issues because redemption required bringing banknotes to home offices that were at distant locations from major centers of commerce.

The Suffolk Bank induced interior banks to keep permanent deposits in Boston. Permanent deposits became permanent restraints on inflationary issues because the Suffolk Bank had sufficient notes on deposit to force bankruptcy by carrying them to home offices for redemption. Furthermore, by statute law, bank stockholders had unlimited liability to redeem banknotes of bankrupt banks. By 1825 New England had a reliable banknote currency due to the legislature's policy of incorporating only banks where entrepreneurs actually possessed capital and because the Suffolk Bank restrained credit creation. By this date the second Bank of the United States was exercising similar credit restraints on state-chartered banks in the rest of the nation.

Internal Improvements

Economic development was inseparably linked to internal improvements in transportation: first turnpikes, second steamboats, third canals, and fourth railroads. The key to understanding economic development in the United States from independence (1783) to the beginning of the Civil War (1861) was that most improvements in transportation were due to policies adopted by state governments.

The early republic did not lack men of vision who advocated constructing a national transportation infrastructure. Jefferson's secretary of the treasury, Albert Gallatin, submitted a report to the Senate in 1808. He proposed an ambitious plan for the national government to build a system of roads and canals to facilitate interstate commerce. Principal among the proposed canals were ones through the neck of Cape Cod in Massachusetts, across central New Jersey from New York harbor to the Delaware River, through the neck of the eastern shore of Maryland to Chesapeake Bay, and south from Norfolk (Virginia) through the Dismal swamp. In addition, canals would be built westward from Albany, New York to the Great Lakes, and up the Potomac River. Nothing came of his plan because Jefferson's and Madison's foreign policies and the War of 1812 bankrupted the national government.

The two principal areas of state action were credit creation (incorporation of banks) and building or subsidizing the construction of transportation projects. During the first thirty years of the nineteenth century, state governments funded the full costs of most of the largest internal improvement projects (canals). The value of the bonds sold to fund these projects were guaranteed by the taxing power of states. Turnpikes were the most common local internal improvement project. State governments encouraged their construction by local entrepreneurs using local bank credit. Alternatively, state funds were used to supply a portion of construction costs.

State legislatures actively encouraged entrepreneurial investments by favorable statutes. By far the most important was credit supplied by state chartered banks. Other important encouragements were cheap and easy procedures for incorporation, limited liability for investors, granting power of eminent domain to corporations, and appropriations to purchase corporate shares in selected banks and internal improvement corporations.

"The South nearly always opposed internal improvements at federal expense." There were three principal reasons for southern opposition to national funding. (1) The South had large numbers of navigable rivers. After 1816, steamboats of all sizes were built that could reach most areas where cotton was the principal marketed crop. (2) Subsidies voted by Congress for constructing internal improvement projects would have required increased tariff revenues and this would have increased prices for imported manufactured products that were consumed in the South, particularly the cheapest products consumed by slaves. (3) Subsidies voted by Congress for internal improvements in northern states would have accelerated the migration of northern farmers to the frontier. The third reason is discussed in detail in chapter eight.[6]

There were four exceptions to southern opposition to congressional appropriations to improve transportation. The first exception was rivers and harbors improvements. Congressional appropriations funded the removal of obstructions (log jams and sand bars) from the upper portions of many rivers to improve navigability. By 1840, there were more than 550 steamboats operating on rivers in the trans-Appalachian west, not counting those operating on the Great Lakes. Along the low lying coasts of the Carolinas, Georgia, and the Gulf Coast, smaller harbors had to be dredged and larger harbors had to have bars removed that accumulated when river flows were insufficient to prevent their deposition. Finally, lighthouses were built on dangerous shoals or at entrances of the principal harbors in order to increase the safety of ships engaged in maritime commerce.

The second exception was funding the construction of the national road that was built from Cumberland, Maryland to the Ohio River at Wheeling, Virginia in 1818, and later extended into central Ohio. Its funding ended in 1828 because President Andrew Jackson opposed further appropriations of national funds for building internal improvement projects.

The third exception was land grants to state governments to construct internal improvement projects. Land grants did not require taxation. Congress granted new states in the trans-Appalachian west a percentage of funds from land sales within their borders (usually 5%). The first grant was to Ohio in 1802, but the amount of money received was small in relation to needs. These funds were often poorly allocated by state governments because of political influence. Many projects were built with minimal reference to their value to interstate commerce. In the 1820s land from the public domain was granted to the governments of Ohio and Indiana to build trunkline turnpikes; and similar grants were made to help build canals in the 1830s. Grants for canal construction were usually alternate sections of land (one square mile) for five miles on either side of the route.

Congress greatly enlarged its land grant policy in 1850 in order to encourage the construction of railroads that would carry interstate commerce. The first was in 1850 to states that then conveyed it to the Illinois Central and Mobile and Ohio railroads. These grants were passed by Congress because the railroads would facilitate commerce between slave and free states. Political leaders in northern and slave states could agree that railroads encouraged internal settlement

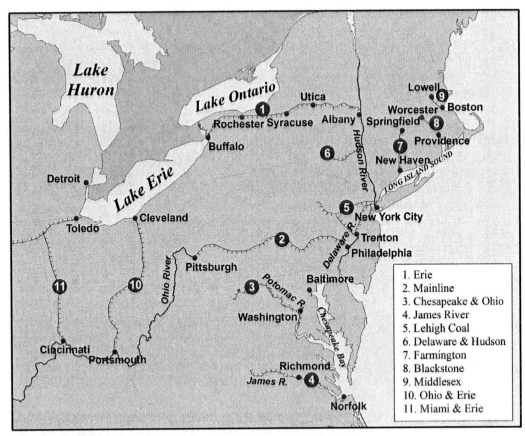

Figure 6.1 Trunkline canals and navigable rivers, 1850. Map by Yu Zhou. Reproduced with permission.

because they made cultivation profitable on land distant from water transportation. During the 1850s, Congress granted a total of 8.9 million hectares (twenty-two million acres) to eleven states so they could convey the land to railroad corporations. More than 60 percent of the land grants were to Michigan, Illinois, Wisconsin, Iowa, Missouri, and Minnesota. Furthermore, Congress authorized railroads to use land in the public domain to build rights-of-way.

The fourth exception was the general survey statute passed by Congress in 1824. It authorized the president to use army engineers (graduates of the United States Military Academy) to survey rights-of-way for roads and canals for military and postal purposes. By extension during the 1830s, army personnel surveyed rights-of-way for railroads and located places where bridges could be built. The act was repealed in 1838 because its activities were too often an integral part of specific internal improvement projects. Critics claimed that this was using national resources for purposes that were state concerns. Army engineers refocused their activities in the 1840s and 1850s and searched for passes in the western mountains that could be used by transcontinental railroads.

Turnpikes were the first business corporation to be incorporated in large numbers after the War for Independence. For the first forty years of the nineteenth century, they were the most numerous business corporations in the United States. The need for improved overland transportation was very great, and the success of the Philadelphia–Lancaster turnpike, incorporated by the Pennsylvania legislature in 1792, indicated that turnpikes could be highly profitable investments if they were built from places where water transportation was available to interior commercial centers. Farmers invested in them to raise land values and businessmen invested in them to extend the trading radiuses of the cities and villages where they lived, not necessarily because they were expected to be profitable investments.

Joseph A. Durrenberger, quoting John B. McMaster, summarizes how the construction of toll roads and toll bridges accelerated economic development after 1800. "The heaviest taxes that could have been laid would not have sufficed to build half the roads or build half the bridges that were required" to change the direction of American commerce from production for export to production for domestic consumption. Local entrepreneurs had to fund most turnpike investments. Complementing the incorporation of turnpike and toll bridge corporations was the incorporation of stagecoach, canal, and steamboat corporations (operating on inland waters), and dock and wharf corporations. These corporations had a franchise relationship with state or local governments and, where required, they were granted the power of eminent domain.[7]

The earliest canals were built without government aid. The first was started in 1793 and completed in 1800. It went north from Charleston, South Carolina to the Santee River. The second was the Middlesex Canal that went north from Boston to the Merrimack River. Construction began in 1794 and was completed in 1803. In both cases, the estuaries of these rivers lacked a usable harbor. Thereafter, a number of feeder canals extended service of the Middlesex Canal into New Hampshire. Its major traffic was timber for shipbuilding and lumber for house construction in Boston. The principal products carried on the Santee Canal was cotton, rice, and wood products. Neither canal was profitable. The Middlesex Canal froze during the winter and its textile traffic to Lowell was preempted by the Boston and Lowell Railroad in the mid-1830s, and the traffic of the Santee Canal was limited and seasonal.

Four other canals in Pennsylvania were built without government aid. Between 1820 and 1825 the Schuylkill Canal was built west from Philadelphia to the anthracite coal deposits near Pottsville. It was immediately profitable and three other coal carrying canals were built soon afterwards: Lehigh, Union, and Delaware and Hudson. The Delaware and Hudson supplied coal for steamboats operating on the Hudson River and Long Island Sound, for iron smelting, for steam engines that powered the rolling mills at Troy, and for space heating in New York City. All coal carrying canals were highly profitable.

Between 1817 and 1825, the New York legislature funded construction of the Erie Canal from Albany to Buffalo. It was financed by selling bonds whose face value and interest were guaranteed by tax revenues—if revenue from traffic was insufficient. Revenue was always sufficient. The success of the Erie Canal induced Pennsylvania to build a trans-Appalachian canal. Construction began in 1826 and was completed in 1834. Like the Erie Canal, it was built with funds raised by selling bonds whose value was guaranteed by tax revenues. It had an impossible route through mountainous areas and was a financial failure.

Many states established boards of public works (internal improvement boards) to provide funds for private companies to build turnpikes, toll bridges, canals, and other improvements in transportation. In the language of the time, they were mixed corporations. Results were highly variable because, in many states, political influence was the principal criteria for funding projects. Frequently, turnpikes were built in remote places and were seldom linked into trunklines. In the terminology of the time, using political influence to build unconnected infrastructure projects in remote places was corruption.

Virginia established a board of public works in 1816 in order to coordinate internal improvement projects and help fund them. State funding was always conditional on the Virginia legislature approving the route or location of a project. In approved projects, private investors had to contribute 60 percent of the capital and the board contributed 40 percent. The state lacked adequate funds for its share in several important projects so it induced several banks to purchase shares in these projects as the price for receiving a charter. The funds Virginia contributed to infrastructure projects came from selling bonds, not from cumulative profits of operating turnpikes, toll bridges, and canals.

By 1831 private investment capital was no longer forthcoming in Virginia because of the low volume of traffic on most turnpikes and toll bridges. In that year Virginia increased its share of construction costs to 60 percent of the capital costs for projects approved by the legislature. The necessity for increased state funding indicates that Virginia turnpikes carried less commercial traffic than northern turnpikes, even though Virginia was the second most populous state in 1820.

The Virginia board of public works (1) borrowed on the credit of the state to get capital for its contributions to improvement projects, (2) built roads in the western part of Virginia entirely at state expense, and (3) managed canal construction and operation. All of the canals built in Virginia received very large state appropriations and none were profitable. This compares to the Erie Canal where revenues were more than adequate to fund the initial cost of construction, deepen it, and build an extensive network of feeder canals. Most other slave states were much less successful than Virginia in subsidizing internal improvement projects.

The large volume of traffic carried by the Erie Canal was indicative of why a high percentage of turnpikes in northern states were built without public funds. Yeomen and farmers in northern states marketed foodstuffs and other commodities throughout the year. This compares to slave states where white peasant households marketed small quantities of exchange commodity crops once a year. Far fewer canals and turnpikes were built in slave states because there was less commercial traffic.[8]

Most canals were built with funds obtained by bonded indebtedness. The ability to sell internal improvement bonds depended on state legislatures guaranteeing annual interest payments and repayment of the principal at their year of maturity. This guarantee was necessary to sell bonds because of the risk of insufficient revenues. During the 1820s and 1830s, large amounts of internal improvement bonds were sold in Europe because bonds of the national government had a high credit rating. European investors were impressed by the frugality of the national government and the annual reductions in the national debt. The high credit rating of U.S. bonds was transferred to state bonds that funded the construction of transportation projects to develop visibly abundant resources.

European investors were equally impressed by the earnings of the Erie Canal and the coal carrying canals of Pennsylvania. By 1840, about forty million dollars of state bonds were owned by European investors, mainly British. During the severe depression from 1839 to 1842, five states repudiated their debts. The electorates in these states rejected heavy taxation in the depths of the depression to pay interest on internal improvement bonds that yielded inadequate revenues. Debt repudiation is investigated in the next chapter.

Factory Manufacturing

Colonial legislatures were familiar with the advantages of incorporation for towns, counties, and cities. Incorporation of municipalities allowed constantly changing governing bodies (by election or appointment) to manage real property (county courthouses) linked to the public services they performed. It was a short step from there to incorporate religious congregations, colleges, and libraries because the public functions they performed required ownership of real property and management by governing bodies with constantly changing memberships. An extension of this was the incorporation of business corporations to provide fire and marine insurance as services to urban households and export merchants. Likewise, loan officers of land banks were incorporated for each county because they were authorized to hold mortgages on agricultural land that was collateral for long-term credit extended to cultivators.

Immediately after independence, state legislatures readily incorporated businesses with limited liability if they did not compete with businesses that had been organized as single proprietorships and partnerships during the colonial era. Tanneries, gristmills, sawmills, shipyards, and partnerships of export merchants were not granted charters of incorporations with limited liability because limited liability would have conferred an unfair competitive advantage on new entrants into these businesses. New businesses, however, that required larger capital investments supplied by multiple owners, like banks, or businesses to exploit new and untried technologies (mechanical spinning and weaving) were readily granted charters of incorporation with limited liability for investors.

State governments were the principal catalyst for encouraging entrepreneurs to organize corporations to use mechanically powered machinery to manufacture products that were imported. The success of factory manufacturing, like state encouragement for investments in internal improvement projects, was strongly stimulated by credit provided by state-chartered banks.

Factory manufacturing of cotton thread in the United States began with the arrival of Samuel Slater in New York City in January 1790. He was twenty-one years old and brought with him his indentures as a mechanic (engineer) that he had acquired while working for Richard Arkwright, the inventor of machinery that used water power to mechanically spin multiple cotton threads. American entrepreneurs were active in Philadelphia, New York City, Boston, and other places trying to build machinery to spin cotton thread, however, they had no engineering drawings. British mill owners vigilantly protected their technical advantage and the British government fully cooperated by inspecting the baggage of any person they suspected of emigrating with specialized tools or drawings. Slater brought no engineering drawings with him. They were in his memory.

Immediately after arrival he inspected spinning machinery built by local mechanics for the New York Manufacturing Company. It was junk. He then answered an advertisement of Moses Brown, a merchant in Providence, Rhode Island who wanted to hire a skilled mechanic to build spinning machinery. Brown invited Slater to Providence to inspect spinning machinery built by local mechanics. It was junk. New machinery had to be built. Brown invited him to do it and offered Slater an attractive contract. He hired Slater and several local craftsmen with basic mechanical skills to help him. If the machinery Slater built was successful, he would receive half of the proceeds from the sale of thread.

Production began in December 1790, using cotton from the Caribbean. The machinery was powered by a water wheel in a small mill (converted from fulling) at a waterfall on the Blackstone River. His machinery was successful. The thread was coarse but strong and highly suitable for weaving sailcloth, canvas tents, and making durable clothing desired by cultivators.

Production from Slater's first mill supplied local hand loom weavers on the putting out system. Weavers received thread on credit and the woven cloth was purchased by agents at an agreed price providing the cloth was of requisite quality. Most weavers were yeomen cultivators during the summer and autumn but became part-time weavers during the spring, and full-time weavers during the winter. Slater also recruited full-time weavers who lived in the village that grew around the mill. They worked under supervision in rooms attached to the mill.

In 1798 Slater organized his own company with a large amount of capital supplied by local merchants. The mill was built on a new waterpower site just across the boundary in Massachusetts. The Massachusetts legislature was anxious to attract a new industry and granted incorporation with limited liability and exemption from taxation for seven years. When the second mill came into production the thread was consigned to agents in Connecticut and Massachusetts who had groups of weavers to whom they supplied thread. A third spinning mill was built on a new site in 1806. It was financed by Slater, Brown, and other merchants. By 1807 thread from Slater's mills were being consigned to agents in Maine and as far south as Philadelphia for distribution to local weavers.

Each subsequent mill in which Slater had an interest had investors who were investors in earlier mills, but with different proportions of ownership. Slater's partners were responsible for purchasing raw cotton, marketing thread, and marketing cloth woven from it on hand looms, and then by mechanical looms. Slater was responsible for building spinning machinery, managing the mills, and recruiting labor.

In the meantime, the first group of mechanics trained by Slater to build spinning machinery followed his example. They became entrepreneurs. Like Slater, they had no money so they offered their skills to merchants who financed the building of spinning machinery. New mills continued to be built in New England by this cloning process and improvements were continually borrowed from Britain by attracting mechanics trained in British mills. Advertisements in British newspapers informed them of opportunities awaiting them in America.

The nine years following enactment of the Nonimportation Act (April 1806) to the end of the War of 1812 (December 1814) were years of spectacular growth in textile manufacturing. Many small gristmills, sawmills, and fulling mills were converted to spinning mills. The embargo followed by war was a hugely successful protective tariff. American textile manufacturers had the American market to themselves.

The legislatures of Massachusetts, Rhode Island, Connecticut, New York, and Pennsylvania quickly responded to entrepreneurs who wanted to manufacture products that were no longer imported. It passed charters of incorporation on request. In 1811, the New York legislature went one step further. It passed a general incorporation statute for businesses it had previously incorporated by individual statutes. "It allowed five or more persons to self-incorporate for manufacturing woolen, cotton, and linen textiles, and for making glass, bar iron, steel, anchors, nail rods, hoop iron, and iron mongery from ore, sheet lead, shot, and white and red lead." It was based on two earlier noncontroversial general incorporation statutes for organizations that performed essential public services: religious congregations (1784) and academies and colleges (1787). It was in effect for five years, long enough to supply local demand until imports resumed.[9]

Incorporation was a cheap legal process. Investors had to file a copy of the articles of incorporation with the secretary of state. Capitalization was limited to one hundred thousand dollars and corporations had a life of twenty years. The statute was actively used. Between 1811 and 1815, about 210 incorporations were registered. At least half of the incorporations were spinning mills. After the end of the war (1815), the New York legislature broadened its provisions "to cover makers of clay and earthenware products, and in the following year, coverage was extended to makers of pins, ale, porter, and beer, and extracting lead from ores." In 1821 the statute was made permanent and coverage was further extended to makers of coarse salt in the western part of the state. During the same period, the Massachusetts legislature incorporated eighty-nine spinning mills, but not all of them became operational.

The first fully modern general incorporation statute was passed by the Connecticut legislature in 1837. Three or more persons could "incorporate for the purpose of engaging in and carrying on any kind of manufacturing or mechanical or mining or quarrying or any other lawful business." This statute is indicative of how noncontroversial manufacturing corporations had become in northern states. In more general terms, all businesses were viewed as performing a public service because they created employment, and it was recognized that factory employment was a highly efficient way of creating new taxable wealth.[10]

Increased textile production was the most dramatic result of ending most imports before and during the War of 1812. In 1808, there were about fifteen spinning mills with 8,000 spindles operating in the United States. By 1810 there were about eighty-seven mills with about 31,000 spindles and a year later, there were 80,000 spindles in operation. By 1815, there were ninety-four spinning mills operating in New England alone. The surge in textile manufacturing was important for two reasons. First, mechanization of textile production was the beginning of the factory system of manufacturing in the United States. Second, mechanization of textile production showed the possibilities of an import substitution policy because the embargo (1807), Nonimportation Act of 1809, and war acted as a high protective tariff.

It is enormously ironic that the surge in factory manufacturing between 1807 and 1815 took place during the administrations of presidents Jefferson and Madison. Both presidents were committed to a policy of free trade in which the United States exported agrarian commodities and imported a high percentage of the manufactured products it consumed.

Peace brought huge prosperity for American cotton cultivators. British mills paid high prices for cotton because power looms were rapidly replacing hand looms, and British spinning machines produced finer thread than could be made in the United States. British textiles flooded the U.S. market. A high percentage of American spinners became bankrupt. Surviving producers were new mills with competent managers. Like Slater's mills, they specialized in spinning heavy thread. The surviving mill operators petitioned Congress to save the infant industry until American entrepreneurs were able to acquire the technology to mechanically weave cloth.

In 1815 the New York legislature tried to preserve the spinning machinery of bankrupt mills from passing into the hands of creditors who would neglect it or junk it. "Machinery, raw materials, and inventories were exempted from distress sale." If spinning machinery remained in the hands of bankrupt operators, it would be available to operate again after a protective tariff raised prices. The state legislature further acted to preserve New York's new manufacturing sector. In 1817 "the legislature exempted from state and local taxation the machinery, inventory and buildings of all manufacturers of thread and cloth."[11]

The wartime experience of excessively high prices, followed by postwar competitive pressures impelled Congress to pass a protective tariff in 1816. One of its purposes was to buy time until power looms could supply the American market. Producers of heavy sheeting received maximum protection under the 1816 tariff. Imports were taxed 25 percent of their value. Textiles were not the only manufactured product receiving protection. Glass and earthenware paid 20 percent; hats, writing paper, and rolled or hammered iron shapes paid 30 percent; men's leather boots paid $1.50 a pair; and iron nails paid 3 cents a pound.

At the same time that American spinners were experiencing intense competition from British textiles, the first power looms in the United States began producing heavy cotton sheeting. The technology to build power looms was acquired by industrial espionage. Francis Cabot Lowell visited Britain between 1810 and 1812, ostensibly for reasons of health. He was thirty-five years old, came from a leading family of Boston merchants, and had made a comfortable fortune from the import-export business in years before the embargo and Nonmportation Act of 1809. Business was at a standstill, and he saw an opportunity to make a new fortune by acquiring the technology of power looms. Lowell had considerable mathematical and mechanical skills. Before leaving for Britain, he visited spinning mills in Massachusetts and Rhode Island, and carefully examined several experimental power looms built by American mechanics that had not achieved commercial production.

While in Britain, he visited several mills where the most recent power looms were in production. He told the owners that when normal imports resumed, he would be an agent to market their cloth in the United States. After seeing British power looms in operation, he made drawings of parts and the arrangements of moving parts that he knew had to be incorporated into a successful loom. After returning to Boston, he used his social standing and commercial vision to mobilize unemployed capital from other import-export merchants (later know as the Boston Associates). Like Lowell, they saw an opportunity for American manufacturers to capture the American market if he could build a commercially successful power loom.

They organized the Boston Manufacturing Company. From its inception it was highly capitalized. It was designed to produce heavy cotton sheeting because the merchants who invested in the company knew that heavy cloth had a large market in New England and the rest of the country.

The first step was to build a machine shop, then build a new, large mill on the falls of the Charles River, at Waltham, fourteen kilometers west of Boston. When the building was complete, spinning machinery was purchased, installed, and put into operation. Spinning began in November 1813, but power looms were not operational until the following December. The Boston Manufacturing Company was an integrated operation. Spinning and weaving were done in one building. Raw cotton entered at one end and cloth emerged at the other end. Production began shortly before British textiles flooded the American market; however, the initial looms continued to be modified and were not in full commercial production until 1817.

Operations were profitable from the beginning and were highly profitable by 1820. One of the investors in the Boston Manufacturing Company estimated that the mill would have been profitable without tariff protection, but the tariff made it highly profitable. A second but highly predictable result of the Tariff of 1816 was that the high profits earned by the Boston Manufacturing Company invited competition. By 1823 competition lowered the prices of textiles, but high profit margins were sustained by lower prices for raw cotton and improved weaving and spinning technology. A high percentage of these improvements were due to the continual arrival of British mechanics and economies of scale in newer and larger mills.

The high profits of the Boston Manufacturing Company allowed the Boston Associates to undertake a major industrial project at Pawtucket Falls on the Merrimack River (forty kilometers north of Boston). A dam was built above the falls to raise the head of water and a canal was built to carry water to mill sites. Raw cotton arrived on the Middlesex Canal and cloth made the return trip to Boston. A new village was founded at the factory site. It was Lowell, Massachusetts. The first mill went into production in 1824 and in the next ten years a total of ten mills were built until all of the available waterpower was utilized.

All of the mills were owned by the Boston Associates but with different percentages of capital contributions. They were built on a standardized plan and went three steps further in integration. They had facilities to bleach, dye, and print cloth. Between 1825 and 1835, the number of spindles increased from 11,000 to 120,000. The mills, machine shop, and related textile processing facilities were linked to Boston by a railroad completed in 1835. They formed the first industrial complex in the United States.

The Lowell shop began to diversify. Two products became important sources of revenue: building railroad locomotives after 1835, and building water turbines after 1838. Water turbines had their first application in France in 1827. Turbines extracted more power from falling water than wheels and had less ice buildup during the winter. The first turbine was installed at Lowell in 1838 and was marginally successful. Work continued and, in 1844, a highly successful turbine became operational. It extracted 78 percent of the available power from falling water compared to 60 percent for the most efficient wheels. The adoption of water turbines meant that the same flow of water could power 30 percent more spindles or looms.

Labor recruitment was a serious problem from the opening of Slater's first mill in 1790. Three types of labor were needed (1) full-time mill hands, (2) children to attend operating machinery, (3) supervisors. Until about 1820, immigrants from Britain were a considerable percentage of full-time mill laborers and supervisory personnel. In the United States, like in Britain, a high percentage of persons attending machines were children seven to twelve years old, and a high percentage of children were girls. Their nimble fingers were efficient at tying broken threads and handing empty spools to mill hands to put on spinning machines. By 1830, children under the age of sixteen were about 40 percent of laborers in small textile mills. They worked twelve hours a day, six days a week, the same as adults.

Slater and other pioneer entrepreneurs built small mills at scattered locations and employed the children of local yeomen cultivators who lived in villages near mills. Slater and other pioneer mill owners preferred to hire whole families, especially those with many children. Daily absentee rates were about 15 percent and the annual labor turnover rate was about 50 percent. In the 1840s and 1850s, annual labor turnover rates increased to about 100 percent.

There is indirect evidence for the cause of higher labor turnovers. During these decades, immigrants increasingly replaced the children of yeomen cultivators as mill workers. In 1860 the average age of males who headed cultivating households in towns where mills were located was fifty-three. Almost all cultivators were landowners of long residence, but they had few resident children to inherit their land. Their children had grown to maturity and moved west to where fertile land was available in larger units, or they moved to towns and cities in New England. By 1860 immigrants were 36 percent of a much larger workforce than was employed in 1830. A high percentage was displaced Irish peasants, and they were an unstable work force compared to the children of New England cultivators.

The mills of the Boston Associates at Waltham and Lowell used a different strategy to recruit labor. They built boarding houses and employed young women to tend operating machines. They were recruited by agents and by word-of-mouth. The boarding houses were built and managed by the companies; and access to them was tightly controlled. Matrons who managed them acted as surrogate parents. This arrangement created confidence among yeomen cultivators that their daughters would not be demoralized by factory employment. Almost all of the young women attracted to mill employment were literate, and they performed efficient labor.

It was, however, a transient labor force. About 50 percent were employed for three years or less. They came to escape the boredom of rural life, to accumulate money to purchase some luxury items, to accumulate money to help a brother attend Harvard collage, and to accumulate money to marry and purchase more fertile land in the west. In both strategies of labor recruitment, labor costs were controlled by laying off unneeded laborers. This was not a serious social problem because they returned to the households of their parents and resumed cultivating chores until they were rehired or married. In normal years, turnover rates were somewhere between 20 and 35 percent.

In the consecutive poor crop years of 1839–1841, Irish immigration surged and during the famine years of 1845 and 1846 it became a flood. The flood continued until normal harvests resumed in 1852. Irish immigrants arrived with no money and had to accept wage employment as close to tidewater as possible. The arrival of the Irish alleviated an increasing shortage of labor in New England textile mills. Beginning in the mid-1830s, and especially in the 1840s, there was a prolonged westward migration of New England cultivators to New York, Ohio, Michigan, and further west. They sought more fertile land in larger units.

Factory production in the United States could not have been sustained without the establishment of a machine tool industry. One of the first producers of machine tools was the Lowell shop that built the machinery for the mills of the Boston Associates. After building the machinery used in the Lowell mills, the Lowell shop began building textile machinery for other New England mills in order to keep their skilled laborers employed. Innovations were continually incorporated into newer machinery. The innovations went in two directions—higher operating speeds, and fewer people to operate them. By the mid-1820s there were interregional shipments of textile machinery.

After the mid-1820s, textile machinery began to be built on rigid cast iron frames that could sustain faster operating speeds and better dampen vibrations. This significantly lowered maintenance costs. Among the first components to be replaced were wooden drive shafts with multiple shivs on them to turn the belts that powered spindles and looms. Iron drive shafts were lighter, stronger, revolved at higher speeds, had fewer vibrations, and were easier to lubricate.

With increasing use of iron and diversification into steam locomotives, it became imperative for the Lowell machine shop to have a foundry. One was built in 1840, and, at the same time the machine shop was made into an independent company. It was no longer tied to the textile mills of the Boston Associates. It was also divided into three divisions that made (1) machine tools, (2) railroad locomotives, and (3) hydraulic machinery.

By 1830 integrated American textile mills making heavy cotton sheeting had higher per capita production than equivalent mills in Britain, and much higher per capita production than most European mills. British mills, however, dominated the production of finer fabrics and these textiles were imported in large quantities.

The higher productivity of American mills was possible because they were powered by belts instead of the British practice of using gears. American machinists of the 1830s did not have the skills to make gears that efficiently meshed at high speeds. This technical disadvantage was compensated by powering machines with belts because they could be run at higher speeds. Belt drives contributed to rapid obsolescence because machinery wore out more quickly, but frequent replacement increased productivity because replacement machines had technical innovations that made them more efficient.

The American practice of frequent replacement contrasted to British practices. Machines with slower speeds were kept in production when higher-speed machines were available. This reduced capital spending which was a more important consideration for British manufacturers than lower labor costs. Postponed capital spending and lower per capita production made unit costs higher, but higher quality fabrics could bear these costs. In the competitive environment of the United States in the 1830s, the heavy sheeting that was the principal product of American mills required lower labor costs to be competitive with British products.

David J. Jeremy's *Transatlantic Industrial Revolution* documents the rapid diffusion of textile technology in the United States, and particularly the diffusion out of New England to New York and Pennsylvania. By 1845 American machinists could design and build textile machinery for many applications that were somewhere near equal to British machines. American machines were cruder in design but their higher speeds gave greater productivity for heavier fabrics.

Jeremy's study also documents the near absence of textile mills in slave states. This is strongly confirmed by Thomas C. Cochran's *Frontiers of Change: Early Industrialism in America*. Chapter 4 is an overview of industrial beginnings in the United States to 1825. For all practical purposes, the slave states and their version of an agrarian republic, was an industrial void.

Eli Whitney's invention of the cotton gin in 1793 revolutionized southern agriculture because it made cotton cultivation very profitable. It was very profitable because there was an instant market in Britain for all of the cotton they could grow. Raw cotton was the bottleneck in expanding Britain's cotton textile industry. In 1792 southern planters had grown 910 metric tons of upland cotton but much of it was unsold because of the difficulty of separating fiber from seeds. United States cotton exports were only 62 metric tons, and almost all of it was the tropical variety grown on the Sea Islands along the coasts of Georgia and South Carolina.

Most of Britain's raw cotton imports came from Caribbean colonies and elsewhere, but excess spinning capacity was available to increase production of cotton cloth. In 1790, all cotton thread in England was mechanically spun. A few experimental power looms wove cotton cloth. The supply of raw cotton, however, was inadequate because tropical plants had low yields. A temperate climate variety of cotton (upland cotton) had much higher yields and stronger fibers but, unlike the tropical variety, its fibers were difficult to separate from its seeds. The cotton gin ended this production bottleneck.

By 1831 the cotton revolution had impacted global commerce. U.S. cultivators produced 175,000 metric tons of cotton out of the estimated 372,000 metric tons that entered world commerce, and almost all of it was upland cotton. In 1831 raw cotton constituted 35 percent of the value of all U.S. exports and a year later it constituted 40 percent. By 1860 cotton accounted for 57 percent of the value of U.S. exports and earned a high percentage of the foreign exchange that was used to purchase rails and other capital equipment in Europe.

Eli Whitney invented the cotton gin on a plantation in Georgia. Plantation owners instantly recognized that using slave labor to cultivate cotton could make them rich. Whitney could not establish a factory in Georgia to manufacture gins because there were neither persons with sufficient mechanical skills nor persons willing to become full-time paid laborers. He returned to Connecticut. On the way he stopped at Philadelphia (the temporary capital) and applied for a patent. The secretary of state administered the patent office. The secretary of state was Thomas Jefferson, and he was strongly interested in the successful manufacture of cotton gins because cotton would be a highly profitable crop for an agrarian republic. Jefferson was especially interested in building small machines for yeomen cultivators. Whitney was more interested in building larger machines for plantations or village businessmen with money to purchase them.

Whitney built a factory in Connecticut and proceeded to manufacture cotton gins as fast as possible, but he made a huge mistake in business strategy. On the basis of his patents, he tried to collect a 20 percent toll from the gins he manufactured and sold. It was immediately resisted. After the gin was seen in operation, it was easy to copy and many persons began building them.

There was a general evasion of licensing fees and tolls whenever a gin not built by Whitney went into operation. Whitney tried to regain control by lawsuits but they were expensive and counterproductive because they took time from what should have been his principal concern: manufacturing gins as fast as possible, selling them, and licensing other manufacturers to do the same.

Whitney had all the advantages in producing gins because he assembled a reliable work force and produced component parts by a uniformity system. He made interchangeable parts for the various sized gins he manufactured. This was relatively easy because the early gins were mostly made of wood and a whole array of wood working power tools were available in Connecticut. In the earliest gins calibration was not critical. Three or four millimeters of tolerance was sufficient.

Before any of his lawsuits were settled, Whitney radically changed direction of his business interests. On the eve of the undeclared naval war with France in 1798, he applied to the War Department to build muskets. In mid-1798, he signed a contract to deliver ten thousand muskets by September 1800. When he signed the contract, he had neither a factory nor the machine tools, nor the laborers to shape metal parts.

He was awarded the contract because of his reputation as a machine builder and because congress was desperate to have muskets for a possible war. The two armories at Springfield and Harpers Ferry could not produce sufficient numbers. Whitney's contract was one of twenty-six awarded to arms makers in 1798. They were to make a total of 30,200 muskets. One of Whitney's principal selling points was that he planned to manufacture on the uniformity system. He planned to make all of the parts interchangeable, as was his practice in manufacturing cotton gins. Manufacturing interchangeable parts for muskets would be done by machines rather than skilled gunsmiths.

Whitney was more interested in the process of producing muskets than in the product itself. For him, the challenge was building the machinery that could make interchangeable parts. The purpose was to eliminate the labor of filing, tapping, bending, and fitting that was required to assemble muskets made by gunsmiths. The process of making interchangeable parts required instruments that could measure the dimensions of parts with complex shapes. For the most part, these machines and measuring devices were designed and made by Whitney.

Whitney never claimed to be the inventor of the uniformity system. He knew he was not the only persons with this idea. In fact, he was duplicating a French arsenal that made muskets with interchangeable parts. Whitney had heard about it but never visited it. What he did claim was inventing the machines (cutting, grinding, boring, stamping, measuring) that made it possible for complex shaped metal parts to be made with uniform dimensions. He borrowed some of his ideas for machine tools from the Springfield and Harpers Ferry armories, and from other gun and clock manufacturers in New England. The designs of the machine tools made in his shop are unknown because he never patented them. This was a legacy of his bad experience with the cotton gin patent.

He divided the manufacturing process into many small operations. Each employee operated one machine that performed one step in making each part. In theory, the final assembly could be done with unskilled labor instead of gunsmiths who had to know when and where to tap, bend, or file in order to make the parts fit. He put into practice Adam Smith's concept of the division of labor as a means of achieving economies of scale that were essential for mass production.

Whitney could not complete his contract on time and the War Department granted an extension, and then more extensions. He delivered the first five hundred muskets in September 1801. They were enthusiastically accepted. He did not complete his contract until January 1809. At its completion, he owned a factory and a complete set of machine tools, and had no debts. Because of the strained relations with Britain and France, he expected the War Department to renew the contract, but it was not renewed. He kept his factory operating by securing contracts with the governments of New York and Connecticut to manufacture muskets for state militias. When President Madison's inept diplomacy blundered the United States into the War of 1812, the national government needed all of the muskets U.S. manufacturers could produce. Whitney's factory was available.

Whitney had close relationships with machinists at the Springfield and Harpers Ferry armories. They shared technical information and there was a continual exchange of personnel. Whitney's relationship with Harpers Ferry was especially valuable because, after the War of 1812, it evolved into an experimental laboratory for developing new machinery to shape iron and steel parts.

Whitney also had good relations with the War Department until his death in 1825. In 1822, he signed a contract to deliver three hundred muskets annually, beginning in 1824. The price included sufficient development costs to replace old machinery and develop more efficient machinery. In other words, the War Department recognized that continuous production required continuous replacement of machine tools so that operating capital was not consumed. In his lifetime Whitney did not quite achieve interchangeability, but he came close. Machine tool makers who followed in his footsteps made it a reality in 1828 at the Harpers Ferry arsenal in Virginia.

The most prominent machinist at Harpers Ferry was John H. Hall. He was a New Englander who stood on the shoulders of Whitney. He was hired in 1819 as an assistant armorer in order to supervise the manufacture of breech loading rifles. He was hired because he had filled a government contract in 1817 for one hundred breech loading rifles of his design. In 1820 he was assigned a separate workshop and directed to manufacture one thousand breech loading rifles. He completed the order in 1824 and continued to receive orders for more. The costs of Hall's rifles were always high because he was not given a large enough building nor enough manpower to manufacture them in sufficient quantities to achieve economies of scale. Production, however, was not the principal purpose of his shop.

Like Whitney, his principal interest was inventing machine tools or improving existing ones until they could make interchangeable parts. He built lathes and boring machines that operated at three thousand revolutions per minute with belt transmissions. These machines had no vibrations so that parts made from templates had uniform dimensions. In 1828 his machines made interchangeable parts.

Hall used part of the budget of the workshop to train men to operate the machine tools he built. Between 1819 and 1835, over one-third of his budget was devoted to building experimental machine tools or ways to improve the performance of existing machine tools. During these years, Hall employed over half of the workers in his shop to build machine tools. There was one machinist for each production worker.

Hall was in continuous communication with Whitney, Simeon North, Samuel Colt, the Springfield armory, and other gun manufacturers in New England and Pennsylvania. These manufacturers freely visited his operation. Hall was at the center of a network of cooperation and transference of technology where all manufacturers who participated could freely borrow technical improvements from each other. By 1836 breech loading rifles were being made by at least three other manufacturers in the United States. The U.S. army never adopted breech loading rifles because no serviceable cartridges were available. Brass cartridges were not invented until after the Civil War (after 1865). Nor did states purchase them for their militia because, in the hands of untrained men mobilized to fight Indian wars, they had a tendency to jam.

The tools Hall invented or improved were available for copying without licensing fees. The machinists he trained adapted them to build many new kinds of capital equipment. Many of the men he trained migrated to the trans-Appalachian west where they established factories at Pittsburgh, Cincinnati, Louisville, and New Orleans. The principal product they manufactured was boilers and other operating parts for steamboats and railroad locomotives, but at New Orleans they manufactured stationary steam engines to power machinery used to make sugar. Hall's superiors in the ordinance department approved of using Hall's workshop as a technical laboratory to train the machinists who helped accelerate the industrial revolution.

Eli Whitney, John H. Hall, Samuel Slater, the machinists at the Lowell shop and the two arsenals made three major contributions to United States economic development. First, Whitney's cotton gin enabled cotton to become the principal export crop of the agrarian republic. Second, these men designed and built machine tools that were essential for generating and transmitting power needed for factory production. Third, the sequence of manufacturing operations developed by these men made possible economies of scale. In the process of manufacturing cotton gins, muskets, rifles, spinning machinery, and power looms these men trained a generation of machinists (engineers) who launched the Industrial Revolution in the United States.

The accomplishments of American manufacturers and machine tool makers were exhibited in London at the Crystal Palace Exhibition in 1851. At first they attracted little attention, but when trained machinists began examining and testing American made products they were impressed. Their principal interest was the uniformity system (interchangeable parts) in the manufacture of small arms. Exhibits of Colt firearms, agricultural machinery (McCormick's reaper), locks, wood working machinery, machine tools, and textile machinery attracted prolonged interest. American innovations and applications of metal milling machines and turret lathes clearly reduced the amount of artisan labor needed to make many metal products, especially small arms.

In 1853 the British government sent two highly qualified engineers to inspect factory production in America. Two things impressed them: (1) the public education systems in states where manufacturing was concentrated, and (2) the employment of many machines in factory manufacturing. Instead of having one expensive machine that could perform many operations, the practice of American factories was to have many small, cheap machines to perform a single operation. These machines were attended by one person who was a semi-skilled operator; and they were always sequenced so that the parts they produced could be assembled with minimal waste motion. The technology of making small arms with interchangeable parts was quickly borrowed by British manufacturers.

The Crystal Palace Exhibition was an indication that American factory production and the tools that made factory production possible had come a long way since 1830. By 1850 it was clear to knowledgeable European observers that the United States was on the brink of becoming a major manufacturing nation. It was a manufacturing sector that could not yet compete with British and European manufacturers in the world market, but could increasingly supply domestic demand for a wide variety of manufactured products.

Literacy

As industrialization began to impact New England, the educational system developed during the colonial era was increasingly obsolescent. Colonial education taught functional literacy to the children of cultivators in small school districts. The new villages that formed around textile mills did not easily fit into this system; nor did the influx of Irish immigrants during the 1830s, 1840s, and 1850s. Some mill owners established schools during the 1820s for the children of mill hands who were full-time employees. This, however, was not a general practice. Nor was it a general practice to provide schools for children who were employed in the mills but were not children of adult employees.

As early as 1814 the Massachusetts legislature investigated the extent of schooling for children employed in incorporated manufactories. Nothing was done. In 1825 another investigation of thirty-five villages with textile mills indicated that many of them lacked schools, or that schooling was inadequate. The following are samples of replies received from mill owners: "no schooling if employed; three months schooling; Sunday school; evening school at expense of company; as much opportunity for schooling as can be expected." The investigation concluded that "some further legislative provision may hereafter become necessary," but no remedial legislation was enacted.[12]

During the 1830s, it was increasingly apparent that children who were full-time factory laborers were not being taught functional literacy. The worst offenders were mill owners who wanted to reduce labor turnover. If parents with several children employed in a mill withdrew one child for three months of schooling, the owners threatened to discharge the father and all of his children.

Massachusetts was the first state to try to remedy the educational deficiencies of children employed in factories. In the eyes of Massachusetts legislators, child labor in factories was acceptable because child labor was the norm in households of yeomen cultivators. Wage labor employment of child labor was an educational problem, not a labor problem. The principal concern of legislators was to ensure that children working in factories had the same opportunities to acquire functional literacy as children of cultivators.

In 1837 the Massachusetts legislature established a state board of education and made it compulsory for villages to fund common schools for children laboring in factories. Children under the age of fifteen were prohibited from employment in factories unless they had attended school for at least three months in the previous year. The law was enforced with little opposition in manufacturing cities like Lowell, but for the first few years it was evaded with little difficulty by the owners of many small spinning mills at interior water power sites.

Horace Mann, president of the state senate, was appointed director of the state board of education in 1837 and served until 1848. He was responsible for restructuring primary education in Massachusetts so that all children had free primary schooling for a sufficient number of years to become functionally literate. The reforms he promoted had two objectives: (1) establish normal schools to improve teaching methods, and (2) concentrate improved teaching methods in villages and cities where factories and immigrant laborers were concentrated. The reforms he institutionalized became the model for many other states.

The first step in creating free public school systems in northern states was the enactment of statutes during the 1830s that permitted villages and cities to levy property taxes to fund free common schools. Thereafter, centralizing control of common school districts was done in a step-by-step process. The second step was supplying matching funds (from state school funds) to supplement local tax funds. The purpose of matching funds was to induce local school boards to extend the school year, introduce new curriculums, have graded class rooms, and reduce inequalities between rural and village schooling. The third step was creating state and county superintendents of schools. The fourth was supervising how local school districts spent education funds.

The educational reforms instituted by Mann were strongly influenced by Prussian educational policies. Many persons in the United States, as well as Mann, recognized that local control of education did not adequately prepare children for the increasingly complex commercial culture that was evolving in Massachusetts and elsewhere in the country.

During the 1830s, the Prussian government undertook a policy of accelerated industrialization. Prussian political leaders understood that universal functional literacy was essential if, in thirty or forty years, Prussia was to equal the industrial capacity of Britain. A policy of accelerated industrialization required an educational system that selected intelligent and motivated students for secondary education and universities.

The essential ingredients of Prussian education were:

1. Free primary schooling
2. Professional teachers trained in specialized colleges
3. Paying teachers sufficient salaries so that teaching was recognized as a profession
4. A longer school year than was customary for teaching literacy to the children of cultivators
5. Generous funding to build schools
6. Establishment of a department of the central government to manage a national system
7. Supervision at the classroom level to ensure quality instruction
8. A curriculum designed to inculcate a strong national identity
9. A curriculum that introduced knowledge of technology and science
10. Secular instruction

Inculcating national identity was of great interest to the French government. The French government commissioned a person to observe and analyze the operation of the Prussian school system. His report was translated into English in 1834. It had an immediate impact on Mann in Massachusetts and Henry Barnard in Connecticut, and others interested in creating state-funded common school systems for much the same reasons that Prussia was restructuring its education system. The French observer was impressed by:

> The stupendous efficiency of Prussian schooling, the spectacle of national authority over education, its centralized, secularized control, its trained and expert teachers, its up-to-date methods, its planning, financing, and supervising, and finally, its bold and frank employment of the school as an instrument for national ends. To the American school reformer's ears much of this was music…With a change here and an alteration there, to bring it into consonance with the American culture, Mann was convinced that it might be put into an effective use in the campaign for better schools.[13]

A new kind of literacy was required for the evolving industrial culture that Mann observed. The old reasons for teaching literacy, in order to read the Bible and conduct commercial transactions, were inadequate for maximizing the production of new wealth. The simple functional literacy taught in common schools did not adequately prepare children for factory labor, nor for learning technical and scientific skills, nor for living in villages and cities, nor for the social mobility that was increasingly possible. Six years of regular attendance in common schools was usually sufficient to teach functional literacy provided the child had continual practice in reading.

The new social and economic environment that was transforming Massachusetts and New England required a new type of education. Life was different in factory villages and cities where children were bombarded with choices that did not exist in rural areas. These choices had to do with (1) the meaning of the world around them, (2) understanding the need for increased government services, (3) how decisions are made, (4) what constitutes merit, (5) rewards for merit, (6) learning the value of new types of labor, and (7) have a positive attitude toward social change. Modern educators call it knowledge acquiring education. It is the curriculum of contemporary urban commercial cultures.

Education in New England had to be remodeled in order to effectively function during the stresses of industrialization, urbanization, and multi-ethnic cities. Remodeling required (1) additional taxation, (2) centralized management of educational funds, (3) uniformity in the length of the school year, (4) establishing teacher training colleges, (5) professional teachers in primary schools, (6) high enough salaries to retain teacher services for many years, (7) secularization to facilitate learning new technologies and sciences, and (8) compulsory attendance statutes so that immigrant households, who controlled wages earned by their children, would be adequately prepared for life in an urban commercial culture. In 1852 the Massachusetts legislature passed a statute requiring compulsory attendance for children of common school age. New York followed in 1853.

There was strong clerical opposition to establishing state and county superintendents of schools because new curriculums were secular. Clerics called them godless; however, the division of the New England church into Unitarians and Trinitarians helped facilitate the process, and Irish immigration confirmed the process. Irish clerics sought state funding for schools they established; however, sectarian neutrality was the only workable solution. Neutrality meant secular and secular meant teaching civic responsibility within the creed of republican governance. This was the only way that all Christian denominations and ethnic groups could be accommodated.

The New York legislature reached this conclusion in 1842 when it passed legislation prohibiting state funding of sectarian schools. It required a constitutional amendment in Massachusetts to institutionalize this policy. Its passage in 1853 prohibited religious schools from receiving tax funds. Other states quickly followed the lead of New York and Massachusetts.

Mann visited Europe in 1843 to see how Prussia and other European nations were creating centralized education systems. The report he wrote became a guide for reforms (public school revival) enacted in many northern states during the next twenty years. While he was director of the Massachusetts board of education, a fund was established to pay for an additional month of common school instruction. Increased local taxation was induced by matching state funds in order to pay higher teacher salaries, attract more motivated persons and, in the process, reduce turnover rates. Whenever possible, Mann persuaded rural school districts to consolidate (union schools) and provide free, standardized textbooks instead of each family supplying their children with a book to be used as a text. During his tenure, three normal colleges were established to train teachers, and public high schools were established to supplement private academies.

None of these improvements were possible without increased taxation, plus an immense amount of travel by county superintendents and state superintendents to persuade rural school districts that improved literacy skills were essential in an age of increasing social, economic, and geographic mobility. By 1850 most northern states had state-wide systems of primary schools but participation in the system was usually voluntary; although, receiving state funds was a strong inducement.

Cities were the first to respond to the opportunity to receive matching state funds because city residents recognized that teaching literacy should be embedded in knowledge acquiring education. City electorates were willing to pay higher taxes than rural districts to acquire the services of trained teachers. Cities also had commercial property that could bear higher taxation. Although rural school districts wanted state funding, they were slow to avail themselves of the opportunity because they were reluctant to increase taxation and accept state supervision of how money was spent.

Not until the mid-1850s did sixteen of the thirty-one states delegate authority to secretaries of state or state superintendents of common schools to supervise teaching practices and audit expenditures. By the 1860s tax funded, free common schools were institutionalized in northern states, but universal functional literacy was not achieved in most states because attendance was not compulsory. Many households did not insist on regular attendance of their children, and the single most important variable for acquiring literacy is regular attendance between the ages of six and twelve. Nonetheless, in northern states in 1860, functional literacy was somewhere near 90 percent for persons thirty years old or younger, if born in the United States.

The ferment that created free, state-wide common school systems in northern states was, for the most part, absent in slave states. Some persons in some southern states made strenuous efforts to establish state-wide systems of common schools but white peasant landowners and slave owning planters preferred low land taxation to universal literacy for whites.

Divergent Land Use

After independence, divergent policies of economic development in free and slave states became much more visible than during the colonial era. Divergence, however, did not become a source of political conflict until after 1815. The principal source of conflict was the disposal of agricultural land from the national public domain. In two previous sections of this chapter I have described two sources of national political conflict: (1) creating bank credit, and (2) funding internal improvement projects. Both of these conflicts were compromised by deferring to state governments. Land conveyance policies from the national domain could not be resolved by deferring to state governments because state governments did not exist.

The ultimate questions were (1) *Should vacant land be allocated to free labor households?* (2) *Should vacant land be allocated to cultivators using slave labor?*

After the end of the War of 1812, there was a huge surge of migration to the frontier. By 1820, 2.4 million people were living in the trans-Appalachian west but this population supported almost no urbanization. Pittsburgh, Cincinnati, Louisville, and St. Louis were villages. Only New Orleans was a city. After 1816, New Orleans had the expectation of being the largest city in the United States because of the proliferation of steamboat traffic on rivers flowing into the Mississippi River. Steamboats operating on the Tennessee, Cumberland, Ohio, Missouri, and Mississippi rivers funneled the commerce of trans-Appalachian states to New Orleans, and the richest part of that commerce was cotton.

Steamboats also led to rapid settlement of Missouri Territory by the sons of pioneering families already resident in the trans-Appalachian west. By 1818 Missouri's population was large enough to apply for admission as a state. Missouri was not a cotton producing territory. In 1818, northern political leaders were willing to concede that cotton cultivation was best done with slave labor, but they insisted that food and feed grain cultivation and accompanying livestock husbandry was most efficiently done by free labor farmers.

When enabling legislation was debated in the House of Representatives, a northern congressman introduced an amendment prohibiting slaves from being brought into Missouri after it became a state, and that all children born to slave parents already in Missouri would be emancipated when they reached the age of twenty-five. This amendment was motivated by two beliefs that were gaining strength in northern states: (1) slavery was evil, and (2) vacant land in the trans-Mississippi west should be used to provide homesteads for the sons of white farmers in eastern states.

When enabling legislation was debated in the senate, the anti-slavery amendment was deleted. The House of Representatives refused to concur and Missouri was not admitted as a state. When enabling legislation was reintroduced in the next session, a compromise was arranged to overcome northern opposition to the geographical expansion of slavery and, by extension, dampen debate on the place of slave labor in American agriculture. The compromise had two parts. First, Maine and Missouri were admitted as states in 1820. Missouri entered as a slave state and Maine as a free state. Second, slavery was prohibited in the Louisiana Purchase north of 36:30 degrees latitude. For the moment, the dual admissions of Missouri and Maine preserved a balance of twelve free and twelve slave states in the Senate. Political leaders in slave states saw the equal number of senators from slave and free states as protection against further anti-slavery legislation by Congress.

Two fundamental issues were involved in the Missouri controversy. The obvious was (1) *Who would derive the greatest benefits from acquiring land in the national public domain?* The less obvious was (2) *What was the social value of agricultural labor?*

Four assumptions are hidden in the second question. The first assumption is that agricultural labor has a high social value. Persons who perform agricultural labor should receive full market value for the commodities they produce because the money incomes they earn from producing commodities for sale on anonymous markets allows them to improve their material welfare. This is socially desirable.

The second assumption is that commercially motivated agricultural labor is the most valuable form of labor. Persons who perform commercial labor norms in agriculture confer great benefits on themselves and society. In the context of 1820, commercial labor norms applied to cultivation was absolutely necessary to transform the trans-Appalachian wilderness into a commercial culture of abundance and comfort.

The third assumption is opposite the second assumption. Agricultural labor has a low social value because slaves must be coerced to perform commercial labor norms. Implicit in this assumption is that subsistence labor in agriculture is the human norm. The evidence for this assumption was the subsistence labor norms of the white peasant majority living in slave states.

The fourth assumption is that patterns of land ownership control governance. Political leaders of slave states believed that republican governance required an elite of large landowners (and slaveowners) to govern a white peasantry that had high rates of illiteracy and a low percentage of landownership. Citizens in northern states believed that the strongest foundation for republican governance was a high percentage of literate households owning the land they cultivated.

After the Missouri controversy, agrarian policies continued to have strong support in northern and southern states, but for divergent reasons. Northern states increasingly favored policies that increased the size and scope of the domestic market. The two best indicators of the northern version of an agrarian republic were investments in transportation projects and the rapid increase of manufacturing in factories. Northern states remained agrarian but manufactured products were increasingly produced in factories. Southern political leaders believed that the domestic market for manufactured products should be supplied by imports because they were cheaper, and because rootless wage laborers crowded into cities were politically unstable.

After the Missouri controversy, perceptive political leaders in slave states understood that competitive settlement of the trans-Mississippi west was a competition that the North would win because there were more white cultivators in northern states than in slave states. In 1820, the population of the United States was 9.6 million. The total white population was 7.8 million. Northern states had a total population of 5.1 million, almost all of them white. Slave states had a population of 4.4 million (46% of total population), but 37 percent (1.6 million) were slaves, with highs of 52 percent in South Carolina and 43 percent in Virginia. Sixty-four percent of the white population lived in free states, 36 percent in slave states. In both sections of the nation whites were overwhelmingly cultivators.[14]

Sometime in the future, northern cultivators would demand preference for their children to acquire land in the national public domain, and sometime in the future the northern urban democracy would resent national policies shaped to the advantage of agrarians, particularly southern agrarians. Northern cultivators would demand the exclusion of slavery from all territories and the northern urban democracy would demand policies to encourage the creation of new forms of wealth. When this happened, senators and representative from northern states would vote to exclude slavery from trans-Mississippi territories. All future states would be free labor states and the way prepared for the extinction of slavery by constitutional amendment. The agrarian economies of southern states would collapse and governing elites would lose their status.

In his seventh-seventh year (1820), Thomas Jefferson clearly saw the future. The geographic expansion of slavery was the "momentous question" facing the republic. It was "like a fire-bell in the night. I considered it at once as the knell of the Union. It is hushed, indeed for the moment. But this is a reprieve only, not a final sentence." Although Jefferson recognized that national unity was in jeopardy, his observation was devoid of moral content. He refused to judge the morality of slave labor. He refused to condemn the potential division of the nation that would destroy the moral authority of the world's only representative republic,. He refused to condemn the political aggression of many political leaders in slave states that had the potential for destroying the political unity that was necessary to create a continental empire, as well as destroying governance by consent that sustained the vision of many Europeans political leaders who were contesting the power of authoritarian regimes.[15]

By 1830 the two democracies had highly visible differences in labor systems, land holding patterns, amounts of urbanization, number of factories, and literacy rates. In the next thirty years these differences would widen into a chasm.

Banks and Railroads

This chapter describes and analyzes economic development between 1830 and 1860. It focuses on banking/credit, and railroad finance/construction because these two policies of political economy accelerated manufacturing and urbanization. During these thirty years, credit from American banks and imports of European capital were essential for constructing railroads. Railroads were essential to accelerate the commercialization of culture because they speeded agricultural commodities to American cities for consumption and to port cities for export. Equally important, during the 1850s, banks and railroads interacted to accelerate factory manufacturing in the United States.

By 1860 it was desirable to have a national solution for problems in banking/credit and railroad/transportation because state policies were conspicuously inadequate for maximizing the production of new wealth on a continental scale. A high percentage of business and political leaders in northern states knew that a much stronger and energetic central government was required to initiate and sustain policies of national economic development.

Put in other terms, by 1860 policies of economic development initiated by states were inadequate to create a continental empire that could produce infinite amounts of new wealth. Political leaders in slave states rejected national policies of economic development because they could not control them. They clearly understood that national policies favored paid labor, industrialization, and urbanization. Just as clearly they understood that agriculture dependent on slave labor needed political/constitutional protection; and this protection required the national government to remain weak. Perpetuating national weakness required that the two principal engines of economic development—banks and railroads—remain under state control.

Banks

Congress incorporated the second Bank of the United States in 1816 to be a central bank. Within one year of its incorporation the bank established eighteen branches, eleven of them in slave states. The bank's principal function was creating a reliable currency by restraining the lending practices of state banks. This meant preventing inflation. Instead, during 1816 and 1817, the branches in slave states participated in inflationary lending fueled by the high price of cotton. The branches behaved like the development banks incorporated by state legislatures. A principal purpose was to finance the purchase land in the trans-Appalachian west and slaves to cultivate it. The price of cotton declined in 1818 and collapsed in 1819. The Bank of the United States teetered on the edge of bankruptcy.

New management saved the bank by enforcing a severe credit contraction. In the process, the lands of many planters were foreclosed. The political cost was high. A large segment of the population, particularly agrarians, lost confidence in its usefulness. The return of normal business conditions in 1822 coincided with the bank performing its intended purpose—preventing inflation by restraining the credit practices of state banks.

For the next twelve years it performed this function with efficiency but its efficiency was increasingly resented because it "stood too much in the way of credit expansion to suit popular interests." Although many cultivators in northern states loudly opposed the operation of the bank, as well as all state chartered banks, the bank's "effective adversaries were not farmers but businessmen." Most credit for local development came from state chartered banks. Local businessmen wanted more credit and more credit could quickly be obtained by state legislatures incorporating more banks.[1]

The Bank War

The election of Andrew Jackson as president in 1828 and his reelection in 1832 was a death sentence for the Bank of the United States. During his first administration, Jackson was increasingly under the influence of Martin Van Buren, and much of his influence was directed against the Bank of the United States. In numerous public statements Jackson indicated that he believed the bank was unconstitutional and he would oppose reincorporating it when its charter expired in 1836. Van Buren used his influence among congressmen from northern states, especially those from New York, to support the president's intention.

Van Buren was one of the principal spokesmen for businessmen opposed to rechartering the bank. These business interests were (1) New York City banks, (2) state chartered development banks, and (3) political leaders in slave states who wanted to diminish the power of the national government because a small and weak national government would help protect slavery from increasing northern political power based on a rapidly expanding industrial base.

When Martin Van Buren went to Washington, first as secretary of state in 1828, and then as vice-president (1832–1836), he brought with him the northern version of states' rights in banking and transportation policies, but especially banking. Northern businessmen would manage the economic development of their states with minimal support from the national government. From previous discussions with political leaders in slave states, Van Buren knew that this policy was acceptable to them. Van Buren understood that protection of slavery was the real reasons why southern political leaders endorsed the Bank War and he willingly supported states rights on southern terms because he needed their support for his presidential ambitions.

Congressmen who opposed Jackson's policies in general and his opposition to the bank in particular, decided to make reincorporating the bank the principal issue in Jackson's campaign for reelection in 1832. Henry Clay was nominated by a congressional caucus to oppose him and agreed that this was a good issue to further his presidential ambitions. Friends of Clay rushed a reincorporating statute through Congress in the expectation that Jackson would veto it. They believed that a veto would seriously impair Jackson's bid for reelection. The veto message, according to Bray Hammond, was "legalistic, demagogic, and full of sham. Its economic reasoning was…beneath contempt." Nonetheless, the veto was popular and Jackson was reelected president in November.[2]

Jackson recommended that the national government sell its shares of the bank. This was equally popular because it would be the first step in separating the national government from all business corporations. A principal tenant of Jacksonian democracy was that business policy was a state prerogative, especially banking. State legislatures increasingly translated this into a corporate laissez-faire business policy.

The Bank of the United States ceased restraining the credit practices of state banks in 1834. Thereafter, states were responsible for restraining the credit practices of banks incorporated by their legislatures. Frequently there was no restraint, and lack of restraints was often coupled with state legislatures incorporating new banks in excess of the credit needs of agrarian commerce. In other words, a high percentage of new banks were speculative.

An inflationary spiral began in 1834. In that year the United States had 506 banks; in 1835 there were 704; in 1837 there were 788; and in 1840 there were 901. In 1830 there were 329 state banks that had a banknote circulation of sixty-one million dollars; in 1840 they circulated 358 million.[3]

In part, the increase in banknote credit was propelled by increasing cotton prices. L. nd sales in the trans-Appalachian west rapidly increased between 1830 and 1836 and a high proportion were in slave states in order to increase cotton cultivation. Cotton exports tripled between 1830 and 1836 and cotton prices remained high until 1839. What happened in slave states happened to a similar extent in states north of the Ohio River, particularly in Ohio and Indiana after the completion of the canal systems in the mid-1830s.

The great triggering event for the depression that began in 1839 was a precipitous decline in the price of cotton. At the beginning of 1839, the price of cotton was 37.5 cents per kilo (17 cents a pound); by 1840 it had declined to 16.5 cents per kilo (7.5 cents per pound). "The depression from 1839 to 1843 was one of the most severe in our history."[4]

New York City banks opposed reincorporating the Bank of the United States because its headquarters was in Philadelphia. When the bank was rechartered in 1816, Philadelphia was the principal port city of the United States. By 1830 New York City was the nation's principal port city. Over half of the tariff revenue of the United States was collected in the port of New York. If the Bank of the United States ceased being the depository for this revenue, it would have to be deposited elsewhere. Elsewhere meant banks in New York City. Deposits of government revenues would greatly increase the lending capacities and profits of those banks. In the process, the commercial vigor of Philadelphia would be diminished and New York City would consolidate its status as the financial capital of the nation.

State chartered banks strongly desired the end of the Bank of the United States because it restrained the creation of development credit. More credit was especially desired by entrepreneurs in the rapidly growing river cities of Pittsburgh, Cincinnati, Louisville, St. Louis, and Detroit, as well as in rapidly growing villages along the Erie Canal in New York and along canals in Pennsylvania, Ohio, and Indiana.

New banks were chartered to serve the needs of specific businesses: farmers and planters' banks served the needs of commercial cultivators; exchange banks served the needs of wholesale merchants, particularly those who assembled cotton for export; merchants' banks served the needs of export merchants; mechanics' banks served the needs of artisans and craftsmen; manufacturers' banks served the needs of factory manufacturers; shoe and leather dealers' banks served the needs of shoemakers; and canal and railroad banks served the needs of transportation. Until the Panic of 1837, and the depression that followed in 1839, state legislatures were eager to incorporate banks to serve these needs.

After the demise of the Bank of the United States in 1836, the preponderance of political and economic power resided with states. By the mid-1850s, there was a confusing mixture of state banking policies that made it increasingly difficult to do business across state lines when railroads were rapidly creating interregional markets.

Between 1820 and 1860, six banking policies operated in states: (1) central banking in New England administered by the Suffolk Bank in Boston, (2) the safety fund in New York operating after 1829, (3) the free banking systems operating in New York and other states after 1838, (4) monopoly banks (with regional offices) incorporated by state legislatures, (5) specie banks (banks that circulated banknotes backed by specie reserves) that were individually incorporated by state legislatures; (6) no banks because state constitutions prohibited legislatures from incorporating banks.

Suffolk System

Beginning in 1818, the Suffolk Bank of Boston acted as the central bank of New England. It regulated the credit practices of banks in interior villages by requiring them to keep a permanent deposit of their banknotes with the Suffolk Bank. If an interior bank issued too many banknotes, the Suffolk Bank, after accepting them for deposit, would carry them to the head office of the bank and demand that they be exchanged for specie. If these banks were unable to redeem them, the Suffolk Bank initiated bankruptcy proceedings. The threat of bankruptcy restrained excessive issues of banknote. The Suffolk system ensured that banknotes of all New England banks circulated at par.

President Jackson's veto of the charter of the Bank of the United States in 1832 was a license for all states to incorporate more banks. Massachusetts was no exception. Between 1836–1837 the Massachusetts legislature chartered thirty-two new banks (seventy-eight between 1830 and 1837). Too many banks were chartered in too short a time for the Suffolk Bank to adequately restrain their credit practices. New England experienced banknote inflation. In May 1837 all New England banks suspended specie redemption of their banknotes and many bankruptcies followed. A year later, surviving New England banks resumed specie redemption. The Suffolk Bank and its successor continued a central banking function until the beginning of the Civil War in 1861. The banknotes of the five hundred banks in New England in 1860 circulated at par.

Safety Fund

The Safety Fund statute was passed by the New York legislature in 1829. It insured the banknotes of state chartered banks so that noteholders would receive full face value if a bank became bankrupt. All state chartered banks were required to annually contribute 0.5 percent of their paid-in capital until they contributed 3 percent. The Safety Fund taxed bank capital instead of banknotes, which forced the largest banks in New York City to subsidize the banknotes issued by interior banks. New York City banks objected to the Safety Fund because they issued relatively few banknotes. Most of their loans were made by crediting customer accounts who then wrote checks against the deposit.

The first purpose of the Safety Fund was to mute agrarian and artisan apprehension over increasing amounts of banknotes in circulation. The second purpose was equalizing business opportunities. This was best served by a multitude of local banks that allocated credit to local entrepreneurs. The third and most important purpose was to cement the alliance of banks and politics as it had evolved in New York in the 1820s under the leadership of Martin Van Buren. Only after agrarian suspicions were allayed could the legislature increase the number of banks. Charters were allocated to party loyalists and businessmen with acceptable political credentials.

Credit restraint was not a purpose of the Safety Fund. It did nothing to restrain the credit practices of New York banks, particularly the lending practices of banks at remote locations. A high percentage of Safety Fund banks incorporated after 1833 had a large element of speculation in them rather than serving the needs of local commerce. The principal purpose of the Safety Fund was to bring political order to the process of bank incorporation. Political order meant perpetuating the election of New York Jeffersonians led by Martin Van Buren, who committed the New York party to supporting the presidential ambitions of Andrew Jackson. Immediately after its passage:

> bills were introduced to recharter twenty-eight operating banks and charter thirty-two new ones. Of these sixty applications, the legislature rechartered sixteen and incorporated eleven new banks. In subsequent years, most operating banks were rechartered and, dur-

ing the years when President Andrew Jackson was making war upon the Bank of the United States (1833–1836), twenty-eight new banks were incorporated. Between 1829 and 1838 the legislature incorporated or reincorporated 93 banks. All of them had to contribute to the safety fund.[5]

Incorporation of new banks was the opportunity to reward Jefferson/Jackson businessmen, but party loyalty was insufficient political weight to obtain a charter. New York's Constitution of 1821 required a two-thirds majority of both houses of the legislature to incorporate banks. The incorporation process had to be managed through the legislature. Jefferson/Jackson legislators were the managers. In order to mobilize a two-thirds majority, shares had to be allocated to state senators and representatives (by purchase or gift). Soon after incorporation legislators usually sold their shares. After passage of the Safety Fund statute, Van Buren resigned and became President Andrew Jackson's secretary of state. When Van Buren went to Washington he took his states' right bank policy with him.

Van Buren was successively state senator, state attorney general, U. S. senator, governor of New York, secretary of state, ambassador to England, vice-president of the United States in the second administration of Andrew Jackson, and successor to Jackson as president of the United States.

The profitability of the Erie Canal generated revenues greatly in excess of maintenance expenses and interest payments on bonds. The obvious use of these funds was increasing the lending capacities of politically friendly banks by depositing canal revenue in them, supplemented by long-term loans. By the end of 1833, seventeen banks in villages along the route of the canal had received deposits. By 1837, thirty-one banks received deposits, and fifty-two received long-term loans. Loans and deposits of canal revenue increased the ability of recipient banks to make loans to local businessmen. Many banks made highly speculative loans, and, after these ventures became bankrupt, their banknotes remained in circulation because the Safety Fund guaranteed their face value. This currency exerted inflationary pressures, especially if the banknotes were from banks at remote locations.

Inflation caused by excessive banknote credit caused a split in the New York Democratic Party. The dissidents were called locofocos and were concentrated in New York City. A high percentage of them were tradesmen, artisans, and retail merchants. They were seriously hurt by inflation because they were frequently paid with banknotes (at their face value) that were issued by banks at remote locations. When these notes were deposited in New York City banks, they were highly discounted and tradesmen, artisans, and retail merchants failed to receive fair value for their products and services.

Small urban businessmen wanted an end to the politics of incorporating banks in remote locations whose principal function was to issue banknotes to circulate at distant localities. They insisted on a reliable currency to conduct day-to-day business; and this currency would come from local banks with trustworthy managers.

The Safety Fund sustained public confidence in the value of New York's banknote currency until the depression of 1839–1842. Eleven banks failed between 1840 and 1842, and the Safety Fund became bankrupt because of flawed language in the statute. Wording made the fund liable for paying depositors as well as holders of banknote currency. This was not the intent. The intent was to guarantee the full face value of banknotes.

In 1845 the legislature corrected the flaw and limited the fund's liability to banknotes, as originally intended. The correction, however, was too late to save the fund from bankruptcy. The fund did not have enough money to pay both noteholders and depositors. These debts were paid by the state in 1845 by the issuance of state bonds. Continued bank failures after 1845 kept the fund bankrupt until it quietly expired in 1866.

Free Banks

The free banking statute was passed by the New York legislature in 1838 after having been rejected in 1837. It was a general incorporation statute for banks that operated the same way as the 1811 general incorporation statute for manufacturing corporations. The 1811 statute opened profit making opportunities in manufacturing to an entrepreneurial democracy. The free banking statute did the same. Entry into the banking business was free from political influence because the rules for entry were known in advance. It was designed to supply abundant credit for local entrepreneurs on a nonpolitical basis.

The basic requirement for entering the banking business was sufficient paid-in capital to guarantee the value of banknotes. Investors in free banks had to deposit securities worth 100 percent of the value of banknotes they issued, and all banknotes circulated by free banks were printed by the state and had registration numbers. There was no limitation on the number of banks that could be incorporated, nor on the volume of banknotes they could issue as long as there were securities backing them. Acceptable securities were United States bonds, bonds of the state of New York or the bonds of any other state approved by the comptroller, or mortgages on unencumbered productive land within New York. Mortgages were soon removed from acceptable securities because they were insufficiently liquid. The comptroller held the bonds in trust.

Free banks were required to have a minimal capitalization of one hundred thousand dollars and keep a specie reserve of 12.5 percent of the banknotes they issued. This requirement was repealed two years later. Thereafter, the creation of banknote credit by free banks depended on purchasing government bonds. The use of bonds for collateral removed an inflexible restraint (specie) on the creation of banknote credit and, at the same time, provided a currency that the public trusted. Several New York City banks reincorporated under its provisions because they could dispense with a specie reserve; and it offered limited liability for stockholders until it was replaced by double liability in the constitution of 1846.

Free banks had a perpetual life, and there were no limits on long-term and short-term credit. A clause in the statute forbid Safety Fund banks from circulating notes less than five dollars after 1841. Thereafter, free banks had the exclusive privilege of putting smaller denomination banknotes in circulation. These banknotes were the currency for daily business transactions and were seldom redeemed for specie. The general incorporation statute for banks was the ultimate corporate laissez faire legislation.

Democratic Party loyalists strongly objected to its passage and, after its enactment, used the courts to try and have it declared unconstitutional. They had three very strong arguments: (1) the Constitution of 1821 did not authorize the incorporation of an indefinite number of banks, only a number judged expedient by the legislature; (2) free banks were called associations (this was a legal fiction because they were corporations by another name); (3) the 1838 statute was not passed by two-thirds of all elected legislators in both houses of the legislature—only by two-thirds of those present.

The Court of Errors (the highest court of New York) sustained the statute's constitutionality because, by the time the court rendered its decision (1842), the Safety Fund was bankrupt. Furthermore, if the free banking statute had been ruled unconstitutional, it would have been interpreted as sustaining the monopoly of a system that failed to protect the value of banknotes. The justices accurately read the latest election returns and did not challenge the statute's popularity. During the first three years of its operation, 167 applications were filed, although only 89 new banks went into operation. By 1849 there were 111 operating free banks in New York, and ten years later there were 274.

As soon as the free banking statute became operational, the officers of the larger banks in New York City organized the Bank of Commerce. Its purpose was to discount the notes of free and Safety Fund banks in order to restrain their credit practices. Like the Suffolk Bank, it functioned as a central bank for banks in New York and northern New Jersey. The banknotes of well managed banks were discounted 0.25 to 0.5 percent when presented for deposit, but the notes of speculative banks were highly discounted.

The frontier state of Michigan is the best example of the dangers of free banking without credit restraints. In 1837 the state legislature passed a nearly identical statute to the free banking bill introduced in the New York legislature that year, but rejected by the legislators. Most free banks in Michigan were organized by merchants and land speculators who wanted to use the credit banks created. In most banks, a high percentage of loans were made to the officers, directors, and stockholders.

To receive a charter, promoters had to deposit "good and sufficient security" approved by the auditor general. A bank could open for business with only 30 percent of its securities paid-in. Acceptable securities were Michigan bonds and mortgages on land. County assessors were generous in land appraisals. Unimproved land purchased a year or two previously for $1.25 an acre was valued at $10 per acre, and town lots were given similar inflated values.

The Panic of 1837 occurred soon after its passage. A special session of the legislature in November 1837 prohibited incorporations after May 1838. This was a window of opportunity for speculators to incorporate banks at remote localities (in the domain of wildcats) until a special session of the legislature permanently suspended the statute's operation in January 1838. The special legislative session also established an independent bank commission to audit the accounts of free banks. Audits showed that most of the banknotes issued by free banks were worthless because the mortgages deposited with the auditor general were on unimproved land. When foreclosed, this land could not be sold on a distressed market.

Like the New York statute, free banks in Michigan were called associations in order to circumvent a constitutional limitation that required a two-thirds vote of elected legislators to incorporate each bank. Its constitutionality was challenged by businessmen who wanted to escape bad debts. Unlike the New York court, the Michigan Supreme Court ruled the statute unconstitutional and its contracts void. Businessmen were released from a morass of entangling debts that would have slowed economic development.

> Michigan's attempt to accelerate its development through free banking foundered because too much credit was created with too few restraints, and the disruptive effects were felt by most Michigan citizens…Farmers preferred to do without local credit facilities rather than conduct business with an unreliable currency. They believed that financial stability and orderly growth could be achieved by drastically limiting the number of banks of issue and by escaping the burden of bad debts through repudiation.[6]

After the fiasco of the free banking statute, the Michigan electorate had an enormous revulsion against banks. Of the sixty-seven banks incorporated in Michigan after statehood (1837), only one continued in business until the Constitutional Convention of 1850. Most Democrat and Whig delegates to the convention strongly favored authorizing banks because businessmen needed local sources of credit. They also realized that there had to be substantial limitations on credit creation to get the constitution ratified by referendum because there would be strong opposition from agrarians. The constitution authorized the incorporation of banks by a general statute with banknote currency backed by state bonds. There were, however, two debilitating provisions, First, bank officers and stockholders had unlimited liability. Second, a free banking statute had to be passed by a referendum.

With the completion of two cross–peninsula railroads in the 1850s and their entry into Chicago in 1852, and the completion of a railroad between Detroit and Toledo, Michigan businessmen in small towns along these routes needed much more credit and a reliable local currency to replace banknotes issued by free banks in Ohio and Indiana that were the usual medium of exchange. After the newly organized Republican Party gained control of the legislature and elected the governor in 1854, its leadership was cautious. Not until 1857 was a general incorporation statute for banks passed by the legislature. It was approved by a referendum in 1858. Only one bank was organized under its provisions because the state constitution required unlimited liability for bank officers and stockholders.

In the legislative session of 1859, the Republican majority passed a constitutional amendment requiring double liability for bank officers and stockholders. It was approved by a referendum in 1860 but no banks were incorporated under its provisions. Not until Congress passed the National Banking Act 1863 (during the Civil War) did Michigan get adequate banking facilities. Five national banks were immediately incorporated, and Michigan, finally, got adequate currency and credit for its businessmen.

Monopoly Banks

The constitutions of the new states of Indiana (1816), Illinois (1819), and Missouri (1821) authorized the legislatures to incorporate monopoly banks with branches. Incorporation of other banks were prohibited. It was assumed that the charters of these banks would be based on the charter of the second Bank of the United States. Only the Indiana legislature acted on the monopoly authorization. A Bank of Indiana was incorporated in 1817 but was bankrupt by 1821. It was not reincorporated until 1834. The state contributed half of its capitalization, appointed the president, and audited its operations twice a year. It had thirteen autonomous branch offices to service regional credit needs. Its lending practices were not politically manipulated. The Illinois legislature incorporated the Bank of Illinois in 1835, but political interventions in its lending practices caused its bankruptcy in 1842. For the next ten years Illinois was without an incorporated bank.

The Missouri legislature incorporated a monopoly bank in 1837 with two-thirds of its capital contributed by the state. It had five branch offices and, like the Indiana bank, served the credit and currency needs of the regions they served. In 1857 there was a clear need for more bank credit in Missouri. St. Louis was the eighth largest city in the United States and the center for steamboat traffic on the upper Mississippi and Missouri rivers. In addition, the city had been connected to Chicago and eastern cities by railroads.

Missouri's constitution was amended to end the monopoly of the Bank of Missouri, but the legislature did not pass a free banking statute. It incorporated nine new banks with each bank required to establish at least two branches. The banks had to maintain specie reserves of one-third of the banknotes they put into circulation. By 1859 the nine banks had a total of forty-one branches. Seven of the banks had head offices in St. Louis where business was concentrated. The Bank of Missouri continued in business until the state sold its interest in 1866 and its ten branches reincorporated with national charters.

Specie Banks

For lack of a better term, these were banks that were required to keep reserves of specie in their vaults to back a percentage of the banknote currency they put into circulation. Specie reserves were usually a high percentage of the banknotes they circulated. They were incorporated one at a time by state legislatures, either on their commercial or political merits. Specie banks usually specialized in short-term credit but, frequently, loans were continually renewed.

The banking system in Louisiana between 1842 and 1853 exemplifies the strengths and weaknesses of specie banking. Many persons were left holding worthless banknotes after the bankruptcy of eleven of the seventeen development banks during the depression from 1839 to 1842, and many planters lost their land by foreclosed mortgages. The political response to these hardships was the banking statute of 1842. Its principal purpose was to supply a reliable currency by requiring banknotes to be backed with a one-third specie reserve. Furthermore, loans were limited to ninety days, and new banks were prohibited from making mortgage loans.

Concern for a reliable currency was carried into the Constitutional Convention of 1845. A clause prohibited the incorporation of new banks and forbid the legislature from renewing the charters of the existing banks. Although the high specie reserves required for incorporation under the 1842 statute supplied Louisiana citizens with a reliable currency, nonetheless, specie was an inflexible basis for supplying New Orleans merchants with sufficient credit to market increasing cotton harvests arriving by steamboats.

New Orleans was a major port, and in 1842 it was the fourth largest city in the United States. A high percentage of the nation's cotton crop passed through its warehouses for export to textile mills in Europe and northern states. City brokers purchased cotton from inland brokers and assembled cargoes, and these transactions required abundant short-term credit. The need for more credit by New Orleans merchants became acute in the 1850s. Increasing amounts of cotton moved upriver to Pittsburgh and onto east–west railroads for marketing in Europe and northern states. Alternatively, cotton moved to Mobile, Alabama over newly built railroads for shipment to northern textile mills or for transshipment to Europe from northern ports.

These diversions were not due to lower transportation costs but the availability of large amounts of credit supplied by banks in New York City and New England at lower interest rates and for longer periods of time. Between 1858 and 1860, the Pennsylvania Railroad, with its trunkline connection from Pittsburgh to Philadelphia, increased its cotton freight from 2,600 metric tons to 13,000 metric tons. Tobacco grown in Kentucky was also diverted eastward.

In order to preserve the competitive advantages of location, New Orleans businessmen had to have more credit. In 1853 the constitutional ban on incorporating banks was repealed and a general incorporation statute was passed by the legislature. It was a copy of New York's general incorporation statute, and four banks were incorporated using its provisions. They provided much needed credit at lower interest rates for New Orleans businessmen who marketed cotton and sugar; and for factors who supplied plantations with supplies.

No Banks

When Texas was annexed in 1845, its constitution prohibited the legislature from incorporating banks. The Constitution of Louisiana, adopted in the same year, prohibited the legislature from incorporating banks. Similar clauses were adopted by the conventions that framed constitutions for Iowa and Arkansas in 1846 and Oregon in 1859. The shortage of a reliable currency in Iowa forced some counties and cities to issue certificates (good for paying taxes) in order to have a currency to conduct local business. Additional currency of dubious quality was supplied by banks incorporated in Nebraska Territory and other states. In 1852, the secretary of the treasury reported that there were no incorporated banks operating in Florida, Arkansas, Texas, Illinois, Iowa, Wisconsin, and California. Seven of the thirty-one states were without incorporated banks.

The new constitution, ratified by the Iowa electorate in 1857, permitted banking provided the statute was ratified by a referendum. Two banking statutes were passed by the legislature and ratified by a referendum: a general incorporation statute for banks and a statute incorporating the Bank of Iowa. No banks were incorporated under the general incorporation statute because of its severe restrictions, but the Bank of Iowa was immediately organized and functioned as a monopoly until 1865. It had fifteen branches. Each branch bank had to keep a 35 percent specie reserve for the banknotes it put into circulation and the maximum length of loans was 120 days. These two provisions were major constraints on lending practices. In 1865 the Bank of Iowa and its branches reincorporated with national charters in order to be able to create more credit.

Triumph of General Incorporation Statutes

When Wisconsin became a state in 1848, its constitution did not prohibit banks, but the legislature did not incorporate banks. Nonetheless, Wisconsin had a bank because the territorial legislature had incorporated the Wisconsin Marine and Fire Insurance Company in 1839. It was authorized to receive deposits and lend money. It immediately went into the banking business and issued circulating certificates based on deposits. These certificates were generally accepted as currency for day-to-day business in Wisconsin. Its charter was repealed by the territorial legislature in 1846, but it continued in the banking business because it was conservatively managed and because a high percentage of its business was in the rapidly growing city of Chicago that needed maximum amounts of credit and a reliable currency. In 1852, it was reincorporated as a bank under the free banking statute passed by the Wisconsin legislature.

In 1849 the legislature of Alabama and in 1850 the legislature of New Jersey enacted general incorporation statutes for banks. The legislatures of Ohio, Illinois, Vermont, and Massachusetts followed in 1851. The Indiana legislature ended the monopoly of the Bank of Indiana in 1852 by passing a general incorporation statute. The legislatures of Connecticut, Wisconsin, and Tennessee also passed general incorporation statutes for banks. Florida and Louisiana followed in 1853. Michigan's legislature passed a second general incorporation statute in 1857, Minnesota passed one in 1858, and Pennsylvania in 1860. No banks were incorporated using the general incorporation statutes in Massachusetts, Vermont, Pennsylvania, Iowa, Alabama, Georgia, and Florida because of excessive restraints. The Tennessee legislature repealed the free banking statute in 1858. The principal restraint of these statutes was unlimited liability for bank officers and stockholders.

All of these statutes were closely based on New York experience where its general incorporation statute was highly successful at creating short-term and long-term credit and a currency that businessmen accepted as reliable because it was backed by government bonds. New York's statute was successful because only the highest rated securities were accepted for backing the currency, and the state printed and numbered all of the banknotes free banks put into circulation.

In Illinois, Indiana, and Wisconsin speculative banks proliferated because state regulators accepted high risk bonds for backing currency and printing banknotes was not supervised. The Wisconsin statute duplicated the disaster of the Michigan statute of 1837. Statutes passed by the Illinois and Indiana legislature were little better. Many Illinois and Indiana free banks became bankrupt during the panic of 1857.

When the Civil War began in April 1861, a high percentage of surviving free banks became bankrupt because state banking commissioners had accepted bonds from slave states as backing for banknote currency. These securities became worthless. These bonds had been purchased at high discounts from the mid-1850s onward because of the risk of impending war. In 1861 there were no incorporated banks doing business in Chicago, and in 1864 only twenty-three banks were operating in Illinois.

An analysis of the evolution of banking practices in New York, Massachusetts, Louisiana, and Michigan is important because they were microcosms for the currency and credit needs of states that were undergoing the stresses of industrialization and urbanization (Massachusetts), and frontier states that needed large amounts of credit to accelerate economic development (Michigan).

The Political Economy of Antebellum Banking

What were the adverse consequences of the demise of the second Bank of the United States? What were the positive contributions of free banks to economic development?

The serious short-term adverse consequences were:

1. The number of banks in the United States increased from four hundred in 1833 to six hundred in 1836, and a high percentage of these banks maximized issuing banknote currency.
2. Credit was highly inflated and its contraction triggered a depression that lasted from 1839 to 1842.
3. Banks issued a confusing hodge-podge of banknotes in many denominations. Many banks issued one, two, three, four, and five dollar banknotes.
4. There was a vast increase in counterfeit banknotes.
5. The officers and directors of many newly incorporated banks engaged in fraudulent practices.
6. Land speculation was the largest use of credit in newly chartered banks in states west of the Appalachian Mountains.
7. A high percentage of newly incorporated banks became bankrupt when the speculative bubble burst.

The long-term adverse consequences were:

1. A weakened national government.
2. A strong public reaction against all banks that caused many frontier states to prohibit the incorporation of banks.
3. The creation of an independent treasury that forced the national government to do business with only gold and silver coins. The result was clumsy fiscal administration and forfeiture of almost all control over currency and credit.
4. Unstable banking systems in many states that hindered the long distance transfer of funds.
5. A disjointed state banking systems in 1860 that was glaringly inadequate for national economic development.

There were six positive consequences that followed the dissolution of the Bank of the United States; however, none of them were directly related to its dissolution:

1. Entry into the banking business was democratized after state legislatures passed general incorporation statutes based on New York's experience.
2. General incorporation statutes based on New York experience freed credit and currency creation from the constraints of a specie reserve.
3. State governments had a much enlarged domestic market for bonds they issued or underwrote because there was a large market for bonds to back the currency of free banks.
4. A high percentage of the bonds issued by states were used to build internal improvement projects.
5. The effect of freeing banks from specie reserves was maximizing credit creation for allocation to local entrepreneurs.
6. Local entrepreneurs were essential for speeding economic development of northern states through the agrarian stage into diversified economies.

Bray Hammond summarizes the impact of New York's free banking statute on national economic development:

> It was a great thing politically. It was all things to all men. It promised more business opportunities, more banks, more money, and protection for the public. It also established a new market for bonds at a time when enthusiasm for public improvements was producing a flood tide of bond issues....Free banking in time became general throughout the country.... It was a program with two underlying aims: first, to advance states rights in the economic field at the cost of federal powers, and, second, to diffuse and expand the opportunities for business enterprise.[7]

The political popularity of New York's free banking systems was its ability to provide a reliable currency for cultivators and abundant credit for local businessmen. Cultivators approved the reliability of its currency and village and city businessmen strongly approved of its ability to create more credit than specie based banking. Examined from a different perspective, credit supplied by free banks democratized credit allocation to small businessmen in rapidly growing cities in northern states. The ability of well-managed free banking systems to supply abundant credit for economic development made it the model for the national banking act of 1863 that mobilized the huge amount of credit required to fight the Civil War—and save the life of the nation.

The governments of slave states had different priorities. The first priority of slave states was providing credit to planters to purchase land and slaves; therefore, a high percentage of the credit created by banks in slave states was locked up in mortgages on land. The result was a continual shortage of short-term credit needed for day-to-day commerce. The second priority was providing sufficient credit for brokers to assemble cotton bales and transport them to market. The third priority was aiding the construction of internal improvements projects.

Frequently, the governments of slave states issued bonds and allocated the funds to banks. Alternatively, state governments underwrote bonds issued by banks. A high percentage of these funds were used to (1) finance the expansion of cotton cultivation (by purchasing land and slaves), (2) supply credit to brokers who assembled cotton bales, (3) short-term credit to transport cotton to port cities for export or for shipment to northern textile mills. By 1838, the states of Louisiana, Mississippi, and Alabama had borrowed thirty-four million dollars to supply capital for their banks.

These banks were often called planters' banks, or planters and merchants' banks. Planters' banks were frequently authorized to establish branches in villages where commercial activity was concentrated during the cotton harvest, but otherwise there was insufficient annual business to support a local bank. Banks were also used to overcome lack of local capital to invest in infrastructure projects by mandating that newly chartered banks purchase shares in a specific turnpike, bridge, or railroad corporation. Many northern state legislatures also used this funding policy as long as banks were individually incorporated. It was a strategy of economic development that avoided taxation.

Railroads

The earliest railroads in the United States were built in the mid-1830s, almost at the same time that railroads demonstrated their carrying capacities in Britain. Most of the earliest railroads were shortlines from tidewater, navigable rivers, or lakes, to inland villages that lacked direct water transportation. They were built to replace stagecoaches in order to speed passengers to where steamboat transportation or canal packets were available.

The earliest roads were built with capital raised from the sale of shares. A high percentage of these shares were purchased by persons living in towns and cities along their routes, or shares were exchanged for labor performed by farmers during the off season, or for supplies like wooden ties, made by farmers during the winter. Engines were underpowered and trains traveled on iron straps nailed to wooden rails. Initially, railroads were considered improved turnpikes, and like turnpikes, a principal reason for purchasing shares was to raise property values along their routes.

Most shortlines were immediately profitable because they serviced the needs of an existing population of commercially motivated cultivators who had money to purchase their services. Their profitability was a strong incentive for promoters to build trunklines that could compete with canals for freight traffic, and for managers of railroads to purchase rolling stock that increased the freight carrying capacities of railroads. During the 1840s and 1850s, all aspects of railroad technology were rapidly improved by borrowing British designs, plus innovations made by American mechanics.

Paralleling technical improvements was the development of management skills needed to operate larger systems. Equally important was the development of financial skills necessary to mobilize the capital required to build second generation roads and reequip the earliest railroads with iron rails, more powerful locomotives, and more rolling stock.

What were the advantages demonstrated by railroad freight transportation? In northern states railroads:

1. operated in all weather after the surfaces of canals, rivers, and lakes froze for one to four months of the year;
2. reduced transshipment costs because they could load products at places of origin and take them directly to places for distribution (more direct routing);
3. arrival of products could be better scheduled;
4. products moved at faster speeds (faster arrivals reduced the cost of maintaining inventories of expensive manufactured products);
5. reduced spoilage of many products that were vulnerable to water damage (flour and textiles), or spoilage during slow transportation (butter), and reduced weight losses of livestock that occurred when driven to market;
6. accelerated the settlement of land that was considered marginal because of its distance from water transportation.

On the following pages I will use the histories of the Boston and Worcester and Boston and Albany railroads to describe the problems that had to be solved in order to build pioneer railroads. The descriptions will show readers how they were promoted, financed, and managed. All pioneer railroads had a similar array of problems. After pioneer railroads had lowered transportation costs for inland towns and demonstrated their profitability, village businessmen as well as farmers in less densely populated districts, wanted railroad service.

Finance

Pioneer railroads owed much to financing canals and building turnpikes. Building canals and railroads required large numbers of laborers who had to work under the close supervision of surveyors. Many of the labor gangs that built northern railroads were composed of farmers who were hired by local contractors to build a kilometer of roadway. These men had to be paid for their labor. The money came from investors who purchased shares of stock or bonds. The means used to mobilize labor to build turnpikes and money to build canals transferred to building railroad rights-of-way.

Financing construction of the Erie Canal was the prototype for financing later large scale infrastructure projects in the United States. The estimated cost of the canal was seven million dollars, all of which had to be borrowed. The money was raised by selling bonds that paid 6 percent interest and had a twenty year maturity. Both the principal and interest were guaranteed (underwritten) by state tax revenues. Construction began in 1817 with funds from the sale of the first of twenty-four bond issues that were needed to complete the canal. The first loan was for two hundred thousand dollars.

Most purchasers of the initial canal bonds were prosperous businessmen who invested one or two thousand dollars. The wealthiest businessmen in New York City were conspicuously absent as subscribers. Before 1822, the largest purchaser of canal bonds was the Savings Bank of New York. In 1821 the bank held about 30 percent of the bonds from the initial issues. Savings banks were semi-philanthropic institutions that originated in Britain in 1810. The first U.S. savings bank was incorporated in Massachusetts in 1817. New York followed in 1819. Savings banks were incorporated to provide city artisans, craftsmen, and retail merchants with a safe place to deposit their working capital and savings. Savings were encouraged by paying interest on deposits.

After 1820, the wealthiest businessmen in New York City began making investments in canal bonds. They became attractive investments because the 150 kilometers of canal in operation in the autumn of 1819 carried considerable traffic. By the autumn of 1822, there were 305 kilometers in operation, and traffic generated sufficient revenue to pay considerable amounts of the funds needed to complete the canal. The projected success of the canal was noted in London where New York export merchants had close commercial ties.

After 1822, British investors were substantial purchasers of canal bonds. The transatlantic market was sufficiently strong so that it was possible to lower interest rates to five percent on subsequent bonds. Investments by European banks and investors accelerated the completion of the canal, and helped reduce borrowings costs. At its completion in 1825, the canal was 585 kilometers in length and was immediately profitable. By 1829, over half of the canal bonds were owned in Europe.

The immediate success of the Erie Canal generated three political responses in New York and other states: (1) building trunkline canals in other states to compete with the Erie Canal for commerce originating in the trans-Appalachian west, (2) building lateral canals to feed traffic into mainline canals, and (3) subsidizing the construction of railroads because they were capable of rapid improvement in speed and carrying capacities, and they could be built where canals could not.

Many shortline railroads were built without state subsidies. First generation railroads connected cities where substantial nonagricultural employment existed. Businessmen invested in them because they wanted faster and more direct transportation for existing passenger and freight traffic than provided by wagons, stagecoaches, canal boats, or steamboats. The desire for railroad transportation by businessmen in long settled communities created enormous pressures on state legislatures to use public credit to mobilize and allocate funds for railroad construction. State governments readily granted this power to railroad promoters after they mobilized initiating amounts of capital from local businessmen; and in all cases, legislatures granted promoters the use of eminent domain to acquire rights-of-way.

Railroads built between 1845 and 1860 were second generation railroads. They were more expensive to build because railroad technology underwent very rapid evolution that made them capable of carrying increasing volumes of freight. In addition, they were capable of operating as long distance trunklines. The most important public contribution was credit. Public credit was in the form of underwriting bonded indebtedness or granting land from the public domain. Between the mid-1830s and 1860, public credit contributed about 30 percent of all construction costs, especially in the trans-Appalachian west where many trunkline railroads were built ahead of settlement.

Only governments could supply requisite amounts of credit, and the only way governments could obtain the credit was by pledging future tax revenues. Pledging tax revenues in the 1840s and 1850s meant pledging tax revenues on agricultural land because agricultural land was the principal form of wealth in all states. State governments, city governments, county governments, village governments, and township governments willingly pledged tax revenues in order to satisfy the insistent demand of their communities for railroad transportation.

Most land taxation, however, was deferred. Governments that underwrote railroad bonds hoped that they would never have to levy land taxes to satisfy these debt obligations because they assumed that railroad revenues would be sufficient to pay annual interest on the bonds and ultimately return the principal to investors.[8]

Taxation of the agricultural sector, however, was not fully deferred. It was disguised. In order to obtain construction funds railroad promoters often accepted discounts on the bonds they sold. A bond with a face value of one thousand dollars, paying 7 percent interest, was sold for eight hundred fifty dollars. Interest, however, was paid on one thousand dollars, for a yield of 8.2 percent interest to investors. Discount financing inflated construction costs, but the railroad was built. In order to pay inflated construction costs, freight rates on agricultural commodities had to be high. In effect, this was a hidden tax. It was a tax that farmers willingly paid because railroad transportation was cheaper than all the alternatives; and lowered transportation costs increased their incomes.

In order to understand the complexities of promoting, financing, and managing pioneer railroads it is best to examine how one regional trunkline was built. That railroad is the Boston and Worcester/Boston and Albany. Most of this story is borrowed from Stephen Salsbury's *The State, The Investor, and The Railroad*.

Boston had a serious commercial problem during the 1820s. In the decade of the 1820s, New York City eclipsed Boston in commercial growth. The value of New York City's foreign commerce was approximately three times the value of Boston's foreign commerce. Part of Boston's continuing decline in the 1830s was attributable to lack of trunkline transportation to the trans-Appalachian west. There was no doubt in the minds of businessmen in Boston, Philadelphia, and Baltimore that the western market would continue its explosive growth.

In the 1830's the commerce of trans-Appalachian states would go in two directions: (1) east via steamboats on the Great Lakes to the Erie Canal with a terminus in New York City, and (2) down stream on the Ohio, Cumberland, Tennessee, Missouri, and Mississippi rivers to New Orleans. *How were the other east coast cities to participate in this commerce?* The immediate response of Philadelphia and Virginia businessmen was to lobby for state funding to build canals into the interior, like the Erie Canal. Lobbying was successful, but the canals were financial failures because they were stopped by a stone wall when they reached the Appalachian mountains.

Railroads were the only alternative. While canals in Virginia and Pennsylvania were being built to dead ends at the Appalachian Mountains, businessmen in Philadelphia and Baltimore were investing in the Pennsylvania and Baltimore and Ohio railroads. The Massachusetts legislature refused to build a canal to the West because it would be frozen four or five months of the year and the Berkshire Mountains in western Massachusetts were as great a barrier to the West as the Appalachian Mountains. Boston's access to western markets had to be by a trunkline railroad from Boston to Albany. After it reached Albany, western agricultural commodities could be transshipped eastward for export or for consumption by residents of cities and towns where manufacturing was concentrated. Trains going westward would carry products manufactured in Massachusetts for transshipment onto the Erie Canal for sale in western markets

The first section in a railroad between Boston and Albany was to Worcester, located seventy kilometers west of Boston. The region immediately surrounding Worcester had many medium sized waterpower sites that were progressively utilized after 1810. Until 1828 its only link to Boston was a turnpike that passed through Worcester on its way to Springfield; however, in that year the Blackstone Canal reached the Worcester region. Businessmen in Providence, Rhode Island funded its construction with the aid of a grant of banking power to the canal company. The Blackstone Canal provided Worcester with a transportation artery but was a financial failure because it could not operate in the winter and soon had railroad competition.

The Boston and Worcester Railroad was incorporated in 1831 with a thirty-year monopoly on railroad transportation between the cities. The legislature incorporated it with the assumption that, in the near future, the same promoters would build westward to Springfield and Albany, and that the roads would operate as a single unit. Construction began in 1832 and the road was completed in the summer of 1835. It was built using a technique borrowed from canal builders. The right-of-way was divided into many small segments and local contractors mobilized the labor of immigrants and local farmers (and their draft animals and equipment) to make cuts and build embankments. Bridges and rock cuts were separate contracts.

The Boston and Worcester also had to acquire land for passenger and freight terminals in Boston. The promoters had purposefully underestimated land and terminal costs because high costs would scare potential investors. When it came time to actually acquire land and build terminal facilities, the costs were higher than expected but the purchase of expensive land was unavoidable.

Rails were purchased in England because American furnaces and rolling mills did not have the capacity to supply them. American furnaces and forges, however, could supply the spikes and fish plates that were used to bolt rails into a continuous line. Rails were expensive because iron products paid a 25 percent tariff. Promoters of several pioneer railroads petitioned Congress in 1830 to remove the tariff as an incentive for investments in railroads. Congress agreed. Between 1830 and 1843 the tariff on iron rails was refunded if the rails were immediately used by railroads.

Worcester had an industrial base. In 1837 it had sixty-seven dispersed mills that spun, wove, and fulled woolen textiles. The demand for textile machinery created a market for iron castings and other iron shapes. A local entrepreneur built a foundry to supply this market. The availability of iron attracted other entrepreneurs who established factories to draw wire and make sieves, axes, scythes, plows, and other iron implements. These factories employed about 2,500 persons. In addition, shoes and boots were manufactured on a putting out system. In 1837, the region around Worcester manufactured 2.35 million pairs. Like the two other shortline railroads in Massachusetts (Boston and Lowell and Boston and Providence) the Boston and Worcester operated between urban commercial centers and like these roads it was entirely built with private capital. All three railroads were instantly profitable because they connected commercial cities.

The Boston and Worcester was capitalized by 10,000 shares with one hundred dollars par value per share. Widespread ownership was encouraged by allowing purchasers to subscribe by paying one dollar per share, but the promoters made it clear that later assessments would be in amounts of twenty dollars to thirty dollars as construction funds were needed. There was no rush to purchase shares. Worcester businessmen were especially negligent, even though they had the most to gain. Most of the initial purchasers were Boston businessmen. In all, 238 persons and institutions purchased shares, and only 18 were from Worcester.

In spite of the success of the Boston and Lowell and Boston and Providence railroads, most the original subscribers sold their shares. When the Worcester began operations in 1835, only forty-one of the original purchasers were still stockholders, and their holdings amounted to only 17 percent of capitalization. A high percentage of the businessmen who were initial purchasers withdrew their capital and invested it in textile mills where profits were 15 percent

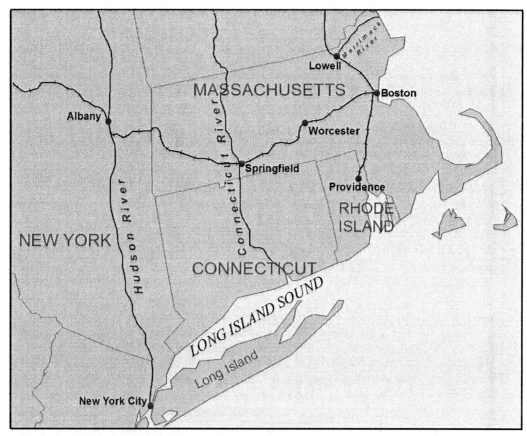

Figure 7.1 Massachusetts Railroads, 1842. Map by Yu Zhou. Reproduced with permission.

per year. They shifted the risks of managing a capital intensive corporation with rapidly evolving technology to others. In 1836, 32 percent of the shares were owned by Boston banks and 45 percent were owned by banks in New York City. New York investors and banks also owned 45 percent of the Boston and Providence Railroad.

The instant profitability of the Boston and Worcester catalyzed businessmen in Springfield and Pittsfield to promote the construction of a railroad westward from Worcester to Albany. Boston businessmen were the principal investors because they wanted to divert some of the export commodities carried on the Erie Canal and Hudson River to themselves. Businessmen in Springfield were especially motivated because the falls on the Connecticut River were harnessed in 1835 to power textiles mills equivalent in size to those at Lowell. These mills were supplied with raw cotton by the Farmington Canal that was built to tap the commerce of central Massachusetts. Construction funds for the canal were supplied by businessmen in Hartford and New Haven, Connecticut. The canal became operational in 1830 but, like the two other New England canals (Middlesex and Blackstone), it became bankrupt soon after railroads were built.

Like the owners of textile mills at Lowell, mill owners in Springfield wanted all weather transportation. The Massachusetts legislature had already passed a charter of incorporation for the Boston and Albany Railroad but it was dormant. Its starting point was Worcester. The Boston and Albany Railroad was capitalized for two million dollars, even though the promoters knew that this was grossly insufficient to build the road to Albany. It was, however, sufficient to build it to Springfield where there was enough traffic to generate enough revenue to attract additional investors needed to build westward. Like the Boston and Worcester, each share had a par value of one hundred dollars.

The initial subscription was five dollars per share. The first offering sold only 13,000 of the 20,000 shares. Boston businessmen purchased 8,500 shares and Springfield investors purchased 4,500. New York City investors shunned the issue because most investors believed it would diminish the commerce of New York City by diverting a substantial portion of Erie Canal traffic to Boston.

The promoters had to democratize selling the remaining 7,000 shares. Between October and December 1835 a publicity blitz sold the remaining shares. When all shares were subscribed, there were 2,800 shareholders. A majority of stockholders owned between one and four shares, but 40 percent of the shares were owned by one hundred investors. Boston residents owned 75 percent of the shares, Springfield residents 10 percent, and 10 percent were owned by residents of smaller towns along the proposed route.

The promoters of the railroad immediately solicited a state subsidy of one million dollars. The Massachusetts legislature was highly receptive. It voted to purchase one million dollars worth of shares with the proviso that private shareholders pay 75 percent of the assessments on their shares before the state paid any assessments on its shares. In April 1836 the state of Massachusetts became the owner of one-third of the railroad. The money to purchase its shares came from selling bonds in London as each assessment came due.

Construction began in January 1837 but immediately encountered difficulties because the Panic of 1837 that occurred in April. It became difficult to collect the fifth five dollar assessment needed to continue grading the roadbed west of Worcester. Simultaneously, engineers increased the estimated costs to at least four million dollars for constructing the road from Springfield to the New York state line. The promoters returned to the state legislature for an additional subsidy of 2.4 million dollars. This equaled 80 percent of the railroad's capitalization. In return the state would get a first mortgage. The compelling reason for requesting this subsidy was "the state can make the loan" because Massachusetts had no substantial debt and a history of fiscal integrity.[9]

In February 1838 the legislature underwrote a loan for 2.1 million dollars. The requirement that shareholders had to pay 75 percent of the par value of their shares was revised downward. The state would not transfer money to the railroad until all shareholders had been assessed thirty dollars on their shares, which required them to pay an additional ten dollars. The bonds were sold in Britain because the export merchants of Boston had good banking connections in London. They found a good market because they were underwritten by the state. They had a thirty-year maturity date and paid 5 percent interest. Thereafter, the state allocated funds in three hundred thousand dollar installments.

Capital from Britain allowed managers to vigorously push construction of the eighty-six kilometers from Worcester to Springfield. This section of the road opened for service in October 1839. After reaching Springfield, a new survey of the route estimated that an additional 1.5 million dollars was required to build the road to the boundary with New York. Promoters returned to the state legislature because the deepening depression produced a severe contraction of credit from local banks. Both contractors who built the right-of-way and shareowners would not or could not fund continuing construction.

Again, the legislature was receptive. In March 1839 it authorized the issuance of 1.2 million dollars of bonds but also required shareholders to pay an additional ten dollar assessment before the state would transfer money to the railroad. These bonds could not be sold in Britain because of the deepening financial crisis in the United States. Boston promoters used them as collateral for loans from Boston and New York banks in order to continue construction. These funds were insufficient to complete the road because the right-of-way through the Berkshire mountains required more rock cuts and higher bridges over watercourses than previous estimates.

In the depth of the depression in 1841, the managers and promoters again returned to the legislature. Their reception was cool. Managers and promoters mounted a state-wide publicity campaign that had the desired results—more state aid. Again, the legislature imposed conditions. Shareholders had to pay an additional twenty dollar assessment, and it authorized only seven hundred thousand dollars of the one million requested. Promoters were forced to return to stockholders at the bottom the depression and collect the full assessment on shares because no more funds were available from the state or from Europe.

After the Boston and Albany reached the boundary with New York, it was sixty-two kilometers from Albany. The New York legislature had already incorporated a company to build a road from Albany to the Massachusetts border, but no money was raised until April 1840 when the city of Albany underwrote one million dollars of bonds. Even in the depression, the city of Albany had no difficulty selling bonds because it was the eastern terminus of the Erie Canal and had a large tax base. The city of Albany used some of this money to purchase control of the franchise, which was then leased to the Boston and Albany. The rest of the funds from the bond issue were used to build the road from Albany to the Massachusetts boundary.

The Boston and Albany became operational in December 1841 by using a short section of rickety tracks built by a shortline railroad that went inland from the Hudson River. Not until early in 1842, did locomotives of the Boston and Albany operate on a right-of-way built to its specifications. It was 310 kilometers in length, including the section in New York, and was the second longest railroad in the United States in 1842.

During construction the Massachusetts legislature underwrote four million dollars of bonds and the city of Albany an additional one million. The state of Massachusetts also owned one million dollars worth of shares. Neither the state of Massachusetts nor the city of Albany incurred losses in underwriting the bonds because the Boston and Albany was a consistently profitable railroad after 1845; and the state of Massachusetts profited from dividends it received on shares it owned.

Management

The management structure of the Boston and Albany was as experimental as railroad technology because management practices developed in textile mills and other factories were not transferable to railroads. In its physical and financial structure, the Boston and Albany Railroad was immensely larger and more complex than any factory. During construction, management decisions were made by a committee of directors who were also the principal promoters and stockholders. All of them had other business interests that took various amounts of their time. Only after the railroad was operational early in 1842 was management concentrated in a president who was a full time employee of the company.

Because of heavy dependence on public credit, there had to be a strong political component in the management of the Boston and Albany. It was immensely useful that the president elected in 1842 had these connections. He had been a member of the Massachusetts legislature from Springfield since 1827 and was president of the senate in 1835. He became a director in 1836 and was a principal member of the management committee that supervised construction.

Prior to construction, the promoters of the Boston and Albany had to decide on a construction strategy. *Should the road be built as cheaply as possible and depend on increasing revenues to gradually upgrade it? Or should they build a first class right-of-way and equip the road with first class equipment?* The promoters decided to build a quality road even though capital costs were probably twice as much as building a road with a narrow right-of-way sharp curves, using light rails that were poorly ballasted, and rolling stock that was moved by underpowered locomotives. Engineers convinced the promoters that flimsy construction was false economy for the intended purpose of the road.

Three factors dictated building a quality road: (1) the eastern terminus was the Boston and Worcester that had been built to the highest existing standards; (2) the road had to be able to carry freight to textile mills and other factories in Springfield and elsewhere along its route, and (3) one of the purposes for building the road was to tap the traffic of the Erie Canal for commodities that could be exported by Boston merchants or consumed in Boston and other industrial cities in Massachusetts. This traffic required a quality right-of-way and the most powerful locomotives to haul freight up the steep grades of the Berkshire mountains. In anticipation of a large volume of freight traffic, all bridges were built to accommodate two tracks, and all embankments and cuts were made wide enough for a second track that would be built when there was sufficient revenue.

When the Boston and Albany was under construction, securing adequate financing dominated the energies of promoters. Acquiring adequate terminal facilities was postponed until after the road was completed. The lack of adequate terminal facilities became a serious problem after completion because freight required terminals at Albany and Boston. At Albany, commodities arriving on the Erie Canal had to be transferred to railroad boxcars, and products manufactured in Massachusetts had to be transferred onto canal boats going west. In Boston, the Boston and Worcester had to build a waterfront terminal for products destined for export. The Boston waterfront terminal would be built on expensive urban land, but its management was reluctant to make this investment until traffic justified it.

The railroad did not enter Albany. It ended on the east bank of the Hudson River opposite Albany. Passengers going west by rail or east to Boston had to disembark and cross the river to make connections. The Boston and Albany did not own a ferry until the summer of 1842. Lack of a bridge at Albany in 1842 was not a serious impediment for freight traffic because most freight arrived in canals boats; however, facilities were inadequate. Revenues would be uncertain until an adequate riverside terminal was built.

After the Boston and Albany was fully operational in early 1842, the two principal responsibilities of the president were financial stability and good relations with the state legislature. Financial stability depended on generating enough revenue to pay the interest on its bonded indebtedness; and enough revenue depended on an adequate rate structure for freight and passengers. Traffic on the partially completed road generated an income of only $49,000 in 1841. Interest payments were $310,000 per year. A reserve fund avoided defaulting on interest payments. It was absolutely essential to increase revenue as quickly as possible to avoid bankruptcy.

The biggest problem was making rate structures for through and local traffic that ensured profitability. Immediately upon completion, there was a contest among four interest groups to have rate structures that benefited them: (1) Boston exporters wanted minimum rates for freight originating at Albany, especially flour; (2) factory owners in Springfield, Pittsfield, and elsewhere along the route, feared that low rates for through traffic would force the railroad to charge excessive rates for local traffic; (3) the managers of the Boston and Worcester railroad wanted a revenue sharing formula that maximized revenue from through traffic; (4) the state of Massachusetts insisted that freight and passenger rates be sufficiently high to pay the annual interest on the four million dollars of bonds that were underwritten by the state.

Directors knew there had to be rate discrimination for freight in order to earn sufficient revenue. Rate discrimination meant that local freight paid more per ton kilometer than through freight because local products had no alternative means of transportation. The directors were very uncertain about a politically acceptable rate structure that would also be profitable. All directors agreed there should be three classes of freight and a special rate for flour. Manufactured products like textiles and shoes paid the highest rate. *What was that rate? What was the special rate for flour?*

The freight rates and passenger fares posted in 1841 were intelligent guesses. A majority of directors believed that freight revenue should pay total operating expenses and passenger fares pay for maintenance and interest on bonded indebtedness. At the end of the first full year of operation (1842), revenue was insufficient to pay interest costs, but it was close. Bank loans prevented bankruptcy. Based on the first year of operation, directors assumed that passenger revenues would exceed freight revenue. This was the revenue structure of the Boston and Worcester. It was a wrong assumption. After 1847 freight revenue was substantially larger.

Before the carrying capacity of the road was fully known, and before it had achieved profitability, directors representing business interests in Boston insisted that the president pursue a policy of competition with Hudson River steamboats. All of the flour arriving at Albany on the Erie Canal was carried by steamboats on the Hudson River to New York City for urban consumption, distribution to coastal cities, and export. Competition required low through rates. They believed this strategy could achieve quick profitability because flour was the highest value commodity (compared to lumber, grain, and salt) carried on the Erie Canal, and it made a disproportionately high contribution to canal revenues. Between 1845 and 1860, flour receipts in Buffalo from western states averaged over one million barrels, plus substantial quantities of flour produced in the state of New York. Boston directors believed that the Boston and Albany was capable of diverting a high percentage of this traffic to Boston where it would contribute to the profits of Boston export merchants.

The president of the Boston and Albany was adamant that the railroad could not win this competition because low rates for through traffic would not produce sufficient revenue to cover financial and operating costs, especially in the early years of the railroad's operation. He believed that profitability was obtainable by serving the needs of towns and cities on its route, not export merchants in Boston. The president made the correct analysis because Boston had already lost primacy to New York City in export–import commerce. Serving the needs of manufacturers located at interior locations would be the principal source of the company's profits. His judgment was overruled, and he was removed from office but returned a year later when the low rate strategy for through traffic was an obvious failure.

High interest payments on its debt and difficult operating conditions over the Berkshire Mountains, especially in the winter, precluded full diversion of the flour trade from steamboats operating on the Hudson and on the protected waters of Long Island Sound. Steamboats on these waters were highly efficient and highly competitive carriers. Nevertheless, flour was an important source of revenue. In any given year during the 1840s and 1850s, between 40 and 50 percent of the flour it carried was delivered to the rapidly growing inland cities where factory employment was rapidly increasing. The rest of the flour went to Boston and supplied between 20 and 25 percent of the flour for local consumption.

The availability of cheap breadstuffs in the communities along the Boston and Albany had the following impacts on the political economy of Massachusetts (and the rest of New England):

1. Cheap flour from the West induced large numbers of cultivators to migrate to western states where larger land units of greater fertility could be purchased from the public domain.
2. Cultivators who remained in New England had to specialize in producing higher value foodstuffs for city consumption. Principal among them were dairy products, fresh meat, vegetables, and fruits.
3. If cultivators opted not to become specialized food producers, they had to take factory jobs or other forms of commercial employment.

4.   During the 1840s and 1850s, the political economy of New England decisively shifted to manufacturing and this shift was sustained by the construction of a network of shortline railroads that, by 1860, were ripe for integration into one or more regional systems.

For the Boston and Worcester, through traffic moving into Boston was a source of additional revenue, but was not essential for its profitability. Local service alone made it profitable. In 1842 it had no debt, paid dividends of 6–8 percent, and generated sufficient revenue to begin double tracking its right-of-way (completed in 1843).

During the initial years of operation, the president of the Boston and Albany wanted the Boston and Worcester to ensure that his railroad had sufficient revenue to pay the interest on its bonded indebtedness. He wanted the two railroads to operate as one system, as the legislature intended when both were incorporated. The Boston and Worcester could ensure this by charging low rates for western traffic that used its tracks to enter Boston. In 1842, at the depth of the depression, the Boston and Worcester accepted lower rates for freight and passenger traffic originating west of Springfield because it was necessary to keep the Boston and Albany from bankruptcy.

It was strongly in the interests of managers of both railroads and the state of Massachusetts to prevent bankruptcy. Bankruptcy would undermine the confidence of European bankers that investments in American railroad bonds were safe if they were underwritten by state governments. If bankruptcy occurred in a leading industrial state with a record of fiscal integrity, then investment risks were much greater in less affluent states. Preventing the bankruptcy of the Boston and Albany was essential for preserving access to European capital to construct future internal improvement projects.

After 1845, the management of the Boston and Worcester changed its policy. An unanticipated increase in freight traffic generated substantial profits for the Boston and Albany and the management of the Boston and Worcester wanted its share. It insisted that all revenue for traffic using its tracks to enter Boston be shared pro-rata, based on the number of kilometers moved on the tracks of each railroad. They also rejected overtures for merger because revenue from Boston and Albany traffic entering Boston would provide funds to guarantee high dividends to its shareholders. A merger did not take place until 1868 after the Boston and Albany threatened to build its own tracks into Boston.

The analysis of the rate making process illustrates a crucial problem that pioneer railroads had to solve when promoters made the transition to managers. *What rates would maximize revenue? What was a safe ratio between capitalization and bonded indebtedness? What formula should be used for revenue sharing with connecting railroads? What should managers do when railroads had to compete with other railroads? What were the advantages and disadvantages to shareholders when shortlines were assembled into systems?* Managers of the Boston and Albany had to resolve these problems after 1845 when the volume of freight and passenger traffic rapidly increased and new railroad construction in the 1850s provided many cities with alternative routes (and lower rates), and when investments in new (expensive) technologies were essential to sustain profitability.

At the same time that the Boston and Albany was experimenting with rate structures and traffic interchange with the Boston and Worcester, the president and directors had to create a management bureaucracy. Departments had to be organized to supervise diverse operations. Some management practices could be borrowed from the three shortlines then operating in Massachusetts, but it was not a direct borrowing. Operations on shortlines could be managed by an active president because he had daily access to operations. This was impossible on the Boston and Albany.

Substantial amounts of authority had to be delegated to persons performing specialized jobs, and thereafter performance had to be supervised from a distance. This required a bureaucracy that fed continuous information to the president and other managers. Information arrived in the form of reports that were submitted at periodic intervals; and these reports had to be in a printed format so that requisite information was immediately visible.

A principal department in the management structure supervised stationmasters who were responsible for selling tickets, dispatching and receiving freight, and procuring wood to fuel the locomotives. Other departments supervised track maintenance and repair of rolling stock. Several spectacular wrecks in its first four years of operation required operating rules defined in great detail and rigidly enforced. There could be no room for error because there were no signals to control trains moving in opposite directions on the single track. Trains were not dispatched by telegraph until the mid-1850s after the New York and Erie Railroad had proven its usefulness in 1851. The basic operating rule was that trains remained on sidings until a scheduled train passed. The second basic rule was that trains moved at slow speeds when descending steep and curving grades because both locomotives and cars had inadequate brakes.

Track maintenance was a continual problem. Maintaining tracks, bridges, and other physical structures was placed in the hands of a superintendent of operations. He was second to the president in the management hierarchy. He divided the railroad into three sections each headed by a roadmaster. Each section was divided into divisions, and within each division daily inspections were required to find mud and rock slides, fallen trees, washouts, or rails that were out of alignment. Misaligned rails were a continual problem during the winter because frost heaves at poorly drained sites moved rails out of alignment.

During the late 1850s, many shortline railroads were built in New England. As these roads became operational, they provided circuitous continuous rail connections between Boston and New York City for passengers and freight. None of these roads were in direct competition with the Boston and Albany but each new link in the growing network captured a little traffic. There was little the Boston and Albany could do to stop the bleeding of traffic.[10]

Finally, and of fundamental importance, management instituted an efficient accounting system because money "transactions were far more numerous than those in a textile mill or on a canal because so many more employees—conductors, freight agents, station agents, and others—handled money." Put in a larger picture, the earliest trunkline railroads, and especially the Boston and Albany, "were literally forced to pioneer the new ways of corporate management...They fashioned the earliest large-scale administrative structures in American business."[11]

After 1845, when increased freight traffic ensured profitability, the Boston and Albany's management paid dividends of 7 and 8 percent and sold an additional 2.15 million dollars of stock to purchase enough rolling stock to move the traffic offered, and begin double tracking its right-of-way from Worcester to Springfield.

During the decade of the 1850s, thirty-five thousand kilometers of new roads were built in the United States.

> The volume of freight carried by a single steamship or pulled by a single locomotive was continuously being enlarged. As a result, in almost no other period in American history did the volume of traffic moved increase so sharply as it did in the dozen years before the civil war.[12]

Increasing freight traffic had many sources (1) increased production of agricultural commodities as more land was brought under cultivation in trans-Appalachian states, (2) flour and grain became increasingly important export commodities, (3) increased production of factory manufactured products, (4) traffic captured from canals and rivers, (5) locomotives that burned coal and could pull longer trains of heavier freight cars at lower costs than locomotives that burned wood, (6) beginning of regional networks due to increased railroad construction.

By 1855 there were thirty-one railroads in the United States with three hundred kilometers or more of operating tracks, or tracks in process of construction, and the size of the Boston and Albany was relatively reduced as were net earnings. In 1855 its net earnings were ninth out of the nineteen longest roads. It was blocked from extending its tracks west of the Hudson River by the New York Central because the New York Central had the largest gross and net earnings of any U.S. railroad. It earned 4.7 times the gross earnings and 5.4 times the net earning of the Boston and Albany.[13]

In all but name, the Boston and Albany became a subsidiary of the New York Central. Its trains were scheduled to meet New York Central trains at Albany where it fed westbound traffic to the New York Central and received eastbound traffic. The two roads merged in 1900.

Technology

Heavy T-rails were used on the Boston and Worcester and the Boston and Albany. They weighed 23 kilos per meter (56.5 pounds per yard) compared to light rails that weighed 14 kilos per meter (35 pounds per yard) or strap iron that was nailed onto wooden rails that were used by many pioneer railroads.

Surprisingly, when the promoters of the Boston and Worcester began searching for motive power in 1832, there were several shops that could manufacture locomotives. Most of them were manufacturers of stationary steam engines. The promoters of the Boston and Worcester decided to equally divide the purchase of locomotive between English and American manufacturers. The two English locomotives were proven performers, but the two American built locomotives were a gamble.

One American locomotive performed to expectations but the other was a failure. When passenger traffic exceeded expectations during the first year of operation, three additional locomotives were ordered: one from England and two from two different American manufacturers. This was the last purchase of English built locomotives because locomotives built for service on English roads frequently had problems operating on American rights-of-way that were not as solidly built and meticulously maintained as roadbeds in England. After 1837, all locomotives were American built because it was easier to make design changes that were suitable to American operating conditions.

Locomotives were being built in Rhode Island, Connecticut, New York, New Jersey, Pennsylvania, and Maryland in 1837, as well as in the machine shop attached to the Lowell textile mills. The first eight engines were built in the Lowell shop. They were small but adequate for service between Worcester and Springfield. More powerful engines were needed for service over the Berkshire Mountains to Albany.

The unanticipated but sustained increase in freight traffic after 1845 strained the resources of the company. Management was forced to rapidly increase the number of locomotives and rolling stock. Among the purchases were seven locomotives built in the shop that supplied the Baltimore and Ohio Railroad. These locomotives were designed to climb the steep grades of the Baltimore and Ohio as it ascended the river valleys of the Appalachian mountains. At the time of their purchase, however, they were untested. They were also designed to burn coal and when converted to wood, which was cheap in western Massachusetts, they lost a high percentage of their power. They were costly failures because many of their drive components were too weak and they continually broke. By 1849 all seven were scrapped.

Thirty-five new locomotives were delivered in 1847 and 1848. In 1846, the Boston and Albany owned forty-three locomotives, sixty-five in 1850, and seventy-two in 1860. New locomotives were more powerful. The Boston and Albany also began doubling the tracks westward to Albany. Heavier rails were used than on the original right-of-way. Not until 1867 was there a double track to Albany. In that year a bridge was built across the Hudson River at Albany and Boston and Albany tracks directly connected to New York Central tracks.

After 1850, the shop at Springfield began building locomotives. The master mechanic suggested building occasional locomotives to keep his skilled mechanics fully employed because the equipment needed to make replacement parts was identical with equipment used to build locomotives. This practice was borrowed from other railroads that had large shops. Furthermore, locomotives built at the Springfield shop could quickly incorporate design changes suggested by operating personnel. Management accepted this proposal and was pleased with the results because the locomotives built in the Springfield shop were equipped with large diameter driving wheels that gave added traction on steep grades. After 1851, about half of the Boston and Albany's new locomotives were built in the Springfield shop.

By 1850 the United States had more kilometers of railroads than Britain or any European nation, and by 1860 New England had a network of shortlines. The profit potential was readily visible for consolidating these roads into a trunkline that directly connected Boston (and Providence) to New York City; however, this was not done until after the close of the Civil War in 1865.

Put in another perspective, by 1860, railroads were poised to capture an increasing percentage of freight carried by canals and steamboats operating on inland waters, but further technical improvements and integration of shortlines into regional and inter-regional systems were necessary to give railroads a decisive advantage.

Inter-Regional Trunkline Systems

The assembly of inter-regional systems began before the assembly of regional systems. Profit potentials were huge if a railroad could capture traffic carried on canals and rivers. In particular, the down river traffic on the Ohio and Missouri rivers, and traffic on the upper Mississippi River would be diverted from New Orleans to east–west railroads with terminals in New York City, Philadelphia, and Baltimore. The reciprocal of diverting agricultural commodities to Atlantic coast cities was carrying increasing amounts of manufactured products to western states. During the 1850s, this meant increasing amounts of domestically manufactured products.

By 1860 seven inter-regional systems were in embryonic form. Four were in northern states, two in slave states, and one ran north–south. The Baltimore and Ohio had connections to Cincinnati and westward to St. Louis. It formed the American Central Line that became operational in 1857. It was composed of four railroads, including the Baltimore and Ohio, and had at least two gauges and three places of transfer. The Pennsylvania Railroad entered Chicago in 1856 when it gained control of the hastily built and financially fragile Pittsburgh, Fort Wayne, and Chicago Railroad. Both railroads used standard gauge and after a bridge was built across the Allegheny River at Pittsburgh in 1858, no transfers were necessary.

The New York Central made connections with the Grand Trunk Railroad running through southern Ontario to Detroit. There it connected to the Michigan Central Railroad. The New York Central also connected with the Lake Shore and Michigan Southern Railroad along the south shore of Lake Erie. The New York Central entered Chicago on the tracks of these railroads in 1852. All of the east–west railroads linked to the New York Central were standard gauge, and by 1860 no transfers were necessary except at the Detroit River. The New York and Erie Railroad was gradually squeezed out of the competition for western traffic because its six-foot gauge was incompatible with standard and other gauges for through freight and passenger service.

The most successful of the east–west trunkline systems in slave states was the South Carolina Railroad that connected with the Georgia Railroad at Augusta. From there, the mainline track went to Atlanta where it connected with the Western and Atlantic going northwest to Chattanooga, and then west to Memphis on the Mississippi River. Another string of shortline railroads went to the Gulf coast. Neither of these routes had a consistent gauge and most shortline feeders were rickety pioneer roads.

The second east–west trunkline railroad in slave states was a failure. It began in Norfolk, Virginia and had six segments that ended in Memphis, Tennessee. It was a financial failure because it had frequent gauge changes, carried insufficient passenger and freight traffic, did not traverse a cotton growing region, and Norfolk had inadequate port facilities and deficient financial services.

The seventh embryonic inter-regional railroad was the Illinois Central that ran the length of Illinois to the Ohio River. There it used steamboats to Columbus, Kentucky in order to link with the northern terminus of the Mobile and Ohio Railroad that ran south to Mobile, Alabama.

In 1860, the New York Central and Erie railroads fed trans-Appalachian commodities into New York City. The Pennsylvania Railroad performed the same function for Philadelphia and the Baltimore and Ohio did the same for Baltimore. Although the South Carolina Railroad fed cotton into Charleston for export, it was overly dependent on cotton for revenue. Just as important, Charleston lacked financial services that could finance direct shipments to Europe or to textile mills in northern states. Northern businessmen or their agents supplied these services.

Most cotton that arrived at Charleston was shipped to New York City and other northern cities where it was carried to Europe on regularly scheduled sailing ships (packets). The same was true for freight arriving at Norfolk and Mobile. In the interior, the Illinois Central helped make Chicago an entrepot for assembling agricultural commodities for shipment to the east and distributing domestically manufactured products in the western Great Lakes region and southward. Most grain going eastward went by water but most flour went by rail, and most manufactured products returned by rail.

Railroads built in the 1850s did not create a national market because of differences in gauges, lack of standardized weights of rails, great variation in the stability of roadbeds, differences in strengths of bridges, lack of agreements to exchange freight, and gaps between the end of one railroad and the next in terminal cities. Most railroads that appear on maps as trunklines did not function as trunkline carriers. By 1860, however, railroads were capable of carrying passengers and distributing some manufactured products (textiles, shoes, boots, edged tools, flour) to all eastern states.

Who Would Manage Inter-Regional Railroads?

The solution was found by experience. During the 1850s it became clear that they would have to be managed by paid professionals who had operating experience because promoters turned managers were usually failures. Henry Varnum Poor, who edited the *American Railroad Journal* from 1849 to 1862, was a consistent critic of management by promoters and an equally strong advocate of paid professional managers (managerial capitalism). This form of management was required for maximum efficiency in railroads, and other businesses where there was a radical separation between owners and managers.

Railroad promoters in the 1850s thought of themselves as building the foundation for a continental nation that would reach the Pacific coast, and they were very public about their intentions. New York businessmen were among the principal promoters. They worked with transplanted New Englanders who built and managed a high percentage of the railroads west of the Appalachian Mountains. A high percentage of New York and New England promoters had a financial background because building railroads and assembling them into systems required huge amounts of money. In 1860 these men were poised to build a railroad across the continent but the Civil War forced a pause in their ambitions.

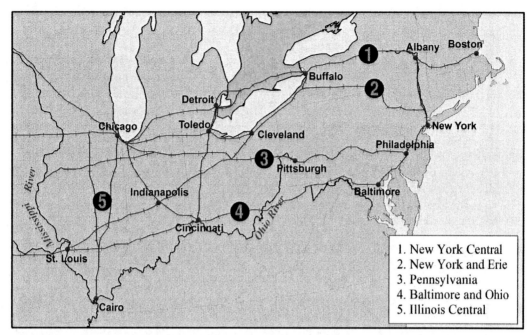

Figure 7.2 Northern Inter-Regional Trunkline Railroad Systems, 1870. Map by Yu Zhou. Reproduced with permission.

I will examine how three embryonic inter-regional systems were assembled before the Civil War and how, during the three decades after the Civil War, railroads created the national market.

New York Central

In 1847 the Erie Canal carried more traffic originating west of the Appalachians than originating in New York, and by 1860 three-quarters of the tonnage carried by the Erie Canal originated in western states. A share of this traffic was waiting to be appropriated by railroads if the ten shortlines paralleling the Erie Canal could be assembled into a trunkline. The ten shortlines were built between 1831 and 1842, almost exclusively with local capital. Seven of the ten roads constituted a trunkline that was 525 kilometers long. Only four of them required the state to underwrite bonds for a total of six hundred thousand dollars. There was great profit potential from consolidation because railroad technology was sufficiently efficient by 1845 to compete with canals for carrying high value freight.

Assembling a trunkline railroad from the ten shortlines required political connections, money, and management skills. Erastus Corning had these skills. He was a banker in Albany, the city's mayor from 1834 to 1837, state senator from 1842 to 1845, a principal leader of the New York Democratic Party, and a principal owner of a rolling mill that made iron rails. He was also president of the 125 kilometer Utica and Schenectady Railroad, one of the shortlines paralleling the Erie Canal, as well as a director of the Hudson River Railroad and the Michigan Central Railroad. In the 1840s Corning negotiated an agreement for uniform scheduling and uniform passenger fares and freight rates on the roads paralleling the Erie Canal.

All were built with strap iron rails and could carry only minimum amounts of freight. Profitability depended on passenger traffic. Trains moved at an average speed twenty-one kilometers per hour and the trip from Albany to Buffalo took twenty-five hours. Between 1844 and 1849 all strap iron rails were replaced with heavy iron rails weighing between twenty-four and twenty-eight kilos per meter (fifty-eight to sixty-seven pounds per yard). Most of them were imported from England. Heavier rails were essential to compete with the Erie Canal for carrying high-value freight. Before this competition could begin canal, tolls had to be removed. The state legislature levied canal tolls during the summer on freight carried by these railroads in order to assure sufficient revenue for the Erie Canal to service its bonded indebtedness. Summer freight rates were prohibitive for most freight. During the winter tolls were removed because the canal was drained for repairs, and the carrying capacities of the railroads were strained to carry all of the traffic offered.

Corning lobbied the New York legislature to end canal tolls. He succeeded in 1851. After they were removed, the ten railroads could utilize unused carrying capacities during the summer to compete with the Erie Canal for high-value freight. Removal of canal tolls also made them ripe for consolidation, and an opportunity for very large capital gains.

The legislature approved consolidation in 1853 by incorporating the New York Central. During the next three years, the railroad was largely rebuilt by straightening curves, reballasting roadbeds, strengthening bridges, double tracking (completed in 1859), enlarging shops, and purchasing more locomotives with increased power; although, they continued to use wood for fuel. Between 1853 and 1856 these improvements were financed by 7.7 million dollars of bonded indebtedness.

The Hudson River Railroad was completed in 1851. It paralleled the west bank of the Hudson River from New York City to Albany. It competed with steamboats for freight and passenger traffic. It was to the advantage of both the Hudson River Railroad and the New York Central to have a working agreement to provide continuous rail service from New York City to Albany and onto Buffalo and cities further west.

This did not happen because steamboat service on the Hudson River was highly competitive, frequent, and comfortable. The New York Central preferred to transfer much of its freight traffic to steamships because commodities for export had easier entry to the docks of the port of New York. The Hudson River Railroad was not a profitable railroad. Not until 1869 did it merge with the New York Central after improved technology made continuous rail travel faster and more comfortable.

There were two routes from Buffalo to the west: (1) across southern Ontario to Detroit, then from Detroit to Chicago using the tracks of the Michigan Central; (2) a railroads being built along the south shore of Lake Erie that would connect with the Michigan Southern and Northern Indiana Railroad for entry into Chicago. At the same time that canal tolls were abolished, the New York legislature authorized the railroads paralleling the canal to invest in securities issued by railroads operating in northern Ohio and Indiana. The investments were made. When the New York Central came into existence in 1853 it could schedule through service to Chicago and westward to three cities located on the Mississippi River.

Immediately after consolidation, both freight and passenger traffic rapidly increased, but freight increased faster. In 1856 freight revenues surpassed passenger revenue, and the New York Central became the largest business corporation in the United States in terms of capitalization and annual revenues. Managers of the Pennsylvania and Baltimore and Ohio railroads pursued similar strategies to capture western commerce by negotiating extensions of service over recently built east–west railroads in Ohio, Indiana, and Illinois. After the Pennsylvania and Baltimore and Ohio railroads entered Chicago in 1856, businessmen in Philadelphia and Baltimore had continuous rail service to Chicago and westward.

South Carolina Railroad

At the time of its incorporation in 1828 its name was the South Carolina Canal and Railroad Company. It was incorporated to build a coastal canal from Charleston to Savannah, or a 218 kilometer railroad from Charleston to Hamburg, South Carolina, located at the headwaters of navigation on the Savannah River, opposite the city of Augusta, Georgia. The railroad would divert cotton bales going down river to Savannah. Promoters were unsure of the motive power: horses or steam. The technique of construction, however, dictated steam. Construction began early in 1831 and it became operational in September 1833.

Construction was flimsy and experimental. Most of the roadbed was built on wooden pilings and trestles with an inclined plane to surmount the steepest grade. The steepest grade, however, was no steeper than the steepest grade on the Boston and Worcester being built at the same time. The rails were wooden with strap iron surfaces (5.5 centimeters wide and 9.5 millimeters thick) nailed onto them. Immediately upon completion, pilings and trestles were found highly susceptible to rot and misalignment when ground became saturated with rainwater. Rebuilding the roadbed with earth cuts and embankments began immediately, but insufficient revenue made replacement of pilings and trestles a slow process.

A principal reason for building on pilings was a "prevailing shortage of labor." When contractors advertised for laborers, "the floating supply proved entirely inadequate" because "native whites of the laboring class were not much attracted by the opportunity" to earn wages. The principal contractor had to "import a large number of white laborers from the north or from Europe." "The number of men at work was continually so small as to keep the impatient members of the company in a state of exasperation." After the railroad became operational, the company had to purchase increasing numbers of slaves to perform maintenance labor.[14]

The railroad's initial cost was nine hundred thousand dollars. Most of the capital came from shares subscribed by Charleston businessmen, but the state loaned one hundred thousand dollars, seventy-five thousand dollars was loaned by individuals, and banks loaned fifty-three thousand dollars. Receipts from the partially completed road were another source of capital. The rest of the capital was obtained by the state underwriting bonds with 7 percent interest. Prior to 1843 all profits were used to upgrade the right-of-way but rebuilding was seriously slowed because shareholders demanded dividends. Small dividends were paid from 1843 to 1849, even after deferred reconstruction reached crisis proportions in 1847.

Accidents that damaged locomotives were occurring with increasing frequency on poorly ballasted strap iron rails. Purchasing iron rails began in 1849 but laying them on the rebuilt roadbed proceeded slowly because of lack of funds. In 1850 shareowners had to pay the remaining twenty-five dollars on their shares or operations would have ceased. Additional funds came from a two million dollar bond issue underwritten by South Carolina to build other railroads in the state. By 1852 strap iron rails were replaced with iron rails weighing twenty-nine kilos per meter. Like those used by northern railroads, iron rails could support more powerful locomotives that could better utilize the carrying capacity of the rebuilt roadbed.

Most of the traffic was bales of cotton—either originating along its route or from trans-shipping bales from the Georgia Railroad that had its eastern terminus in Augusta. Most of the bales carried on the Georgia Railroad went down river to Savannah. In 1845 one hundred forty thousand bales of cotton arrived at Augusta from central Georgia, but the South Carolina Railroad carried only twenty thousand bales to Charleston. Augusta businessmen, allied with steamboat and flatboat operators, successfully blocked most diversion by preventing a bridge being built across the Savannah River so the South Carolina Railroad could connect with the eastern terminus of the Georgia Railroad. Augusta businessmen opposed a connection because it would reduce their business of transshipping cotton bales from the highly productive cotton growing region between Augusta and Atlanta. Lack of a bridge preserved most of the cotton traffic for water transportation.

The rules changed in 1853 when the South Carolina Railroad built a bridge across the Savannah River into Augusta. Its tracks, however, did not directly connect with the tracks of the Georgia Railroad. The city of Augusta would not allow it. Horse drawn wagons delivered freight from the depot of the Georgia Railroad to the depot of the South Carolina Railroad. At the same time, a rail network was in process of construction in Georgia that centered on Atlanta. Cotton brokers in Atlanta wanted a choice of ports for cotton exports. The choices were Savannah and Charleston, but not until 1858 was there continuous rail traffic between Charleston and Atlanta. After rebuilding its roadbed and connecting with the Georgia Railroad, the South Carolina Railroad paid dividends from 1852 to 1860 that averaged more than 8 percent.

The Georgia Railroad was incorporated in 1833 to build westward from Augusta to Athens, Georgia. Businessmen in Augusta, Athens, and other villages subscribed to shares with a par value of 1.5 million dollars. The initial payment was five dollars and subsequent installments were fifteen dollars. The legislature assisted in financing by granting banking privileges in 1835. Construction of the Georgia Railroad began in 1835, but it did not reach Athens until 1841. A mixture of strap iron rails and light iron rails were laid on a narrow roadbed

Like the South Carolina Railroad, construction was slow because white peasants were reluctant to perform wage labor as long as their subsistence needs were satisfied by small amounts of money acquired by growing small amounts of cotton. Construction to Atlanta languished after reaching Athens partly due to a lack of funds during the depth of the depression, but also due to complacent management. "The completion of the Georgia Railroad to Atlanta was …in fact, as great a concern or greater with the citizens of Augusta and Charleston than with the company itself."[15]

Additional finance was required to complete the road to Atlanta. It came from selling shares to businessmen in Augusta and Charleston, from not paying dividends in 1843, 1844, 1845, and from seven hundred thousand dollars of 7 percent bonds underwritten by the state. The extension used light iron rails (16 kilos per meter) and did not reach Atlanta until September 1845. It entered Atlanta one month ahead of the Central of Georgia that was being built inland

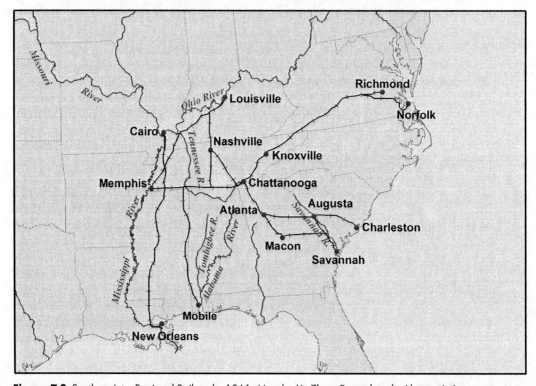

Figure 7.3 Southern Inter-Regional Railroads, 1861. Map by Yu Zhou. Reproduced with permission.

from Savannah. During the next seven years the right-of-way between Atlanta and Augusta (275 kilometers) had to be completely rebuilt to handle the traffic. At the same time, management purchased shares of stock in shortline railroads radiating from Atlanta in order to obtain traffic, but there was never enough traffic except when the cotton harvest was marketed.

The superintendent of the Georgia Railroad accurately measured the lack of diversified commerce in the cotton South in 1859. The company's "engines annually hauled into Atlanta over three thousand empty cars, whose return journey from Augusta was a dead loss to the company." In addition, artificial congestion was created on the single track because a Georgia law "forbade the moving of freight on Sunday."[16]

The Central of Georgia was much like the South Carolina Railroad. It was chartered in 1833 to build either a canal or railroad to the recently settled town of Macon, Georgia and it also was granted banking privileges. Its management saw no urgency for construction and construction did not begin until 1837. Construction was flimsy. The first 214 kilometers used strap iron rails and the remaining 92 kilometers used very light iron rails weighing only 13 kilos per meter. Its construction was plagued by labor shortages. White peasants were reluctant and unreliable laborers and the slaves who were leased from planters to build the right-of-way were available only during periods of slack agricultural labor. The road did not become operational until October 1843 when it reached Macon. In the next two years it was extended 164 kilometers to Atlanta.

The final link in the east–west inter-regional trunkline was the Western and Atlantic Railroad going 222 kilometers northwest from Atlanta to Chattanooga, Tennessee where it connected with an east–west railroad that had its western terminus on the Mississippi River at Memphis. The Western and Atlantic was completely built with state funds. It was incorporated in 1836 but construction did not begin until 1838. Slow construction became slower during the depression and because of a failure to find a market for half of the bonds authorized by the legislature. Nor was there any urgency for construction because the Georgia and Georgia Central railroads did not reach Atlanta until 1845. When completed in 1851, its underpowered engines ran on a patchwork of light rails.

The Western and Atlantic Railroad was built to carry cotton grown in central Tennessee to Memphis for down river transportation to New Orleans, or to Charleston or Savannah. The cotton arrived by steamboats traveling up the Tennessee River to Chattanooga or by rail from feeder roads in Tennessee. Maize grown in central Tennessee, Illinois, and Indiana, plus flour, bacon, and barreled meat from Cincinnati formed a considerable percentage of its traffic. These foodstuffs supplied a growing market in northern and central Georgia because many planters used slave labor to grow enlarged cotton crops instead of growing sufficient food crops to feed them.

An assured food supply was not produced by white peasants in northern Georgia but it was readily obtainable from northern farmers if transportation could deliver it to planters at competitive prices. Steamboats up the Tennessee River to Chattanooga and a railroad from Chattanooga to Atlanta could deliver these foodstuffs. The availability of foodstuffs from northern farmers enabled planters to take advantage of favorable terms of trade for growing enlarged cotton crops.[17]

Most southern railroads were slow to upgrade their rights-of-way and replace obsolescent rolling stock because of inadequate revenue from non-cotton commodities. The most common non-cotton commodities were peanuts, hides, lumber, and highly variable amounts of grain, mostly maize. Railroads did not carry naval stores (turpentine, rosin, tar) to port cities because they were produced on the coastal plain (pine barrens) and moved by wagons to shallow bays, estuaries, and inlets where schooners operating out of New York City, Boston, and other northern seaports carried them to market. Nor did the South Carolina Railroad carry rice because it was grown in ponded fields along tidal estuaries and carried by flatboats to Charleston, Savannah, and Wilmington for milling and packing into casks for export.

Increased revenues largely depended on more land being planted in cotton. Put in a larger perspective, railroads in slave states did not carry continuous volumes of freight because white peasants were not continuous producers of agricultural commodities or artisan products for sale on anonymous markets. Trains going inland carried limited volumes and varieties of manufactured products for consumption by slaves, white peasants, planters, and town residents. Slaves and white peasants were minimal consumers and planters and town residents were a small percentage of the population. On most southern railroads passenger fares generated more revenue than freight.

John F. Stover compared the number of locomotives on southern railroads with those in service on northern trunkline railroads in 1860. The four northern trunklines (New York Central, Pennsylvania, Baltimore and Ohio, New York and Erie) had 876 locomotives in service, which was slightly less than all of the locomotives on all railroads in slave states. In slave states in 1860, there was no east–west trunkline comparable to the four northern trunklines.

Continuous rail travel, however, was possible from the coastal cities of Norfolk, Charleston, and Savannah to cities on the Mississippi River and Gulf of Mexico. Travel, however, required many transfers because southern railroads were about equally divided between standard gauge and 5 foot gauge, plus other gauges. For example, in 1860, there was continuous rail service between Philadelphia and Charleston but passengers had to make at least eight transfers due to changes in gauge. Freight between these cities went by ship.

Railroads in slave states lacked adequate sidings for loading freight. They were only about 10 percent of mainline trackage. Sidings on most northern railroads were 20–33 percent of trunkline trackage. In addition, few southern railroads were double tracked. Double tracking was not essential for railroads whose principal traffic was the seasonal harvest of cotton. After moving cotton to port cities, trains were infrequent compared to northern trunkline railroads because urban residents in slave states were less than ten percent of the population. Urban residents were more likely to use railroads for travel than cotton planters or white peasants.

Stover summarizes the status of railroads in slave states in 1860.

> The railroads of the twelve southern states did not compare with those north of the Potomac and Ohio rivers…Southern lines were generally inferior in construction, rail, motive power, and rolling stock. They tended to have steeper grades, sharper curves, less ballast, and more weakly constructed bridges than those in northern states…Nearly all southern lines were extremely short of passing sidings or secondary track (and were) much inferior in motive power.[18]

The flimsy construction of a high percentage of southern railroads measures only half of the weakness of agrarian economic development. Slave labor states failed to develop sufficient commercial skills to market their crops. The shortage of financial and marketing skills for cotton was an opportunity for northern businessmen to supply these highly profitable services. "The South provided neither the services to market its own exports nor the consumer goods and services to supply its own needs, and had a very high propensity to import." Urban merchants in slave states had two principal functions: (1) forwarding cotton and rice to northern cities for consumption or for export to Europe, and (2) transfering manufactured products that were made and warehoused elsewhere and sent to them for distribution in its trading radius.[19]

Planters and politicians in southern states lamented their dependence on northern businessmen but could do little because cotton planters preferentially invested their considerable profits in buying land and labor (slaves). Purchasing slaves was a huge investment of capital that was unavailable for building sturdy railroads, or accumulating sufficient capital to market the cotton crop, or for training persons with requisite marketing skills.

Another measure of the success of northern businessmen in appropriating the marketing of cotton was the stagnation of population of Charleston, South Carolina. Its population remained stationary compared to the very rapid increase in the populations of northern cities. In 1820, Charleston's population was 24,000 and in 1860 it was 40,000. During these same years, the population of New York City increased from 125,000 to 801,000 and other northern cities had similar increases—including Chicago from zero to 109,000.

These generalizations capture the disparity of economic development policies in slave states and northern states. In northern states, an increasing percentage of the population was wage laborers in factories where they performed commercial labor norms. In slave states, factory production by wage labor was close to nonexistent; therefore, factory made products provided little traffic for southern railroads. It is clear beyond doubt that the economic development of slave states was hugely retarded by the subsistence labor norms of white peasants compared to the commercial labor norms performed by yeomen, farmers, and factory workers in northern states. Nor did the commercial labor norms coerced from slaves compensate for the subsistence labor norms of white peasants.

Illinois Central

The Illinois Central Railroad was incorporated in 1851 to build a standard gauge railroad from Chicago to the Ohio River. At the Ohio River passengers and freight crossed to the northern terminal of the Mobile and Ohio Railroad. Both railroads were conceived as an inter-regional system that would equally benefit northern and southern cultivators and the businessmen who marketed their crops. Promoters of both roads petitioned Congress for assistance because they were assured of bipartisan support.

In September 1850, in accordance with states' rights policies of economic development, Congress granted land to the states of Illinois, Mississippi, and Alabama for them to allocate to the Illinois Central and Mobile and Ohio railroads. State governments would convey alternate sections of land for six miles on both sides of the rights-of-way to these corporations as soon as a segment became operational. Much of the land along their routes was in the public domain and unsold at $1.25 per acre ($2.75 per hectare) because of poor access to water transportation.

The Illinois Central was granted 1.05 million hectares (2.59 million acres) of land. It was part of a national speculation in railroad construction between 1852 and 1857. During these years, 9.1 million hectares (22.5 million acres) of land was conveyed to trans-Appalachian states to aid railroad construction. In addition, 303,000 hectares (750,000 acres) of land was conveyed to Michigan in 1852 to build the Sault Canal to connect Lake Superior to Lake Huron so that the newly discovered iron ore deposits of the Marquette region and the copper mines of the Keweenaw Peninsula had a profitable market.

Like other railroads built in Illinois during the 1850s, long sections of the Illinois Central were built four or five years ahead of demand; therefore, there was a substantial ingredient of speculation in its promotion. The magnitude of speculation is the amount of vacant land that was alienated during the 1850s. In 1849 the public domain in Illinois was 5.6 million hectares (14 million acres). By 1857 less than 40,000 hectares (100,000 acres) remained.

At least 2.4 million hectares (6 million acres) of the public domain in Illinois was acquired by speculators, mostly by purchasing land warrants given to veterans of the Mexican and Indian wars. Warrants were purchased for $1.25 to $2.50 per hectare ($0.50 to $1.15 per acre). Speculators held it until railroads were built within twenty-five kilometers or less from it. Railroad construction in Illinois in the 1850s surpassed all other states. In 1850 Illinois had

175 kilometers of railroad and in 1860 it had 4,490 kilometers. By 1860, six east–west railroads crossed Illinois to the Mississippi River, and one bridge crossed the Mississippi River at Rock Island, Illinois.

The estimated cost of the Illinois Central was 16.5 million dollars but its completed cost was twenty-one million dollars. Initial construction was financed by (1) shares of stock, of which 20 percent of their face value was paid-in at the time of purchase; (2) sale of two million dollars of bonds to the principal promoters but with the provision that calls on capital would be gradual; (3) two million dollars in bonds were underwritten by the Michigan Central Railroad so that the Michigan Central could use Illinois Central tracks to enter Chicago.

Construction began in 1852. The first completed section was a short distance south of Chicago to connect with Michigan Central tracks. The Lake Shore and Michigan Southern Railroad also entered Chicago in 1852 using the tracks of the Rock Island Railroad. These entries provided continuous rail service to New York City. As the railroad was built south, management had a problem not encountered by Indiana and Ohio railroads. There were no trees on the prairies that covered half of the state. In 1855 some locomotives were converted to burn coal and trial runs indicated that coal was one-half the cost of wood. By 1860 half of Illinois Central locomotives were using coal produced from mines along its route.

Completion of the Illinois Central depended on three substantial contributions from Europe. The first was capital. This encountered difficulties because Illinois had defaulted on its debts from 1841 to 1846. Illinois had further impaired its credit by giving preference in payments to some bondholders at the expense of others. Nonetheless, a syndicate of English bankers bought five million dollars of bonds because the bonds were collateralized by the huge land grant instead of being underwritten by state tax revenues. The ownership of vacant land made Illinois Central bonds attractive to European investors. This was a speculative opportunity for bondholders to participate in the profits of land sales.

In order to sweeten bond sales, purchasers were given the right to purchase five shares of stock for each one thousand dollar bond. Purchasers of shares paid-in only a portion of its face value with the assurance that paying the full face value would not be necessary. Funds arrived in ten quarterly installments between July 1852 and October 1854. This loan was of immense value for expediting construction in a predictable way; however, the funds were insufficient to complete the road. Additional capital came from (1) assessments on all shareowners, (2) additional bonds sold to promoters, (3) bonds sold in Europe at discounts, (4) sale of land, and (5) a very large floating debt.

The second essential European contribution was construction labor. There had to be at least six thousand men continually employed, and as many as ten thousand during summer months. One contractor went to Ireland and recruited the men he needed. Immigrant Irish laborers made up the largest component in the labor force from beginning of construction to completion. The second largest was comprised of Germans fleeing the turmoil that followed the failed revolutions of 1848. Labor was also recruited by agents on the docks of New York City. They arrived in Chicago in immigrant coaches attached to regularly scheduled trains. Immigrant laborers had to be continually replaced because of high turnovers. Management tried to retain them by offering to sell land to them on credit, and this succeeded to some extent, especially among German immigrants. Other laborers used the money they earned to establish themselves in Chicago and in other towns along the route.

The third essential European contribution was iron rails from England.

Management wanted to sell its land as quickly as possible but it also wanted the highest prices to aid construction. The state also had an interest in rapid sales because land granted to the Illinois Central paid no taxes until it was sold. Management tried to keep its lands from being accumulated by speculators because they wanted the land adjacent to the railroad cultivated as soon as possible in order to carry harvests to market. Management also wanted to carry lumber to homesteaders to build their houses and barns on the treeless prairie. The intent of management was clear. Rapid sales to actual settlers would increase railroad revenues.

The principal way of attracting farmers was selling land on credit. Mortgages were for seven years but the initial payment was only two years' interest on the purchase price, and the interest rate was only 2 percent. In the third year, purchasers paid one-fifth of the principal plus interest. Sales contracts also stipulated that farmers had to fence and cultivate at least one-tenth of their land during the first year of residence and an additional one-tenth in the five following years. This portion of the sale contract was unenforceable.

The generous credit policy of the Illinois Central had an unavoidable contradiction. Management needed as much money as possible from land sales to complete construction but management had to offer generous credit to attract farmers who were willing to pay high prices for well located land. The very low initial payments by purchasers deferred income from land sales when it was most needed for construction. In addition, sales were delayed between 1852 and 1854 because the land market was saturated with cheaper land being sold by speculators along the projected routes of other railroads that did not receive land grants.

The road was completed in 1856 but was financially vulnerable because it had 3.8 million dollars of floating debt owed to banks and suppliers. The Panic of 1857 pushed it to the edge of bankruptcy because of the failure of management to adequately assess shareholders. The promoters had hoped they could complete the road by paying-in only 50–60 percent of the face value of their shares. Extreme economy prevented bankruptcy. An abundant harvest in 1859 and money from land sales finally created financial stability, and in 1859 the Illinois Central paid its first dividend.

During the 1850s, the Illinois Central sold 518,000 hectares (1.28 million acres) of vacant land for an average price of $26 per hectare ($12 per acre). In 1860 Illinois led the nation in wheat and maize production and Chicago forwarded 700,000 barrels of flour to eastern markets. A high percentage of these commodities were for export. The other substantial market was southern cotton planters who maximized cotton cultivation by reducing the amount of food crops they planted to feed slaves The needed food was purchased from northern farmers.

The Civil War was a serious crisis. Products carried south by the Illinois Central lost their market. Approximately 20 percent of its southbound traffic was flour, preserved meat, and maize going downriver by steamboat from its southern terminus on the Ohio River. These foodstuffs were delivered to river towns for shipment inland where they were purchased by cotton planters to feed slaves, or they went up the Tennessee River to Chattanooga and then by rail to northern and central Georgia for consumption on cotton plantations.

Management solved the loss of the southern market by accepting maize for mortgage payments, less transportation costs to Chicago. After being sold in Chicago, maize went by steamboats to Buffalo, then by the Erie Canal and the Hudson River to New York City. Most of this maize was exported. Accepting maize for mortgage payments was an expedient arrangement but it sustained financial stability in 1861 and 1862 until the national government made large purchases to feed the U.S. Army.

The southern half of the north–south inter-regional system was the Mobile and Ohio Railroad. The problem of the Mobile and Ohio was the same as the South Carolina Railroad. It had limited traffic potential because a high percentage of households along its route were white peasants who produced minimal amounts of cotton and other commodities for sale on anonymous markets. Failure to generate adequate revenues delayed its completion until April 1861, almost five years after the completion of the Illinois Central. Ten days after completion it was bankrupt because that was the day the Civil War began.

Construction began with funds obtained by selling shares to businessmen in the city of

Mobile and other businessmen in Alabama and Mississippi. These funds were supplemented by small loans from the governments of Alabama, Mississippi, and the city of Mobile; and a grant of ten thousand dollars per mile from the Tennessee government. Money was available in Mobile for railroad investment because Mobile overtook Charleston and Savannah as a cotton exporting city in 1840. In 1860, cotton shipments from Mobile were 35 percent of cotton shipments from New Orleans, the nation's leading exporter of cotton.

Cotton brokers in Mobile were largely from New York and New England, and they used credit supplied by New York and Boston banks to market cotton. Two other means were used to retain control of cotton marketing. Ships were designed to carry cotton bales and regular service was established with packet ships. Packet ships sailed on fixed schedules to northern ports whether they were fully loaded or not.

Unlike Charleston and New Orleans, Mobile had no direct commerce with Europe. A high percentage of cotton bales assembled in Mobile went to Boston to supply New England textile mills, and the rest went to New York City where they were exported in packet ships that sailed to Liverpool, England and Havre, France. The principal return cargoes were manufactured products (often iron rails), and immigrants.

Only a small section of the Mobile and Ohio Railroad was in Alabama. Over four hundred kilometers were in Mississippi, where most of its land grant was located. The Mobile and Ohio received no land grants in Kentucky or Tennessee because these two states were originally the western extensions of Virginia and North Carolina. Vacant land in these states belonged to the states and state legislatures made no grants to the Mobile and Ohio.

Construction was seriously slowed by an inability to collateralize its land grant as an inducement for selling bonds in Europe. European bankers were well informed of the glut of cheap land available for settlement in slave states; therefore, land sales failed to contribute predicted amounts of funds for construction. The Graduation Act of 1854 authorized the sale of land in the public domain at prices from 30 cents per hectare to $2.47 per hectare (12.5 cents to 1.00 per acre). These prices

> allowed white peasants to purchase land at give away prices. In Louisiana between 1854 and 1861 over 566,000 hectares (1.4 million acres) were sold at prices ranging from 39.8 cents to $1.85 per hectare (12.5 to 75 cents per acre). Equally large areas of federal land in Mississippi were sold at similar prices.[20]

Texas offered similar bargains to attract settlers. A high percentage of this land was of marginal fertility, as well as being distant from water transportation, but it was adequate for the subsistence aspirations of white peasants. At these prices many white peasant households abandoned eroded land in South Carolina and other seaboard slave states and moved to Mississippi and Texas.

Potential planters with money and credit to purchase land from the Mobile and Ohio Railroad needed slaves to cultivate it. Although land was cheap and cotton prices were high in the 1850s, slaves were expensive. They were expensive because planters were in competition with railroads to purchase slaves. Slaves were preferred for the construction of rights-of-way and maintenance because white peasants were an unpredictable supply of laborers. A high percentage of the rights-of-way of southern railroads were built with rented and purchased slaves.

For example, in 1854 the Montgomery and West Point Railroad in Alabama owned sixty-six slaves and in 1859 and the South Carolina Railroad owned eighty-eight. All of them were males and, if they labored on plantations, they would be prime field hands. Ownership of slaves by railroads provided predictable numbers of laborers but slave ownership was a capital expenditure that detracted from purchasing heavier rails and more powerful locomotives.

Political Economy of Antebellum Railroads

In 1860 there were 49,200 kilometers of operating railroads in the United States and 34,700 (70%) were built in the 1850s. Of the railroads built in the 1850s, 22,800 kilometers were constructed in northern states compared to 11,900 in slave states. All U.S. railroads were poorly integrated in providing passenger and freight service but they were less integrated in slave states than in northern states. In 1860 travelers going inland from tidewater cities could purchase thru tickets on the principal inter-regional systems but changes in trains were frequently due to changes in gauge, lack of bridges, or gaps between the terminals of two railroads in the same town. Lack of integration was inconvenient for passengers but was a serious impediment for freight.

Different gauges were the principal reason for poor integration. There were five principal gauges. In 1860 railroads in fifteen of the thirty-one states had only one gauge, but that gauge could be standard gauge, 5 foot gauge, or 5 feet 6 inches gauge. The other sixteen states had a mixture of gauges. Standard gauge, however, was the gauge for half of the operating railroads and standard gauge railroads were concentrated in northern states.

During the 1850s, an increasing percentage of the population in northeastern states lived in cities. In 1840 there were five cities in the nation with 50,000 or more residents. In 1860 there were sixteen. Most of these cities were in the Northeast where village and city residents were 36 percent of the population. This was also the region with the densest railroad network, and with the heaviest concentration of factories.

Economic development policies implemented in New England and northern states in the 1850s were radically different in scope and purpose from economic development policies in slave states, although, outwardly, they appeared similar. Railroads in northeastern states increasingly served villages and cities by carrying food to urban residents from distant places and returning with manufactured products. In northeastern states, railroad were built to accelerate the creation of a diversified commercial culture that was increasingly urban. In slave states railroads were built to service the limited needs of an agrarian culture.

Policies operating in New York, Massachusetts, and eastern Pennsylvania provided guidance for states west of the Appalachian Mountains and north of the Ohio River to adopt policies that encouraged the creation of urban wealth. Economic development in these states was diversified and diversification was in direct ratio to increased manufacturing. Commerce, manufacturing, and accompanying skills were concentrated in villages and cities.

The best evidence for the dynamic economic development of northern states were the huge investments in transportation projects. Most of these investments were profitable because a very high percentage of cultivators were continuous producers of commodities for market sale, and an increasing percentage of the population were full-time paid laborers working in factories that produced an increasing variety of products for domestic consumption. The geographic expansion of the United States from 1840 to 1860 accelerated divergent economic development between northern and slave states. Free labor states in the trans-Appalachian and trans-Mississippi west duplicated the evolving diversified economies of northern seaboard states.

In contrast, governing elites in slave states were largely indifferent to economic development beyond supplying the transportation and credit needs of planters. New slave states in the trans-Appalachian west duplicated the agrarian economies of seaboard slave states. Governing elites in slave states clearly recognized that diversification and urbanization were implicit threats to an agrarian status quo where more than 90 percent of slaves were agricultural laborers. It was essential that most slaves be agricultural laborers because their conduct was manageable on plantations, but could become conspiratorial in cities. Examined from a different perspective, slave states had two distinct and highly visible agricultural sectors: commercial (concentrated in plantations) and subsistence (the white peasantry). Governing elites in slave states were committed to maintaining this status quo.

Railroad revenues are a broad measure of new wealth creation during the 1850s. Albert Fishlow compiled the revenues of all railroads by regions in 1859 in order to measure the on-going commercial transformation of the United States. The volume of freight moved by railroads in northern states dwarfed the volume of freight moved by railroads in slave states. Revenues of railroads operating in the seven states west of the Appalachian Mountains and north of the Ohio River, were thirty-four million dollars, with freight accounting for eighteen million of those dollars. This compares with revenues of twenty-four million dollars for railroads operating in the eleven slave states, where freight revenues were only thirteen million dollars.

Railroads in trans-Appalachian states north of the Ohio River had 30 percent more revenues than all of the railroads in slave states. In addition, the railroads in the eleven states north of the Potomac River and east of the Appalachian Mountains had sixty million dollars of revenue. Of that sixty million, thirty-four million (56%) was from freight. Freight revenue alone, from northern states was 30 percent larger than the revenues of all railroads in slave states.

Total revenue for railroads in the United States in 1859 was 118 million dollars, of which 94 million dollars (80%) was in northern states. Freight revenue was sixty-three million dollars: of all revenue of northern railroads. Freight revenue in slave states was eleven million dollars: 17 percent of all revenues in slave states. These numbers accurately measure the diversified commerce in northern states compared to restricted commercial activity in slave states.[21]

Competition with Canals

During the 1850s, railroad management, technology, and integration improved, and by 1860 railroads were competing with water transportation for carrying freight. Much of the freight was high value agricultural commodities (flour and cotton) going east and manufactured products going west. Both commodities and manufactured products benefited from faster railroad transportation because there was less handling and less susceptibility to water damage than transportation on rivers, lakes, and canals. Increasingly, most canal traffic was low value bulk commodities: coal, salt, grain, lumber.

In 1858 the Erie Canal carried 1,273,000 tons of western commodities eastward and in 1860 it carried 1.9 million tons going east but only 119,000 tons of merchandise going west. In 1858 the New York Central carried 229,000 tons of freight eastward, the Erie Railroad 224,000 tons, the Baltimore and Ohio 171,000 tons, and the Pennsylvania Railroad 141,000 tons. Although these four railroads carried only 37 percent of the tonnage going east, a high percentage of their traffic was high value commodities. The reciprocal of railroads carrying high value commodities eastward was carrying high value manufactured products westward.

Unlike the canal systems of Ohio and Indiana, the Erie Canal maintained its profitability during the 1850s because it was a funnel for carrying bulk commodities that arrived at Buffalo from Ohio and Indiana canals, and on steamboats from cities along the shores of all of the great lakes. Contemporary political leaders were painfully aware that the Ohio, Indiana, and Pennsylvania canal systems, plus the lateral canals in New York were bankrupt because railroads replaced the older technology of canals before the canals were paid for. These canals were the victims of telescoped technology that was not foreseen when construction began.

The Ohio and Indiana canal systems were state owned and tax revenues were required to pay the interest on the bonds that financed construction. The continuing decline of revenues of the Ohio and Indiana systems in the 1850s forced elected officials in 1860 to ask whether it was worth maintaining operations because revenues were less than the cost of funding the debts incurred to build them. The answer was yes for trunklines—at least for the moment.

The most competent state legislators understood that canals greatly increased the profit-ability for commodities produced at interior locations by bringing markets to cultivators. They also understood that railroads would accelerate and broaden the process of market penetration begun by canals. In spite of declining canal revenues, state legislatures encouraged railroad construction by enacting general incorporation statutes that also granted railroads the power of eminent domain. Powerful lobbies, acting in conjunction with municipalities, not served by water transportation, wanted reduced transportation costs.

Economic historians have tried to measure the impact of canals on economic development before the Civil War. *Were the commercial benefits derived from canal transportation greater than the cost of construction even when the canals operated at a loss?* The answer is yes for trunkline canals. Analyses of tonnages moved on trunkline canals indicates that they conferred economic benefits greater than construction costs because they accelerated the transition of frontier subsistence to diversified economies. The economic impact of many lateral canals is more problematic.

Chapter 7 of Ronald E. Shaw's *Canals for a Nation* is a good summary of how canals helped accelerate economic development and initiate urbanization, especially in states west of the Appalachian Mountains and north of the Ohio River.

State Debts

During the 1820s and 1830s, the national government continually reduced the national debt until it was extinguished in 1835. At the same time, states increased their bonded indebted-ness; slowly in the 1820s and rapidly in the 1830s. Increased state indebtedness was inseparably linked to the construction of internal improvement projects: first turnpikes, then canals, then railroads. By 1860 bonds underwritten by states and municipalities to build railroads dwarfed all other uses of state indebtedness.

State governments could increase their bonded indebtedness in the 1820s and 1830s be-cause most had low debts relative to their tax bases, and their tax bases were rapidly increasing. Low taxation on rapidly increasing tax bases made investments in state bonds appear safe and they appeared to be doubly safe because state governments used their bonded indebtedness to construct turnpikes and canals in the 1820s; canals and railroads in the 1830s, and only railroads after 1845. A variant in slave states was using bonded indebtedness to provide bank capital in order to extend credit to planters for purchasing land and slaves, and then to market the cotton crop.

All of these investments generated revenue that was assumed to be sufficient to pay the annual interest on the bonds. Furthermore, these investments helped increase commercial wealth, which made the bonds doubly safe investments because the new commercial wealth could be taxed to pay the annual interest if an internal improvement project failed to generate sufficient revenue.

State funding of internal improvement projects accelerated after the Erie Canal demon-strated its profitability. Between 1820 and 1830 states contracted twenty-six million dollars of bonded indebtedness, and between 1830 and 1838 state debts increased to 172 million dollars. Of this amount 109 million dollars was used to construct turnpikes, canals, and railroads, principally in northern states; and fifty-four million dollars was allocated to capitalize banks, principally in slave states. In 1838, about half of the bonded indebtedness of states was owned in Europe. By 1843 state bonded indebtedness was 231 million dollars with about 150 million owned in Europe. Selling bonds was facilitated by denominating them in European currencies, usually pounds sterling, with the interest on them being paid in London or elsewhere in Europe.

The depression that began in 1839 and bottomed in 1842 greatly reduced all forms of state revenue and state legislatures were extremely reluctant to levy higher taxes to service their bonded indebtedness. At the end of 1842, Arkansas, Florida Mississippi, and Michigan repudiated some of their bonded indebtedness to the amount of thirteen million dollars. Arkansas, Florida, and Mississippi never redeemed their repudiated debts, and Michigan partially redeemed it after protracted negotiations. Louisiana, Maryland, Indiana, Illinois, and Pennsylvania defaulted on interest payments on some or all of their bonded indebtedness, but all of them eventually paid arrears in interest and resumed paying annual interest.

The biggest defaulter was Pennsylvania. In August 1842, it failed to pay interest on thirty-three million dollars of bonded indebtedness. Ten million of Pennsylvania's debt was owned in the United States and twenty-three million in Europe. Almost all of this debt was incurred building canals, and the largest single source was construction costs of the main line.

The main line was a 575 kilometer combination of canals and railroads between Phila-delphia and Pittsburgh. Its central link was an inclined plane railroad at the Allegheny front where stationary steam engines lifted and lowered canal boats. Building this monstrosity cost twelve million dollars. Other canals cost an additional 6.5 million dollars, and 10.5 million was spent on internal improvement projects that were never completed. All of these debts were underwritten by the state. When the depression began in 1839, revenue from internal improvement projects owned or subsidized by the Pennsylvania government yielded less than one-quarter of the revenue needed to pay the annual interest on bonded indebtedness. Yet the state legislature continued to subsidize construction.

The political response to the debacle of Pennsylvania's internal improvement debts was selling shares it owned because the electorate wanted to raise money to service debts without increasing taxes. In 1842 the state sold its shares in internal improvement corporations. They had a face value of two million dollars, but the state received less than 15 percent of face value. The shares consisted of approximately one million dollars in banks, five hundred thousand dollars in toll bridges and four hundred thousand dollars in four shortline railroads The sale generated insufficient revenue to pay interest on its bonded indebtedness and the state defaulted. Tax increases in 1844 generated sufficient revenue to pay interest in 1845 and extinguish arrears in 1847. Many other states followed the example of Pennsylvania and sold shares in internal improvement projects for what money they could get.

The electorate also wanted the state legislature to end subsidizing the construction of internal improvement projects. The culmination of this policy was the sale of the main line canal/railroad to the Pennsylvania railroad in 1857. The Pennsylvania Railroad immediately integrated the railroad portion of the main line into its inter-regional trunkline. This put a continuous right-of-way under one management from Philadelphia to Pittsburgh. West of Pittsburgh the Pennsylvania Railroad had already negotiated connections to Chicago, which greatly enhanced the ability of Philadelphia businessmen to capture trans-Appalachian commerce.

Previous to 1840, no state constitutions limited the power of state legislatures to contract bonded indebtedness. The revulsion against state subsidies to build internal improvement projects adopted by the Pennsylvania legislature in 1842, was adopted in various forms by nineteen other states prior to 1860. The four most common restraints on debt creation were (1) bonded indebtedness had to be approved by referendum, (2) only a single project could be in one referendum, (3) there was a cap on the amount of indebtedness for each project, and (4) legislatures could not underwrite bonded indebtedness of corporations.

Government subsidies for building railroads and other internal improvement projects did not cease after borrowing limitations were inserted in state constitutions. They changed. State legislators were very careful to preserve the option of municipalities to use their tax bases to subsidize internal improvement projects that contributed to local prosperity. The borrowing power of municipalities (cities, counties, villages) was unaffected by constitutional limitations on debt creation. Debt limitations applied only to state governments.

At the same time (1842–1847), that many states were selling state owned shares in internal improvement corporations and banks, the European market for American bonds strongly revived. It had two causes: (1) United States-Mexican War (1846–1848), and (2) several abortive revolutions in western European nations in 1848. Bonds that were sold to finance the Mexican War had a very high rating for long-term investment because of the previous extinction of the national debt, and bonds sold to finance American railroads, underwritten by state and municipal governments, had high interest rates. These bonds were magnets for capital fleeing political turmoil in Europe.

The availability of European capital in the 1850s helped fuel the boom in railroad construction. Between 1848 and 1852, an estimated sixty million dollars of U.S. bonds were sold to European investors. The good reception by European investors of American bonds induced London bankers in 1852 to establish a public market for them. Bond trading on a continuous basis greatly helped mobilize capital for U. S. railroads.

It also benefited British iron smelters because, from 1849 to 1854, half of the money obtained from bonds sold in Europe was spent in England to purchase rails. In 1854, over two-thirds of the rails used in new railroad construction were imported from Britain. British rolling mills often accepted railroad bonds in partial payment for rails and the London bond market allowed them to convert them to cash when necessary.

Statistics compiled in 1853 for use by U.S. congressmen estimated that the total bonded indebtedness of all state and municipal governments and corporations was 475 million dollars. A high percentage of this indebtedness was underwritten by state governments to construct internal improvements. Of the 475 million, 140 million (29%) was foreign owned, but it could have been substantially more according to an estimate made by a knowledgeable New York banker. Table 7.1 is an official summary of railroad, canal, state, and municipal bonded indebtedness in 1853, and how much was foreign owned.

By 1860 European investors probably owned one hundred million dollars of American railroads bonds. European investors were highly selective in their investments. They preferred the bonds of trunkline railroads, and especially those that could be aggregated into inter-regional trunklines. This usually meant east–west railroads across the Appalachian Mountains to Pittsburgh, Cincinnati, St. Louis, Detroit, Chicago, and westward. These investments were essential for accelerating U.S. economic development because building trunkline railroads was the best possible use of capital to stimulate investments in new manufacturing technologies located in cities.

The small amount of bonded indebtedness of the national government in 1853 (fifty-eight million) relative to the bonded indebtedness of state and municipal governments is an accurate picture of states rights economic development policy. Most of the vision and leadership to build internal improvement projects originated in the states, and the mobilization of the capital needed to complete them was largely dependent on state policies. The national government

Table 7.1 Bonded Indebtedness for Constructing Internal Improvements: 1853

	Total Indebtedness Millions of Dollars	Foreign Owned Millions of Dollars
State Bonds	190	73
County Bonds	14	5
Municipal Bonds	79	16
Railroad Bonds	170	44
Canal Bonds	22	2
Totals	475	140

Source: Adler, Dorothy R. British Investments in American Railways (Charlottesville: University of Virginia Press, 1970) p. 23.

made continuous contributions to all varieties of internal improvement projects but they were largely supplemental; although, for a few projects, like building the Illinois Central Railroad, national contributions were crucial.

Manufacturing and Urbanization

Economic historians generally explain industrialization before 1860 by the conjunction of five factors: (1) friendly state governments, (2) an assured food surplus to feed urban workers, (3) borrowed technologies, (4) high rates of literacy, and (5) organizational efficiency. The weight they give these factors is usually in the above order of importance, with friendly governments and an assured food surplus being silently assumed. Their analysis is correct; although, I would change the order of importance by putting literacy third, organizational efficiency fourth and technology fifth because the profitable application of borrowed and indigenous technology depended on the preexistence of the other four factors.

But regardless of the order, industrialization could not have been sustained unless there were (1) school systems that taught functional literacy that enabled persons to learn new skills, (2) market institutions that induced persons to perform commercial labor norms in agriculture and industry, and (3) saving rates (or bank credit) that could pay workers for labor they performed. All of these factors existed in northern states, especially in New England. All of them did not exist in slave states.

I focus on iron smelting and steam engine technology because they best measure the growth of heavy industry. I especially concentrate on railroads because they were the largest single consumer of iron in the 1840s and 1850s and the most ubiquitous user of steam power. The transportation revolution began with canals, accelerated with steamboats on inland waters, and accelerated again with railroads. Accelerated factory production is directly linked to accelerated transportation. An excellent example of how railroads helped accelerate factory production in Massachusetts in the 1850s is chapter 7 in Jonathan Prude's *The Coming of Industrial Order*.

American smelters and rolling mills supplied the iron straps for the rails of pioneer railroads and almost all of the iron plates for building locomotives. American foundries also supplied the shapes used for manufacturing rolling stock, chairs, and spikes; but they could not supply the demand for solid iron rails. In 1850, 21 percent of iron rails used by U.S. railroads were produced by American rolling mills. By 1860 American smelters and rolling mills supplied 58 percent of the iron rails; however, a considerable percentage of American produced rails were rerolled iron, and a high percentage of re-rolled iron was from imported rails.

In 1850 iron production in the United States was about 600,000 tons and in 1860 it is estimated to have been 900,000 tons. Iron smelting capacity, like textiles, was at the cutting edge of the industrial revolution. Railroads were the largest single consumer of iron, although, they used only about 20 percent of United States production in 1860. Most iron produced in the United States was used to fabricate products with higher value than rails. Fortunately for the United States, smelting capacity existed in Europe to satisfy the U.S. demand for large tonnages of rails. Money to purchase imported rails came from three sources: (1) gold mined in California, (2) foreign exchange earned by cotton and grain exports, and (3) sale of bonds in Britain and Europe.

In 1860, 50 percent of American iron production was in Pennsylvania. Production in Pennsylvania and other states was extremely fragmented. There were at least 150 blast furnaces operating in Pennsylvania, and their capacities were highly variable. To a considerable extent, the capacities of blast furnaces depended on the fuel they used. Furnaces that used anthracite coal usually had the highest smelting capacity: three thousand to ten thousand tons per year.

Furnaces using charcoal usually produced less than three thousand tons per year. The third fuel, just coming into use in western Pennsylvania, was coke made from bituminous coal. Annual production from coke furnaces was highly variable but was usually more than charcoal furnaces and less than anthracite furnaces. During the 1850s, the use of charcoal as a fuel was in steep decline. It was being replaced by anthracite and coke because furnaces using mineral fuels usually had larger capacities, and the largest furnaces often had attached rolling mills that made plates and rails.

Iron ore came from numerous magnetite (iron oxide) deposits in eastern Pennsylvania, northern New Jersey, and northern New York. In central and western Pennsylvania it came from siderite (iron carbonate) nodules found at the base of most coal beds. Wherever coal was mined near water transportation, siderite nodules were a valuable byproduct.

The impact of railroads was far greater than being able to move people and commodities from practically any location to any other location at high speeds. Nathan Rosenberg summarizes. "The transportation revolution was a revolution of steam and iron." "In numerous ways the huge demands of the railroads for steam power, metals, and machinery generated improvements which spilled over into other sectors of the economy which relied on steam and iron technology." The principal other sector was heavy industry.[22]

What constituted heavy industry? Smelting iron is an obvious heavy industry. So are mills that rolled rails and plates, and factories that made engines that powered locomotives, steamboats, and industrial machinery. Building steam engines was an established industry in the United States in 1830. The most obvious use of steam engines before 1840 was powering steamboats operating on inland waters. Less obvious but more numerous were stationary steam engines that powered manufacturing machinery.

Slave states used far fewer stationary steam engines than northern states and they were widely dispersed. A high percentage of them performed agrarian tasks: compressing cotton bales prior to marine shipment; powering cotton gins, crushing sugar cane, milling rice, cracking maize into grits, and sawing lumber. Almost all engines operating in slave states, including those powering steamboats and locomotives, were manufactured in northern states or were imported from England.

In 1838, approximately 1,850 stationary steam engines were operating in the United States. Approximately 550 (30%) operated in slave states, and of this number, 275 (50%) were in Louisiana. Most of them crushed sugar cane. In addition, there were approximately 800 engines powering steamboats, and 350 locomotives. Both steamboats and locomotives were even more concentrated in northern states. Only 22 percent of steamboat operators were based in slave states in 1838.

In the twenty-two years after 1838, the number of stationary steam engines rapidly increased but their use in slave states lagged further and further behind use in northern states. Louisiana was the exception. Louisiana had comparable numbers of operating engines with many northern states but they were almost exclusively used to make sugar. Carroll W. Pursell summarizes their use in slave states: "engines in the South aided but did not seem to create industries."[23]

In 1848 Charleston, South Carolina had 28 operating steam engines in the immediate vicinity. This is far less than the 174 operating in metropolitan Philadelphia and the 133 that were operating in the immediate vicinity of Pittsburgh in 1838 (10 years earlier). Engines in northern cities were mostly used for manufacturing. Some of their uses were pumping water from mines, making rope, rag paper, edged tools, carpets, glass, milling wheat into flour, refining sugar, brewing beer, running printing presses, running machinery in brass and iron foundries, powering machinery that made machine tools, boilers, and locomotives, and supplied supplemental power in textile mills.

After 1845 the scale of urban manufacturing accelerated in northern cities. Larger manufacturers needed suppliers of component parts. These parts were increasingly supplied by artisans who rented rooms (mechanics rooms) in buildings that housed a steam engine that turned a central shaft. Belts transmitted power from the shaft to machines in mechanics rooms where artisans tended grinding wheels that made edged tools, or turned a lathe for making smaller parts for assembly into larger machines; or made small objects of many shapes for a multitude of uses.

The attitude of the governing elites of slave states to new technologies and the use of wage laborers in factories is concisely illustrated by an ordinance passed by the city council of Charleston, South Carolina in 1845. It forbid the use of steam engines within city limits. The leading entrepreneur in South Carolina heaped scorn on the governing elite for looking backward:

> The labor of negroes and blind horses can never supply the place of steam, and this power is withheld lest the smoke of an engine should disturb the delicate nerves of an agriculturalist; or the noise of the mechanic's hammer should break in upon the slumber of a real estate holder or importing merchant.[24]

In the years surveyed in this chapter (1830–1860), steam power applied to inland transportation (rail and water) increased by a magnitude each decade; and the skills to design and build steam engines was overwhelmingly concentrated in northern cities. Like the manufacture of textile machinery, engineering designs and metal fabrication technologies continued to be borrowed from Europe but increasingly American mechanics made innovations that improved efficiencies under operating conditions in America.

Railroads performed another largely hidden function in accelerating industrialization. All railroads required machine shops to maintain and repair rolling stock. The boom of railroad construction in the 1850s required large numbers of maintenance facilities because steam locomotives are high maintenance machines; and other rolling stock required continual repair because of rough roadbeds. As new machine shops were established, mechanics had to be trained to use machine tools to make replacement parts. This was the hidden function of railroads.

Railroad machine shops trained mechanics who were sent to maintenance shops in dispersed villages. Albert Fishlow estimates that machinists with metal fabrication skills were 5 percent of railroad employees in 1860. He further estimates that the total number of machinists maintaining rolling stock was 20 percent more than all machinists employed in building locomotives. The dispersal of machinists in villages had two long-term effects. They were core people in urban growth and they expanded the scope of diversified economies because they could transfer their skills to other industrial applications that used stationary steam engines. Furthermore, stationary engines would be fueled with coal delivered by railroads, and railroads would market the products they produced.[25]

The principal use of coal in 1860 was space heating. Industrial use accounted for about 5 percent of production. It was used by stationary steam engines in cities, in textile mills where steam engines supplemented water power, on steamboats operating on, rivers, lakes and the protected waters of east coast port cities; and in iron smelting and fabrication. Iron smelting and fabrication were its most significant industrial uses. In 1860, a few railroads, like the Illinois Central and Baltimore and Ohio, were using coal for locomotive fuel because wood was unavailable, but the great transition to coal did not take place until the decade of the 1870s when steel replaced iron in boiler construction. Nonetheless, the use of coal in the 1850s established it as the most efficient industrial fuel.

"Compared with growth in the rest of the United States, the South's growth in both manufacturing capital and manufacturing value was miniscule." Per capita value of manufactured products in New England increased from one hundred dollars in 1850 to one hundred and fifty dollars in 1860. During the same decade in slave states, per capita manufactured products increased from about eight dollars to about thirteen dollars. Urbanization in slave states increased at about the same proportion: from 7 percent in 1850 to 9 percent in 1860.[26]

Seen from a different perspective, investments in land and slaves foreclosed investments in manufacturing and starved investments in internal improvement projects. It could not have been otherwise because the creation of a diversified economy was impossible as long as white peasants refused to become full-time wage laborers. White peasants would perform wage labor only when they had to acquire target sums of money. The unskilled labor they performed was the same unskilled labor performed by slaves—moving earth to build railroad rights-of-way or stacking lumber at sawmills. In other words, when white peasants performed wage labor, they performed the same unskilled labor as slaves. This had the effect of denigrating the social value of wage labor.

Summary

The principal accelerant of economic development in the 1840s and 1850s was the symbiotic relationship between credit and railroad construction. Imaginative financing in the United States, supplemented by borrowed European capital, mobilized the enormous amounts of money needed for railroad construction. Imaginative financing was necessary because of the huge shortage of capital in the United States and the chaotic banking systems in many states after the destruction of the second bank of the United States.

The second most important driving force in economic development was the rivalry of east coast cities for the commerce of the interior. Primarily this involved subsidizing the building of canals and railroads to funnel commodities to seaport cities for export or urban consumption. The principal port cities seeking exports were Boston, New York City, Philadelphia, Baltimore, Charleston, Savannah, Mobile, and New Orleans. To a lesser extent, canals and railroads were built to funnel commodities to cities located on rivers and the great lakes: Chicago, Cleveland, Cincinnati, St. Louis, Louisville, and Memphis.

During the depression from 1839 to 1842, many states experienced financial stringencies and had to increase taxes when the electorate could least afford it. In the mid-1840s and 1850s, many state constitutional conventions restrained state legislatures from underwriting bonds for private corporations, often in the form of debt limitations. These restraints, however, were not serious impediments for mobilizing capital from public sources because they did not prohibit state legislatures from giving land or tax exemptions to railroad corporations. Even more important, constitutional restraints did not prohibit municipalities from underwriting bonds issued for railroad construction. When the city of Albany underwrote bonds in 1840 to build the Boston and Albany Railroad from Albany to the Massachusetts boundary, it did what other cities, counties, and villages would do for the rest of the nineteenth century.[27]

European inputs into railroad construction are not usually accorded their importance:

1. Many railroads built in the 1850s required huge investments of European capital for rapid completion. Often these investments had a large speculative content because they traversed districts with sparse populations. It was questionable how soon railroads traversing these districts would provide sufficient revenue to fund construction debts.
2. Rapid completion of these railroads also required large numbers of laborers. European immigrants, mainly from Ireland and Germany, were available when their labor was needed.

3. European iron smelting and rolling mills that supplied rails supplied the essential products that American furnaces and mills could not. During the peak of railroad construction (1851–1857), 45 percent of British iron exports came to the United States as rails.

During the past fifty years several econometric historians have emphasized that water transportation in the 1850s carried two-thirds or more of the tonnage of intra-state and inter-regional freight. Their conclusion is that railroads were not as essential for accelerating industrialization as most historians believed. Econometric historians recognized that railroads diverted high value commodities from water transportation and that some railroads carried substantial amounts of bulk commodities like grain, coal, and lumber. Ultimately, however, they based their interpretation on the overwhelming tonnage of freight carried on water, and the poor integration of trunkline railroads.

This interpretation is misleading because the best way to interpret the impact of railroads on economic development during the 1850s is their linkage to products produced in factories in northern cities. Contemporary northern businessmen had no doubt that the railroads built in the 1850s were a technical breakthrough that accelerated the creation of new wealth. The large tonnage of bulk commodities that continued to be carried by canals, rivers, and other inland waterways do not accurately measure the speed and scope of social change induced by railroad transportation.

Chapter 8

Free Soil

The disposal of the national public domain in the trans-Missouri west was about the social value of labor, although, outwardly, it was an issue of land use. Divergent policies of land use and labor came into direct conflict in western territories. Elsewhere in the nation, states controlled land use policies, labor policies, and policies of economic development. Slave labor was constitutionally safe in states where it was established, unless the states themselves decided to abolish it.

A states' right solution to land use was impossible in the trans-Missouri west because states did not exist. All land was in the national public domain, and therefore, its disposal required a national solution. The contest was between free labor and slave labor for control of national land policy. Northern farmers wanted to use national power (congressional statutes) to prevent the expansion of slave labor agriculture into organized territories in order to allocate land to the sons of northern farmers. Plantation owners wanted to use the power of the national government to guarantee that planters who took slaves into organized territories would be protected by congressional statute, as the first step in organizing state governments that protected slave property.

The contest to control land policies in the national public domain began with the Missouri Question in 1820 and ended with the election of Abraham Lincoln in 1860. The contest was the result of the abundance of vacant land acquired by the United States after independence: the Louisiana Purchase (1803), the annexation of Texas (1845), the division of the Pacific Northwest with Canada (1846), and the land acquired from Mexico after the Mexican War.

This land was a reservoir of future states and future political power. Southern slave owners believed that control of some of this land was essential in order to prevent the unthinkable: peaceful abolition by constitutional amendment. Abolition would end the ability of planters to coerce commercial labor norms from slaves, and this would substantially reduce labor inputs into cultivation. Planter wealth would be greatly reduced, and they would lose their entitlement to govern. Equally unthinkable was that white peasants would have to compete for land use with emancipated black peasants.

As western settlement accelerated in the late 1840s, the long-term implications of land use policies came into clearer focus. The southern variety of agrarian democracy would disappear unless it was preserved within the boundaries of a republic that had a priority of preserving slave labor. The preservation of slave labor required more slave states.

Competing Labor Values

The social objective of northern farmers was to earn money incomes. To do this they had to produce substantial amounts of commodities for market sale. This volume of commodities could only be produced by performing commercial labor norms. Farmers performed all or most of the labor of cultivation. Their labor earned them an income sufficient to enjoy a comfortable level of welfare, an ability to pay taxes to fund common schools, and sufficient additional money to invest in infrastructure projects needed to market their corps. For them, agricultural labor had a high social value.

The social objective of planters was identical with northern farmers except they used slave labor to earn money incomes. Their margin of profit was based on their ability to coerce commercial labor norms from slaves and, at the same time, impose subsistence welfare on them. Planters did little or no agricultural labor.

White peasants did not perform commercial labor norms. Their social objective was enjoying maximum amounts of indolence. They minimized the cultivation of exchange commodity crops (tobacco, cotton, and maize) because the acquisition of money required labor to produce them. Minimizing agricultural labor to produce crops for market sale minimized money acquisition. White peasants also minimized the cultivation of food crops and tried to transfer as much of this labor as possible to their children or, if they were upper strata peasants, to one (or two) slaves they owned.

Both white peasants and the governing elites of slave states assumed that agricultural labor had a low social value because the only cultivators who consistently performed commercial labor norms were slaves, and this labor had to be coerced from them. Put in other terms, neither planters nor white peasants believed in the dignity of labor, and especially they rejected wage labor in factories that required full-time, supervised labor like the supervised labor that planters imposed on slaves.

Embedded in the struggle to control the disposition of the national public domain was the larger issue of the best use of the power of governance. *Should the power of governance be used to create a fully commercial culture that rewarded workers with the full money value of the labor they performed or should the power of governance be used to protect an agrarian culture based on slave labor?* The fundamental issue of the free soil controversy was the contest to create a fully commercial culture in order to encourage the production of new wealth on a continental scale, or using the power of governance to protect a status relationship between planters, white peasants, and slaves in an agrarian culture.

In 1860 the United States was 84 percent rural but 91 percent rural in slave states (75% rural in northern states and 64% rural in New England). Access to land use was an overwhelming concern for the sons of northern and southern cultivators. Political leaders in slave states knew that the future of slavery was ominous because Lincoln's election ended the possibility of adding more slave labor states. His election also signified that new free labor states in the trans-Missouri west would eventually unite with older northern states to pass a constitutional amendment that emancipated slaves.

All political leaders accepted the possibility that slavery could be peacefully ended by a constitutional amendment. This possibility, however, was unthinkable to a large majority of white southerners. Neither white peasants nor governing elites could conceive that emancipated slaves could become a constituent part of American culture. From 1820 to 1860, southern political leaders had ensured the preservation of slavery by control of the national government or by making alliances with northern political leaders in order to neutralize anti-slavery political activity. The election of Lincoln foreclosed these strategies. For a high percentage of political leaders in slave states the only way to preserve slavery was an independent republic.

Democratic Governance

After 1800, and especially after 1820, republican governance in both slave and free states began a rapid evolution toward democratic governance. The transition began in new states in the trans-Appalachian west and worked its way eastward to the original thirteen states and was generally complete by 1845. The paths to democratic governance, however, were divergent. By 1860 there were two highly visible types of democracy in the United States: agrarian and commercial. Both types of governance were by consent.

All states did not have a full complement of statutes and constitutional clauses that created democratic electorates, but most states had most provisions. The general characteristics of democratic governance were:

1. a white male electorate;
2. end of tax payments as a qualification for voting, or if a state levied a poll tax, the effect was universal male suffrage;
3. all state officials were elected;
4. presidential electors were elected by popular vote instead of being appointed by state legislatures;
5. judges were elected for limited terms instead of lifetime appointments;
6. county, city, village, and township offices were elective, but state legislatures often granted the power to exclude nonproperty owners from voting in municipal elections because municipal revenues came from land taxes;
7. legislative representation was apportioned on the basis of population, but there was a variation in slave states. The federal census counted three-fifths of slaves as a basis for apportioning congressional representation. Slave states often retained the three-fifth rule in apportioning representation in state legislatures in order to disproportionately represent the wealth of plantation owners;
8. provisions were made for periodic reapportionment of state legislatures as population distribution changed;
9. state governors were given an unrestricted veto because they were elected by the total electorate. The veto was a restraint on legislative corruption;
10. secret ballots;
11. general incorporation statutes to equalize business opportunities.

Three issues in northern states were not fully resolved before the Civil War: (1) registration of voters to prevent frauds, (2) suffrage for resident aliens who had no experience in self-government, and (3) suffrage for free blacks because of racial antipathy.

Agrarian Democracy

Agrarian democracy was based on Virginia's experience that was popularized by Thomas Jefferson. During the congressional debate in 1848 for establishing a territorial government for Oregon, John C. Calhoun defined the Jeffersonian version of democratic governance.

> No Southern man—not the poorest or the lowest—will under any circumstances, submit to perform menial labor. He has too much pride for that and I rejoice that he has....With us the two great divisions of society are not the rich and the poor, but white and black; and all the former, the poor as well as the rich, belong to the upper class, and are respected and treated as equals if honest and industrious; and hence have a position and pride of character of which neither poverty nor misfortune can deprive them.[1]

This statement recognizes that being white in southern agrarian culture conferred a social status that gave white peasants a claim for a share of governance. Democratic political stability was achieved because both governing elites and white peasants were committed to preserving a democracy that preserved the subsistence labor norms of white peasants and enforced slavery on blacks. It was a democracy that did not achieve democratic prosperity, but that was not its intention.

Large landowners who were also large slaveowners would govern, or governance would be conducted by lawyers who were their surrogates. Planter elites insured that they would continue to govern by retaining property qualifications for candidates for state offices and the state senate. The democratic peasant electorate was given a choice of candidates but not a choice of policies. The principal function of government was to protect property, especially slave property.

After white peasants were enfranchised, they consented to being governed by planter elites because both benefited from a status quo democracy. Governing elites clearly understood that maintaining a status quo democracy depended on protecting the subsistence labor norms of white peasants by low money taxation and maintaining the white peasantry's access to land use.

Five policies sustained democratic governance by consent in slave states: (1) Planters provided sharecropping opportunities for landless white peasant households. This was a policy of racial loyalty. (2) Low prices for land sold from the national and state public domains. (3) Low taxation of agricultural land that benefited both peasant and planters. (4) No expensive tax funded common school systems. (5) Minimal state subsidies for internal improvement projects.

Literacy was not required for a status quo democracy because white peasants did not require literacy to conduct their affairs. Storekeepers who extended subsistence credit would conduct their money transactions. Literacy was the concern of persons engaged in commerce, and white peasants were minimal participants. Few municipalities funded common school systems and state funding of them was meager at best, and often nonexistent.

Commercial Democracy

During the pioneer stage of settlement democracy in states north of the Ohio River was little different from the democracy of trans-Appalachian slave states. In both regions, agriculture was the dominant occupation. Agrarian democracy north of the Ohio River, however, had a hidden difference because the commercial motivation of most cultivating households contained the seeds of a diversified economy.

In northern states, the democracy was composed of a literate population that performed commercial labor norms. Although, ownership of agricultural land was still the principal form of wealth, policies favored by the northern democracy were increasingly shaped by income rather than ownership of agricultural land. Most cultivators sold a high percentage of the crops they grew, and money from the sale of these commodities was the basis for land taxation that funded statewide common school systems.

The functional literacy taught in rural common schools sustained a commercially motivated democracy. School systems were established soon after statehood and steadily expanded with increasing appropriations from state revenues because the commercial democracy understood that literacy was the basic commercial skill and was essential for (1) marketing commodities that were continuously produced, (2) learning how to use new technologies, (3) educating an electorate on policy choices, and (4) equalizing (democratizing) business opportunities. It was a democracy that could be successfully transferred to cities.

Diversified economies became visible in these states during the 1830s and 1840s and rapidly accelerated during the 1850s. Candidates for elective office in diversified economies had to represent more than one constituency in order to be elected. The democracy in states with diversified economies comprehended all persons who were yeomen, farmers, full-time wage laborers, salaried employees, and entrepreneurs. It was the democracy of persons who measured their social security by earning money incomes from the continuous production and sale of commodities and services on anonymous markets.

In most cases money determined who was elected. It was not the money of personal fortunes but the money of competing interest groups that wanted to use the power of governance to shape policies that would enhance the welfare of their constituents. In a commercial democracy, equalized opportunities to earn money incomes were an equalized opportunity for people to improve their welfare, and, if labor was steadily performed, the result would be personal and community prosperity. Steadily performed labor to earn money incomes conferred dignity on people. In addition, money incomes equalized the distribution of wealth compared to slave states where subsistence labor norms equalized the distribution of privation.

Trans-Missouri West

Nine events between 1835 and 1860 defined the contest between free and slave labor cultivation (between plantations and farmers):

1. debate on the gag rule (1835–1837);
2. annexation of Texas (1845);
3. annexation of land from Mexico (1848);
4. organization of the Free Soil political party (1848);
5. California statehood (1850);
6. Kansas-Nebraska Act (1854);
7. organization of the Republican Party (1856);
8. Dred Scott decision of the Supreme Court (1857);
9. election of Abraham Lincoln as president (1860).

In 1835 anti-slavery politicians (and abolitionists) in northern states began to flood congress with petitions to end slavery in the District of Columbia and in organized territories. These were two places where the national government had undoubted power to act. At the same time, abolitionists began using the mail to send southerners large amounts of anti-slavery literature. Political leaders from slave states were in a frenzy of apprehension because they feared this literature might spark a slave rebellion. Southern political leaders were determined to silence this opposition. They succeeded because both houses of Congress passed gag rules requiring all anti-slavery petitions to be laid on the table without reading. Furthermore, southern postmasters refused to deliver abolitionist literature and the postmaster general approved this practice.

During the debate over the passage of the gag rule (1836), John C. Calhoun characterized anti-slavery political activity as war. "The war which abolitionists wage against us is of a very different character, and far more effective. It is a war of religious and political fanaticism…waged not against our lives but our character."[2] In the continuing debate (February 1837), John C. Calhoun clearly saw the future. Slavery was the foundation of southern agrarian culture and slave states would seek independence if northern political leaders persisted in seeking abolition.

> By the necessary course of events, if left to themselves, we would become finally, two people….I hold that in the present state of civilization, where two races of different origin, and distinguished by color, and other physical differences, as well as intellectual, are

brought together, the relation now existing in the slaveholding States between the two, is, instead of an evil, a good—a positive good.[3]

A treaty to annex the Republic of Texas was rejected by the U.S. Senate in 1844 because there were enough senators from northern states to block ratification. Treaties require a two-thirds majority for ratification. These senators did not want an additional slave state. Their vote, however did not represent stonewall opposition because there was strong support to expand the boundaries of the nation. Texas annexation was a necessary step to extend the western boundary to the upper Rio Grande Valley where the authority of the Mexican government was barely acknowledged. The annexation of Texas carried with it the possibility that this region would be annexed in the near future. Texas was annexed by a joint resolution of Congress in 1845 because joint resolutions require only a majority vote.

The United States claimed the boundary claimed by the Republic of Texas. The Mexican government claimed that the boundary of the Republic of Texas was the boundary of the province of Texas. The boundary of the province of Texas was much smaller than the boundary claimed by the Republic of Texas. Neither nation would compromise, and war followed. Anti-slavery congressmen believed that the principal purpose of the war was to annex sufficient land to create more slave states by dividing Texas into several states and then annexing vacant land beyond the western border of Texas.

David Wilmot, a Democratic congressman proposed an amendment to a war appropriation bill in 1846 that: "as an express and fundamental condition to the acquisition of any territory from the Republic of Mexico…neither slavery nor involuntary servitude shall ever exist." David Wilmot represented a rural district in Pennsylvania that strongly believed that vacant land in the West should be reserved for the sons of northern farmers. The words of the proviso were a paraphrase from the Northwest Ordinance of 1787 that excluded slavery from trans-Appalachian territory north of the Ohio River.

The words were not incendiary but southern congressmen reacted as if they were. Calhoun led southern opposition. He claimed that Congress did not have the power to exclude settlers from taking their property into territories. This was a clear right of U.S. citizens because the Constitution recognized slaves as a form of property. After bitter debate, the Wilmot Proviso did not pass because enough northern Democrats voted with their southern colleagues to dampen the issue before the presidential election of 1848. In the peace treaty following the war with Mexico (1848), the United States annexed land to the Pacific Coast, including the province of California. The treaty was quickly ratified.

President James K. Polk decided not to seek reelection in 1848. He had accomplished his objective: the territorial expansion of the United States to the Pacific Ocean in California and Oregon. His retirement set in motion a highly divisive contest for the Democratic presidential nomination. The two principal candidates were former president Martin Van Buren who had opposed the annexation of Texas and the war with Mexico, and Lewis Cass (from Michigan) who led northern opposition to the Wilmot Proviso. Van Buren had a majority of delegates going into the nominating convention, but before a vote was taken the rules were changed. Nomination required a two-thirds vote of delegates. Van Buren could not get two-thirds but Cass could. The two-thirds rule gave Democrats from slave states a veto of all future presidential nominations. This rule prevented the Democratic Party from nominating future candidates who opposed additional slave states.

At the Democratic nominating convention, the credentials committee excluded anti-slavery delegates from New York. The convention then proceeded to nominate Lewis Cass. The rejected delegates withdrew to Utica, New York and nominated Van Buren on a platform to exclude slavery from all territories. They called themselves Free Soil Democrats and immediately set out to expand their appeal by inviting anti-slavery Whigs to coalesce into a party with a broader appeal to the northern electorate. A second convention was held in Buffalo, New York that endorsed Van Buren for the presidency.

The platform of the Free Soil Party contained two phrases that summarized the discontent of an increasing percentage of the population in northern states: "no more slave states and no more slave territories," and "free soil, free speech, free labor, and free men." Van Buren's nomination was expedient for anti-slavery political leaders, but these two phrases carried a message that the northern electorate understood. The expansion of slavery onto vacant land was inimical to diversified economic development because the incentive of paid labor (wage labor) was essential for creating new wealth, whether in the form of larger harvests by farmers or products produced in factories. A continual theme of election rhetoric in northern states was "a vote for Van Buren and Free Soil was a vote to elevate and dignify labor."[4]

In the election of 1848, Van Buren received about 10 percent of the national vote. All of his votes were in northern states where he received 14 percent of the vote. His votes came about equally from Democrats and Whigs.

Immediately after the annexation of territory from Mexico (1848), gold was discovered in California. Placer miners soon discovered that low places in river gravels accumulated gold, often in bonanza quantities. California filled with people overnight, but there was no organized territorial government and it was highly likely that establishing one would be a long and arduous political process. Northern congressmen would insist on applying the Wilmot Proviso: no more slave territories. California could not wait for Congress to act. Newly arrived settlers needed a government. They acted for themselves. They organized a provisional state government, held a constitutional convention, drafted a constitution that excluded slavery, ratified it by referendum, and petitioned Congress for admission as a state without the intermediate status of a territorial government.

Congressional leaders from slave states had to deal with a situation over which they had no control. The admission of California as a free labor state would permanently upset the balance between free labor and slave labor states. In 1850 there were fifteen free labor and fifteen slave labor states. In the immediate future, northern political power would prevent the creation of more slave labor territories and states. Senator John C. Calhoun, in his dying speech, characterized the admission of California as the first step in the political process of overwhelming southern agrarian culture. "We shall know what to do when you reduce the question to submission or resistance."[5]

The admission of California to statehood was an opportunity for southern congressmen to extract concessions from northern congressmen. They wanted a new fugitive slave law that required U.S. marshals to apprehend escaped slaves living in northern states and return them to their owners. They wanted to use the power of the national government to enforce slavery in free labor states because law enforcement agencies in most northern states refused to apprehend escaped slaves. After bitter debates, the compromise was enacted into law. California was admitted as a free labor state, a new fugitive slave law was passed, and territorial governments were established for New Mexico/Arizona and Utah without reference to slavery. This was an implicit rejection of the Wilmot Proviso.

Railroad politics was the genesis of the Kansas-Nebraska Act of 1854. The principal protagonist was Stephen A. Douglas, senator from Illinois. Douglas wanted Congress to grant land from the public domain to build a transcontinental railroad with its eastern terminus in Chicago. He hoped to duplicate his success in getting the national government to grant land, similar to the grant that helped construct the Illinois Central Railroad. Douglas had a serious problem because St. Louis, Memphis, and New Orleans also wanted to be the eastern terminus for a transcontinental railroad.

The first step in building a transcontinental railroad with Chicago as its eastern terminus was encouraging settlement in Nebraska Territory. Nebraska Territory, however, would not attract settlers until it had a government that could record land titles. Furthermore, under the policy of state control of economic development, there had to be a state government to receive a land grant from the national government in order to convey it to a railroad corporation. This was how the Illinois Central Railroad received its land grant. Congressmen from slave labor states would not vote for a territorial government for Nebraska because it was north of latitude 36:30. By terms of the Missouri Compromise, Nebraska Territory would be a free labor territory and become a free labor state.

Establishing a territorial government for Nebraska required the support of congressmen from southern states. The only way to get their support was to repeal the 36:30 provision in the Missouri Compromise and open Nebraska to settlement by slave owners. Douglas knew that opening Nebraska to slavery would have explosive political consequences in northern states. Nonetheless, he supported repeal. In an attempt to soften its effect, Nebraska was divided into two territories: Kansas and Nebraska. It was assumed that Nebraska would be settled by northern farmers migrating from Iowa and that Kansas would be settled by slaveowners migrating from Missouri because Kansas was directly west of Missouri.

After three months of virulent controversy, the 36:30 provision of the Missouri Compromise was repealed and the Kansas-Nebraska Act (1854) established territorial governments for Kansas and Nebraska. It was immediately clear to a large segment of the northern population that only a new political party could prevent the expansion of slave labor onto vacant land. By the nature of the issue, the new political party would be a wholly northern party. Settlers immediately began arriving in Kansas in order to capture control of the territorial government. They would decide for themselves (popular sovereignty) whether they wanted slavery or reject it.

Missouri slaveowners migrated across the border and northern farmers settled in the interior. Northern farmers were permanent settlers compared to the temporary residence of most migrants from Missouri. Missouri migrants did not bring slaves with them because they would be in continual jeopardy. They did, however, bring their rifles and a mini civil war began. (Bleeding Kansas).

The passage of the Kansas-Nebraska Act triggered the spontaneous organization of the Republican Party in a number of northern states. These parties coalesced into a northern party in 1856—in time to nominate a candidate for the presidency. The principal reason for organizing the party was to use the power of the national government to exclude slavery from vacant land, but its appeal was broadened by advocating construction of infrastructure projects at national expense that were beneficial for a commercial democracy. The Republican candidate was defeated; however, the Dred Scott decision by the Supreme Court (1857) hardened public opinion in northern states against attempts by southern political leaders to create more slave states.

The Dred Scott decision validated the claim of southern agrarians that only whites could be national citizens and that Congress had exceeded its authority in 1820 when it prohibited slavery in territory north of 36:30. The Supreme Court went out of its way to declare unconstitutional a statute that was repealed in 1854 by the Kansas-Nebraska Act. The decision denied Congress the power to exclude slavery from territories—the principal reason for the Republican Party's existence.

Election of Lincoln

The election of Abraham Lincoln as president in 1860 broke a deadlock. The Republican Party was a wholly northern party that was committed to using the power of the national government to prevent the expansion of slavery and accelerate the creation of all forms of wealth, especially wealth concentrated in cities. Investments in factories would be encouraged by a protective tariff and the national government would subsidize the construction of a transcontinental railroad by land grants and other forms of funding backed by the credit of the national government.

Two policy statements dealt with land and labor. A Republican controlled Congress would pass a statute that excluded slavery from all territories. The Dred Scott decision would be ignored. The second policy would encourage northern farmers to migrate to western territories by giving them free land in the public domain (Homestead Act). The land and labor policies advocated by the Republican Party defined the fundamental issue of the nation's future.

Would the nation be governed in the interests of a democracy that performed commercial labor norms? Or would governance protect the interests of large landowners who coerced commercial labor norms from slaves and protected the subsistence labor norms of white peasants? If the principal purpose of governance was to encourage the performance of commercial labor norms of landowning farmers and urban paid laborers, then the production of new wealth had infinite possibilities. If the principal purposes of governance were to protect slave labor agriculture and the subsistence labor norms of white peasants, the production of new wealth would be seriously constrained.

In 1860 a high percentage of the northern electorate believed that excluding slavery from the territories was the first step in abolishing slavery. At the Democratic Party's nominating convention in 1860, northern Democratic leaders emphatically rejected the demand made by southern Democratic leaders that they support a congressional statute for a slave code to operate in organized territories. Southern political leaders claimed that such a statute was the logical extension of the Dred Scott decision. Northern Democrats could not consent to using the power of the national government to actively encourage the establishment of slave labor agriculture on vacant land, even when they were indifferent to its operation in slave states.

The Democratic Party split. The northern half of the Democratic Party nominated its candidate and the southern half nominated its candidate. The election of Lincoln was assured. During the election campaign, Lincoln gave a clear warning that if slave states attempted to secede, force would be used to preserve national unity. Lincoln fully agreed with the party's campaign promise "The union must and will be preserved."

Lincoln saw more clearly than most of his contemporaries that national unity had to be preserved for a more universal reason. In 1860, the United States was the world's only democratic republic and the stability of this new form of government was on trial before the world. *Were democratic republics inherently unstable? Or could democratic republics provide the political stability required for nations undergoing the social stresses of industrialization?* Lincoln believed that a democratic republic was the best government for nations that actively undertook the transforming experience of industrialization, and that the United States was the test case for the rest of the world.

After Lincoln's election in November 1860, eleven slave labor states opted for war in April 1861 in order to establish a slave labor republic.

Chapter 9

Civil War

Prior to Lincoln's inauguration as president, both sides were uncertain of what would happen after the slave states confederated into a rival nation. Some northerners believed that the best policy was not to contest secession. Many southerners believed that if Lincoln decided to contest secession, the war would be short because of the enthusiasm of white peasants to fight to preserve their superior racial status.

When Lincoln contested secession, he had to convey a clear message of why the war was being fought. He did. Volunteer soldiers were fighting to preserve national unity. In addition, a high percentage of volunteers in the U.S. Army explicitly understood that the source of southern hostility to the United States government was a commitment to preserve slave labor agriculture at all costs.

Both the white peasantry and governing elites of slave states saw emancipation over the horizon and could not conceive that emancipated slaves could become constituent members of American culture. A higher percentage of white men in slave states enlisted in the Confederate Army than men in northern states enlisted in the U.S. Army. The Civil War was a democratic and popular war. Almost all of the soldiers in both armies were volunteers. The U.S. Army had 1.55 million three year enlistments and the Armies of the Confederacy had 1.08 million.

Volunteers knew exactly why they enlisted. White peasants understood that emancipation would lower their political and social status. Being white would no longer guarantee participation in government, and landless, illiterate, white peasants would have to compete with emancipated, landless, illiterate, black peasants for land use. The commitment of white peasants to preserve slavery was the reason the war lasted four years and was not over until the armies of the confederated slave states were defeated in the field.

Northern men enlisted for a different purpose. The clearest expression of the purpose of the war was President Lincoln's Gettysburg Address delivered on the battlefield in November 1863: "these dead shall not have died in vain—that this nation under God shall have a new birth of freedom." The new birth would be a national republic that was "a government of the people, by the people, for the people." There was no mention of the union, nor of racial limitations on freedom. The weak states' right union that made it possible for slave states to organize a civil war would be replaced by a strong national government so that there would never be another civil war.

Nationalizing Process

During the last months of President James Buchanan's administration, the Republican Party gained control of both houses of congress because congressmen from slave states withdrew after their states seceded. By mid-January 1861, the Republicans had a majority in both houses and they began passing legislation that had been frozen because of opposition by congressmen from slave states. In January 1861, Kansas was admitted as a free labor state and Colorado, Nevada, and Dakota were provided with organized territorial governments. President Buchanan signed these statutes into law during his last month in office. Slavery was not explicitly excluded from these territories because the incoming Lincoln administration would prevent temporary sojourners from establishing governments that protected slavery.

From the moment the war began, the clear intent of the Lincoln administration was to use the exigencies of war to nationalize political institutions and policies of economic development. In the process, as circumstances permitted, the powers of state governments would be diminished and slavery abolished. The two immediate necessities were finding ways to finance the war and mobilize the manpower to prosecute it. All other congressional legislation was subordinate. Nonetheless, during the course of the war, Congress found time to enact nationalizing legislation that reduced the power of state governments in the North and would subordinate them after the war was won.

The following is a list of the principal nationalizing statutes passed by Congress during the Civil War (1861–1865):

1. protective tariff (Morrill Tariff), March 1861;
2. national management of railroads for military purposes when required, February 1862;
3. Legal Tender Act to provide a national currency (greenbacks), February 1862;
4. abolition of slavery in the District of Columbia, April 1862;
5. giving land in the national public domain to actual settlers (Homestead Act), May 1862;
6. abolition of slavery in all territories, June 1862;
7. subsidize building a transcontinental railroad (Pacific Railway Act), July 1862;
8. land grants to states to encourage the establishment of colleges to teach engineering, agricultural technology, and train reserve army officers (Morrill Act), July 1862;
9. recruitment of black soldiers (Militia Act), July 1862;
10. establishing a national banking system (National Banking Act), February 1863 and June 1864;
11. making all men from twenty to forty years of age liable for military service (Conscription Act), March 1863;
12. equal pay for black soldiers, June 1864;
13. subsidizing the building of a second transcontinental railroad (Northern Pacific), July 1864;
14. 2 percent tax on currency issued by state banks, October 1864;
15. thirteenth amendment to the constitution abolishing slavery, so that it could be sent to state legislatures for ratification, January 1865;
16. 10 percent tax on banknotes issued by state banks in order to end their circulation and have a uniform national currency, March 1865;
17. army officers authorized to supervise labor contracts between landowners and emancipated slaves, (Freedmens Bureau), March, 1865.

The remainder of this chapter will focus on taxation and credit creation because they were key policies for prosecuting the war and nationalizing economic development after the war.

Taxation

The protective tariff of March 1861 (Morrill Tariff) was not a tax for revenue because revenue immediately declined when maximum revenue was needed. It fulfilled a commitment of the Republican Party to encourage American manufacturers to produce a higher percentage of products consumed by Americans, particularly products made from iron.

The first two wartime taxes were on incomes and consumer products. The income tax became law in August 1861, but income from interest on U.S. bonds was exempt from state and municipal taxation in order to stimulate sales. The law levied a 3 percent tax on portions of incomes above eight hundred dollars. It was increased in 1862 and 1865 and slightly graduated. Incomes between six hundred dollars and five thousand dollars paid 5 percent, and incomes greater than five thousand dollars paid 10 percent.

The administration and collection of internal taxes was assigned to the Commission of Internal Revenue, but collection was deficient because of extensive evasion and an inadequate bureaucracy. Recruiting and training a bureaucracy was a slow process. Not until 1864, did excise taxes yield enough revenue to pay about 25 percent of current expenditures. During the war, collection of income taxes was below expectations. After the war the tax made a major contribution to national revenue, especially after corporate presidents and elected officials of state and local governments were directed to withhold the tax from the salaries of managers and employees. The law was repealed in 1872.

The secretary of the treasury recommended increased tariffs on consumer products not produced in the United States. Among them were coffee, tea, sugar, rubber, silk, and brandy. These taxes were not for protection. They were for revenue, but the revenue they yielded was totally inadequate for the exigencies of war because the secretary of the treasury believed that new taxation should be limited to the amount needed to pay interest on new bonded indebtedness. He believed that borrowing should finance the war.

Congress had more faith than the secretary of the treasury in the willingness of the northern democracy to be taxed. In July 1862 excise taxes were levied on liquor, beer, tobacco products, bank capital, bank deposits, and corporation dividends. Stamp taxes were levied on the sale of stocks and bonds, bills of lading, insurance policies, bills of exchange, telegrams, and many other varieties of commercial paper and legal documents.

Manufactured products were taxed at 3 percent of their value and the gross receipts of railroad corporations, ferryboat franchises, toll bridge franchises, and steamboat companies were taxed at rates varying from 1.5 to 3.0 percent. The tax on manufactured products was collected at the place of manufacture, and was the largest single source of excise revenue. In 1863, 1864, and 1865 rates were raised and new products and services taxed. In addition, inheritances of liquid assets greater than one thousand dollars were taxed at 0.75 to 5 percent but inherited real property was not taxed.

The principal manufacturing industries that paid taxes were textiles, leather products, paper, soap, sugar refineries, iron products, coal mines, and oil refineries. These taxes were on products consumed by the northern democracy, and many of them had been previously taxed by state legislatures. Most rates were low and calculated to yield maximum revenue. All taxes levied by Congress had to be paid with national currency issued by the Treasury Department (greenbacks, treasury notes, certificates of indebtedness). Both businessmen and the general public were being trained to use a national currency and experience its commercial advantages.

Bonded Indebtedness

During the four years of war, neither Congress nor U.S. bankers attempted to sell bonds to European investors. Funding the cost of the war depended entirely on tax revenues and credit mobilized in the United States.

The first order of business in the special session of Congress (July 1, 1861) was to increase national revenue; and the principal means of doing this was selling war bonds. Taxes passed at this time were supplemental. Sixteen days after it met, Congress authorized the sale of 250 million dollars of bonds with a complex mixture of interest rates and maturity dates. The largest part of the bonds carried 7.3 percent interest and matured in twenty years with interest paid in gold coins. Immediate expenses would be paid with money obtained by selling one-year treasury notes paying 3.65 percent interest, with the option of being converted into twenty-year bonds with 7.3 percent interest.

A month after its passage, the secretary of the treasury realized the amount was entirely inadequate to fund the rapid military build-up that was recognized as essential for prosecuting the war. Congress approved an additional 150 million dollars of bonds at 7.3 percent with a three-year maturity date. From the moment of its passage, this amount was inadequate for funding military operations. The secretary of the treasury was forced to issue 33 million in demand notes. Demand notes meant they could be redeemed for gold coins on demand. They were, in fact, legal tender currency that paid interest.

In December, in order to conserve its gold coins and pay interest on U.S. bonds, the secretary of the treasury and the principal banks suspended specie redemption of banknote currency. From this date, revenues and expenditures were entirely in paper. This simplified revenue collection and expenditures, provided there was a long-term financial plan—but there was no plan.

Until there was a plan, finances were sustained by temporary expedients and legal tender currency (greenbacks) issued in February 1862, June 1862, and March 1863. The usual expedients were treasury notes and certificates of indebtedness with maturity dates of one, two, or three years with 6 percent compound interest. Not until mid-1863 were finances put on a predictable basis.

Congress authorized the issuance of all bonds requested by the secretary of the treasury, but the bonds had to be marketed. Bankers did their share but they did not have the ability to democratize sales. This was done by Jay Cooke, a Philadelphia banker who sold bonds like merchants sold manufactured products. He hired 2,500 agents and advertised that it was the patriotic duty for all households to purchase at least one bond. Bonds were sold across the counter of village stores in denominations as small as fifty dollars. His tactic was highly successful.

By July 1863 increased tax collection and bond sales relieved financial pressure, and by October 1864 the national government's finances were on a firm foundation. Fiscal stability was achieved by increased bond sales by Jay Cooke and bonds purchased by banks chartered under the national banking act of February 1863. In 1863 Cooke sold 200 million dollars of three-year treasury notes that paid 7.3 percent interest. These notes were attractive investment because, after the defeat of confederate armies, they could be converted into twenty-year, 6 percent bonds, with interest paid in gold. Patriotic bond purchasers would be rewarded.

Banks and Currency

Preserving the agrarian bias of the national government had been a key policy of the political leaders of slave states. They had strongly supported retaining the independent treasury statute passed in 1846 because it forced the national government to conduct most of its business in cash. As long as the independent treasury operated, the finances of the national government were hand-to-hand, and the national government was correspondingly weak. Political leaders in slave-labor states were determined to keep the national government financially weak because it reduced the ability of the northern majority to abolish slavery.

During 1861, the secretary of the treasury managed to mobilize sufficient credit to fund the military build-up, but it required one financial expedient after another. By the end of the year, the Suffolk System in New England and the free banking system of New York were strained to their capacities to mobilize credit for war use, and banking elsewhere in the United States was a morass of inefficiency. More credit had to be generated elsewhere. Elsewhere was the Legal Tender Act passed by Congress in February 1862.

Legal tender currency (greenbacks) was printing press money. It was passed because the secretary of the treasury had failed to present Congress with a comprehensive program of taxation. Printing paper currency was the only way of obtaining the requisite money to finance military operations. The statute authorized the treasury department to emit 150 million dollars of greenbacks. Interest was not paid on them. They were money because the national government said they were money.

Greenbacks were lawful money for paying all public and private debts, except interest on U.S. bonds and the tariff. These two payments had to be made with gold coins or in treasury notes that could be redeemed for gold coins. Insufficient tax revenues and the slow sale of bonds forced the secretary of the treasury to ask Congress to authorize an additional 150 million dollars in June 1862. Necessity forced the printing of more greenbacks because tax revenues and bond sales were inadequate during the rest of 1862; and by December the treasury was having difficulties accumulating enough money to pay soldiers. The solution was the emission of an additional 150 million dollars of greenback currency in March 1863.

Greenbacks were inherently inflationary. During the war, the value of greenbacks continually declined relative to gold. In 1862, on average, it took 113 greenbacks to purchase 100 dollar of gold coins; in 1863, 145 greenbacks; in 1864, 203; and in 1865, 157. Six percent U.S. bonds purchased with greenbacks earned almost 9 percent interest in 1863, over 12 percent interest in 1864, and over 9 percent in 1865, if the gold coins received in interest were converted into greenbacks. Conversion was widely practiced because greenbacks became the usual money of commerce.

During 1863, the secretary of the treasury encouraged the conversion of short-term interest bearing treasury notes and certificates of indebtedness into long-term bonds because they frequently circulated as currency and, like greenbacks, they were a source of inflation. In addition, these short-term obligations had to be refinanced at their maturity dates and there was no way of predicting that this could be done without excessive interest rates. The best way to remove them from the money supply was to convert them into long-term bonds. At the same time, the national government gained some predictability in finance.

In his annual reports to Congress in December 1861 and 1862, the secretary of the treasury recommended the passage of a national banking statute based on New York's experience with free banks. The currency circulated by free banks in New York was uniform, numbered, and printed by the state. It was accepted by farmers and urban businessmen because it was backed by securities that had a market value.

The market value of bonds held by the New York state government to back the value of currency issued by free banks depended on state or municipal governments using their tax base to underwrite bonds to build infrastructure projects. If free banks purchased more bonds, they could increase banknote credit that could be extended to businessmen. New York's free banking system was a flexible and expansive system of credit creation. This was its attraction to the secretary of the treasury in 1861 and 1862. By January 1863 the secretary of the treasury was running out of options and Congress was receptive to a national banking system that would replace the financial expediencies that had, so far, financed the war.

The principal reason for creating a national banking system was to provide a market for U.S. bonds. The exigencies of war were the opportunity to nationalize credit creation and allocate a large part of it to the national government for military use. If the national banking system operated as intended, the banknote credit created by national banks would be directly tied to the credit needs of the national government. The secretary of the treasury estimated that the market for bonds needed to capitalize national banks would be 250 million dollars. Even a fraction of this amount in 1863 would make a substantial contribution to wartime expenditures.

There were four other reasons for creating a national banking system in 1863.

1. National banks would issue a uniform national currency that was instantly recognizable, had a known value, and was acceptable to northern agrarians. Endemic counterfeiting of banknotes issued by state banks generated strong popular support for a national banknote currency. In January 1862 there were 1,496 banks in northern states that issued 7,000 varieties of banknote currency.
2. National banks would be safe deposits for excise taxes. Collectors were very reluctant to deposit national revenue in state chartered banks in which the national government exercised little control. Funds deposited in national banks would be under national control.
3. National banks would be incorporated in states that had highly restrictive banking laws of agrarian origin. These states had a shortage of credit for businessmen. Ohio and Michigan (among many states) needed more banking facilities, but new banks were not forthcoming from state legislatures.
4. National banks would equalize opportunities for entrepreneurs to enter the banking business, especially to provide credit for small town businessmen.

Charters for national banks were for twenty years. They could be obtained by five or more businessmen in towns with population of less than six thousand if they invested fifty thousand dollars of acceptable securities, of which thirty thousand dollars had to be U.S. bonds. In towns with populations greater than six thousand but less than fifty thousand, the minimum capitalization was one hundred thousand dollars; and in cities with more than fifty thousand, the minimum capitalization was two hundred thousand. National banks were required to purchase U.S. bonds to the amount of one-third of their paid-in capital, but the minimum amount was thirty thousand dollars. These bonds had to be deposited with the comptroller of the currency and were collateral for the issuance of banknotes equal to 90 percent of their value. Banknotes issued by national banks were legal tender for all public and private debts, except payment of tariffs and interest on U.S. bonds. Like free banks in New York, stockholders had double liability.

National banks in seventeen designated cities had to keep currency reserves (greenbacks, treasury notes) equal to 25 percent of the value of their deposits to insure that deposits could be converted into cash on demand. Banks in medium-sized cities were also required to keep a 25 percent reserve but half could be deposited in New York City banks where it earned interest. The smallest banks in the smallest towns had to keep a currency reserve of 15 percent of deposits/banknotes, but 9 percent could be deposited one of the seventeen designated cities where it earned interest. Deposits made by national banks in the largest cities, and especially in New York City, concentrated credit available for military expenditures.

Finally, an attempt was made to induce state chartered banks to reincorporate as national banks by imposing a 2 percent tax on the banknote currency they issued. Reincorporation was slow. By October 1863, there were only sixty-six national banks. These banks had purchased less than four million dollars of U.S. bonds. A year later, there were 508 national banks that had purchased 108 million dollars of U.S. bonds.

Conversion of state banks to national banks was slow because most state governments placed fewer restraints on the credit practices of state chartered banks. National banks had more stringent restraints on credit practices. Not until Congress levied a 10 percent tax on banknotes issued by state banks (March 1865) did conversion accelerate. Between March and October 1865, the number of national banks increased to 1,513, and they purchased 171 million dollars of U.S. bonds. One year later there were 1,644 national banks that had purchased 280 million dollars of U.S. bonds.

When the last state banknotes were withdrawn from circulation in 1866, the United States had a national currency. It consisted of coins, greenbacks, and banknotes of national banks. In order to contain wartime inflation, Congress limited the amount of greenbacks that could be put into circulation to 300 million dollars. This was the estimated amount of currency needed to provide for normal business transactions.

Summary

The actual cost of the war is difficult to estimate but it was in excess of four billion dollars. Bonded indebtedness provided about 65 percent of the revenue, taxation about 20 percent, and greenbacks about 15 percent. In addition, there was fifty million dollars of fractional currency that was issued after inflation drove small coins from circulation; there were also large expenditures by state governments in 1861 and 1862 before Congress enacted sufficient loan and tax legislation to support a fully national army. State expenditures were in excess of one hundred ten million dollars but, until 1892, only forty-four million had been funded by the national government.

In the first year of the war, expenditures of the national government were more than seven times greater than annual prewar expenditures; and by 1865 they were twenty times greater. The amount of credit that was mobilized was directly related to very low ante-bellum taxation and the latent tax resources of the diversified economies of northern states. In August 1865, four months after the end of the war, the bonded indebtedness of the national government was 2.84 billion dollars. Annual interest obligations were 133 million dollars.

Interest payments dictated that congress continue many taxes until the war debt was funded into bonds with long maturity dates so that annual budgets could be made more predictable. Funding was accomplished within five years, and by 1872 most wartime excise taxes were repealed. Successful funding made U.S. government bonds attractive to European investors. By 1867 approximately 350 million dollars were owned in Europe.

The significance of the war debt is that it was created without excessive strain on political stability or excessive inflation. After the war Congress had to decide whether the national government should (1) revert to minimal governance and minimal taxation that had served the needs of the agricultural majority in the antebellum economy, or (2) retain the ability of the national government to create huge amounts of credit for allocation to businesses that would accelerate national economic development.

Chapter 10

Creating the National Market

The Civil War was the real American revolution. Slavery was ended, states rights were ended, and national unity preserved. The Thirteenth Amendment (1865) abolished slavery, the Fourteenth Amendment (1868) constitutionalized national political supremacy, and the Fifteenth Amendment (1870) was designed to create a national democratic electorate that included freedmen (emancipated slaves). After the three war amendments were ratified, states exercised only as much power as Congress assigned to them. These amendments assured creation of a national market that would not be impeded by states rights interests. The amendments were equally essential for the global greatness of the United States in the twentieth century.

Wartime legislation created a national currency and established a national banking system that exerted centralized control over credit creation and allocation. Wartime necessity also demonstrated that huge amounts of credit could be created from domestic sources. After the war these instruments were available for peacetime use. The Republican Party was determined to use them for two principal purposes: (1) maximize the creation of industrial wealth, and (2) settle a continent.

The measure of Republican determination to use national power to accelerate industrialization was congressional reaction to President Andrew Johnson's postwar program for restoring civil governments to ex-slave states after the end of hostilities. After Lincoln was assassinated in April 1865, he was succeeded by Vice President Andrew Johnson. Andrew Johnson was chosen the Republican Party's vice-presidential candidate in 1864 because he was a war Democrat. He had been U.S. senator from Tennessee and refused to support secession. He denounced the traitorous conduct of all state officials who supported secession. Lincoln appointed him war governor of Tennessee after the U.S. Army occupied most of the state. He served with great bravery in a very dangerous situation.

After hostilities ceased, Johnson used none of the executive power (war power) used by Lincoln to conduct the war. Congress approved using these powers to elect manageable governments in ex-slave states. Instead, Johnson believed that the end of hostilities automatically constituted peace. Based on this assumption, he allowed the prewar electorate (that had actively waged war against the United States to the point of exhaustion) to elect wartime leaders to local and state offices, and to Congress. Six months after hostilities ceased, the civil governments of ex-slave states were controlled by pardoned traitors. Johnson allowed this to happen because he was an agrarian Democrat who wanted to restore the states right republic as it existed before the war, but without slavery.

Johnson's program for restoring civil governments in ex-slave labor states was unacceptable to Congress. In the first session of Congress after the end of hostilities (December 1865), none of the men elected to Congress from ex-slave states were seated. In the congressional elections of 1866 Republicans gained overwhelming control of both houses of Congress. They proceeded to replace the civil governments that had been organized under presidential authority and had governed for over a year. The First Reconstruction Act (March 1867) declared that no legal governments existed in ten ex-slave states. Tennessee was excepted.

These states were divided into five military districts, each commanded by a general. Army officers were instructed to organize constitutional conventions. Delegates were to be elected by a new electorate consisting of freedmen who were specifically enfranchised, and whites who had not participated in the war. All whites who held office in the wartime governments of ex-slave states or had served in the armies of the confederated slave states were disfranchised. Voting by freedmen was supervised by officers in the army of occupation, and by army officers who staffed the Freedmens Bureau.

State constitutions framed by these conventions had to enfranchise freedmen and disfranchise persons who had participated in the war. One more step was required. State legislatures had to ratify the Fourteenth Amendment. Only after ratification would representatives and senators from ex-slave states be admitted to Congress.

The Republican Party intended to retain control of the national government for the foreseeable future. The political power that was poured into ex-slave states by the congressional program of reconstruction would be managed from Washington. It would be used to preserve the policies of economic development that were enacted into law during the war. Even if Republicans lost control of several northern states where they had tenuous majorities, their policies of economic development would be protected from serious modification or repeal by managing the new electorates they installed in ex-slave states.

The foreseeable future ended in 1877 when white southern political leaders gained full control of the governments of ex-slave states. Northern support for the Republican Party had slowly ebbed after 1870 because of corruption in the national government that was amplified by corruption in the governance of ex-slave states, where too many incompetent and opportunistic men were elected to public office. The depression of 1873 further disillusioned the northern electorate. Republicans lost control of the House of Representatives in 1874. Agrarian discontent was also increasing in northern states, particularly in the trans-Mississippi west. A northern agricultural party (the Greenback Party) ran a presidential candidate in 1876. Agrarian opposition to Republican policies of economic development will be described and analyzed in the next chapter.

The persistence of the depression into 1876 was ominous. Democratic control of Congress and the presidency would mean that Congress could substantially modify or repeal Republican policies of economic development, and a Democratic president would sign them into law. Above all else, the Republican Party had to retain the presidency. If a Democratic congress passed adverse legislation, the president could veto it and Republican policies of economic development would continue to operate.

Republican Party leaders knew that the presidential election of 1876 would be close. It was closer than predicted. It appeared the Democratic presidential candidate won, but Republican Party leaders salvaged the presidency by making a deal with some southern Democratic congressmen. These congressmen would consent to counting electoral votes the way Republicans wanted them counted because they supported Republican policies of national economic development, provided ex-slave states got their share of subsidies for internal improvement projects.

In return for a favorable vote, a Republican president would (1) withdraw the army of occupation, (2) silently consent to disfranchising the black electorate, (3) Republican congressmen would vote for a land grant to build a transcontinental railroad with a southern terminus, (4) Republican congressmen would vote to increase appropriations to build other infrastructure projects in capital starved southern states, and (5) the Republican president would allocate large numbers of patronage jobs to cooperating southern Democrats. The Republican presidential candidate was elected by one electoral vote.

The southern Democratic congressmen who consented to the election of a Republican president were called redeemers because they negotiated an end to national management of elections in ex-slave states. The Democratic governors who succeeded Republican governors were in no hurry to disfranchise the black electorate. They voted Republican, and rapid disfranchisement would irritate the northern Republican electorate. Redeemers had a more important target. They wanted to control the Democratic parties in their states. Their leadership was acceptable to white peasants because they would enforce white supremacy in social relations. The policies of white supremacy and eventual disfranchisement would keep the Democratic Party in office in ex-slave states for the foreseeable future.

Implementing Republication Development Policies

Three principal policies shaped industrialization after 1865: (1) railroads, (2) tariffs, (3) currency.

Railroads were expensive to build, and when they were built ahead of demand (transcontinental railroads) they required very large subsidies from the national government. Furthermore, most railroads in ex-slave states were partially destroyed by warfare and everywhere maintenance was neglected. Huge investments were required to restore service and expand the network.

Tariffs meant protective tariffs. Protective tariffs were designed to help the urban-industrial sector of the economy by insuring high profit margins and high rates of capital accumulation for manufacturers of products consumed in the agricultural sector of the economy.

Currency policies are best understood as a contest between inflationary and deflationary policies. Inflation helped the agricultural sector and deflation helped the urban-industrial sector of the economy.

In the following sections, the reader must remember that rural residents were a majority of the population until 1915. There were, however, two statistics that qualified demographic numbers: (1) a high percentage of the population of ex-slave states were peasants who were economically inert, and (2) urban wealth surpassed rural wealth by about 1875 and, thereafter, increased at an extremely rapid rate compared to agricultural wealth. A high percent of new wealth was industrial and was highly concentrated in northern cities.

From 1865 onward, an increasing percentage of the food crops grown in the United States were consumed in U.S. cities. The agricultural and urban/industrial sectors were increasingly integrated by inter-regional trunkline railroads and their branches. The 50,000 kilometers of railroads in the United States in 1861 became 305,000 kilometers in 1900. Between 1865 and 1900 a national railroad network was built. The rapid construction of trunkline railroads after the Civil War and their integration into regional and inter-regional systems was the principal reason that a national market of continental dimensions was a reality by 1895. In other words, the completion of the national railroad network coincided with the creation of the national market.

The creation of a national market for almost all products and services was the great accomplishment of the Republican program of economic development. In all elections after the

Civil War, the principal purposes of Republican Party governance were preserving policies that encouraged the creation of the national market and production of industrial wealth.

The principal constituency of the Democratic Party was agricultural, and they wanted only as much government subsidies for economic development as would serve agrarian needs. Preferably, these subsidies would be supplied by state and local governments where there were better restraints on speculation and fraud. The urban constituency of the Democratic Party did not oppose rapid industrialization, but they were ambivalent about using all the power available to the national government to promote the production of new wealth.

Railroads

The precursor of the national market was the completion of a national telegraph network in states east of the Missouri River prior to the Civil War. Its principal business was transmitting commodity prices and other business information to newspapers, and dispatching railroad trains. A transcontinental line was completed in October 1861.

Railroads, however, made the national market a reality. The most dramatic project was building the first transcontinental railroad. Congress passed the Pacific Railway Act in 1862, but little work was done until after the war. Subsidizing its construction was a political decision designed to nationalize new states in the trans-Missouri west. Some historians have estimated that it was built ten years ahead of demand; however, its early completion created a demand for services that were not fully anticipated.

By statute law (January 1863), Congress mandated that transcontinental railroads use standard gauge. This was the gauge of a high percentage of railroads north of the Ohio and Potomac rivers, and this would mean that trans-Missouri traffic could move eastward with minimal transshipment costs. In effect, mandating standard gauge for transcontinental railroads was a mandate for all railroads in the United States change to standard gauge. A uniform gauge was fundamental to creating a national market.

The first transcontinental railroad was built in two parts. The Union Pacific built westward from Omaha, Nebraska and the Central Pacific eastward from Sacramento, California. The two roads would meet at an indefinite location. Construction began in the summer of 1865 and the two roads joined in May 1869 in northern Utah territory. The principal source of labor for building westward was demobilized veterans of the U.S. Army and Irish immigrants. The principal source of manpower for eastward construction was Chinese immigrants.

Both roads received very large land grants and equally large money subsidies. Land grants were alternate sections of land for ten miles on either side of the roads. Each completed mile was a claim to ten square miles of land (25,900 hectares); therefore, speed of construction was the first priority. The land would be sold as soon as possible and the funds used for construction or to upgrade the initial right-of-way. Together, the Union Pacific and Central Pacific were granted 9.7 million hectares (24 million acres).

Much of the initial construction was flagrantly substandard. Upgrading meant reballasting rights-of-way that had been built on sand, replacing wooden bridges with steel bridges, reducing or eliminating curves, building higher landfills across valleys or deepening cuts through hills in order to reduce grades, increasing the number of sidings, building snow sheds over the right-of-way in the Sierra mountains in order to maintain winter service, and exploring for coals deposits in order to have local sources of fuel.

The money that funded actual construction came from thirty-year United States bonds with 6 percent interest. Subsidies varied with the terrain. Construction of the right-of-way on prairies was subsidized at the rate of sixteen thousand dollars per mile, thirty-two thousand

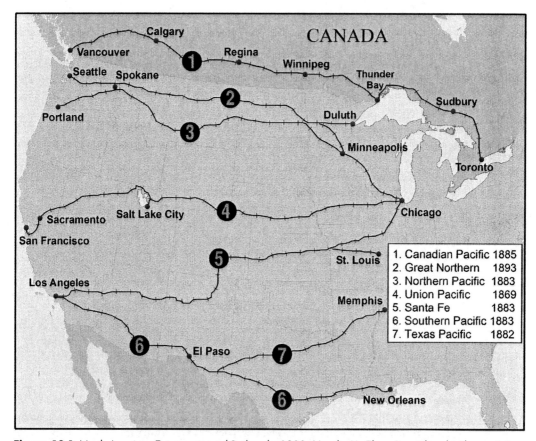

Figure 10.1 North American Transcontinental Railroads, 1900. Map by Yo Zhou. Reproduced with permission.

dollars per mile on intermountain plateaus, and forty-eight thousand dollars per mile over mountains or to bore tunnels through them. Money was not transferred to the railroads until a government inspector certified that 20 miles (32 kilometers) of rails could support commercial traffic. The Union Pacific received 27.2 million dollars of money subsidies and the Central Pacific 25.8 million.

Three additional transcontinental railroads received land grants: Northern Pacific, Atlantic and Pacific, and Texas Pacific. Construction of the Northern Pacific began in 1870. Its eastern terminus was Minneapolis, Minnesota and its western terminus was Seattle, Washington. It received a grant of alternate sections of land for 20 miles on either side of its right-of-way, but received no money subsidy. It was granted 15.8 million hectares (39 million acres) of land. Funds for construction came from bonds backed by a first mortgage on land grants.

Construction began in 1870, but bankruptcy stopped construction in the middle of the Dakota Territory in 1873. Reorganization and profits allowed westward construction to resume in 1878, but not until 1880 was the road sufficiently profitable to attract forty million dollars of bonded indebtedness needed to complete the road to the Pacific Coast. Construction was from both ends. Mainly Chinese laborers built eastward and largely immigrant laborers built westward through the Dakota Territory. Rails were joined at Helena in the Montana territory in 1883.

The third transcontinental railroad to receive land grants was the Atlantic and Pacific. It became bankrupt during the 1873 depression and was acquired by the Santa Fe Railroad, which was building west from Kansas City, Missouri. It was completed in Los Angles, California in 1883. The fourth transcontinental railroad to receive land grants was the Texas Pacific with eastern terminuses in Dallas, Texas and New Orleans, Louisiana. It received its land grant in 1871 but became bankrupt in the panic of 1873. It never built its right-of-way outside of Texas and never claimed its land grant. Its route was completed by the Southern Pacific Railroad building eastward from Los Angles without benefit of a land grant or money subsidy from the national government. The juncture took place east of El Paso, Texas in 1882.

Altogether, the national government granted 53 million hectares of land (131 million acres) from the public domain to subsidize railroad construction. Almost 90 percent was west of the Mississippi River. Sale of railroad land did not take place until it was surveyed. Most sales were delayed, often for many years, although all land grant railroads wanted to sell land as quickly as possible in order to have people producing commodities that would use rail services.

The fifth United States transcontinental railroad was the Great Northern. It was built westward from Grand Forks, Dakota Territory without a land grant or money subsidy from the national government. Construction began in 1884 and it entered Seattle in 1893. A sixth transcontinental railroad, the Canadian Pacific, was built just north of the United States–Canadian border. It received large subsidies from the Canadian government and reached the uninhabited site of Vancouver, British Columbia in 1885.

The principal beneficiaries of the standard gauge east–west trunkline railroads were the eastern seaboard cities north of the Potomac. Much of the export commodities produced in the trans-Mississippi west could move to East Coast port cities without transshipment, instead of going down the Missouri and Mississippi rivers to New Orleans. A similar diversion of traffic originating in Illinois, Indiana, and Ohio had taken place during the late 1850s.

By 1880, 80 percent of U.S. railroads had standard gauge because many southern railroads were changed to standard gauge after the war, when they came under control of northern businessmen who supplied funds to rebuild and reequip them. Half of the remainder had a gauge of 4 feet 9 inches, which for all practical purposes did not hinder traffic interchange with standard gauge railroads. The remaining 10 percent was 5 foot gauge, almost all of which was in southern states.

Several technologies were used to make interchanges of rolling stock on railroads with different gauges. Many railroads equipped their rolling stock with compromise wheels. They had rolling surfaces 12 centimeters wide (5 inches) so they could operate on standard gauge tracks and 4 foot 10 inch tracks. Three other technologies made it possible to interchange with 5 foot, 5 foot 10 inch, and 6 foot gauges: (1) axels were designed to have wheels slide on them to fit several gauges, (2) hoists lifted box cars and passenger cars off of their wheels and rolled wheels of a different gauge under them, (3) laying a third rail so that cars with different gauges could operate on the same roadbed. Laying a third rail was usually preliminary to changing to standard gauge.

In February 1886 representatives of railroads with 5 foot gauges met in Atlanta and made plans to change to standard gauge. The change was made in June 1886. After the change, the national market was a reality.

Other physical improvements maximized efficiency. Principal among them were replacement of iron rails by steel rails. Steel rails were heavier and stronger and could support heavier locomotives and freight cars. Coal replaced wood as fuel for locomotives. Coal burning locomotives equipped with steel fireboxes and steel boiler tubes were much more powerful because they produced higher steam temperatures and pressures. They could pull more freight cars of larger capacity. Other physical improvements were double tracking, terminal yards, standardized couplings, standardized brakes, bridges across major rivers, replacement of wooden truss bridges with steel truss bridges, cross-town linkages, and belt railways around major inland cities to facilitate through traffic.

Four operating procedures enhanced efficiency:

1. Fast freight companies moved through traffic on the rails of several railroads to reach a final destination. Ownership of freight cars by fast freight companies relieved railroads of some of the capital expenses of replacing obsolete rolling stock at a time when profits were needed to replace iron rails with steel rails and purchase more powerful locomotives.
2. Bills of lading routed products to their final destinations. Revenues were shared with participating roads. Similar ticketing speeded passengers to their destinations without changes of cars when traveling on the tracks of several railroads.
3. A national pool of freight cars assured that cars would be available when traffic was offered. Owners of cars received daily rent when they were not on the owner's tracks.
4. Time zones, adopted in 1883, improved the scheduling of freight trains and assured compatible arrival and departure times at interchanges, especially for passenger trains.

The political dimensions that accompanied the creation of the national railroad network were (1) building inter-regional systems;, (2) destructive competition, (3) rate pools, (4) agrarian discontent with rate structures for agricultural commodities, (5) frequent bankruptcies, (6) regulation by the national government.

System Building

The purpose of building systems was to create profitable rate structures. Profitable rate structures were best maintained by reducing or eliminating competition within a railroad's territory. In an era when general incorporation statutes for railroads encouraged maximum construction, regional systems were always threatened by speculative promoters assembling shortlines into new trunklines to compete in territories already served by established trunklines.

The first systems were assembled in the late 1850s. The nucleus of a system was a trunkline that served the businessmen in one terminal city, usually a seaport or river port. They became inter-regional by alliances with railroads that connected interior cities, usually in other states. After 1865 railroad managers wanted to convert alliances into a corporation under one management. This was done by mergers, purchasing a controlling interest, or negotiating leases of franchises. They also wanted to enter two or more terminal cities in search of additional traffic. After a terminal city had competitive freight rates from two or more trunklines (for delivering agricultural commodities and distributing manufactured products), businessmen in these cities could choose competitive rates if services were complementary.

By 1880 speculative construction of trunkline railroads was a serious problem east of the Mississippi because it weakened the financial structures of existing trunkline railroads. Between 1882 and 1886, 43,000 kilometers (27,000 miles) of new railroads were built without a corresponding increase in traffic. Average freight rates declined by 20 percent.

In 1885 there were three trunkline railroads that served Chicago: the Pennsylvania, New York Central, and Baltimore and Ohio. These railroads were solidly built. Two more were in process of assembly. Five trunkline railroads would create an environment for destructive competition. Promoters/speculators were assembling the two new roads from shortlines that they linked together by building additional shortlines. Their purpose was to force established trunkline systems to purchase them at inflated prices. Managers of existing trunklines strongly resisted pressures to purchase them because resultant over-capitalization would increase vulnerability to bankruptcy during declines in business activity.

Management

After 1850 most new railroad construction was financed by bonded indebtedness. After the Civil War this was practically the only way new railroads were built. The greatly enlarged bond market that had mobilized funds to prosecute the war was available to fund construction of a national rail network and provide working capital for new and enlarged factories. Even with a greatly expanded capital market, building the American railroad network in the 35 years between 1865 and 1900 required a huge infusion of European capital. Most of it was British, and like British railroad investments in the 1850s, most of it was invested in trunklines.

The two great attractions of American railroad bonds were high interest rates and discounted prices at initial offering. In 1898 British investors owned about 1.7 billion dollars of U.S. stocks and bonds. Other European investors probably owned an additional 400 million. These investments were portfolio investments that European banks held for their clients. European bankers were not active participants in management but many placed a watchdog person on the board of directors.

The bonds that financed construction of the first transcontinental railroad were sold at full face value because they were underwritten by the national government. Many of the other trunkline railroads built after 1865 were speculative to a greater or lesser degree. In order to attract purchasers, a one thousand dollar bond bearing 7 percent interest was sold for eight hundred or nine hundred dollars. As a further inducement to purchasers, five or ten shares of stock accompanied the sale of each one thousand dollar bond. Interest payments would be on the full face value of the bond. Seven percent bonds that were sold for nine hundred dollars had a real interest rate of 7.75 percent; if sold for eight hundred dollars, the real interest rate was 8.75 percent. Discounting the sale of construction bonds seriously inflated capital costs.

Between 1865 and 1900, 254,000 kilometers (158,000 miles) of railroads were built. In 1890 a high percentage of these roads had fragile capital structures due to (1) selling discounted construction bonds, (2) inadequate traffic, (3) destructive competition. Destructive competition had many forms: discounting published rates, assigning lower categories to freight, rebates to preferred customers, special contracts for large customers, and drawbacks where favored customers were given a percentage of the rate charged to competitors.

Several devices were tried to end destructive competition. The most common was pools. Pools were agreements among competing railroads to charge the same rates for the same classes of commodities and products going to the same destinations. There were variants: some pools divided the available traffic by assigning percentages to participating roads, others shared revenue regardless of the railroad that carried the product.

The first pool was organized in Iowa in 1870 to share agricultural commodities traffic going to Chicago. By 1874 it had failed. In 1875, thirty-two southern railroads formed a pool that was successful until 1886. Its success was due to the financial weaknesses of most southern railroads. No southern railroad had sufficient revenue to encroach on the territories of neighboring railroads without jeopardizing their own fragile capital structures.

The first pool east of the Mississippi River and north of the Ohio River was organized in 1874 by the president of the New York Central Railroad. Its purpose was to prevent further declines in freight rates during the depression that began in 1873. Within six months it failed because freight agents of the New York Central and Pennsylvania railroads continued to give rebates to preferred customers. Although railroad presidents could not agree to end destructive competition, they did agree to reduce costs by reducing wages by 10 percent.

The explosive reaction was unanticipated. In July 1877 there was a general strike of the employees of the affected railroads. The intensity of resentment ignited riots in which large amounts of railroad property were destroyed, especially rolling stock. Railroad presidents made two responses (1) a call for the protection of railroad property by a reorganized national guard to replace inept state militias, and (2) organization of another pool. It lasted two months.

The return of prosperity in 1879 initiated a rate war between major trunkline systems serving New York City, Philadelphia, and Baltimore. In 1881 the New York Central slashed rates on most commodities and products by 50 percent to retain its traffic from encroachment by the Pennsylvania and Baltimore and Ohio railroads. Freight rates in eastern states declined 50 percent between 1882 and 1886.

An increasing percentage of pools organized after 1879 had their principal application to intercity traffic. Rate competition increasingly originated in cities because multiple entries of trunkline systems gave merchants and factory owners a choice of carriers for their products. These pools indicated that increasing percentages of railroad revenues came from intercity freight traffic of manufactured products.

After 1880 the national market began a rapid evolution into the national urban market. In 1880 28 percent of the U.S. population was urban (living in villages and cities with populations of at least 2,500 people). By 1890 40 percent of the U.S. population was urban and in 1915 urban residents became a majority of the population. Seen from another perspective, railroads that had been built to serve agrarian interests and were paid for by transporting agricultural commodities increasingly began to serve urban industrial interests.

Regulation

Agrarian discontent, the Great Strike of 1877, and the inability of railroad managers to prevent destructive competition was a shout into the ears of railroad managers for rules governing rate structures. Railroads needed protection. Protection had to come from the national government because many state legislatures were controlled by agrarians who wanted freight rates for agricultural commodities comparable to freight rates for manufactured products moving between cities. "The lines of railways are no longer to be considered merely state organizations, and under state control, but national in their character."[1]

The completion of the national railroad network by 1900 was a spectacular achievement, but it lacked a solid financial foundation. The two principal weaknesses were overcapitalization and mismanagement by promoter/speculators. Little could be done to stop building speculative railroads as long as: (1) urban businessmen opposed any form of national regulation that would end competitive freight rates, (2) general incorporation statutes for railroads continued to operate, and (3) promoter/speculators could build rights-of-way on vacant western land in order to establish territory for a future system.

Managers were unanimous that the national government had to protect railroads from hostile state legislatures controlled by agrarians and from destructive competition among themselves. They wanted Congress to enact legislation that would make freight rates negotiated among a pool of railroads legally enforceable by the courts, thus overcoming the fundamental weakness of pools. Rates set by pools were not legally enforceable. Without legal enforcement, they were short-lived. By 1882 most managers of trunkline railroad systems wanted the national government to protect their earnings because "it is absolutely required for the public interest." But they wanted protection (regulation) on their own terms.[2]

Many states had railroad commissions that regulated rates for agricultural commodities with varying degrees of effectiveness, but they did little to restrain destructive competition for intercity traffic. In 1886 destructive competition among the principal trunkline systems reached crisis proportions. Managers of impacted roads positively supported a national railroad regulatory commission—with the assumption that men friendly to railroad interests would staff it.

At his point the Supreme Court forced Congress to act. It declared unconstitutional an

Illinois statute of agrarian origin that fixed rates for commodities going from villages in Illinois to New York City. The court made the obvious interpretation. The Illinois statute invaded the power of the national government to regulate interstate commerce. Both public opinion and the ambiguities created by the decision catalyzed the enactment of legislation that Congress had been contemplating for the previous ten years. All parties agreed that the inability of railroad managers to control destructive competition required a political remedy. The delay was due to railroad managers wanting a remedy on their own terms. They got it.

Congress established the Interstate Commerce Commission (ICC) in 1887. The scope of its authority was a composite of powers exercised by state railroad commissions. Railroads were required to publish rate schedules and were prohibited from making rebates from published rates. The law also prohibited pools as restraints on trade. The commission was given authority to issue cease and desist orders, if investigation substantiated that railroads were charging unreasonable rates. Railroads were required to charge reasonable and just rates, but reasonable and just was not defined. In other words, Congress delegated interpretation of what were unreasonable freight rates to the commission, and ultimately to the courts, because the ICC was not explicitly given the power to fix rates.

Railroad managers were happy with the prohibition of rebates but less happy about the prohibition of pools. Nonetheless, the ICC was their creature because the five men who constituted the commission were appointed by the president. It was certain that presidential appointees would protect railroads from hostile legislation passed by state legislatures controlled by agrarians. Beyond that, the ICC had serious problems because the Supreme Court reduced the effectiveness of the ICC.

The Supreme Court was unwilling to empower the ICC to make rates without explicit authorization by Congress. Congress could have delegated this power to the ICC because rate making power was explicitly delegated to state railroad commission by state legislatures. Even without an explicit delegation of rate making power by Congress, the ambiguous wording of the statute could have been interpreted as congressional intent. The Court did not make this interpretation because it wanted to be the ultimate protector of railroad earnings (and the national market), not the ICC.

The Court limited the power of the ICC to investigating complaints of destructive competition and declaring these rates unreasonable. Thereafter railroad managers had to revise rate structures in accordance with the Court's guideline of "fair return on a fair evaluation of the investment." Rate making was therefore a judicial question. "Fair return on a fair evaluation" was a guideline that was as ambiguous as "reasonable and just," but it allowed the Court to usurp the implied power of the ICC and set reasonable rates.

Nonetheless, the limited supervision that the Court allowed the ICC, especially after the numerous bankruptcies after 1893, helped stabilize railroad revenues and strongly contributed to the ability of railroads to upgrade services. Finally, in 1906, Congress specifically gave rate making powers to the ICC (the Hepburn Act), along with the power of enforcement. The Court concurred. Rate making became a nonjudicial process.

Bankruptcy

The ICC, however, did not function alone in increasing the efficiency of the national railroad network. Four other events increased its efficiency and, by extension, increased the efficiency of the national market. These events were (1) large numbers of railroad bankruptcies during the depression that began in 1893, (2) installation of new management by bankruptcy trustees, (3) consolidation of many railroads into larger systems, and (4) creation of groups of regional and inter-regional railroad systems.

A high percentage of railroads built after 1865 were speculative. They were speculative when they were (1) built too far ahead of settlement to generate sufficient revenue to pay interest on bonded indebtedness, (2) assembled from shortlines to compete with established trunkline systems, or (3) promoters retained management control by keeping a majority of shares of stock in their hands. Management control allowed promoters to generously reward themselves with bonds for their promotional services. Dividends on shares of stock had last call on earning, but this was acceptable to promoters because their profits came from selling bonds they awarded themselves.

Most speculative railroads were overcapitalized. Overcapitalization was seriously aggravated by destructive competition. By the mid-1880s there were numerous signs of impending disaster. Early in 1889 J. P. Morgan, the leading investment banker in New York City, called a meeting of the presidents of twenty-two trans-Mississippi railroads for the purpose of ending rate wars, and, more broadly, to help the regulatory function of the ICC. ICC commissioners were present. They wanted railroad executives to create a rate organization (pool by another name) that would make rates that the ICC would enforce as reasonable and just. If investigation found that a member railroad was engaging in destructive competition, the ICC would issue a cease and desist order. Shortly afterward, Morgan presided over a similar meeting of the presidents of ten eastern railroads to organize a similar association. Both organizations lasted less than six months.

Before 1893 neither the ICC nor investment bankers like J.P. Morgan were able to force railroad managers to act in their own best interests. The cumulative effects of destructive competition were weak financial structures for a high percentage of railroad systems, which made them very vulnerable to bankruptcy when there were downturns in business activity.

The depression that began in 1893 and lasted to 1896 devastated the national railroad network. During the summer of 1893, seventy-four railroads became bankrupt, and by the end of 1894, 104 were bankrupt, including the Union Pacific, Northern Pacific, and New York and Erie. The seventy-four railroads that became bankrupt in 1893 had 43,000 kilometers of track. Between 1894 and 1898 railroads with an additional 65,000 kilometers of track became bankrupt. Between 1884 and 1896 over four hundred railroad corporations because bankrupt, most of them after 1893. This was one-quarter of total railroad capitalization. At the same time over six hundred banks became bankrupt. The ICC could do nothing about bankruptcy. Bankruptcy was controlled by another set of laws.

The depression of 1893 was, in effect, a house cleaning of speculative railroad finance. Large numbers of bankruptcies created opportunities to revalue bonded indebtedness, reduce destructive competition, and reduce the excessive number of railroads. Financial restructuring and consolidation proceeded in tandem.

What was the process of financial restructuring? Receivers were appointed by national courts and management was placed in their hands. Generally, receivers were bankers that supplied money to keep the road operating. They created a voting trust composed of representatives of a railroad's principal creditors and then installed a new management team.

Bankers then did their work:

1. Floating debts were capitalized with new shares of stock.
2. Bonded indebtedness was revalued and capital structures simplified by reducing the classes of bonds and reducing interest rates. Bonds of one thousand dollars face value were revalued to nine hundred dollars, or eight hundred dollars, or seven hundred dollars to conform to a railroads earning capacity.
3. Emergency funds were created to repair physical damages to rights-of-way due to storms, wrecks, and other emergencies.

4. Better access to terminal cities was obtained by purchasing shortlines or building them.
5. Bankrupt railroads were merged to create larger systems.
6. Moratoriums in interest and dividends were imposed until roads were on a solid operating basis.
7. Bankers placed one or more of their representatives on the board of directors after voting trusts expired. They were there to exercise continual surveillance of management policies in order to protect the interests of bondholders and stockholders.

During bankruptcy proceedings, if a one thousand dollar bond was revalued to eight hundred dollars the owner would often receive ten shares of stock. If the railroad became profitable, stockholders would benefit from dividends. First call on profits was interest on revalued bonds. If there were no additional profits, there would be no dividends on common stock. The purpose of expanding equity was to reduce fixed costs so that there was greater assurance that earnings during business downturns were sufficient to pay interest on the revalued bonds.

By 1906 about three-quarters of U.S. railroad trackage was controlled by eight groups. Each group was built around one major trunkline, or railroads in a group depended on one bank to supply credit and advise management. Groupings were maintained by interlocking directorates where very large amounts of power were exercised by bank representatives on the boards of directors. They were there to (1) stop rebates and destructive competition among railroads within their group, (2) stabilize earnings, (3) facilitate the interchange of traffic, and (4) prevent speculative activities by managers that would jeopardize earnings needed to pay interest on bonded indebtedness.

The smallest of the eight groups controlled 25,000 kilometers of tracks and the largest 40,000 kilometers. Railroads in California (Central Pacific, Southern Pacific, Western Pacific) were not part of bankruptcies after 1893 because, from the time of their construction, they had overlapping ownership and interlocking boards of directors. There was no destructive competition in California.

During these years New York City became a financial center rivaling London, based on its ability to fund the Civil War debt and raise capital for railroad construction. Between 1870 and 1890 railroad capitalization increased from 2.5 billion to 10 billion dollars. This could not have happened if the national banking system had been dismantled after the Civil War, as advocated by many agrarians. Agrarians disliked the national banking system because it restrained inflation and it helped mobilize capital from the agrarian sector so it could be allocated to the urban industrial sector. This is discussed in the next chapter.

Tariff

Between 1870 and 1900 most of the revenue of the national government came from the tariff. During these years it became increasingly protective. The Morrill Tariff of 1861 was designed to give broad protection to the emerging urban/industrial sector concentrated in Pennsylvania, New York, and New England, but after the Civil War it also benefited the rapidly industrializing states north of the Ohio River and east of the Mississippi River. These were states that had developed diversified economies before the Civil War.

After 1870 the tariff lost whatever coherence it had in 1861. Tariff rates and products protected had little relationship to competition from specific foreign countries; and tariffs were increasingly focused on specific products. Lobbyists were employed to influence congressmen to provide protection for an increasing variety of manufactured products (and some agricultural commodities). "The protective tariff stimulated the political organization of American business into industrial and commercial associations more than any other government policy in the late nineteenth century."[3]

The core constituencies of the protective tariff were iron smelters and their successors, integrated steel mills. American manufacturers of iron and steel products claimed that the protective tariff accelerated industrial investments. They claimed that without protection, investments needed to make new products would be delayed, and in many cases, substantially delayed. Furthermore, new urban industries provided jobs with higher wages and higher incomes for workers than less capitalized industries like tanneries and sawmills.

I will examine the origins of integrated steel mills in the United States. Sustaining industrialization required the replacement of iron by steel. Steel was the metal of the future because of its strength and versatility compared to iron. The United States required a steel industry as soon as possible and the protective tariff helped accumulate the capital needed to build steel mills.

Production of steel by Bessemer converters began in the United States in 1869–1870. It was contemporary with British steel production by the Bessemer process. Thereafter, until 1890, a high percentage of steel produced in the United States was used by railroads in the form of rails, steel castings for railroad rolling stock, plates to make locomotive boilers, I-beams to build stronger railroad bridges, and for a rapidly expanding variety of other uses.

Before 1870 steel rails paid a tariff of 45 percent of their value (fifty dollars per ton was an average price in Britain). The tariff revision of 1870 changed the tariff to twenty-eight dollars per ton. This was a slight increase based on the British price for steel rails. After 1870 the price of steel rails in Britain began a steady decline because of technological innovations and increased scale of production. By 1877 the price of steel produced in Britain was thirty-one dollars per ton, a decline of 40 percent. In the United States, on average, production costs declined even faster. The tariff of twenty-eight dollars per ton was almost 100 percent of the value of British produced steel rails and American steel mills could charge high prices. Railroads built in the 1870s and 1880s used expensive steel rails made in the United States.

The tariff revision of 1883 lowered the tax on steel rails to seventeen dollars per ton. Profits, however, remained high during the 1880s because 115,000 kilometers (72,000 miles) of new railroads were built. A high percentage of profits were reinvested to expand existing steel mills, and high profits stimulated investments in new mills to supply railroad steel. The capital to build them came from domestic sources.

A significant percentage of the trunkline railroads built in the 1880s were financed by bonds sold in Europe and in Britain. These funds made possible the extremely rapid completion of the national railroad network and, at the same time, freed American capital for investment in factories that produced new products like barbed wire, agricultural implements, all diameters of water pipes for cities, and I-beams to construct bridges and high rise buildings.

Rapid industrialization required agriculture to make a disproportionately large capital contribution to build railroads and a steel industry. The high price of steel, sustained by the protective tariff, substantially increased the costs for building post-Civil War railroads. Servicing high bonded indebtedness required high freight rates for harvests, especially for harvests from the prairies of central Illinois and the high plains of Kansas, Nebraska, and Texas where there was no alternative means of transportation. Railroads built with high priced steel rails could charge high rates for transporting harvests, and they did, because cultivators on the high plains had no choice. They could not market their crops without railroad transportation.

Republican Party leaders were not concerned that the high price of steel for new railroad construction had to be paid by the agricultural sector. It was the explicit policy of the Republican Party to force the agricultural sector to subsidize industrialization because it was in the national interest to accelerate industrialization and concentrate it in cities.

The Republican Party's rationale for a policy of protection changed during the 1880s. It was no longer to protect infant industries. It was a commitment to encourage the production of new wealth by the commercialization of new technologies. There were increasing numbers of new technologies that had to be encouraged because the commercialization of these technologies was being encouraged by European governments. The United States was engaged in an international race to be competitive in exploiting the potential of these technologies.

The protective tariff was a major political issue in the 1880s because of continuing surplus revenue. In the early 1880s the surplus revenue was used to reduce the Civil War debt and provide generous pensions for veterans who served in the U.S. Army during the Civil War. Revenue surpluses, however, continued into the late 1880s. *The obvious question was how to use the surplus?* Most Democratic congressmen wanted to lower the tariff in order to reduce the price of many manufactured products consumed in the agricultural sector of the economy. Republican Party leaders were determined to retain protection because it was a hidden tax that transferred capital from the agricultural sector to the industrial sector. This transfer was essential for sustaining a policy of accelerated industrialization.

In order to generate broader support for protective tariffs for manufactured products, two agricultural commodities received substantial protection. They were wool and sugar. Wool was one of the few agricultural commodities that could benefit from protection. Wool producers were concentrated in northern states and were reliable Republican voters. Australia was the principal exporter of raw wool in the last half of the nineteenth century. The United States had a substantial capacity to produce wool. Early in the nineteenth century it was one of several commodities produced by farmers and yeomen cultivators in northern states. Railroads, however, changed the pattern of wool production. The change began in the 1840s when cheap wheat from the trans-Appalachian west forced many cultivators in New England and New York to migrate to western states in search of more fertile land. Many of the cultivators who did not migrate changed land use to sheep grazing. New England was a substantial producer of wool.

During the Civil War there was a precipitous drop in cotton available to northern textile mills. The need for uniforms forced the United States government to turn to wool. After the war, the resumption of cotton cultivation bankrupted many woolen mills. The remaining mills petitioned for protection—as did sheep grazers who saw the domestic market shrink and, at the same time, experienced severe competition from Australian wool. In 1866, sheep grazers and manufacturers of woolen cloth united to petition for protection. Support for a wool tariff was broadly distributed in the agricultural sector, and support for a tariff on woolen cloth was concentrated in Pennsylvania, New York, and New England, where most mills were located. Wool and woolen cloth received tariff protection by Congress in March 1867.

The political base for protection broadened after the mid-1880s when railroads began crossing inter-mountain basins in the West and cattle and sheep grazers followed. Even though grazers used public land they were a long way from markets. Protection made sheep grazing profitable and provided a commodity that could be carried on transcontinental railroads to eastern textile mills. Sheep grazers and textile mills that made heavy woolen cloth (blankets) and carpets were significant interest groups that favored protection for raw wool and heavy woolen fabrics.

Sugar was protected for economic reasons. Louisiana sugar plantations supplied only a small percentage of the American market, and production costs were high compared to sugar cane grown in Cuba and Brazil. The real purpose of the high tariff was revenue. American consumers were willing to pay a high price for sugar. Only incidentally were Louisiana sugar producers protected.

In 1895, the United States was the world's largest producer of steel. The United States was also the largest producer of industrial products and had the largest national market of industrial nations. The protective tariff did what it was intended to do. It helped mobilize capital from the agricultural sector so that it could be allocated to the industrial sector, particularly the steel industry. By 1900, the United States was no longer a developing nation and the protective tariff lost its significance as a policy of economic development.

Currency

At the end of 1866 there was about 390 million dollars of legal tender currency (greenbacks) in circulation. They were the national currency used for most day to day business transactions. From the perspective of Congress, they were the preferred currency because no interest was paid on them; therefore, they were not a burden on tax revenues. They averaged 71 percent of the purchasing power of gold coins. By 1867, the agricultural sector of the economy came to realize the value of greenbacks because they could be used to make payments on mortgages with inflated dollars. Farmers believed that mortgages made in inflated dollars should be repaid in inflated dollars.

Railroads also had an interest in retaining greenbacks in circulation. Railroads derived most of their revenue in greenbacks and they wanted to pay interest on their bonded indebtedness in greenbacks, especially bonds contracted during the 1850s that specified interest payments in gold coins. In 1867 gold coins had an average premium of 38 percent over greenbacks, and in 1868 the premium averaged 33 percent. If railroads and farmers were forced to pay interest on bonds and mortgages in gold coins or equivalent money, this would precipitate large numbers of foreclosures and bankruptcies.

Other beneficiaries of greenback currency were owners of U.S. bonds purchased during the Civil War. The 5 percent interest they received was paid in gold coins. If the gold coins were converted into greenbacks, their real interest rate was 6.6 percent. Owners of bonds with 7.3 percent interest received 9.7 percent interest if gold coins were converted into greenbacks.

U.S. bonds were especially valuable investments for national banks. In addition to a high real interest rate, when gold coins were converted into greenbacks, U.S. bonds had additional value in the 1860s and 1870s. Ninety percent of the value of U.S. bonds owned by national banks could be converted into banknotes that were loaned to earn additional interest. Furthermore, because national banks were concentrated in northern cities, the credit they created was preferentially available in the urban/industrial sector. In February 1868 Congress passed legislation preventing further retirement of greenbacks. The 356 million dollars of greenbacks in circulation were to be retained in circulation.

In 1870 the U.S. Supreme Court declared unconstitutional the legal tender act of 1862 as it applied to contracts made before its passage. If these contracts specified repayment in gold dollars, they had to repaid in gold dollars. In the meantime, Congress enlarged the Supreme Court to nine members (from seven). President Ulysses S. Grant appointed two new justices (one a leading railroad lawyer). Both favored reversal of the 1870 decision. The second legal tender case in 1871 reversed the 1870 decision and validated the use of greenbacks to pay all public and private debts, except tariffs and interest on U.S. bonds.

The second legal tender case confirmed the power of the national government to control all aspects of the currency. Politically, it confirmed the power of Congress to inflate the currency by any means Congress thought expedient. In spite of this, the second legal tender case did not stop a policy of deflation. Another, more politically potent policy operated to compel slow deflation. That policy was United States participation in the international gold standard.

The international gold standard came into being in the second half of the nineteenth century because it facilitated international commerce and the international transfer of capital. A significant American contribution to European industrialization was cheap food to feed urban industrial workers and cheap cotton to manufacture clothing for them. The gold standard facilitated wheat and cotton purchases by European nations, as well as facilitating the transfer of capital to the United States to build railroads.

After the second legal tender case, deflation continued until January 1, 1879 when gold coins and greenbacks and national banknotes attained par. Thereafter, deflation continued to the end of the nineteenth century. From 1866 to 1899 approximately 300 million dollars of greenbacks were in annual circulation. During these same years, the banknotes of the national banks averaged 250 million in annual circulation, but there were substantial annual fluctuations in their circulation in the 1880s. Silver certificates and gold and silver coins added to the money supply but never enough to cause inflation. In a very rough measurement of the money supply, circulation increased from approximately 670 million dollars in 1866 to 1.85 billion dollars in 1899.

During these thirty-three years, the money supply tripled but the economy quadrupled and the wholesale price index declined from wartime inflation of 190 in 1866, to 99 in 1884, and to 85 in 1899. From 1879, when gold and paper currency reached par, the policy of all presidents and majorities in both houses of Congress was to restrict the volume of currency to amounts that could be safely redeemed for gold coins on demand. Redemption of paper currency for gold coins on demand compelled deflation because there was a finite supply of gold. Although the world supply of gold rapidly increased after 1886 following discoveries at Witwatersrand, South Africa, inflation was not possible as long as the principal industrial nations redeemed their currencies for gold on demand.

The combination of a slowly increasing money supply (based on new gold discoveries), the development of deposit banking, rapid industrial growth, and steadily declining prices for manufactured products and food meant that currency gradually appreciated in value. This was deflation. Deflation operated strongly in favor of holders of bonds and mortgages on agricultural land because the fixed annual interest payments were in dollars that were appreciating in purchasing power. The appreciating dollar had the effect of extracting capital from the agricultural sector, either as interest payments on mortgages, or as the high freight rates necessary to service the bonded indebtedness of railroads built with high priced steel, or as higher interest rates on loans to small town businessmen than loans to city businessmen.

In summary, four policies sponsored by the Republican Party adversely affected agrarian welfare: (1) the high cost of railroad transportation for agricultural commodities because railroads built after 1870 were built with high-priced steel rails. Money to pay interest on the bonded indebtedness that purchased them had to come from high transportation rates for agricultural commodities; (2) a monetary policy of deflation; and (3) a concentration of credit resources in cities by the national banking system where it could be allocated to urban industries. A fourth event that adversely affected agrarian welfare was steadily declining commodity prices. Republican policies had no control over this, but the combination of declining commodity prices and a deflationary monetary policy intensified agrarian discontent.

What interest group was penalized by deflation? What interest group benefited from deflation? The short answers are (1) the agricultural sector was penalized by deflation, and (2) the urban/industrial sector benefited from deflation. During the years of deflation, wage rates of industrial workers remained the same. The same wages had increased purchasing power and at the same time food and rent became cheaper. Unlike farmers who owned their land and houses, urban workers rented their homes, and competition in housing tended to reduce rents.

The next chapter will examine why farmers wanted inflation and how they sought to obtain it.

Chapter 11

Agrarian Discontent

The cause of agrarian discontent was a prolonged decline in commodity prices.

Both grain and cotton cultivators wanted to increase prices by an inflationary monetary policy because domestic prices were dictated by prices on the international market (see Table 11.1).

Settlement of the trans-Missouri west after 1865 rapidly increased the size of wheat harvests. Production nearly tripled from 235 million bushels in 1870 to 650 million bushels in 1900. Yields remained stationary at 30 to 32 bushels per hectare (12 to 13 bushels per acre). Increased production was wholly due to more land under cultivation, increasing from 7.7 million hectares (19 million acres) in 1870 to approximately 18.2 million hectares (45 million acres) in 1900.

Increased cotton harvests were comparable to wheat because of the rapid expansion of cultivation in Texas, Arkansas, and elsewhere in southern states after 1865. Cotton harvests increased from 4.3 million bales in 1870 to over 9.5 million bales in 1900. Like wheat, cotton yields per hectare remained stationary: 1.2 bales in 1870, 1.0 bales in 1880, 1.0 bales in 1890, and 1.1 bales in 1900.

At the same time that the United States was exporting about 30 percent of its wheat harvest (see Table 11.2), Russia, Australia, and Argentina were increasing their wheat exports; and cotton exports were increasing from Egypt and India. Inflating the domestic prices for wheat and cotton would have lessened the competitive advantage of American commodities on the international market but, more importantly, inflation would not benefit the industrial sector

Table 11.1 Average Market Prices in Cents for Select Commodities

Years	Cotton-pounds	Maize-bushels	Wheat-bushels
1870–1873	15.1	43.1	106.7
1874–1877	11.1	40.9	94.4
1878–1881	9.5	43.1	100.6
1882–1885	9.1	39.8	80.2
1886–1889	8.3	35.9	74.8
1890–1893	7.8	41.7	70.9
1894–1897	5.8	29.7	63.3

Source: Hicks, John D. *The Populist Revolt: A History of the Farmer's Alliance and the People's Party* (Omaha: University of Nebraska Press, 1961) p. 56. (See also Shannon, Fred A. *The Farmers Last Frontier: Agriculture, 1860–1897* (New York: Rinehart, 1959), p. 415, 417, and Buck, Solon J. *The Granger Movement: A Study of Agricultural Organization and Its Political, Economic and Social Manifestations, 1870–1880* (Omaha: University of Nebraska Press, 1963) p. 29–30 for other price lists.

Table 11.2 Percentage of Select Commodities Exported

Year	Wheat	Cotton
1870	22	67
1880	37	65
1890	26	67
1900	34	64

Source: Shannon, Fred A. *The Farmers Last Frontier: Agriculture, 1860–1897* (New York: Rinehart, 1959) p. 415, 417.

of the economy. It would increase food and clothing prices for city residents and destabilize a wage scale and cost of living index that minimized urban unrest. Cheap food and cheap cotton textiles were major contributors to the rapid industrialization of the United States.

Grain Farmers

Grain farmers wanted to increase their annual money incomes in order to repay long-term debts incurred to purchase land (mortgages), wagons, cultivation implements, draft animals, livestock, barbed wire fencing, bored wells, and to build frame houses and barns. These were expensive capital investments and annual payments on them became increasingly difficult with declining grain prices.

Farmers were further squeezed by the national monetary policy of deflation. Between 1870 and 1890 the purchasing power of the dollar increased about 45 percent. Fixed mortgage payments on farms were made with these dollars and these payments deprived farmers of the use of dollars that were appreciating in purchasing power. Grain farmers sought two political remedies: (1) inflation, (2) regulation of railroad rates. In 1868 they successfully lobbied Congress to mandate that 356 million dollars of greenback currency be retained in circulation. They thought that this legislation would prolong wartime inflation. It did not because the rapidly growing economy needed more money. They then sought to induce state legislatures to pass legislation to force railroads to make rate schedules favorable to agricultural interests.

Farmers converted the Grange (a farmer fraternal organization) into a lobby to pressure state legislatures to reduce rates for transportation and storage of grain. Railroads always charged higher rates for short hauls from agricultural villages to terminal cities because operating costs for short hauls of small volumes of freight from numerous villages were more expensive than moving long trains of through traffic. Railroads could charge higher rates because there was no competition in small villages along their tracks. They charged what the traffic would bear. Grain farmers wanted transportation rates on a pro-rata basis. If a carload of grain moved a short distance to a terminal city, the cost of moving it should be proportional to the distance traveled. Conversely, if a carload moved a long distance to a terminal city, the rate should be proportionally higher.

Grange lobbying was successful in getting the Illinois legislature to establish an independent railroad commission in 1873. It was given the power to make rates for grain transportation and storage if the commissioners considered them too high. Other states established similar commissions with similar powers in order to benefit farmers and mercantile interests within the state.

Alternatively, state legislatures passed statutes mandating favorable rate schedules for agricultural commodities. If rate schedules made by railroad commission or by statutes crossed state borders, restraining orders from courts usually overturned them because regulating interstate commerce by a single state was an invasion of the power of the national government to regulate interstate commerce. Continual attempts by state railroad commissions and state legislatures to regulate railroad rate structures for the benefit of farmers threatened to fragment the national market before it was fully formed. This was one of the reasons that compelled Congress to establish the Interstate Commerce Commission in 1887.

The Grange also lobbied Congress to change national monetary policy from deflation to inflation by printing greenbacks in excess of the 356 million dollars in circulation. Inflation was a much more popular policy than regulating railroad rates because state-by-state railroad regulation was a slow process. Inflation had greater popularity after the depression of 1873 because it could be rapidly implemented by congressional legislation, and its results would be equally rapid.

In 1876 farmer discontent had outgrown the Grange. Direct political action became the preferred means of expressing discontent. Inflationists organized the Greenback Party and nominated a presidential candidate and numerous congressional candidates. When Grange activists became Greenback Party organizers, the Grange dissolved as a lobby. The Greenback presidential candidate received about 1 percent of the vote in 1876; however, in the congressional election of 1878 Greenback candidates received over one million votes and fourteen Greenback candidates were elected to Congress. Three were from the cotton South and the rest from Corn Belt and frontier wheat states where the Grange had its principal membership. In the next election (1880), ten representatives were elected.

During the 1880s inflationists changed their focus. The emphasis went from printing indefinite amounts of paper currency to minting unlimited amounts of silver dollar coins. The shift to silver dollar coins was possible because of the discovery of bonanza deposits of silver ore at Leadville, Colorado; Butte, Montana; and scattered mining districts in Utah and Nevada. American silver flooded the world market at a time when many European nations were demonetizing silver. The price of silver went into steady decline. Western mine operators wanted a market for their silver. In 1878, congressmen from western states joined agrarian congressmen to pass legislation requiring the treasury department to purchase at least two million ounces of silver per month at market prices and mint it into silver dollar coins.

Greenback and agrarian Democratic congressmen were eager to implement inflation with silver dollar coins. The coins were minted but the secretary of the treasury had discretionary power to withhold them from circulation. Subsequent treasury secretaries opted to circulate minimum amounts in order to retain the convertibility of paper currency and silver dollar coins into gold coins on demand. Convertibility could be maintained only if treasury secretaries limited the circulation of silver dollar coins, which they did. This was the gold standard.

Cotton Peasants

Peasants in the cotton South (black and white) had a different agenda. They wanted to maintain the subsistence social order, and the subsistence social order did not depend on money incomes. It was defined by two institutions: subsistence labor norms and the furnish . The furnish was personal credit (subsistence credit) supplied by storekeepers. A high percentage of subsistence cultivators were sharecroppers who contracted with landowners to cultivate ten to twenty hectares. They acquired land use by cultivating an agreed hectarage of cotton and sharing the harvest with landowners. If a sharecrop household owned a draft animal (usually a mule) and cultivation implements, half of the harvest went to landowners. If a household owned no draft animals or cultivation implements and these were supplied by landowners, landowners received two-thirds of the cotton harvest. Sharecrop households were also responsible for growing or procuring all of the food for their households.

Sharecrop cultivators were minimal producers of commodities for market sale. In the cotton South they usually acquired money once a year. It came from the sale of the cotton crop. The sale was conducted by landowners or their agents (usually gin operators). Both landowners and storekeepers had liens on the cotton harvest. Crop liens were legally enforceable because state laws validated annual oral contracts between illiterate sharecroppers and landowners and storekeepers. After landowners received their share from gin operators, storekeepers had first claim on sufficient amounts of the remaining harvest to pay the furnish of the previous year. Any remaining money went to the peasant household.

The furnish allowed illiterate households cultivating cotton to acquire limited amounts of manufactured items (clothing, shoes, edged tools) and food. No cash was involved. Acquisition of manufactured products was by money of account. If the storekeeper's share of the cotton harvest was insufficient to fully pay the furnish, the debt was carried to the next year. More often than not, however, sharecroppers defaulted by moving to the next county

The furnish was not a money income. Peasants seldom handled cash money because they seldom acquired cash as long as their subsistence needs were satisfied by the furnish. Because sharecroppers owned no land and possessed few material objects that could be used as collateral, interest on the furnish was high. Money-of-account prices were 25 to 50 percent higher than cash prices, which converts into annual interest rates of 30 to 100 percent.

Peasants believed that storekeepers were the local agents of city bankers (soulless money corporations). This was accurate because storekeepers depended on bank credit to maintain their inventories. Peasants believed that storekeepers should continue to supply annual furnishes in customary amounts, regardless of the market price of cotton. This would allow them to continue to perform subsistence labor norms. Peasants believed that the insistence of storekeepers on full payments of furnishes in years of declining prices was a conspiracy to deprive them of "independence." Independence was a euphemism for subsistence labor norms.

Declining cotton prices in the 1880s and 1890s meant that customary amounts of subsistence labor were no longer sufficient to produce harvests that would pay for customary amounts of a furnish. If cotton peasants were to enjoy a customary level of subsistence welfare, they had to acquire more money. There were four ways: (1) increase labor inputs into cotton cultivation to produce larger harvests, (2) grow all, or almost all, of the food households consumed instead of relying on the furnish to supply a high percentage of food, (3) performing wage labor, and (4) inflation.

The first three ways of acquiring money required the performance of more labor. Cotton peasants believed that performing more than customary amounts of labor was a form of victimization. It was a threat to Jeffersonian democracy because preserving their independence was the proper goal of governance. According to their reasoning, waging four years of war to establish the confederated slave states of America did not change the purpose of governance. The purpose of governance remained the same: preserving the subsistence labor norms of a white peasant democracy.

Most peasant households did not grow enough food to supply household needs. Contemporary studies in the 1880s and 1890s calculated 25–30 percent of the food consumed by peasant households was acquired from the furnish. When cotton prices were high, favorable terms of trade between cotton and maize meal and preserved meat (salted or smoked pork or beef), imported from northern states, allowed households to minimize the labor of food production.

Reducing household food production was a conscious decision of peasant households because sharecrop land units were always large enough for households to grow all of their food if they expended the labor. As long as food could be procured from storekeepers by favorable terms of trade for cotton, most peasant households did not expend the labor to be self-sufficient in food production.

The practice of minimizing food production did not make peasants poor. Poor is a term that measures welfare in commercial cultures where households have low money incomes. Peasants are subsistent. Cotton peasants measured their social security by control of land use and access to a furnish. They believed that an acceptable level of subsistence welfare was obtainable by a fixed amount of labor in a normal crop year.

As long as they controlled land use (as sharecroppers) and cotton prices were stable, they could control the amount of agricultural labor they performed. Additional labor to increase the size of cotton harvests or performing interludes of wage labor (to acquire cash money) had a lower social value than preserving subsistence labor norms that Jeffersonian rhetoric translated into independence.[1]

Cotton peasants (white and black) were extremely reluctant to expend more labor to grow an enlarged cotton harvest or be self-sufficient in food production. The alternative was accepting smaller furnishes and a lower level of subsistence welfare. Most peasant households accepted a lower level of subsistence welfare rather than perform interludes of wage labor or perform more than customary amounts of agricultural labor. If, however, there was a political remedy to increase cotton prices or restore customary amounts of the furnish, they eagerly supported it.

Cotton peasants joined alliances that lobbied for the national government to subsidize subsistence credit. Cash loans made by the national government to cotton peasants immediately after the harvest would enable them to purchase food and manufactured products at cheap cash prices. Their perpetual indebtedness to storekeepers would end.

"The national government would lend money direct to the people at a low rate of interest, not to exceed two percent per annum, on non-perishable farm products." Farm commodities would be stored in cotton and grain warehouses in counties where the commodities were grown. The warehouses were called sub-treasuries because they stored the nation's principal wealth. According to agrarian rhetoric, agricultural commodities were the proper measure of a nation's wealth.[2]

The first alliance was organized in Texas in 1877. It was for whites only. Owners of bank stock, lawyers, rural storekeepers and their clerks, and owners of dry goods and hardware stores in villages were specifically excluded from membership. Between 1877 and 1887 the Texas Alliance absorbed similar organizations in cotton growing states and changed its name to Southern Alliance. In addition to lobbying the national government to subsidize subsistence credit, the Southern Alliance had two subsidiary issues: (1) a more rigid enforcement of white supremacy, and (2) disfranchisement of black peasants.

At the same time, similar alliances were organized in the frontier wheat producing states of Kansas, Nebraska, and Minnesota, and in the Dakota Territory. In 1889–1890 the Kansas and Dakota Alliances joined the Southern Alliance because they shared the same rhetoric of being victimized by the deflationary monetary policy of the national government. A similar movement took place in the maize producing states in the Midwest. The first farmers alliance in the Midwest was organized in 1880. By 1882 it had grown into the Northern Alliance and claimed 100,000 members.

Inflation was the principal objective of the Northern Alliance. It would be the means of reducing the number of foreclosures because declining grain prices precluded farmers from making mortgage payments. Farm mortgages required payments of fixed sums of money, with fixed rates of interest, for a fixed number of years. Paying annual interest and repaying the principal with inflated currency would benefit them. The debts of southern peasants were of a different order. They were annual, personal, for indefinite amounts of money, with no fixed interest rate. Inflation was of less benefit to peasants. Although inflation would increase the price they received for cotton, the price of manufactured products they consumed would increase in tandem with cotton.

In 1889, the Southern and Northern Alliances held a joint convention in St. Louis, Missouri for purposes of merging. Delegates from the Knights of Labor were invited. It was immediately clear that delegates from the Southern Alliance did not speak the same language as the Knights of Labor. Using the fiscal resources of the national government to subsidize furnishes for cotton peasants in order to allow them to escape performing wage labor was directly opposed to the purpose of organized labor.

The Knights of Labor represented wage laborers. The message of the Knights was clear: wage labor conferred dignity on workers. They had little sympathy for peasants who wished to escape wage labor, and no sympathy for using tax resources to subsidize furnishes. National resources should preferentially be used to improve urban infrastructures where wage laborers lived.

Delegations from the Northern Alliance also had a fundamental difference with delegates from the Southern Alliance. The principal goal of the Northern Alliance was clear and obtainable: inflation to increase the annual money incomes of farmers. Delegates from the Northern Alliance also knew there was no chance of Congress passing legislation to subsidize furnishes. Northern and Southern Alliance delegates had further differences. Southern delegates were indifferent to railroad regulation and northern delegates were indifferent or hostile to black disfranchisement and increasing the scope of white supremacy. The merger was not consummated but they did agree on the necessity of an inflationary monetary policy.

The greatest success of the Southern Alliance in the congressional elections of 1890 was in Kansas, where the only message was inflation. The electoral success in Kansas was a catalyst for splitting the Southern Alliance. Half of the members wanted to retain its original purpose of lobbying in state capitals and in Washington, D.C. The other half wanted to convert the Southern Alliance into a political party. Lobbyists knew that if the Southern Alliance sponsored a political party, it would cease to exist because members would focus their energies on electoral politics and stop paying dues.

After the merger of the Kansas and Nebraska Alliances with the Southern Alliance in 1889–1890, the political half of the Southern Alliance was dominated by northern farmers, especially Kansas wheat farmers. At the annual meeting of the leadership council in December 1890 (in Ocala, Florida), the Kansas contingent tried to commit the Alliance to organizing the Peoples' Party. They failed. Nevertheless, the Kansas contingent, supported by delegates representing northern farmers issued a call for an organizing convention to be held in Cincinnati, Ohio in May 1891.

The annual meeting of the Northern Alliance, held in Omaha, Nebraska in January 1891, endorsed holding the organizing convention in Cincinnati. The Cincinnati convention attracted a heterogeneous collection of self-appointed discontents. After acrimonious debate, the formal organization of the People's Party was postponed to the election years of 1892; although, in fact, the party came into being.

The regularly scheduled meeting of the leadership council of the Southern Alliance was held in November 1891 in Indianapolis, Indiana. The council successfully prevented efforts of activists to get the leadership council to endorse the People's Party as its political agent. At this point, the leadership of the Southern Alliance called for a unity convention to be held in St. Louis, Missouri in February 1892. The convention committed the Southern and Northern Alliances to organizing the People's Party. It was dominated by northern and western farmers, with Kansas sending the largest delegation. The demands adopted reflected their priorities. The first demand of frontier farmers was inflation.

After adjournment, while delegates were still in their seats, political activists issued a call to attend a convention to be held in Omaha, Nebraska in July to nominate a presidential candidate for the People's party. The convention nominated James B. Weaver. He had been the Greenback Party's presidential nominee in 1880. He was from Iowa and had been a general in the U.S. Army during the Civil War. He had minimal appeal to white southern peasants. For Weaver, the only issue was inflation.

Northern farmers, led by Kansas activists, hijacked control of the Southern Alliance from cotton peasants and made it serve their priority of inflation. They were able to gain control of the Populist Party because farmers had money to contribute to candidates. Cotton peasants gave little money to Populist candidates because they had little to give. Calculations of incomes by region indicate that per capita money incomes in 1880 in New England were 141 percent of the national average, in midwestern states they were exactly the national average, and in plains states (where the only industry was railroads) per capita incomes were 90 percent of the national average. Southern states had 50 percent of national average and incomes were highly concentrated in large landowners—who gave no money to Populist candidates.[3]

Populism

The glue of the Populist coalition was the shared belief that they were victims of low commodity prices. Leaders of the Populist Party believed that inflation would restore the welfare of cotton peasants, frontier wheat farmers, midwestern maize farmers, and western irrigation farmers. Both grain farmers and cotton peasants claimed that deflationary monetary policies benefited urban industry at the expense of agriculture. This was an accurate assessment of the policy of deflation. Western silver miners had a similar grievance—low prices. They wanted the national government to subsidize high prices by coining silver into money.

In 1892 the Peoples Party had varying strengths in southern, midwestern, and western states, and almost no support in industrial states and cities. In states where it had electoral strength, Populists leaders had to build coalitions with either the Democratic or Republican parties. This was the only way they could influence national monetary policies. The party's greatest strength was in wheat and cotton producing states, with lesser strength in Corn Belt states. Western mine operators contributed cash to fund the campaign.

Most Democratic Party leaders in cotton states rejected coalitions with Populists because this would be the first step in replacing themselves. Democratic Party leaders were not going to allow this to happen. They clearly understood that increasing commercial wealth depended on retaining control of governance in the interests of commercially motivated planters and businessmen. If a southern state was controlled by Populists, it would lose momentum in attracting investments in manufacturing tobacco products and textiles. In the late 1880s commercially motivated persons were a minority of the population of southern states, but peasant disfranchisement could convert the commercially motivated minority into a majority.

Democratic Party leaders pursued two strategies to repel attempts by Populists to gain control of state governments. The first strategy was adopting many policies favored by Populists. The second was disfranchising as many peasants as possible. Many policies favored by Populists were included in Democratic Party platforms before the presidential election of 1892: (1) inflation, (2) graduated income taxes because this tax would be paid by city residents, (3) popular election of U.S. senators, and 4) excluding aliens from owning agricultural land.

The racism of white peasants made it politically expedient to extinguish the black electorate. This was a highly popular policy with white peasants because disfranchisement satisfied a desire for legalizing white supremacy. Race was the only advantage that a high percentage of white peasants had over black peasants because, in fact, there was little measurable difference between white and black peasant labor norms and per capita production of cotton. Furthermore, white sharecroppers hoped to gain access to more fertile land because white landowners would allocate land to them in preference to black sharecroppers. It did not always operate this way.

After emancipation, landowners no longer practiced racial loyalty with white peasants because white peasants were no longer necessary to preserve slavery. Emancipation ended the prewar democracy where white peasants and planters had an equal interest in preserving slavery. Emancipation made landless black and landless white peasants equals as sharecrop cultivators. Landowners wanted upper strata peasants of either race as sharecrop tenants because they would produce larger harvests and larger shares for landowners. Black peasants were as stratified as white peasants and landowners knew this.

The Democratic Party's advocacy of disfranchisement sent a powerful message to white peasants because the national platform of the Populist Party was silent on disfranchising black voters. Disfranchisement, however, contained a hidden agenda that Populist leaders did not fully perceive. The means of legally disfranchising black peasants could also be used to disfranchise white peasants. White peasants assumed that disfranchising procedures would be used only on blacks. Democratic Party leaders thought otherwise.

After the black electorate was extinguished, it was equally expedient to disfranchise as many white peasants as possible in order to reduce the Populist vote. By 1892, in some ex-slave states, the white electorate was reduced as much as 50 percent of its 1885 numbers.

How were black and white peasants legally disfranchised? In most southern states it was achieved by a bundle of statutes and constitutional amendments. Southern state legislatures, controlled by commercially motivated Democrats, adopted some or all of the following means: (1) poll taxes, (2) literacy tests, (3) voter registration, (4) printed ballots marked in secret, (5) constitutional amendments defining voting qualifications in order to put repeal beyond the reach of state legislatures if Populists gained temporary control, (6) gerrymandering, and; (7) malapportionment. Democratic Party leaders pursued disfranchisement with great vigor after the election of 1892.

The poll tax was the most effective way of reducing the white peasant electorate. An article in the Georgia constitution of 1877 made the poll tax voluntary, but its payment was a requirement for voting. It immediately reduced the black and white peasant electorate and made Georgia relatively immune to Populist challenges to the governing elite. Democratic governing elites in other southern states noted the results.

The second most effective way of reducing the white peasant electorate was literacy tests because literacy was a broad measure of commercial motivation. Statutes requiring literacy tests for voting were often borrowed word-for-word from statutes in northern states where they were used to exclude illiterate immigrants from voting. Registration procedures and secret (written) ballots were also tests of literacy. Literacy was further enforced by forbidding persons to accompany voters into booths to instruct them how to vote. By 1896, in most southern states, these procedures had substantially reduced the white peasant electorate, and the black electorate was reduced to a mere percent of its former numbers.

Thereafter, Democratic governing elites ignored the Republican Party and the few black voters who passed literacy tests. These blacks voted Republican and were no threat to contesting control of the state's Democratic Party. Without its black electorate, state Republican parties were too small to be effective coalition partners with Populists. Democratic Party leaders consolidated their power of governance by sponsoring primary elections to choose candidates. Only whites were allowed to vote in Democratic primary elections that chose candidates for state and local offices.

Democratic Party leaders managed primary elections for their advantage by scheduling elections on days when a maximum number of urban voters would participate and a minimum number of rural voters would participate. Planting and harvesting seasons were preferred times. This strategy ensured that governing elites exercised considerable control over nominations. White primaries allowed whites to disagree among themselves over using the powers of governance for agrarian or commercial purposes. After the mass disfranchisement of black peasants, white primary elections were the real elections in ex-slave states.

Between 1892 and 1896 the focus of agrarian discontent strongly shifted to northern states because of the substantial electoral success of Populist candidates with inflation as the principal issue. In the election of 1892 a coalition of Populist and Democrats elected governors in Kansas, Colorado, and North Dakota and three U.S. senators, and gave the Populist presidential candidate 22 electoral votes (of 444). In many rural districts in northern and western states similar coalitions elected many candidates.

Results of the 1892 election demonstrated that inflation was the only issue that could elect candidates. The problem facing leaders of the Populist Party was how to retain the Populist/Democratic coalition of 1892 so that it could elect more congressmen in 1894 and 1896. The depression that began in 1893 was the opportunity for Populist leaders and the agrarian wing of the Democratic Party to claim that inflation would restore prosperity to both the rural and urban sectors of the economy. The Populist coalition held together for the congressional election of 1894.

The presidential nominating convention of the Democratic Party in 1896 was controlled by inflationists, who nominated William Jennings Bryan for the presidency. His prospects for election seemed favorable because the majority of the U.S. population was rural (and remained so until 1915). Bryan, however, did not recognize that the influence of industrial wealth extended far into rural areas surrounding cities. For example, in the Midwest, a high percentage of farms had no mortgages and a high percentage of the maize they grew was fed to hogs or used to fatten cattle. The meat they produced was consumed in nearby cities and meat prices were profitable.

After Bryan's nomination, Populist Party leaders in northern states were hugely enthusiastic to nominate him as their candidate, and they did. At the Populist nominating convention he received 75 percent of the votes of delegates and the Populist Party merged into oblivion. All of the Texas delegates, however, voted against Bryan's nomination because he strenuously opposed the sub-treasury plan. The Texas delegation clearly understood that inflation, without an equal commitment to subsidize the furnish (sub-treasury plan), would confer minimal benefits on peasants. When the Texas delegation returned home, they were political orphans. The Populist Party ceased to exist just as the Southern Alliance had ceased to exist after 1892 when the Populist Party replaced its lobbying function.

Most historians interpret Populism as a reform movement because they believe what Populists said about themselves. Historians make two assumptions when they interpret Populists as reformers: (1) all Populists had the same social goals, and (2) policies favored by Populists were beneficial for both rural and urban America. This perspective comes from lumping southern, northern, and western Populists into a party that they claimed shared the same vision of how the national government should equalize the welfare of its citizens.

In my opinion, it requires intellectual gymnastics slightly short of levitation to claim that western silver miners, western irrigation farmers, frontier wheat farmers, Corn Belt farmers, and cotton peasants shared a vision of how government and society should operate. In my opinion, expedience was the only reason that the Populist Party maintained its cohesion from 1892 to 1896.

The Populist Party was inherently unstable because the grievances of grain farmers and cotton peasants were fundamentally different. Western irrigation farmers, frontier wheat farmers, Corn Belt farmers, and silver miners were not challenging the market economy and the commercial ethic that guided its operation. They fully supported the operation of a market economy in normal times. Their grievance was that the national (and international) commercial systems were not operating to their fair benefit because they were not receiving adequate prices for the commodities they produced.

The grievances of cotton peasants were of a different order. They rejected the ethic of commercial institutions that demanded sufficient paid labor to earn money incomes in order to make timely money payments for the products and services they consumed. White southern peasants who supported Populist policies rejected the compulsions of a market economy that forced silver miners and city laborers to perform continuous paid labor in order to earn money incomes. Cotton peasants rejected the fundamental requirement of commercial cultures: that households measure their social security by money incomes.

All historians who have studied southern Populism and analyzed Populist votes by district tell their readers that white Populists voters were highly concentrated in districts with the lowest per capita production of marketable crops, lowest land values, and that white households in these districts had very high rates of illiteracy.

Southern Populist leaders always claimed that cultivators were the purest strand of Jeffersonian democracy and were, therefore, the foundation of American democracy. If white southern peasants were the purest Jeffersonian democrats, as I believe they were, then southern peasants and their leaders were political, social, and economic anachronisms in a nation governed in the interests of commercial institutions. If we believe what southern Populist leaders said about the behavior of their constituents, as I believe we should, then southern Populist leaders were not reformers. They were reactionaries.[4]

Election of 1896

A record number of voters cast ballots in the 1896 election, and Bryan lost by the biggest margin in any election after the Civil War. The largest single reason for his defeat was he had little to say to wage laborers and urban problems. Cities were hostile territory because this is where banks and industrial corporations were located,. "On the one side stand the corporate interests of the nation, its moneyed institutions, its aggregations of wealth and capital, imperious, arrogant, compassionless…They demand the Democratic Party become their agent to execute their merciless decrees." On the opposite side were the "work-worn and dust-begrimed" farmers begging the Democratic Party to be their champion. Bryan's strategy to get the Democratic presidential nomination was to polarize the party, and he used the same strategy in the general election.[5]

His twin messages were inflation and lower tariffs, but inflation dominated his message. His message of inflation and its benefits was beamed to the agricultural sector of the economy. In Bryan's rhetoric, "the great cities rest upon our broad and fertile prairies. Burn down your cities and leave your farms, and your cities will spring up again as if by magic." The most important U.S. citizens were cultivators because they were "the producing masses of this nation." The second category of U.S. citizens was "the commercial interests" who served the needs of cultivators. The third category of U.S. citizens was "laboring interests." They worked in factories. In the election of 1900 the Democratic Party again nominated Bryan for the presidency. His message was similar to that of 1896 and he lost. He was nominated a third time in 1908 and lost again.[6]

The Republican candidate for the presidency in 1896 was William McKinley. His message was directed to city residents in general and industrial workers in particular. Republican Party leaders recognized that the commercially motivated agrarian democracy of northern states had been seamlessly transferred to industrial cities. The defeat of Bryan for a second time in 1900 made it clear that the future of American democracy was in cities. The defeat of Bryan for the third time in 1908 confirmed the obvious. The only place where Jeffersonian agrarianism survived was in the peasant South.

Republican Party leaders claimed that McKinley was the advance agent of prosperity because he authored the McKinley Tariff in 1890, which was highly protective. After the beginning of the 1893 depression, the tariff was lowered by Congress, which had Democratic majorities. Republicans claimed that restoring urban prosperity depended on restoring the protective tariff and preserving sound money guaranteed by the gold standard.

Urban residents and factory workers benefited from sound money. Deflation meant that the same wages could purchase more goods and services with the same amount of money. The welfare of wage laborers had increased since 1865 because of the increased purchasing power of the dollar. Inflation would destabilize a cost of living index that benefited urban residents because, during inflation, wages would not increase as fast as the cost of living. McKinley's message was clear. The protective tariff created urban employment, sound money preserved the purchasing power of the dollar, and the gold standard institutionalized sound money.

If Congress opted for an inflationary monetary policy, gold coins would be replaced by a flood of paper currency and 378 million dollars of silver dollar coins. The minting of these coins was mandated by the Silver Purchase Act of 1878 but treasury secretaries appointed by Republican presidents and the secretaries appointed by President Grover Cleveland withheld them from circulation because this amount of new money could not be redeemed for gold coins on demand. If they circulated, the United States would be forced off of the gold standard and inflation would ensue.

The inflationary policy favored by Bryan split the Republican and Democratic parties. Inflationary Republican congressmen, mostly from western states, supported Bryan. Sound money Democrats, mostly in northeastern states, and especially in New York, voted for McKinley, and this realignment become permanent. Many urban Democrats who had been ambivalent about using the full power of the national government to accelerate industrialization realized that only the Republican Party could repel agrarian policies that would restrain the creation of new wealth.

Chapter 12

Accelerated Industrialization

Accelerated industrialization began in the United States in 1865 and was complete by 1900. Thereafter, the economy evolved to serve the needs of a consumer culture. U.S. industrial production passed that of Britain in 1885. By 1914 annual production was eight times larger than in 1865 and equaled the combined industrial production of Britain, France, and Germany. Between 1865 and 1914, the gross national product of the United States increased at an average rate of 4 percent per year. The new wealth created between 1865 and 1900 was produced by a population that was only 2.8 times larger than in 1865. The United States was enormously successful at catch-up industrialization.

In addition, the United States settled a continent. The 1890 census showed that there was no continuous line in the trans-Missouri west beyond which there were less than two civilized persons per square mile. The frontier vanished. The United States was a continental nation. The simultaneous achievements of becoming the world's leading industrial nation and settling a continent were not accidental.

Many of the institutions that propelled rapid industrialization were largely invisible. Foremost among them were:

1. a belief that the principal purpose of national and state governments was to serve the needs of commerce;
2. cheap and efficient national and state governments;
3. high rates of literacy among American born whites in northern states;
4. an abundance of entrepreneurs;
5. laws that protected corporate and individual wealth;
6. contract laws that were predictable and were enforced by friendly courts;
7. a fluid social structure in cities;
8. high geographic mobility (people moved to where there was employment);
9. peace.

Principal among the polices that encouraged industrial investments were:

1. lack of restraints on mobilizing capital;
2. low interest rates from 1870 to 1910;
3. no corporate or personal incomes taxes;
4. general incorporation statutes for all varieties of businesses;
5. state bankruptcy laws that favored debtors;

6. development of investment banking;
7. few restraints on mergers;
8. capital borrowed from Europe to build trunkline railroads;
9. open immigration to provide industrial labor;
10. laboring for ten to twelve hours per day, six days a week;
11. minimal funding of government social services;
12. cheap food to feed city residents;
13. a miniature national bureaucracy and a miniature army and navy funded by miniature appropriations.

The fundamental foundation for industrialization is the performance of commercial labor norms by full-time paid laborers. Their efficiency is strongly enhanced by literacy because literate workers quickly learn new skills. By 1875 the southern transportation and banking infrastructures that had disintegrated during the Civil War were restored and were in process of being integrated into the national market; however, they rested on a weak foundation because southern states had a huge shortage of capital and human skills. The greatest shortage was literate persons who were commercially motivated. Illiteracy was pervasive and, for all practical purposes, the ex-slave states were a peasant society.

High rates of illiteracy were related to high labor turnovers in the cotton textile mills and tobacco processing factories that were established after the Civil War. In textile mills, labor turnovers were as high as 175 percent per year because 20–40 percent of workers were always rotating between subsistence cultivation and wage labor. For nine or ten months peasants grew enough food to feed their families and then migrated to mill towns to perform variable periods of wage labor in order to acquire target sums of money to purchase clothing and metal tools. After making these purchases they returned to subsistence cultivation. The availability of land for subsistence cultivation meant that southern peasants were not forced to become full-time wage laborers, and few of them did.

The focus of the following sections is almost exclusively on northern states where full-time paid labor was performed by urban residents.

Government

Compared to the size of the U.S. economy and especially to the size of industrial production, the national and state governments were very small until 1900. After that date they began to increase in size as the national and state governments funded more social welfare programs and increased regulation of the economy.

National

"In 1901 the president's staff consisted of a secretary, two assistant secretaries, two executive clerks, four lesser clerks or telegraphers, and a few doorkeepers and messengers." Most policy decisions were made by congressional leaders. Presidents were mostly concerned with party matters. Chief among them was patronage.[1]

Rapid turnovers in bureaucratic personnel after each presidential election prevented the formation of a tenured bureaucracy. Not until 1883 (the Pendleton Act) were government employees hired on the basis of passing civil service examinations. The Pendleton Act had minimal impact during the first twelve years of operation because the act delegated power to the president to extend civil service protection to employees at his discretion. Outgoing presidents extended civil service protection to their appointees, but if they quit or retired replacements had to pass civil service examinations. By 1900, 100,000 civil servants were protected.

The post office had more employees than any other department of the national government—56,000 in 1880, 95,000 in 1890, and 136,000 in 1900. In 1880 the post office accounted for 56 percent of the employees of the national government, 61 percent in 1890, and 57 percent in 1900. In most years revenues made the post office self-supporting, or nearly so; and during these years it was the largest business in the United States.

The Bureau of Agriculture was elevated to a cabinet level department in 1889. It should have rapidly grown in importance, however, it had little immediate impact on alleviating agricultural distress that culminated in organizing the Populist Party. Instead, it slowly expanded by conducting investigations, undertaking crop research, and assembling information. Its effectiveness had to wait for stronger presidential leadership.

In spite of intense political activity to enact an inflationary monetary policy and regulate railroad freight rates, there was little pressure from Congress to expand the power and scope of national governance. The electorate preferred a political status quo in spite of the persistence of the issue of inflation. During the 1880s, on most policy issues, the status quo became a stalemate. In the House of Representatives, "all business was done either under unanimous consent or on a motion to suspend the rules by a two-thirds vote, which in practice enabled a minority to prevent legislation....The only way to do business inside the rules is to suspend the rules....The object of the rules appears to be to prevent the transaction of business."[2]

The best evidence for satisfaction with status quo governance was the congressional consensus to repay the Civil War debt. It was steadily reduced from 1870 to 1892. A government with minimal income relative to taxable wealth, and using that income for debt reduction, was a government with minimal aspirations. In electoral terms during these years, no party had a mandate for changing the social and economic policies of the national government.

Local satisfaction with status quo governance worked strongly in favor of the Republican Party because it was a condition that lent itself to defending the three industrializing policies put in place during the Civil War: the protective tariff, the national banking system, and the subsidization of railroad construction to create a national market. These policies were continually approved by the electorate, sometimes by narrow margins. The reciprocal was that most policies favored by agrarians were rejected.

A second condition that helped the Republican Party defend its policies of economic development was the small revenues of the national government. Congress was not tempted to increase spending because low taxation policies had bipartisan support. Before 1900, low taxation by the national and state governments aided capital accumulation in the hands of persons and corporations that could more efficiently invest it than alternative investments available to the national government.

More revenue was readily available to the national government from an income tax; however, additional revenue was not needed because the national government had surplus revenue in the 1880s. This revenue was used to pay interest on the national debt and fund pensions for Civil War veterans. In 1880, 57 percent of national revenues were used for these two purposes, in 1890 these two expenditures accounted for 45 percent of the national budget, and in 1900 they accounted for 35 percent. Only after 1900 did tax revenues of the national government increase, but they lagged far behind rapidly increasing national wealth.

The revenue surplus changed in the 1890s. The depression of 1893 and reduced revenues from lowered tariffs caused a deficit in national revenue. In order to supply the necessary revenue, in August 1894 Congress passed a 2 percent tax on personal and corporate incomes in excess of four thousand dollars. It was strongly supported by agrarians because it would shift taxation to cities.

The constitutionality of the tax was immediately challenged and the Supreme Court immediately accepted jurisdiction. In April 1895, in *Pollock v. Farmers Loan and Trust Company*, the court declared it unconstitutional. It was a collusive suit because both parties wanted the tax declared unconstitutional. The Supreme Court knew this but accepted jurisdiction and wrote an opinion even though internal rules prohibited the Court from accepting collusive cases. The decision clearly indicated that a majority of Supreme Court justices considered themselves as the ultimate guardians of industrial wealth from assault by agrarians who would vote for Populist Party candidates.[3]

The *Pollock* decision was totally unrealistic because the urban democracy increasingly desired expensive social service and farmers desired improved (paved) roads, irrigation systems, and hydroelectric dams on western rivers (funded by matching state appropriations). Furthermore, the cost of future wars among industrial nations would dwarf previous costs. In every session of Congress after 1905, legislation was introduced to levy an income tax, or initiate the process of amending the Constitution to overrule the *Pollock* decision. In 1907 president Theodore Roosevelt recommended levying an income tax. In 1909 Congress adopted a constitutional amendment and sent it to the states for ratification. Most states acted immediately and it was added to the Constitution in 1913.

State

Status quo governance was especially strong in rural America. The agrarian democracy in northern and southern states preferred cheap and simple governance. Generally, state governance before 1900 was dominated by localisms, and in most states this meant preserving a status quo. In most northern states, local welfare was visibly improving. In most southern states, the commercially motivated governing elites also wanted their variation of the status quo because they wanted no interference by the national government while they reduced the black electorate, enforced the sanctions of the black caste system (white supremacy), and disfranchised white peasants who were inclined to vote Populist.

Congress approved disfranchisement and acquiesced to white supremacy. The Supreme Court assented to enforcement of the black caste system with the doctrine of "separate but equal" in *Plessy v. Ferguson* in 1896. All presidents, all sessions of Congress, and the Supreme Court assented to the primacy of localism as long as national policies accelerating industrialization continued to operate without significant modification.

All state legislatures were malapportioned. As cities multiplied and grew, state legislatures were not reapportioned. Rural interests dominated state legislatures and the rural electorate wanted governments that were cheap and simple. Rural status quo governance had a price. Taxation of real property (land, homes, stores, and factories) provided two-thirds of state revenue in 1900. On average, 75 percent of real property was taxed at its local value while only 40 percent of intangible wealth (stocks, bonds, and other financial instruments) were taxed at market value. Large amounts of intangible wealth escaped taxation.

State governments were forced to search for additional revenue during and after the depression of 1893; and to keep searching for more revenue because cities desired increasing services from state governments. The obvious place to acquire additional revenue was corporate taxation. This was not new. Bank capital had been taxed almost as soon as banks were incorporated, but industrial corporations successfully resisted equalized taxation of their property compared to taxation of other real property. It was a slow process to transfer revenue from real property to fairly assessed industrial property. In the late 1880s taxation of corporation property produced about 25 percent of state revenue. By 1900 it contributed about 33 percent.

Urban

Urban residents were seriously underrepresented in all state legislatures in 1890, but this was not seen as a serious problem because cities had a high percentage of illiterate foreign-born residents who had no experience in representative government. Urbanization was also part of localism in governance. In 1890 over 80 percent of all city residents lived in northeastern and north-central states. For the most part, state legislatures delegated power to city governments to solve their problems, but often with limitations on bonded indebtedness.

The surge of urbanization from 1870 to 1910 created huge problems in financing housing, public health, public transportation, education, and law enforcement. In 1870, 25 percent of the U.S. population was urban. By 1910, 45 percent was urban. During these years, the U.S. population increased from forty million to ninety-two million. Investments in housing and public transportation facilities were supplied by individuals and corporations, but funding for public health services (potable water, sewers, and garbage collection), education, and policing were by municipal governments.

During the surge of urbanization, there is no question that most mayors of the largest cities used the power of governance to enrich themselves and their political supporters. The usual way was to award contracts to political supporters to pave streets, dig sewers, and build municipal office buildings. Similarly, franchises were awarded to friendly corporations to manufacture producer gas, build street railways, provide telephone service, and generate and distribute electricity. Limitations on municipal debts forced mayors to turn to private investors to build these infrastructure facilities—and mayors enthusiastically accepted the opportunities to award franchises to their friends and accept gifts of stock in these franchises.

In many ways, however, corruption associated with awarding franchises and contracts was a small part of the story of urbanization because these corrupt practices succeeded in getting city infrastructures built, usually without excessive cost. At the same time, school systems were enlarged to begin the process of Americanizing the children of immigrants.

Big city mayors performed another function that rivaled the importance of building infrastructure facilities. "Machine politicians often seemed the only persons in the community who took a positive interest in their plight....They mediated between bewildered new immigrants and the harsh impersonalities of the law." Frequently, they found jobs and housing for persons or families that were otherwise without resources, or provided relief for persons or families that were temporarily destitute. By providing aid to immigrants and then controlling their votes, big city mayors began the process of teaching them the function and purpose of democratic governance.[4]

Before 1900 most state legislatures were content to delegate most of the problems of city governance to mayors because cities were just another local government. City mayors, who created political organization to retain power, strongly approved of the autonomy (indifference) that rural-dominated state legislatures accorded city problems. The autonomy of city governance was an opportunity to levy higher taxes and state legislators were happy to allow city governments to levy them. By the mid-1920s, northern states and cities had equalized assessments and reformed collection procedures so that industrial corporations and other businesses paid, on average, about 40 percent of state and city tax revenues.

Literacy

During the 1880s and 1890s, state funding of education steadily increased in northern states. By 1900 between 25 and 33 percent of all state revenues were appropriated for education; nonetheless, the amount of state and local revenue for education did not keep pace with increasing population, increasing urbanization, and the need for secondary education (high schools) in cities.

Compared to northern states, education funding in southern states was a disaster. Before the Civil War, households that wanted literate children hired tutors or paid tuition to a teacher who taught neighborhood children. This made literacy an artifact of commercial motivation because white peasants were indifferent to teaching literacy to their children. Low taxes had a much higher priority than literacy because money to pay taxes had to be acquired by wage labor or expending the labor to grow enlarged crops (cotton) for market sale. Before the Civil War only North Carolina had a common school system. It was poorly funded and did not survive the war.

After the Civil War, teaching literacy in southern states began from a substantially smaller tax base because of wartime destruction of property and reduced state and local revenues. Per capita production of all agricultural commodities substantially declined because after emancipation, freedmen (black peasants) reverted to subsistence labor norms like white peasants. The increase in subsistence cultivation reduced the tax base. At the same time, freedmen were candidates for learning literacy.

Republican Party governance (Reconstruction) in ex-slave states (between 1865 and 1876) established common school systems for both white and black peasants. It was a heroic task because revenues were inadequate and former slaveowners were indifferent to teaching literacy to white peasants, and there was active and sometimes violent opposition from white peasants for funding common schools for blacks. Nonetheless, common school systems were established and survived, even though funding was anemic for whites and at famine levels for blacks.[5]

In 1900 the average school year in southern states was about one hundred days, but school years for black children were substantially shorter. Enrollment averaged about 60 percent of eligible children and was substantially less for black children; and attendance for both races of children was haphazard at best. Only about one-third of school aged children (six to fourteen) were in daily attendance. In North Carolina in 1900, the average annual expenditure was $1.65 per school aged child. School facilities were equally deficient. The value of schoolhouses in 1900 was $1.64 per school aged child, and teachers were paid, on average, $82 per year.

Common schools for whites in southern states received four or five times the funding of common schools for blacks. Different levels of funding for white and black schools were further intensified by higher levels of funding for urban schools. Urban residents understood that literacy was necessary for urban commerce; therefore, they approved higher local taxes to fund their schools. In 1900 southern cities were largely white. In every respect, funding for black education was less.

There are many estimates of illiteracy rates in southern states in 1900. All of them are high. They were high even when taken from official statistics that always minimized illiteracy. I estimate that the illiteracy rate for southern whites in 1900 was somewhere in the neighborhood of 50 percent and black illiteracy was probably more than 80 percent. Rural rates were much higher than city rates. Blacks were penalized on two counts: racism and living in overwhelmingly rural areas. They were powerless to secure fair funding for common schools because the white primaries of the Democratic Party excluded them from the budget making process at both state and local levels.

Landowners understood that illiteracy was a very large barrier to urban migration. Landowners knew that white and black peasants rejected urban migration because city residence required continuous wage labor. As long as land was available for subsistence cultivation, southern peasants preferred the minimal labor of subsistence cultivation. Illiteracy benefited landowners because it helped preserve a reservoir of sharecrop peasants to cultivate their land. Landowners in the postwar cotton South were as much part of subsistence agriculture as peasants themselves.

Between 1880 and 1900, increased funding of free elementary and secondary education accurately measured the value of literacy in northern commercial culture. Increased per capita funding was a measure of the effort made to teach literacy to the children of immigrants. In Massachusetts in 1900, school property averaged $60 per school aged child and teachers had an average annual salary of $566. In Massachusetts, annual funding for each school-aged child was $21 and school years averaged 189 days. School years, however, were longer in cities than in rural areas. Even in Kansas, an almost totally agricultural state where farmer incomes had seriously declined in the 1890s, teacher salaries averaged $236 per year.

In 1900 lengths of school years, investments in school buildings, and teacher salaries in northern states were magnitudes greater than in southern states. In almost all northern states attendance was compulsory but difficult to enforce in urban ethnic neighborhoods where a high percentage of parents were illiterate in their native languages, as well as English. Many of these households were ambivalent about school attendance because wages from child labor contributed to household incomes.

Three school systems coevolved in northern states to teach mass functional literacy to diverse populations—rural, urban, and parochial. By 1900 rural, one room schools began to be consolidated into township or county school systems with horse drawn carriages taking students to larger, centrally located schools where classes were graded. Attendance improved and learning accelerated.

During the same years, many urban school systems had to be cleansed of patronage appointed teachers who were marginally qualified. Increasingly, professional educators staffed state boards of education and actively worked to replace patronage appointed county superintendents of schools. State boards also used the power of matching funds to induce the adoption of standard textbooks and lobbied legislatures to appropriate funds to make them free. Standard textbooks had a second function. They were the means of prescribing uniform curriculums.

The literacy that was taught in uniform curriculums was through a lens that emphasized that good citizenship required performing wage labor or earning money incomes within the context of the political and commercial institutions of the United States. The political and economic success of the United States was due to its democratic institutions, and the continuing prosperity of the United States depended on literate workers who were willing to labor to improve their personal material welfare. This was a curriculum of social efficiency (secular neutrality) that would transform diverse ethnic immigrants into productive United States citizens. Citizens who wanted to integrate religious belief into the fabric of American culture did it as individuals.

Many Roman Catholics and some Lutherans objected to the social efficiency curriculums of public schools. The individualism and secular neutrality in public school curriculums was an incentive to establish parochial schools. Some wanted a religious content to education specific to their beliefs. Parochial schools were established in the 1880s in order to teach literacy through a lens of supernatural belief that was to guide the conduct of society.

Generally, the curriculum laws in northern states required that a majority of hours of instruction be in English and that religious instruction be a minimal part of curriculums. At the same time that curriculum laws were enacted, certification was required for both public and parochial school teachers. After 1880, certification was increasingly based on attending a normal school (teachers college). Certification was a major step in converting teaching into a recognized profession.

City school systems required a broader tax base than rural school districts. The obvious source of increased revenue was taxation of corporate property. In 1890 taxation of corporate property produced about 30 percent of revenue in northern states. By 1900 about one-third of state revenues came from taxing corporate property. Municipal governments shared taxation of corporate property, and considerable amounts of this local revenue was invested in high schools. After 1880 these revenues were often used to convert private academies into tax-supported high schools.

The academic curriculums of high schools and their high cost of operation generated considerable taxpayer opposition. A principal source of opposition was taxpayers who claimed they were undemocratic institutions because they were for the benefit of persons who could afford to send their children to private academies. Similar criticism was aimed at curriculums where a major component was learning Latin and Greek.

The most effective reply to the supposed nondemocratic funding policies of high schools was that enrollment was open and attendance was free. High school education was an opportunity for upward mobility that was open to the democracy; therefore, high schools were valuable democratic institutions. The second criticism carried more weight. Learning Latin and Greek had little relevance to either governance or business in the United States. These subjects were steadily omitted from high school curriculums and replaced by history, geography, science, and modern languages.

Almost all tax-supported high schools were in northern cities, and their curriculums were broadly preparatory for college, but at highly variable levels of competence. Standards for admission to college were equally variable, and until public high schools and private academies had curriculums with some degree of standardization, admission to colleges was by examination.

Standardizing curriculums and increasing state funding meant that communities lost substantial control over education. This raised a fundamental question. *What was the purpose of education beyond teaching functional literacy?* This question returns to the coevolution of three school systems in northern states after the Civil War. Rural schools were content with teaching functional literacy in common schools.

Primary education in cities had to be different. Unlike rural students, urban students were continually bombarded with new experiences that had to be understood.

> City schools must explain more to students than village schools because there are many more uses for literacy in cities. City schooling is knowledge acquiring education. This is very different from the functional literacy taught in villages (because) all commercial cultures require a high percentage of city residents to be educated beyond functional literacy.[6]

In cities knowledge acquiring education had to have an extended dimension. High schools had to be established because large business corporations needed persons who could learn the skills of office management. The earliest free high schools were in larger cities where entry level jobs for business management were concentrated. Beginning in the mid-1880s, high school education began replacing on-the-job training for managers. During the early 1890s, enrollment levels were less than 10 percent of students from primary schools, and graduation rates were less, especially for males.

After 1895, high school graduation was an increasingly important credential for being hired to learn office and management skills in large business corporations. The concentration of free high schools in cities was an opportunity for the children of European immigrants to seek and secure jobs with high pay scales. Cities were the place of commercial opportunity, and a high percentage of these opportunities went to persons who were educated in urban schools and who were the children of European immigrants.

Mobilizing Capital

Where did the capital come from to accelerate industrialization? And how was it mobilized and allocated? There were eight sources of capital. The most important source was the agricultural sector. The seven others were (1) concentration of bank reserves in big city banks, especially in New York City banks; (2) development of investment banking; (3) overseas borrowing, mainly from Britain; (4) credit from local banks to local entrepreneurs; (5) protective tariff; (6) no national taxation of corporate profits; and (7) few corporate welfare expenses.

Agriculture

The following polices mobilized capital from the agricultural sector and preferentially allocated it to urban industries: (1) deflation, (2) high freight rates for agricultural commodities compared to competitive freight rates for intercity transportation of manufactured products, (3) protective tariffs that raised prices of manufactured products consumed by cultivators, and (4) the national banking system that concentrated deposits from small town banks in large cities. The following agrarian contributions helped accelerate industrialization: (1) declining prices for wheat and maize that translated into cheap breadstuffs and meat for city residents, and (2) continuous urban migration by the literate sons of northern farmers capable of being trained as skilled laborers and clerical staffs for businesses.

One measure of the success of extracting capital from the agricultural sector was the declining percentage of agricultural products in the gross national product (GNP). In 1870 the United States was about 75 percent rural, and agricultural commodities were about 53 percent of the GNP. In 1900 agricultural commodities were only about 33 percent of the GNP, and declining rapidly. The declining percentage of agricultural commodities as a percentage of GNP occurred at the same time that huge amounts of new land were brought under cultivation.

Between 1860 and 1900, approximately 175 million hectares (431 million acres) was transferred from the public domain to farmers, ranchers, and railroads. A parallel measurement was the increase in the number of farms, from two million in 1860 to 5.7 million in 1900. The westward expansion of agriculture was a very impressive achievement that strongly contributed to national economic development; however, the increase in urban industrial wealth was greater than the increase in agricultural wealth. This was a much more impressive achievement.

Continuous deflation from 1865 to 1896 corresponded with continuously declining prices for agricultural commodities. Little could be done to stop price declines because immense amounts of new land were being brought under cultivation in Russia, Australia, and Argentina and this grain was grown for export. The U.S. government was committed to the same policy by encouraging homesteading on land in the public domain or land purchased from railroads. Homesteading required money, usually more money than pioneer households possessed. Mortgages supplied the money to build houses or barns and drill water wells, while pioneer households supplied livestock and cultivation implements.

After 1865, mortgage payments on agricultural land had to be made with dollars that gradually increased in purchasing power. Although maturity dates for mortgages on agricultural land were usually short (three to five years), if interest and some of the principal was annually paid, mortgages were renewed so that short-term mortgages became long-term mortgages. Payments made with appreciating dollars magnified interest rates to 8–9 percent for frontier grain farmers. These were high interest rates compared to 5–6 percent interest rates on midwestern farms that practiced diversified agriculture and were less vulnerable to droughts. In the United States in 1890, 38 percent of farms were mortgaged, but it was 60 percent in Kansas and 54 percent in Nebraska and other frontier grain states. High interest rates paid with appreciating dollars transferred capital to banks, where it was available for loans to manufacturing corporations.

For the first ten years of its operation (1863–1873), the national banking system restrained the incorporation of new state banks because the 10 percent tax on banknote currency issued by state banks (1866) ended their circulation and reduced profits. In 1863 there were 1,466 state banks, but in 1873 there were only 277. During this decade the number of national banks increased from zero to 1,968. Most of the new banks were in northern states because ex-slave states had dissipated huge amounts of capital in waging war. Their economies were desperately short of capital for investment in banks. Frontier states were also deficient in capital. After 1873 the number of new state banks slowly increased as southern agriculture recovered and wheat farming expanded westward. Many of the new state banks incorporated between 1874 and 1884 served agriculture by making mortgages on agricultural land.

National banks in small towns served the needs of town businessmen and only indirectly the needs of agriculture because they were prohibited from making mortgages on agricultural land. These banks had two uses for their capital and deposits: (1) Most of their loans were made to town businessmen and substantial farmers. They were noncollateralized. (2) From 1870 to 1895 state and national banks in small towns kept high balances in city banks because the demand for rural credit peaked at planting and harvest. During the rest of the year these banks had idle funds. Idle funds were deposited in city banks because they received 2 percent interest; otherwise, they would be inert in bank vaults. Adjusted to risk considerations, it was safer to deposit funds in city banks rather than lending to less credit worthy businessmen and farmers.

Deposits in city banks drained funds from the agricultural sector because declining commodity prices increased risks of default. In the larger cities, and especially in New York City, these deposits provided credit to industry and commerce, usually in the form of working capital. This was an efficient allocation of credit for the national policy of accelerating industrialization.

Investment Banking

Investment bankers mobilized capital from diverse sources in order to allocate to capital intensive projects. They did not issue national banknote currency, accept deposits, or make commercial loans. American investment banking began in the 1850s when several banks in seaboard cities began specializing in mobilizing capital for railroad construction. From the beginning, American investment bankers reached out to Europe to obtain capital.

After 1868, when the Civil War debt was funded, European investment bankers resumed investments in bonds of the national government because they paid 5 or 6 percent interest in gold. Suddenly they were A-grade investments. They were purchased in large amounts at substantial discounts. In 1869 European investors owned one billion dollars of war bonds. German investors were the largest purchasers. At the same time, European bankers evaluated investment opportunities in trunkline railroads. The Civil War had temporarily stopped European investments in U.S. railroad bonds because most railroad construction was suspended, and European investors purchased few war bonds.

The preservation of national unity changed the perception of European investment bankers. They liked the high interest rates, especially the bonds of railroads with large land grants that had transcontinental ambitions. By the late 1870s, the principal business of American investment bankers and their European agents was underwriting new issues of railroad bonds.

Seven investment banks dominated the underwriting and trading of railroad bonds, although there were many smaller participants. Three of the largest investment banks were American and four were British. American investment bankers established close agency relationships with European investment bankers, especially those in Britain. In the process they acquired new underwriting and marketing skills. Prior to 1890, most of the business of American investment bankers was funding railroad construction or providing funds that allowed bankrupt railroads to operate. After 1895, they increasingly underwrote issues of stocks and bonds of manufacturing corporations.

The business they conducted was very large. In 1876 British investments in U.S. railroads was 486 million dollars, in 1900 it was about two billion dollars, and in 1913 about three billion dollars. The largest American investment bankers had London offices and British investment bankers had New York, Philadelphia, or Boston agents. Investment bankers in Paris, Frankfort, and Amsterdam also had American agents. American railroads bonds were routinely traded on European exchanges on a par with local securities. In 1914 long-term European investments in the United States were estimated at 7.1 billion dollars. Of this amount, 4.1 billion was invested in railroad securities; and 66 percent was owned in Britain as portfolio investments.

European investors (and speculators) also sought profit making opportunities by acquiring vacant land. Land speculation was particularly attractive to European investors because of the abundance, cheapness, and availability of land in large units with clear titles. Railroad land was especially attractive because vacant land in the trans-Missouri west would acquire value after it was traversed by railroads. Railroads were eager to sell their land grants as soon as possible because they needed money to build rights-of-way and purchase rolling stock.

The only way purchasers could earn speculative profits was to recruit settlers. Railroads were eager to settle farmers along their routes in order to produce commodities they could transport to markets, and territorial and state governments wanted railroads to sell land because it did not generate taxes until it was sold. Recurring railroad bankruptcies clearly showed why European investors preferred purchasing the bonds of land grant railroads because receivers willingly exchanged defaulted bonds for vacant land as part of financial restructuring.

Direct foreign investment in manufacturing was the second largest source of European capital during the fifty years after the end of the Civil War (1865–1914). European corporations that built factories in the United States usually had the assistance of European bankers, but not necessarily investment bankers. These bankers acted as conduits for transferring capital. Factories were built in the United States because the protective tariff precluded profitable exports. In order to retain American markets, manufacturing had to be done in the United States. European corporations that built factories in the United States sent managers to the United States to build and manage them. Direct foreign investments often involved transferring new or improved technologies to the United States. In the process of construction, European managers usually adopted the American practice of using more machines and less labor.

One of the best documented builders of factories in the United State was a manufacturer of specialty steel. The company used the crucible process to make the same products they made in Sheffield, England. These were alloy steels of superior hardness, resistance to heat, and durability of edges needed to saw wood, plow, or cut, bore, or bend low carbon steel into a multitude of shapes.

European investor/speculators also contributed significant amounts of capital to mining after railroads entered the inter-mountain West. The capital for these investments may or may not have been mobilized by investment bankers. British investors were especially attracted to gold and silver mining and German investors were attracted to copper and other nonferrous metals because of a potential shortage of them in rapidly industrializing Europe. These investments were made before 1900. After 1900, new technologies in earth moving and mineral recovery made it possible to mine very large, low-grade copper deposits in the United States (and Chile). Capital for these open pit mines came from the United States.

Immigrants and Migrants

There were four migrations within the United States between 1865 and 1914. Two were agricultural and two were urban. The agricultural ones were (1) replication of subsistence agriculture by black and white peasants migrating to vacant lands in Texas, Arkansas, and Oklahoma; and (2) expansion of grain farming on prairie land in Kansas and its western extension, and irrigated farming in intermountain river valleys. The two urban migrations were (1) the sons of northern farmers migrating to cities in search of employment, and (2) displaced European peasants crossing the Atlantic to perform unskilled urban labor.

A fifth migration never happened. It was the nonmigration of southern peasants (black and white) to northern cities seeking full-time wage labor employment. In 1890 the black population of New York City was 1.6 percent, Boston was 1.8 percent, Philadelphia 3.8 percent, Pittsburgh 3.3 percent, Cleveland 1.1 percent, Detroit 1.7 percent, and Chicago 1.3 percent. In 1910 the percentages were less than double 1890 percentages. As long as land was available for subsistence cultivation in ex-slave states, black and white peasants rejected urban migration to perform full-time wage labor.

The children of southern peasant households (white and black) could have acquired literacy if their parents had migrated to northern cities and become full-time wage laborers. Southern peasants, however, did not migrate to northern cities in any significant numbers. Southern peasants had little interest in upward mobility for themselves or for their children as long as they had access to land use. The nonmigration of southern peasants to northern cities in the 1870s, 1880s, 1890s, and 1900s was an enormous missed opportunity for the upward mobility of their children.

The abundant unskilled industrial jobs in northern cities were performed by European immigrants; and their children attended adequately funded school that taught functional literacy. By default, the abundant commercial opportunities available in cities that required literacy went to the children of immigrant wage laborers.

Immigration from Europe almost ceased after 1914 due to World War I. Northern industries searched for other sources of unskilled labor. They recruited a steady stream of migrants from southern states. In 1910, 89 percent of blacks lived in the South but by 1920, only 85 percent of blacks lived in southern states. The available evidence indicates that blacks who migrated to northern cities had a higher rate of functional literacy than those who remained.

Literate blacks probably constituted about 60 percent of the migrants after 1914, and white migrants had an estimated literacy rate of 90 percent. It is clear that literate migrants after 1915 actively sought full-time wage labor. Like European immigrants who preceded them to northern cities, migration was an opportunity for a better life. Both black and white peasant were like European immigrants with whom they mingled. They had to adjust to the discipline of full-time wage labor.

European Immigration

This section concentrates on European immigrants because their labor was responsible for creating very large amounts of new wealth compared to the economically inert peasantry of the cotton South. European peasants who migrated to European cities faced an uncertain future, but if they remained in their villages they faced persistent hunger; therefore, they emigrated. Displaced European peasants knew that they would have to perform full-time wage labor in America. Three themes dominate letters written from the United States to family members remaining in European villages: (1) wages were high and savings were possible; (2) earning money required ten hours of labor for six days a week; and (3) food was abundant and cheap, including meat.

Between 1820 and 1879, the United States absorbed about 8.5 million European immigrants. About 7.5 million (88%) came from northwest Europe (Ireland, England, Scotland, and Germany). Between 1880 and 1914, the United States absorbed more than 20 million additional European immigrants. In these thirty years, northwest Europe continued to supply the same number of immigrants as in the previous sixty years, but Scandinavian immigration increased from about 4 percent to over 20 percent.

A high percentage of German and Scandinavian immigrants who arrived after 1870 were literate, came with some money, and intended to become permanent residents. They usually came as families and often had some experience working for wages in cities. The voyage across the Atlantic was an extension of urban migration in their own country. Most became city residents, although some moved to the frontier, purchased cheap land, and hoped they could acquire pioneering skills from their neighbors.

The Irish were the first European peasantry to arrive in a surge. It began with a strong flow during the hungry years of the mid-1830s and became an avalanche during the famine years from 1845 to 1850. The famine was most intense in the least commercialized west, a region with the highest population density. This group was poorly prepared for immigration. A high percentage were seriously malnourished when they boarded ships and many were destitute when they arrived. They clustered in port cities because they had no money to travel inland. Boston was a favored destination because it was the closest large American city to Ireland.

These immigrants performed unskilled wage labor in waterfront warehouses or building construction; dug ditches for water, sewer, or gas pipes; or moved short distances inland to work in textile mills, shoe factories, or moving earth to build canals and railroad rights-of-way. What happened in Boston also happened in New York City and Philadelphia.

Between 1880 and 1914, 12 million immigrants came from Poland, Hungary, Italy, Greece and other nation of eastern and southern Europe. They immigrated because the governments of these nations initiated policies to commercialize agriculture. These nations did not have enough urban employment for displaced peasants and the central governments of these nations tacitly encouraged emigration because (1) displaced peasants were potential sources of political unrest if they remained at home, and (2) remittances of gold dollars were a substantial source of foreign exchange that was needed for capital investments. The largest single group came from southern Italy and Sicily, and the second largest group was Polish.

Peasant immigrants who intended to be permanent residents emigrated to escape hunger because (1) partible inheritance in southern Italy and Russian Poland reduced cultivation units to small sizes that could not supply subsistence amounts of food in poor crop years, and (2) political pressure to commercialize agriculture (in German Poland and Hungary) made them superfluous persons. Others emigrated with the intent of earning money and returning to their home villages to purchase land and sharecrop it. They would build new homes and retire by subsisting on money from the sale of their share of the crops. "Whenever there is a chance to buy a piece of land a man leaves his wife at home and goes to America."[7]

Most of these immigrants settled in industrial cities where they were employed as unskilled laborers in heavy industry, railroad track maintenance, and other industrial jobs. In 1890 the population of New York City was 42 percent foreign born, 35 percent of Boston's residents were foreign born, the percentage in Philadelphia was 25 percent, Pittsburgh was 30 percent, Cleveland 37 percent, Detroit 39 percent, and Chicago 41 percent.

Displaced peasants from eastern and southern Europe usually knew exactly where they were going when they left their home villages. They had friends in the United States who gave them specific directions how to get to their place of employment after they arrived. Large industrial corporations did not recruit laborers, because letters from immigrants to their home villages sustained immigration. Competitive steamship companies provided cheap immigrant fares, and when combined with prepaid tickets, crossing the Atlantic was affordable to all who wanted to emigrate. In 1856 more than 95 percent of immigrants arrived in sailing ships after voyages of six to eight weeks. By 1893, 97 percent arrived in steamships, and the crossing took nine to twelve days. Steamships converted the Atlantic into a highway to America (and back again), instead of the last barrier to be crossed.

From another perspective, cheap steamship tickets made it possible for European peasants to become migrant laborers instead of permanent residents. There were very large seasonal migrations of peasants from eastern and southern Europe to perform seasonal agricultural labor (planting, harvest) on farms and vineyards in Germany, France, and elsewhere; or perform short periods of wage labor in textile and other factories until they acquired target sums of money. For these immigrants, the voyage to the United States was an extension of migratory paid labor in Europe. They came for the specific purpose of saving target sums of money in order to improve their welfare in their home villages, or marry there, or retire there.

In a social sense, returned immigrants were looking backward. They came to the United States to accumulate target sums of money in order to return to their home villages and live as upper strata peasants. From deficient statistics compiled from many sources, scholars estimate that between 25 and 33 percent of all immigrants from 1880 to 1930 returned to Europe after a short residence (one to three years) or a longer residence (three to ten years).

Those who immigrated with intent to remain (a large majority), did so because, whatever their experiences as industrial laborers in the United States, their long-term welfare was better than they could expect in home villages or as wage laborers in European cities. They accepted the commercial labor norms of American industrial culture because the European alternatives were worse. Furthermore, many families anticipated that their children would have substantial commercial opportunities in American cities because upward mobility in America was an accepted social norm.

> Thousands of immigrants saw America for what it actually was. A promise, perhaps, but one to be redeemed at the price of terribly hard work, dismal living conditions, recurrent insecurity, and deteriorating health—a price much steeper than they had imagined in Europe.[8]

Immigration from England, Scotland, and Wales was continuous. It was nearly invisible because they spoke English, a high percentage were literate, and many came with money. Other immigrant groups with high rates of literacy were Bohemians (Czech Republic) and Jews. They emigrated in search of commercial opportunities and to escape religious persecution. A high percentage of Bohemians were covert Protestants who wanted to escape paying taxes to support the Roman Catholic Church.

Jews from the Russian part of Poland and from Russia itself came from a literate subculture in a sea of illiterate peasants. They lived in towns and cities and were attracted to American cities by the commercial opportunities that were highly favorably compared to their circumscribed status in Europe. They had urban skills (tailoring was the most common), and they came as families. They were induced to flee by officially tolerated pogroms and they had no intention of returning. They recognized that upward mobility required learning the English language as soon as possible because it was the language of business, and parents of these households wanted their children to be fluent.

How rapid was upward mobility? It varied among immigrant groups according to the rates of literacy they brought from Europe and their experience in Europe as full-time paid laborers, and especially their experience as urban wage laborers. A significant percentage of children of literate immigrant groups (second generation) entered the middle class; however, not until the third generation did they homogenize into American commercial culture. For illiterate immigrant groups from eastern and southern Europe, homogenization took one or two generations longer.

Thomas Kessner succinctly summarizes the different goals of commercially motivated immigrants and peasant immigrants. Jewish immigrants "often measured their success by the achievements of their children. Tremendous pressure was placed on children to fulfill the ambitions of their parents....These pressures were generally expressed as economic goals." Households of illiterate peasant immigrants often had a different priority. In peasant societies the function of children is to perform agricultural labor at the earliest age. Urban residence in the United States had little effect on this social value.

School enrollment competed with parental desire for small increments to family income that was possible from child labor. "Children were expected to hold jobs and contribute to family income. They entered the job market before they could train for high status careers. Consequently, the second generation generally settled into manual labor." This behavior transferred the subsistence social values of peasant villages to cities, but it was monetized. Monetized subsistence usually lasted only during the second generation.[9]

Accelerated Industrialization in the United States would not have been possible without the labor of immigrants who arrived after 1880. In 1900 a U.S. government survey found that 73 percent of Italian, Slavic, and Hungarian immigrants were concentrated in the largest cities in seven industrial states. These seven states produced 61 percent of American manufactured and mined products. In another perspective, between 1899 and 1910 young single males aged fourteen to forty-four constituted about 75 percent of immigrants from eastern and southern Europe. They were of prime working age. The cost of raising them to working age had been made by their parents and their home villages. The United States was a huge beneficiary of their labor because their labor was instantly available where and when it was needed.

American Urban Migration

There are many high quality scholarly studies of European immigration to U.S. cities during the surge from 1880 to 1914. There are several high quality studies of the migration of southern blacks to cities (after 1914), but there are no comparable studies of the urban migration of the sons of northern farmers. This is very strange because this migration was comparable in numbers to European immigrants becoming permanent city residents. As near as can be calculated, eleven million rural residents migrated to cities between 1880 and 1910. A high percentage were young, and they found their first employment in nearby small towns. After varying periods of employment, they moved to larger cities

The reasons given for this migration are probably accurate, and the job categories that historians assume they filled are probably accurate as well, but there is a total lack detail of as to where they fit into the process of industrialization. The general reasons for the migration were (1) higher rural birthrates; (2) rapid increase in the mechanization of cultivation; (3) low prices for agricultural commodities; and (4) ease of entry into urban employment because they were literate, spoke English, were commercially motivated, and they understood the wide range of employment opportunities available to them. Their migration was vital to the success of accelerated industrialization.

The agricultural frontier is the usual focus of historians who write about internal migration in the United States. This migration has been intensively studied because it was a geographically dramatic event. But in terms of the numbers of migrants and the new wealth they helped create, the migration of the sons of northern farmers to cities was of equal or greater significance. For every son of a northern farmer who migrated to the agricultural frontier, ten migrated to cities seeking employment.

Clearly, in 1900 ex-slave states were not part of accelerated industrialization. In 1900 only about 4 percent of the adult populations of southern states were wage laborers, and city residents were about 15 percent of the population. At that time manufactured products produced in southern states were about 10 percent of the national product, about the same as in 1860. The five principal industries in southern states in 1900 were cotton textiles, tobacco products, lumber, iron and steel (at Birmingham, Alabama), with accompanying coal mining.

Protection of Property

During the years of accelerated industrialization (1865–1900) the national judiciary, capped by the Supreme Court, acted with great energy to protect industrial wealth from what the Court considered to be arbitrary legislation that was often of agrarian origin. During these years neither the presidents nor Congress had a coherent vision of how the national government should function in the transforming events of industrialization and urbanization.

The best measures of lack of vision were the four issues that generated continuous controversy: inflation, protective tariff, national protection of the black electorate, and the proper relationship between business and government. All four issues were stalemated in Congress and the president followed. In this situation, the Court filled a policy vacuum.

In 1883 the Supreme Court sanctioned white supremacy in ex-slave states (*Civil Rights Cases*) by declaring unconstitutional the Civil Rights Act passed by Congress in 1875. The Civil Rights Act of 1875 was designed to use national power to protect the black electorate. By extension, the court sanctioned the disfranchisement of large numbers of white peasants. Reducing the black and white peasant electorates had the highly desirable effect of reducing electorates that were in process of being mobilized (by Populists) in order to enact legislation that would restrict or repeal policies that were accelerating industrialization. The policy stalemate gave the Supreme Court great latitude to protect industrial wealth on its own terms, and a high percentage of residents of northern cities approved of the Court's decisions.

How did the Supreme Court protect industrial wealth? The Court based its assumption of power on the "due process of law" clauses in the Fifth Amendment (ratified in 1791) and the first section of the Fourteenth Amendment (ratified in 1868). The Fourteenth Amendment ended states' rights, and after its ratification states exercised only as much power as the national government consigned to them. The conventional meaning of "due process of law" was that individuals had procedural safeguards in the conduct of judicial hearing and trials to prevent arbitrary conduct by law enforcement authorities.

The Supreme Court changed the meaning from procedural safeguards for individuals to substantial protection of industrial wealth from unreasonable legislation by Congress and state legislatures. "Substantive due process actually endowed the courts with a kind of quasi-legislative power." The "due process of law offered immunity to private property and vested interests against unreasonable social legislation." The Supreme Court decided what was unreasonable.[10]

The Court used the clear grant of power to the national government in the Fourteenth Amendment to protect their vision of the industrial future of the United States. The United States would be a great industrial nation, and, during the transforming process, new wealth had to be protected from agrarian assault. In order to continue the accumulation of capital and its productive investment, the Court had to preserve the policies that encouraged commercial diversification in northern states prior to the Civil War. These were the policies the Republican controlled Congress enacted into law during the Civil War.

The justices understood the industrialization process because they had participated in it during their youth, and they protected these policies from what they considered to be unreasonable legislation in (1) labor relations, (2) business regulation, and (3) public health legislation.

Labor Relations

The Court's decisions were based on what it considered to be excessive use of police power in matters affecting industrialization. Two examples will show how the Supreme Court filled a vacuum policy in matters of labor relations at a time when industrial corporations were in the process of becoming big by consolidation. The two examples are injunctions in strikes and the doctrine of freedom of contract

The Pullman strike of 1894 was the first use of an injunction in a strike affecting a vital part of the national market. The Pullman Company was a major supplier of railroad equipment. The strike was caused by a 20 percent reduction of worker wages but continuing high salaries for managers and continued payment of regular dividends. Workers organized a union and began a strike. When no wage agreement was forthcoming, striking workers began using violence to obstruct interstate railroad traffic.

The attorney general of the United States sought an injunction to force union leaders to order an end to obstructing interstate commerce. Union leaders did not or could not stop violence and they were convicted of contempt of court and imprisoned. From this experience it was clear that court injunctions were not a satisfactory way of adjudicating labor disputes in industries, especially in industries vital to the operation of the national market.

The freedom of contract doctrine was an imaginative creation of the Supreme Court. The doctrine was created by expanding the due process of law clause of the Fourteenth Amendment. The court said that due process also guaranteed individuals the right to live and work wherever they could find employment. Chief among the guarantees was the freedom to enter into contracts for labor that maximized personal benefits. The court had a purpose in creating the freedom of contract doctrine. "The concept of freedom of contract was to be used after 1900 mainly to invalidate state laws regulating conditions of labor" because the court believed these statutes reduced profits from private property and added excessive costs to production.[11]

The culmination of the Supreme Court's assumption of the power to define unreasonable labor relations came in 1908 when it declared unconstitutional a congressional statute that prohibited "yellow dog" contracts, which required prospective employees to sign contracts that they would not join a labor union. The reasoning behind the Court's decision was that employees must have freedom to contract their labor, and prohibiting yellow dog contracts limited that freedom. In the name of freedom of choice the Court granted industrial corporations the power to prevent employees from joining labor unions—in a situation where individuals had minimal bargaining power with large corporations.

Business Regulation

Two examples will indicate how the Supreme Court filled the vacuum created by the policy stalemate in Congress that produced ambiguously worded regulatory statues. The two most important examples are the 1887 statue that established in the Interstate Commerce Commission (ICC) and the Sherman Anti-Trust Act of 1890 that attempted to prohibit the organization of cartels and monopolies by mergers.

Congress established the ICC in order to prevent state railroad commissions and state legislatures from regulating interstate freight rates to the advantage of a state's farmers and village storekeepers. The ICC was approved by most railroad managers because a single national agency could rationalize interstate freight rates—or so railroad managers believed. The ICC was not explicitly granted rate-making power, but it was granted the power to issue cease and desist orders if railroads violated any provision of the law. One of the provisions was that railroads had to charge reasonable and just rates.

This implied that after an order was issued to cease charging unreasonable rates, the ICC could fix reasonable rates, but again this was not an explicit grant of power. In other words, the principal function of the ICC was poorly defined in the statute that created it. Ambiguity was intentional. Ambiguity was the congressional response to the continuing policy stalemate in Congress as it applied to problems arising from agrarian discontent and accelerated industrialization. The congressional response was, let the courts decide.

In a series of cases, the Supreme Court was unwilling to grant rate making powers to the ICC (by implication) because Congress could have made an explicit grant of power. State legislatures explicitly granted rate making powers to state railroad commissions. Furthermore, the court was highly suspicious of the quasi-judicial power granted to the ICC to determine reasonable and just railroad rates. The Court wanted to be the ultimate protector of railroad earnings because railroads sustained the national market.

In 1890, three years after the ICC was established, the court said that the reasonableness of railroad rates fixed by state railroad commissions was a judicial question. Thereafter, all rates set by the ICC and state railroad commissions were subject to judicial review. The Court would decide the reasonableness of railroad rates. In effect, the Court assumed quasi-legislative powers and in doing so usurped the quasi-legislative power that Congress had delegated to the ICC.

The creation of giant manufacturing corporations began in the 1880s. The usual way to create them was by mergers. Once mergers began in an industry, the objective of many managers was to create a monopoly to control prices and prevent destructive competition. Alternatively, mergers created oligopolies. Oligopolies were two, three, or four giant corporations in an industry that could reduce destructive competition and accumulate capital to efficiently service the national market. The creation of giant manufacturing corporations followed in the footsteps of creating giant railroad systems.

Like the creation of giant railroad systems, with monopolistic power to set rates in the territories they served, giant manufacturing corporations were a source of public apprehension because they appeared so suddenly. A related source of public apprehension was the great wealth owned by the few people who owned stock in monopoly or oligopolistic corporations—and this wealth was concentrated in cities.

The Sherman Anti-Trust statute did not prohibit mergers but made illegal "every contract, combination in the form of trust or otherwise, or conspiracy in restraint of trade or commerce among the several states." What did this mean? There was no definition of restraint of trade, nor of conspiracy, nor of what constituted a monopoly. It is clear from the debate in Congress that the authors of the statute wanted ambiguity. They intended the courts to interpret the statute, and they assumed the interpretation would be based on experience in British common law. In effect, the ambiguity of the statute granted the Supreme Court the power to decide what constituted harmful restraints of trade.

In 1895 the attorney general of the United States initiated a lawsuit to dissolve the American Sugar Refining Company, which had been formed in 1892 by merging or otherwise absorbing forty sugar refineries so that it controlled in excess of 90 percent of the U. S. market. A Supreme Court decision in 1895 (*United States v. E. C. Knight Co*) was a combination of great clarity and great ambiguity. The great clarity was the Court's refusal to recognize the American Sugar Refining Company as a monopoly that restrained commerce.

The great ambiguity was a sharp distinction between commerce and manufacturing—even when manufactured products were produced to be sold on the national market. In the words of the majority opinion, "commerce succeeds to manufacture and is not a part of it." Manufacturing corporations were not part of interstate commerce, even when they were monopolies; therefore, they were beyond congressional regulation. Presumably only railroads and other forms of interstate transportation were interstate commerce and could be regulated by Congress.[12]

As we have seen in the first part of this section, the Court was reluctant to give Congress the power to regulate railroads, and was equally reluctant to give Congress the power to regulate big manufacturing corporations, even when they were monopolies. The Supreme Court saw with greater clarity than members of Congress that the national market that came into being in their lifetimes needed big business corporations for efficient operation. Railroad transportation was most efficient when integrated into big systems. Manufacturing was also most efficient when technologies of mass production could achieve economies of scale; therefore, the Supreme Court used the rule of reason to protect big business corporations.

The rule of reason was little different from President Theodore Roosevelt's opinion that there were good and bad big business corporations, based on their behavior in the national market. Big corporations were good when they used the efficiencies of mass production and economies of scale to lower prices on consumer products. Big corporations were bad when they used collusion (restraints of trade) to maintain high markups on the products they made.

Public Health

The Supreme Court's decisions on public health merge with its decisions on hours of labor. The leading decision on the Court's attitude toward public health was *Lochner v. New York* in 1905. The decision declared unconstitutional a New York statute that limited hours of labor for bakers to ten hours per day and sixty hours per week. The basis for the Court's reasoning was freedom of contract. The majority opinion stated: "There is no reasonable ground for interfering with the liberty of persons or the right of free contract by determining the hours of labor in the occupation of a baker." The Court rejected the contention that long hours of labor in food preparation might constitute a health hazard if tired bakers allowed dirt to become mixed with dough. "The safety…of the public…is not in the slightest degree affected by such an act."[13]

The majority of justices were trained before germs were identified as human pathogens. The *Lochner* decision cited a decision by a New York court (*In re Jacobs*, 1885) as a precedent. The New York court had unanimously declared unconstitutional a New York statute prohibiting making cigars in crowded rooms in New York City tenements. Cigar making in the 1880s was a home industry, usually done by immigrants. Hand rolling cigars invariably littered floors with scarps of tobacco, and because they were made in living quarters where children were in and out of rooms, they were usually unsanitary. The New York court ignored unsanitary conditions and said that the statute had no relation to the health of residents. It was unconstitutional because it infringed on a man's right to earn an honest livelihood and it deprived building owners of profits from his property.

The *Lochner* decision was incompatible with an 1898 decision where the Court approved a Utah statute that fixed eight hours as the working day in mines, smelters, and refineries. These jobs required heavy labor and were dangerous, and the justices recognized that fatigue in dangerous workplaces caused excessive accidents and mortalities. Where the justices had experience with heavy labor, as most of them did in their youths, they recognized that limits on hours of labor for dangerous jobs were desirable. The justices approved the Utah statute because the majority said that freedom of contract did not apply in all situations.

The inconsistencies of their decisions were an embarrassment. Three years after the *Lochner* decision (1908), the court silently overruled it. It upheld a 1903 Oregon statute that prohibited employing women for more than ten hours per day in laundries and in factories where heavy machinery was operating.

The Court passed judgment on national and state legislation based on their experience, not on the experience of state legislators or congressmen, or increasing numbers of municipal officials and third parties who wanted to use the power of governance to improve working conditions in factories and living conditions in cities. In the 1890s these reformers had minimal impact on the justices of the Supreme Court because public health statutes had to agree with the experiences of the justices.

Bankruptcy

The Constitution granted Congress the power to pass bankruptcy statutes. Congress did not act until 1800 and the statute passed in that year applied only to merchants. It was unpopular because its provisions favored creditors instead of debtors. Only creditors could initiate bank-ruptcy proceedings. Its intended purpose was to provide a procedure for creditors of merchants trading overseas to obtain fair shares of assets when wartime captures bankrupted merchants. It was repealed in 1803 because it was strongly opposed by agrarians who purchased land on credit. Banks and other creditors used the statute to initiate forecloses of mortgages. After foreclosure, the labor expended to bring new land under cultivation was uncompensated.

Agrarians strongly favored state bankruptcy statutes that favored debtors because they excluded most household assets from seizure in bankruptcy proceedings. State bankruptcy stat-utes were often supplemented by stay laws that granted moratoriums of six to twelve months in mortgage payments during periods of financial stringency. Stay laws gave temporary protection to landowners from forced sale at sacrifice prices. During this respite, they could negotiate better terms of sale for their land or return to financial solvency. Stay laws were a temporary expedi-ent that did not give agrarians what they wanted most. Agrarians wanted instant debt relief by voluntary bankruptcy laws that terminated all debts rather than fair treatment of creditors. This would allow them to resume cultivation without the burden of unpayable debts.

This was reasonable in a culture that was becoming fully commercial. Much of the credit that banks extended to agrarians and other businesses in the 1830s came from newly incorporated banks. Many of them had little or no real assets. In other words, many debts of cultivators were incurred from weak or fraudulent banks operating in a highly inflationary economy. Dividing the assets of legally bankrupt persons would enrich speculative bankers. The best policy was to cancel these debts because people who were relieved of debts could resume normal commercial activities. Their unencumbered labor would stimulate the revival of commerce.

A second bankruptcy statute was passed by Congress in 1841, at the depth of the depres-sion. Debtors disliked it because state lien laws were preserved and creditors disliked it because of high legal costs. It was repealed in 1842. Congress passed the third national bankruptcy law in 1867, primarily for the relief of debtors. It was poorly drafted and costly to administer, although its voluntary bankruptcy procedures provided agrarian relief during the depression that began in 1873.

In spite of its imperfections, it survived because it was amended to allow businesses that were legally bankrupt, but otherwise viable, to propose plans to their creditors to settle debts over several years. Creditors thus had opportunities for full repayment with the return of prosperity. The alternative was to lose most of the value of their loans from forced bankruptcy sales at the bottom of depressions. It was repealed after the return of prosperity in 1878 be-cause creditors disliked its excessive legal costs and the easy procedure for debtors to declare themselves bankrupt.

Rapid increases in manufacturing and the equally rapid expansion of the national market created an urgency for a new bankruptcy statute to replace the spasmodic operation of national laws during depressions. The need for a national procedure was acute for railroads because rail-roads had to continue to operate after excessive debts or inadequate revenues forced them into bankruptcy. National courts assumed the power to ensure their continued operation without congressional authorization. Nobody objected.

Court supervised receiverships were especially approved by owners of railroad securities because national courts had no intention of changing the structure of management, finance, or relationships to the national or state governments. Receivership was not the first step in nationalization. The principal interest of court appointed receivers was restoring the financial health of railroads (see chapter 10).

Agrarian opposition, however, remained strong and the policy stalemate in Congress during the 1880s prevented new bankruptcy legislation from being passed. Not until the 1893 depres-sion, followed by the election of 1896, was the stalemate permanently ended. The election of

1896 was one of the few in U.S. history where the issues were clear. *Would national power be used to govern in the interests of agrarians? Or would national power be used to govern in the interests of industry and cities?* William McKinley was elected president and both houses of congress were controlled by Republicans. The issue was decided. The power of Congress, the presidency, and the courts would govern in the interests of industry and cities.

Businesses serving the national market wanted uniform rules governing bankruptcy, and Congress was eager to act. In 1898 Congress passed a statute that was carefully drafted and continues to operate. It allows all persons (but not corporations) to seek voluntary bankruptcy. Involuntary bankruptcy could not be forced on wage laborers or farmers. Furthermore, wage laborers had a priority claim on the assets of bankrupt corporations (workman liens) for wages earned within three months of bankruptcy. The law became noncontroversial because it accepted exemptions that state legislatures had written into their bankruptcy laws. People who petitioned for voluntary bankruptcy would not be dispossessed of their homes and other property necessary to maintain households. Corporations, like railroads, that were part of the national infrastructure could petition for temporary bankruptcy until improved business and/or new management returned them to profitability.

The 1898 bankruptcy statute was a success because it recognized that in fully commercial cultures lenders must assume most of the risks in making loans. If lenders used poor judgment by extending credit to speculative enterprises, or to persons with minimal management or technical skills, they must assume most or all of the loss. The principal purpose of personal bankruptcy laws in fully commercial cultures is debt relief—exactly as desired by agrarians—because overhanging debts are a huge restraint on normal commercial activities.

> The chief interest of the nation lies in the continuance of a man's business and the conservation of his property for the benefit of creditors and himself, and not in the sale and distribution of his assets among his creditors…Forced sale of property and stoppage of a business in times of depression constitute loss to the nation at large, as well as to the individual debtors and creditors. [14]

Progressive Governance

The principal purpose of progressive governance was governing in the interests of industry and cities, rather than statusquo governance preferred by rural electorates. The election of 1896 was decisive in committing the president and Congress to active governance in the interests of cities. This brought the two elective branches into line with the Supreme Court, which had consistently used its power to protect the industrial policies put into place during the Civil War from agrarian encroachment. The Supreme Court, however, was extremely reluctant to give up the power it had accumulated in the 1870s, 1880, and 1890s. Put in other terms, Supreme Court justices were reluctant to (1) defer to policies that Congress enacted into statute law, and (2) give up power to shape industrialization policies based on their experience.

After 1900, the strong leadership of presidents Theodore Roosevelt and Woodrow Wilson propelled enactments of legislation that were beneficial to urban residents and industrial laborers. The experiences of these presidents were very different from the experiences of justices who composed the Supreme Court.

Presidential leadership was encouraged by the ratification of the Seventeenth Amendment in 1913, which provided for the popular election of U.S. senators. Transferring the election of U. S. senators from state legislatures to a popular vote gave greater weight to urban electorates, because all state legislatures were malapportioned in favor of rural electorates. Popularly elected senators were more receptive to business regulation, social welfare legislation, and public health legislation desired by urban residents. At the same time, popularly elected senators would be less influenced by agrarians.

The House of Representatives passed the Seventeenth Amendment in 1893, 1894, 1898, 1900, and 1902, but it always died in the Senate. The stalemate was broken when state legislatures authorized holding preferential primaries for senate candidates, with state legislatures obligated to elect the winner. By 1912, twenty-nine states had preferential primaries for senators. A year later the Seventeenth Amendment was ratified by three-quarters of the state legislatures.

What congressional legislation was desired by the urban electorate? How would the Supreme Court react to presidential leadership that challenged the Court's practice of protecting industrial wealth on their terms? After 1896, the following four issues were important to the urban electorate: (1) freight rate structures fixed by the ICC, (2) eight hour work day for paid laborers, (3) compensation from a national fund for injuries incurred while working, and (4) enforcement of the Sherman Anti-Trust Act.

Urban residents wanted the ICC to have rate-fixing power because, after 1896, the national railroad network was primarily serving cities. City manufacturers did not necessarily want the lowest freight rates, nor competitive freight rates. They wanted predictable freight rates so they could compete on a level playing field with manufacturers of the same or similar products. A concurrent issue was lower freight rates for agricultural commodities; and both would be achieved by a reinvigorated ICC. The national courts had to be excluded from reviewing freight rates set by the ICC.

President Theodore Roosevelt strongly lobbied Congress to pass the requisite legislation, which it did in 1906 (Hepburn Act). It did not totally exclude the national courts from the review process but, in clear language, the ICC was granted rate-making powers after it had conducted an investigation and found unreasonable rates. *How would the courts interpret their power of review?* The national courts were happy to extract themselves from the morass of judicial determinations of reasonable freight rates. "The courts inexpertly had judged transportation by criteria which, however precious in jurisprudence, bore little relation to economics."[15]

The retreat of the Supreme Court from judicial review of the rate-making process was the signal for Congress to grant original rate making powers to the ICC. The requisite legislation was passed in 1910 (Mann-Elkins Act) and the Court sustained this grant of power in 1914. Theodore Roosevelt's strong leadership in making the ICC into an effective regulatory agency was a necessary first step in creating "efficient federal controls for the positive government of an industrial society.... Only continuous, disinterested administrative action,... not intermittent lawsuits or intermittent legislation,... could properly direct the development of American industrial society."[16]

The Supreme Court's confirmation of the ICC to regulate complex businesses serving the national market was a signal for Congress to establish more independent commissions. In steady succession Congress established commissions and the Court sustained their power. President Woodrow Wilson lobbied Congress for commissions to regulate the national banking system (Federal Reserve Board, 1913); regulate competition that was threatened by monopoly practices of large corporations (Federal Trade Commission, 1914); Federal Tariff Commission to recommend changes in trade policies (1916); Federal Farm Loan Board (1916) to supply more and cheaper credit to farmers from nationally chartered land banks. A high percentage of loans from the Federal Loan Board were used to refinance farm mortgages with lower interest rates and more years to repay. Congress also established the Railroad Labor Board (1920) to put mediation of labor disputes on a continuing basis as the best way to prevent strikes that would paralyze the operation of the national market.

During the rest of the 1920s and 1930s, numerous commissions were established to supervise other complex industries. Among the most important were the Federal Power Commission established in 1920 to regulate the generation of hydroelectric power and its transmission across state boundaries. Its jurisdiction was later expanded to regulate electricity generated by coal fired generating facilities. The Federal Radio Commission was established in 1927, and evolved into the Federal Communications Commission in 1934. It allocated broadcasting rights to radio corporations. The Civil Aeronautics Board was established in 1938 to encourage and supervise the creation of a national network of airline passenger corporations.

The Supreme Court, however, refused to restrain itself from contesting Congress and the president on labor legislation. In matters of labor, the Supreme Court continued to protect the industrial sector on its own terms. In other words, its decisions had the effect of substituting its concept of good industrial policy for policies defined by congressional statutes. In 1906 Congress enacted legislation transferring liability for industrial accidents to employers in all corporations engaged in interstate commerce. No longer could railroads and other interstate carriers claim that accidents were due to negligence of fellow workers.

In a 5 to 4 decision, the Supreme Court ruled it unconstitutional because it included all employees of transportation companies rather than those directly involved in moving products. The minority of justices thought this reasoning specious. Congress passed a second employer liability statute in 1908, and the Court validated it in 1912. Seemingly, the Court now accepted broad power by Congress to regulate labor in all aspects of interstate commerce.

In 1916, President Woodrow Wilson addressed Congress and requested immediate passage of a statute establishing eight hours as the working day for railroad employees. The immediate reason was a threatened national strike that would paralyze business. The compelling reason was the enormous number of deaths in the railroad industry. In 1907 over 4,500 railroad workers died in accidents. A high percentage of these deaths occurred at night, near the end of ten hours of labor when fatigued men were working among heavy moving equipment.

The application of an eight hour work day for railroad workers was the best way to blunt potential Supreme Court opposition to labor legislation for other industries. In 1917 the Supreme Court accepted the eight hour day for railroad employees by a vote of 5 to 4. Three of the four dissenting justices, however, believed the statute was unconstitutional because the regulation of hours of labor was not a proper exercise of regulating interstate commerce—even for railroads that were the prime movers of products in interstate trade. The Supreme Court still believed that hours of labor was a voluntary contract between individuals and employers except for special circumstances. Three of the special circumstances were underground miners, railroad workers, and women. Child labor was not a special circumstance.

In 1916 Congress passed a statute prohibiting from interstate commerce products made in factories using child labor. Child labor was defined as factory employment of children under fourteen years of age, or labor performed by children between the ages of fourteen and sixteen, if their labor was more than eight hours per day, six days a week, or at night. Chief among employers of child labor were coal mines, where young boys picked slate from lump coal moving on conveyors and textile mills. Agricultural labor (children who cultivated and harvested cotton) was specifically excluded from coverage.

Products produced by child labor were not dangerous but the employment of children usually removed them from school before they were literate or, alternatively, restricted their opportunities to use recently acquired functional literacy. They usually reverted to illiteracy. State legislation to end child labor was always linked to its regressive effects on teaching literacy. Labor unions, the quintessential urban organization, always supported child labor legislation.

In 1918 the Supreme Court, in a 5 to 4 decision, ruled the child labor statute unconstitutional. The majority said that the statute was not a regulation of commerce but a prohibition of commerce. The majority refused to look at the harmful social effects of child labor. Congress tried again in 1919. The second child labor statute had the same purpose as the first, but instead of an outright prohibition, the second statute levied a 10 percent tax on factories employing child labor. In 1922 the Supreme Court declared it unconstitutional because it would prohibit commerce instead of raising revenue. During these same years (1918), the Court validated the meat inspection statute of 1906 that excluded spoiled and adulterated meat from interstate commerce because wholesome meat was necessary for public health.

In one area of policy, however, the Supreme Court ensured that Congress and the president did not overreact to public concern about giant industrial corporations that resulted from mergers. Congress had addressed public concern by passing the Sherman Anti-Trust Act in 1890 but the statute, as previously noted, used words that gave the Supreme Court wide latitude for interpretation. The statute did not prohibit mergers. In effect, the Supreme Court could define what constituted restraints on interstate commerce and what mergers were reasonable to make production more efficient to service the national market. The Supreme Court clearly recognized that giant industrial corporations were efficient accumulators of capital and efficient in servicing the national market.

In 1895 the Supreme Court signaled its intention to protect large manufacturing corporations because they ended destructive competition. Large corporations that could exert some degree of control over prices were beneficial because they reduced the waste associated with bankruptcies. Capital accumulated by more predictable prices and profits was available for reinvestment in improved technologies or larger factories that could take advantage of economies of scale.

The first opportunity for the Supreme Court to interpret the Sherman Anti-Trust Act was *United States v. E. C. Knight Co.* in 1895. The attorney general of the United States began a lawsuit to dismantle the American Sugar Refining Company that had been organized in 1892 by merging more than forty sugar refiners. The American Sugar Refining Company was a monopoly because it controlled more than 90 percent of the refining capacity in the United States. The attorney general attempted to dismantle the monopoly into its premerger parts. This was a high profile lawsuit because a successful outcome would lower the price of a common product of household consumption.

The Supreme Court denied the government's claim that the sugar refining monopoly restrained commerce. The majority opinion made a sharp distinction between manufacturing and commerce: "commerce succeeds to manufacturing, and is not part of it." According to the majority opinion, the Sherman Act applied only to combinations that restrained interstate commerce and the sugar refining monopoly was not in interstate commerce. It was in manufacturing. Mergers that created giant manufacturing corporations had only an indirect effect on commerce; therefore, they were not comprehended by the Sherman Act. Presumably, the Sherman Act applied only to railroads or other corporations that actually moved commodities in interstate trade.[17]

The Court's unrealistic distinction between manufacturing and commerce created a twilight zone in which neither Congress nor state legislatures could act with certainty. Only the Supreme Court, at the top of the national judiciary, could act with certainty. *What rationale would guide decisions of the Supreme Court to limit the size of manufacturing corporations?* The Court invented the rule of reason.

The attorney general of the United States began a law suit to dismantle the Standard Oil Company and American Tobacco Company into their component parts. Unlike the sugar monopoly, both were organized as holding companies that could be interpreted as combinations. Like the sugar monopoly, Standard Oil and American Tobacco companies controlled 90 percent of the production and marketing of petroleum and tobacco products.

Two lower court decisions in 1911 ordered the dismantling of the Standard Oil Company and the American Tobacco Company. On appeal, the Supreme Court approved dismantling the Standard Oil Company because it was an unreasonable combination; but only required the American Tobacco Company to reorganize. Presumably the American Tobacco Company was a half-reasonable combination. The Standard Oil and American Tobacco decisions established the rule of reason as the Court's guideline for deciding whether giant manufacturing corporations were reasonable and ought to continue in business, or were unreasonable and ought to be dismantled.

In many ways the Standard Oil decision was a hollow victory for the government because the Standard Oil monopoly was crumbling. The oil business was transformed by the discovery of the first prolific oil reservoir on the Gulf Coast of Texas (Spindletop, 1901). The first six wells produced more oil in one day than all of the other oil wells in the world. None of this oil was owned or controlled by Standard Oil.

After the discovery of Spindletop, the focus of the oil industry shifted from refining and marketing to exploring for new reservoirs, and many were quickly discovered. After about 1910, most of the oil produced from newly discovered reservoirs would be refined into gasoline to fuel automobiles, or used as crude oil to replace coal as a locomotive fuel, or propel ships; as well as refining kerosene, lubricating oil, and grease that were essential for lubricating railroad locomotives, railroad rolling stock, and industrial machinery. By 1911 gasoline to fuel automobiles was a large market—on its way to becoming a huge market that one company could not control.

After 1911, it was virtually impossible for the attorney general of the United States to prosecute giant manufacturing corporations, even if they were monopolies. Furthermore, it was soon demonstrated that promoters of monopoly corporations could not charge monopoly prices for any length of time because monopoly corporations had two serious weaknesses. First, they usually had fragile financial structures because the merger process was expensive. Second, charging monopoly prices encouraged new corporations to enter production. Price competition was soon restored. Supreme Court decisions that sustained the integrity of giant manufacturing corporations had the tacit consent of Congress and presidents because they rationalized fragmented industries.

Examined from a different perspective, mergers speeded the transition from a multitude of small manufacturing corporations to oligopolistic competition. Oligopolistic competition often occurred when monopoly corporations became bankrupt, as most of them did. In the cases of dismantling the Standard Oil and American Tobacco monopolies, the result was a small number of large successor corporations that competed in the national market by other means than destructive competition. The new competition was based on advertising and brand names. This was the pattern of production and marketing in other advanced industrial nations because oligopolistic competition was the most efficient way to produce manufactured products for domestic consumption and sale on the global market that rapidly expanded after 1900.

Chapter 13

Big Business

The purpose of business corporations is to make profits by productively employing resources over a long period of time. The purpose of big business corporations is to do this on a very large scale. Corporations become big by (1) investing internal savings supplemented by bank credit, (2) mergers, (3) using new technologies, and (4) using old technologies in a more efficient way. Big business requires a radical separation between owners and managers; therefore, corporate governance must be done by paid professionals. This is managerial capitalism.

The management structure of big businesses must be hierarchical so that failed managers can be replaced and successful managers promoted on their abilities to coordinate the activities of other persons in the management structure and define successful strategies to remain profitable. Markets for products manufactured by big businesses are national, or more likely international. "Big business arose and triumphed because it was the most effective instrument yet devised to organize and coordinate productive economic activities in a nation where material progress was the purpose of life."[1]

Railroads were the first big business in the United States. Some were big businesses by 1860. Other big businesses in 1860 were the Erie Canal, the U.S. Post Office, and Western Union Telegraph Corporation. By 1866 Western Union monopolized telegraphic communication. It was formed by merging northern telegraph companies and acquiring the franchises of southern telegraph companies that ceased operations due to destruction during the Civil War. Monopoly prices for telegraphic communication were not a significant public issue because most of its revenue came from transmitting commercial information for railroads, banks, newspapers, and other businesses.

This chapter focuses on big manufacturing corporations. They abruptly entered the business structure of the United States after 1885, although the Standard Oil Company achieved monopoly status in 1879 and became instantly notorious because of alleged high prices charged to consumers. Big manufacturing corporations made products in large factories where there were central sources of power, large numbers of employees, a complex division of labor, and a high percentage of workers who operated specialized machinery. These factories made new products (electric lighting, electric motors for street railways, automobiles) or old products in new ways (steel, lubricating oil).

Production in large factories steadily increased after 1870. Several factors contributed to concentrating production in large factories: (1) mergers, (2) profitability of economies of scale, (3) increased purchasing power of urban residents, (4) a rapidly expanding national market, (5) availability of capital for investment in new technologies, (6) optimal efficiency of oligopolistic competition, and (7) protective tariff.

Big business was big urban business. The efficiency of mass production and economies of scale were directly related to the rapid urbanization of the United States after 1870. In 1870, 25 percent of the population was urban. In 1910, 45 percent was urban, but the nation's population had increased from thirty-eight million in 1870 to ninety-two million in 1910. In 1910 forty-two million people lived in cities, which was four million more people than the total population of the United States in 1870.

Unlike contemporary peasant nations, urbanization in the United States was directly linked to a rapid increase in industrial wealth, and an equally rapid increase in per capita incomes. Robert Higgs estimates that the gross national product increased at an average rate of 4 percent per year between 1865 and 1908. During these same years (1870–1900) average per capita incomes increased from $237 to $482, at a time when the purchasing power of the dollar was increasing (deflation).

Albert Rees estimated that hourly wages for industrial workers increased 28 percent between 1890 and 1914. He further estimates that 77 percent of increased wages were spent on consumer products, human services, and housing, and 23 percent on increased leisure (ten hours to nine hours of labor per day in a six day work week). The average annual rate of wage increase was 1.3 percent during these years, and the annual per capita increase of production per industrial worker was 2.1 percent. On average, per capita production of industrial workers increased faster than wages.

How was this capital surplus used? The best estimate is that it had two principal uses—purchasing much larger amounts of machinery that increased per capita productivity and paying dividends to shareholders. Between 1890 and 1914, the use of more machinery in mass production technologies, combined with a stable or slightly rising cost of living, made possible increases in hourly wages and real incomes. The increasing real income of industrial workers during these years was the preamble to the emergence of a consumer culture in the 1920s.[2]

New wealth was concentrated in cities in northern and western states, where disciplined wage labor was performed. Ex-slave states with a high percentage of peasants in their populations were marginal participants in the production of new industrial wealth.

Mergers

"The merger movement was the most important single episode in the evolution of the modern industrial enterprise in the United States from the 1880s to the 1940s." A great surge began near the end of the 1893 depression (1895) and continued for ten years. It reached its peak between 1895 and 1899 when there were ninety-two mergers in major industries. The principal goal of mergers was to stabilize prices.[3]

Mergers themselves did not insure profitability, nor did investments in large factories using mass production technologies. Few mergers organized by investment bankers were financially successful unless managers were able to "create an organization that was able to coordinate a high-volume flow of materials through the process of production and distribution, from suppliers of raw materials to the ultimate consumer."[4]

The desire to merge was often propelled by necessity, and the principal necessity was ending destructive competition. Mergers usually followed the failure of cartels and other means to sustain adequate profitability in markets that were rapidly increasing in size and integration. Between the mid-1870s and the mid-1890s, local markets were telescoped into regional markets, and regional markets were telescoped into the national market. During the 1880s, when the national railroad network was rapidly expanding, industrial corporations faced destructive competition during the same years that railroads were experiencing destructive competition in rates.

Railroads tried pools to control destructive competition, but Congress refused to legalize them because they were restraints on trade. Almost all pools failed. The strongest railroads began leasing franchises to create inter-regional systems, and this had some success in reducing rate wars, but real relief did not come until there were large numbers of bankruptcies in the mid-1890s. During this crisis, investment bankers, acting as receivers, forced mergers. This reduced destructive competition but it was not ended until the Mann-Elkins Act (1910) granted the ICC rate making powers. Thereafter, the ICC became the honest broker for the railroad industry.

The depression that began in 1893 lasted for three years and generated destructive competition among manufacturing corporations that had large debts, especially in new industries. Managers of these corporations pursued a strategy of continuing optimum production because it was essential to generate revenue to service their debts. They believed that reduced production would cause bankruptcy sooner than continuing optimum production and selling at reduced prices that did not generate sufficient revenue to replace obsolescent machinery. This was destructive competition.

Manufacturing corporations tried to control destructive competition by organizing cartels. Congress refused to legalize them because, like railroad pools, they were restraints on trade. Without legal enforcement cartels were like railroad pools. They had short lives. More imaginative businessmen then organized trusts. Owners of several competing corporations put all their stock in the hands of a board of trustees and received trust certificates of equivalent value. Boards of trustees became, in effect, boards of directors with full powers of management, and holders of trust certificates were converted into shareholders. The constituent corporations were managed as a single unit and the chairman of the board of trustees had the power to consolidate and rationalize production by closing inefficient factories and enlarging and modernizing the most efficient or best located factories.

Trusts, however, had a serious weakness. They were not single legal entities where responsibility for ownership and management were clearly located. Legal complications were inevitable when a trustee died, had a policy disagreement or conflict of interest with the majority of trustees. As a result, there was not any sure way of legally transferring ownership of shares.

New York City, Philadelphia, and New Jersey businessmen lobbied the New Jersey legislature to legalize a simple solution. In 1889 the New Jersey legislature amended its general incorporation statute to allow any manufacturing corporation incorporated in New Jersey to hold shares in any manufacturing corporation in any state. Corporations whose only asset were shares of stock in other corporations were called holding companies. Headquarters and governance of holding companies incorporated in New Jersey could be located across the Hudson River in New York City or across the Delaware River in Philadelphia, or in any city in the United States.

Similar statutes were soon passed by the legislatures of Delaware, New York, and Pennsylvania. Holding companies were ideal vehicles for combining many small manufacturing corporations into large ones in order to reduce destructive competition. After 1889, holding companies were used to organize mergers. Most trusts were immediately reorganized as holding companies and reorganized again into operating companies with a centralized management structure.

The Sherman Anti-Trust statute was the congressional response to the New Jersey statute. It was passed in order to allay public fear that holding companies were a legal encouragement for the creation of monopolies, especially monopolies that manufactured consumer products.

Monopolies that produced consumer products were not in the public interest. The ambiguous wording of the Sherman Act left interpretation of what constituted the public interest to the national judiciary. The only clear purpose of the Sherman Act was what it did not do. It did not prohibit mergers, and the Supreme Court interpreted this omission as a license to protect all varieties of mergers, even when they created monopolies of consumer products (*U.S. v. E.C. Knight Co.* 1895).

Most mergers were organized by converting trade associations into holding companies. The most successful mergers controlled between 40 and 70 percent of production in their industries. Attempts to achieve monopoly (90% or more of productive capacity in an industry) were usually financially unstable because (1) high debts were incurred to acquire marginally profitable corporations for inclusion in the merger, and (2) high monopoly prices invited new entrants.

The momentum of the merger movement was sustained by the evolution of the capital market. Investment bankers like J. P. Morgan, who were highly successful at reorganizing the capital structures of bankrupt railroads and then welding them into regional systems, observed that large manufacturing corporations created by mergers before 1893 had remained more profitable than railroads during the depression. These mergers were organized by owner/managers. Owner/managers were responsible for most mergers before 1896.

Mergers organized by the owners of participating corporations accurately valued the assets of participating corporations and new shares of stock were issued accordingly. The most successful mergers were nine corporations or less with funds supplied, where necessary, by local bankers. These mergers usually excluded corporations that had obsolescent machinery, poor locations, and high production costs.

Investment bankers saw a new market for their services and they were responsible for most mergers from 1896 to 1914. They would promote mergers of manufacturing corporations by becoming the financial intermediaries to create a dominant corporation in an industry. From the perspective of investment bankers, the best mergers were those that included 10 or more corporations that controlled 40 percent or more of the productive capacity of an industry. Mergers organized by investment bankers tended to be less stable than those organized by owner/managers because bankers tended to inflate the assets of participating corporations in order to induce a high percentage of corporations in an industry to join the combination.

Investment bankers who brokered mergers issued new common and preferred stock to the owners of participating corporations. Preferred shares represented the actual value of the assets of participating corporations and common shares represented the speculative success of the merger. Shares of common stock were sold to the investing public or to savings banks and insurance companies.

Investment bankers clearly saw three positive results of their work. (1) A national market was created for shares of industrial corporations. They joined the existing national market for railroad securities. (2) Industrial shares substantially enlarged the capital market of the United States. (3) Mergers were used to create oligopolistic competition because oligopolistic competition was the most effective way of ending destructive competition.

Stabilized earnings did not automatically happen after mergers. About one-third of big businesses created by mergers became bankrupt within five years of organization. Their inflated capital structures made them unstable during business downturns, and the promoters, who became managers failed to reorganize them into operating corporations with centralized managements. Another 20 percent of mergers were only marginally profitable because managers failed to convert bigness into dominance within their industry.

Dominance was achieved by (1) centralizing management in order to rationalize production, (2) investing in technologies of mass production in order to achieve economies of scale, (3) closely integrating production with sales and distribution, and (4) producing products at sufficiently low prices to exclude new entrants. To achieve dominance, large factories had to be built to achieve economies of scale, and the production of these factories had to be marketed by the company's sales organization. The strategies that created dominant corporations forced other corporations in the industry to duplicate the management strategies of the dominant corporation. If they did not, they became bankrupt.

After one corporation in an industry achieved dominance, surviving corporations engaged in oligopolistic competition. Oligopolistic competition was based on (1) productive efficiency that was more or less equal among companies in the industry; (2) sales and distribution organizations that were more or less equally efficient among competing companies; (3) producing and selling products of known quality or durability; (4) continuing to make improvements in their products. Price differences were rarely a decisive factor in increasing market share. "Modern business enterprise became a viable institution only after the visible hand of management proved to be more efficient than the invisible hand of market forces in coordinating the flow of materials through the economy."[5]

The visible hand was a managerial hierarchy capable of planning and monitoring complex activities in regional, national, and international markets. By 1900 it was clear that the visible hand of management ended the worst forms of destructive competition after mergers established oligopolistic competition.

Management

After a merger of many corporations, the big business that resulted was a ramshackle collection of factories with highly variable management skills, profitability, and market shares. The only common denominator was that all factories were in the same industry. The merger that created a big business did not automatically make it a dominant corporation. A big business could never become dominant until management was centralized and hierarchically organized, and production and distribution were integrated. Small and inefficient factories had to be closed and production concentrated in large factories at the best locations using the most productive technologies.

Simultaneously, staff functions (sales, distribution, purchasing, power supply, and engineering) had to be concentrated in departments that performed these single functions. After restructuring was complete, a big business had economies of scale that achieved a large competitive advantage over the remaining (smaller) corporations in an industry. Undertaking restructuring was the job of organization builders. Organization building required very different skills than those possessed by most entrepreneur/owner/managers. The transfer of corporate governance to organization builders signifies the transition to managerial capitalism.

Managerial capitalism became essential after the mid-1880s when mass production by continuous process technologies became possible in many industries; and managerial capitalism became mandatory during the 1890s when large-scale mergers created big businesses. Mass production required concentrating production in big factories built for that purpose in order to fully realize economies of scale. When factories had one hundred to two hundred employees, owner/managers delegated hiring and supervision of labor practices to foremen. Owner/managers personally knew the foremen and could supervise their practices, but this was impossible when factories had two thousand or more employees and had high labor turnovers. Big factories had to be managed by different practices than those that operated in small factories. Management had to be done by professionals.

Although, the principal incentive to merge was ending destructive competition, the creation of a big business did not automatically solve the competition problem. Big businesses created by mergers had to be converted into dominant corporations. It was strongly in the interests of an industry to have a dominant corporation that could establish price leadership. Price leadership was really price discipline and price discipline was essential for ending destructive competition. A big business did not become dominant until it could enforce price leadership, and price leadership depended on achieving economies of scale.

Two practices were successful in enforcing price discipline. First, during downturns in business, dominant corporations reduced prices for their products, but not below the cost of production. A corporation voluntarily lost market share to smaller competitors that sold at lower prices. These businesses continued to operate at optimum levels but often sold their products below the cost of production. When a dominant corporation lost too much market share, it drastically reduced prices until it regained market share. This tactic taught managers of competing corporations that it was better to voluntarily reduce production during downturns in business and price its products above the cost of production.

Second, during downturns in business, dominant corporations reduced production by laying off workers and continued to sell its product for normal prices, or slightly reduced prices. It continued to be profitable because it maintained sufficient production to achieve economies of scale, but with fewer employees. Smaller corporations could not risk destructive competition by selling below the cost of production because the dominant business had unused productive capacity and could outlast them in a price war.

The purpose of price leadership was to establish oligopolistic competition. Oligopoly pricing was established when all corporations in an industry reduced costs by laying off workers rather than trying to increase market share by reducing prices below the cost of production. Oligopolistic competition ended destructive competition.

In order to maximize production, big factories had a multitude of operations under one roof. Paid professional managers were essential for mass production, just as they were essential for managing the trunkline railroad systems that were assembled in the 1850s. The first step in managing big factories was partitioning management responsibilities. Management responsibilities were delegated to professionals who were trained or hired to direct production in big factories that had a multitude of operations of differing complexities under one roof.

Two essential duties of professional managers were implementing technical changes and coordinating the uninterrupted flows of processing operations. Mass production depended on (1) more efficient machinery, (2) the use of more energy from a central source in order to power machines, and (3) using semi-finished parts or raw materials that had predictable qualities so that operating speeds of machines could be increased and waste reduced. Long interruptions in production or frequent short interruptions were disastrous for profitability.

The profitability of mass production depended on promoting persons into management on the merits of their performance in implementing technical changes. Technical changes usually required workers being trained to use specialized machinery. Foremen, who controlled hiring, were unable to recruit workers in a consistent way who were capable of implementing technical changes. Professional managers had to exert centralized control over hiring by substituting their procedures for the informal hiring practices by foremen. Labor recruitment, especially recruitment of skilled labor, became one of the more important jobs of professional managers.

> When those breakthroughs came, the increases in the speed of output were spectacular. In all these manufacturing establishments, the coordination of high-volume flow through several processes of production, led to the hiring of a staff of salaried managers and the development of modern factory procedures and organization.[6]

If managers synchronized all the variables of new technologies that were necessary for mass production, the same number of workers using the same machines could increase the number of products produced during a work day.

Lower unit costs resulted from an intensification of the speed of materials through an establishment rather than from enlarging its size. They came more from organization and technical innovations that increased the velocity of throughput than from adding more men and machines.[7]

In 1900 Daniel Nelson counted seventy-nine factories in the United States with more than two thousand employees. Fifteen were steel mills and seventeen manufactured heavy steel products (ships, locomotives, railroad cars, and pipes) or simple steel products (wire and saws). There were fifteen textile/carpet mills (the original factories) with over two thousand employees.[8]

Distribution

Mass production required a national sales organization that could reach the ultimate consumer. It also needed railroads because they were the means of mass distribution. The completion of the national railroad network between the mid-1880s and the mid-1890s and the adoption of one gauge made possible two developments: (1) the creation of big businesses with several factories, and (2) new channels of distribution that bypassed wholesale agents. New channels of distribution were greatly facilitated after 1880 by the invention of the telephone, which gave instant communication in cities for the distribution of manufactured consumer products. During the 1880s cities became the most profitable markets for mass produced consumer products.

In order to stay in business, wholesale merchants had to become jobbers. Wholesale merchants accepted delivery of batches of products on credit supplied by manufacturers and sold them on commission. Jobbers purchased batches of products directly from manufacturers using local credit and sold them to their account. Ownership of products was an opportunity to make higher profits than the 2.5 to 5.0 percent on commission sales.

Manufacturers transferred the acquisition of credit to jobbers. This freed the credit resources of manufacturing corporations for other purposes. The shift to local credit and the single national currency and a national banking system greatly facilitated the interstate transfer of funds. The speed of communication and the reliability of railroad transportation made it possible to substantially lower the costs of maintaining inventories. When speed of delivery and reliable local credit supplied by national banks were combined with access to instant price information supplied by telegraphs and telephones, risks of price fluctuations were reduced. The conversion of wholesale merchants into jobbers was complete by the mid-1870s.

The most successful wholesale jobbers became very large businesses. Many of them, like Marshall Field, opened large department stores in the central business districts of the largest cities. These stores were evidence of the rapidly increasing purchasing power of urban residents. Other mass retailers like J.C. Penny and Sears began buying directly from manufacturers and selling to consumers in chains of stores and from mail order catalogs. By the mid-1890s, the highly visible success of wholesale jobbers was incentive for both retail merchants and manufacturers of consumer products to enter the business of distribution. Entry was frequently done by purchasing a jobbing business and retaining the former owner as manager.

Manufacturers of packaged consumer products wanted to bypass wholesale jobbers because they found that many local and regional jobbers were unprepared to distribute the large volume of products that continuous process machinery could produce. Jobbers could not be relied on to maintain adequate inventories so that consumer demand could always be satisfied. Some of the consumer products that were first produced by continuous process machinery in the 1880s and 1890s were cigarettes, matches, photographic film, soap, wheat flour, condensed milk, canned vegetables, fruit, and soup. All of these products were made in large factories using expensive machinery. Low cost production and the ability to sell products cheaply depended on speed in processing and speed in distribution.

The business strategy of these corporations was to sell their products for low, fixed prices and accept low profit margins on a high volume of sales. Profits were made on volume, not markups. Seen from a different perspective, manufacturers of consumer products achieved economies of scale in distribution by organizing their own sales and distribution organizations. Managers of big retail businesses benefited because they could bargain for reduced prices for bulk purchases.

Almost instantly, managers of sales and distribution of mass produced consumer products linked their product to brand names publicized by large advertisement budgets in weekly and monthly magazines. After cheap wood pulp newsprint became available during the 1890s, advertising budgets expanded to daily newspapers. Undertaking distribution had a further advantage. Production could be better matched with consumption. When there were downturns in business and warehouse inventories increased, this was a clear signal to reduce production.

It was equally essential for manufacturers of machinery used in households or retail businesses to undertake national distribution because people wanted to test their operation before purchase. Among these machines were typewriters, scales, cash registers, sewing machines, and agricultural implements. Purchasers also wanted to be assured that spare parts and repair technicians were available. Efficient distribution was achieved by establishing dealerships that sold only the machinery of one company (agricultural implements, automobiles), or regional sales organizations supervised by salaried managers who delivered products from regional warehouses to retailers as needed. These warehouses also stocked spare parts.

An essential duty of regional sales/distribution managers was to collect money after sales were made. A steady cash flow for corporations that mass produced consumer products ensured that production would increase without the corporation becoming dependent on finance capital.

Barriers to Entry

It was strongly in the interest of dominant corporations in an industry to exclude entry of new corporations. Examined from another perspective, excluding new entries in an industry was essential for establishing oligopolistic competition. Oligopolies made the national market more predictable and orderly, and this benefited both employment and the collection of tax revenues.

Dominant corporations used six strategies to create barriers to entry:

1. economies of scale in production and distribution;
2. closely integrating sales and distribution organizations so that they could service the national market;
3. pricing policies during downturns in business that induced competing corporations to lay off workers to reduce costs rather than engaging in destructive competition to try and increase market shares;
4. controlling sources of raw materials;
5. licensing agreements for patents that allowed orderly entry;
6. extracting rebates from railroads until this practice was prohibited and enforced.

Creating a national sales organization was a very effective way of discouraging new competition and a strategy that generated no political opposition. Potential entrants could purchase the necessary machinery with little difficulty and hire persons to manage operations but national sales and distribution organizations were expensive to create. New entrants could use wholesale jobbers for distribution but wholesale jobbers were unreliable agents for consumer products because they usually distributed the products of competitors and they preferred satisfactory markups instead of striving for high volume sales; and they often failed to fill orders on time.

The two most substantial barriers to new entrants were low prices and consumer loyalty. Low prices were possible by mass production and consumer loyalty was sustained by high advertising budgets for brand name products. "Of all the new types of business organizations formed in the United States after 1840, none were more complex than those that integrated mass production with mass distribution." The businesses that achieved mass production and mass distribution were the leaders in producing a consumer culture during the 1920s.[9]

The rest of this chapter will examine how, by 1914, four industries were dominated by a small number of big corporations created by mergers. They were steel, petroleum, electrical equipment manufacturing, and automobiles. In four different ways these industries evolved into oligopolies that became the pattern for the U.S. economy during the twentieth century.

Steel

Before 1870, iron smelting, iron refining, and iron fabrication in Pennsylvania and elsewhere were highly fragmented. There was no integration in one corporation of smelting in blast furnaces, refining in forges, and fabrication of shapes in rolling mills and foundries. Smelting, refining, and fabrication were three separate industries done at widely scattered locations.

Pennsylvania had 295 blast furnaces in 1850. Somewhere between 150 and 180 were operational. Average weekly production in furnaces using charcoal was 25 tons. Furnaces using anthracite coal or coke produced 70 to 80 tons per week. Charcoal fueled furnaces employed between 55 and 65 men and anthracite furnaces employed over 100 men. In 1840, almost all blast furnaces used charcoal as fuel, but by 1850 over half used anthracite or coke. By 1860 two-thirds were using anthracite or coke, and by 1870 coke was the usual fuel. The change in fuel from charcoal to anthracite to coke was coupled with building larger furnaces and increasing furnace temperatures. Output per furnace increased.

Eastern Pennsylvania had 118 forges, 6 bloomeries, and 56 rolling mills in 1850. In western Pennsylvania there were 3 forges, and 23 rolling mills. Average employment in bloomeries and forges was between 20 and 30.

Molten iron as it comes from the blast furnace is called pig iron. It has a high content of dissolved carbon. Forges remove carbon by a relatively simple process, and the result is pure iron. Steel is iron with a low carbon content. Converting iron into steel required a highly specialized and expensive refining process.

Before 1868, the uses of steel were limited to expensive edged tools—knives, prairie plows, shovels, saws to cut wood, and guns. Before 1870, the United States was not self-sufficient in steel production. This changed after 1868 when the Bessemer converter made it possible to mass produce steel. In the next twenty years, Bessemer steel replaced iron in most fabricated products made from iron, and most shapes cast from pig iron. Especially, steel rails replaced iron rails.

Steel production was essentially a new industry, although it used most of the technologies of iron smelting and fabrication. It was a new industry because it required substantially higher capitalization for entry, replaced most uses of iron, and was capable of economies of scale. Chapter 10 described the huge market for steel that was clearly visible if steel became cheap enough to replace iron rails and iron plates and tubes in locomotive boilers. Steel plates and tubes could contain much higher pressures needed to generate the power to pull longer trains of freight cars of increased carrying capacity. Steel made it possible to increase economies of scale in railroad transportation by several magnitudes.

In 1865 Andrew Carnegie resigned his senior management job with the Pennsylvania Railroad and transferred his interests to manufacturing. His two principal investments were in corporations that built iron bridges to carry railroad traffic over major rivers and a blast furnace that produced iron to roll into rails and beams for bridges. He also made several trips to Europe to market railroad bonds that were used to finance the rapidly expanding U.S. railroad network. While in Europe, he visited blast furnaces and observed Bessemer converters making steel.

On the basis of his experiences as a railroad manager, salesman of railroad bonds, and knowledge of the strength and durability of steel rails, he clearly understood that Bessemer steel was the metal of the future. The small trackage of steel rails in the 1860s demonstrated their strength and durability. The few steel rails in place were on heavily traveled main lines, especially on sharp curves where there was extreme wear on iron rails. Iron rails at these locations had to be replaced every six months. On mainline tracks with few curves, iron rails were usually replaced after four years.

The steel rails that replaced iron rails had little wear after several years of service. It was clear that steel rails would last at least twenty years without replacement and could carry much heavier freight cars. Savings in maintenance and rail replacement would be huge, and the speed of trains could be exponentially increased with more powerful locomotives that had boilers made with steel.

Carnegie envisioned producing steel in an integrated factory by a continuous series of operations beginning with smelting iron ore in blast furnaces, moving molten pig iron to Bessemer converters, and then rolling the steel into semi-finished shapes like rails, boiler plates, and bridge beams, or making the heavy castings required for marine and stationary steam engines. All of these operations, if they were concentrated in one factory under centralized management, could achieve economies of scale and speed of output that guaranteed large profits.

In 1872 Carnegie decided to concentrate all of his energies on the production of Bessemer steel. He had no difficulty raising capital from his business associates and began building a large, integrated steel mill on vacant land. Its principal product would be rails and other products used by railroads. The first investment was a state of the art blast furnace that was much larger than British counterparts. Next to it were Bessemer converters that were also larger than British counterparts. Next to the converters were facilities to produce ingots, billets, slabs, and other intermediate shapes.

Construction was done during the depression (1873–1875) and costs were below estimates. Production began in 1875. He used no new technologies, but the large capacity and physical arrangement of machinery achieved economies of scale. His blast furnaces were more than twice the size of average British furnaces and their output was three times that of the average British furnace.

His furnaces were driven. They had a shorter productive life than British furnaces, and when they wore out they were replaced with larger furnaces. Hard driving and frequent replacement forced other steel mills to follow this practice because it produced cheap steel compared to the British practice of making equipment last as long as possible, even when machinery was obsolescent and more productive machinery was available. On average, the output of blast furnaces and Bessemer converters in U.S. mills were 50 percent greater than British mills.

Bessemer converters were also much larger in integrated American mills than in British mills and they were also driven. Steel production from Bessemer converters in integrated American mills was at least ten times greater than production using pre-Bessemer technologies. In 1880 the cost of converting pig iron to steel by the Bessemer process was twice the cost of producing pig iron. By 1883 steel made in Bessemer converters that was rolled into rails cost the same as iron rails. Iron rails ceased being manufactured except for street railways in cities that used horse drawn cars.

Profits from economies of scale in Carnegie's mill were enhanced by minimal capital debts and a hierarchical management structure that Carnegie transferred from railroads. It was a management structure he had helped create while employed by the Pennsylvania Railroad.

What was Carnegie management strategy? The most important element was hiring the most experienced and successful managers from other iron/steel mills. It was strongly hierarchical with clearly defined areas of authority so that individual performance could be accurately evaluated. Once hired, these managers were delegated full authority to supervise their assigned operation. Carnegie made efficient managers into junior partners if they performed to expectations. Success was measured by controlling costs and costs were quantified by cost accounting.

Cost accounting was the means of evaluating the performance of managers. "Watch the costs and the profits will take care of themselves." The basis of cost accounting was continuous written reports on amounts of daily and weekly production; with additional reports on other problems that hindered or speeded production. From the beginning of production, the hiring and training of managers was impersonal. Carnegie knew only the most senior managers. Carnegie created a bureaucracy in the steel industry similar to the bureaucracy that made the Pennsylvania Railroad the most efficiently managed railroad in the 1850s and 1860s. The immediate success of Carnegie Steel was a highly visible model of managerial capitalism.[10]

From the moment of first integrated production in 1875, Carnegie Steel was the dominant producer in the industry and was profitable from the beginning of production. Estimated profits were 25 percent per year during its first five years of production. Competitors were numerous in spite of large capital investments needed to build integrated mills. The boom in railroad construction after 1878 attracted ten new entrants but not all of them were integrated. New mills were built because the market was there and because in 1878 the protective tariff was 100 percent of the price of steel rails.

In 1880 steel production in the United States was 1.2 million tons and 1.0 million tons was rolled. Rails were 85 percent of all rolled steel. Between 1880 and 1885 steel production increased 28 percent, and in the next four years (1885–1889) there were eighteen new entrants in Bessemer steel production. Nonetheless, rails steadily declined as a percentage of rolled steel products. In 1885 they were 70 percent and in 1900 they were 30 percent; although, production of steel rails in 1900 was 2.5 times greater than in 1885. Original iron rails had to be replaced with heavier steel rails to carry heavier locomotives that pulled longer trains with substantially heavier freight cars. In addition, many mainlines were double tracked.

During the 1880s and 1890s, the scale of production continually increased. Increased blast furnace capacity was achieved by building taller furnaces, using the best coke for fuel, enlarging stoves to heat air to higher temperatures and using more powerful engines to blast it into furnaces. Layout was a less visible way of lowering costs. Molten steel from Bessemer converters was poured into ingots and allowed to solidify, but, before it lost its heat, ingots were moved to rolling machinery and shaped into rails and other shapes. Full cooling was avoided because reheating cold steel to rolling temperature is expensive.

At the same time, Bessemer converters were slowly being replaced by open hearth furnaces because the open hearth process removed phosphorous from molten pig iron during the process of refining it to steel. Small amounts of phosphorous weakens steel, and Bessemer converters could not remove it. The open hearth process also reduced waste because the air blown through the molten iron in Bessemer converters oxidized substantial amounts of metallic iron. In 1900 two-thirds of U.S. steel production was Bessemer but it continually declined in the next ten years. By 1911 two-thirds of the steel made in the United States was produced in open hearth furnaces.

At least two integrated steel mills built before 1880 became bankrupt within five years of beginning production. At least two entrants after 1885 became bankrupt and were purchased by Carnegie Steel. Several additional new mills were financially unstable because they were organized by promoter/investment bankers. They were over capitalized and poorly managed.

The only way many late entrants could survive was by merger and investment bankers, like J. P. Morgan, were essential brokers. A high percentage of these mergers took place between 1895 and 1900. The larger competitors of Carnegie Steel sought to neutralize his low production costs by integrating into manufacturing finished products like wire, plates, sheets, and pipes. Horizontal integration into higher priced semi-finished and finished shapes would force Carnegie Steel to do the same. Carnegie did not want to undertake this competitive battle. In 1899 he wanted to retire and give his fortune away while he was still alive. Nonetheless, he made plans to manufacture semi-finished and finished shapes.

This decision forced J. P. Morgan to seek an accommodation with Carnegie. Above all, Morgan wanted to avoid destructive competition. A new steel company that Morgan had helped capitalize in order to compete with Carnegie, would be severely hurt by a protracted price war. It was, therefore, strongly in the interest of Morgan to end destructive competition before it began. Morgan knew Carnegie wanted to retire so he asked Carnegie how much he wanted for his assets. Carnegie named his price. It was 480 million dollars. In January 1901, Morgan purchased Carnegie Steel at this price.

Thereafter, Morgan used Carnegie Steel as the nucleus to organize United States Steel Corporation by multiple mergers with other integrated steel mills, numerous manufacturers of semi-finished products, sources of raw materials, and transportation. The horizontal dimensions of the merger included a large number of manufacturers of semi-finished products (wire, tubes, beams, and plates of all thicknesses). The vertical dimensions of the merger included coal mines, coke ovens, iron ore mines, iron ore boats on the Great Lakes, and two shortline railroads. The assets that went into U.S. Steel had an estimated value of 880 million dollars.

These assets were represented by bonds and preferred stock bearing 5 percent interest. They went to the owners of corporations included in the merger. U.S. Steel, however, was capitalized at 1.4 billion dollars. In other words, the Morgan Bank issued over 500 million dollars of common stock that had minimal earning capacity because it had last call on earnings. The common stock was water. It represented the speculative success of the merger. The speculation, however, was a reasonable projection of the future demand for steel. Steel production in the United States increased from 9.2 million tons in 1900 to 21.3 million tons in 1914.

The Morgan Bank underwrote the shares of common stock. They were quickly purchased because U.S. Steel controlled two-thirds of United States steel production. The expectation was that destructive competition was ended and earning would be sufficient to pay dividends on common stock. The owners of the companies included in the merger and the Morgan Bank made very large speculative profits. After the creation of United States Steel Corporation, the number of steel producers in the United States was reduced to twelve.

Over the next twenty-five years, U.S. Steel gradually lost market share in a rapidly growing market for steel. This was an intentional policy. There were two reasons for voluntarily losing market share: (1) maintaining price stability in the industry, and (2) avoiding anti-trust prosecution by the attorney general of the United States.

Rationalization of production and management began immediately after the merger—but only to a point. The principal policies that guided senior managers of U.S. Steel were scheduling production and setting prices; otherwise, many of the constituent corporations in the merger retained their pre-merger management structures. Senior managers installed by the Morgan Bank abandoned Carnegie's policy of maintaining optimum production in order to take advantage of economies of scale. They adopted a policy of price stabilization.

In order to maintain price stability, production was reduced at U.S. Steel when there were downturns in business because U.S. Steel refused to engage in destructive competition. This policy allowed other steel producers to continue to operate furnaces, Bessemer converters, open hearths, and fabrication operations at optimum capacity and profit accordingly. The stabilized profits resulting from stabilized prices was an opportunity for other steel producers to make large capital investments in new machinery of high productivity. By 1914, they could match the economies of scale that operated at U.S. Steel. The steel industry became an oligopoly with U.S. Steel as the dominant producer.

Petroleum

The petroleum industry originated in the United States. It began in 1858 with the discovery of crude oil reservoirs in the northwestern corner of Pennsylvania. A large domestic and foreign market already existed for products that could be made from petroleum. Kerosene replaced coal oil and whale oil for household lighting; petroleum wax replaced bees wax for candles; and crude oil itself replaced animal fat for lubricating the hubs of wagon wheels; and petroleum grease replaced animal fat lubricating the moving parts of locomotives, railroad rolling stock, and the moving parts of stationary and marine steam engines. Kerosene accounted for 90 percent of the products produced from crude oil in the 1860s and 1870s.

Oil recovered in Pennsylvania was easily refined into these products by using enlarged versions of whiskey stills. Technical innovations soon converted distillation into a semi-continuous process that was rapidly up-scaled. In 1865 John D. Rockefeller, a wholesale merchant in Cleveland, Ohio recognized the potential of petroleum products. He became a partner in a local refinery, then bought it, and then organized a partnership in 1870 and built a new refinery. It was incorporated as Standard Oil Company. The new refinery used the newest technology for refining and was the largest in the world, although it produced only 5 percent of the nation's petroleum products. It had the lowest costs in the industry and instantly achieved economies of scale.

In 1870 the refining capacity of the United States was at least double the annual production of crude oil. Excessive refining capacity was a formula for destructive competition. Rockefeller was determined to consolidate the refining business in order to match production with consumption, as the only way to stabilize profits. He did this by using his productive advantage to: (1) gain control of the other refineries in the Cleveland area, (2) negotiate rebates from railroads for transporting crude oil from Pennsylvania to his Cleveland refineries, and (3) negotiate rebates for refined products that were transported to places of consumption.

After Rockefeller gained control of the refineries in Cleveland, he embarked on a program to control national refining and distribution as a means of obtaining satisfactory prices. He obtained rebates from railroads by guaranteeing substantial daily traffic in crude oil coming from Pennsylvania and refined products destined for domestic consumption and export. The three trunkline railroads that offered rebates were the Pennsylvania, New York Central, and Erie. In return for rebates, 45 percent of the traffic would be carried on the Pennsylvania railroad and 27.5 percent each on the New York Central and Erie. The three railroads were pleased with this contract because it gave them a predictable volume of traffic to schedule trains as well as generating predictable revenues.

All three of these railroads had terminals at tidewater. This was essential for a successful consolidation because two-thirds of U.S. refinery production was destined for export, and 70 percent of exports went to Europe. Control of domestic refining and dominance of the export market allowed Standard Oil to control export prices, and export prices became the price for petroleum products designated for domestic consumption. In 1880 refined petroleum products were the fourth most valuable export after cotton, wheat, and preserved meat. Petroleum products were 20 percent of the value of cotton, the largest U.S. export.

Rockefeller tried to convert the National Refiners Association into a cartel that could induce refiners to limit production. Rockefeller was the association's director. The association collapsed in 1873 and destructive competition resumed. It was clear to Rockefeller that consolidation was required to match refinery capacity with consumption.

Refiners that refused to join Standard Oil were shown the details of the rebate agreement that Rockefeller had negotiated with the railroads. This agreement specified that all refineries that were not controlled by Standard Oil would pay the full published price schedule for the transportation of crude oil and refined products. Furthermore, part of the published price they paid to railroads would be rebated to Standard Oil.

The combination of economies of scale in refining and railroad rebates meant that Standard Oil could sell its products at half the prices charged by other refiners and still be profitable. This was a very powerful lever that induced the owners of more than 30 refineries to exchange shares of stock (usually a majority) for shares in the Standard Oil cartel (alliance). If they accepted participation in the Standard Oil cartel, they would earn stabilized profits; if they rejected participation, Standard Oil would bankrupt them by ruinously low prices in their marketing area.

In 1873 Standard Oil controlled about 10 percent of U.S. refining capacity. After it gained control of the largest refinery in New York City in 1876, it controlled somewhere between 30 and 40 percent of U.S. production. By 1878 it controlled 90 percent. After monopoly control was established, Standard Oil was a hodge-podge of small, inefficient refineries, large efficient refineries, poorly located refineries, fully owned refineries, majority owned refineries, leased refineries, and companies that controlled groups of regional refineries.

The consolidation of the 1870s was not a merger. It was an interlocking alliance managed by the dominant refiner, Rockefeller. There was no central management to integrate production and distribution, but Rockefeller controlled enough shares of stock in each refinery so that he could allocate market shares to each one. In this sense, Standard Oil was a cartel because all refiners remained in business, but ownership of shares gave Rockefeller the power to control the production of each refinery.

In 1882 management was centralized and production and distribution were integrated by reorganizing the alliance into a trust. All refiners in the alliance were required to convert their remaining shares into certificates of the Standard Oil trust at a valuation of their assets made by Standard Oil. In effect they became shareholders with the organizers of Standard Oil owning a majority of certificates and supplying most of the senior managers.

Senior managers were appointed to:

1. purchase crude oil;
2. improve the technology of refining;
3. market the several products produced from petroleum;
4. distribute them in the national market;
5. make large investments in railroad tank cars and bulk storage tanks along railroad tracks;
6. build ocean going tankers;
7. create an international marketing organization that operated in several nations as joint ventures or as wholly owned subsidiaries;
8. close unneeded refining capacity. Management did not yet perceive that backward integration into exploration for crude oil was essential for long-term profitability.

In the next four years (1882–1886), the fifty-three refineries were reduced to twenty-two and production of kerosene was concentrated in the three largest refineries located in northern New Jersey, Philadelphia, and Cleveland. Pipelines supplied them with crude oil. Because of the importance of exports, refineries in northern New Jersey produced 45 percent of Standard Oil's production. In 1882 sixteen smaller refineries were converted to producing specialty products: naphtha, lubricating oil, grease, tar, and wax. Four years later their number was reduced to eleven. Finally, corporate headquarters was moved to New York City because over two-thirds of U.S. production of kerosene and almost one-third of lubricating oil were exported.

Owners of oil wells were the principal losers in the creation of the Standard Oil monopoly because they had to accept the prices offered by Standard Oil. They responded to low crude oil prices by building a pipeline from northwest Pennsylvania to tidewater in northern New Jersey. The pipeline supplied a new refinery with an assured supply of crude oil. The pipeline was completed in 1879. It greatly lowered the cost of transporting crude oil. Cheap pipeline transportation of crude oil to a new, highly efficient refinery preserved 10 percent of the U.S. market for products made by corporations not part of the Standard Oil monopoly.

The cost effectiveness of pipeline transportation impelled two responses by Standard Oil—it built its own pipeline and a very large and efficient refinery at a tidewater location in northern New Jersey, and management energetically entered the international market, particularly the European market.

Rising demand for kerosene and other petroleum products, coupled with the depletion of oil reservoirs in northwest Pennsylvania, forced management to face the reality that their refineries must have assured supplies of crude oil. The problem of adequate supplies was solved by the discovery of the Lima-Indiana oil field (straddling the Ohio-Indiana border) in the mid-1880s. It was a prolific source of oil. The discovery of the Lima-Indiana field was an opportunity seized by Standard Oil. In 1889 it purchased the Ohio Oil Company and became a major producer of crude oil that was transported by pipeline to a new, large refinery in northern Indiana that supplied markets in western states. Three years later Standard Oil was producing about one-third of the nation's crude oil.

By the mid-1890s, Standard Oil was a fully integrated company. It controlled a high percentage of crude oil needed by its refineries; owned a network of pipelines, a flotilla of tankers to carry refined products to Europe; and it marketed consumer products with the Standard Oil brand name. Because Standard Oil had successfully restructured the petroleum industry before holding companies became legal, there was no urgency in converting the trust into a holding company. The conversion was delayed until 1899.

The discovery of bonanza quantities of crude oil in the Spindletop reservoir in 1901 initiated the end of the Standard Oil monopoly. Spindletop was at tidewater on the Gulf Coast of Texas. The first six wells produced more oil in one day than all of the other wells in the world. None of it was controlled by Standard Oil. Oil from Spindletop could be cheaply transported in ocean going tankers to refineries located along the East Coast of the United States and to Europe. The Spindletop discovery was followed by discoveries of additional prolific reservoirs in Texas and southern California. These discoveries, and similar discoveries elsewhere in the United States (and the world) were compelling evidence that petroleum was an abundant source of cheap power.

Within ten years of the discovery of Spindletop, the U.S. market for petroleum products underwent a revolutionary change. Consumption rapidly increased in the form of gasoline to fuel automobiles, and unrefined crude oil replaced coal to power steamships and locomotives (in Texas).

The breakup of Standard Oil into thirty-eight constituent companies that was ordered by the Supreme Court in 1911 (*Standard Oil Co. v. United States*) had minimal effect on the oligopolistic structure of the U.S. petroleum industry. Between 1901 and 1910, eight integrated corporations entered the U.S. market, including Shell Oil Company owned by Anglo-Dutch investors. They were joined by the five integrated petroleum companies that emerged from the dissolution of Standard Oil. All of these companies had access to abundant supplies of cheap crude from prolific reservoirs like Spindletop. By 1917, thirteen petroleum companies were among the 278 largest industrial corporations in the United States, and the petroleum industry was engaging in oligopolistic competition.

Electrical Equipment

Telegraphy was the first large-scale use of electricity. By 1870 the United States had a national telegraph network, but electricity to operate it was supplied by batteries. The technology did not exist to generate large amounts of electricity that could be harnessed to heavy usage. This changed after 1875 with the invention of the dynamo that could generate large amounts of electricity on demand. An urban market already existed for electricity that could be mass produced. City residents were supplied with both outdoor and indoor lighting by producer gas, a manufactured gas that was piped to offices and homes for indoor lighting and cooking. It was also used for street lighting in the largest cities. By 1875 there were over four hundred corporations in the United States manufacturing gas and all of them were in cities.

Arc lighting (controlled spark) was a means of converting electricity to light. In 1875 the ability to convert electricity into light was thirty-five years old, but was unused because there was no technology to generate sufficient electricity, nor was there technology to produce a steady and predictable flow of electricity. By 1879, the technology of arc lighting was sufficiently improved, simplified, and cheap so that it had a specialized market for outside lighting. It could not be used indoors because melted carbon that dripped from the arc was a fire hazard if it fell on wood floors.

Entry into manufacturing arc lighting equipment and dynamos was open to all entrepreneurs because basic patents had expired. Only improvements were patentable. Many companies entered the business of manufacturing and installing arc lighting equipment. By 1880 arc lighting was operating in a number of cities, including New York, Boston, and Philadelphia. In 1883 there were 6,000 arc lights in operation, and by 1885, 96,000 had been installed and arc lighting had displaced outdoor lighting using producer gas. By 1897, 325,000 were in operation.

Four parallel developments were occurring in the 1880s: (1) Thomas A. Edison was inventing a system for indoor incandescent lighting, (2) facilities were being built to generate electricity, (3) experiments were being made to transmit electricity long distances using alternating current, and (4) organizers replaced inventors as managers of the electrical equipment manufacturing industry. By 1889, ten years after the first successful application of electricity to arc lighting, manufacturing electrical equipment was a big business.

Electricity suddenly appeared in U.S. cities. All levels of government recognized that manufacturers of electrical equipment had to be big because big investments were needed to build factories and train people to operate the most sophisticated technologies of the era. Likewise, electrical generating facilities had to be sufficiently large to supply large numbers of city customers. Furthermore, technical innovations had to be continuous in order to increase the efficiency of generation and distribution of electricity.

Thomas A. Edison's first industrial skill was a telegrapher. He became interested in improving its operation and made several inventions while working in the financial district of New York City. He sold them for substantial sums of money and retired in 1876 in order to become a full-time inventor. Using his own money, he built a small laboratory at Menlo Park, a village in northern New Jersey that was within long commuting distance from the financial district of New York City

Edison knew there was a huge market for better lighting in the offices of city businesses and residences, and he focused his experiments on solving a problem that he knew had a solution. He knew that if he solved the technical problems of indoor incandescent lighting, money would be available from the investment bankers of Wall Street where he previously worked. He also knew that very little of the technology of arc lighting was transferable to incandescent lighting, and that he could not create a system alone. He needed large amounts of money to hire experts.

Edison estimated it would require three or four years to invent the technology of a workable commercial system. He approached the senior managers and large shareholders of Western Union Telegraph Company and other businesses related to telegraphy, including a partner of the Morgan Bank. In 1878 twelve investors incorporated the Edison Electric Light Company and designated Edison to direct the research of experts he hired. Many were Europeans. The company's two purposes were to finance the invention of a system of indoor incandescent lighting that was commercially viable, and retain ownership of the patents of the component parts that were essential for operation. The original and subsequent investors contributed half a million dollars. Edison could not have been successful without very strong financial backing from Wall Street investors and bankers.

An experimental system became operational in December 1879. It was immediately decided to put a small system in commercial operation in the financial district (Wall Street) of New York City. Corporations were organized to manufacture component parts: dynamos, light bulbs, sockets, switches, fuses, voltage regulators, meters, and insulation for transmission wires. Generators were designed to produce enough electricity to replace 16,000 gas lights that were in use in the financial district. Edison charged the same price for electric lighting as gas companies charged for gas lighting. The system became operational in September 1882 and by April 1883 new customers exceeded generating capacity. By 1888 there were 185 generating facilities in operation in the United States but they averaged only 2,080 lights because most of them used direct current that had a transmission radius of about 1 kilometer from generating facilities. The largest generating facility was in New York City. It lit 41,000 lights.

The highly visible success of indoor incandescent lighting in New York City propelled very rapid changes in production and management. The several manufacturers of component parts produced under license from Edison Electric Light Company were consolidated into Edison General Electric in 1889. The merger of 1889 was brokered by the Morgan Bank, and in a subsequent reorganization, management was placed in the hands of organizers. Thomas Edison was excluded from management decisions, although he remained a director. New managers centralized production of the various products, sales, financing sales, and research.

George Westinghouse was a contemporary of Edison. In 1880 he was already a wealthy manufacturer of railroad equipment. In 1881 after inspecting the signaling practices of British railroads, he added electrically operated signal devices to his products. He was increasingly attracted to the industrial potential of electricity, and in 1884 he organized the Union Switch and Signal Company in order to manufacture electrically operated signal devices for railroads. Westinghouse recognized, as Edison did not, that the expansion of incandescent lighting depended on larger generating facilities than the miniature ones then in operation; and that larger generation facilities were only possible by transmitting electricity long distances. This required the use of alternating current.

The generation and transmission of alternating current was the key to future increases in the use of electricity. This was clear in 1885 because Edison's system in New York City using direct current could not be efficiently transmitted more than two kilometers from generating facilities because, even with the best insulation, there was excessive leakage. Like Edison, Westinghouse hired experts to solve the problem of long distance transmission of electricity by using alternating current, and, like Edison, many of the experts were Europeans.

They were successful in developing a transformer that could convert the high voltages used for the long distance transmission of alternating current into low voltage electricity that was used for indoor incandescent lighting. On the basis of the success of this technology, the Westinghouse Electric Company was incorporated in 1886. The company immediately established a laboratory staffed with full-time engineers to improve all aspects of electricity generation and transmission.

The first commercial application was in Buffalo, New York at the end of 1886. It was highly successful and within six months Westinghouse had orders for 25 municipal systems; and by 1890, 350 generating facilities were in operation that averaged 2,000 lights per station. By 1890 Edison and Westinghouse had built about the same number of generating facilities, but the long-term advantage was with Westinghouse because his generating facilities used alternating current that could transmit electricity over much longer distances without excessive leakage of energy. They could achieve economies of scale because they could service larger areas.

From the beginning of manufacturing, Edison General Electric sold systems on the basis of geographic franchises—usually towns and cities—and accepted 25 to 30 percent of the sale price as fully paid stock in the franchise. General Electric, the successor corporation to Edison General Electric, continued this sales policy because it tied the sale of replacement equipment to General Electric. General Electric charged higher prices for replacement equipment than competitors, but its equipment was higher quality and carried guarantees of repair and performance to engineering specifications.

The earliest systems sold by Westinghouse were for cash with few restrictions on purchasing replacement equipment. By 1895, however, Westinghouse changed its sales strategy. Franchises were obtained from municipal governments and Westinghouse built generating facilities and strung networks of wires to consumers. After it was tested, it was sold to local investors. Like General Electric, Westinghouse guaranteed repair and performance to engineering specifications. These guarantees were essential for selling equipment. These guarantees could not be made until both companies had access to each others patents.

Both companies wanted to avoid a morass of prolonged litigation over patent infringements. There were two options—merger and cross-licensing of patents (patent pool). The Morgan Bank took the initiative to broker a mutually satisfactory agreement on both options. Westinghouse was not interested in a merger with Edison General Electric, but other principal manufacturers welcomed consolidation. The result was the creation of General Electric Corporation in 1892. After the merger the principal remaining competitors were Westinghouse, Siemens, and Western Electric.

A court decision in December 1892 sustained the Edison patent for incandescent light bulbs and General Electric began legal action to end non-licensed manufacturing by Westinghouse and other companies. General Electric began litigation even though the basic patent on Edison's light bulb expired in 1894. General Electric wanted to collect licensing fees on the subsequent improvements that made the Edison bulb technologically superior to all others. In 1896 General Electric reached a licensing/price agreement with 16 producers of light bulbs, including Westinghouse. Thereafter, General Electric had 50 percent of the national market and became the price leader. Westinghouse had 15 percent and followed the pricing policy of General Electric.

In the same year General Electric and Westinghouse agreed that the best way to end litigation over patent infringements was a cross-licensing agreement because there was a strong desire by managers of both companies to manufacture the best possible product—and not manufacture inferior products in order to circumvent patents. Furthermore, both companies wanted to manufacture a full complement of electrical equipment and this required using the patents owned by both companies. An agreement was reached in March 1896.

General Electric patents were calculated to represent 62 percent of the value of the patents owned by both companies. The agreement was to last for fifteen years. The patent pool made it easier for both General Electric and Westinghouse to initiate litigation against smaller companies for patent infringement.

The patent pool did not include dividing market shares between the companies, and it had little effect on prices. Prices continued to be competitive within a range that was necessary to continuously finance research needed to improve product reliability in the most technologically complex industry in the world.

Two additional urban markets awaited capture by electricity: (1) traction motors replacing steam engines operating on elevated railways and horses pulling passenger cars on street railways, and (2) electric motors replacing small steam engines that were used in various urban manufacturing processes. Electric traction grew out of Edison's interest in electric motors to replace small stationary steam engines in cities. Edison knew that electricity for lighting would increase at night but large amounts of generating capacity were unused during the day. Daytime use of electricity by electrified street railways and electric motors in manufacturing would substantially increase revenues.

Edison conducted experiments with electric traction motors to the point of building two short experimental railways at Menlo Park, but he never had the time to carry the project to completion. In two trials in 1883 and 1884, electric locomotives successfully pulled trains of passenger cars, but the owners of urban railroad franchises (street and elevated) showed little interest because of the high cost of transmitting electricity to locomotives.

Other persons in the United States and Europe were interested in traction motors for urban transportation. Batteries were tried and failed because they lacked power to climb hills, needed continual repair on rough tracks, and had limited lives. By 1888–1889, overhead wires with electricity transmitted to motors by trolley wheels solved the problem of supplying electricity to traction motors, but continual experiments did not produce a reliable motor. Several shortlines operated for a while, but without commercial success.

Frank J. Sprague, a graduate of the United States Naval Academy, perfected traction motors. In 1882 the U.S. Navy sent him to Europe to attend an international industrial exposition to evaluate dynamos that could supply electricity to power equipment on warships. He observed the latest electrical technologies of Europe and wrote a long report for the navy. On his return, he was hired by Edison to install generators. Sprague knew that Edison's time was totally consumed in improving incandescent lighting and that producing and marketing electric motors was a distant second interests. While working for Edison, he used as much time as possible to develop a reliable electric motor.

Sprague resigned from Edison General Electric in 1884 to devote full-time to develop traction motors and large electric motors capable of industrial application. With a partner who supplied funds, in November 1884 they incorporated the Sprague Electric Railway and Motor Company. The first success was improved industrial motors. They were manufactured by Edison General Electric and they found instant use to power printing presses, passenger and freight elevators, and belts that transmitted power to industrial machinery.

The instant profitability of manufacturing industrial electric motors allowed him to change the focus of his experiments to traction motors to power the cars of street railways. For Sprague, this meant replacing the smoky steam engines that operated on elevated tracks in New York City. Elevated trains were an obvious use of electrical traction motors because: (1) power could be transmitted on a third rail without danger to pedestrians, (2) elevated railroads had fewer stops than street railways, and (3) tracks were carefully built and better maintained.

The demonstration he made in late 1886 was highly successful but the owner of the four New York City elevated railroads rejected replacement of steam power.

Sprague then sought to electrify a street railway and signed a contract in May 1887 to build a generating facility and electrify 19 kilometers of track in Richmond, Virginia. It was an experimental project that took a year to put into reliable service. Completion of the railroad cost twice as much as the contract price but high profits from manufacturing electric motors sustained the operation until technical weaknesses were rectified. The success of the Richmond Street Railway Company created a surge in demand, especially after he invited potential buyers to Richmond to demonstrate its reliability.

Eighteen months after the Richmond Street Railway began operation, there were 180 street railways using electric power or in process of converting to electric power. They operated on 1,930 kilometers of track with nearly 2,000 passenger cars providing service. In 1889 Sprague Railway Company was merged with Edison General Electric. After the acquisition of Sprague Electric Railway and Motor Company, Edison General Electric became the technical leaders in the business of manufacturing electric and traction motors; and this leadership carried over into the 1892 merger that created General Electric.

In 1890 George Westinghouse desperately wanted to enter the traction motor business because he recognized that there was a huge market in rapidly urbanizing America. Westinghouse had to engage in catch-up technology. In 1890 there were 13,000 kilometers of street railways in the United States and only 2,100 were electrified. In 1902 there were 35,000 kilometers of street railways and all were electrified.

By early 1891, Westinghouse engineers had designed and his factories were producing reliable traction motors. When General Electric was formed in 1892, manufacturing traction motors was a duopoly of Westinghouse and General Electric. The intense competition between General Electric and Westinghouse from 1892 to 1900 resulted in rapid improvements in operating efficiencies of traction motors designed for street railways, elevated railways, subways, and inter-urban railways.

Niagara Falls

In 1890 Niagara Falls was the largest potential source of hydroelectric power in the United States, and it was near the center of the nation's urban population. Its only use was to power water turbines that transmitted mechanical power to five or six paper and flour mills. American engineers had been highly successful in designing water turbines that could convert small and medium flows of water with low heads into mechanical power to operate textile machinery, make paper, saw logs, and grind grain; however, designing equipment to harness the prodigious flow of water over Niagara Falls, and its high head, was beyond their capabilities.

By 1890, it was obvious to many that urban and industrial use of electricity would increase at an accelerating rate. Nobody could predict the rate but knowledgeable persons knew the market was huge. It was also clear by 1890 that water turbines that produced mechanical power could be converted to generate electricity. Niagara Falls was an electricity bonanza waiting to be developed, but there were two very large problems— money and technology. It would be expensive to divert water from the Niagara River at the top of the falls into canals built along the rim of the gorge to carry it to where it would fall seventy to eighty meters in tubes to turbines located at the base of the cliff at river level. Obtaining money for this construction was only half the problem.

American engineers did not have the experience or theoretical training to design large generators, nor turbines that had blades that could withstand the pressure of eighty meters of falling water, nor large diameter tubes to contain water falling eighty meters. The design skills resided in Europe, particularly in Switzerland where high heads of water under high pressure from mountain reservoirs were used to generate a high percentage of the electricity used in Swiss cities. Theoretical calculations and design had to be done in Europe, but building the generators, turbines, and tubes was done in the United States.

J. P. Morgan was one of several investment bankers who recognized the power potential of Niagara Falls. All of them were willing to mobilize very large amounts of capital to build a hydroelectric infrastructure that could produce far more power than any other generating facility in the United States. The scale of investment required an engineering study and an evaluation of the best way to transmit electricity to Buffalo, forty kilometers away where reciprocating steam engines supplied most of the power used by manufacturing corporations. These engines were candidates for replacement by electricity generated at the falls.

Investment bankers like Morgan were fully aware that the technology of electricity transmission was changing very rapidly. After continuous consultations from 1891 to 1893, the decision was made to install generators that generated alternating current. Both General Electric and Westinghouse were requested to submit bids for generators. Because of its lead in developing alternating current, Westinghouse was awarded the contract in October 1893. The first electricity was produced in August 1895.

The two largest consumers were aluminum smelting and manufacturing artificial abrasives. The Pittsburgh Reduction Company (renamed Aluminum Company of America—ALCOA) smelted aluminum oxide into metal and the Carborundum Corporation made silicon carbide, a more efficient abrasive than quartz sand or crushed garnets. Within two years, additional factories were built to manufacture other products requiring large amounts of electricity. Some of these products were calcium carbide (used to make acetylene), caustic soda, and chlorine gas.

Before cheap electric power was available at Niagara Falls, the commercial possibilities of electrochemistry were experimental. Availability of large amounts of hydroelectric power at Niagara Falls propelled experimental technology to commercial production. The location of electrochemical manufacturing at Niagara Falls was not foreseen by the investors in the Niagara Falls generating facility but was greatly welcomed because these industries consumed electricity for twenty-four hours a day, every day of the year.

The decision to generate alternating current at Niagara Falls had significance beyond the mega-potential of Niagara Falls. It was a decision that dictated that future investments in generating electricity would be large central generating facilities that could achieve economies of scale. Central generation of electricity depended on three technologies that were contemporaneous with generating hydroelectricity at Niagara Falls: (1) ability to transmit electricity long distances by alternating current, (2) ability to transform high voltage current used in long distance transmission into low voltage current for factory and household consumption, and (3) steam turbines to generate electricity. Only coal fired steam turbines could generate electricity in places where hydroelectricity was unavailable, and only alternating current could transmit electricity for tens of kilometers without excessive leakage.

In 1900 electricity was a minor source of power in manufacturing. It supplied about 5 percent of power needs and only one-third of this power came from central generating facilities. In the next twenty-five years, the building of large centralized generating facilities was a growth industry comparable to automobile manufacturing. During the 1920s, the availability of cheap electricity in cities and cheap automobiles for rural residents were the most visible evidence of an emerging consumer culture.

Automobiles

The internal combustion engine was developed in Europe, where many men recognized that a compact engine could power personal vehicles. It had great potential to fill a need that could not be satisfied by railroad locomotives and street railways. During the early 1890s, several engines successfully powered passenger vehicles (automobiles) on city streets. Several American engineers and promoters were as optimistic as their European counterparts that manufacturing automobiles could be a highly profitable business if internal combustion engines could be made mechanically reliable. In 1900 European and American automobile manufacturers began from a technological base that was approximately equal.

Between 1900 and 1915, there were over one hundred manufacturers of automobiles in the United States. During these same years, there was an extremely rapid acceleration in demand. In spite of this demand, a high percentage of entrants became bankrupt. The manufacturers that survived used three strategies to achieve economies of scale: (1) mass production, (2) mergers, and (3) franchised dealers. Henry Ford used the technologies of mass production to become big and William C. Durant of General Motors used mergers to become big. Both companies built national sales organizations of franchised dealers who sold directly to consumers; and by 1920 there was oligopolistic competition.

The explosive increase in automobile ownership in the United States after 1905 was almost entirely due to the ability of American manufacturers to mass produce low-priced automobiles. Pre-eminent among these manufacturers was Henry Ford. In 1905 Britain, France, and Germany had a total 81,000 automobiles in operation and the United States had 74,000. By 1913 Europeans had 426,000 in operation and the United States had 1,258,000. Annual production in the United States was 4.3 million in 1926. In Europe it was 495,000. In 1927, 19 million of the 23.4 million families in the United States owned a new or used automobile. Of the 27.4 million automobiles built since 1909, over 12 million were made by Ford. The automobile was the most visible sign that the United States had become a consumer culture.[11]

Henry Ford

Henry Ford was born in 1863 on a farm a short distance west of Detroit. As a youth, he hated the huge amount of hand labor required for farming and the never-ending care required to keep draft horses healthy. At age sixteen he went to Detroit where his mechanical aptitude secured an apprenticeship as a machinist at Detroit Drydock Company. He rapidly acquired the skills of a master mechanic and was hired by Edison Illuminating Company of Detroit where he was rapidly promoted to senior engineer. By 1896, he was high enough in the management structure to be invited to New York City for the annual dinner for senior managers of Edison franchises. There he met Thomas Edison.

While employed at Detroit Edison, Ford experimented with internal combustion engines to power automobiles. He built his first engine in 1893. Then he built an automobile around it. It had its first road test in 1896. In August 1899 he resigned from Detroit Edison in order to devote full time to perfecting his automobile. At the same time, he and several investors incorporated the Detroit Automobile Company with capital of fifteen thousand dollars. The company produced about twenty-five automobiles but was bankrupt in 1900.

In 1901 Ford and another set of investors incorporated the Henry Ford Motor Company. They invested thirty thousand dollars. Ford's title was engineer but he did not have management control and he resigned in 1902. The third Ford Motor Company was incorporated in 1903. Ford had 25 percent ownership and eleven other Detroit investors owned the rest. The invested capital was twenty-eight thousand dollars. The company's immediate profitability allowed Ford to progressively buy out other investors. By 1906, he owned 58 percent of the company's stock and could manage the company the way he wanted.

Ford stopped making luxury models and used the company's resources to produce a cheap automobile. It sold as fast as it was produced and Ford Motor Company sales increased from

1.5 million dollars in 1906 to 5.8 million dollars in 1907. During 1907 Ford concentrated on redesigning his cheap automobile so that it could operate on rough and rutted rural roads, and was simple to maintain.

The auto he designed was the Model T. It was introduced in October 1908 and was an instant best seller. Over ten thousand were sold in the first year of production, which made Ford the leading automobile manufacturer in the United States. In 1909 Ford decided that the Model T would be the only model produced by Ford Motor Company and, in order to lower production costs and the sale price, he froze the design. The design remained frozen for eighteen years. The Model T was light weight with a highly reliable four cylinder gasoline engine mounted on a strong steel frame, and its large diameter wheels allowed it to operate in snow and in the furrows of muddy rural roads. It was designed to replace farm carriages pulled by horses and, by extension, end rural isolation.

Henry Ford and his engineers then concentrated on production efficiency to satisfy demand, because production was the principal restraint on corporate growth. The national market for automobiles was Ford's for the taking. Observers of production in Ford factories "saw unprecedented seeking after a kind of truth, the ultimate of productive efficiency which lay hidden beneath traditional and conventional modes of work. Ford was a complete, if careful, revolutionary."[12]

Ford adopted a moving assembly line that subsequently became the standard method for mass producing durable consumer products for mass consumption. The moving assembly line brought the task to workers who were spaced at regular intervals where they attached component parts to the frame. The assembly line moved at waist level so that there was no lost motion in stooping and lifting. It was a carefully planned sequence of conveyors, rollways, and gravity slides that brought component parts (brakes, steering wheels, axels, transmissions, and engines) to workers who performed only one task in the production process, and they did that task for the whole working day.

Ford manufactured a high percentage of component parts. They were mass produced by specialized machinery designed to perform only one operation. Using single-purpose machines reduced waste because handling was reduced. Damage or mistakes in measurements or alignments were most likely to occur during frequent handling.

The successful operation of the moving assembly line required a new factory designed for that purpose. Ford built the factory in 1910 and it achieved optimum production in 1913. It was immensely successful at lowering the time (and cost) of production. Assembly time for automobiles was reduced from 12 hours to 2.5 hours and by the spring of 1914 it was 1.5 hours. By 1914, daily production by the Detroit assembly line was 1,000 automobiles per day.

Between 1910 and 1915, Ford built twenty-seven assembly lines in twenty-seven cities, because it was cheaper to transport parts to local assembly lines than to ship completed automobiles. Managers of these assembly factories were delegated responsibility for recruiting and supervising franchised dealers, as well as carrying adequate inventories of spare parts.

Costs savings were passed on to Ford workers and to consumers in general. In 1913 the price of a Model T was $500 and in 1916 it was $345. In that year Ford produced 577,000 Model Ts, which was 50 percent of U.S. auto production. In January 1914 Henry Ford doubled wages to $5 per day for an 8 hour day. Higher wages for industrial workers rewarded their productivity and made it possible for them to purchase Model Ts. High wages also attracted the most productive workers. Henry Ford claimed, with a large amount of truth, that high wages were cost efficient because they reduced labor turnover.

The rapid growth of Ford Motor Company was self-financed. The Model T was sold for cash and the cash flow was adequate to finance expansion without bank loans. Profits were also adequate to undertake vertical integration. In 1919 Henry Ford began building a steel mill to supply castings, sheets, and other shapes required for manufacturing most of the component parts of the Model T. The steel mill and parts factories were closely integrated with an adjacent factory that assembled the Model T. The production process was rigid but enormously efficient in producing an automobile that had not changed for ten years.

The short depression of 1920–1921 seriously reduced cash flow. Ford survived by (1) lowering prices, (2) firing one-third of his administrative and production personnel, and (3) using the credit worthiness of his dealers and suppliers with local banks. Dealers continued to accept new automobiles and pay cash for them using their credit with local banks, and parts suppliers extended credit for ninety days or longer. Henry Ford also used the downturn in business to buy, at discounted prices, the remaining shares of Ford Motor Company from the original investors. After 1920, Henry Ford had complete ownership. When prosperity returned in 1921, the reduced overhead from the reduced number of employees produced twice as many autos as in the depression year of 1920. The Model T supplied 55 percent of the U.S. market and profits soared. In 1923 Ford produced 1.6 million Model T's, which was 46 percent of national sales. It sold for $295.

Ford's survival of the depression, followed by increased profitability and market dominance increased Henry Ford's confidence that he and three or four personally loyal managers could administer the company. He fired many senior managers who warned him of changing market conditions and the increasing obsolescence of the Model T. They warned him that the lowest price was a declining incentive to purchase the Model T in a consumer culture. Among those fired were William S. Knudsen, who later became president of General Motors.

In 1922 Henry Ford described his company's management structure: "The Ford factories and enterprises have no organization, no specific duties attaching to any position, no line of succession or of authority, very few titles, and no conferences." In other words, there was no systematic management hierarchy and no clear channel to acquire market information from Ford dealers or of problems within the company.[13]

Henry Ford's desire to be self-sufficient in producing component parts had huge hidden dangers. The least danger was the rigidity of the production system that precluded incremental improvements in style and performance. The biggest danger, however, was the failure of Henry Ford to recognize the significance of the replacement market. When it came time for families to replace their Model T, they frequently purchased an upscale model from a competing manufacturer. Families with increased disposable incomes, especially urban families, wanted choices, and Ford Motor Company did not offer choices. Henry Ford's rejection of market analysis abdicated competition in the replacement market.

Model T sales began a steady decline in 1924. Henry Ford ignored dealer complaints about the lack of upscale models to compete with General Motors and other manufacturers, and not until 1928 did he organize a credit subsidiary to finance installment purchases. General Motors filled the market that Ford vacated. In 1924 it had 18 percent of the national market; in 1927 it had captured 43 percent. General Motors replaced Ford as the dominant corporation in the automobile manufacturing industry.

In 1927 Ford had to face the obvious. The Model T was an antique. His response was bizarre. He closed thirty-four assembly factories in the United States while his parts factories retooled to produce the model A. Closure of assembly factories lasted a minimum of six months. In 1927 Ford's share of the national market fell to 9 percent and Ford lost a high percentage of its most experienced dealers.

The model A replaced the Model T. It was an excellently engineered auto that incorporated the most up-to-date features, but cession of production gave market leadership to General Motors and Ford continued to lose market share. In 1937, near the end of the Great

Depression, General Motors had 41 percent of the U.S. market, Chrysler 25 percent, and Ford 21 percent.

The Model T was immensely successful for satisfying a family's need for their first automobile. It was also the most obvious durable consumer product in the consumer culture that emerged in the 1920s. The consumer culture was based on mass production, electricity generation, cheap gasoline, rising wages, rising worker productivity, and a reduction of working hours to eight hours per day five days a week. Henry Ford was a leader in four of these events: mass production, increased worker productivity, higher wages, and reduced hours of labor.

General Motors

Like Henry Ford, William C. Durant was convinced there was a mass market for automobiles. In order to supply mass demand, manufacturing corporations had to be big, and the quickest way to become big was by mergers. Durant had experience in this strategy. He and a partner organized a carriage business at Flint, Michigan in 1885. Flint was an optimum location because it was near an abundant supply of mature oak and maple trees and this wood was preferred for building carriages.

Durant was a super salesman. He used two strategies to achieve rapid growth: (1) organizing a national network of dealers, and (2) organizing a network of part suppliers in and around Flint. They made bodies, wheels, axels, upholstery, springs, steel and brass fittings that his factory assembled into many models. By 1900, his company was the largest carriage maker in the United States.

In 1904 it became obvious to him that the future was horseless carriages. He purchased a bankrupt auto maker in Flint (Buick) and used the same strategy of expansion that made him the largest manufacturer of carriages. He built an assembly factory in Flint and encouraged manufacturers of component parts to establish their factories in and around Flint. At the same time, he began organizing a network of dealers. In the year Durant purchased Buick it produced twenty-eight autos. In 1908 it produced 8,800 and was the largest auto manufacturer in the nation. Ford produced 6,100 autos and was the second largest manufacturer of autos.

In order to become big enough to sell on the mass market that he knew existed, Durant's strategy was to merge a number of the most efficient automobile manufacturers into a holding company. In 1908 he incorporated General Motors to be the vehicle for acquiring auto manufacturers. Within two years General Motors acquired ten automobile and parts manufacturers, three truck manufacturers, and ten manufacturers of component parts. The focus of his acquisitions was marketing. Only companies with regional and national sales organizations were acquired.

Like Ford, Durant did not use the services of investment bankers. Acquisitions were made by exchanging shares of stock. Durant tried to acquire Ford Motor Company, but Henry Ford rejected Durant's offer because he wanted cash. Like Ford, Durant neglected management. He failed to create an organization that could exert centralized control over the combination he created. Centralized control was essential to integrate parts makers, engineering design, and assembly of autos in order to achieve economies of scale. Acquired corporations remained divisions that were managed with a high degree of autonomy.

Finance was hand-to-mouth. There was no cash reserve because Durant assumed that there would be no decline in demand. In 1910 there was a blip in demand and General Motors lacked money to pay suppliers and workers. He was forced to borrow. In return he had to sign a five-year voting trust that gave bankers control of General Motors. The principal interest of bankers was to put General Motors on a strong financial base rather than continue rapid expansion of production to the extent that revenues allowed. Walter P. Chrysler was hired from American

Locomotive Company to manage Buick and he rationalized its engineering, and production technologies. He borrowed much from Henry Ford.

After Durant was excluded from management, he acquired a small auto manufacturing company—Chevrolet—and rapidly increased its size by mergers and its sales by adding dealers. Chevrolet was the vehicle used by Durant to regain control of General Motors, and after he was restored to the presidency, Chevrolet was merged into General Motors. Durant was able to regain control of General Motors because he convinced Pierre du Pont to purchase shares of General Motors stock. Durant did the same. When the trust expired in 1915, Durant and du Pont controlled General Motors. In 1916 General Motors rewarded the du Ponts for their investment by paying a dividend of fifty dollars per share from earnings accumulated by the bankers while they managed General Motors.

After resuming the presidency, Durant continued to acquire parts manufacturers (roller bearings, radiators, horns, and lighting systems) that were required to build upscale automobiles. They were combined into a parts division and Alfred P. Sloan was placed in charge. Sloan was the former owner of a roller bearing manufacturer acquired by General Motors.

Durant made a first step in rationalizing management by dissolving the holding company and grouping the various corporations into divisions. General Motors became an operating company but the operating divisions lacked centralized control in finance, purchasing (inventory control), engineering, and marketing. The operating divisions were largely autonomous.

Du Pont Corporation greatly increased its investment in General Motors after 1918. It had a huge amount of cash from wartime profits making explosives, and it needed an investment because of the sudden contraction in the explosives market. The treasurer of Du Pont Corporation became the treasurer of General Motors, but overall management remained in the hands of Durant and he continued to acquire companies that made automotive parts. Durant was also closely attentive to customer needs. In 1919 General Motors organized a consumer credit division in order to finance the purchase of autos on the installment plan.

Durant's policy of continuous expansion by merger abruptly stopped in the late summer of 1920. General Motors faced bankruptcy because of a precipitous drop in sales that was intensified by lack of management control of purchasing. Huge inventories of parts had been accumulated by the assembly divisions based on Durant's assumption that there was no limit to the immediate market for autos. Eventually eighty-four million dollars of parts inventories had to be written off as a dead loss. Durant resigned the presidency. Fiscal solvency was restored by a cash infusion from Du Pont Corporation and a loan from the Morgan Bank.

After finances were stabilized, Pierre du Pont began to reorganize General Motor's management structure. It took four years. Reorganization was done by university trained engineers. Both Pierre du Pont and Alfred P. Sloan were graduates of M.I.T. Sloan had urged Durant to institute centralized cost controls and actively coordinate the policies of the assembly and parts divisions. He had submitted a reorganization plan in 1919 but Durant ignored it. After Durant's resignation, Sloan was appointed operating vice president and assigned the job of restructuring management. In 1923 he was appointed president.

Sloan's plan retained the autonomy of the assembly divisions that sold the several models produced by General Motors, but each division was assigned a niche market. Chevrolet was to complete with the Model T but have a higher price and more comfort and style. Cadillac was to compete with smaller manufacturers of luxury automobiles. The marketing guideline was a car for every price and purpose. Price was important for selling autos but it was not the only concern of an increasing percentage of purchasers. They wanted a little comfort and a little style; and they wanted General Motors to help finance the purchase of new autos.

The replacement market in the rapidly growing consumer culture of the 1920s required: (1) product differentiation, (2) mass advertising, (3) consumer financing, (4) improved dealer relations, and (5) recognition that the market for used cars was an integral part of the automobile industry.

In the new management structure, an executive committee exercised general supervision over all assembly and staff divisions. The executive committee met at regular intervals and was advisory to the president. In order to have current information, new channels of communication were created between the executive committee and managers of the assembly divisions. The executive committee consisted of the president of General Motors and vice president of finance (in charge of budget making, accounting, consumer finance, taxation, dividends), and the managers of the assembly divisions. The executive committee made all strategic and budgetary decisions. Vice presidents of other divisions (purchasing, parts, dealer relations, and research) were part of the staff. They were invited to meetings of the executive committee when information was needed and policy decisions of the executive committee had to be implemented.

The management structure created by Sloan resembled the line and staff functions that commands and deploys an army equipped with a large variety of modern weapons. It had two great advantages. (1) The principal function of the executive committee was to see the big picture and make policy decisions accordingly. In order to make policy decisions, regular channels of internal communication gave the executive committee large amounts of information gathered by staff personnel and the managers of the assembly divisions. (2) Vice presidents of the staff divisions were delegated large amounts of autonomy to solve problems within the overall strategy formulated by the executive committee. General Motor's management structure was widely copied by other big businesses that encompassed a large number of diverse operations in national and international markets.

Chapter 14

Consumer Culture

The basis of consumer culture is the mass production of consumer products. Behind the technical ability to mass produce consumer products is the assumption that an abundance of material possessions and human services is politically and socially desirable. In order to obtain abundance, all persons of employable age should perform full-time paid labor to earn wages, salaries, or entrepreneurial profits. Furthermore, the abundance that is possible by full-time paid labor should be shared on an equalized basis. In other words, the purpose of mass production is mass consumption, and mass production is only possible by a labor force composed of full-time paid laborers who earn enough money to purchase an adequate share of the products they produce. Full employment and consumer cultures are reciprocals.

A consumer culture became a reality in the United States between the end of World War I in November 1918 and the congressional elections of November 1930. It was the first consumer culture to evolve from the industrial revolution. The usual measures of a consumer culture are (1) full-time paid labor employment; (2) eight hours of labor per day, five days a week; (3) mass production of consumer durable products; (4) electric power available in most homes; (5) urbanization; (6) abundant leisure activities; and (7) abundant food (especially meat).

In the 1920s economic growth and the consumer culture were co-events. Between 1921 and 1929, industrial production increased approximately 90 percent, wages of industrial workers increased about 17 percent, and the wholesale price index remained stationary. The increased industrial production was done by a labor force that did not increase in size. There were 8.4 million industrial workers in 1919 and 8.3 million in 1929. During the 1920s, significantly more manufactured products were produced by fewer persons.

Higher average incomes earned by industrial workers increased disposable incomes. Higher incomes were spent two ways: purchasing durable consumer products, including housing; and using additional human services (vacation travel, entertainment, and health care). Employment in human services increased 7.6 percent.[1]

Reduced Hours of Labor

The beginning of reduced hours of industrial labor began in 1912 when Congress made eight hours of labor per day mandatory for government contracts. In 1912, however, government contracts were a small percentage of the economy. In 1916 Congress made the eight-hour day mandatory for railroad workers. In the meantime (1914), Henry Ford reduced hours of labor to eight hours. After the United States entered World War I in April 1917, government contracts became a significant percentage of the economy, and industry rapidly adopted the eight-hour day, often with four additional hours on Saturday. All labor in excess of forty hours per week was paid a 50 percent bonus (time and a half for overtime). During the war most laborers worked fifty hours per week.

The shortage of labor in the command economy that mobilized the industrial resources of the United States to produce military supplies and equipment created an overnight shortage of labor. Coupled with a national policy of eight hours per day, industrial wages soared. In the nineteen months that the United States was at war, real wages in manufacturing increased one-third more than consumer prices. The short depression of 1920–1921 sharply increased unemployment but had little effect on wage rates. With the return of industrial prosperity, industrial workers and salaried employees retained the increased purchasing power they obtained during the war.

Electrical Power

After 1910, building central generating facilities and distribution systems was a huge growth industry, as well as being the most technically complex industry in the United States. "The capital demands of the American utilities during the 1920s, when many regional systems were under construction, exceeded those of the railroads during the decades of their most rapid expansion." By 1920 all urban businesses and most businesses in small towns had indoor electric lighting, and by 1930 it was almost universal for residential housing in cities and towns. During the 1920s, electricity use in the United States more than doubled.[2]

After 1905, electric motors rapidly replaced reciprocating steam engines that turned overhead drive shafts that turned belts that transmitted power to machines. Stationary steam engines in factories were scrapped in direct relation to electrification. Industrial dependence on stationary steam engines had lasted fifty years. Stationary steam engines produced half of the industrial power in the United States in 1870. The other half was produced by water wheels or water turbines; and all of this power was mechanically transmitted to machines. In 1909 electric motors supplied 25 percent of the power used by industry; in 1919, 55 percent, and in 1929 they supplied 82 percent to an industrial base that had undergone rapid expansion.[3]

Reciprocating steam engines were ponderous and inefficient in converting coal to electricity. They were similar to steam locomotives, but instead of turning drive wheels they turned shafts that turned belts that turned the rotors of generators. They were expensive to operate and their vibrations and weight of moving parts limited revolution per minute. This put an upper limit on the amount of power that reciprocating engines could generate and kept electricity prices high. Lower prices required economies of scale in generation and this required new technology. It was available. The new technology was steam turbines, a technology borrowed from Europe.

Steam turbines had four huge advantages over reciprocating engines: (1) capital costs were lower, (2) they were much more efficient at converting coal into electricity, (3) they were capable of increased size with no foreseeable upper limit, and (4) they were capable of major improvements in thermal efficiency. The first steam turbine generators in the United States became operational in Chicago in 1903. They were over 110 percent larger than the largest generators powered by steam engines. Two years later (1905) these generators were replaced by generators that produced 400 percent more power than the largest generators powered by reciprocating steam engines. Thereafter, steam turbines, like alternating current, became the standard technologies of the industry because they made possible economies of scale.

From the beginning of electricity generation in the largest cities, generating facilities were highly fragmented because the earliest generating facilities produced only direct current. The maximum distance of transmission of direct current was one to two kilometers. Beyond this distance there were excessive losses of energy. City councils awarded a multitude of franchises to serve the needs of neighborhoods in exactly the way they awarded franchise for street railways. Generating facilities were a mixture of franchises owned by local investors, municipally owned generators, and isolated facilities producing power for one factory. Even franchises that generated alternating current (that could be transmitted long distances) were not integrated into networks for distribution to where demand was greatest. The business of generating electricity desperately needed consolidation, because economies of scale could not be financed by small franchises.

Samuel Insull is the best known consolidator of electricity generating franchises, but many other organizers understood the potential of economies of scale in generating and distributing electricity. Insull had been personal secretary to Thomas Edison in the 1880s and then manager of the Edison General Electric factory that built dynamos (generators). He resigned after the merger created General Electric (1892) and accepted the presidency of Chicago Edison. Chicago Edison was one of 18 generating facilities in Chicago that sold electricity. In addition, there were 498 isolated systems. Altogether, these facilities lit 273,600 electric lights, 16,415 arc lights, and supplied power for an indeterminate number of electric motors.

This was a chaotic situation that required a political and technological solution. Chicago Edison was best placed to consolidate electricity generation because it was the principal supplier of electricity to businesses in the city center where demand was concentrated. Insull was acutely aware that Chicago Edison's future growth was restrained by franchises that supplied electricity to neighborhoods surrounding the central business district. Many of these franchises used Westinghouse technology to generate alternating current, and they were better situated than Chicago Edison to supply the accelerating demand for electric lights in residential housing and to power motors in manufacturing industries. Between 1892 and 1898, Insull used his considerable political skills to gain approval from Chicago politicians to purchase all of the generating franchises within the city.

Reorganization of electricity generation was a five-part process: (1) consolidate the franchises within the city of Chicago into a monopoly corporation; (2) generate and distribute electricity with the most modern, large scale technologies in order to achieve economies of scale; (3) sell electricity as cheaply as possible to industrial, commercial, and residential consumers because the demand was there; (4) incorporate a holding company in order to create a regional system by consolidating the franchises that served small towns in northern Illinois; and (5) incorporate additional holding companies in other regions to assemble franchises on the basis of experience in Chicago and northern Illinois.

By 1898 Chicago Edison had a monopoly for selling electricity within Chicago. As envisioned by Insull and other organizers, central generating facilities would create natural monopolies in the regions they served. Monopoly franchises would prevent destructive competition, capital investments would be optimized, and economies of scale would be initiated. Insull and others used the political process to endorse consolidation. In order to make natural monopolies acceptable to the public, Insull invited state regulation. He correctly believed that establishing state regulatory commissions, as was previously done for railroads, was the best way to dampen political opposition to creating monopoly corporations that sold electricity to households.

There were two very serious technological restraints on economies of scale and geographic expansion. The electricity generated by Chicago Edison was direct current that could not be efficiently transmitted more than two kilometers from a central generating facility; and its central generating facilities used reciprocating engines.

One serious handicap was overcome in 1896 by the invention of the rotary converter. It converted direct current into alternating current and made the generation of direct current and alternating current compatible. Direct current generated by the existing facilities of Chicago Edison could be converted to alternating current and transmitted long distances. It allowed Chicago Edison's direct current generators to continue to operate until they were replaced by generators producing alternating current.

The second handicap was not overcome until 1903 when generators powered by steam turbines became operational. In the meantime, generating costs using reciprocating engines were sufficiently high so that many isolated generating facilities remained in operation. Real economies of scale had to wait until steam turbines replaced reciprocating engines and high voltage transmission using alternating current could distribute electricity to all potential users. Steam turbine generators became operational after 1905 and Chicago Edison aggressively sought new consumers. Put in other terms, "turbines were, in effect, supply in search of demand."[4]

By 1908, 65 percent of the power generated in Chicago was used by streetcars, elevated, and interurban trains. Traction companies no longer generated their own power because it was too expensive. The ability of steam turbines in central generating facilities to produce more electricity than was immediately used in Chicago allowed Chicago Edison to lower prices for all classes of consumers in order to encourage consumption. This was the vision of Samuel Insull—cheap electricity to encourage household consumption and industrial expansion.

The distribution network that Insull organized to serve Chicago was complete in 1910. Immediately afterward (1911–1914), Chicago Edison acquired control of the fragmented street and elevated railroad franchises in Chicago. Soon afterward, he gained control of the electrified interurban railroads that carried passengers into the city from the suburbs. After these acquisitions, Chicago Edison still had surplus generating capacity and it needed new customers. They were available in large numbers in small towns in northern Illinois.

After Chicago Edison acquired the franchises of small towns, their generating facilities were converted into substations that transformed the high voltages arriving from central generating facilities to lower voltages for distribution to consumers. Long distance transmission using high voltages made it possible to sell electricity in small towns at prices that were comparable to prices charged to city residents. Insull fully intended that the generation and distribution systems he organized in Chicago and northern Illinois should be models for other organizers.

Three national developments occurred during the 1920s: (1) accelerated consolidation to build regional systems, (2) mobilization of huge amounts of capital to build central generating facilities needed by regional systems, and (3) vastly increased efficiency of electricity generation.

Consolidation

Holding companies were the means of merging numerous small town franchises into operating corporations that were sufficiently large to build central generating facilities, and especially where consolidation would form a natural monopoly. A simple message gained political approval for consolidation: economy of scale was the only way to generate and distribute cheap electricity.

The need for consolidation was overwhelming. Large cities had a multitude of small franchises that generated direct current. This limited service to a radius of two kilometers from the generator. The demand for electricity was increasing as fast as generating and distribution systems could be built. This created an insatiable demand for investment capital because generating electricity is a capital intensive industry.

Holding companies were an efficient nongovernmental solution because they could (1) consolidate fragmented franchises and merge them into regional systems, (2) mobilize capital, (3) supply technically competent engineers and managers, and (4) connect adjoining systems in order to transfer power to where it was most needed. Holding companies also had staffs of skilled persons who could increase sales, make rates that maximized revenues, and manage debts in order to create stable capital structures.

The need for consolidation became acute during World War I because the demand for power surged. Power generation needed rationalization in order to maximize production from existing facilities and allocate it to where it was most needed. Some utilities had to ration power to household consumers in order to supply industrial needs. Between 1912 and 1919, sales by Chicago Edison doubled. In other systems (during the same years), demand tripled. During the 1920s, the demand for electric power increased 9 percent per year.

The earliest holding companies were organized in the late 1890s to merge small franchises in order to increase the number of customers required to build a central generating facility. They were organized by diverse organizations: (1) the principal manufacturers of electrical equipment (General Electric and Westinghouse) that accepted bonds from utility companies as partial payment; (2) utility companies in larger cities that expanded into the suburbs as Chicago Edison did; (3) consulting businesses that contracted to supply management, engineering, and financial services; (4) investment bankers; and (5) managers of adjacent franchises who merged operations in order to improve their capacity to borrow.

There was no systematic way that holding companies assembled franchises. It was an opportunistic process and sometime involved competitive bidding that was often inflationary. The nucleus of many franchises in medium sized towns was an electrified streetcar franchise that often became an interurban line that connected adjacent towns. They sold electricity to households as a byproduct and when rail service ceased in the evening, no electricity was generated for household consumption. Most of these franchises used obsolescent generators and the electricity they sold to households was expensive, as well as not being continuously available. Few people argued with consolidation if it guaranteed continuous service and lower prices.

Management control was obtained by purchasing a block of common stock. Only common stock had voting rights. Holding companies did not usually purchase a majority because it was unnecessary for control. The principal job of managers installed by holding companies was to increase the number of customers, connect with neighboring utilities, contain costs, and create stable capital structures. A common formula was (1) 60 percent of capitalization was bonded indebtedness that had first call on earnings, (2) 20–25 percent was preferred stock that had second call on earnings, and (3) 20–25 percent was common stock that had third call on earnings.

The number of regional holding companies rapidly increased after the end of World War I because of their ability to raise capital. Holding companies mobilized capital by issuing bonds and preferred stock based on the total earning capacities of the franchises they merged into a single operating company. The highly favorable prospect for increasing profits was the incentive for investment bankers to underwrite and sell bonds and shares of stock in holding companies. Capital mobilized by holding companies was invested in higher capacity generating equipment and distribution systems.

For example, in 1928 Samuel Insull was president of the Middle West Utilities Company. It was a holding company of national scope that controlled twenty-seven regional holding companies that controlled over two hundred franchises of various sizes that produced about 8 percent of the nation's electrical power. He was also president of all of the holding companies controlled by Chicago Edison, or by one of its subsidiaries.

As soon as one holding company acquired a sufficient number of franchises and merged them into a new operating company, Insull installed technically competent managers who could integrate them into a regional distribution system. If a central generating facility did not exist, one was built as soon as a sufficient numbers of franchises were consolidated to justify its construction.

In 1921, 74 utilities (each composed of several or many franchise) were consolidated into regional systems; in 1922, 285 were consolidated; and in 1926, 1,029 were consolidated. Between 1919 and 1929, 4,329 public utilities were consolidated. By 1930, ten holding companies of national scope controlled over 70 percent of the nation's generating capacity; and in 1932, sixteen holding companies with a national scope controlled over 75 percent of the nation's generating capacity.[5] The electrification of urban and suburban residences was virtually complete by 1930.

During the 1920s, electrification of rural households lagged far behind urban and suburban markets. In 1930 rural electrification in the most prosperous agricultural districts of the nation extended only short distances from towns. A high percentage of northern farmers were marginal participants in the consumer culture (except for automobiles and telephones), and the rural South was largely untouched. Utility companies refused to build rural distribution lines because rural lines had too few customers, and declining farm incomes limited the ability of farmers to fund cooperatives to build transmission lines. Furthermore, rural households used only one-half the power of urban and suburban households.

The Great Depression that began late in 1930 created enormous stresses on the financial structures of utility holding companies because industrial consumption of electric power declined for the next three years, although residential usage continued to increase and continued to increase throughout the depression. The frail financial structures of many holding companies collapsed. A large contributing factor was the way in which many holding companies had been assembled. Holding companies with assets in non-contiguous operating companies were most vulnerable because the utilities they controlled were small, often had obsolescent generating equipment, and lacked connections to adjoining utilities.

As the depression deepened and investigations exposed many highly speculative financial practices, there were increasing public doubts about the ability of holding companies to manage inter-regional transmission of electricity. Investigations by the Federal Trade Commission came to two conclusions. First, holding companies were effective instruments for organizing regional systems by merging small franchises into utilities large enough to achieve economies of scale in generation and distribution. Second, holding companies were financially fragile if they acquired widely separated franchises with small customer bases. Fragmented utility franchises could not achieve economies of scale and were candidates for bankruptcy during downturns in business.

Congress acted on this evaluation in 1935 by passing the Public Utility Holding Company Act. It legalized natural monopolies if the monopoly was large enough to achieve economies of scale in electricity generation. If a holding company did not control enough contiguous franchises to consolidate into an operating company with sufficient revenues to build central generating facilities, it had to divest them.

Mobilization of Capital

During the 1920s, there was an insatiable demand for capital to purchase generating equipment and reequip older systems. Unlike the railroad building era in the second half of the nineteenth century, almost all the capital was mobilized in the United States. The three principal ways of mobilizing capital were retained earnings, credit supplied by manufacturers of electrical equipment, and the sale of securities (in holding companies) by investment bankers.

State legislatures helped mobilize the needed capital. After 1918, many state legislatures copied a 1912 New York statute that authorized corporations to sell shares with no par value. Prior to this statute, state laws required shares of stock to have a face value (par value), usually one hundred dollars. Most initial purchasers of shares did not pay the full face value. Shares were purchased with a partial payment of the face value, but purchasers were legally liable to pay the full face value if the corporation needed more capital than the initial payment. If they failed to pay, their shares were forfeited. Shares that had money obligations attached were often difficult to sell.

Issuing shares with no par value allowed underwriters to sell shares for their speculative value (potential for future dividends). The market determined the value of shares. This made shares in new corporations easier to sell and trade. Shares with no par value that were marketed at low initial prices reached new groups of investors and helped democratize ownership of shares.

Frequently, bonds and shares of stock of small franchises had no market value because they were locally owned. A market had to be created for them. To make a market they had to be consolidated with other small franchises and recapitalized. After consolidation, the portfolios of most regional holding companies had a bewildering variety of common stock, preferred stock, and bonds, and it was difficult to evaluate their earning capacities. In other words, the financial structures of many regional holding companies were a financial tangle. The capital structures of regional holding companies had to be simplified, and this was done by exchanging old bonds and shares of stock for new ones.

Regional holding companies were a means of recapitalization. Portfolios of bonds owned by equipment manufacturers, local banks, and individuals were exchanged for the bonds and shares of stock of regional holding companies. Based on a larger customer base, investment bankers underwrote additional bonds and shares of stock to finance the construction of central generating facilities, as well as the acquisition of controlling interests in additional small franchises. New bonds issued by regional holding companies usually had lower interest rates compared to the original bonds because they had a market value. Their market values were based on a visible earning potential because of the larger geographic areas they served.

Most of the value of common stock of new operating utilities created by consolidation was speculative. It was speculative in the sense that the use of electricity was expected to increase at a high rate for the foreseeable future. In time, common stock would acquire substance because regional holding companies could (1) mobilize capital to build new central generating facilities to service its market, (2) better allocate existing generating capacity, and (3) earn much larger profits than the combined profits of many small, unconsolidated franchises. The much larger profits earned by operating companies created by consolidation could easily pay interest on bonds and preferred stock; and the residual profits would pay high dividends on common stock.

The opportunity for large speculative profits in a rapidly growing industry was an opportunity for holding companies with a national scope to aggregate regional holding companies. Holding companies of a national scope would become holding companies of regional holding companies. After they gained control of regional holding companies, national holding companies performed three principal functions: (1) bringing order to the finances of regional holding companies by simplifying their capital structures, (2) increasing access to additional capital, and (3) providing a wide variety of technical and management services. These highly useful services were provided by long-term contracts (often lucrative), or by receiving shares of common stock, or by a combination of these payments.

Seen from a different perspective, holding companies with a national scope were at the top of complex financial pyramids that resulted from opportunistic control of regional holding companies. Like regional holding companies, national holding companies acquired control of regional holding companies by accepting shares of common stock for services rendered, especially financial services. If the prospects were good for a rapid increase in revenues, national holding companies often purchased large blocks of stock, often at concessionary prices. Frequently these shares paid dividends of 20 percent or more on the purchase price.[6]

Efficiency

Managers of operating companies created by consolidation required access to the most productive generators in a technology that was rapidly changing. During the 1920s, the efficiency of converting coal to electricity by steam turbines in central generating facilities increased an average of 80 percent. For example, in 1900 electricity generated by reciprocating steam engines required an average of 3.1 kilos of coal to generate one kilowatt hour of electricity. In 1920 steam turbines required 1.37 kilos, and in 1930 it was less than 800 grams.

The highest efficiencies were achieved in the newest generating facilities that had the largest boilers, largest turbines, and highest pressures obtained by superheating steam. Additional power was extracted from turbines that was wasted ten years previously. Exhaust steam from high pressure turbines was fed into low pressure turbines that extracted the last energy before steam was condensed and reused.[7]

The use of high voltages to transmit electricity long distances was solved in the European Alps and in California where hydroelectric dams were built in mountainous terrain. Long-distance transmission meant 150 kilometers or more from dam sites to cities. Dams at high elevations in Switzerland and California diverted river water into tubes that carried it to where there was a precipitous drop to turbines. These turbines generated large amounts of power from limited flows because the water entered the turbines under very high pressure. Between 1912 and 1920, hydroelectric power supplied a high percentage of California's electricity needs. In effect, these dams were very large central generating facilities.

In densely populated eastern states, the same technology was used during the 1920s to transmit electric power from large thermal generating facilities that were built after many small franchises were consolidated into regional systems. Thermal generating facilities required cooling water, and they were usually built on a major river or on the shore of one of the Great Lakes. Transmission distance to major cities from these facilities was usually less than one hundred kilometers, but longer transmission distances were necessary when the transmission lines of regional utilities were connected into interregional grids that were essential for optimizing the distribution of power.

Consumer Products

The two most visible products of American consumer culture are automobiles and advertising. In cultures of scarcity, advertising provides information on the availability of manufactured products. Scarcity of products assures an instant market when a product becomes available. Advertising is minimal. In consumer cultures, scarcity of products is replaced by an abundance of products manufactured by mass production technologies. After this happens manufacturers must make their product continuously visible to consumers and, at the same time, differentiate it from competing products of similar value and utility. Manufacturers must create brand names and advertise them in several medias in order to sustain mass appeal. "That is why it is valid to regard advertising as distinctively the institution of abundance."[8]

The three categories of consumer products are durable, invisible, and expendable. Automobiles are the most visible durable consumer product. Most other durable consumer products are used in homes. Like a high percentage of automobiles in the 1920s, they were purchased using consumer credit (installment buying). Electricity and consumer credit are the principal invisible consumer products. Neither electricity nor consumer credit are usually considered consumer products but both rank with automobiles as a measure of a consumer culture. Food, soap, clothing, and nonprescriptive medicines are the principal expendable consumer products.

Indoor electric lighting in urban housing was a huge stimulus to use electricity to power machines that could reduce household labor. In 1925 over 90 percent of residences in Chicago were electrified and other major cities reached this percentage by 1930. Among the first electricity powered durable products purchased by households were irons, vacuum cleaners, and toasters. At a later date washing machines and refrigerators were purchased. By 1928 the President's committee on economic change estimated that 15.3 million irons, 6.8 million vacuum cleaners, 5 million washing machines, and 4.5 million toasters were owned by American households.[9]

The availability of electricity also made it possible to acquire less visible durable consumer products. Telephones were the first. In 1900, 1.3 million telephones were in operation, most of them in cities. In 1930, 20.2 million were in use, and in regions of commercial agriculture a high percentage of farms had them. Entertainment also entered homes with radios and phonographs.

Agriculture

The agricultural sector was increasingly prosperous after 1900 because prices steadily increased; and during World War I (1914–1918), prices of agricultural commodities doubled. During these years, a high percentage of farmers contracted debts to purchase more land, more implements, and make other improvements. Inflated commodity prices ended abruptly in 1920. The steep drop in prices was due to the return of normal harvests in Europe and increased cotton cultivation in tropical colonies of European nations. During the rest of the 1920s, the price of agricultural commodities slowly declined.

At the same time, the efficiency of cultivation in the commercial sector improved because gasoline powered tractors began replacing horses. Tractor ownership increased from 246,000 in 1920 to 920,000 in 1930, an increase of 370 percent. Ownership of farm trucks similarly increased in numbers and percentage. After horses were replaced, pastures were converted to cultivation. During the 1920s, harvests of food and feed grains increased 9 percent and the efficiency of agricultural labor increased 15 percent, mostly due to the reduced time it took to plow, plant, and harvest by using tractors and implements powered by tractors. At the same time, thirteen million acres of marginal land were withdrawn from cultivation.[10]

During the 1920s, over one million rural residents migrated to cities and became permanent residents. They found commercial and industrial employment because European immigration had been reduced to a trickle by legislation in 1921 and 1924. Most migrants to the cities came from northern farms, and they found employment because they were literate. Few permanent residents came from the subsistence sector of southern agriculture. When they did, a high percentage came as sojourners who labored long enough to acquire target sums of money before returning home to practice subsistence agriculture. One of their principal jobs was maintaining railroad tracks, the same jobs performed by many European peasant immigrants immediately after their arrival.

Larger harvests by grain farmers did not translate into increased incomes because global prices of all agricultural commodities declined. Incomes of grain farmers and cotton planters could not avoid price declines because a high percentage of these commodities were exported and international prices dictated domestic prices. Congressmen from agricultural states continually tried to get the U.S. government to intervene in agriculture in order to subsidize commodity prices.

Their favorite program was subsidizing exports. The national government would purchase agricultural commodities at artificially high prices in order to raise prices for commodities consumed in the United States. The surplus acquired by the national government would be exported and sold below world market prices (concessionary prices). Farmers succeeded in lobbying Congress to pass such legislation in 1927 (the McNary-Haugen Bill) but President Calvin Coolidge vetoed it for the right reason. Increasing commodity prices would have encouraged production and magnified the problems of the agricultural sector rather than helping to solve them.

The Agricultural Marketing Act of June 1929 established the Federal Farm Board. Its intended purpose was to increase farm incomes by encouraging farmers to organize cooperative marketing organizations. After the stock market crash in October 1929, the Farm Board was forced to loan money to cotton and wheat cooperatives in order to underwrite commodity loans that had been made by local banks; otherwise, these banks faced bankruptcy. The Federal Farm Board did not prevent continuing declines in commodity prices, and the loans it had underwritten were not paid. It became the owners of the commodities. In 1931 it owned one-third of the national wheat supply, for which there was no market. It was bankrupt and board members could see only one solution to excessive commodity production—the national government must use compulsion to limit production, as the only means of increasing prices.

Employment

Employment is a wholly commercial term. It signifies that social security is obtained by full-time paid labor to earn money incomes from wages, salaries, or entrepreneurial profits. Employment is about persons who continuously labor in the commercial sector. Employed people are permanent town and city residents or, alternatively, they are farmers who continuously labor to produce agricultural commodities for market sale (grain, livestock, dairy products, and vegetables or fruit for urban consumption). The social security of permanent city residents and farmers depends on earning money incomes. If they earn large incomes, they are rich. If they earn small incomes, they are poor.

White and black peasants in the cotton South were not employed because their social security was not dependent on earning money incomes. Their social security depended on control of land use as sharecroppers, leaseholders, or landowners. Control of land use meant they could control their labor expenditures. In practice this meant reducing agricultural labor expenditures to subsistence amounts. They grew only enough food for household consumption and planted three or four additional hectares of a market crop (cotton or tobacco) to acquire target sums of money sufficient to purchase a few manufactured items such as clothing, metal tools, and food items like coffee and sugar (or molasses). After these needs were satisfied, they ceased to labor.

Southern peasants were not poor, they were subsistent. They were largely outside the commercial sector and entirely outside the consumer culture. Because they were nonparticipants in the consumer culture, and because they were largely disfranchised by the electoral laws of southern states, this discussion of employment ignores them.[11]

Sustaining consumer cultures requires full-time wage labor employment because this is essential for the mass production of consumer products. The reciprocal of mass production is mass consumption. Full employment means full-time paid labor employment in cities. Without employment, cities become sinks of destitution. In consumer cultures, one of the principal functions of governance is to sustain full-time paid labor employment in cities.

In the largest industrial cities, a high percentage of residents in the 1920s were European immigrants, or the children of European immigrants who arrived in the United States during the 1880s and 1890s. The children of immigrants attended city schools and were literate. They had employment opportunities that were not available to their parents. They competed on even terms with the literate sons of northern farmers who migrated to cities because they lived where employment opportunities were concentrated. If they had education beyond primary schools, they were better prepared to take advantage of urban employment opportunities than the sons of northern farmers. The American melting pot in the 1920s was equalized opportunities for urban employment.

The prosperity of the 1920s was real. On average, households purchased 23 percent more consumer durable products in 1929 than in 1923, and 26 percent more human services. On average, the standard of living of city residents increased faster than the welfare of farmers. Urban prosperity was sustained by abundant credit and low interest rates by the Federal Reserve Board that was supplemented by low taxation of personal wealth. Production of durable consumer products steadily increased, especially residential housing and commercial office buildings.

Business leaders claimed, with a large amount of accuracy, that they created the urban/industrial prosperity of the 1920s. The elections of 1920, 1924, and 1928 endorsed their claim that they were responsible for creating full employment, cheap government, and the consumer culture. The nomination of Herbert C. Hoover for the presidency in 1928 reflected this claim. He had been secretary of commerce since 1921, serving in the administrations of Warren G. Harding and Calvin Coolidge. The *Wall Street Journal* accurately summarized the alliance of urban businessmen and the national government. "Never before, here or anywhere else, has a government been so completely fused with business."[12]

The economy in the 1920s had many weaknesses that have been intensively investigated by economists. The most serious weakness was the instability of the nation's banking system. It should have been recognized in the 1920s, but it was not. Bank bankruptcies were continuing events. The fewest number occurred in 1922 when 367 banks failed. The highest number occurred in 1926 when 976 banks closed their doors. In 1929, 659 banks failed.

A high percentage of these failures had known causes. There were too many banks in small towns with inadequate capital, permissive lending policies, and limited clienteles of credit worthy residents. In 1874 there were 2,331 banks in the United States, in 1885 there were 3,704 banks, in 1900 there were 8,738, and in 1914 there were 25,016. By 1914, 70 percent of all banks were state chartered because there were fewer restraints on credit practices. The principal problems of small town banks were (1) inadequate state supervision, (2) a high concentration of loan portfolios in agricultural land, (3) declining commodity prices, (4) magnified by inadequate management skills, and (5) state laws that prohibited branch banking.

Consolidating small town banks by mergers or by holding companies (similar to electric utility holding companies), could have strengthened rural banking by supplying better trained managers who would be more selective in extending credit to applicants.

The most serious weakness of the banking system, however, was a gradual loss of liquidity, especially state chartered banks. Liquidity loss was measured by a gradual decline in the percentage of commercial loans and a gradual increase in the number of loans collateralize by investment securities (bonds, shares of stock). Loans on investment securities increased 121 percent and real estate loans increased 178 percent. Many investment securities used as collateral were of questionable value. This trend was aggravated by the failure of the Federal Reserve Board to restrain brokers from funneling money into stock market and real estate speculation.

When the correction of stock market speculation occurred in October-November 1929, "the banking system no longer underwent a short, but paralyzing, period of deflation. Instead, it went through a prolonged liquidation attended by groups of disastrous failures." Investment securities owned by banks had to be sold, often for unrealistically low prices. There was no vigorous intervention by the Federal Reserve Board or other government agencies to stop bankruptcy of sound banks that temporarily lost liquidity.[13]

President Hoover and his closest advisors expected the speculative bubble to burst. When stock and real estate prices plummeted, they believed that the proper policy was to use credit allocation by the Federal Reserve Board to cushion its impact but, otherwise, let the slump run its course. They assumed that the stock market crash and subsequent decline in commodity prices would be self-correcting, as had happened in the depression of 1920–1921.

Immediately after the crash, Hoover worked hard to cushion its deflationary impact. His political style was to deal with the people he knew best. He held a series of White House conferences in late November 1929 with the presidents of major railroads, leading representatives of the construction industry, presidents of leading manufacturing corporations, presidents of the largest electric utilities, leaders of farm organizations, and labor leaders. Hoover believed that depressed business conditions would last until inflated values were liquidated. He estimated it would take a year. After these conferences ended, his message was assurance of future prosperity.

He recommended that business leaders temporarily shorten the work week, accelerate construction of planned capital investment projects, and avoid wage cuts or strikes. The national government undertook its share of policy initiatives to help restore business confidence. Congress reduced corporate income taxes by one percent, appropriated funds for public works to be managed by state and city governments, attempted to stabilize the prices of agricultural commodities with funds provided to the Federal Farm Board, and the Federal Reserve Board reduced the rediscount rate from 4.5 to 3.5 percent.

Nonetheless, in April 1930 there were 3 million unemployed and by the end of the year there were at least 4.3 million unemployed. This was 8.7 percent of the work force. In terms of unemployment rates, the 8.7 percent in 1929–1930 was similar to the 11.9 percent in the depression of 1920–1921. The social impact of unemployment in 1930 was considerable but not disastrous; many families had second or third members who were employed and did not depend on one breadwinner. The Republican Party suffered losses in the congressional election of November 1930, but there was no repudiation of Hoover's policies.

Was the 1929–1930 situation different from the 1920–1921 situation? "No one, not even the president, could see clearly what the true situation was or what would be the consequences of alternative courses of action. Though Hoover knew the weaknesses of the European economies better than most, even he could not gauge their vulnerability." Furthermore, Hoover and his advisors "underrated the weakness of the banking system."[14]

Hoover should have recognized the weaknesses of the banking system because (1) bank bankruptcies totaled over five thousand during the 1920s; (2) concentration of bank bankruptcies in the agricultural sector; and (3) extreme fragmentation of banking. In his tenure as secretary of commerce, he approved of consolidating manufacturing corporations into large corporations in order to achieve oligopolistic competition. Minimal consolidation occurred in the banking business when it was clearly recognized that larger banks with diverse loan portfolios could better maintain liquidity.

After January 1931 it was clear that the 1929–1930 depression was not the same as the 1920–1921 depression; nor was it self-correcting. From January 1931 to the inauguration of Franklin D. Roosevelt as president in March 1933, employment in industry and commerce continually declined until 24.9 percent of the labor force was unemployed. The years 1931, 1932, and 1933 were disastrous.

Why was there a plunge in industrial production after 1930? What were the weaknesses that created this disaster and why was the economy not self-correcting? There is no agreement among economists and historians on ranking the weaknesses that caused the disaster. Economists and historians agree on only three interpretations: there were multiple causes for the Great Depression; all of the policies of the New Deal failed to end the Great Depression; it ended when the United States began rearming in 1941 because it was increasingly possible, if not probable, that the United States would become involved in the European war. The rest of this chapter is my interpretation of why the Great Depression persisted from 1931 to 1941.

Great Depression

Some economists have concluded that weaknesses in the domestic and international economies in the 1920s were insufficient to cause business paralysis after 1930. I believe that this is an accurate assessment. The depression of 1929–1930 deepened into the Great Depression because the national government did not sufficiently implement interventionalist policies to sustain the consumer culture. When it did intervene, its policies were hesitant and insufficient. They were one step behind events.

For most owners of shares of stock, the spectacular decline in the value of stocks in October-November 1929 produced paper losses. Most persons who owned stock could afford these losses. They may have felt poor, but they were not poor as long as they were employed. Their response was predictable. Most households restrained spending, and this restraint persisted as long as unemployment continued to increase. Restrained spending continued during 1930 because President Hoover's recovery policies seemed without effect. The reduced consumer spending that persisted into 1931 initiated destructive competition that accelerated the number of unemployed and bankruptcies.

In Peter Temin's judgment, "The large decline in consumption expenditures for both durable and non-durable goods in 1930 had a profoundly depressing effect for the economy." According to his analysis, the combination of a rapid decline in consumption spending and a decline in the value of exports in 1930 precluded self-correction. In the immediate years after World War I, United States bankers made very large loans to European nations to revive peacetime industry and trade. The loaned funds returned to the United States to purchase capital equipment. In the late 1920s, similar loans were not made because they were unneeded and high tariffs substantially reduced imports and the ability of our trading partners to acquire dollars with which to purchase products produced in the United States. When self-correction did not begin in the second half of 1930, only the national government could inject purchasing power into the economy to sustain consumer and business confidence. It was not forthcoming.[15]

In my judgment, the depression years of 1929 and 1930 that deepened into the Great Depression happened because the economic policies of the Hoover administration were based on the highly successful policies that had achieved rapid industrialization. This phase of economic development, however, was completed by 1900. In the 1920s the United States was the paramount industrial nation in the world. It was, however, unprepared for global leadership in politics and commerce. This was leadership the United States could have had for the taking after the end of World War I. Instead, president Warren G. Harding called for a return to normalcy. Normalcy was the obsolete policies of political economy that had propelled rapid industrialization.[16]

United States involvement in World War I demonstrated that distance no longer insulated the United States from economic and political events in Europe. Hoover had a better understanding of this than Harding or Coolidge who preceded him, but he could not break the mold of his experience as secretary of commerce. During eight years as secretary (1921–1929), he used his prestige and administrative skills to actively promote national prosperity that helped create a consumer culture that was the envy of the rest of the world. This achievement was guided by a simple formula of political economy: enact into law the policies that business leaders believed were best for business because these policies had been hugely successful in the immediate past.

What were these policies? The principal ones were (1) low taxation of business incomes; (2) abundant bank credit on the assumption that businessmen were more productive investors than governments; (3) regulation of industrial practices on terms acceptable to the industries being regulated; (4) minimal tax funded social services and welfare programs because they were state and municipal problems; (5) a small, cheap national government; and (6) protective tariff.

In 1920 these policies were obsolete for four reasons.

1. A majority of the population was urban. Unemployed city residents could not return to family farms because there were no family farms. Sustaining an urban consumer culture required urban employment.
2. Prolonged unemployment for urban households often meant destitution because savings and private charities were insufficient to mitigate unemployment during depressions.
3. The U.S. economy was a major participant in the global economy. Imports from Europe had been a major factor in the postwar revival of global commerce, even though foreign trade was a relatively small percentage of total U.S. commerce.
4. Imports of consumer products at competitive prices helped sustain a consumer culture, as well as providing foreign exchange so that our trading partners could purchase products produced in the United States.

In 1929 the United States produced 40 percent of the manufactured products produced by industrial nations. Most of the U.S. production was consumed in the United States. Reduced purchases of the manufactured products from other industrialized nations impacted their economies far more seriously than the U.S. economy. The more the U.S. participated in the global economy, the greater the energizing effects on the economies of our trading partners—like ripples on water expanding from the center.

When Hoover became president in January 1929, he was committed to retaining the old policies of political economy that he had successfully administered during the 1920s. He was an engineer by training who preferred to formulate policies with advice from business leaders and technocrats like himself. It was difficult for him to believe that U.S. business leaders did not know what national policies were best for their interest and best for the national interest. It was equally difficult for him to believe that the old political economy of economic development was obsolete. This made it difficult for him to adopt new policies in our relations with industrial nations because he did not fully perceive that these policies had to be global in scope.

The best examples of Hoover's commitment to the old formula of political economy was his support for the high rates of the Fordney-McCumber Tariff of 1922 and the higher rates in the Smoot-Hawley Tariff that he signed into law in June 1930. These tariffs took no cognizance that the United States had become the great creditor nation. In order to purchase U.S. commodities and manufactured products, foreign nations had to sell products in the United States. Increased international trade was required so that foreign nations could repay the credit extended to them by the U.S. government, as well as the credit extended by American businesses that helped revive global commerce after World War I.

Neither the Fordney-McCumber and Smoot-Hawley tariffs took cognizance that the governments of many European nations were unstable in the aftermath of World War I, and that increased trade would enhance their political stability by helping create employment. Especially, the Smoot-Hawley Tariff was a great self-inflicted wound. Between 1929 and the end of 1932 the value of world trade declined 60 percent and that of the United States declined 75 percent. Hoover's experience in international affairs should have recognized that high tariffs were counter-productive to consumer cultures.

Three additional events indicate Hoover's commitment to obsolete policies of political economy.

First, in July 1932 Hoover vetoed the Garner-Wagner Bill that would have provided destitute households with relief money directly from the national government. It would also have funded an extensive public works program under the direct supervision of the national government. Hoover opposed empowering the national government to provide direct relief to long-term unemployed. Instead, state and local governments would create employment by originating and managing self-help projects with funds supplied by the national government. He believed that local control was necessary to preserve local responsibility for community welfare.

Immediately after the veto, Congress passed an unemployment relief program that Hoover approved. It authorized loans to state and municipal governments to begin construction of public works projects on the basis of long-term self-liquidation. Most state and local governments were less prepared than the national government to immediately begin self-help projects; immediacy was crucial to relieve destitution.

Second, in July 1932 Hoover also vetoed a bill that would have established nationally funded employment agencies in states that did not have them. The reason he gave was that unemployment was a state problem. It is difficult to understand his reasoning when there were at least twelve million unemployed and American business activity had declined about 50 percent since April 1930. Unemployment was the overwhelming concern of the nation. The long-term unemployed looked to the national government for help because they knew that state and local agencies were totally inadequate to reduce unemployment.

Third, the Reconstruction Finance Corporation (RFC) was established in February 1932. Hoover approved the RFC because its purpose was to make loans to banks, railroads, life insurance companies, building and loan societies, and farm loan associations in order to prevent their bankruptcy. These loans were highly desirable. Nobody can fault Hoover for sponsoring the use of the superior financial power of the national government to prevent the collapse of the commercial infrastructure.

Building new infrastructure projects by state and municipal governments was also highly desirable, but the RFC frustrated the intent of the law by using excessive caution in approving projects, and, when projects were approved, the expenditures of RFC funds did not compensate for reductions in state funding of public works projects because of declining state revenues. The RFC did nothing to inject new funds into the economy. Its managers conceived its purpose as defensive—to prevent further deterioration of the economy.

That, however, was not the political significance of the RFC. The political significance was that Hoover rejected direct linkage of the national government to individuals whose labor made the national market a reality. He believed that individuals should be linked to the national government through business corporations that organized and managed the national market or through state and local governments because state and local governments were better able to provide for individual welfare. Both of these linkages precluded a quick response to economic crisis.

After the Great Depression began late in 1930, new policies of political economy were required to sustain the consumer culture. *What were the new policies?* The short answer is massive fiscal intervention by the national government in the peacetime economy. There were, however, few guidelines of how it should be done; and before it could be fully implemented three changes in political thinking were required.

First, the electorate had to accept the doctrine that governments often make more intelligent spending decisions than businessmen. In other words, a fundamental weakness of the business-dominated culture of the 1920s was a mind-set that government should be the junior partner of business. During years of normal business activity, the national government should be an equal partner with business in managing the economy, and in times of crisis it must be the senior partner. During downturns in business, central governments must intervene in the economy to sustain consumer cultures, and the intervention must be large and quickly executed to prevent a downward spiral of business and consumer confidence. It is a matter of political and economic expediency how the national government injects money into the economy to sustain employment and consumer purchasing power.

Where to intervene is a major problem. How to intervene is another problem, and priorities of intervention are an additional problem. There were few peacetime guidelines in 1930, although the command economy instituted during World War I was an example of what could be quickly done because it effectively mobilized U.S. manpower and material resources during the nineteen months the United States was at war. In order to make intervention politically acceptable, presidential leadership must be articulate and highly visible. This was not Herbert Hoover's style of leadership.

Second, small, frugal governments are poorly equipped to deal with financial crises in urban, industrial, and consumer cultures. Big governments are required because of the complexity and scope of problems to sustain employment in urban industries. Sustaining employment in times of crisis requires energetic governance and complex management of finances. The key policy is deficit spending that quickly injects purchasing power into the economy.

In 1930 cheap credit was available but little used. A quick injection of purchasing power would have been the trigger mechanism to sustain incomes of urban residents; however, neither president Hoover nor Congress could jettison the mind-set that a balanced budget was essential for restoring business confidence. Hoover summarized this mind-set: "We cannot squander ourselves into prosperity."[17]

Third, there must be an income floor to sustain the social security of urban households to prevent destitution. A floor can be created by initiating numerous infrastructure construction projects, minimum wages, unemployment benefits for various lengths of time, various varieties of relief payments, or by providing minimum pensions for retired urban residents.

"Before 1930 most Americans viewed the private enterprise economy as essentially self-regulating." They believed that the best policy of the national government "was to encourage private enterprise which was to be constrained by government's regulatory powers only when excessive market power threatened the public well-being. The Great Depression of the 1930s changed public perceptions of the economic role of government."[18]

Why did the depression persist long after it reached bottom in 1933? This is the story of the presidency of Franklin D. Roosevelt and the New Deal.

New Deal

"The legacy of the Great Depression is the New Deal—the first, decisive intervention of the federal government into the operation of the national economy." The peacetime interventions of the New Deal established the principle that active interventionalist policies of the national government are necessary to sustain consumer cultures.[19]

The campaign rhetoric of Franklin D. Roosevelt in 1932 was ambiguous and contradictory, but economic conditions assured his election. On one hand he said, "The country demands bold, persistent experimentation." He also said, "I regard reduction in Federal spending as one of the most important issues of this campaign. In my opinion, it is the most direct and effective contribution that government can make to business." There was little certainty how Roosevelt would use the power of the presidency and national government to reduce unemployment and restore a measure of prosperity, but the paralysis of government between Roosevelt's election in November 1932 and his inauguration on March 4, 1933 generated a popular expectation that there would be energetic leadership.[20]

The electorate was not disappointed. During the first one hundred days of his administration, large numbers of newly elected congressmen were eager to enact his recommendations into law. Almost all of this legislation was conceived as emergency measures.

Unlike Herbert Hoover, President Franklin Roosevelt understood that the political economy of economic development no longer worked in a consumer culture. Sustaining a consumer culture required new policies of political economy and new legislation to institutionalize them. Roosevelt knew that the national government had to vastly expand its power of governance in order to ameliorate destitution and restore industrial productivity. He understood that there had to be fundamental changes in the power of governance and he endorsed the necessary legislation; however, he was seldom sure of how many of these policies would restore prosperity.

In the months following passage of the emergency legislation that stabilized the banking system and agricultural prices, he was acutely aware that he had no overall plan on how to proceed further. He approved many commercial and social experiments. A high percentage of them were failures. Nonetheless, in matters of fundamental institutional change he followed the advice of his most knowledgeable advisors.

Three statutes institutionalized the political economy of the consumer culture: (1) the Banking Act of 1935 centralized control of credit so that the national government had enough power to manage the money supply, (2) the Social Security Act of 1935 provided incomes for the long-term unemployed and pensions for persons who retired from businesses that participated in the national market, and (3) the Wagner Act of 1935 gave sufficient bargaining power to unionized industrial workers to participate on equalized terms with management and government in formulating policies that equalized incomes. This was a first step in a better distribution of manufactured products that were the most visible aspect of the consumer culture.

Banks

Between the election of Franklin D. Roosevelt in November 1932 and his inauguration in March 1933, the economy was in paralysis. During these four months, business activity declined to about 50 percent of what it was in April 1930. The great menace to recovery was the increasing instability of the banking system. Its instability was measured by the number of bankruptcies. In 1929 there were 23,972 banks in the United States. As the depression deepened, the number of bankruptcies increased. There were 1,345 bank bankruptcies in 1930, 2,298 in 1931, and 1,456 in 1932.

When Franklin Roosevelt was inaugurated, more than 20 percent of the nation's banks had become bankrupt since the stock market crash. A high percentage of bankruptcies were state chartered banks. Most were in small towns, but in 1931 increasing numbers of city banks closed their doors. Loans from the Reconstruction Finance Corporation prevented the bankruptcy of many of the largest city banks. In mid-January 1933 increasing numbers of depositors began withdrawing their money from banks. In February withdrawals became a panic. Depositors wanted gold coins, not paper money.

The governors of Nevada and Louisiana were the first to act. They ordered the closing of all banks in their states. This brought a high percentage of business to a stand-still. On February 14, 1933, the governor of Michigan did the same. After the action by the Michigan governor, other governors followed. The collapse of the banking system was complete when the governor of New York issued a proclamation closing all of the banks in the financial center of United States. By the time of Franklin D. Roosevelt's inauguration on March 4, 1933, twenty-two state governors had closed banks (bank holidays) in their states for varying lengths of time.

One of the first acts of President Roosevelt was to close all of the nation's banks for four days during which preliminary audits were conducted. This executive order was issued on March 6. At the same time, a special session of Congress assembled. On the first day of the session (March 9, 1933), Congress passed the Emergency Banking Act.

The Act granted the president broad powers to regulate currency, credit, and foreign exchange. An executive order prohibited the export of gold unless licensed by the secretary of the treasury. In April 1933 the president issued another executive order requiring all citizens to exchange gold coins and paper currency backed by gold for greenbacks (printing press money), or silver dollar coins, or silver certificates (currency backed by silver). The United States was off of the gold standard and Congress approved by a joint resolution in June. In the future, the United States would have a currency free from the constraints that the gold standard imposed on credit creation. The currency would be managed and it could be quickly inflated.

The emergency banking act also delegated sweeping powers to the comptroller of the currency to reorganize all national banks that were capable of doing business if an injection of capital could restore liquidity. The liquid capital was provided by loans from the Reconstruction Finance Corporation. Between March 11 and 15, nearly 70 percent of pre-holiday banks reopened. If banks were judged incapable of doing business, they were closed. When all audits were completed, approximately, four thousand banks did not reopen for business. The bank holiday and the work of bank auditors had the desired effect.

Money that had been withdrawn in a panic was redeposited in reopened banks; nonetheless, it continued to be hoarded, even after deposits were protected by the Federal Deposit Insurance Corporation. People hoarded money in bank accounts (excessive savings) because of fear of unemployment, which continued until 1941. Fear of unemployment ended in 1941 because the national government injected huge amounts of money into the economy to begin rearming prior to our entry into WW II.

The best evidence for hoarding money was the greatly reduced velocity of money. The annual turnover of deposits in commercial banks in 1929 was about 30 percent; in 1934 it was 16 percent, and in 1940 it was about 13 percent. Money on deposit was available for spending but it was not spent. Demand deposits in 1940 were 50 percent greater than in 1929. Money on deposit was available to support credit for businessmen and for investment in new businesses, but it was not used.[21]

Following the Emergency Banking Act (June 1933) Congress made six significant structural changes in the banking system.

1. Commercial banking was separated from investment banking. All commercial banks were prohibited from underwriting new corporate stocks and bonds because too many issues during the 1920s had been highly speculative. Bank managers often persuaded depositors to invest in them and depositors lost their savings.
2. There was one exception. Commercial banks could underwrite state and municipal bonds because their investment grade was a matter of public record.
3. Higher capitalization was required for national banks because it helped retain liquidity, and managers were prohibited from receiving loans from the banks they managed.
4. National banks were authorized to engage in branch banking if state laws permitted.
5. Loans that were collateralized with investment securities were limited.
6. The Federal Deposit Insurance Corporation (FDIC) was established to insure deposits in all national banks and those state banks that submitted to national regulation. Bankrupt banks could not use insured deposits to pay the bank's debts. This legislation was designed to end panic withdrawals of deposits—and it did. Congress made the FDIC a wholly owned government corporation in 1935.

In 1935 Congress restructured the Federal Reserve Board in order to make it a central bank. It was delegated authority to set reserve requirements for all member banks and rediscount rates; however, all state banks were not required to be members of the system and, thereby be regulated by the national government. Most of these banks were in small towns serving farmer clienteles.

Agriculture

Following the passage of the Emergency Banking Act in 1933, bills were introduced that were designed to restore the purchasing power of the agricultural sector, provide emergency relief funds for the destitute, reduce competition among industrial corporations, and inflate the currency in order to raise domestic prices. Congress made agriculture its first priority in order to dampen threats of rural violence.

Congress passed the Agricultural Adjustment Act (AAA) in May. It was conceived as emergency legislation for the principal purpose of increasing the prices of commodities in order to increase farm incomes. Its authors, however, assumed that after the immediate crisis some form of AAA would continue to operate. Congress stipulated that the restrictions on planting and marketing would terminate when the agricultural emergency was over; and that the president would make this decision. "No president ever has so found and proclaimed, and this massive federal intervention in agriculture has remained in place come rain or shine ever since 1933." The AAA gave planters and farmers what they wanted: increased incomes based on subsidized prices.[22]

The principal means of raising prices was to reduce the number of hectares under cultivation and the number of livestock raised for slaughter. The provisions of the AAA applied to commodities that could be stored without wastage (grain, cotton, tobacco), plus pork and milk. At later dates peanuts, sugar beets, sugar cane, potatoes, and flax were added. The goal was to balance production and consumption in order to obtain prices equal to average prices that prevailed from 1909 to 1914 (parity prices). Landowning planters and farmers who contracted to reduce cultivation were paid for nonproduction with revenue generated by taxing food processors. The principal food processors were cotton gins, flour mills, tobacco warehouses, and slaughterhouses. Higher food prices were passed on to consumers.

When the secretary of agriculture ordered a huge reduction in cotton cultivation and hog production in 1933, landowning planters and farmers were happy to comply. The incentive for plowing under planted cotton fields was an immediate cash payment for the estimated value of the cotton that would not be harvested. No planter would receive these payments unless they contracted to reduce cotton plantings in 1934 and 1935. Four million hectares (ten million acres) of planted cotton and 4,800 hectares of tobacco were plowed under.

Northern farmers reduced livestock numbers by slaughtering 6 million piglets and 220,000 breeding sows. The piglets and hogs were purchased by the government at premium prices. In return for premium prices, hog farmers had to contract to reduce maize planting by 20–30 percent in 1934 and 1935. The calculated reduction in the 1933 harvest did not occur because the reduced hectarage was more carefully weeded, and fertilizer that would have been applied extensively was applied intensively. In following years, committees of local landowners assigned the number of hectares that participating planters and farmers could cultivate.[23]

County committees were usually staffed by the largest, most efficient farmers and planters. They allotted the number of hectares each household could cultivate and the area of land that received a cash subsidy for noncultivation. Agricultural organizations that represented smaller farmers criticized this procedure because subsidies were based on the area of land not cultivated, not on the income needed by households of small farmers. In the long run, this policy would force small farmers to sell their land and migrate to cities. The secretary of agriculture and the director of the AAA strongly supported the allotment powers of country committees because long-term reduction of agricultural production was one of the goals of the AAA. The best way to achieve it was by reducing the number of small farmers.

In October 1933 an executive order established the Commodity Credit Corporation (CCC) to guarantee bank loans on commodities, especially cotton. Loans on the 1933 cotton harvest were ten cents per pound, which was substantially above the market price. Loans were made only to planters who contracted to reduce cotton planting by 40 percent in 1934 and 1935. Without these loans the projected price of the 1933 cotton harvest was five or six cents a pound, the same as the disastrously low price of the 1932 harvest. During the first three years of operation, production was not brought into balance with domestic consumption and exports. The CCC became owner of huge commodity surpluses (especially cotton), because farmers and planters defaulted on their loans.

The AAA was quickly followed by a statute establishing the Farm Credit Administration in June 1933. It supplied credit to refinance farm mortgages at lower interest rates for an increased number of years to reduce the amount of monthly payments. Lower payments over more years would reduce the number of foreclosures. Within eighteen months, 20 percent of all farms that had mortgages refinanced them with the Farm Credit Administration. The Home Owners Refinancing Act did the same for city homeowners who had mortgages vulnerable to foreclosure. By 1935, about 20 percent of all urban homes that had mortgages were refinanced.

In January 1936 the Supreme Court declared the AAA unconstitutional. Congressional and presidential response to the invalidation of the AAA was strongly negative. In the next two years, most of the AAA was reenacted into law in slightly different form because its programs were strongly supported by farmers and planters. In February 1936 Congress passed the Soil Conservation and Domestic Allotment Act. Its purpose was exactly the same as the AAA—to reduce the number of hectares under cultivation in order to reduce commodity surpluses. Landowners were paid to lease 15 percent of their cultivated land to the U.S. government. The leased land was immediately fallowed and became part of the soil conservation program administered by the department of agriculture.

In an abrupt about-face in 1937, the Supreme Court validated all of the revised AAA programs. In 1938 Congress passed a second, more comprehensive AAA statute designed to further reduce harvests. If two-thirds of farmers and planters approved of marketing quotas (usually a formality), the secretary of agriculture was delegated authority to impose quotas on them. Only contracting farmers and planters qualified for subsidy prices for their harvests. The statute contained prohibitive taxation on cultivators who marketed harvests in excess of their quotas.

The programs of the revised AAA had the desired effect. A combination of reduced planting, reduced livestock production, and subsidies nearly tripled net agricultural income between 1932 and 1940. In 1932 net agricultural income was 2.8 billion dollars. In 1937 it had increased to 6.2 billion dollars and by 1940 net farm income was over 8.0 billion dollars.

This price level was acceptable to efficient farmers in northern states because mechanization, the use of more fertilizers, and increased planting of hybrid maize increased yields and lowered the costs of production. In contrast, large parts of southern agriculture remained at a depressed level of subsistence welfare because the subsidies of new AAA legislation were designed to help planters. Only small ameliorations in welfare trickled down to sharecrop peasants.

During the 1930s, per hectare yields of cotton and maize in southern states were at subsistence levels because white and black peasantry continued to cultivate cotton and maize with subsistence labor norms. Both planters and peasants had minimal interest in mechanization. Planters accepted subsistence labor norms and the subsistence sized harvests grown by sharecroppers as long as they controlled agricultural labor. Planter control of local government ensured their control of agricultural labor.

The adoption of hybrid maize in southern states was slow because peasant households had minimal interest in maximizing maize yields. Cultivating hybrid maize required purchasing seed and much more labor than local varieties because it had to be planted as early as possible, required fertilization, and had to be intensively weeded in order to produce maximum yields. If this labor was not done, yields were less than local varieties.

Peasant households wanted maize that had a good taste when grains were cracked into grits, and they wanted tall plants that shaded competing weeds into attenuation. Yields of these varieties were low but they reduced the labor of weeding. This was a more important consideration for peasants because they acquired their target sums of money by cultivating cotton or tobacco.

In contrast, farmers in the Corn Belt states of Ohio, Indiana, Illinois, Missouri, Iowa, and Nebraska rapidly adopted hybrid maize and yields dramatically increased. Not until the late 1940s did southern landowners begin to plant hybrid maize in considerable amounts. It was adopted because fully mechanized cotton cultivation displaced peasants from the land. Land that was planted in cotton and maize was cultivated by farmers and they adopted the same cultivation practices as Corn Belt farmers. They wanted maximum yields in order to maximize incomes. The complement of fully mechanizing cotton and maize cultivation in southern states was that by 1958, almost two million hectares (4.9 million acres) of marginal land ceased being planted in cotton.[24]

Industry

Congress passed legislation establishing the National Industrial Recovery Administration (NIRA) in June 1933. It was an emergency agency that was expected to expire in two years or sooner if the president proclaimed an end to the emergency or if a joint resolution by Congress declared the emergency was over. However, it was not mandated to expire.

The NIRA was designed to revive industry by fair competition codes (pricing agreements) that would end destructive competition. The codes would ensure that prices were sufficiently high to pay the overhead expenses of factories that had large amounts of idle capacity. Fair competition codes were most easily negotiated in industries that were dominated by a few large corporations. In effect, they endorsed oligopolistic competition, which was what managers of large business corporations tried to obtain in the 1920s.

The fair competition codes for each industry were generally written by lawyers from trade associations who were paid by the largest companies in the industry. By law, the codes had to be written by consultations among lawyers representing government, business, and organized labor in each industry, with additional inputs from consumer groups. Labor leaders, however, made minor inputs and there were almost no input from consumer groups.

After codes were written, a public hearing was held in which interest groups could suggest amendments or deletions. After public hearings were concluded and subsequent changes made, codes became law after President Roosevelt signed them. Signed codes were enforceable in federal courts. It was impossible to write codes for all industries in the time available because the political agenda of President Roosevelt was immediate action. If industry leaders used delaying tactics, the president was authorized to impose a code on an industry.

In July 1933 all businesses were asked to subscribe to a blanket code that had provisions that would be included in all codes for all industries. Most of its provisions dealt with employment. Businesses agreed not to hire any person under sixteen years of age and to pay clerical and service workers wages of fifteen dollars per week in cities and twelve dollars per week in small towns.

There was also a minimum wage of forty cents an hour for industrial workers and a maximum work week of thirty-five hours. Higher hourly wages were retained for skilled workers.

Workers in mass production industries were authorized to organize their own unions in order to bargain collectively for higher wages and improved working conditions. This provision voided yellow dog contracts. Furthermore, the national government prohibited company managers from interfering with organizing activities. Within several months, 2.3 million businesses with a total of 16 million employees worked under provisions of blanket codes. These provisions are examined in greater detail in the Industrial Labor section in this chapter.

Businesses that subscribed to blanket codes, with its minimum wage provision, usually lost a competitive advantage with businesses that did not subscribe to the blanket code. Therefore, there was an accelerated effort to get industrial codes approved as soon as possible so that, when the president signed a code into law, it was imposed on all businesses in an industry. Quickly, there were 557 industrial codes, 189 supplementary codes, and 19 codes in food-related businesses that were shared with the AAA.

There was no way in which uniformity of regulation could be achieved. Altogether, there were 1,000 provisions to regulate 150 trade practices in 150 industries. In this formative period, two outcomes were possible: bureaucratic chaos or manipulative control of codes by the largest businesses in an industry. Manipulative control won and the largest businesses wrote large parts of fair competition codes to their advantage.

Proponents of NIRA called the codes industrial self-government. After a fashion this was correct. They codified business practices that were largely hidden during the 1920s and made these practices compulsory on all businesses in an industry. In theory, the NIRA would manage the national market in order to end business cycles. In theory, the NIRA would be the honest broker between industry, labor, and consumers in order to extend the benefits of the consumer culture to the maximum number of people. In reality, the codes closely resembled old fashioned cartels. In May 1935 the Supreme Court unanimously declared the NIRA unconstitutional.

The trade statute of 1934 was companion to the NIRA in the attempt to revive industrial production by increasing exports. Congress authorized the president to negotiate tariff reductions up to 50 percent on products where both nations would benefit. The president was authorized to proclaim agreements into law without formal congressional approval. The statute was to be in effect for three years but Congress reenacted it in 1937, 1940, and 1943. After the end of World War II, U.S. trade policies were governed by new rules that were more international in scope. These rules are examined in the next chapter.

The effect of the 1934 statute was that Congress voluntarily refrained from levying tariffs on specific products because the international trade in industrial products had become too complex. Secretary of State Cordell Hull made tariff reductions a high priority during his tenure because he strongly believed that trade barriers among industrial nations contributed to war and that freer trade among industrial nations was the best insurance for peace. He concluded bilateral agreements with twenty-seven nations that resulted in reducing rates an average of 44 percent.[25]

The trade statute of 1934 and programs extracted from the NIRA as separate statutes had three long-term impacts on the national economy. (1) Industrial competition never again became destructive. In one way or another (usually by approving mergers), the national government has encouraged oligopolistic competition. (2) Reluctantly, U.S. business leaders accepted the national government as the senior partner in the management of the national market. (3) After the mid-1960s, business leaders accepted the national government as the dominant partner in the management of their interests in the global market.

Social Welfare

On the same day President Roosevelt signed the AAA into law, he also signed the Federal Emergency Relief Act (FERA). The act was a direct repudiation of the relief policies of the Hoover administration. The national government accepted responsibility for the ultimate welfare of its citizens when, through no fault of their own, they became destitute because of long-term unemployment. Persons who received FERA assistance and were capable of labor were employed on projects that were prioritized and supervised by state authorities, but they were employees of the national government and received minimum wages. Persons who were incapable of labor due to age, disease, or women with young children, also received assistance.

In order to get the program into operation as soon as possible, huge amounts of authority were delegated to President Roosevelt. He appointed Harry Hopkins as administrator. Hopkins had been director of relief for the state of New York when Roosevelt was governor. Hopkins understood the urgency of the situation. Households facing destitution had to have an income as soon as possible. They especially needed an income to carry them through the coming winter while state governments were deciding what projects to fund.

Roosevelt issued an executive order authorizing Hopkins to organize the Civil Works Administration (CWA). By mid-January 1934, the CWA had 4.2 million workers on its payroll. Its principal projects were improving streets and roads, building bridges, building airports and municipal buildings, and providing salaries for teachers in urban and rural school districts that were bankrupt.

The CWA provided enough employment to enough households to avoid the worst forms of privation. President Roosevelt ordered the CWA disbanded as soon as warmer weather returned because many of its projects were make-work and generated growing criticism. The CWA went out of existence in mid-April 1934. Incomplete projects were turned over to FERA, which by this time had a bureaucracy that was large enough to manage relief programs of national scope.

Hopkins had little sympathy for destitution in the rural South. The observers he sent reported that FERA funds were wasted when allocated to evicted sharecrop households. Relief payments to these households provided a better level of subsistence welfare than when they were sharecroppers. Relief payments allowed most households of evicted sharecroppers to reject performing agricultural labor during the plowing, planting, and harvesting seasons when planters needed supplemental labor. Hopkins believed the AAA should fund rural relief in the South. He wanted FERA funds used for the relief of the urban unemployed. He knew that they were eager to end temporary employment whenever they found full-time employment.[26]

President Roosevelt's message to Congress in January 1935 was important for two reasons: the New Deal had not cured the Great Depression, and there was a continuing need to mitigate urban destitution. Unemployment had decreased from about 25 percent of the work force in 1933 to 20 percent in 1935. The FERA was clearly a temporary agency that had to continue to operate because the number of unemployed remained at disaster levels during 1934 and 1935. In 1935 Congress funded a relief program with the largest single appropriation up to that time, and delegated huge amounts of authority to the president to manage it.

President Roosevelt and his closest advisors knew that only the national government had "sufficient power and credit to meet this situation. We have assumed this task and we shall not shrink from it in the future." Huge amounts of deficit spending were required. The former truism that a small, frugal national government was best for the nation was in process of replacement. The ability of national relief programs to prevent the destitution of many families changed public perceptions of governance. Larger governments were desirable if they could deliver essential welfare services.[27]

Two senior advisors to the president competed to control the expenditures of relief funds. They were Harry Hopkins and Secretary of the Interior Harold L. Ickes. Ickes wanted to use the funds to build capital improvement projects and Hopkins wanted to use the funds for less ambitious projects. Hopkins won because his projects could provide instant employment while the projects advocated by Ickes required long lead times in engineering design. Furthermore, leaders of the American Federation of Labor feared that the projects advocated by Ickes would undercut union wage scales in the construction industry because of a policy of employing the maximum number of persons with the available funds. The projects favored by Hopkins did not threaten organized labor because a high percentage of them were disguised relief payments.

There were, however, many infrastructure projects that were built with funds from the 1935 relief appropriation. Among the most important was constructing power lines in order to bring electricity to rural households. The Rural Electrification Administration (REA) was created by executive order in May 1935 and was authorized to lend 100 percent of the costs of construction to rural cooperatives. Electricity was essential for bringing rural households into the consumer culture—as soon they had sufficient incomes to purchase durable consumer product for household use. Until farms had electricity, barn and household labor was little changed from the nineteenth century. It was labor intensive, and this was a stonewall limitation on increasing productivity. By 1940, 40 percent of U.S. farms had electricity and 90 percent were electrified by 1950.

Investment Securities

Congress passed the federal securities statute in June 1933, and the securities exchange statute one year later. The 1934 statute established the Securities Exchange Commission (SEC), an independent regulatory agency. Its two principal purposes were to (1) compel full disclosure for the intended use of new issues of stocks and bonds and assess the risks, and (2) regulate stock market exchanges to prevent price manipulation by brokers.

All stock exchanges had to be licensed by the SEC and trading had to follow prescribed rules. Furthermore, the Federal Reserve Board was empowered to regulate the credit practices of investment bankers and stock brokers in order to curb speculation. The SEC had no power to initiate criminal proceedings against persons or corporations that engaged in fraudulent practices. Prosecutions were made by the attorney general at the recommendation of the SEC, but the attorney general had discretion to prosecute or not.

From its inception, the SEC was highly successful in ensuring that investment bankers made full and fair disclosures of the material facts underlying issues before they were offered to investors. All new issues required printed prospectuses of the material facts and other relevant information. The SEC was equally successful in enforcing rules of fair trading on exchanges and over-the-counter sales. Its early successes invited Congress to expand it authority to regulate the capital structures of public utility holding companies and the reorganized capital structures of corporations emerging from bankruptcy.

Recidivist Court

Given the circumstances in 1933, preservation of the consumer culture required immediate large-scale intervention in the economy by the national government. Many of the New Deal programs in 1933, 1934, and 1935 were hastily drafted, seriously flawed, wasteful, and had minimal impact on reducing high unemployment rates; but they did stop the decline in industrial production.

The interventionalist policies of the New Deal generated a strong negative response by the Supreme Court because a majority of justices were committed to the 1920s policy of passive governance. Two of the most important rejections were the NIRA and AAA. The NIRA was judged to be unconstitutional because Congress delegated excessive legislative power to the president. The AAA was judged unconstitutional because the tax on processors to generate revenue to pay farmers for withdrawing part of their land from cultivation was not a tax for revenue but the first step "to impose federal regulation upon any phase of economic life merely by purchasing compliance."[28]

The immediate response of President Roosevelt and Congress to the invalidation of the NIRA was a sigh of relief. It had proved unworkable and an embarrassment to its proponents because managers from the largest corporations in an industry used their knowledge of the complexities of mass production and mass distribution to guide administrative decisions for their benefit. Pricing policies preferred by the largest corporations frequently made it difficult for smaller corporations to earn adequate profit margins. There were, however, programs to be salvaged. Most of these programs dealt with industrial labor, and they are discussed in the next section.

In the meantime, in November 1936 Roosevelt was reelected president by an overwhelming majority of popular and electoral votes. The first item on his agenda was increasing the number of justices on the Supreme Court from nine to fifteen. The additional judges he would appoint would validate New Deal legislation. A majority of judges read the election returns and made an abrupt about face in 1937 by validating New Deal legislation.

Many of the programs validated were only marginally different from programs that had been judged unconstitutional in the previous three years. Chief among the programs that the court found constitutional were programs designed to increase farmer and planter incomes by various forms of subsidies combined with criminal penalties for farmers who refused to reduce the number of hectares they cultivated. The court packing plan died in Congress. Thereafter, retirements allowed President Roosevelt to appoint judges who were sympathetic to active governance.

Industrial Labor

Labor leaders had a clear agenda of programs they wanted enacted into law; and President Roosevelt made certain that their agenda was written into the NIRA statute. The following were the principal provisions in the agenda of industrial labor:

1. Employees must have a legal right to organize and select their representatives to negotiate contracts with employers.
2. The bargaining process had to be free of interference or restraint by employers.
3. No person seeking employment would be required to join a union sponsored by the company as a condition of employment.
4. Employers had to pay minimum wages for unskilled workers.
5. Child labor under the age of sixteen was prohibited. Most codes adopted a work week of eight hours per day, five days a week, but some adopted a work week of thirty-five hours.

Two months after the NIRA was declared unconstitutional (July 1935), the labor provisions of NIRA were put into a separate bill that Congress enacted into law (Wagner Act). It established the National Labor Relations Board (NLRB), an independent commission that (1) protected union organizers who were engaged in recruiting new members; (2) forbid unfair labor practices that hindered organizational activities; (3) conducted votes on whether employees in a factory or all the employees of a company wanted an independent union to represent their interests; (4) supervised the election of officers for independent unions; and (5) after certification of a majority vote favoring an independent union, the union had the power to bargain for all of a company's employees (collective bargaining).

The principal unfair labor practices were (1) financial support for company unions; (2) interfering with organizational activities; (3) hiring employees who would join company sponsored unions, or firing employees who favored membership in independent unions; (4) discrimination against employees who complained about company practices that discouraged unionization; and (5) refusal to bargain collectively with elected union representatives. Although not delegated the authority to mediate contract negotiations in order to prevent or settle strikes, the NLRB often assumed this function.

Under the protection of the Wagner Act, independent unions rapidly increased membership. In 1933 they had 2.9 million members; 3.8 million in 1935; and 8.5 million in 1939. In 6 years almost 6 million employees were recruited into independent unions; and independent unions became a potent political interest group that strongly favored interventionalist policies to help procure increasing incomes for its members.[29]

The new political influence of organized labor translated the unfair labor practices defined in the Wagner Act (1935) into the Fair Labor Standards Act (1938). The Fair Labor Standards Act was a positive claim on the national government to institutionalize labor practices commensurate with a consumer culture. It mandated a work week of eight hours per day, five days a week with a pay bonus of 50 percent for additional hours of labor (time and a half for overtime). A minimum wage was established for industrial workers and child labor (industrial workers under sixteen years of age) was prohibited. From the perspective of union leaders, the most important part of the Fair Labor Standards Act was the sections defining wages and hours. Enforcement was safely located in the department of labor; and it had its own budget that guaranteed its independence.

Social Security

After the congressional election of 1934, presidential advisors urged Roosevelt to use the increased Democratic majority in Congress to enact legislation that would institutionalize a national system of unemployment insurance in order to mitigate the worst effects of urban unemployment, and provide supplementary pensions to persons who retired from paid labor. They urged presidential action because the Congress that assembled in January 1935 would look to the president for leadership and it would be highly receptive to this legislation.

Congress passed the Social Security Act in August 1935. It had four principal programs: (1) unemployment insurance;(2) pensions for persons who retired at age 65; (3) funds supplied to state governments to support destitute persons who were blind, crippled, or otherwise incapable of full-time paid labor; (4) funding agencies that provided public health services, vocational rehabilitation, and maternity and child care. Funds for unemployment compensation were accumulated by taxes on the payrolls of all businesses with 8 or more employees. Farmers, planters, agricultural laborers, teachers, persons employed in transportation, and government employees were exempt from participation. Unemployment compensation was administered by the states because of variable wage scales in different regions of the nation.

The old age pension program was administered by the national government without the intermediary of state governments or business corporations. Funding came from a payroll tax paid by employers and a tax on employee wages paid by employees. Pension payments were uniform throughout the nation, but monthly payments were based on the amount of money recipients had contributed. Only persons with employment records received retirement incomes. In 1939 the scope of Social Security was expanded to provide pensions to survivors of deceased workers who had contributed to the fund. Thereafter, the number and scope of welfare services increased with the ability of increased tax revenues to pay for them.

The Social Security Administration institutionalized welfare services that came directly from the national government. It is the foundation of the welfare state. The authors of the Social Security Act clearly saw that nationally funded social services would tie American citizens more closely to the national government than to state governments because the national government's superior financial resources could fund desired services that state governments could not.

Summary

New Deal policies of political economy did not end the Great Depression; however, they started recovery with a minimal increase in employment in 1934. Thereafter, recovery stalled for six years. In 1934 the unemployment rate was 21 percent of the labor force. In 1938 it was 19 percent, in 1940 it was 14 percent, and in 1941 it was 10 percent, about what it was in 1930 before the economy plunged into the Great Depression. *Why were New Deal policies of political economy so ineffective?*

In 1935 expenditures of the national government were 6.5 billion dollars and in 1936 expenditures were 8.5 billion dollars, a one-year increase of 30 percent. Thereafter until 1940, expenditures of the national government stayed about the same or slightly increased. In 1941 national expenditures increased to 13.3 billion, a one-year increase of 46 percent.[30]

The huge injection of money in the economy in 1941 was the beginning of rearming in preparation for entry into World War II. Most people recognized that increased military spending was essential for the national interest. They also recognized that military spending would escalate in the foreseeable future and employment rates would proportionately increase. The sustained injection of purchasing power in the economy, beginning in 1941, overcame reservations that businessmen had about increasing investments in capital equipment. It signaled businessmen to resume optimal production of durable consumer products because the prospect of full employment was also the prospect for returning consumer spending. Consumers would stop hoarding money when they knew employment was always available.

Two policies are essential for sustaining business and consumer confidence during periods of business slowdown. First, central governments must always be ready to use interventional fiscal policies because, as the Great Depression showed, consumer cultures are fragile social structures. Second, fiscal intervention must be large-scale, immediate, and when necessary, sustained. President Roosevelt and most other New Deal leaders, and especially economists, did not fully understand the magnitude of intervention that was required until preparation for war forced large-scale fiscal intervention.

Chapter 15

The Global Business Economy

The focus of this chapter is the competitiveness of the industrial sector of the U.S. economy in the global market because the national market, as it existed in 1955, no longer exists. Trade in agricultural commodities is a separate category of global commerce, as is trade with peasant nations. I ignore these two categories because manufactured products have been more than 80 percent of global commerce since 1920. This is true even in the current era of massive movements of crude oil in global commerce.

After the end of World War II, the United States was the preeminent industrial nation. The great uncertainty was how the United States would act in world affairs. *Would the United States withdraw into its protective shell as it did after World War I? Or would the United States assume world political and economic leadership that was for the taking?* President Franklin D. Roosevelt strongly supported ending the imperial commercial rivalries that had contributed to igniting World Wars I and II and he strongly favored policies that would closely integrate the commercial policies of industrial nations after the war; but he died in April 1945, one month before the end of the war in Europe.

Would his successor, Harry S. Truman, use the power of the United States to guide cooperative policies that would replace imperial commercial rivalries? The answer was yes. It was also yes for Dwight D. Eisenhower, Truman's successor to the presidency in 1952. The United States would use its preeminent political and industrial power to revive industrial production in Western Europe and encourage production of additional industrial wealth wherever governments were receptive.

Eisenhower also accepted the New Deal policy that the national government was ultimately responsible for sustaining high levels of employment by using the fiscal powers at its disposal. This meant high levels of deficit spending in order to sustain full employment. The acceptance of this fiscal policy created a political consensus. Leaders of the Democratic and Republican parties agreed that the national government was the senior partner in the management of the domestic economy. Both parties also reached consensus on policies of defense. Western European nations and Japan had to be protected from Soviet imperial ambitions, a policy that was necessary to prevent future wars.

In the immediate aftermath of World War II, six principal policies guided U.S. conduct:

1. maximizing the commercial integration of the principal industrial nations as the best way to prevent future wars;
2. creating stable governments in Western European nations and Japan by achieving full employment as soon as possible;

3. restoring full industrial employment as the best way to neutralize the appeal of the Soviet variety of Marxist socialism;

4. reindustrialize Western Europe to provide markets for manufactured products made in the United States;

5. remove U.S. trade barriers so that the U.S. market was freely accessible to products of European and Japanese manufacture because access to the U.S. market was essential to put the global market on a sustaining basis;

6. favorable terms of trade for products manufactured in Europe and Japan would strongly contribute to sustaining the American consumer culture.

It was also clear beyond doubt, that an overwhelming majority of citizens in the industrial nations of Western Europe and Japan wanted their version of a consumer culture. It was equally clear that policies that maximized international trade would help create a consumer culture in these nations.

New Commercial Institutions

In the four years following the end of World War II (1945–1949), the political leaders of Western European nations and the United States knew that the political uncertainty and economic disruptions caused by the war was a one-time opportunity to create a new system of global commerce that would fairly balance its benefits among the principal industrial nations. Its long-term goal was simple. Cooperative management of commerce on a global scale would tie the economies of the principal industrial nations so tightly together that waging war among them would be impossible. A global business economy was the best guarantee for future peace.[1]

The building process had to be initiated by the United States; however, the political leaders of Western European nations had to do at least 50 percent of the building because two world wars had originated there. It was immediately clear that the economic integration of Western Europe would need a huge injection of capital and an equally large amount of protection to make it work. Both capital and protection had only one source—the United States. The United States was in a preeminent position to provide solutions to these problems because it was the preeminent industrial nation.

In the broadest understanding of political economy, there were four major problems that required simultaneous solutions: (1) how to protect Western Europe and Japan from possible Soviet aggression after the Soviet Union isolated itself from participating in global commerce, (2) how to incorporate Germany and Japan into a new political and economic system without creating long-term military threats to their neighbors, (3) how to reindustrialize Western Europe and Japan, and (4) how to revive international trade without reviving imperial commercial rivalries.[2]

The creation of the consumer culture in Western European nations and Japan could not have happened unless cooperative international institutions were created that removed barriers to trade. These institutions extended the visible hand of political economy that created oligopolistic competition in advanced industrial nations to creating the global market. Six principal cooperative institutions have been created since the end of WW II.

1. The Bretton Woods Agreement was the first cooperative institution to help revive international commerce. It was an agreement among thirty-two nations to conduct international financial transactions by a set of rules. It was negotiated in July 1944, and its provisions became operational in December 1946. The purpose of the agreement was to provide maximum

liquidity among the world's currencies in order to stimulate the revival of commerce among industrial nations. Maximum liquidity meant that all currencies were freely convertible into all other currencies. "All participants agreed that stability in the value of national currencies and full convertibility would help prevent the reappearance of imperial commercial rivalries." The U.S. dollar was the only currency that was fully convertible into all other currencies. It was, therefore, the foundation for reviving global commerce.[3]

Reviving global commerce was facilitated by fixed exchange rates of the U.S. dollar with all currencies outside the Soviet sphere of influence. Fixed exchange rates translated into low inflation, price stability, and the ability of businessmen in Western European nations and Japan to have predictable costs for capital investments. By 1955 all of the currencies of Western European nations were fully convertible among themselves, and in 1959 they were fully convertible into U.S. dollars. Convertibility was possible because industrial production of Western European nations had reached pre-World War II levels.

2. The common market was the second cooperative institution that helped achieve consumer cultures in participating nations. Its organization and management was totally due to the vision and skills of European political leaders, with strong encouragement from the United States. It began with the organization of the European Coal and Steel Community in July 1952. It removed all barriers to production and distribution of these products. Its success immediately generated planning for closer market integration for manufactured products, but not for agriculture.

The Treaty of Rome in 1957 established a common market among six nations in Western Europe that underwent continual expansion after 1973. The extraordinary success of the common market in accelerating industrial production hugely benefited all participating European nations. The highly visible increases in welfare by lowered trade barriers produced a consumer culture by 1970. The success of the common market was an incentive to lower trade barriers among all nations. Especially, the United States, Canada, and Australia would be beneficiaries in proportion to the volume of their international trade because lowered trade barriers would help sustain their consumer cultures.

Seen from a different perspective, by 1970 the original nations of the common market consumed a similar array of products and services that had created the consumer culture in the United States in the 1920s, and these products and services were available at competitive prices. During the years of catch-up industrialization, the nations of the common market were becoming rich in terms of income available for purchasing consumer products and social services.

Economists are fond of pointing out that, during these years, the United States produced a reduced percentage of the world's industrial products. In 1963 the United States produced 40 percent of the world's industrial products. By 1977 the U.S. share of global production had declined to 37 percent. Common market nations also had a declining share of the world's industrial production. Their production declined from 27 percent in 1963 to 24 percent in 1977. Other nations, especially Japan but also Brazil and South Korea, increased their share of world industrial production. Between 1960 and 1977 the annual increase in output per hour of labor in the United States averaged about 3 percent. During these same years, output per hour of labor in Japan and common market nations (except Britain) increased an average of about 6 percent, and hourly wages of workers increased proportionately.

It appeared as if the United States was falling behind in the creation of new industrial wealth and consumer products. This was emphatically not the case! Other nations were catching-up. As common market nations and Japan successfully pursued catch-up industrialization, the United States was a huge beneficiary because an increasing volume of consumer products was being produced for export at competitive prices; and exports of these products to the United States helped sustain U.S. consumer culture.[4]

3. The International Monetary Fund (IMF) was the third cooperative institution designed to create a new global economy. It became operational in March 1947, with the United States as the largest contributor of capital. Its purpose was to supervise exchange rates and provide loans to the industrial nations of Western Europe when they had temporary balance of payment problems. Loans from the IMF would restore liquidity, which was essential for sustaining production for export.

The IMF did not fulfill this function because of inadequate capitalization. Instead, liquidity for international trade was supplied by eurodollars held by the central banks of common market nations. Central banks acquired U.S. dollars from defense spending by the United States to support NATO. They remained in Europe and supplied liquidity for trade within the common market. The IMF reinvented its mission. It became the new imperial power that supervised the financial policies of peasant nations. This mission was subsidized by the principal industrial nations in order to prevent the dissolution of central governments in these nations, and consequent anarchy.

4. The General Agreement on Tariffs and Trade (GATT) was the fourth cooperative institution designed to create a new global economy. It became operational in January 1948. The first draft was made in the U.S. State Department in 1945 and it was amended and adopted in Geneva, Switzerland in October 1947. Twenty-three nations signed. Its purpose was to broker multilateral reductions of tariffs, reduce or eliminate non-tariff trade barriers, and act as a mediator in trade disputes. Reciprocity was the basis for removing barriers, and the basis of reciprocity was favorable terms of trade for products that nations produced for export markets.

5. The World Bank was the fifth cooperative institution designed to create a new global economy. It became operational in June 1946. Most of its capital was supplied by the United States. Delegates to the Bretton Woods conference envisioned a multinational bank to make loans to Western European nations to repair railroads, roads, bridges, and electricity generating facilities. From its inception it lacked sufficient capital and was mainly a supplementary source of funds to help reindustrialize Western European nations. After 1950, it began shifting its lending practices to post-colonial nations in order to build basic infrastructure projects. It had a close working relationship with the IMF. Its lending practices made it increasingly peripheral to the expanding global economy in industrial and consumer products because the projects it funded were closely related to the production of low priced export commodities produced in peasant nations rather than of high priced manufactured products produced by industrial nations.

6. Regional trade agreements were the sixth cooperative institution designed to lower trade barriers. The common market was the most successful and became an equal partner with the United States in managing the global market. Other important regional trade agreements are the North American Free Trade Agreement (NAFTA) between the United States, Canada, and Mexico; Commonwealth of Independent States (CIS) that is designed to retain the commercial unity of former Soviet republics, now independent nations; Mercado Comun del Sur (MERCOSUR) to eliminate trade barriers between Brazil, Argentina, Paraguay, and Uruguay.

The New Competition

During the five years following the end of World War II (1945–1950), the United States dominated global industrial production and trade. In 1953 the United States produced 29 percent of the global trade in manufactured products. By 1976 the U.S. share had declined to 13 percent. This occurred because the rebuilt manufacturing facilities of common market nations and Japan effectively competed with U.S. manufactured products. That is only half of the picture. The competition was taking place in a global market with a vastly increased volume of trade. The 29 percent of global commerce in manufactured products in 1953 was 29 percent of 37 billion dollars (10.7 billion dollars). The 13 percent in 1976 was 13 percent of 585 billion dollars (76 billion dollars).

After 1970, the global market for manufactured products was increasingly propelled by direct foreign investments by multinational corporations. Most of these investments were in industrial nations. In 1970 U.S. corporations made direct foreign investments of 78 billion dollars and in 1977 it was 148 billion dollars. Sixty-five percent of these investments were in common market nations and Canada. A similar strategy guided investments of foreign multinational corporations. In 1970 foreign based multinational corporations invested 13 billion dollars in the United States. In 1977 it was 34 billion, and 90 percent of the 34 billion dollars was made by corporations with headquarters in common market nations, Canada, and Japan.[5]

A high percentage of direct foreign investments made by multinational corporations are made where investments were safe (in other industrial nations). After direct foreign investments are made, production is free from non-tariff trade barriers that the governments of many industrial nations (including the United States) erect to protect domestic industries from intense international competition.

Parallel to the rapid increases in direct foreign investments made by multinational corporations, were corporate mergers across national boundaries. During the 1970s, multinational corporations based in the common market and Japan reached technological par with U.S. multinational corporations. Thereafter, they rapidly increased their competitive presence in the United States and in the global market. Mergers that created multinational corporations were a quick way to increase an ability to compete in the global market. Because of the complexities of trade relations that evolved after 1970, the governments of the principal industrial nations placed few restraints on multinational mergers. This is the new competition.

Mergers to create multinational corporations were a repetition, on a global scale, of the merger movement in the United States from 1890 to 1930. Most industrial mergers in the United States created corporations large enough to service the national market, and a high percentage of these of mergers had close relationships with investment banks. Most multinational mergers after 1970 created corporations large enough to compete in the global market, and they also had close relations with banks. After 1970, the United States became another participant in the global market. It was the biggest participant but it was not the dominant participant it had been in 1960.

Political leaders in industrial nations learned that multinational corporations were very efficient in transferring technology and superior management practices. Profits earned by multinational corporations were a nonpolitical issue because the most important contributions of direct foreign investments were transferring technologies and management skills, creating employment, and contributing tax revenues to sustain social service programs. Many products made by direct foreign investments were for intra-corporate use or global distribution. Component parts were made in one nation and assembled elsewhere, or brand name products were produced for sale in the global market. National markets in advanced industrial nations became increasingly difficult to define.

After 1970, five principal trends defined competition in the U.S. domestic market:

1. Foreign corporations increased direct investment to manufacture products for sale in the United States.
2. These investments internalized international competition.
3. Mergers of banks and insurance corporations increased in tandem with mergers of industrial corporations in order to effectively compete in the global market.
4. Multinational corporations headquartered in industrial nations tended to create oligopolistic

competition on a global scale for an increasing number of manufactured products and related services.

5. Global oligopolistic competition made the anti-trust laws of the United States largely irrelevant or counter-productive.

During the 1990s, four events accelerated mergers to create global corporations:

1. Between 1985 and 1990, world income increased by about 6 percent per year and international trade increased about 9 percent per year. The largest contribution to increased global commerce was probably the enormous increase in direct foreign investments. During these years, it increased at average annual rates of between 23 and 29 percent.
2. The end of the cold war in 1991.
3. GATT transforming itself into the World Trade Organization (WTO) in 1995.
4. Mergers between multinational corporations became commercially advantageous because "the perception of senior managers of many big corporations in large national markets was that they could be squeezed into niche markets unless they produced a wider range of products or services at competitive prices for sale on the rapidly evolving global market."[6]

The dynamics of the global market create continual stresses in the economies of industrial nations; therefore, protection has not ended. All industrial nations continue to protect some industries because it is politically expedient. Protection is obtained by negotiating orderly marketing agreements (OMA) or voluntary export restraints (VER). OMAs are between two or more nations where one limits the volume of exports of specific products for a specified number of years. The assumption behind them is that protection will generate sufficiently high profits for domestic manufacturers to replace obsolescent technologies as well as restructure management. The WTO does what it can to prevent OMAs from becoming permanent trade restrictions.

The great lesson learned by political and business leaders in advanced industrial nations (United States, European Union, and Japan) is that multinational corporations have reduced national commercial rivalries to manageable proportions. Commercial rivalry is between multinational corporations with a global scope, not rival political empires. The rules governing international commerce have been assigned to the WTO, IMF, and regional trade agreements where disputes are resolved by negotiations. It is not a level playing field but it is as close as is politically possible.

Losers in Global Competition

Steel

Between 1950 and 1975, the U.S. integrated steel industry (from mining iron ore to producing semi-finished shapes) declined from world leader to obsolescence. The cause was simple. Managers of most integrated steel mills deferred investing in new technologies that would substantially lower production costs. The three most important new technologies were basic oxygen furnaces (BOF) replacing open hearths, continuous casting of slabs that bypassed casting ingots, and electric furnaces operated by minimills that melted scrap steel into the lowest grades of slabs, bars, and rods that are shaped by end users. These investments were essential if steel made in integrated steel mills in the United States was to be competitive with imported steel in the domestic market.

After the mid-1960s, imports of low carbon steel supplied about 15 percent of the U.S.

market that increased to about 20 percent by 1988. Most imported steel came from new integrated mills in Japan that were built on vacant land at tidewater. These mills had large capacity blast furnaces, used basic oxygen furnaces (BOF), and continuous casting. The layout of the mills had production moving in one direction—from unloading ships carrying iron ore and coking coal, to blast furnaces, to BOFs, to continuous casting of slabs, to rolling mills and foundries, to warehousing semi-finished shapes where they could be transported by rail or water to ultimate consumers.

U.S. market share of steel produced in integrated steel mills declined from 92 percent in 1956, to 68 percent in 1979, to 58 percent in 1988. Alloy and stainless steels accounted for about 7 percent of the U.S. market. They continued to be competitively priced with imported equivalents.

After the mid-1960s, steel was the largest export industry in Japan and retained its rank until 1977. By 1970 Japanese steel production was 93 million tons. Three years later it was 119 million tons. Thereafter, annual production averaged over 100 million tons. By 1973 Japan was exporting over 25 million tons of steel in various shapes, plus the steel used to build ships and automobiles that were exported.

In a free global market the cost efficiency of Japanese steel producers could dictate prices. Those prices would bankrupt large numbers of obsolescent mills in the United States, Canada, and common market nations because of the efficiency of their technology. Between 1968 and 1974, managers of Japanese steel mills invested 14.2 billion dollars; steel producers in common market nations invested 14.3 billion dollars, and U.S. steel producers invested 12.0 billion dollars. The funds invested by U.S. and common market steel mills were not efficiently allocated. Many U.S. steel mills grafted BOFs onto obsolescent rolling mills, or continuous casting machinery onto obsolescent open hearth furnaces. Patchwork investments did not produce steel with competitive prices. "The Japanese advantage in production efficiency can be attributed largely to consistently shrewd investment decisions and technological adaptation geared to the rigors of world export market standards."[7]

There are a number of ways of measuring comparative efficiency. The best measure was Japanese practices because Japanese steelmakers had substantially lower costs than most integrated mills in the United States and common market nations. In 1977 Japanese steel producers had 25 blast furnaces capable of annual productions of 2 million tons. The United States had no blast furnaces capable of producing 2 million tons of steel. Most U.S. blast furnaces produced less than 1 million tons annually. Japanese steel producers used about 460 kilos of coke to produce one ton of crude steel and U.S. furnaces used about 650 kilos.

On average in 1978, Japanese mills converted 100 tons of crude steel into 78 to 87 tons of finished shapes. The average in integrated mills in the United States was 68 to 73 tons into finished shapes. Japanese steel mills produced, on average, 400 tons of crude steel per year per employee. The average in the United States was 250 tons. This directly translated into lower labor costs. Labor accounted for 12 percent of the cost of a ton of crude steel in Japan. In the United States it was 35 percent.

U.S. mills had some advantages. Coking coal and metallurgical limestone were cheaper and were located on the doorsteps of most mills. Most mills were located in the middle of a large market of steel consumers, and they had the advantage of using iron ore pellets as blast furnace feed. Pellets reduced throughput time in blast furnaces by about 50 percent. But these advantages were not sufficient to overcome the small size of most blast furnaces and poor layout of most integrated mills. Few integrated mills in the United States in 1970 had a continuous series of operations that moved in one direction at one site; and almost no integrated steel mills in the United States had junked open hearth refining and adopted BOFs and continuous casting.

In the late 1960s the managers of integrated mills pursued two strategies to maintain oligopolistic competition among themselves. Investments in new technologies were deferred and, when Japanese competition became intense, they sought protection from imports. Managers deferred investments in new technologies in order to preserve open hearth production until the furnaces wore out. Only then did they invest in BOFs. Managers of integrated mills were equally slow to invest in continuous casting and made almost no investments in electric furnaces.

Managers of integrated mills abdicated a large share of the domestic market to minimills that use electric furnaces to recycle locally available scrap. Minimills are small, geographically dispersed, and make low quality steel. The usual capacities are between two hundred thousand and six hundred thousand tons per year. Only a few exceed one million tons. They are built to serve local markets for a narrow range of shapes that do not require high quality steel. The principal products they produce are concrete reinforcing rods, rods for drawing into wire, strips for spiral welding into pipes, and small billets used by foundries and other fabricators. Producing a limited number of shapes for a limited geographic market allowed them to achieve economies of scale with small scale facilities that had low capital costs.

During the 1960s, minimills were nearly invisible. In 1960 they produced two million tons of steel and integrated mills produced ninety-seven million tons. In 1985 minimills produced seventeen million tons and integrated mills produced seventy million tons. In 1980 about 25 percent of U.S. steel production came from minimills and by 1986 they produced about 36 percent of domestically produced steel. In 2000 they produced about 45 percent of domestic production. In 1986 there were fifty-eight minimills in the United States and at least twelve of those were joint ventures with foreign partners or were foreign owned. Minimill steel was competitively priced with Japanese imports.

Minimills rapidly increased their share of the U.S. market because newer electric furnaces had larger capacities and used substantially less power. Furnaces were seamlessly integrated with continuous casting, and rolling mills. In 2001 the largest minimill corporation was Nucor. It had eight widely dispersed mills that produced eleven million tons annually. This was nearly as much as was produced by U.S. Steel, the largest integrated mill that produced thirteen million tons annually.

Minimills have been consistently profitable because they had high rates of capacity utilization. In 1986 only 54 percent of U.S. blast furnace capacity was in production but 80 percent of minimill capacity was in production. Minimills also had substantially lower labor costs. Wages averaged about 75 percent of wages in integrated steel mills and there were no rigid work rules. Most minimills were not unionized. Minimills used about 2.4 man hours to produce one ton of steel in 1985 compared to about 3.5 hours in integrated mills.

The failure of managers of integrated mills to replace open hearth and ingot technology as soon as possible forced managers to petition the national government for orderly marketing agreements (OMA) with Japan and common market nations. This strategy was fully supported by the steel workers union. Managers of integrated mills claimed that Japanese and common market producers were dumping steel on the U.S. market. This was unfair competition.

Japanese producers did not dump steel because the price of steel they sold in the United States was the same price charged customers in their home markets, plus transportation costs. "When the major U.S. steel producers focused on fairness of import penetration they masked their failure to manage the transition from old to new rules of competitiveness" that were based on investments in more productive technologies.[8]

Petitions for protection were highly successful. The long-term effect of protection, however, was to delay restructuring of the steel industry into fewer producers at the best locations. The OMAs negotiated in the late 1960s assumed that managers of integrated steel mills would use stabilized profits to invest in new technologies. During the six years they operated, managers did make substantial investments in new technologies but not at a rate that made steel competitive with global market prices. Protection maintained high prices for steel destined for domestic consumption, but the global market was supplied by cheaper steel from Japan.

What occurred in the mid-1960s in the United States occurred in the mid-1970s in the common market. Japanese imports into common market nations were restricted in 1972, then allowed to lapse, but were reinstated in 1975. In 1975 production in mills in the common market declined to 65 percent of capacity and destructive competition forced an average price decline of 35 percent. The threat of increased Japanese imports threatened further destabilization.

In 1976 the common market and Japan negotiated a voluntary export restraint agreement (VER) that limited Japanese imports to common market nations. In a desperate effort to prevent additional declines in production, common market steel producers began dumping steel in the United States. Steel production and marketing in the common market and the United States was in wild disarray.

In 1977 the common market formulated a policy (Davignon Plan) for the orderly closure of obsolescent mills, teaching new skills to laid-off workers, encouraging mergers among more efficient mills, and subsidizing replacement of obsolescent technologies with more efficient technologies. The Davignon Plan established a basic price system for steel produced by integrated mills in common market nations. The Davignon Plan was called "organized free trade" but was, in fact, a cartel for preserving market shares of integrated steel mills in common market nations by limiting imports. The preservation of market shares and adequate profit margins assumed that the managers of integrated steel mills would accelerate capital investments to increase productive efficiency.

Both the United States and common market had to devise ways for domestic steel producers to retain market shares in a contracting market as well as prevent steel being dumped in each other's markets. In 1978 U.S. negotiators proposed a trigger mechanism for prices on eighty-four steel products and shapes. The trigger mechanism was the U.S. equivalent of the common market's basic price system (Davignon Plan). Both mechanisms had quotas on steel imports that were subsequently defined in VERs. The trigger pricing mechanism was accepted by Japan and became operational in mid-1978. It lasted until 1982. The base for trigger pricing was estimated production costs in Japan, plus 10 percent for overhead expenses, an 8 percent profit margin, and transportation costs. Prices below this estimated cost would trigger countervailing duties.[9]

The trigger price mechanism in the United States and the basic price system in the common market attempted to solve two dilemmas. First, *How could a political commitment to free trade be harmonized with very strong political pressures to protect an industry that a high percentage of political leaders considered the foundation of industrial culture?* They could not be harmonized. A euphemism had to be used. The euphemism was adjustment strategy. Neither the United States government nor the managers of the common market could unilaterally implement an adjustment strategy. It had to be formulated by multilateral negotiations with Japan and other exporters of steel; otherwise, these nations would enact retaliatory restraints on trade for other products.

Second, *How to manage a steep decline in steel usage because domestic markets were contracting?* Plastics and aluminum were substituting for steel. Beverage containers are the best example, but it was equally true for autos, especially fuel efficient autos that required reduced weight. In 1973 the U.S. produced 136 million tons of steel, of which 21 million tons were used by the automotive industry. In 1986 production had declined to 74 millions tons, of which 10 million tons were used by auto manufacturers. A similar but lesser decline in production and consumption occurred in common market nations.

The trigger mechanism and subsequent VERs established high floor prices that were close to the list prices of shapes made in integrated mills in the United States. The basic price system of the Davignon Plan did the same for obsolescent integrated steel mills in common market nations. Closures of obsolescent mills in the United States and in common market nations were delayed as long as possible during the 1970s because simultaneous closures would have created surges of unemployment in affected cities. Closures occurred only when subsidies were insufficient to keep them operational. Fourteen obsolescent mills in poor locations in the United States were closed in 1977 and their facilities scrapped, and in November 1979 U.S. Steel closed fifteen steel fabricating factories. More closures followed in the 1980s.

A committee representing government, industry, and labor was established to monitor the operation of trigger pricing. Trigger pricing had four effects:

1. Price competition was eliminated in the U.S. market because foreign steel was prevented from competing with lower prices.
2. Many marginal steel producers and fabricators continued in business.
3. U.S. industries that used large amounts of steel to make products for sale on the global market, like manufacturers of heavy earth moving machinery, were severely penalized by high domestic steel prices.
4. The national government became the highly visible senior partner in managing the survival of integrated steel production in the United States. In effect, most integrated steel companies became clients of the national government.

Profits from subsidized prices during the 1960s, 1970s, and 1980s were not invested in a way to make steel competitive with imports. A principal reason for the persistence of high-production costs was management's adoption of the strategy of diversification. For example, U.S. Steel acquired Marathon Oil Company. Marathon was consistently profitable and its profits were invested in petrochemicals while steel production was marginally profitable or lost money. Managers of integrated steel mills used approximately 15 percent of subsidized profits for diversification.

The extent of obsolescence in U.S. integrated mills was measured by the difference between production capacity and operating rates. In the boom year of 1973, the United States had the capacity to produce of 141 million tons of steel from 182 blast furnaces. These furnaces operated at 97 percent of capacity and produced 136 million tons. In the depressed year of 1986, capacity was 116 million tons from 85 blast furnaces; however, only 42 furnaces were in production. U.S. blast furnaces operated at only 53 percent of capacity. In 1986 U.S. industries consumed 91 million tons of steel and only 74 million tons were produced in the United States. Imports were 17 million tons. Of the 74 million tons produced in the United States, about 47 million tons were produced by integrated mills. Minimills produced about 27 million tons, which was about 35 percent of domestic production. Integrated steel companies had over 40 million tons of obsolescent capacity.

Common market nations had a similar problem in the 1980s. They also had over forty million tons of obsolescent capacity. Steel consuming industries in common market nations (like those in the United States) were penalized by high steel prices maintained by the Davignon Plan. Noncompetitive steel prices in the United States and common market nations gave a substantial competitive advantage to Japanese and Korean automobile manufacturers that used sheet steel that was 25 to 30 percent cheaper than steel produced in the United States or common market nations. Put in broader perspective, restraints on steel imports from Japan, Korea, and elsewhere increased domestic prices of products, like automobiles, that were made with expensive steel produced in the United States.

Between 1985 and 1988, surviving integrated steel mills adopted BOFs and continuous casting. During these years, the most efficient U.S. integrated mills reduced labor costs so that the man hours required to produce one ton of steel declined from 3.47 to 2.87 hours. Employment in the steel industry declined from 509,000 in 1973 to 163,000 in 1987. By 1988 the most efficient integrated mills were producing slab steel somewhere near the cost of Japanese mills. In order to prevent additional unemployment in steel mills, import quotas were renewed in 1989. This subsidy was ended in 1992. In spite of the increased efficiency of integrated mills, the U.S. imported 23 million tons of steel in 2001. The managers of integrated mills and union leaders lobbied for renewed protection for a large number of shapes. President George Bush assented in March 2002.

For the past forty years (1960–2000), production in integrated steel mills in the United States is a history of the failure of management and government policy. Management failed to make adequate and timely investments in technologies that could have reduced labor costs and made integrated mills globally competitive. Nor did the national government, as senior partner in the integrated steel industry, actively induce the closing of more obsolescent mills and encourage mergers among the most efficient mills.

The failure of management and government policies means that in 2005 there are no national steel industries in the United States, Canada, and the European Union in the sense that integrated steel mills within national borders are owned by companies headquartered in that nation. Steel production in the United States and Canada has lost its national character because many bankrupt integrated mills have been purchased in whole or in part by multinational corporations.

Global competition in slabs, semi-finished shapes, and manufactured products with a high steel content, will intensify during the second decade of the twenty-first century because the newest integrated steel mills in Brazil are joint ventures with Japanese, Korean, and European Union steel corporations. Slab steel produced by these mills will have a high content of Japanese expertise. The newest mills in China will produce cheaper slab steel than made in Japan, Korea, European Union, and the United States because labor costs are significantly lower.

Automobiles

In 1955 U.S. auto manufacturers supplied 96 percent of the American market. In 1987 Japanese and European imports supplied 30 percent of the U.S. market.

The oil shocks of 1973 and 1979 had a huge effect on the automotive industry because the price of gasoline increased twelve times over 1970 prices. The U.S. automotive industry was completely unprepared for it. A high percentage of U.S. production during the 1970s and 1980s was big autos with high fuel consumption. Smaller autos made by Japanese manufacturers were much more fuel efficient and were competitively priced. They also had engineering features that improved safety and performance (high compression four cylinder engines, front wheel drive, disk brakes, fuel injection, all wheel steering, radial tires, quartz headlights, and electric powered windshield wipers). These improved technologies gave Japanese automobiles a big advantage in the U.S. market.

Technical innovations were not the only source of superior performance of Japanese autos. Japanese automakers reorganized assembly line labor. It began with workers being indoctrinated with company loyalty. In return for company loyalty, workers were assured lifetime jobs with high enough incomes to enjoy the benefits of a consumer culture. Assembly line workers were then trained to share the responsibilities for producing an auto that was competitive on the global market. Assembly line workers knew that global competitiveness was essential for the assurance of lifetime employment.

What were some of the responsibilities workers assumed? They could reject component parts that were seen to be defective, they could stop the assembly line if they found defective workmanship, they were trained to work at several work stations on the assembly line in order to reduce boredom and the possibility of repetitive mistakes, and they were strongly encouraged to make suggestions to improve production efficiency. These procedures were highly effective in reducing the installation of defective parts and reducing the amount of defective workmanship that had to be repaired in costly secondary operations.

In the big picture, Japanese managers had different production priorities than U.S. managers. U.S. managers wanted maximum assembly line production. Japanese managers wanted quality production and they accepted smaller numbers of autos being produced per shift, but these autos had very low percentages of defective parts and workmanship. This practice significantly lowered production costs and produced better built autos that had significantly lower maintenance costs than autos produced on the assembly lines of U.S. automakers.

The strategy of quality production was borrowed from the United States. It was not part of Japanese management practices before the World War II. Quality production required three new practices: (1) there had to be hands-on leadership by all levels of management. Put another way, managers had to be visibly seen by production workers as part of a team. (2) Production workers had to be actively and continually motivated to work as a team. (3) Engineers had to incessantly strive to improve all phases of production technology that economized labor.

In 1950 Japan had to reestablish export markets in order to purchase food and the machinery that was necessary to rebuild its industrial infrastructure. Reestablishing permanent export markets required quality products. "This was a difficult challenge for top management in Japan." Put in a different perspective, Japanese managers had "to help people to work smarter, not harder." In practice this meant:

1. "Cease dependence on inspection to achieve quality. Eliminate the need for inspection by building quality into the product in the first place."
2. "End the practice of awarding business on the basis of price tag. Move toward a single supplier for any one item on a long-term relationship of loyalty and trust."
3. "Eliminate quotas on the factory floor. Eliminate management by numerical goals. Substitute leadership."
4. "Institute a vigorous program of education and self-improvement."[10]

In the 1970s and 1980s, Japanese automakers had much closer relations with manufacturers of component parts. They had fewer suppliers and assisted them to increase engineering performance. The U.S. practice, until managers learned otherwise in the 1980s, was to purchase from many suppliers, mostly on a cost basis. In many ways, relations between automakers and suppliers were more adversarial than cooperative.

The competitive advantage of Japanese manufacturers was further enhanced by management that was clearly more efficient in: (1) greater use of automated material handling, (2) fewer defective parts, and (3) lower absenteeism. Japanese autos were built with the same process technology used by U.S. manufacturers but Japanese management was clearly superior in applying this technology. They continually experimented with better arrangements of productive processes. One of the principal results of experimentation was the development of just-in-time delivery of component parts to automobile assembly lines. Just-in-time delivery generated huge savings by reducing inventory costs.

One of the best measurements of productivity is the number of autos produced per worker per year. In 1960 the average worker at Ford produced fourteen autos. At Toyota the average number was fifteen. In 1970 the respective numbers were twelve and thirty-right; and in 1980 the respective numbers were fifteen and fifty-eight. A significant part of the static productivity of U.S. workers during the 1960s and 1970s was inflexible work rules that labor unions forced into contracts. Management accepted counter-productive work rules because higher costs could be passed on to consumers as long as there was no foreign competition.

In 1970 Japanese auto production surpassed U.S. auto production. This was a wake-up call for managers of the U.S. automotive industry. In 1976 imported autos supplied 20 percent of the U.S. market and by 1980 they supplied about 30 percent. Most imports came from Japan. The wake-up call became a scream for help after Chrysler lost 1 billion dollars in 1979 and 1.7 billion dollars in 1980. In 1980 Ford lost 1.5 billion dollars and General Motors 760 million.

Chrysler was saved from bankruptcy by a loan guaranteed by the U.S. government. During 1979 and 1980, Chrysler reduced it labor force by half, closed one-third of its factories, negotiated wage concessions from the union and price concessions from component suppliers. Ford and General Motors closed similar numbers of factories, reduced similar numbers of employees, and negotiated wage concession in order to return to profitability.

Managers of U.S. automotive corporations, with strong support from labor unions, claimed that recovery from the losses of 1979, 1980, and 1981 required protection in the form of restrictions on imports. The national government was receptive, as it had been receptive to the trigger mechanism on steel in 1978. In 1981 the U.S. government negotiated a voluntary export restraint agreement (VER) with Japan. The Japanese government used its influence to induce Japanese automakers to reduce exports of fuel efficient autos to the United States.

Export restrictions were put in the form of a VER in order to circumvent the rules of the General Agreement on Tariffs and Trade (GATT). Japanese manufacturers agreed to limit exports to 1.68 million vehicles or about 16.5 percent of the U.S. market instead of the two million autos it sold in the United States in 1980. Quotas gradually increased to 2.3 million in 1985 when the VER expired. Thereafter, Japanese automakers restricted imports to this number while they built assembly factories in the United States.

The auto VER had four consequences. Three were predictable and the fourth was not:

1. It was predictable that U.S. auto manufacturers would increase prices because of reduced competition, which they did.
2. The price of imported autos also increased and Japanese automakers used increased profits to build assembly factories in the United States in order to escape the export quotas of the VER.
3. It was also predictable that U.S. automotive corporations would seek joint ventures with Japanese automakers so that U.S. managers could acquire superior Japanese management skills. By 1990 eight Japanese automakers had assembly lines in the United States and Canada that had the capacity to annually produce two million autos. After the formation of the European Union in 1992, Japanese automakers expanded the number of their assembly lines in Europe. In both the United States and European Union, Japanese parts manufacturers also made investments in order to supply the assembly lines of Japanese automakers.
4. The unforeseen consequence of the VER was that Japanese manufacturers moved upscale where there were no restraints on exports. They designed mid-sized and luxury models to compete with the core production of U.S. automakers. Within a decade U.S. automakers had competition from Japanese automakers in the entire range of models they produced.

The VER agreement of 1981 allowed U.S. manufacturers time to make changes in engineering technologies, production procedures, and labor relations necessary to reduce costs, but the return of U.S. automakers to profitability in 1983 was not competitive profitability. It was subsidized profitability that depended on substantially less competition from imported autos.

The subsidized profits of U.S. automakers after 1983 allowed the managers of U.S. automobile corporations to duplicate the strategy of the managers of U.S. steel mills. They pursued a policy of diversification. In 1984 General Motors acquired Electronic Data Systems for 2.5 billion dollars; a year later (1985) Ford acquired Hughes Aircraft for 5 billion dollars, and

Chrysler acquired Gulfstream Aerospace for 636 million dollars and Electrospace Systems for 367 million. Ford and Chrysler also acquired financial corporations.

Policies of diversification for auto manufacturers seemed to assume that subsidized profits from VERs were a permanent part of U.S. trade policy. They were not. They quietly expired because, by 1990, Japanese automakers in the United States assembled and sold in excess of 1.5 million autos and had the capacity to build 2.7 million. During the 1990s, annual imports from Japan declined to an average about 800,000 autos per year.

Autos manufactured by Japanese companies in the United States forced U.S. automakers into real price competition because of the superior performance of autos assembled by Japanese companies in the United States. On a smaller scale, in 1991 Japanese automakers supplied 11 percent of the European market (26 percent in nations without VERs), and also forced European automakers to become price competitive.

In 1988 General Motors Corporation president Roger Smith placed the blame for the reduced market share of GM on his predecessors. "The main reason for Japanese efficiency is not to be found in exchange rates, differential tax burdens, or other external factors....but management of both people and work processes." From 1950 to the mid-1970s the U.S. auto industry was in technical hibernation. The oligopoly of U.S. manufacturers neglected innovations because U.S. auto producers had settled on a strategy of mass producing autos with a frozen design. Designs were not as frozen as Henry Ford's Model T in the 1920s but, nonetheless, they seriously lagged in incorporating improved technologies.[11]

During the 1980s, U.S. automakers made substantial improvements in productivity but most assembly operations were less efficient than Japanese assembly lines. In 1990 an average of twenty-five man hours were required by most U.S. automakers to assemble one auto, but Japanese automakers in the United States required only twenty-one man hours, a 15 percent advantage. There were, however, several assembly lines of U.S. automakers that duplicated man hours per auto of Japanese automakers. U.S. automakers avoided some of the competitive pressures to reduce prices because of the successes of minivans and sports-utility vehicles (SUV). By 1999, SUVs had 19 percent of the U.S. market and minimal competition from Japanese and European automakers.

The best evidence for the faltering performance of U.S. automakers was the buyout of Chrysler by Daimler-Benz in 1998. As John E. Kwoka observed, "Daimler's acquisition of Chrysler was part of a broader trend toward alliances and acquisitions among international auto companies. Daimler also proceeded to acquire Mitsubishi, the fourth largest Japanese car company in 2000....Other prominent arrangements include GM's equity purchase in Fiat and Daewoo, and its acquisition of Saab; and Ford's purchase of Volvo and Renault's takeover of Nissan."[12] These alliances and acquisitions are attempts by surviving automaker to increase market shares in the global market that managers perceive as necessary for survival.

There is also a new entry in the global market. In 1986 Korean made autos entered the United States. In 1995 imports were one hundred thousand vehicles that increased to three hundred thousand in 2001. Korean made autos had 3 percent of the U.S. market. Hyundai alone had 1.9 percent, which was more than Mercury, Saturn, Mitsubishi, and Mazda.

In 2005 the assembly lines of all corporations manufacturing automobiles in the United States use components that are manufactured in several nations. Autos with American and Japanese names have an increasing content of components that are international in origin. It is difficult to tell where the steel came from, where components were manufactured, and where the autos will be sold.

In addition, on the immediate horizon, there is a new dimension to global competition. It is probable that in fifteen years, hybrid autos with batteries charged by internal combustion engines will dominate urban markets because they get 18 to 25 kilometers per liter (45 to 60 miles per gallon). In 2005 hybrid autos were about 25 percent more expensive than autos with conventional engines but there are customer waiting to purchase them. The race is on to see which automaker can produce them at competitive prices.

Winners in Global Competition

Computers

The first generation of electronic computers was built for specific purposes during the 1940s. Most were purchased by the national government for use by the census bureau, weather bureau, ordinance bureau, and military uses. They were hand wired and were programmed to perform specific functions for which they were designed. Government funding, especially for military uses, was essential for development. The earliest computers were ponderous machines that used vacuum tubes. Vacuum tubes are inefficient in switching electric circuits because they have short operating lives and use large amounts of electricity.

International Business Machines (IBM) immediately recognized that electronic computing could be used to enhance the efficiency of its main products: punch card tabulating and data processing machines. It immediately began intensive research to computerize them. It delivered its first electronic computer in 1953. Vacuum tubes were used in its circuitry. The first models evolved into mainframe computers that were designed to perform specific functions for the military, science, and business. Military uses (space program, ballistic missiles, designing nuclear powered submarines and supersonic aircraft) accounted for a high percentage of the market for mainframe computers. By 1956 IBM derived 75 percent of its revenue from manufacturing mainframe computers for sale in the national market that totaled 269 million dollars.

IBM dominated the electronic computer business because it developed a wide range of peripheral equipment to apply to many problems; and IBM's management emphasized customer service. IBM's management recognized that optimal business usage of computers required salesmen to teach potential customers how to use them and then be available for consultation. IBM did everything possible to make computers user friendly.

The second generation of computers replaced vacuum tubes with transistors. Transistors are on-off switches (digital) made of crystals of elements that have dielectric properties. Crystals of dielectric elements can conduct electric currents or resist electric currents if one current at one voltage is used to regulate the flow of another current with a different voltage. AT&T funded research in transistors in order to find a replacement for vacuum tubes.

Transistors can operate at very high speeds and use minimal electrical power. They were invented in 1947 in Bell Telephone laboratories. The first transistor was made from germanium but germanium is a scarce and expensive element and loses its dielectric properties at elevated temperatures. The invention of the silicon transistor in 1954 had two huge advantages over germanium transistors. They operate at higher temperatures and silicon is a cheap and readily available element.

The patent for transistors conferred a licensing monopoly on AT&T. In order to forestall anti-trust litigation for charging high royalties that would restrict replacement of vacuum tubes in radios and television receivers, the management of AT&T licensed all applicants for twenty-five thousand dollars. The license was free from future royalty payments. Licensing without paying royalties ensured that many companies would search for better ways to manufacture transistors and expand their usage. AT&T telecommunication technology would benefit from research done by other companies. As soon as the technology was developed to mass produce silicon transistors, they replaced vacuum tubes in telephone switching and computer circuitry.

The invention of integrated circuits in 1958 vastly lowered the price of silicon transistors as soon as engineering problems of mass production were perfected. The engineering break-through occurred in 1962 when integrated circuits could be etched on silicon transistors. Silicon transistors were first used in computers in 1963. The value of installed computers increased from 1 billion dollars in 1959 to 6 billion dollars in 1965. IBM retained market dominance of mainframe computers with about 65 percent of sales in 1965. Using its dominant position in the U.S. market, it vigorously expanded into the global market. By 1969, 35 percent of its revenue came from international sales.

During the 1960s, the computer industry divided into four streams:

1. Super computers designed to process numbers at the highest speed. Their principal uses were military, science, and government.
2. Mainframe computers for managing large amounts of business information. They became essential for making airline reservations, distributing seats on individual flights, and scheduling flights. They were equally essential for making payrolls, billing, and inventory control. Most corporations rented time on mainframe computers to do these tasks.
3. Fast input-output computers to perform only one function in the daily conduct of business (calculators and cash registers).
4. Minicomputers that used low performance components with little or no peripheral equip-ment in order to operate one machine. During the 1960s, the rapidly increasing use of minicomputers to operate machinery and conduct day-to-day business transactions was the opportunity for many corporations to enter the computer business.

The third generation of computer technology began after 1965 with the replacement of expensive germanium transistors with integrated circuits etched on silicon chips and wafers. Modern computers could not exist without integrated circuits. Integrated circuits were invented in the laboratories of Texas Instruments and Fairchild Semiconductor in 1958. They were im-mediately installed in computers for military use because of their light weight, reliability, and durability.

In 1961 IBM produced seven different mainframe computers. All had separate architec-tures that did not interface with each other. It was absolutely essential to make operations of all IBM mainframe computers compatible in order to allow jobs to be seamlessly transferred from one computer to another. Compatibility was achieved by writing software programs. IBM's software programs set an industry standard for communications between computers with dif-ferent architectures because in 1970 IBM had 70 percent of the global market for mainframes. Compatibility achieved economies of scale in designing computers for business applications.

The fourth generation of computers began with the invention of memory chips in 1970 and microprocessor chips in 1971, plus the availability of off-the-shelf integrated circuits. Several U.S. manufacturers became suppliers of standardized integrated circuits for sale to any manufacturer of minicomputers designed to operate machinery, or for installation in consumer electronic products (television receivers, calculators, cash registers, and printers).

The first integrated circuit contained two transistors on a silicon microchip about 1.5 square centimeters in area. Each subsequent year the number of transistors that could be etched on silicon microchips increased by magnitudes. In 1965 about 1,000 transistors could be etched on a microchip that was 100 square millimeters in area. By 1989 1 million transistors could be etched on a microchip about 7 square centimeters in area. In 1993 3.1 million could be etched on larger silicon wafer; in 1997 7.5 million; and in 1999 9.5 million.

In 1975 U.S. manufacturers of transistor devices had 98 percent of the U.S. market, 78 percent of the European market, but only 20 percent of the Japanese market. This situation could not last. The technology of designing and manufacturing all varieties of transistor devices was technology that many industrial nations wanted within their borders. At the same time, it was in the interest of U.S. manufacturers to preserve their lead in research in order to reduce global competition for as long as possible.

Minicomputers

The development of minicomputers using off-the-shelf integrated circuits and silicon chips was the opportunity for many companies to enter the low priced end of the computer industry. Off-the-shelf components greatly reduced capital costs for entering the computer business. Digital Equipment Corporation marketed the first minicomputer in 1965. "It was a high-speed computer, built for real-time, integrative operations, designed to be used on a dedicated basis, and its modularity permitted it to be easily interfaced with other equipment." In other words, it could control the operations of a large variety of machines if it had programs to guide it. Software programs had to be written for each dedicated use. IBM did not compete in this market.[13]

Entry into the minicomputer business focused on developing new applications. Manufacturers of minicomputers did little basic research. They left that to universities and manufacturers of transistors. There were many entries into minicomputer manufacturing during the 1970s, each seeking a competitive advantage in a fragmented market where manufacturers did not, for the most part, compete with each other in a company's niche market. A principal function of minicomputer manufacturers was to write programs that gave their computers a competitive advantage in the niche they sought to fill. Programs often cost more than computer hardware, and writing programs rapidly became a specialized business.

Research and engineering technology to produce transistors and integrated circuits are hugely expensive. Companies making integrated circuits have research costs that are 10 percent of revenues; and the cost of machines that etch integrated circuits onto silicon chips and wafers are an additional 30 percent of revenues. There was, however, a huge market for integrated circuits because they were small, could be used to program many tasks, used minimal amount of electricity, and could be mass produced.

Two locations had concentrations of businesses engaged in research to increase the speed of transistor devices and fabricate them into increasingly complex circuits. Both locations were near or adjacent to universities that had world class physics departments. The universities were Massachusetts Institute of Technology (MIT) and Harvard in metropolitan Boston, and Stanford University south of San Francisco, California. The industrial parks around Stanford soon outnumbered the industrial parks in the Boston area. The concentration of research and development companies near Stanford University became known as Silicon Valley. Between 1960 and 1975, Silicon Valley became an intense science-technology-business environment that was extremely successful in exchanging information (and personnel) needed to develop new technologies and rapidly bring them into commercial production.

The rapid evolution of computer design and production technology reduced the importance of patents and copyrights. Research had two principal focuses: (1) produce obsolescence as quickly as possible, and (2) improve production technology in order to reduce wastage in the exacting process of manufacturing integrated circuits. Lawsuits over patent and copyright infringements were usually counterproductive because manufacturers and programmers could always show that their product had sufficient innovations that differentiated it from patented devices or copyrighted programs. Continuing profits in manufacturing integrated circuits and writing software programs depended on proprietary skills developed by continuous research, not legal protection.

After 1980 mainframe computers were a rapidly declining percentage of domestic sales because large numbers of minicomputers could be linked to perform many of the functions of mainframe computers. Arrays of minicomputers operated much of the telecommunication revolution that replaced copper wires with fiber optics; and that further evolved into cell phone networks with each cell phone containing an integrated circuit. "The 1980s marked the passage from an era of large, centralized computer installations to a world in which vast numbers of more inexpensive machines, distributed widely among users" were linked into networks that were more flexible and cheaper to operate than mainframe computers.[14]

Personal Computers

From the beginning, U.S. manufacturers have dominated the global market for personal computers. The first personal computer was produced at the end of 1974, but a mass market did not begin until after 1978 with the introduction of the Apple II. Apple II was contemporaneous with the introduction of spread sheets for business uses and desk top printers. Thereafter, the manufacture of personal computers was a highly competitive business. The appeal of personal computers is the number and variety of data processing functions they can perform after software programs are downloaded into memory chips. In 1981 sales were approximately 2 billion dollars, which increased to 31 billion dollars in 1987, and 60 billion dollars in 1990.

Foremost among competitors was IBM. It entered the personal computer business in 1981. Its computer was cheap and its architecture was reliable, but it was rushed into production. IBM "bought almost all the hardware and software components from others, assembled a product, and put the IBM name on it. Because the product embodied virtually no proprietary hardware or software, the architecture was fully open."

This was a clearly thought out strategy. IBM's management anticipated "a dramatic explosion in the demand for personal computers" that would make IBM architecture "the internationally accepted standard for all desk top computing." It used integrated circuits and memory chips manufactured by Intel and a software program written by Microsoft (that became Windows in 1984). "In this way, Intel and Microsoft received what became the most lucrative franchise in the history of American business." The sale of personal computers increased from 344,000 in 1981 to 3.2 million in 1985. Both Intel and Microsoft used the success of IBM's personal computer (and its clones) to become global leaders in manufacturing transistor devices and writing software programs for personal computers.[15]

The reliable architecture of IBM computers was an invitation for other corporations to build clones. They appeared within a year of IBM's initial marketing and rapidly displaced IBM from leadership in the personal computer market. Competition was intense with about 200 companies making clones. Profit margins were squeezed. The survivors (Dell, Compaq, Gateway, and several Japanese companies) had managements that made the decision to concentrate on reducing production costs and advertise in order to sell to a mass market. Personal computers were marketed as another consumer electronic product.

By 1986 IBM's market share of personal computers had declined to 25 percent, and by 1993 it was 12 percent. Apple Computer (Macintosh after 1984) experienced similar competitive pressure. Its market share shrank to about 9 percent. The real winners in the personal computer market were manufacturers of integrated circuits and memory chips and creators of software programs, especially Windows. The Windows operating system allowed users to accept new programs if they were compatible. It did not matter who wrote the programs. Windows is an open system in contrast to Apple, a closed system. Apple retains full control of it's architecture and software and this discourages third parties from writing programs to increase the number of functions its computers can perform.

In 1993 IBM lost 8 billion dollars because its mainframe business continued to shrink.

New management saved it from further losses by shifting research emphasis to network systems but retaining an emphasis on integrated solutions for its business customers. As early as 1985, Apple was in serious financial difficulties. Its profits were only 45 million dollars on sales of 1.9 billion dollars. Its financial health was precarious and by 1995 it was hemorrhaging money. In 1997 Microsoft invested 150 million dollars in Apple to ensure its survival. In return for Microsoft's investment, Apple ended protracted litigation over copyright infringement that a federal judge had already ruled was not an infringement.

IBM personal computers and its clones that used Windows could perform an increasing number of word processing functions as well as receiving and transmitting graphics. Microsoft's revenues were 16 million dollars in 1981 when its operating system was first used in IBM personal computers. In 1985 revenues were 140 million dollars; 1.1 billion dollars in 1990 (with versions in thirteen languages that provided over 50% of Microsoft's revenues); 2.7 billion in 1992; 5.9 billion in 1995, 22.9 billion in 2000, and 36.8 billion dollars in 2004. Independent programmers began writing software that was compatible with Windows and this trend accelerated after the 1992 update, and further accelerated with future updates. Microsoft Windows, however, had captured the global software market for personal computers.

Intel is a similar story. Revenues doubled from 2 billion dollars in 1987 to 4 billion in 1990 and profits increased from 248 million dollars to 650 million. In 1990 Intel produced over 70 percent of the microprocessors used in personal computers, laptops, and other personal products. In 1991 IBM organized a consortium to develop a proprietary microprocessor. Intel's marketing of the Pentium processor in 1993, that was compatible with Windows and other operating systems eclipsed IBM sponsored competition. In 1994 Intel had 74 percent of the global market for microprocessors and IBM's microprocessor had 12 percent, which was about its share of the U.S. market for personal computers.

IBM's investment in developing a microprocessor for its personal computers was not a failure. Neither was it a success. IBM abandoned its policy of close working relations with Intel—to its disadvantage. Intel continued to consult manufacturers of IBM clones and produce clearly superior microprocessors.

Internet

The Internet came into being in 1969 when the National Science Foundation linked computers in U.S. research laboratories into a network where stored information could be retrieved and routed to other computers through a central supercomputer. The Internet was a means of instantaneous communication between computers used by scientists doing research in government laboratories and on government funded projects at major universities, as well as for engineers designing military hardware. The Internet became international in 1972 and shortly afterwards was opened to nongovernment users. By 1988 there were approximately six million users but access to the internet was fragmented among several providers that were not interlinked.

In 1990 an American physicist working at CERN (European Particle Physics Laboratory) wrote a program that made it possible for owners of personal computers to access the Internet. The popularity of personal computers was further increased in 1993 by a software program that could transmit pictures. Popularity was further increased in 1994 when Netscape invented a browser that provided easy access to all Internet Web sites. The browser was almost instantly linked to search engines (Google, Lexus, Ask Jeeves) that could locate all Web sites. Popularity of personal computers was further increased in 1995 when Sun Microsystems released a software program (Java) that could access the principal operating systems (Windows, Apple, and Unix). The demand for personal computers exploded.

Several U.S. telecommunication companies recognized the commercial possibilities of the internet because it was a way for wholesalers and retailers to come into direct contact with customers. Among them were Sprint, MCI, CompuServe, Prodigy, and AOL. They began to actively sell access services that used the Netscape browser. In one year Netscape went from a startup company to a company with 2.9 billion dollars in revenue. Microsoft was astonished by the near instantaneous growth of the internet. There was no internet browser in Windows and Windows did not offer a browser (Internet Explorer) until 1996. In order to be competitive with an inferior product (compared to Netscape), Internet Explorer was made a free feature of Windows. Thereafter it was improved until it became competitive with Netscape and other browsers. In 1998 Netscape also became free, and in 2000 Netscape merged with AOL in an exchange of stock worth 4.3 billion dollars.

Overnight, the Internet became the World Wide Web (www) because it could send and receive messages and transmit pictures between computers anywhere in the world that had access to electric power, or to any computer that had sufficiently powerful batteries to receive and transmit signals relayed from satellites. The incomparably large amount of free commercial information that is instantly available on the internet created an information superhighway of global proportions that has accelerated the integration of the global market and greatly contributed to the efficiency of consumer cultures.

Global Competition

Beginning about 1960, European nations and Japan realized the impact that computers would have in business, science, and government. They had to engage in catch-up technology if they were to have substantial computer industries. They made strenuous efforts but European researchers were only marginally successful. In 1974 there were 165,000 mainframe computers in use in the United States; and Europe and Japan together had 75,000. About 80 percent of the installed computers in Europe were U.S. made, as were 45 percent in Japan.

Japanese researchers were much more successful in developing advanced computer technology because they seized an opportunity offered to them in 1971. The chief designer for IBM's newest mainframe computer resigned in 1970 to go into business for himself. He was convinced that he could produce a clone mainframe at much lower cost. He failed to raise the requisite capital in the United States so he approached Fujitsu, a major Japanese computer manufacturer that was having great difficulty building clones of older IBM mainframes. Fujitsu acquired the needed technology and was adequately funded by Japan's Ministry of International Trade and Industry (MITI). By 1976 Fujitsu had developed a low end mainframe computer that was competitive on the global market with equivalent IBM computers.

By 1980 other Japanese computer manufacturers were also producing mainframe clones using technology developed with research funds supplied by MITI. European attempts at catch-up technology collapsed between 1975 and 1982. Thereafter, only the United States and Japan had a sufficiently large knowledge base to continue research in advanced computer architecture. Nevertheless, corporations headquartered in common market nations acquired the desired technology to produce mainframe computers because U.S. and Japanese corporations licensed technology and made direct foreign investments.[16]

In addition, many U.S. makers of integrated circuits were purchased by European manufacturers of electronic equipment. These corporations wanted in-house suppliers of integrated circuits and research staffs dedicated to improving the performance of the products they manufactured. IBM purchased a controlling interest in one transistor/integrated circuit manufacturer. Philips from the Netherlands, Siemens from Germany, and Schlumberger from France did the same.

Between 1969 and 1974, U.S. corporations established eighteen wholly owned factories in Europe and twenty-eight joint ventures. Like Japanese automakers who maintained their share of the U.S. market by making direct investments in factories in the United States, U.S. computer makers did the same in common market nations. Only after 1980 did European transistors and integrated circuit manufacturers begin to supply some of the needs of European manufacturers; and this was mainly done by internationalizing the costs of research and production.

The Japanese market was entirely different. "The Japanese strategy was avowedly one of import substitution through the creation and promotion of indigenous suppliers." Government funding for transistor research was available because MITI accurately assessed future uses of integrated circuits of standard design. Usage would rapidly increase because there was a rapidly increasing global market for consumer electronic products. MITI used two strategies of catch-up technology: (1) It negotiated licensing agreements for U.S. patents and then allocated usage among Japanese manufacturers of semiconductors and integrated circuits; (2) In return for funding research and development, MITI insisted that Japanese manufacturers allocate projects among themselves and share the results of their research.[17]

From 1960 onward, these two strategies were strongly supported by a policy of protecting infant manufacturers of transistors from competition from the United States; preventing direct foreign investment by U.S. corporations; and preventing joint ventures where majority control was owned by U.S. corporations. "The government…used all of the weapons at its disposal to force foreign firms to transfer their technology to Japanese partners on the best possible terms for the latter."[18]

During the 1960s, government policies, acting through MITI and Nippon Telegraph and Telephone, effectively limited the U.S. share of the Japanese transistor market to 20 percent. The 20 percent was concentrated in the most advanced silicon chips while Japanese manufacturers concentrated on how to produce standardized integrated circuits for consumer electronics (radios, television, tape recorders, audio equipment, and calculators).

Results were impressive. By 1967 Japanese production of transistors surpassed U.S. production. In 1968 consumer electronic products used 60 percent of the semiconductors made by Japanese companies. In the 1970s MITI shifted its focus to funding the development of memory chips, integrated circuits, and other semiconductor devices used in computers. By 1975 the performances of Japanese integrated circuits of standard design (off-the-shelf products) were comparable with similar integrated circuits manufactured in the United States.

By 1976 the Japanese government had eliminated most tariff barriers but protection persisted. Protection was transferred to non-tariff barriers:

1. Vertical integration (keiretsu) of Japanese companies was maintained by cross-shareholding that prevented foreign companies from purchasing or acquiring majority control of Japanese companies in order to gain entry to the Japanese market.
2. Cross-shareholding was a source of research funds to develop new products for the domestic and export markets.
3. The national government continued the policy of rejecting direct foreign investments by U.S. corporations in computer related technologies.
4. The domestic market was protected from export competition by certification of new products based on design, not performance; and when design specifications were attained, certification was frequently delayed by bureaucratic resistance.
5. Government purchases were always from Japanese companies without public bidding, like purchases by the U.S. government of mainframe and supercomputers. Like the U.S. government, the Japanese government paid high prices for mainframe and supercomputers manufactured in Japan in order to subsidize continuing research.

In the United States a high percentage of subsidized research was military related. Subsidized research in Japan was based on an accurate assessment of increasing uses of computers to operate machinery, consumer electronics, and personal computers. By 1980 production of integrated circuits, memory chips, and other transistor devices reached parity in quality with U.S. manufacturers; although, Japanese researchers had not yet succeeded in matching the technology of wafer design and system architecture needed to enhance computer performance.

By the mid-1980s Japanese exports of integrated circuits and other transistor devices were seriously undercutting prices of similar devices manufactured in the United States. A large part of the ability of Japanese manufacturers to undersell U.S. producers was due to a shift in MITI sponsored research in the late 1970s. Research focused on improving the technology of etching integrated circuits onto silicon chips and wafers.

Japanese manufacturers of transistor devices maximized automation in the fabrication of large wafers, with fabrication taking place in ultra-clean rooms using ultra-pure silicon. Manufacturing was concentrated in large factories where continual monitoring of quality control, similar to quality control practiced by Japanese automakers, significantly improved the percentage of chips and wafers that passed final testing. Furthermore, Japanese manufacturers of integrated circuits worked closely with manufacturers of products that used transistors to control the operation of machines they made. In contrast, U.S. manufacturers of transistor devices seldom had enduring relations with manufacturers of integrated circuits.

Again, results were impressive. On average, 68 percent of silicon wafers produced by Japanese manufacturers were without flaws compared to 25 percent produced by U.S. manufacturers. The difference in production costs was dramatic. On average, wafers made by U.S. manufacturers cost $11.83. Japanese made wafers cost $3.31. Between 1985 and 1990 the U.S. share of open market sales of transistors in the global market declined from 58 percent to 37 percent. During these same years, the Japanese share of global sales increased from 26 percent to 49 percent.

U.S. manufacturers of integrated circuits accused Japanese manufacturers of engaging in destructive competition (dumping) to gain market share in the United States. This was a half truth at best. There was a major slump in the market for transistor devices in 1974–1975. U.S. manufacturers reduced capital investments from 410 million dollars in 1974 to 194 million dollars in 1975. Japanese manufacturers did not reduce capital investments and when demand surged in 1978 there was a serious shortage of U.S. production capacity that was filled by Japanese manufacturers. By 1980 Japanese manufacturers supplied 40 percent of the U.S. market and retained it because of low manufacturing costs. Advanced Micro Devices, Intel, Mostek, Motorola, and National Semiconductor withdrew from manufacturing off-the-shelf integrated circuits.

In 1986 trade talks began on a monthly basis between the U.S. Department of Commerce and MITI. The purpose was to speed agreement on a Semiconductor Trade Agreement (STA) that would stabilize market shares and profits. In order to speed negotiations, the U.S. government levied tariffs on specific Japanese manufacturers of integrated circuits and memory chips: Hitachi 11.9 percent, Mitsubishi 13.4 percent, NEC 22.8 percent, and Oki 35.3 percent. This was allowed under a provision in the GATT if an investigation indicated dumping. The STA was signed in September 1986.

The STA was for five years and had four parts:

1. Tariffs on Japanese imports would be rescinded when a system was in place to estimate manufacturing costs and monitor export prices of semiconductor devices sold in the United States and in sixteen other nations.
2. MITI would control prices and quantities of exports to other nations in order to prevent a gray market by transshipments from second nations to the United States.

3. European manufacturers of transistor devices also filed an antidumping complaint to prevent Japanese manufacturers from dumping in common market nations where manufacturing transistor devices for personal computers was still an infant industry. European manufacturers produced only 10 to 12 percent of global production of transistor devices.
4. Open the Japanese market for U.S. and European manufacturers of integrated circuits with a five year goal of 20 percent of the Japanese market being supplied by imports. Japanese manufacturers were very unhappy because they did not want the Japanese market opened to imports from the United States or elsewhere.[19]

After the STA became operational, Japanese manufacturers followed the same strategy as Japanese automakers in order to preserve their market share. They established factories in the United States. By 1994 there were sixteen factories. After establishing factories, eight Japanese transistor manufacturers negotiated joint ventures with U.S. research companies for sharing development and production costs. A convergence in business strategies followed. First, surviving U.S. manufacturers of off-the-shelf transistor devices adopted the Japanese practice of closely integrating research with the technology of production in order to improve yields and lower costs. Second, users of transistor devices developed closer relationships with research companies and suppliers of peripheral equipment, as was done by IBM.[20]

Two precedents were set by the STA: (1) The United States Department of Commerce would create the floor prices by advising Japanese manufacturers what prices to charge in order to avoid an investigation of dumping. (2) MITI would allocate percentages of exports to Japanese manufacturers. Thereafter, MITI used its full persuasive power (a command in all but name) to reduce 1987 production of transistor devices by 32 percent in order "to extricate themselves from the inclination toward excessive competition, as can be seen from the rivalry among ten companies in one market."[21]

Japanese manufacturers agreed that managed production was essential to prevent trade friction. They also understood that their best interests were served by adequate prices to sustain research; and that the best way to obtain adequate prices was a managed global market. In effect, the U.S. department of commerce and MITI became managing partners in a global cartel in the production of off-the-shelf integrated circuits, memory chips, and other transistor devices used in computers.

The U.S.-Japanese STA was an opportunity for Japanese and U.S. manufacturers to enjoy high prices during the rapidly growing market for personal computers during the second half of 1987. By the end of 1987 Japanese and U.S. manufacturers were operating at near capacity, and by mid-1988 prices in Europe and the United States for transistor devices were substantially above floor prices set by the U.S.-Japanese STA.

Neither Japanese nor U.S. manufacturers increased investments to fully satisfy the demand because they would have too much excess capacity if the optimistic market projected for personal computers failed to materialize. "Investment patterns in semiconductors have been lumpy, producing chronic booms and busts, with excess capacity emerging approximately every five years." Overcapacity was a serious problem because the design of transistor devices was undergoing rapid evolution.[22]

A further variable in global pricing was the entry of Samsung (of Korea) into the transistor market in 1989, a time when the market for personal computers reached a plateau. Samsung was determined to become a major supplier in the global transistor market, and by 1991 it was the leading producer of off-the-shelf chips of low capacity. Chips made by Samsung and other Korean chipmakers gained market share by lower prices. The principal market for Korean transistor devices were markets where Japanese products dominated; although, some entered the Japanese market. The entry of Samsung transistor devices into the global market had the potential for creating another cycle of unstable prices.

Japanese manufacturers did not slash prices. Instead, they reduced production of low capacity transistor devices and increased production of the next generation of higher capacity wafers that measurably increased the speed and memory capacity of personal computers. In 1991 both domestic consumption and exports of transistor devices were less than projections. Japanese manufacturers conceded market shares to Korean manufacturers of low capacity clips, and when the 1986 STA between the United States and Japan expired, it was renewed without controversy as was a similar version for the common market.

Both the United States and common market countries then filed a dumping complaint against Korean manufacturers. Investigation in the United States did not prove dumping; however, investigation in the common market did, and a 10 percent tariff was levied on transistor devices. Both disputes were resolved in 1993 when Korean manufacturers agreed to follow the same rules followed by Japanese manufacturers for transistor devices that entered the United States and the European Union. In effect, Korean manufacturers joined the cartel that managed the global market for transistor devices used in computers.[23]

Senior Partners

The increased number of multinational corporations makes it impossible to write national economic histories after 1960. This is true for the United States as well as for the European Union. This final section is an attempt to put the political economy that governs the conduct of the principal industrial nations into the context of the global market as it operates in 2005. Examined from a different perspective, the economic history of the United States since 1960 can only be understood in a global context.

The global market requires that central governments of industrial nations perform two essential functions: (1) promote and protect comparative advantages of national industries, and (2) reduce frictions in the operation of the global market. Central governments can be highly visible in defining commercial priorities, as in Japan, France, and Germany, or they can respond to imbalances in international trade when they occur. This is the usual U.S. policy. Both cases, however, require that central governments be the senior partner in corporate governance if a nation's businesses are to be competitive in the global market. The senior partner may be silent, as is usual in the United States, or provide active guidance as is the case of Japan. In both instances, however, the central government is the senior partner.

The best example is Japan. The success of Japan's Ministry of International Trade and Industry is the measure for similar policies in other nations trying to accelerate production and increase trade within the rules of WTO. MITI promoted comparative advantages in four Japanese industries where none previously existed: steel, automobiles, consumer electronics, and transistor devices for computers. Japanese advantages in global commerce after World War II were policy induced and fairly won.

Competitive prices for these four products did not depend on cheap labor or cheap raw materials. Competitive production was achieved by a strategic policy managed by the national government that perceived opportunities in the global market that came into focus in the 1960s. Competitive production in these export industries was fueled by abundant credit, and much of the credit came from the central government or from bank loans underwritten by the central government.

In 1950 the Japanese steel industry was small (5 million tons), technologically obsolescent, and in shambles. It had no domestic source of iron ore and only a small amount of poor quality coking coal. All ore and most coking coal had to be imported. This was not a significant barrier to expansion because raw materials were readily available on the global market. New steel mills were built at tidewater to facilitate imports of raw materials and the export of semi-finished shapes.

Initial production concentrated on heavy plates and beams used in shipbuilding, because there was a rapidly growing demand for tankers to carry crude oil from the Persian Gulf to global markets. At a later date, sheet steel would become a major product as the automobile industry increased its penetration of U.S. and other markets. By the late 1960s semi-finished steel shapes had captured the West Coast market of the United States, and thereafter entered the rest of the U.S. market. Between 1966 and 1972, Japanese steel production increased at an annual rate of 23 percent until it reached 100 million tons per year.

After the decision was made to build a new steel industry, production and marketing was done by the managers of steel corporations. There were, however, three situations where the central government continued to guide corporate decisions: (1) building additional capacity, (2) inducing managers to restrain exports when exports created political tensions, and (3) inducing managers of steel mills to share reductions in output during years of recession—in order to prevent destructive competition.

The postwar Japanese automobile industry also began from a small manufacturing base and deficient technical expertise. It used identical technologies that were available to U.S. and European automakers but with an invisible difference. The invisible difference was management. Japanese managers concentrated their energies on the manufacturing process. Just in time delivery of component parts receives undue credit for lowering costs. It was important, but of much greater importance was including workers in the process of manufacturing quality products. Managers of Japanese automakers had read W. Edwards Deming who had demonstrated that if workers are motivated to produce military equipment, as they were during WWII, they would actively help produce quality products. Workers were more than workers. They were part of a team that could produce measurable social benefits for society and themselves.

Seen from the perspective of Japanese business leaders in the steel and automobile industries, these two industries had limited markets in Japan. In the case of steel, the future was a replacement market after light rails of railroads were replaced with heavier rails, cities were rebuilt, and the needs of shipbuilders were satisfied. Likewise, the domestic market for automobiles and trucks would be a replacement market after domestic demands was satisfied. The limitations of a replacement market did not happen.

Policy makers in MITI clearly understood the opportunities of the global market. This was a secondary concern of U.S. industrial leaders and European political and industrial leaders. The U.S. market for steel and autos was large and unchallenged and European political and industrial leaders were immersed in integrating European nations into a common market. The policies of political economy defined by MITI and guided by the allocation of credit nullified the advantages of nations that were better endowed with raw materials and technical expertise.[24]

During the 1970s trade relations between the United States, the common market, and Japan were evolving in tandem. Clearly defined national markets were disappearing because multinational corporations were rapidly increasing in number. At the same time, Japanese capacity to export an increasing variety of products at competitive prices made Japan an equal participant in the management of the global market. Management of the global market was increasingly assigned to GATT (that became the World Trade Organization after 1995). During the 1970s, the global market came into being because the volume and value of trade in industrial products and related services increased at a rate that exceeded the best expectations of the architects of the institutions that govern the global market.

At the same time, competition in the global market created huge stresses in the economies of all of the principal industrial nations. These stresses were absorbed in three ways: (1) encouraging the creation of multinational corporations that made direct foreign investment, (2) negotiating restraints on imports for specific products for limited numbers of years, and (3) ending the manufacture of some products because there was little hope they could ever be produced at competitive prices. All industrial nations adopted these policies. The first two were adopted when it was politically expedient to prevent too many corporate bankruptcies at one time, or to downsize an industry by stages. The third policy was unavoidable and caused unavoidable stress.

In 1953 Congress prompted President Dwight D. Eisenhower to formulate a comprehensive trade policy to conduct multilateral negotiations to reduce tariffs. Congress and the president agreed that such a policy could not be effectively administered by the state department because it was fully engaged in cold war diplomacy. Nor could it be done by the commerce department because it focused on domestic commercial problems. A trade commission was established by Congress and its chairman joined Eisenhower's inner circle of advisors.

The enormous success of the common market in the 1960s forced President John F. Kennedy to seek increased authority to negotiate tariff reductions in order to make U.S.-manufactured products as competitive in the global market as comparable products manufactured in common market nations. Congress acted in 1962. By the early 1970s, however, the rapidly increasing volume of global commerce made it advisable for the president to actively seek elimination of nontariff trade barriers. The trade statute of 1934 (see previous chapter) did not apply to nontariff barriers like licensing, inspections, domestic subsidies, and import quotas. Congress established the office of special representative for trade negotiations in 1974 to deal with nontariff trade barriers. It was located in the office of the president.

Congress insisted that agreements negotiated by the special trade representative receive congressional approval for each agreement because many congressmen had businesses in their districts that would be affected—positively or negatively—by changes in trade policies. Securing congressional approval could lead to infinite delays and final approval would be problematic. Counterparts of the U.S. trade representative would reject serious negotiations when the results of their labor were in doubt. A compromise procedure was passed in 1979. The statute was drafted by the office of special trade representative working very closely with appropriate members of Congress. Agreements negotiated by the special trade representative were submitted to the president. If he accepted them he submitted them to Congress. Congress could not amend agreements and had sixty days to approve or reject them with a yes or no vote. If approved they became law.

The 1979 statute had three beneficial effects:

1. It greatly reduced the possibilities of Congress passing legislation to protect specific industries. This preserved the bargaining power of the special trade representative.
2. The deadline for accepting or rejecting agreements prevented delaying tactics.
3. A yes or no vote deflected pressure on congressmen from businesses in their districts that sought protection. Congressmen could claim that an agreement encouraged sales for other businesses in his district. The speed that non-tariff trade agreements got congressional approval (or disapproval), compared to other types of legislation, made this procedure fast track.

Normally, nontariff agreements were designed to reduce trade barriers but they could also be used to erect trade barriers—and they were. In the case of steel, automobiles, and transistor devices, the president instructed the special trade representative to negotiate voluntary restraints on exports (VERs) to allow time for these industries to adopt more efficient technologies and management practices that were essential for survival in the global market.[25]

An equivalent of MITI does not exist in the U.S. government; nonetheless, on some occasions in some industries, the national government provides active guidance. The best example is subsidies for the infant computer industry that were underwritten by military related contracts. In 2005 there are five strands to industrial guidance: (1) defense related projects, (2) opening foreign markets that are protected by nontariff barriers, (3) subsidizing research to speed commercial applications of new technologies, (4) preserving corporations that are too big to fail, and (5) subsidizing urban building construction.

1. Funding military related projects is done by the Defense Advanced Research Projects Agency. It hires private companies and university personnel to do research related to military needs.
2. Political pressure was required to induce the Japanese government to accede to opening their domestic market to imports from the United States. These agreements removed licensing procedures and other nontariff barriers that prevented products like transistor devices and auto parts, and services like banking, from entering the Japanese market. The office of special trade representative performs these negotiations.
3. Research grants by the national government are divided into experimental and commercial categories. Both government owned laboratories and universities are funded to do experimental and commercial research. Experimental research does not involve immediate application. For example, the National Science Foundation (NSF) funds projects to find new ways of understanding the mechanics of plate tectonics and the national institute of health funds the search for new instruments for medical diagnosis. Commercial research focuses on applications of known technologies. Three examples are searching for more high temperature superconductor alloys; experimenting with ways to fabricate existing superconductor alloys so they can be used to transmit and store electrical power; and applying molecules of carbon 60 to new uses (nanotechnology). The NSF and National Institute of Health (NIH) fund these projects.
4. There are several examples of rescuing large corporation by large infusions of tax money because they were too big to fail. This was not a new policy. Congress incorporated the Reconstruction Finance Corporation in 1932 in order to prevent the bankruptcy of banks, railroads, and other infrastructure corporations during the depths of the Great Depression. These corporations were the vertebrae of the industrial economy and without their continued operation the economy would self-destruct.

During the height of the cold war and the impact of increasing competition in the global market, several large corporations had to be rescued from bankruptcy. Lockheed Aircraft Company was rescued in 1971, mainly because it was a principal defense contractor. In 1976 truck competition on interstate highways magnified by excessive regulation, pushed the Penn Central Railroad into bankruptcy. It was the principal carrier in northeastern states. It was rescued by a large infusion of tax money. At the same time, five smaller railroads were merged to create a regional railroad system named Conrail. When Conrail returned to profitability it was sold to the investing public.

In 1979 Chrysler Motors had to be rescued with a huge infusion of money. In 1983 Continental Illinois Bank was saved from bankruptcy by being purchased by the Federal Deposit Insurance Corporation. The FDIC managed the bank for eight years and returned it to profitability and then sold it to the investing public.

5.   The Housing and Community Development Act passed by Congress in 1977 made grants to cities to subsidize new construction in order to restore commercial vitality to city centers. During the twelve years it operated (1977–1989), it expended 4.6 billion dollars, but these subsidies attracted more than 30 billion dollars of private investment. Two-thirds of the funds were used for commercial buildings. Combined with changes in the tax code in 1981, the subsidies were highly successful in promoting urban construction and renovating older buildings.

With the exception of funding military related projects, the guidance of the economy by the national government is spasmodic and reactive. Unlike MITI in Japan and similar government agencies in France and Germany, there is no central guidance for investment priorities for industries that increasingly participate in the global market. By default, multinational corporations are the principal U.S. agents for competing in the global market.

> They seek and select strategic alliances on the basis of their own interests instead of promoting certain foreign policy goals. Their interests dictate that they team up with those candidates who can pool internal know-how, human resources, and capital needed for carrying on radical innovation. They also seek partners which can share market risks, provide market access, and allow them to recover R&D costs. In their selection criteria, therefore, national identity and past historical animosities do not have any place.[26]

U.S. business leaders prefer arms-length relations with the national government (except during crises) because they fear excessive regulation, especially when jobs are transferred to nations with lower labor costs. In their experience, noncrisis guidance by the U.S. government is not always based on consultation and cooperation.

Five empirical observations guide policy making by the central governments of the principal industrial nations:

1.   There are few inherent comparative advantages in industrial production that cannot be overcome by nations that pursue coherent policies of political economy.
2.   Central governments of industrial nations must exercise continual vigilance to reduce or prevent non-tariff barriers in manufactured products or commercial services because all industrial nations have interest groups that continually seek advantages by other means than price or quality of their products.
3.   The principal industrial nations must manage trade in some products in order to reduce social stresses caused by radical changes in technology and dislocations caused by severe changes in terms of trade. Principal among advantages in terms of trade are lower labor costs.
4.   Managed trade is essential for promoting direct foreign investment, preventing destructive competition, and reducing political friction.
5.   The global market is a very competitive place for products manufactured by industrial nations.

The Immediate Future

What is the projection for the growth of the global market during the next ten years? Growth will be large and very rapid, but United States participation in it is not so easy to project; however, it is clear that the future of the U.S. economy is inseparably linked to the global market.

This assessment is based on the increasing participation of China and Russia in international trade, and the smaller participation of India. All three nations have national transportation infrastructures that operate with variable efficiency. All three nations have the capacity to generate large amounts of electric power and allocate it to commercial users with varying efficiency. All three nations have educational systems that train large numbers of technical personnel and employ them with varying efficiency. All three nations are learning, with varying efficiency, how to be effective competitors in the global market.

As of 2006 China is the most effective new participant in the global market because its large pool of cheap labor is being efficiently harnessed to light industry. To a very considerable degree, this has happened because businessmen in Hong Kong, Taiwan, Singapore, and expatriate Chinese businessmen from elsewhere already have the skills to compete in the global market. Their skills give them bargaining power with Chinese political authorities to establish manufacturing operation that confer highly visible mutual benefits.

Russia has an equal potential with China for developing into a major participant in the global market. It would be a supplier of raw materials and engineered equipment and machinery. Russia is on a rapidly ascending learning curve to navigate the intricacies of the global market.

India has two impediments for effective participation in the global market. Its food surplus is problematic in most crop years and this limits the number of people that can be transferred from the agricultural sector to the commercial sector, and its rural population is overwhelmingly illiterate. This is an enormous restraint on labor flexibility. Finally, physical labor has a low social value in the Hindu Caste System and this is an even greater restraint on production than a problematic food supply and illiteracy.

How will the increasing manufacturing capacities of these three nations and the new members of the European Union impact the ability of U.S. businessmen to compete in the global market? If the U.S. economy remains robust, there will probably be minimal impact at least until accelerated deficit spending further erodes the value of the dollar against the euro and other better managed currencies.

Offsetting this to a considerable extent is the rapidly growing middle classes in the three big nations and the new members of the European Union that are evolving consumer cultures. The middle classes of these nations will purchase the same array of durable consumer products that were purchased by the original consumer cultures in the United States and Western Europe. The U.S. and Western European economies will no longer be alone in sustaining consumer cultures. In this situation, the existing strength of the U.S. economy will continue to effectively compete in the global market, but the market will be considerably larger.

NOTES

Chapter 1

1. Seavoy, Ronald E. *Famine in Peasant Societies* (Westport, CT: Greenwood Press, 1986), 22 (quote).
2. Seavoy, Ronald E. *Famine in Peasant Societies*, 31–32.
3. Innes, Stephen ed. *Work and Labor in Early America* (Chapel Hill: University of North Carolina Press, 1988), 4–5.
4. Seavoy, Ronald E. *Famine in Peasant Societies* (Westport, CT: Greenwood Press, 1986), 104 (quote).
5. Seavoy, Ronald E. *Famine in Peasant Societies*, 105 (quote).
6. Seavoy, Ronald E. *Famine in Peasant Societies*, 104–105 (quote).
7. Seavoy, Ronald E. *Famine in Peasant Societies*, 105 (quote).
8. Hill, Christopher. "Pottage for Freeborn Englishmen: Attitudes to Wage-Labour," in *Change and Continuity in Seventeenth-Century England*, ed. Christopher Hill, (Cambridge, MA: Harvard University Press, 1975), 220, 221 (quotes).
9. Horn, James. "Servant Emigration to the Chesapeake in the Seventeenth Century," in *The Chesapeake in the Seventeenth Century*, eds. Thad W. Tate and David L. Ammerman, (New York: Norton, 1980), 81 (quote).
10. Kussmaul, Ann. *Servants in Husbandry in Early Modern England* (Cambridge, MA: Harvard University Press, 1981), 23 (quote).
11. Seavoy, Ronald E. *Famine in Peasant Societies* (Westport, CT: Greenwood Press, 1986), 107 (quote).
12. Seavoy, Ronald E., *Famine in Peasant Societies*, 75 (quote).
13. Seavoy, Ronald E. *Origins and Growth of the Global Economy: From the Fifteenth Century Onward* (Westport, CT: Praeger, 2003), 76 (quote).
14. Graham, Ian C. *Colonists from Scotland: Emigration to North America, 1707–1783* (Ithaca, NY: Cornell University Press, 1956), chapters 2, 3, 4; 46 (quote).

Chapter 2

1. Galenson, David W. *White Servitude in Colonial America* (Cambridge, MA: Harvard University Press, 1982), 5 (quote).
2. Morgan, Kenneth. *Slavery and Servitude in Colonial North America* (New York University Press, 2001), 45–46, 48, 52, 57–58.
3. Horn, James. "Servant Emigration to the Chesapeake in the Seventeenth Century," in *The Chesapeake in the Seventeenth Century*, eds. Thad W. Tate and David L. Ammerman, (New York: Norton, 1980), 56 (quote).
4. Craven, Wesley F. *Dissolution of the Virginia Company: The Failure of a Colonial Experiment* (Gloucester, MA: Peter Smith Publications, 1964), chapter 6. Edmund Morgan, "The Labor Problem in Jamestown" in Alan L. Karras, and John R. McNeill, eds. *Atlantic American Societies: From Columbus through Abolition, 1492–1888* (New York, Routledge, 1992)
5. Menard, Russell R. "British Migration to the Chesapeake Colonies in the Seventeenth Century," in *Colonial Chesapeake Society*, eds. Lois G. Carr, Philip D. Morgan, and Jean B. Russo, 103–105; 121 (Chapel Hill: University of North Carolina Press, 1991).
6. Menard, Russell R. "From Servant to Freeholder: Status Mobility and Property Accumulation in Seventeenth-Century Maryland," *William and Mary Quarterly*, 30 (1973) 37–64. Wertenbaker, Thomas J. *The Planters of Colonial Virginia* (New York: Russell and Russell, 1959), chapter 3.
7. Carr, Lois G. and Menard, Russell R. "Immigration and Opportunity: The Freedman in Early Colonial Maryland," in *The Chesapeake in the Seventeenth Century*, eds. Thad W. Tate and David L. Ammerman, eds. (New York: Norton, 1980), 221. Stiverson, Gregory A. *Poverty in a Land of Plenty* (Baltimore: The Johns Hopkins University Press, 1997) chapters 2, 5. Seavoy, Ronald E. *The American Peasantry: Southern Agricultural Labor and Its Legacy, 1850–1995* (Westport, CT: Greenwood Press, 1998), 241–242.

8. Seavoy, Ronald E. *The American Peasantry: Southern Agricultural Labor and Its Legacy, 1850–1995* (Westport, CT: Greenwood Press, 1998), 238 (quote).

9. Seavoy, Ronald E., *The American Peasantry*, 400–416.

10. Kelly, Kevin P., "In Dispersed Country Plantations: Settlement Patterns in Seventeenth Century Surry County, Virginia," in *The Chesapeake in the Seventeenth Century*, eds. Thad W. Tate and David L. Ammerman, (New York: W. W. Norton & Company, 1980), 197. Wycoff, Vetrees J. "Land Prices in Seventeenth-Century Maryland," *American Economic Review*, 28 (1938).

11. Menard, Russell R. "From Servant to Freeholder: Status, Mobility, and Land Accumulation in Seventeenth-Century Maryland," *William and Mary Quarterly* 30 (1973), 61.

12. Craven, Wesley F. *The Southern Colonies in the Seventeenth Century* (New York: Norton, 1980), 200 (quote).

13. McKinley, Albert E. *The Suffrage Franchise in the Thirteen Colonies in America* (Gin & Co., 1905), 62–65; 61 (quote).

14. Bishop, Cortlandt F. *History of Elections in the American Colonies* (New York: Columbia College, 1893), 71 (quote).

15. McKinley, Albert E. *The Suffrage Franchise in the Thirteen English Colonies* (Gin & Co., 1905), 34 (quote). Bishop, Cortlandt F. *History of Elections in the American Colonies* (New York: Columbia College, 1893), 70 (quote).

16. Bailyn, Bernard, "Politics and Social Structure in Virginia," in *Colonial America: Essays in Politics and Social Development*, ed. Stanley N. Katz, (New York: McGraw-Hill, 1992), 143 (quote).

17. Bacon, Nathaniel "Nathaniel Bacon's Victory over the Indian, April 1676," in *The Old Dominion in the Seventeenth Century*, ed., Warren M. Billings, (Chapel Hill: University of North Carolina Press, 1975), 267 (quote).

18. Seavoy, Ronald E. "Slave Plantations in the United States: How They were Managed," *Plantation Society in the Americas*, 4, 1997. Ransom, Roger L. and Sutch, Richard. *One Kind of Freedom* (Cambridge University Press, 2001), 151.

19. Davis, Ralph. "English Foreign Trade, 1700–1774," in *The Growth of English Overseas Trade in the Seventeenth and Eighteenth Centuries*, ed. Walter E. Minchinton, (New York: Metheun, 1969), 111–116; see appendix (tobacco).

20. Carman, Harry J. ed. *American Husbandry* (New York: Columbia University Press, 1993) chapter 15. Seavoy, Ronald E. *The American Peasantry: Southern Agricultural Labor and Its Legacy, 1850–1995* (Westport, CT: Greenwood Press, 1998), 55, 61–63, 238–241.

21. Rutman, Darrett B. and Rutman, Anita. *A Place in Time* (New York: W. W. Norton & Company, 1984), 188 (quote).

22. Beeman, Richard R. *The Evolution of the Southern Backcountry: A Case study of Lunenberg County, Virginia, 1746–1832* (Philadelphia: University of Pennsylvania Press, 1985),. 178–179 (quote).

23. Wells, Guy F. *Parish Education in Colonial Virginia* (New York: Teacher's College Press, 1923),. 28 (quote).

24. Seavoy, Ronald E. *Subsistence and Economic Development* (Westport, CT: Praeger, 2000), 66 (quote).

25. Bruce, Philip A. *Economic History of Virginia in the Seventeenth Century*, (New York: Macmillan, 1907). Vol 2, 408 (quote), 410 (quote). Isaac, Rhys *The Transformation of Virginia, 1740–1790* (Chapel Hill: University of North Carolina Press, 1999), 121–124.

26. Fischer, David H. *Albion's Seed: Four British Folkways in America* (New York: Oxford University Press, 1991) 345–348, 347 (quote). Lawrence A. Cremin, *American Education: The Colonial Experience, 1607–1783* (New York: Harper & Row, 1970), 178, 183.

27. Beeman, Richard R.. *The Evolution of the Southern Backcountry: A Case Study of Lunenburg County, Virginia, 1746–1832* (Philadelphia: University of Pennsylvania Press, 1985), 206 (quote).

Chapter 3

1. Fischer, David H. *Albion's Seed: Four British Folkways in America* (New York: Oxford University Press, 1991), 177–180, 179 (quote).

2. Innes, Stephen. *Creating the Commonwealth: The Economic Culture of Puritan New England* (New York, Norton, 1995), 71–99, 146–150, 84 (quote), 85 (quote).

3. Greven, Philip J. *Four Generations: Population, Land, and Family in Colonial Andover, Massachusetts* (Ithaca, NY: Cornell University Press, 1970), 104–109. Kenneth A. Lockridge, "The Population of Dedham, Massachusetts, 1636–1736," *Economic History Review*, 19 (1966): 330–332.

4. Main, Jackson T. *Society and Economy in Colonial Connecticut* (Princeton, NJ: Princeton University Press, 1985), 241.

5. Demos, John. "Notes on Life in Plymouth Colony," *William and Mary Quarterly*, 22, (1965). Greven, Philip J. "Family Structure in Seventeenth-Century Andover, Massachusetts," *William and Mary Quarterly*, 23 (1966).

6. Powell, Sumner C. *Puritan Village: The Formation of a New England Town* (Middletown, CT: Wesleyan University Press, 1970), 82 (quote), 93 (quote).

7. Morison, Samuel E. *Builders of the Bay Colony* (Boston, Houghton Mifflin, 1930), 93–95.

8. Bailyn, Bernard. *The New England Merchants in the Seventeenth Century* (Cambridge, MA: Harvard University Press, 1979),. 139, 159–160, 176–177, 139 (quote). Heyrman, Christine L. *Commerce and Culture* (New York: Norton, 1986) chapters 2 and 6. Withey, Lynne. *Urban Growth in Colonial Rhode Island: Newport and Providence in the Eighteenth Century* (Albany: State University of New York Press, 1984), chapter 2.

9. Bailyn, Bernard. *The New England Merchants in the Seventeenth Century* (Cambridge, MA: Harvard University Press, 1979), 192 (quote)

10. Lockridge, Kenneth A. Alan Kreider, "The Evolution of Massachusetts Town Government, 1640–1740," *William and Mary Quarterly*, 23 (1966): 556–561; 550 (quote).

11. Bailyn, Bernard. *The New England Merchants in the Seventeenth Century* (Cambridge, MA: Harvard University Press, 1979) 170, 176–177, 194–195.

12. Akagi, Roy H. *The Town Proprietors of the New England Colonies: A Study of their Development, Organization, Activities, and Controversies* (Philadelphia: Robert P. Smith, 1963), 76 (quote).

13. Lockridge, Kenneth A. "Land, Population, and the Evolution of New England Society, 1630–1790," *Past and Present*, 39 (1968): 72.

14. Lockridge, Kenneth A. "Land Population and the Evolution of New England Society, 1630–1790: and an Afterthought," *Past and Present*, 39 (1968). Reprinted in Stanley N. Katz, *Colonial America: Essays in Politics and Social Development* (New York: McGraw-Hill, 2000), 476. McCusker, John J., and Menard, Russell R. *The Economy of British America, 1607–1789* (Chapel Hill: University of North Carolina Press, 1991), 325–326.

15. Zuckerman, Michael. "The Social Context of Democracy in Massachusetts," *William and Mary Quarterly*, 25 (1968): 529 (quote). Daniels, Bruce C., *The Connecticut Town: Growth and Development, 1635–1790* (Middletown, CT: Wesleyan University Press, 1979) chapter 6. Grant, Charles S. *Democracy in the Connecticut Frontier Town of Kent* (New York: Norton, 1972), chapters 3 and 9.

16. Douglas L. Jones, "Poverty and Vagabondage: The Process of Survival in Eighteenth-Century Massachusetts," *New England Historical and Genealogical Register*, 133 (1979) .

17. Withey, Lynne *Urban Growth in Colonial Rhode Island: Newport and Providence in the Eighteenth Century* (Albany: State University Press of New York, 1984), 52–71.

18. Small, Walter H. *Early New England Schools* (Boston: Ginn and Company, 1914), 344 (quote).

19. Seybolt, Robert F. *Apprenticeship and Apprenticeship Education in Colonial New England and New York* (Salem, NH: Ayer Publishing, 1969), 37 (quote).

20. Wright, Louis B. and Fowler, Elaine W. eds. *English Colonization of North America* (London: Edward Arnold Publishers, 1968), 86 (quote).

21. Seybolt, Robert F. *Apprenticeship and Apprenticeship Education in Colonial New England and New York* (Salem, NH: Ayer Publishing, 1969), 53 (quote). Innes, Stephen. *Creating the Commonwealth: The Economic Culture of Puritan New England* (New York: W. W. Norton & Company, 1995), 150–159.

22. Updegraff, Harlan. *The Origin of the Moving School in Massachusetts* (New York: Teacher's College Press, 1908), 87 (quote), 91 (quote).

23. Seavoy, Ronald E. *The Origins of the American Business Corporation* (Westport, CT: Greenwood Publishing, 1982), 15–18.

24. Main, Jackson T. *Society and Economy in Colonial Connecticut* (Princeton, NJ: Princeton University Press, 1985), 313 (quote). Lockridge, Kenneth A. *Literacy in Colonial New England: An Enquiry into the Social Context of Literacy in the Early Modern West* (New York: Norton, 1974), 58–69.

25. Tolles, Frederick B. *Meeting House and Counting House* (New York: Norton, 1963), 39–44.

26. Wolf, Stephanie G. *Urban Village* (Princeton, NJ: Princeton University Press, 1980), chapters 1, 2.

27. Faust, Albert B. *The German Element in the United States* (New York: Steuben Society, 1927), 131–139.

28. Seavoy, Ronald E. *Famine in Peasant Societies* (Westport, CT: Greenwood Publishing, 1986), 297–312. Bailyn, Bernard *Voyagers to the West: A Passage in the Peopling of America on the Eve of Revolution* (New York: Vintage, 1988), 36–37, 43–44.

29. Dickson, R. J. *Ulster Immigration to Colonial America, 1718–1775* (Belfast: Ulster Historical Foundation, 1976), 225.

30. Lemon, James T. *The Best Poor Man's Country: A Geographical Study of Early Southeastern Pennsylvania* (Baltimore: Johns Hopkins University Press, 1972), 11.

31. Woody, Thomas *Early Quaker Education in Pennsylvania* (New York: Teacher's College Press, 1920), 30–31 (quotes). Wright, Louis B. and Fowler, Elaine W. eds. *English Colonization of North America* (London: Edward Arnold Publishers, 1968), 97–102.

Chapter 4

1. Dickerson, Oliver M. *The Navigation Acts and the American Revolution* (Philadelphia: University of Pennsylvania Press, 1974), 21 (quote).

2. Henretta, James A. "*Salutary Neglect*": *The American Colonies in the First Half of the 18th Century* (New York: Arlington House, 1975), 65–66, 317–318, 324, 344. Greene, Jack P. *The Quest for Power: The Lower Houses of Assembly in Southern Royal Colonies, 1689–1776* (New York: Norton, 1972), chapters 1, 2. Seavoy, Ronald E. *Origins and Growth of the Global Economy: From the Fifteenth Century Onward* (Westport, CT: Praeger, 2003), chapter 2.

3. Johnson, Emory R. *History of Domestic and Foreign Commerce of the United States* (New York: Burt Franklin, 1964), Vol. 1, chapter 6, table 7, 118–121. Shepherd, James F. and Walton, Gary M. *Shipping, Maritime Trade and the Economic*

Development of Colonial North America (Cambridge: Cambridge University Press, 1972), chapters 6, 7; table 7.1; appendix 4, tables 2, 3, 4, 5, 9, 12, 13; appendix 6. Davis, Ralph. "English Foreign Trade, 1700–1774," in *The Growth of English Overseas Trade in the Seventeenth and Eighteenth Centuries,* ed., Walter E. Minchinton, (New York: Methuen, 1969).

4. McCusker, John J., and Menard, Russell R. *The Economy of British America 1607–1789* (Chapel Hill: University of North Carolina Press, 1991), 192; 108 (table 5.2); 130 (table 6.1); 174 (table 8.2); 199 (table 9.3).

5. Price, Jacob M. "Buchanan and Simpson, 1759–1763: A Different Kind of Glasgow Firm Trading to the Chesapeake," *William and Mary Quarterly,* 40 (1983); Price, Jacob M. "Economic Function and Growth of American Port Towns in the Eighteenth Century," *Perspectives in American History,* 8 (1974): 165; appendix E.

6. Johnson, Emory R. *History of Domestic and Foreign Commerce of the United States* (New York: Burt Franklin, 1964), Vol. l, chapter 6, table 7.

7. Bailyn, Bernard. *Voyagers to the West: A Passage in the Peopling of America on the Eve of Revolution* (New York: Vintage, 198) chapter 7. Price, Jacob M. "Economic Function and the Growth of American Port Towns in the Eighteenth Century," *Perspectives in American History,* 8 (1974): appendix F.

8. Labaree, Leonard W. *Royal Government in America: A Study of the British Colonial System before 1783* (New Haven: Yale University Press, 1930, 1958), 283–311.

9. Kemmerer, Donald L. "The Colonial Loan-Office System in New Jersey," *Journal of Political Economy* 47 (1939) .

10. Leslie V. Brock, *The Currency of the American Colonies, 1700–1764* (New York: Arno Press, 1975), 271. Baxter, William T. *The House of Hancock: Business in Boston, 1724–1775* (Cambridge, MA: Harvard University Press, 1945),16–34.

11. Ernst, Joseph A. *Money and Politics in America, 1755–1775: A Study in the Currency Act of 1764 and the Political Economy of Revolution* (Chapel Hill: University of North Carolina Press), 79 (quote).

12. Ernst, Joseph A., *Money and Politics in America, 1755–1775,* 92 (quote). Brock, Leslie V. *The Currency of the American Colonies, 1700–1764: A Study in the Colonial Finance and Imperial Relations* (New York: Arno Press, 1975), 508 (quote).

13. Morgan, Edmund S., and Morgan, Helen M. *The Stamp Act Crisis: Prologue to Revolution* (Chapel Hill: University of North Carolina Press, 1995), 96, 117, 139–144.

Chapter 5

1. Miller, John C. *The Federalist Era, 1789–1801* (Long Grove, IL: Waveland Press, 1998), 76 (quote).

2. Jefferson, Thomas. *Notes on the State of Virginia* (Chapel Hill: University of North Carolina Press, 1996 [originally published in 1781]), 157–158 (quote).

3. Jefferson, Thomas. *Notes on the State of Virginia,* 85, 86 (quotes).

Chapter 6

1. Schumpeter, Joseph A. *Capitalism, Socialism and Democracy* (New York: Harper Perennial, 1962), 132 (quote).

2. Lamb, Robert K. "The Entrepreneur and the Community," in *Men in Business,* ed. Miller, William (Westport, CT: Greenwood Press, 1979), 116 (quote).

3. Seavoy, Ronald E. *The Origins of the American Business Corporation* (Westport, CT: Greenwood Publishing, 1982), 46–51.

4. Adams, Henry. *History of the United States of America; During the Second Administration of Thomas Jefferson* (New York: Charles Scribner's Sons, 1903), Vol. 2, 282.

5. Seavoy, Ronald E. *The Origins of the American Business Corporation* (Westport, CT: Greenwood Publishing, 1982), 57 (quote).

6. Bruchey, Stuart W., *The Wealth of the Nation: An Economic History of the United States* (New York, Harper Row, 1988), 39 (quote).

7. Durrenberger, Joseph A. *Turnpikes: A Study of the Toll Road Movement in the Middle Atlantic States and Maryland* (Southern Stationary and Printing Co., 1931), 96 (quote).

8. Segal, Harvey M. "Cycles of Canal Construction," in Goodrich, Carter ed. *Canals and American Economic Development* (New York: Columbia University Press, 1961), 211–213, table 4; 278.

9. Seavoy, Ronald E. *The Origins of the American Business Corporation* (Westport, CT: Greenwood Publishing, 1982), 65 (quote).

10. Seavoy, Ronald E., *The Origins of the American Business Corporation,* 66, 111 (quotes).

11. Seavoy, Ronald E., *The Origins of the American Business* Corporation, 67, 68 (quotes).

12. Ware, Caroline F. *The Early New England Cotton Manufacture: A Study in Industrial Beginnings* (Johnson Reprint Corp., 1966), 283 (quote).

13. Meyer, Adolphe E. *An Education History of the American People* (New York: McGraw-Hill, 1967), 157 (quote).

14. Walker, Francis A., ed. *A Compendium of the Ninth Census: June 1, 1870* (New York: Arno Press, 1976), table l, 8–9; table 2, 11; table 3, 13.

15. Cunningham, Noble E. *The Presidency of James Monroe* (Lawrence, KS: University of Kansas Press, 1996), 104 (quote).

Chapter 7

1. Hammond, Bray, *Banks and Politics in America* (Princeton, NJ: Princeton University Press, 1957), 287 (quote).
2. Hammond, Bray, *Banks and Politics in America*, 405 (quote).
3. Dewey, Davis R. *Financial History of the United States* (New York: Longmans Green, 1928), 225.
4. North, Douglass C. *The Economic Growth of the United States* (New York: Norton , 1966), 190 (quote).
5. Seavoy, Ronald E. *The Origins of the American Business Corporation* (Westport, CT: Greenwood Publishing, 1982): 119 (quote).
6. Seavoy, Ronald E. "Borrowed Laws to Speed Development: Michigan, 1835–1863," *Michigan History*, 59 (1975): 50 (quote).
7. Hammond, Bray, *Banks and Politics in America* (Princeton NJ: Princeton University Press, 1957), 596, 598 (quotes).
8. Pierce, Harry H. , *Railroads of New York*, (Cambridge, MA: Harvard University Press, 1953), chapters 2, 3, 4.
9. Salsbury, Stephen, *The State, the Investor, and the Railroad: A Study of Government Aid, 1826–1875* (National Technical Information Service, 1982), 146..
10. Salsbury, Stephen, 245, 270 (maps of New England's skeletal railroad network in 1851).
11. Chandler, Alfred D. ed. *The Railroads: The Nations First Big Business* (Salem. NH: Ayer Publishing, 1981), 98 (quotes).
12. Chandler, Alfred D. *The Railroads: The Nations First Big Business*, 8 (quote).
13. Chandler, Alfred D. *The Railroads: The Nations First Big Business*, 4–6 (maps of railroad construction outside of New England between 1849 and 1854); 13, 16.
14. Phillips, Ulrich B. *A History of Transportation in the Eastern Cotton Belt to 1860* (New York: Octagon Books, 1968), 149–150 (quotes).
15. Phillips, Ulrich B., *A History of Transporation in the Eastern Cotton Belt to 1860*, 241 (quote).
16. Phillips, Ulrich B., *A History of Transportation in the Eastern Cotton Belt*, 250 (quote). Seavoy, Ronald E. *The American Peasantry: Southern Agricultural Labor and Its Legacy, 1850–1995* (Westport, CT: Greenwood Press, 1998), 253–256.
17. Seavoy, Ronald E. *The American Peasantry*, 23–30, 248–258.
18. Stover, John F. *Iron Road to the West: American Railroads in the 1850s* (New York: Columbia University Press, 1978), 89–90 (quotes), 188–189.
19. North, Douglass C. *The Economic Growth of the United State* (New York: Norton , 1966), 67 (quote).
20. Seavoy, Ronald E. *The American Peasantry: Southern Agricultural Labor and Its Legacy, 1850–1995* (Westport, CT: Greenwood Press, 1998), 246 (quote).
21. Fishlow, Albert. *American Railroads and the Transformation of the Ante-Bellum Economy* (Cambridge, MA: Harvard University Press, 1965), 337.
22. Rosenberg, Nathan. "The Economic Consequence of Technological Change, 1830–1880," in *Technology in Western Civilization*, eds. Melvin Kranzberg and Carroll W. Pursell, (New York, Oxford University Press, 1987), 521–522 (quotes).
23. Carroll W. Pursell, *Early Stationary Steam Engines in America* (Washington, D.C.: Smithsonian Institution Press, 1969), 73 (quote), 88–89.
24. Pursell, Carroll W. *Early Stationary Steam Engines in America*, 78 (quote).
25. Fishlow, Albert. *American Railroads and the Transformation of the Ante-Bellum Economy* (Cambridge, MA: Harvard University Press, 1965), 154–156.
26. Schweikart, Larry. *Banking in the American South from the Age of Jackson to Reconstruction* (Baton Rouge: Louisiana State University Press, 1987), 255 (quote).
27. Four books document the crucial contribution that public finance contributed to the rapid construction of transportation arteries in the United States. These books are: George R. Taylor, *The Transportation Revolution;* Carter Goodrich, *Government Promotion of American Canals and Railroads;* Harry H. Pierce, *Railroads of New York: A Study of Government Aid;* Louis Hartz, *Economic Policy and Democratic Thought: Pennsylvania.* Many more books do the same, either as broad studies or as individual studies like Stephen Salsbury, *The State, The Investor and the Railroad.*

Chapter 8

1. Goodrich, Carter ed. *The Government and the Economy, 1783–1861* (Indianapolis, IN: Bobbs-Merrill, 1967), 458 (quote).
2. McLaughlin, Andrew C. *A Constitutional History of the United States* (Greenwich, CT: Appleton-Century-Crofts, 1961), 482–483 (quote).
3. McLaughlin, Andrew C. *A Constitutional History of the United States*, 489–490 (quote).
4. Rayback, Jospeh G., *Free Soil: The Election of 1848* (Lexington: University of Kentucky Press, 1970), 265 (quote).
5. Hamilton, Holman, *Prologue to Conflict: The Crisis and Compromise of 1850* (New York: Norton, 1964), 73 (quote).

Chapter 10

1. Kolko, Gabriel, *Railroads and Regulation, 1877–1916* (New York: Norton, 1970), 14 (quote).

2. Kolko, Gabriel, *Railroads and Regulation, 1877–1916*, 27 (quote).
3. Bensel, Richard F. *The Political Economy of American Industrialization, 1877–1900* (Cambridge: Cambridge University Press, 2000), 459 (quote).

Chapter 11

1. Ransom, Roger L. and Richard Sutch, *One Kind of Freedom: The Economic Consequences of Emancipation* (Cambridge: Cambridge University Press, 1977), 151–162.
2. Seavoy, Ronald E. *The American Peasantry: Southern Agricultural Labor and Its Legacy, 1850–1995* (Westport, CT: Greenwood Press, 1998), 304 (quote).
3. Easterlin, Richard A. "Regional Income Trends, 1840–1950," in *American Economic History*, ed. Seymour E. Harris (New York: McGraw-Hill, 1961), 528..
4. Seavoy, Ronald E. *The American Peasantry: Southern Agricultural Labor and Its Legacy, 1850–1995* (Westport, CT: Greenwood Press, 1998), 312–313.
5. Sundquist, James L. *Dynamics of the Party System: Alignment and Realignment of Political Parties in the United States* (Washington, D.C.: Brooking Institution Press, 1983), 123–124 (quote from congressional speech, August 1893).
6. Bryan, William J. "Cross of Gold speech," in Commager, Henry S., ed., *Documents of American History* (New York Appleton-Century-Crofts, 1958) document 342, concluding paragraph, July, 8, 1896 (quotes).

Chapter 12

1. Morton Keller, *Affairs of State: Public Life in Late Nineteenth Century-America* (Cambridge: Belknap Press, 1979), 298 (quote).
2. Binkley, Wilfred E. *President and Congress* (New York: Alfred Knopf, 1947), 219 (quote).
3. Kelly, Alfred H., and Harbison, Winfred A. *The American Constitution* (New York: W. W. Norton & Company, 1990), 566–577, 622–626.
4. Garraty, John A. *The New Commonwealth, 1877–1890* (New York: Harper & Row, 1968), 218 (quote).
5. Harlan, Louis R. *Separate but Unequal: Public School Campaigns and Racism in the Southern Seaboard States, 1901–1915* (Chapel Hill: University of North Carolina Press, 1958), chapter 1.
6. Seavoy, Ronald E. *Subsistence and Economic Development* (Westwood, CT: Praeger, 2000), 76–77 (quote).
7. Wyman, Mark. *Round-Trip to America: Immigrants Return to Europe, 1880–1930* (Ithaca, NY: Cornell University Press), 3 (quote).
8. Morawska, Eva. *For Bread With Butter: The Life-Worlds of East Central Europeans in Johnstown, Pennsylvania, 1890–1940* (Cambridge: Cambridge University Press, 2004), 112 (quote).
9. Kessner, Thomas, *The Golden Door: Italian and Jewish Immigrant Mobility in New York City* (New York: Oxford University Press, 1977), 94–95 (quotes).
10. Kelly, Alfred H., and Harbison, Winfred A. *The American Constitution* (New York: Norton, 1990), 515, 524 (quotes).
11. Kelly, Alfred H., and Harbison, Winfred A. *The Amercian Constitution*, 523 (quote).
12. Kelly, Alfred H., and Harbison, Winfred A. *The American Constitution*, 556–564, 560–561 (quotes).
13. Kelly, Alfred H., and Harbison, Winfred A. *The American Constitution*, 541–546, 528 (quote).
14. Warren, Charles *Bankruptcy in United States History* (New York: Da Capo Press, 1972), 144 (quote).
15. Blum, John M. *The Republican Roosevelt* (New York, Atheneum 1962), 104 (quote).
16. Blum, John M. *The Republican Roosevelt*, 105 (quote).
17. Kelly, Alfred H., and Harbison, Winfred A. *The American Constitution* (New York: Norton , 1990), 556–564, 608–610.

Chapter 13

1. Porter, Glenn. *The Rise of Big Business, 1860–1920* (Arlington Heights: IL, Harlan Davidson, 1992), 117 (quote).
2. Rees, Albert. *Real Wages in Manufacturing, 1890–1914* (Princeton, NJ: Princeton University Press, 1961), 120, table 44. Higgs, Robert. *The Transformation of the American Economy, 1865–1914* (New York: John Wiley & Sons, 1971), 19.
3. Chandler, Alfred D. *Scale and Scope: The Dynamics of Industrial Capitalism* (Cambridge, MA: Belknap Press, 2004), 79 (quote).
4. Chandler, Alfred D. *The Visible Hand: The Managerial Revolution in American Business* (Cambridge, MA: Belknap Press, 1993), 338–339 (quote).
5. Chandler, Alfred D. *The Visible Hand*, 339 (quote).
6. Chandler, Alfred D. *The Visible Hand*, 240 (quote).
7. Chandler, Alfred D., *The Visible Hand*, 257 (quote).
8. Daniel Nelson, *Managers and Workers: Origins of the Twentieth-Century Factory System in the United States, 1880–1920* (Madison: University of Wisconsin Press, 1995), 8–9, (table 3).
9. Chandler, Alfred D. *The Visible Hand: The Managerial Revolution in American Business* (Cambridge, MA: Belknap Press, 1993), 376 (quote).

10. Livesay, Harold C. *Andrew Carnegie and the Rise of Big Business* (New York: Longman, 1999), 101 (quote).
11. Chandler, Alfred D. *Giant Enterprise: Ford, General Motors and the Automobile Industry* (New York: Harcourt, Brace and World, 1964), 4, 107.
12. Hughes, Jonathan R. *The Vital Few: The Entrepreneur and American Economic Progress* (New York: Oxford University Press, 1986), 327 (quote).
13. Chandler, Alfred D. *Giant Enterprise: Ford, General Motors and the Automobile Industry* (New York: Harcourt, Brace and World, 1964), 15 (quote).

Chapter 14
1. Hughes, Jonathan R. *American Economic History* (Boston, MA: Addison Wesley, 2002) 446–447. Soule, George H. *Prosperity Decade: From War to Depression, 1917–1929* (New York: Harper & Row, 1968), 214–215.
2. Hughes, Thomas P. *Networks of Power: Electrification in Western Society, 1880–1930* (Baltimore: Johns Hopkins University Press, 1993), 365 (quote).
3. Schurr, Sam H., and Netschert, Bruce C. *Energy in the American Economy* (Westport, CT: Greenwood Publishing, 1977), 55, 180–181, 186–189.
4. Hughes, Thomas P. *Networks of Power: Electrification in Western Society, 1880–1930* (Baltimore: Johns Hopkins University Press, 1993), 364 (quote).
5. Soule, George H. *Prosperity Decade: From War to Depression, 1917–1929* (New York: Harper & Row, 1968), 142. Hughes, Thomas P. *Networks of Power: Electrification in Western Society, 1880–1930* (Baltimore: Johns Hopkins University Press, 1993), 392–401.
6. Soule, George H. *Prosperity Decade: From War to Depression, 1917–1929* (New York: Harper & Row, 1968), 182–186, 303.
7. Report of the Committee on Recent Economic Changes. *Recent Economic Changes in the United States* (New York: McGraw-Hill, 1929), Vol 1, 130–133.
8. Potter, David M. *People of Plenty* (Chicago: University of Chicago Press, 1954), 175 (quote).
9. Report of the Committee on Recent Economic Changes. *Recent Economic Changes in the United States* (New York: McGraw-Hill, 1929), Vol 1, 325.
10. Barger, Harold, and Landsberg, Hans H. *American Agriculture, 1899–1939* (National Bureau of Economic Research, 1942), 201–217.
11. Seavoy, Ronald E. *The American Peasantry: Southern Agricultural Labor and Its Legacy, 1850–1995* (Westport, CT: Greenwood Press, 1998), chapters 6, 10.
12. William F. Leuchtenburg, *The Perils of Prosperity* (Chicago: University of Chicago Press, 1958), 103 (quote).
13. Studenski, Paul, Krooss, Herman E. *Financial History of the United States* (New York: McGraw-Hill, 1963), 334–343, 337 (quotes).
14. Davis, Joseph S., *The World Between the Wars: An Economist's Perspective* (Baltimore: Johns Hopkins University Press, 1975), 205–206 (quotes).
15. Temin, Peter. *Did Monetary Forces Cause the Great Depression?* (New York: Norton , 1976), 65, 74–75, 172 (quote).
16. Kindleberger, Charles P. *The World Depression, 1929–1939* (Berkeley: University of California Press, 1986), 291–298.
17. Davis, Joseph S. *The World Between the Wars: An Economist's Perspective* (Baltimore: Johns Hopkins University Press, 1975), 288 (quote).
18. George, Peter J. *The Emergence of Industrial America: Strategic Factors in American Economic Growth Since 1870* (Albany: State University of New York Press, 1982), 165 (quote).
19. George, Peter J. *The Emergence of Industrial America*, 191–192 (quote).
20. Leuchtenburg, William E. *Franklin D. Roosevelt and the New Deal* (New York: Harper Perennial, 1963), 5, 11 (quotes).
21. Studenski, Paul, and Krooss, Herman E. *Financial History of the United States* (Beard Books, 2003), 394.
22. Higgs, Robert, *Crisis and Leviathan: Critical Episodes in the Growth of the American Government* (New York: Oxford University Press, 1987), 177 (quote).
23. Seavoy, Ronald E. *The American Peasantry: Southern Agricultural Labor and Its Legacy, 1850–1995* (Westport, CT: Greenwood Press, 1998), 425–439.
24. Seavoy, Ronald E. *The American Peasantry*, 480.
25. Destler, I. M. *American Trade Politics*, 4th ed. (Institute for International Economics, 2005), 11–20.
26. Seavoy, Ronald E. *The American Peasantry: Southern Agricultural Labor and Its Legacy, 1850–1995* (Westport, CT: Greenwood Press, 1998), 434, 458–460.
27. Mitchell, Broadus. *Depression Decade: From New Era through the New Deal, 1929–1941* (Austin, TX: Holt, Rinehart and Winston, 1966), 319 (quote).
28. Kelly, Alfred H., and Harbison, Winfred A. *The American Constitution* (New York: Norton, 1990), 749 (quote).
29. Mitchell, Broadus. *Depression Decade: From New Era through the New Deal, 1929–1941* (Austin, TX: Holt, Rinehart and Winston, 1966), 271–274.

30. Hughes, Jonathan R. *American Economic History* (Boston, MA: Addison Wesley, 2002), 467–469.

Chapter 15
1. Seavoy, Ronald E. *Origins and Growth of the Global Economy: From the Fifteenth Century Onward* (Westport, CT: Praeger, 2003), 184–204, 256–264.
2. Seavoy, Ronald E. *Origins and Growth of the Global Economy*, 185 (quote).
3. Seavoy, Ronald E. *Origins and Growth of the Global Economy*, 186 (quote).
4. Freeman, Richard B. "The Evolution of the American Labor Market, 1948–1980," 355 (table 5.3); Branson, William H. "Trends in United States International Trade and Investment since World War II", 187–197 (tables 3.2, 3.3, 3.9) in Feldstein, Martin S., ed. *The American Economy in Transition* (Chicago: University of Chicago Press, 1980).
5. Branson, William H. "Trends in United States International Trade and Investment since World War II," 189, 195–196, 240–247, 545, fn 17, (tables 3.13, 3.30, 3.36, 3.37, 3.42).
6. Seavoy, Ronald E. *Origins and Growth of the Global Economy: From the Fifteenth Century Onward* (Westport, CT: Praeger, 2003), 258 (quote).
7. Jones, Kent. *Politics vs. Economics in World Steel Trade* (London: Allan & Unwin, 1986), 111 (quote), 117–118, 123–124, 138–144.
8. Borrus, Michael "The Politics of Competitive Erosion of the U.S. Steel Industry" in *American Industry in International Competition: Government Policies and Corporate Strategies,* John Zysman and Laura D. Tyson, eds. (Ithaca, NY: Cornell University Press, 1983), 83 (quote).
9. Lima, Jose G. H. *Restructuring the U.S. Steel Industry: Semi-Finished Steel Imports, International Integration, and U.S. Adaptation* (Boulder, CO: Westview Press, 1991), 18–24, 30, 63–65, 69, 103, 117–118, 152–154.
10. Deming, W. Edwards *Out of Crisis* (Cambridge, MA: MIT Press, 1982), 5, 8, 23–24 (quotes).
11. Adams, Walter and Brock, James W. "The Automobile Industry," in *The Structure of American Industry*, ed. Walter Adams (New York: Macmillan, 1990), 115 (quote).
12. Kwoka, John E. "Automobiles: Product, Process, and the Decline of U.S. Dominance," in *Industrial Studies,* Larry L. Duetsch, ed. (Armonk, NY: M. E. Sharpe, 2002), 21 (quote).
13. Dorfman, Nancy S. *Innovation and Market Structure* (Cambridge, MA: Ballinger Publishing Company, 1987), 103 (quote).
14. Flamm, Kenneth S., *Creating the Computer: Government, Industry, and High Technology* (Washington D.C.: Brookings Institution Press, 1988), 239 (quote).
15. Rohlfs, Jeffrey H. *Bandwagon Effect in High-Technology Industries* (Cambridge, MA: MIT Press, 2003), 123 (quote). Chandler, Alfred D. *Inventing the Electronic Century* (New York: Free Press, 2001), 137 (quotes), 138.
16. Chandler, Alfred D. *Inventing the Electric Century*, 110–113. Chandler, Alfred D. "The Information Age in Historical Perspective," in *A Nation Transformed by Information: How Information has Shaped the United States from Colonial Times to the Present,* eds. Alfred D. Chandler and James W. Cortada, (New York: Oxford University Press, 2000), 29–30.
17. Tyson, Laura D. *Who's Bashing Whom: Trade Conflict in High-Technology Industries* (Washington, DC, Institute of International Economics, 1992), 66–71, 76–82, 92 (quote).
18. Flamm, Kenneth S. *Mismanaged Trade?: Strategic Policy and the Semiconductor Industry* (Washington, D.C.: Brooking Institution Press, 1996), 124 (quote).
19. Flamm, Kenneth S. *Mismanaged Trade*, 171–174.
20. Angel, David P. *Restructuring for Innovation: The Remaking of the U.S. Semiconductor* (New York: Guilford Press, 1994) 65–86. Chandler, Alfred D. *Inventing the Electronic Century* (New York: Free Press, 2001), 122–131.
21. Flamm, Kenneth S., *Mismanaged Trade?: Strategic Policy and the Semiconductor Industry* (Washington, D.C.: Brooking Institution Press, 1996), 185–186 (quote).
22. Tyson, Laura D. *Who's Bashing Whom: Trade Conflict in High-Technology Industries* (Institute of International Economics, 1992), 89 (quote).
23. Flamm, Kenneth S., *Mismanaged Trade?: Strategic Policy and the Semiconductor Industry* (Washington, D.C.: Brooking Institution Press, 1996), 212–226. Angel, David P. *Restructuring for Innovation: The Remaking of the U.S. Semiconductor,* 177–183.
24. Magaziner, Ira C., and Hout, Thomas M. *Japanese Industrial Policy,* (Berkeley, CA: Institute of International Studies, 1980), 56–60. Bingham, Richard D. *Industrial Policy American Style: From Hamilton to HDTV* (Armonk, NY: M. E. Sharpe, 1998), 152–160.
25. Destler, I. M. *American Trade Politics*, 4th ed. (Washington, D.C.: Institute for International Economics, 2005), 12–27, 71–76, 200–212.
26. Yang, Xiaohua. *Globalization of the Automobile Industry: The United States, Japan, and the People's Republic of China* (Westport, CT: Praeger, 1995), 195 (quote).

BIBLIOGRAPHY

Abbate, Janet. *Inventing the Internet.* Cambridge, MA: MIT Press, 1999, chapter 6.

Adams, Henry. *History of the United States of America During the Second Administration of Thomas Jefferson,* Vol. 2. New York: Scribners, 1931 (reprint of 1890 edition), chapters 7–12.

Adams, Henry. *History of the United States of America During the First Administration of James Madison.* New York: Scribners, 1931 (reprint of 1890 edition), Vol. 1, chapter 9, Vol. 2, chapters 10, 11.

Adams, Walter, and Mueller, Hans. "The Steel Industry." In *The Structure of American Industry,* edited by Walter Adams and Hans Mueller. New York: Macmillan, 1990.

Adams, Walter, and James W. Brock. "The Automobile Industry." In *The Structure of American Industry,* edited by Walter Adams. New York: Macmillan, 1990.

Adler, Dorothy R. *British Investments in American Railways, 1834–1898,* Part 1. Charlottesville: University Press of Virginia, 1970.

Akagi, Roy H. *The Town Proprietors of the New England Colonies: A Study of their Development, Organization, Activities and Controversies, 1620–1770.* Gloucester, MA: Peter Smith, 1963 (reprint of 1924 edition).

Albion, Robert G. *The Rise of New York Port: 1815–1860.* New York: Scribners, 1970 (reprint of 1939 edition).

Allen, Gardner W. *Our Naval War with France.* Boston: Houghton Mifflin, 1909.

Allen, Frederick L. *The Big Change: America Transforms Itself, 1900–1950.* New York: Harper, 1952, chapter 10.

Ambrose, Stephen E. *Nothing Like it in the World: The Men who Built the Transcontinental Railroad, 1863–1869.* New York: Touchstone Books, 2001.

Angel, David P. *Restructuring for Innovation: The Remaking of the U.S. Semiconductor Industry.* New York: Guilford Press, 1994.

Aydelotte, Frank. *Elizabethan Rogues and Vagabonds.* Oxford: Clarendon Press, 1913; chapters 1, 2, 3.

Baer, Christopher T. *Canals and Railroads of the Mid-Atlantic States, 1800–1860.* Wilmington, DE: Eleutherian Mills-Hagley Foundation, Regional Economic History Center, 1981.

Bailyn, Bernard. *The New England Merchants in the Seventeenth Century.* New York: Harper Torchbooks, 1964 (reprint of 1955 edition).

Bailyn, Bernard. "Politics and Social Structure in Virginia." In *Colonial America: Essays in Politics and Social Development,* edited by Stanley N. Katz. Boston: Little, Brown, 1971; reprinted from J. M. Smith, ed. *Seventeenth Century America.*

Bailyn, Bernard. *Education in the Forming of American Society.* New York: Norton, 1972.

Bailyn, Bernard. *Voyagers to the West: A Passage in the Peopling of America on the Eve of the Revolution.* New York: Vintage Books, 1988.

Baker, George P. *The Formation of the New England Railroad Systems: A Study of Railroad Combination in the Nineteenth Century.* Cambridge, MA: Harvard University Press, 1949.

Ballagh, James C. *White Servitude in the Colony of Virginia: A Study of the System of Indentured Labor in the American Colonies.* Baltimore: John Hopkins University Press, 1895.

Barger, Harold, and Hans H. Landsberg. *American Agriculture, 1899–1939: A Study of Output, Employment, and Productivity.* New York: National Bureau of Economic Research, 1942, chapter 5.

Barnett, Donald F., Robert W. Crandall. *Up from the Ashes: The Rise of the Steel Minimill in the United States.* Washington, DC: Brookings Institution, 1986.

Barnett, Donald F., and Robert W. Crandall. "Steel: Decline and Renewal." In *Industry Studies,* edited by Larry L. Duetsch, Armonk, NY: M. E. Sharpe, 2002.

Barrett, Don C. *The Greenbacks and Resumption of Specie Payments, 1862–1879.* Cambridge, MA: Harvard University Press, 1931, chapters 1, 2, 3.

Baxter, William T. *The House of Hancock: Business in Boston, 1724–1775.* Cambridge, MA: Harvard University Press, 1945, chapters 2, 4.

Becker, Robert A. *Revolution, Reform, and the Politics of American Taxation, 1763–1783.* Baton Rouge: Louisiana State University Press, 1980.

Beeman, Richard R. *The Evolution of the Southern Backcountry: A Case Study of Lunenburg County, Virginia, 1746–1832*. Philadelphia: University of Pennsylvania Press, 1984, chapter 7.

Beer, George L. *The Origins of the British Colonial System, 1578–1600*. New York: Macmillan, 1922, chapters 4, 5, 6.

Beier, A. L. "Vagrants and the Social Order in Elizabethan England." *Past and Present* no. 64 1974.

Bemis, Samuel F. *Jay's Treaty: A Study in Commerce and Diplomacy*. New York: Macmillan, 1924, chapter 8.

Bemis, Samuel F. *Pinckney's Treaty: A Study of America's Advantage from Europe's Distress*. Baltimore: Johns Hopkins University Press, 1926, chapter 12.

Bensel, Richard F. *The Political Economy of American Industrialization, 1877–1900*. Cambridge: Cambridge University Press, 2000, chapter 7.

Berggren, Christian, Masami Nomura. *The Resilience of Corporate Japan: New Strategies and Personnel Practices*. London: Paul Chapman Publishing, 1997, chapters 4, 6, 7, 9.

Berkowitz, Edward D., and Kim McQuaid. *Creating the Welfare State: The Political Economy of Twentieth-Century Reform*. New York: Praeger, 1988, chapter 9.

Bernhard, Virginia. "Poverty and the Social Order in Seventeenth-Century Virginia." *Virginia Magazine of History and Biography* 85 (1977).

Bernstein, Marver H. *Regulating Business by Independent Commission*. Princeton, NJ: Princeton University Press, 1955, chapters 1, 2.

Bidwell, Percy W., and John I. Falconer. *History of Agriculture in the Northern United States, 1660–1860*. New York: Peter Smith, 1941 (reprint of 1925 edition, chapters 7, 8, 9).

Billings, Warren M. "The Growth of Political Institutions in Virginia, 1634 to 1676." *William and Mary Quarterly* 31 (1974).

Billings, Warren M., ed. *The Old Dominion in the Seventeenth Century: A Documentary History of Virginia, 1606–1689*. Chapel Hill: University of North Carolina Press, 1975, chapter 1, no. 8 "Starving Time;" chapter 3.

Billings, Warren M., John E. Selby, and Thad W. Tate. *Colonial Virginia: A History*. White Plains, NY: KTO Press, 1986, chapters 6, 9.

Bingham, Richard D. *Industrial Policy American Style: From Hamilton to HDTV*. Armonk, NY: Sharpe, 1998, chapters 6, 7, 8.

Bining, Arthur C. *British Regulation of the Colonial Iron Industry*. Philadelphia: University of Pennsylvania Press, 1933.

Binkley, Wilfred E. *President and Congress*. New York: Vintage Books, 1962; revision of 1937 edition.

Bishop, Cortlandt F. *History of Elections in the American Colonies*. New York: Columbia College, 1893.

Blue, Frederick J. *The Free Soilers: Third Party Politics, 1848–1854*. Urbana: University of Illinois Press, 1973.

Blum, John M. *The Republican Roosevelt*. New York: Atheneum, 1962 (reprint of 1954 edition; chapters 6, 7; 87–105).

Bodenhorn, Howard. *State Banking in Early America: A New Economic History*. New York: Oxford University Press, 2003, chapters 6–10; 97–105.

Bolton, Charles C. *Poor Whites of the Antebellum South: Tenants and Laborers in Central North Carolina and Northeast Mississippi*. Durham, NC: Duke University Press, 1994, chapters 3, 6.

Borrus, Michael. "The Politics of Competitive Erosion in the U.S. Steel Industry." In *American Industry in International Competition: Government Policies and Corporate Strategies*, edited by John Zysman and Laura D. Tyson. Ithaca, NY: Cornell University Press, 1983.

Borrus, Michael, James E. Millstein, and John Zysman. "Trade and Development in the Semiconductor Industry: Japanese Challenge and American Response." In *American Industry in International Competition: Government Policies and Corporate Strategies, edited by* John Zysman, Laura D. Tyson. Ithaca, NY: Cornell University Press, 1983.

Boyer, Charles S. *Early Forges and Furnaces in New Jersey*. Philadelphia: University of Pennsylvania Press, 1931.

Branson, William H. "Trends in United States International Trade and Investment since World War II." In *The American Economy in Transition*, edited by Martin S. Feldstein. Chicago: University of Chicago Press, 1980.

Bridenbaugh, Carl. *The Colonial Craftsman*. New York: New York University Press, 1950, chapters 2, 3, 4.

Bridenbaugh, Carl. *Vexed and Troubled Englishmen, 1590–1642*. New York: Oxford University Press, 1968, chapter 12.

Bridenbaugh, Carl. *Fat Mutton and Liberty of Conscience: Society in Rhode Island, 1636–1690*. New York: Atheneum, 1976, chapter 5.

Bright, Arthur A. *The Electric-Lamp Industry: Technological Change and Economic Development from 1800 to 1947*. New York: Macmillan, 1949, chapter 4.

Brock, Gerald W. *The U.S. Computer Industry: A Study of Market Power*. Cambridge: Ballinger Publishing, 1975.

Brock, Leslie V. *The Currency of the American Colonies, 1700–1764*. New York: Arno Press, 1975, chapter 2.

Brody, David. *Steelworkers in America: The Nonunion Era*. Harper Torchbooks, 1969, chapters 1, 2.

Brown, John K. *The Baldwin Locomotive Works, 1831–1915: A Study in American Industrial Practice*. Baltimore: John Hopkins University Press, 1995, chapter 1.

Brown, B. Katherine. "Puritan Democracy in Dedham Massachusetts: Another Case Study." *William and Mary Quarterly* 24 (1967).

Brown, Robert E. *Middle-Class Democracy and the Revolution in Massachusetts, 1691–1780*. Ithaca: Cornell University Press, 1955, 12–20.

Bruce, Philip A. *Economic History of Virginia in the Seventeenth Century.* New York: Macmillan, 1907, chapter 17.

Bruce, Philip A. *Institutional History of Virginia in the Seventeenth Century.* New York: Putnam, 1910; part 2, chapters 1–8, 18; part 3, chapters 4–10.

Bruchey, Stuart. *The Roots of American Economic Growth, 1607–1861: An Essay on Social Causation.* New York: Harper Row, 1965, chapter 4.

Bruchey, Stuart. *The Wealth of the Nation: An Economic History of the United States* New York: Harper Row, 1988, chapter 3.

Bryant, Lynwood. "The Beginnings of the Internal-Combustion Engine." In *Technology in Western Civilization: The Emergence of Modern Industrial Society, Earliest Times to 1900,* edited by Melvin Kranzberg, and Carroll W. Pursell. New York: Oxford University Press, 1967.

Buck, Solon J. *The Granger Movement: A Study of Agricultural Organization and its Political, Economic and Social Manifestations, 1870–1880.* Lincoln: University of Nebraska Press, n.d. (reprint of 1913 edition).

Calder, Lendol G. "From Consumptive Credit to Consumer Credit: E. R Seligman and the Moral Justification of Consumer Debt." *Essays in Economic and Business History* 14 (1996).

Cameron, Edward M. *Samuel Slater: Father of American Manufactures.* Freeport: Bond Wheelwright Company, 1960.

Campbell, Edward G. *The Reorganization of the American Railroad System, 1893–1900: A Study of the Effects of the Panic of 1893, the Ensuing Depression, and the First Years of Recovery on Railroad Organization and Financing.* New York: Columbia University Press, 1938.

Campbell, John L., J. Rogers Hollingsworth, and Leon N. Lindberg, eds. *Governance of the American Economy.* Cambridge: Cambridge University Press, 1991.

Carman, Harry J. ed. *American Husbandry.* Port Washington, NJ: Kennikat Press, 1964 (reprint of 1939 edition that was a reprint of 1775 edition, chapter 12).

Carr, Lois G., and Russell R. Menard. "Immigration and Opportunity: The Freedman in Early Colonial Maryland." In *The Chesapeake in the Seventeenth Century: Essays in Anglo-American Society,* edited by Thad W. Tate and David L. Ammerman, Chapel Hill: University of North Carolina Press, 1979.

Carr, Lois G., Philip D. Morgan, and Jean B. Russo, eds. *Colonial Chesapeake Society.* Chapel Hill: University of North Carolina Press, 1988.

Carr, Lois G., and Russell R. Menard. "Land, Labor, and Economies of Scale in Early Maryland: Some Limits to Growth in the Chesapeake System of Husbandry." *Journal of Economic History* 49 (1989).

Carr, Lois G., Russell R. Menard, and Lorena S. Walsh. *Robert Cole's World: Agriculture and Society in Early Maryland.* Chapel Hill: University of North Carolina Press, 1991.

Carrier, Lyman. *Agriculture in Virginia, 1607–1699.* Williamsburg, VA: Celebration Corporation, 1957.

Carrier, Lyman. *The Beginnings of Agriculture in America.* New York: McGraw-Hill, 1923, chapters 12, 13, 14, 15.

Carroll, Charles F. *The Timber Economy of Puritan New England.* Providence, RI: Brown University Press, 1973, chapters 4, 5, 6, 7.

Chandler, Alfred D. "Henry Varnum Poor: Philosopher of Management." In *Men in Business: Essays on the Historical Role of the Entrepreneur,* edited by William Miller. New York: Harper Torchbooks, 1952.

Chandler, Alfred D. *Strategy and Structure: Chapters in the History of the Industrial Enterprise.* Cambridge, MA: M.I.T. Press, 1962, chapters 1, 3.

Chandler, Alfred D., ed. *Giant Enterprise: Ford, General Motors, and the Automobile Industry.* New York: Harcourt, Brace, World, 1964.

Chandler, Alfred D., ed. *The Railroads: The Nation's First Big Business.* New York: Harcourt Brace World, 1965, parts 1, 2, 3.

Chandler, Alfred D. "Anthracite Coal and the Beginning of the Industrial Revolution in the United States." *Business History Review* 46 (1972)

Chandler, Alfred D. *The Visible Hand: The Managerial Revolution in American Business.* Cambridge, MA: Harvard University Press, 1977.

Chandler, Alfred D. "The Emergence of Managerial Capitalism." *Business History Review* 58 (1984).

Chandler, Alfred D., and Richard S. Tedlow. *The Coming of Managerial Capitalism: A Casebook on the History of American Economic Institutions .* Homewood, IL: Irwin, 1985, cases 9, 10, 11.

Chandler, Alfred D. *Scale and Scope: The Dynamics of Industrial Capitalism.* Cambridge, MA: Harvard University Press, 1990, chapters 2, 3, 4.

Chandler, Alfred D., and James W. Cortada, eds. *A Nation Transformed by Information: How Information has Shaped the United States from Colonial Times to the Present.* New York: Oxford University Press, 2000, chapters 1, 6, 7.

Chandler, Alfred D. *Inventing the Electronic Century: The Epic Story of the Consumer Electronics and Computer Industries.* New York: Free Press, 2001.

Cheape, Charles W. *Moving the Masses: Urban Public Transit in New York, Boston, and Philadelphia, 1880–1912.* Cambridge, MA: Harvard University Press, 1980.

Clark, John G. *The Grain Trade in the Old Northwes.* Urbana: University of Illinois Press, 1966, chapters 10, 11.

Clemens, Paul G. E. *The Atlantic Economy and Colonial Maryland's Eastern Shore: From Tobacco to Grain.* Ithaca, NY: Cornell University Press, 1980, chapter 6.

Clemens, Paul G. E., and Lucy Simler. "Rural Labor and the Farm Household in Chester County, Pennsylvania, 1750–1820." In *Work and Labor in Early America,* edited by Stephen Innes. Chapel Hill: University of North Carolina Press, 1988.

Cochran, Thomas C. *Railroad Leaders, 1845–1890: The Business Mind in America.* Cambridge, MA: Harvard University Press, 1953, chapter 2.

Cochran, Thomas C. *Frontiers of Change: Early Industrialism in America.* New York: Oxford University Press, 1981, chapter 4, 6.

Cohen, David S. *The Dutch American Farm.* New York: New York University Press, 1992, chapter 4.

Cohen, Patricia C. *A Calculating People: The Spread of Numeracy in Early America.* Chicago: University of Chicago Press, 1985.

Coleman, Peter J. *The Transformation of Rhode Island, 1790–1860.* Providence, RI: Brown University Press, 1963, chapters 3, 4.

Conrad, James L. "Drive that Branch: Samuel Slater, the Power Loom, and the Writing of America's Textile History." *Technology and Culture* 36 (1995).

Cook, Edward M. "Social Behavior and Changing Values in Dedham, Massachusetts, 1700–1775." *William and Mary Quarterly* 27 (1970).

Cook, Edward M. *The Fathers of the Towns: Leadership and Community Structure in Eighteenth-Century New England.* Baltimore: Johns Hopkins University Press, 1976.

Cooke, Jacob E., ed. *The Reports of Alexander Hamilton.* New York: Harper Torchbooks, 1964.

Corless, Carlton J. *Main Line of Mid-America: The Story of the Illinois Central.* New York: Creative Age Press, 1950, chapters 7, 8, 9.

Cortner, Richard C. *The Apportionment Cases.* New York: Norton, 1970; chapter 1.

Cowhey, Peter F., and Jonathan D. Aronson. *Managing the World Economy: The Consequences of Corporate Alliances.* New York: Council of Foreign Relations Press, 1993.

Craven, Avery O. *Soil Exhaustion as a Factor in the Agricultural History of Virginia and Maryland, 1606–1860.* Gloucester, MA: Peter Smith, 1965 (reprint of 1926 edition; chapter 2).

Craven, Wesley F. *The Southern Colonies in the Seventeenth Century, 1607–1689.* Baton Rouge: Louisiana State University Press, 1949, chapters 5, 6, 10.

Craven, Wesley F. *Dissolution of the Virginia Company: The Failure of a Colonial Experiment.* Gloucester, MA: Peter Smith, 1964 (reprint of 1932 edition).

Cremin, Lawrence A. *The American Common School: An Historical Conception.* New York: Columbia University Press, 1951.

Cremin, Lawrence A. ed. *The Republic and the School: Horace Mann on the Education of Free Men.* New York: Columbia University Press, 1957.

Cremin, Lawrence A. *American Education: The Colonial Experience, 1607–1783.* New York: Harper Torchbooks, 1970, chapter 6.

Cunningham, Noble E. *The Presidency of James Monroe.* Lawrence: University of Kansas Press, 1996; chapter 7.

Daniels, Bruce C. "The Political Structure of Local Government in Colonial Connecticut." In *Town and Country: Essays on the Structure of Local Government in the American Colonies,* edited by Bruce C. Daniels. Middletown, CT: Wesleyan University Press, 1978.

Daniels, Bruce C. *The Connecticut Town: Growth and Development, 1635–1790.* Middleton, CT: Wesleyan University Press, 1979.

Daniels, Bruce C. "Economic Development in Colonial and Revolutionary Connecticut" *William and Mary Quarterly* 37 (1980).

Davis, Joseph S. *The World Between the Wars, 1919–1939: An Economist's View.* Baltimore: Johns Hopkins University Press, 1975.

Davis, Ralph. "English Foreign Trade, 1700–1774." In *The Growth of English Overseas Trade in the Seventeenth and Eighteenth Centuries,* edited by Walter E. Minchinton, London: Methuen, 1969.

DeConde, Alexander. *This Affair of Louisiana.* New York: Scribners, 1976, chapters 9, 10, 11.

Deming, W. Edwards, *Out of Crisis.* Cambridge, MA: MIT Center for Advanced Engineering, 1982, chapters 1, 2.

Demos, John. "Notes on Life in Plymouth Colony." *William and Mary Quarterly* 22 (1965).

Destler, I. M. *American Trade Politics.* Washington: Institute for International Economics, 1992, chapters 2, 4, 8.

Dewey, Davis R. *Financial History of the United States.* New York: Longmans Green 1928.

Dickerson, Oliver M. *The Navigation Acts and the American Revolution.* New York: Barnes, 1963 (reprint of 1951 edition).

Dickson, R. J. *Ulster Emigration to Colonial America, 1718–1775.* London: Routledge and Kegan Paul, 1966.

Doerflinger, Thomas. *A Vigorous Spirit of Enterprise: Merchants and Economic Development in Revolutionary Philadelphia.* New York: Norton, 1987.

Dorfman, Nancy S. *Innovation and Market Structure: Lessons from the Computer and Semiconductor Industries.* Cambridge: Ballinger Publishing, 1987.

Dunn, Richard S. *Puritans and Yankees: The Winthrop Dynasty of New England, 1630–1717.* New York: Norton, 1971 (reprint of 1962 edition).

Dunn, Richard S. "After Tobacco: The Slave Labour Pattern on a Large Chesapeake Grain-and-Livestock Plantation in the Early Nineteenth Century." In *The Early Modern Atlantic Economy*, edited by John J. McCusker, and Kenneth Morgan Cambridge: Cambridge University Press, 2000.

Durrenberger, Jospeh A. *Turnpikes: A Study of the Toll Road Movement in the Middle Atlantic States and Maryland*. Valdosta: Southern Stationary and Printing Company, 1931.

Earle, Carville V. *The Evolution of a Tidewater Settlement System: All Hallow's Parish Maryland, 1650–1783*. Chicago: University of Chicago Department of Geography Research Paper 170, 1975.

Easterlin, Richard A. "Regional Income Trends, 1840–1950." In *American Economic History*, edited by Seymour E. Harris. New York: McGraw-Hill, 1961.

Egnal, Marc. "The Origins of the Revolution in Virginia: A Reinterpretation" *William and Mary Quarterly* 37 (1980).

English, William B. "Understanding the Costs of Sovereign Default: American State Debts in the 1840s" *American Economic Review* 86 (1996).

Ernst, Joseph A. "Genesis of the Currency Act of 1764: Virginia Paper Money and the Protection of British Investment" *William and Mary Quarterly* 22 (1965).

Ernst, Joseph A. *Money and Politics in America, 1755–1775*. Chapel Hill: University of North Carolina Press, 1973.

Ewing, John S., and Nancy P. Norton. *Broadlooms and Businessmen: A History of the Bigelow-Sanford Carpet Company*. Cambridge, MA: Harvard University Press, 1955, chapter 1.

Faust, Albert B. *The German Element in the United States*. New York: Steuben Society of America, 1927; reprint of 1909 edition, chapter 5.

Fehrenbacher, Don E. *The Slaveholding Republic: An Account of the United States Government's Relations to Slavery*. New York: Oxford University Press, 2001, chapter 10.

Feldstein, Martin S., ed. *The American Economy in Transition*. Chicago: University of Chicago Press, 1980.

Ferguson, Elmer James. "Currency Finance: An Interpretation of Colonial Monetary Practices" *William and Mary Quarterly* 10 (1953).

Ferguson, Elmer James. *The Power of the Purse: A History of Public Finance, 1776–1790*, Chapel Hill: University of North Carolina Press, 1961, chapters 4, 13, 14.

Ferguson, Eugene S. "The Steam Engine before 1830;" "Metallurgical and Machine-Tool Developments;" "Steam Transportation." In *Technology in Western Civilization*, Vol. 1, edited by Melvin Kranzberg and Carroll W. Pursell. New York: Oxford University Press, 1967.

Fischer, David H. *Albion's Seed: Four British Folkways in America*. New York: Oxford University Press, 1989, chapters 1, 2; 224–246.

Fishlow, Albert. *American Railroads and the Transformation of the Ante-Bellum Economy*. Cambridge: Harvard University Press, 1965.

Fisk, Carl R. "The English Parish and Education at the Beginning of American Colonization." *School Review* 23 (1915).

Flamm, Kenneth S. *Targeting the Computer: Government Support and International Competition*. Washington: Brookings Institution, 1987, chapters 3, 5.

Flamm, Kenneth S. *Creating the Computer: Government, Industry, and High Technology*. Washington, DC: Brookings Institution, 1988.

Flamm, Kenneth S. *Mismanaged Trade? Strategic Policy and the Semiconductor Industry*. Washington, DC: Brookings Institution, 1996, chapters 2, 4.

Fletcher, Stevenson W. *Pennsylvania Agriculture and Country Life, 1640–1840*. Harrisburg: Pennsylvania Historical and Museum Commission, 1950, chapters 4, 5, 13.

Foner, Eric. *Free Soil, Free Labor, Free Men: The Ideology of the Republican Party Before the Civil War*. London, Oxford University Press, 1970, chapters 1, 2.

Ford, Henry J. *The Scotch-Irish in America*. New York: Arno Press (reprint of 1915 edition).

Foster, Stephen. "The Massachusetts Franchise in the Seventeenth Century" *William and Mary Quarterly* 24 (1967).

Foster, Stephen. *Their Solitary Way: The Puritan Social Ethic in the First Century of Settlement in New England*. New Haven, CT: Yale University Press, 1971, chapter 5, appendix A.

Freeman, Richard B. "The Evolution of the American Labor Market, 1948–1980." In *The American Economy in Transition*, edited by Martin S. Feldstein. Chicago: University of Chicago Press, 1980.

Friedman, Karen J. "Victualling Colonial Boston." *Agricultural History* 47 (1973).

Friedman, Lawrence M. *A History of American Law*. New York: Touchstone Book, 1974, 238–243, 480–482.

Galenson, David W. *White Servitude in Colonial America: An Economic Analysis* Cambridge: Cambridge University Press, 1981.

Garraty, John A. *The New Commonwealth, 1877–1890*. New York: Harper Torchbooks, 1968, chapters 5, 6.

Gates, Paul W. *The Illinois Central Railroad and its Colonization Work* .Cambridge: Harvard University Press, 1934.

George, Peter J. *The Emergence of Industrial America: Strategic Factors in American Economic Growth Since 1870*. Albany: State University of New York, 1982, chapter 8.

Gibb, George S. *The Saco-Lowell Shops*. Cambridge, MA: Harvard University Press, 1950, chapters 1, 2, 3.

Gilmore, William J. *Reading Becomes a Necessity of Life: Material and Cultural Life in Rural New England, 1780–1835*. Knoxville: University of Tennessee Press, 1989, chapters 2, 3.

Golab, Caroline. *Immigrant Destinations*. Philadelphia: Temple University Press, 1977.

Goldenberg, Joseph A. *Shipbuilding in Colonial America*. Charlottesville: University Press of Virginia, 1976.

Goodrich, Carter. *Government Promotion of American Canals and Railroads, 1800–1890*. New York: Columbia University Press, 1960.

Goodrich, Carter. *Canals and American Economic Development*. New York: Columbia University Press, 1961.

Goodrich, Carter, ed. *The Government and the Economy, 1783–1861*. Indianapolis: Bobbs-Merrill, 1967, part 8, no. 42.

Gordon, Robert B. *American Iron, 1607–1900*. Baltimore: Johns Hopkins University Press, 1996, chapters 3–9.

Gottlieb, Peter. *Making Their Own Way: Southern Blacks Migration to Pittsburgh, 1916–1930*. Urbana: University of Illinois Press, 1987, 29–31, 43–46, 55–59, 90–101.

Graham, Ian C. *Colonists from Scotland: Emigration to North America, 1707–1783*. Ithaca, NY: Cornell University Press, 1956, chapters 2, 3.

Grant, Charles S. *Democracy in the Connecticut Frontier Town of Kent*. New York: Norton, 1972.

Green, Constance M. *Eli Whitney and the Birth of American Technology*. New York: Harper Collins Publisher, 1956.

Green, George D. "Louisiana, 1804–1861." In *Banking and Economic Development: Some Lessons of History*, edited by Rondo Cameron. New York: Oxford University Press, 1972.

Greene, Jack P. "Foundations of Political Power in the Virginia House of Burgesses, 1720–1776." *William and Mary Quarterly* 16 (1959).

Greene, Jack P., ed. *Great Britain and the American Colonies, 1606–1763*. New York: Harper Paperbacks, 1970, introduction.

Greene, Jack P. *The Quest for Power: The Lower Houses of Assembly in the Southern Royal Colonies, 1689–1776*. New York: Norton Library, 1972 (reprint of 1963 edition).

Greene, Jack P. *Pursuits of Happiness: The Social Development of Early Modern British Colonies and the Formation of American Culture*. Chapel Hill: University of North Carolina Press, 1988, chapters 3, 6.

Greene, Jack P. "The Currency Act of 1764 in Metropolitan-Colonial Relations, 1764–1776." In *Negotiated Authorities: Essays in Colonial Political and Constitutional History*, edited by Jack P. Greene. Charlottesville: University Press of Virginia, 1994.

Greven, Philip J. "Family Structure in Seventeenth-Century Andover, Massachusetts." *William and Mary Quarterly* 23 (1966).

Greven, Philip J. *Four Generations: Population, Land, and Family in Colonial Andover, Massachusetts*. Ithaca, NY: Cornell University Press, 1970.

Griffith, Lucille. *The Virginia House of Burgesses, 1750–1774*. University, AL: University of Alabama Press, 1968.

Grodinsky, Julius. *The Iowa Pool: A Study in Railroad Competition, 1870–1884*. Chicago: University of Chicago Press, 1950.

Grodinsky, Julius. *Transcontinental Railway Strategy, 1869–1893: A Study of Businessmen*. Philadelphia: University of Pennsylvania Press, 1962.

Gutman, Herbert G. "The Reality of the Rags-to Riches Myth: The Case of the Paterson New Jersey Locomotive, Iron, and Machinery Manufacturers, 1830–1880." In *Nineteenth-Century Cities: Essays in the New Urban History*, edited by Stephan Thernstrom, and Richard Sennett. New Haven, CT: Yale University Press, 1969.

Hahn, Steven H. *The Roots of Southern Populism: Yeoman Farmers and the Transformation of the Georgia Upcountry, 1850–1890*. New York: Oxford University Press, 1983, chapters 4, 5, 6.

Haites, Erik F., James Mak, and Gary M. Walton. *Western River Transportation: The Era of Early Internal Development, 1810–1860*. Baltimore: Johns Hopkins University Press, 1975; chapter 7.

Hall, Jacquelyn D. et al. *Like a Family: The Making of a Southern Cotton Mill World*. New York: Norton, 1989, chapter 4.

Haller, William. *The Puritan Frontier: Town-Planting in New England Colonial Development, 1630–1660*. New York: AMS Press, 1968 (reprint of 1951 edition).

Hamilton, Holman. *Prologue to Conflict: The Crisis and Compromise of 1850*. New York: Norton, 1964.

Hammond, Bray. *Banks and Politics in America from the Revolution to the Civil War*. Princeton, NJ: Princeton University Press, 1957.

Hammond, Bray. *Sovereignty and an Empty Purse: Banks and Politics in the Civil War*. Princeton, NJ: Princeton University Press, 1970.

Harlan, Louis R. *Separate and Unequal: Public School Campaigns and Racism in the Southern Seaboard States, 1901–1915*. New York: Atheneum, 1968 (reprint of 1958 edition; chapter 1).

Hartz, Louis. *Economic Policy and Democratic Thought: Pennsylvania, 1776–1860*. Chicago: Quadrangle Books, 1968 (reprint of 1948 edition; chapters 2, 3, 4).

Hawke, David F. *Nuts and Bolts of the Past: A History of American Technology, 1776–1860*. New York: Harper and Row, 1988.

Hazard, Blanche E. *The Organization of the Boot and Shoe Industry in Massachusetts before 1875*. Cambridge, MA: Harvard University Press, 1921, chapters 1–5.

Hecht, Irene W. D. "The Virginia Muster of 1624/5 as a Source for Demographic History" *William and Mary Quarterly* 30 (1973).

Henretta, James A. "Economic Development and Social Structure in Colonial Boston." *William and Mary Quarterly* 22 (1965).

Henretta, James A. *Salutary Neglect: Colonial Administration Under the Duke of Newcastle.* Princeton, NJ: Princeton University Press, 1972.

Hepburn, A. Barton. *A History of Currency in the United States.* New York: Augustus Kelley Publishers, 1967 (reprint of 1924 edition; chapters 11, 12, 13, 16, 20).

Herndon, Ruth W. *Unwelcome Americans: Living on the Margin in Early New England.* Philadelphia: University of Pennsylvania Press, 2001.

Heyrman, Christine L. *Commerce and Culture: The Maritime Communities of Colonial Massachusetts, 1690–1750.* New York: Norton, 1984, chapters 2, 6.

Hibbard, Benjamin H. *A History of the Public Land Policies.* Madison: University of Wisconsin Press, 1965 (reprint of 1924 edition; chapters 3, 4).

Hicks, John D. *Republican Ascendancy, 1921–1933.* New York: Harper, 1960.

Hicks, John D. *The Populist Revolt: A History of the Farmers Alliance and the Peoples Party.* Lincoln: University of Nebraska Press, 1961 (reprint of 1931 edition).

Higgs, Robert. *The Transformation of the American Economy, 1865–1914: Essays in Interpretation.* New York: Wiley, 1971, chapter 2.

Higgs, Robert. *Crisis and Leviathan: Critical Episodes in the Growth of American Government.* New York: Oxford University Press, 1987, chapters 2, 8.

Hill, Christopher. "Pottage for Freeborn Englishmen: Attitudes to Wage-Labour." In *Change and Continuity in Seventeenth-Century England*, edited by Christopher Hill, Cambridge, MA: Harvard University Press, 1975.

Hill, Forest G. *Roads, Rails and Waterways: The Army Engineers and Early Transportation.* Norman: University of Oklahoma Press, 1957.

Hogan, William T. *World Steel in the 1980s: A Case of Survival.* Lexington, KY: Lexington Books, 1983, chapters 3, 4.

Hoogenboom, Ari A., and Olive Hoogenboom, *A History of the ICC: From Panacea to Palliative.* New York: Norton, 1976, chapters 1, 2.

Horn, James P. P. "Servant Emigration to the Chesapeake in the Seventeenth Century." In *The Chesapeake in the Seventeenth Century: Essays in Anglo-American Society,* edited by Thad W. Tate and David L. Ammerman. Chapel Hill: University of North Carolina Press, 1979.

Horn, James P. P. "Adapting to a New World: A Comparative Study of Local Society in England and Maryland, 1650–1700." In *Colonial Chesapeake Society,* edited by Lois G. Carr, Philip D. Morgan, and Jean B. Russo. Chapel Hill: University of North Carolina Press, 1988.

Horn, James P. P. "Moving on in the New World: Migration and Out-Migration in the Seventeenth-Century Chesapeake." In *Migration and Society in Early Modern England,* edited by Peter Clark, and David Souden. Totowa, NJ: Barnes and Noble, 1988.

Houndshell, David A. "The System: Theory and Practice." In *Yankee Enterprise: The Rise of the American System of Manufactures,* edited by Otto Mayr, and Robert C. Post. Washington: Smithsonian Institution Press, 1981.

Hounshell, David A. *From the American System to Mass Production, 1800–1932: The Development of Manufacturing Technology in the United States.* Baltimore: Johns Hopkins University Press, 1984, chapters 1, 6, 7.

Hughes, Jonathan R. T. *The Vital Few: The Entrepreneur and American Economic Progress.* New York: Oxford University Press, 1986, chapters 7, 23 24, 25.

Hughes, Jonathan R. T. *American Economic History.* Glenview, IL: Scott Foresman, 1990, chapters 23, 24, 25.

Hughes, Thomas P. *Networks of Power: Electrification in Western Society, 1880–1930.* Baltimore: Johns Hopkins University Press, 1983, chapters 8, 10, 13; 429–443.

Hugins, Walter. *Jacksonian Democracy and the Working Class: A Study of the New York Workingmens Movement, 1829–1837.* Stanford: Stanford University Press, 1960; chapter 9.

Hungerford, Edward. *Men and Iron: The History of the New York Central.* New York: Crowell, 1938, chapters 4, 5, 6, 7, 9.

Hunter, Louis C. *Steamboats on the Western Rivers.* New York: Octagon Books, 1969 (reprint of 1949 edition; chapters 6, 7, 12).

Hunter, Louis C. *A History of Industrial Power in the United States, 1780–1930: Waterpower in the Century of the Steam Engine,* Vol. 1. Charlottesville: University Press of Virginia, 1979.

Innes, Stephen. "Land Tenancy and Social Order in Springfield, Massachusetts, 1652 to 1702." *William and Mary Quarterly* 35 (1978).

Innes, Stephen, ed. *Work and Labor in Early America.* Chapel Hill: University of North Carolina Press, 1988, introduction, chapters 1, 2, 3.

Innes, Stephen. *Creating the Commonwealth: The Economic Culture of Puritan New England.* New York: Norton, 199, chapters 6, 7.

Isaac, Rhys. *The Transformation of Virginia, 1740–1790.* Chapel Hill: University of North Carolina Press, 1982, chapter 6.

Jackson, George L. *The Development of School Support in Colonial Massachusetts.* New York: Columbia University Press, 1909.

James, John A. *Money and Capital Markets in Postbellum America.* Princeton, NJ: Princeton University Press, 1978, chapters 2, 4.

Jefferson, Thomas. *Notes on the State of Virginia.* New York: Harper Torchbooks, 1964; reprint of 1785 edition.

Jeremy, David J. *Transatlantic Industrial Revolution: The Diffusion of Textile Technologies Between Britain and America, 1790–1830s.* Cambridge, MA: MIT Press, 1981.

Jernegan, Marcus W. "Slavery and the Beginnings of Industrialism in the American Colonies" *American Historical Review* 25 (1920).

John, Arthur H. "Aspects of English Economic Growth in the First Half of the Eighteenth Century." In *The Growth of English Overseas Trade in the Seventeenth and Eighteenth Centuries*, edited by Walter E. Minchinton. London: Methuen, 1969.

Johnson, Arthur M., and Barry E. Supple. *Boston Capitalists and Western Railroads: A Study in the Nineteenth-Century Railroad Investment Process.* Cambridge, MA: Harvard University Press, 1967.

Johnson, Emory R. *History of Domestic and Foreign Commerce of the United States*, Vol. 1. New York: Burt Franklin, 1964; reprint of 1915 edition; chapters 4, 5, 6.

Johnson, Keach. "The Baltimore Company Seeks English Markets: A Study of the Anglo-American Iron Trade, 1731–1755." *William and Mary Quarterly* 16 (1959).

Jones, Douglas L. "Poverty and Vagabondage: The Process of Survival in Eighteenth-Century Massachusetts." *New England Historical and Genealogical Register* 133 (1979).

Jones, Kent. *Politics vs Economics in World Steel Trade.* London: Allen and Unwin, 1986, chapters 5, 6, 7.

Jones, Stanley L. *The Presidential Election of 1896.* Madison: University of Wisconsin Press, 1964, chapters 5, 6, 13, 23.

Jonnes, Jill. *Empires of Light: Edison, Tesla, Westinghouse, and the Race to Electrify the World.* New York: Random House, 2003, chapters 11, 12.

Kaestle, Carl F. *The Evolution of an Urban School System: New York City, 1750–1850.* Cambridge MA: Harvard University Press, 1973, chapters 6, 7.

Kaestle, Carl F. *Pillars of the Republic: Common Schools and American Society, 1780–1848.* New York: Hill and Wang, 1983, chapters 6, 7, 8, 9.

Karras, Alan L., and John R. McNeill, eds. *Atlantic American Societies from Columbus through Abolition, 1492–1888.* New York: Routledge, 1992.

Kars, Marjoleine. *Breaking Loose Together: The Regulator Rebellion in Pre-Revolutionary North Carolina.* Chapel Hill: University of North Carolina Press, 2002.

Katz, Stanley N., ed. *Colonial America: Essays in Politics and Social Development.* Boston: Little, Brown, 1971.

Kay, Marvin L.M. "The Payment of Provincial and Local Taxes in North Carolina, 1748–1771." *William and Mary Quarterly* 26 (1969).

Keller, Morton. *Affairs of State: Public Life in the Late Nineteenth Century.* Cambridge, MA: Belknap Press, 1977, chapters 8, 9, 10, 11.

Kelly Alfred H., and Winfred A. Harbison, *The American Constitution: Its Origins and Development.* New York: Norton, 1970, chapters 19, 20, 21, 22, 23, 27, 28.

Kelly, Kevin P. "In Dispersed Country Plantations: Settlement Patterns in Seventeenth-Century Surry County Virginia" In *The Chesapeake in the Seventeenth Century: Essays on Anglo-American Society*, edited by Thad W. Tate and David L. Ammerman. Chapel Hill: University of North Carolina Press, 1979.

Kemmerer, Donald L. "The Colonial Loan-Office System in New Jersey." *Journal of Political Economy* 47 (1939).

Kemp, William W. *The Support of Schools in Colonial New York by the Society for the Propagation of the Gospel in Foreign Parts.* New York: Columbia University Press, 1913, chapter 5.

Kessner, Thomas. *The Golden Door: Italian and Jewish Immigrant Mobility in New York City, 1880–1915.* New York: Oxford University Press, 1977, chapters 2, 3, 4.

Kindleberger, Charles P. *The World in Depression, 1929–1939.* Berkeley: University of California Press, 1973, chapter 14.

Kirkland, Edward C. *Men, Cities, and Transportation: A Study in New England History, 1820–1900.* Cambridge, MA: Harvard University Press, 1948.

Kirkland, Edward C. *Industry Comes of Age: Business, Labor, and Public Policy, 1860–1897.* New York: Holt, Rinehart, Winston, 1962.

Klebaner, Benjamin J. "State-Chartered American Commercial Banks, 1781–1801." *Business History Review* 53 (1979).

Klein, Maury. "Coming Full Circle: The Study of Big Business Since 1950." *Enterprise and Society* 2 (2001).

Klett, Guy S. *Presbyterians in Colonial Pennsylvania.* Philadelphia: University of Pennsylvania Press, 1937, chapters 1, 2, 11.

Klier, Thomas H. "Lean Manufacturing: Understanding a New Manufacturing System." In *The Multinational Enterprise in Transition: Strategies for Global Competitiveness*, edited by Phillip D. Grubb, and Dara Khambata. Princeton, NJ: Darwin Press, 1993.

Klingaman, David C. "Food Surpluses and Deficits in the American Colonies, 1768–1772." *Journal of Economic History* 31 (1971).

Kolko, Gabriel. *Railroads and Regulation.* New York: Norton, 1970 (reprint of 1965 edition).

Kolp, John G. *Gentlemen and Freeholders: Electoral Politics in Colonial Virginia.* Baltimore: John Hopkins University Press, 1998, chapter 2.

Kranzberg, Melvin, and Carroll W. Pursell, eds. *Technology in Western Civilization*. New York: Oxford University Press, 1987.

Krug, Edward A. *The Shaping of the American High School, 1880–1920*. Madison: University of Wisconsin Press, 1969, chapters 1, 11.

Kulik, Gary, Robert Parks, and Theodore Z. Penn, eds. *The New England Mill Village, 1790–1860*. Cambridge, MA: MIT Press, 1982.

Kussmaul, Ann. *Servants in Husbandry in Early Modern England*. Cambridge: Cambridge University Press, 1981; chapters 1, 2, 3.

Kwoka, John E. "Automobiles: Products, Process, and the Decline of U.S. Dominance." In *Industry Studies*, edited by Larry L. Duetsch. Armonk, NY: Sharpe, 2002.

Labaree, Leonard W. *Royal Government in America: A Study of the British Colonial System Before 1783*. New Haven, CT: Yale University Press, 1930; chapter 7.

Lamb, Robert K. "The Entrepreneur and the Community." In *Men in Business: Essays on the Historical Role of Entrepreneurs*, edited by William Miller. New York: Harper Torchbooks, 1952.

Lamoreaux, Naomi R. *The Great Merger Movement in American Business, 1895–1904*. Cambridge: Cambridge University Press, 1985.

Land, Aubrey C. "Economic Behavior in a Planting Society: The Eighteenth-Century Chesapeake." *Journal of Southern History* 33 (1967).

Langdon, George D. *Pilgrim Colony: A History of New Plymouth, 1620–1691*. New Haven, CT: Yale University Press, 1966, chapters 4, 7, 11.

La Vopa, Anthony J. *Prussian Schoolteachers: Profession and Office, 1763–1848*. Chapel Hill: University of North Carolina Press, 1980, chapters 3, 4, 5.

Lazerson, Marvin, *Origins of the Urban School: Public Education in Massachusetts, 1870–1915*. Cambridge, MA: Harvard University Press, 1971, chapters 1, 7, 9.

Lee, Charles R. "Public Poor Relief and the Massachusetts Community, 1620–1715." *New England Quarterly* 55 (1982).

Lemon, James T. *The Best Poor Man's Country: A Geographical Study of Early Southeastern Pennsylvania*. Baltimore: Johns Hopkins University Press, 1972, chapters 1, 2.

Leuchtenburg, William E. *The Perils of Prosperity, 1914–1932*. Chicago: University of Chicago Press, 1958, chapters 10, 13.

Leuchtenburg, William E. *Franklin D. Roosevelt and the New Deal, 1932–1940*. New York: Harper and Row, 1963.

Lima, Jose G. H. *Restructuring the U.S. Steel Industry: Semi-Finished Steel Imports, International Integration, and U.S. Adaptation*. Boulder, CO: Westview Press, 1991.

Livesay, Harold C. *Andrew Carnegie and the Rise of Big Business*. Boston: Little, Brown, 1975.

Lockridge, Kenneth A., Alan Kreider. "The Evolution of Massachusetts Town Government, 1640–1740." *William and Mary Quarterly* 23 (1966).

Lockridge, Kenneth A. "The Population of Dedham, Massachusetts, 1630–1736." *Economic History Review* 19 (1966).

Lockridge, Kenneth A. "Land, Population and the Evolution of New England Society, 1630–1790: and an Afterthought." *Past and Present* no. 39 (1968).

Lockridge, Kenneth A. *A New England Town: The First Hundred Years: Dedham, Massachusetts, 1636–1736*. New York: Norton, 1970.

Lockridge, Kenneth A. *Literacy in Colonial New England: An Enquiry into the Social Context of Literacy in the Early Modern West*. New York: Norton, 1974.

Lodge, George C. *Perestroika for America: Restructuring U.S. Business-Government Relations for Competitiveness in the World Economy*. Boston: Harvard Business School Press, 1990; chapters 3, 5, 6.

Lydon, James G. "Fish and Flour for Gold: Southern Europe and the Colonial American Balance of Payments." *Business History Review* 39 (1965).

McCormac, Eugene I. *White Servitude in Maryland*. Baltimore: Johns Hopkins University Press, 1904.

McCusker, John J., Russell R. Menard. *The Economy of British North America, 1607–1789*. Chapel Hill: University of North Carolina Press, 1985.

McDonald, Forrest. *Insull*. Chicago: University of Chicago Press, 1962.

MacGill, Caroline E. *History of Transportation in the United States before 1860*. New York: Peter Smith, 1948 (reprint of 1916 edition).

McGouldrick, Paul F. *New England Textiles in the Nineteenth Century: Profits and Investment*. Cambridge, MA: Harvard University Press, 1968, chapter 2.

McGrane, Reginald C. *Foreign Bondholders and American State Debts*. New York: Macmillan, 1935, chapters 1, 4, 13.

McKelvey, Blake. *The Urbanization of America, 1860–1915*. New Brunswick, NJ: Rutgers University Press, 1963, chapter 4.

McKinley, Albert E. *The Suffrage Franchise in the Thirteen English Colonies in America*. Philadelphia: Ginn, 1905, chapters 2, 3.

McKitrick, Eric L. *Andrew Johnson and Reconstruction*. Chicago: University of Chicago Press, 1960, 314–318, 439–443.

McLaughlin, Andrew C. *The Confederation and the Constitution, 1783–1789*. New York: Collier Books, 1962 (reprint of 1905 edition).

McLaughlin, Andrew C. *The Foundations of American Constitutionalism.* Greenwich, CT: Fawcett Publications, 1961 (reprint of 1932 edition; chapters 4, 6).

McLaughlin, Andrew C. *A Constitutional History of the United States.* New York: Appleton-Century-Crofts, 1963 (reprint of 1935 edition; chapters 35, 40).

McMahon, Sarah F. "A Comfortable Subsistence: The Changing Composition of Diet in Rural New England, 1620–1840." *William and Mary Quarterly* 42 (1985).

McManis, Douglas R. *Colonial New England: A Historical Geography.* New York: Oxford University Press, 1975, 53–66.

McMaster, John B. *A History of the People of the United States,* Vol. 8. New York: Appleton, 1926, chapters 84–93.

Magaziner, Ira C., and Thomas M. Hout. *Japanese Industrial Policy.* Berkeley, CA: Institute of International Studies, 1980.

Magaziner, Ira C., and Robert B. Reich. *Minding America's Business: The Decline and Rise of the American Economy.* New York: Harcourt Brace Jovanovich, 1982, chapters 13, 20, 21, 22, 23.

Main, Jackson T. *Society and Economy in Colonial Connecticut.* Princeton, NJ: Princeton University Press, 1985.

Majewski, John A. *A House Dividing: Economic Development in Pennsylvania and Virginia before the Civil War.* Cambridge: Cambridge University Press, 2000, chapter 5.

Malerba, Franco. *The Semiconductor Business: The Economics of Rapid Growth and Decline.* Madison: University of Wisconsin Press, 1985, chapters 1, 2.

Margo, Robert A. *Race and Schooling in the South, 1880–1950: An Economic History.* Chicago: University of Chicago Press, 1990, chapters 2, 3, 7.

Martin, Albro. "The Troubled Subject of Railroad Regulation in the Gilded Age—A Reappraisal." *Journal of American History* 61 (1974).

Martin, John F. *Profits in the Wilderness: Entrepreneurship and the Founding of New England Towns in the Seventeenth Century.* Chapel Hill: University of North Carolina Press, 1991.

Mathews, Lois K. *The Expansion of New England: The Spread of New England Settlement and Institutions to the Mississippi River, 1620–1865.* New York: Russell and Russell, 1962, chapters 6, 7.

Mayr, Otto, Robert C. Post, eds. *Yankee Enterprise: The rise of the American System of Manufacturing.* Washington, DC: Smithsonian Institution Press, 1981.

Menard, Russell R. "From Servant to Freeholder: Status, Mobility, and Property Accumulation in Seventeenth-Century Maryland." *William and Mary Quarterly* 30 (1973).

Menard, Russell R., Lois G. Carr, and Lorena S. Walsh. "A Small Planter's Profits: The Cole Estate and the Growth of the Early Chesapeake Economy." *William and Mary Quarterly* 40 (1983).

Menard, Russell R. "British Migration to the Chesapeake Colonies in the Seventeenth Century." In *Colonial Chesapeake Society,* edited by Lois G. Carr, Philip D. Morgan, and Jean B. Russo. Chapel Hill: University of North Carolina Press, 1988.

Meyer, Adolphe E. *An Educational History of the American People.* New York: McGraw-Hill, 1957, chapters 7, 8, 9.

Middlekauff, Robert. *Ancients and Axioms: Secondary Education in Eighteenth-Century New England.* New Haven, CT: Yale University Press, 1963.

Middleton, William D. *The Interurban Era.* Milwaukee, WS: Kalmbach Publishing, 1961.

Miller, George H. *Railroads and the Granger Laws.* Madison: University of Wisconsin Press, 1971.

Miller, John C. *Alexander Hamilton and the Growth of the New Nation.* New York: Harper Torchbooks, 1959.

Miller, John C. *The Federalist Era, 1789–1801.* New York: Harper Torchbooks, 1960.

Miller, Nathan. *The Enterprise of a Free People: Aspects of Economic Development in New York State During the Canal Period, 1792–1838.* Ithaca, NY: Cornell University Press, 1962, chapters 5, 6, 7, 8.

Minchinton, Walter E., ed. *The Growth of English Overseas Trade in the Seventeenth and Eighteenth Centuries.* London: Methuen, 1969.

Misa, Thomas J. *A Nation of Steel: The Making of Modern America, 1865–1925.* Baltimore: Johns Hopkins University Press, 199, chapter 4.

Mitchell, Broadus. *Depression Decade: From New Era through New Deal, 1929–1941.* New York: Rinehart, 1958.

Mohl, Raymond A. *The New City: Urban America in the Industrial Age, 1860–1920.* Arlington Heights, IL: Harlan Davidson, 1985.

Monkkonen, Eric H. *The Local State: Public Money and American Cities.* Palo Alto, CA: Stanford University Press, 1995, chapters 3, 4.

Moore, Glover. *The Missouri Controversy, 1819–1821.* Lexington: University of Kentucky Press, 1953.

Morawska, Ewa. *For Bread With Butter: The Life-Worlds of East Central Europeans in Johnstown, Pennsylvania, 1890–1940.* Cambridge. MA: Cambridge University Press, 1985.

Morawska, Ewa. "From Myth to Reality: America in the Eyes of East European Peasant Migrant Laborers." In *Distant Magnets: Expectations and Realities in the Immigrant Experience, 1840–1930,* edited by Dirk Hoerder, and Horst Rossler. New York: Holmes and Meier, 1993, chapters 1–4.

Morgan, Edmund S., and Helen M. Morgan. *The Stamp Act Crisis: Prologue to Revolution.* New York: Collier Books, 1962 (reprint of 1953 edition).

Morgan, Edmund. "The Labor Problem in Jamestown." In *Atlantic American Societies: From Columbus Through Abolition,*

1492–1888, edited by Alan L. Karras, John R. McNeill. London: Routledge, 1992 (reprinted from *American Historical Review* 76, 1971).

Morgan, Kenneth. *Slavery and Servitude in Colonial North America: A Short History*. New York: New York University Press, 2000, chapter 3.

Morison, Samuel E. *Builders of the Bay Colony*. Boston: Houghton Mifflin, 1930.

Morison, Samuel E. *The Maritime History of Massachusetts, 1783–1860*. Boston: Houghton Mifflin, 1961, chapter 13.

Morris, Richard B. *Studies in the History of American Law: With Special Reference to the Seventeenth and Eighteenth Centuries*. New York: Columbia University Press, 1930, chapter 2; 69–82.

Morris, Richard B. *Government and Labor in Early America*. New York: Columbia University Press, 1946; chapter 8; 500–508.

Mulhern, James. *A History of Secondary Education in Pennsylvania*. New York: Arno Press, 1969 (reprint of 1933 edition; chapters 1, 2, 3, 4).

Nash, Gary B. "Poverty and Poor Relief in Pre-Revolutionary Philadelphia." *William and Mary Quarterly* 20 (1963).

Nelson, Daniel. *Managers and Workers: Origins of the Twentieth-Century Factory System in the United States, 1880–1920*. Madison: University of Wisconsin Press, 1995.

Nettels, Curtis P. *The Money Supply of the American Colonies before 1720*. New York: Augustus Kelley, 1964 (reprint of 1934 edition; chapters 8, 10).

Ng, Kenneth. "Free Banking Laws and Barriers to Entry into Banking, 1838–1860." *Journal of Economic History* 48 (1988).

North, Douglass C. *The Economic Growth of the United States, 1790–1860*. New York: Norton, 1966 (reprint of 1961 edition; chapters 3–6, 13).

North, Douglass C. *Growth and Welfare in the American Past: A New Economic History*. Englewood Cliffs, NJ: Prentice-Hall, 1966.

Nugent, Walter T. K. *Crossings: The Great Transatlantic Migrations, 1870–1914*. Bloomington: Indiana University Press, 1995.

Okimoto, Daniel I. *Between MITI and the Market: Japanese Industrial Policy for High Technology*. Palo Alto, CA: Stanford University Press, 1989, chapters 2, 3.

Olmsted, Frederick L. *The Slave States*. New York: Capricorn Books, 1959; reprints from 1856 and 1857 editions, 69–71, 86–87, 107–110, 200–206, 249–254, 270–274.

Osgood, Herbert L. *The American Colonies in the Seventeenth Century*. Gloucester, MA: Peter Smith, 1957 (reprint of 1904 edition; vol. 1, chapters 11, 12).

Ostrander, Gilman M. "The Colonial Molasses Trade." *Agricultural History*. 30 (1956).

Palmer, Bruce. *Man Over Money: The Southern Populists Critique of American Capitalism*. Chapel Hill: University of North Carolina Press, 1980.

Papenfuse, Edward C. "Planter Behavior and Economic Opportunity in a Staple Economy." *Agricultural History* 46 (1972).

Paskoff, Paul F. *Industrial Evolution: Organization, Structure, and Growth of the Pennsylvania Iron Industry, 1750–1860*. Baltimore: Johns Hopkins University Press, 1983.

Passer, Harold C. *The Electrical Manufacturers, 1875–1900: A Study in Competition, Entrepreneurship, Technical Change, and Economic Growth*. Cambridge, MA: Harvard University Press, 1953.

Passer, Harold C. "Frank Julian Sprague: Father of Electric Traction." In *Men in Business: Essays on the Historical Role of the Entrepreneur*, edited by William Miller. New York: Harper Torchbooks, 1967.

Percy, David O. "Ax or Plow? Significant Colonial Landscape Alternation Rates in the Maryland and Virginia Tidewater." *Agricultural History* 6 (1992).

Perkins, Edwin J. *American Public Finance and Financial Services, 1700–1815*. Columbus: Ohio State University Press, 1994.

Perrin, Noel, Kenneth Breisch, and Serge Hambourg. *Mills and Factories of New England*. New York: Harry N. Abrams Publishers, 1988.

Phillips, Ulrich B. *A History of Transportation in the Eastern Cotton Belt to 1860*. New York: Octagon Books, 1968 (reprint of 1908 edition; chapter 3).

Pierce, Harry H. *Railroads of New York: A Study of Government Aid, 1826–1875*. Cambridge, MA: Harvard University Press, 1953.

Platt, Harold L. *The Electric City: Energy and the Growth of the Chicago Area, 1880–1930*. Chicago: University of Chicago Press, 1991.

Porter, Glenn, and Harold C. Livesay. *Merchants and Manufacturers: Studies in the Changing Structure of Nineteenth-Century Marketing*. Baltimore: Johns Hopkins University Press, 1971. chapter 6.

Porter, Glenn. *The Rise of Big Business, 1860–1920*. Arlington Heights, IL: Harlan Davidson, 1992; revision of 1973 edition.

Potter, David M. *People of Plenty: Economic Abundance and the American Character*. Chicago: University of Chicago Press, 1954. chapter 8.

Potter, David M. *The Impending Crisis, 1848–1861*. New York: Harper Torchbooks, 1976, chapters 7, 9, 10, 16.

Potter, Jim. *The American Economy Between the World Wars*. New York: Wiley, 1974.

Powell, Sumner C. *Puritan Village: The Formation of a New England Town*. Middleton: Wesleyan University Press, 1963.

Price, Jacob M. "Economic Function and Growth of American Port Towns in the Eighteenth Century." *Perspectives in American History* 8 (1974).

Price, Jacob M. *Capital and Credit in British Overseas Trade: The View from the Chesapeake, 1700–1776*. Cambridge, MA: Harvard University Press, 1980, chapters 5, 6.

Price, Jacob M. "Buchanan and Simpson, 1759–1763: A Different Kind of Glasgow Firm Trading in the Chesapeake." *William and Mary Quarterly* 40 (1983).

Prude, Jonathan. *The Coming of Industrial Order: Town and Factory Life in Rural Massachusetts, 1810–1860*. New York: Cambridge University Press, 1985, chapter 7.

Pruitt, Bettye H. "Self-Sufficiency and the Agricultural Economy of Eighteenth-Century Massachusetts." *William and Mary Quarterly* 41 (1984).

Pursell, Carroll W. *Early Stationary Steam Engines in America: A Study in the Migration of Technology*. Washington, DC: Smithsonian Institution Press, 1969.

Rainbolt, John C. "The alteration in the Relationship Between Leadership and Constituents in Virginia, 1660–1720." *William and Mary Quarterly* 27 (1970).

Ransom, Roger L., and Richard Sutch. *One Kind of Freedom: The Economic Consequences of Emancipation*. Cambridge: Cambridge University Press, 1977, chapters 5, 8, 151–159.

Ratchford, Benjamin U. *American State Debts*. Durham, NC: Duke University Press, 1941, chapters 4, 5, 6.

Rayback, Joseph G. *Free Soil: The Election of 1848*. Lexington: University Press of Kentucky, 1970.

Reavis, William A. "The Maryland Gentry and Social Mobility, 1637–1676." *William and Mary Quarterly* 14 (1957).

Rees, Albert. *Real Wages in Manufacturing, 1890–1914*. Princeton, NJ: Princeton University Press, 1961, chapter 5; table 44.

Report of the Committee on Recent Economic Changes. *Recent Economic Changes in the United States*. New York: McGraw-Hill, 1929, Vol. 1, chapter 2, part 2.

Riegel, Robert E. *The Story of the Western Railroads*. New York: Macmillan, 1926.

Riegler, Claudius H. "Scandinavian Migrants Images and the Americanization of the Work Process." In *Distant Magnets: Expectations and Realities in the Immigrant Experience, 1840–1930*, edited by Dirk Hoerder, and Horst Rossler. New York: Holmes and Meier, 1993.

Robbins, Michael W. *The Principio Company: Iron-Making in Colonial Maryland, 1720–1781*. Washington, DC: Smithsonian Institution dissertation, 1972, (University Microfilms, 1979), chapters 1, 2.

Rohlfs, Jeffrey H. *Bandwagon Effects in High-Technology Industries*. Cambridge, MA: MIT Press, 2001, chapters 11, 13.

Rohrbough, Malcolm J. *The Land Office Business: The Settlement and Administration of American Public Lands, 1789–1837*. New York: Oxford University Press, 1968, chapters 1, 2.

Rosenberg, Nathan, ed. *The American System of Manufactures: The Report of the Committee on the Machinery of the United States 1855*. Edinburgh: Edinburgh University Press, 1969, introduction.

Rosenberg, Nathan. "The Economic Consequence of Technological Change, 1830–1880." In *Technology in Western Civilization*, edited by Melvin Kranzberg, and Carroll W. Pursell. New York: Oxford University Press, 1987.

Rubin, Julius. *Canal or Railroad? Imitation and Innovation in the Response to the Erie Canal in Philadelphia, Baltimore, and Boston*. Philadelphia, Transactions of the American Philosophical Society, New Series, 1961, vol. 51, part 7

Russo, Jean B. "Self-Sufficiency and Local Exchange: Free Craftsmen in the Rural Chesapeake Economy." In *Colonial Chesapeake Society*, edited by Lois G. Carr, Philip D. Morgan, and Jean B. Russo. Chapel Hill: University of North Carolina Press, 1988.

Rutland, Robert A. *The Birth of the Bill of Rights, 1776–1791*. New York: Collier Books, 1962 (reprint of 1955 edition; chapters 6, 7).

Rutman, Darrett B. "Governor Winthrop's Garden Crop: The Significance of Agriculture in the Early Commerce of Massachusetts Bay." *William and Mary Quarterly* 20 (1963).

Rutman, Darrett B. *Husbandmen of Plymouth: Farms and Villages in the Old Colony, 1620–1692*. Boston: Beacon Press, 1967.

Rutman, Darrett B., and Anita H. Rutman. *A Place in Time: Middlesex County, Virginia, 1650–1750*. New York: Norton, 1984; 166–167.

Salerno, Anthony. "The Social Background of Seventeenth-Century Emigration to America." *Journal of British Studies* 19 (1979).

Salinger, Sharon V. *To Serve Well and Faithfully: Labor and Indentured Servants in Pennsylvania, 1682–1800*. Cambridge: Cambridge University Press, 1987.

Salsbury, Stephen. *The State, the Investor, and the Railroad: The Boston and Albany, 1825–1867*. Cambridge, MA: Harvard University Press, 1967.

Scheiber, Harry N. *Ohio Canal Era: A Case Study of Government and the Economy, 1820–1861*. Athens: Ohio University Press, 1969, parts 1, 2.

Scherrer, Christoph. "Governance of the Steel Industry: What Caused the Disintegration of the Oligopoly." In *Governance of the American Economy*, edited by John L. Campbell, J. Rogers Hollingsworth, and Leon N. Lindberg. Cambridge: Cambridge University Press, 1991.

Schumpeter, Joseph A. *Capitalism, Socialism and Democracy*. New York: Harper, 1942.

Schurr, Sam H., and Bruce C. Netschert. *Energy in the American Economy, 1850–1975: An Economic Study of its History and Prospects*. Baltimore: Johns Hopkins University Press, 1960, chapters 3, 4.

Schweikart, Larry. *Banking in the American South from the Age of Jackson to Reconstruction.* Baton Rouge: Louisiana State University Press, 1987, chapters 5, 6.

Schweitzer, Mary M. "Economic Regulation and the Colonial Economy: The Maryland Tobacco Inspection Act of 1747." *Journal of Economic History* 40 (1980).

Sears, Stephen W. *The Automobile in America.* New York: American Heritage Publishing, 1977.

Seavoy, Ronald E. "Borrowed Laws to Speed Development: Michigan, 1835–1863." *Michigan History* 59 (1975).

Seavoy, Ronald E. "The Organization of the Republican Party in Michigan, 1846–1854." *The Old Northwest* 6 (1980–1981).

Seavoy, Ronald E. *The Origins of the American Business Corporation, 1784–1855, Broadening the Concept of Public Service During Industrialization.* Westport, CT: Greenwood Press, 1982.

Seavoy, Ronald E. *Famine in Peasant Societies.* Westport, CT: Greenwood Press, 1986; chapters 1, 2, 5.

Seavoy, Ronald E. "The Constitutionalization of Laissez-Faire Business Policy in the United States." *Essays in Economic and Business History* 9 (1991).

Seavoy, Ronald E. "Slave Plantations in the United States: How They were Managed." *Plantation Society in the Americas* 4 (1997).

Seavoy, Ronald E. *The American Peasantry: Southern Agricultural Labor and its Legacy, 1850–1995: A Study in Political Economy.* Westport, CT: Greenwood Press, 1998, chapters 6–12; 223–229, 322–324, 328–360.

Seavoy, Ronald E. *Subsistence and Economic Development.* Westport, CT: Praeger, 2000; chapter 3.

Seavoy, Ronald E. *Origins and Growth of the Global Economy, From the Fifteenth Century Onward.* Westport, CT: Praeger, 2003, chapters 1, 2, 5, 6.

Segal, Harvey H. "Canals and Economic Development." In *Canals and American Economic Developmen*, edited by Carter Goodrich. New York: Columbia University Press, 1961.

Seybolt, Robert F. *Apprenticeship and Apprenticeship Education in Colonial New England and New York.* New York: Columbia University Press, 1917.

Seybolt, Robert F. *The Public Schools of Colonial Boston, 1635–1775.* Cambridge, MA: Harvard University Press, 1935.

Seybolt, Robert F. *The Private Schools of Colonial Boston.* Cambridge, MA: Harvard University Press, 1935.

Shade, William G. *Banks or No Banks: The Money Issue in Western Politics, 1832–1865.* Detroit, MI: Wayne State University Press, 1972, chapters 4–7.

Shannon, Fred A. *The Farmers Last Frontier: Agriculture, 1860–1897.* New York: Holt, Rinehart, Winston, 1963 (reprint of 1945 edition; chapter 6).

Sharkey, Robert P. *Money, Class, and Party: An Economic Study of Civil War and Reconstruction.* Baltimore: Johns Hopkins University Press, 1959.

Shaw, Ronald E. *Erie Water West: A History of the Erie Canal, 1792–1854.* Lexington: University of Kentucky Press, 1966, chapter 4.

Shaw, Ronald E. *Canals for a Nation: The Canal Era in the United States, 1790–1860.* Lexington: University Press of Kentucky, 1990, chapter 7.

Shelton, Cynthia J. *The Mills of Manayunk: Industrialization and Social Conflict in the Philadelphia Region, 1787–1837.* Baltimore: Johns Hopkins University Press, 1986; chapters 2–3.

Shepherd, James F. "Commodity Exports from the British North American Colonies to Overseas Areas, 1768–1772." *Explorations in Economic History,* vol. 8, 1970.

Shepherd, James F., and Gary M. Walton. *Shipping, Maritime Trade, and the Economic Development of Colonial North America.* Cambridge: Cambridge University Press, 1972; chapters 6, 7; appendix, table 1.

Shimokawa, Koichi. *The Japanese Automobile Industry: A Business History.* London: Athlone Press, 1994, chapters 1, 3.

Slack, Paul A. "Vagrants and Vagrancy in England, 1598–1664." In *Migration and Society in Early Modern England,* edited by Peter Clark, and David Souden. Totowa, NJ: Barnes and Noble, 1988.

Small, Walter H. *Early New England Schools.* Boston: Ginn, 1914.

Smith. Merritt R. *Harpers Ferry Armory and the New Technology: The Challenge of Change.* Ithaca, NY: Cornell University Press, 1977.

Soltow, Lee, and Edward Stevens. *The Rise of Literacy and the Common School in the United States: A Socioeconomic Analysis to 1870.* Chicago: University of Chicago Press, 1981, chapters 2, 4–5.

Souden, David. "Rogues, Whores, and Vagabonds? Indentured Servant Emigration to North America and the Case of Mid Seventeenth-Century Bristol." In *Migration and Society in Early Modern England,* edited by Peter Clark, and David Souden. Totowa, NJ: Barnes and Noble, 1988.

Soule, George H. *Prosperity Decade: From War to Depression 1917–1929.* New York: Rinehart, 1947.

Spufford, Margaret. *Contrasting Communities: English Villagers in the Sixteenth and Seventeenth Centuries.* Cambridge: Cambridge University Press, 1974; Part 1, chapters 6–8.

Stanwood, Edward. *American Tariff Controversies in the Nineteenth Century.* Boston: Houghton, Mifflin, 1904, chapter 16.

Stein, Herbert. *The Fiscal Revolution in America.* Washington, DC: AEI Press, 1990, chapter 11.

Stevens, Frank W. *The Beginnings of the New York Central Railroad.* New York: Putnam, 1926.

Stiverson, Gregory A. *Poverty in a Land of Plenty: Tenancy in Eighteenth-Century Maryland.* Baltimore: Johns Hopkins University Press, 1977, chapters 2, 5.

345

Stone, Lawrence. "The Educational Revolution in England, 1560–1640." *Past and Present*, no. 28 (1964).

Stover, John F. *The Railroads of the South, 1865–1900: A Study in Finance and Control.* Chapel Hill: University of North Carolina Press, 1955.

Stover, John F. *American Railroads.* Chicago: University of Chicago Press, 1961.

Stover, John F. *Iron Road to the West: American Railroads in the 1850s.* New York: Columbia University Press, 1978.

Studenski, Paul, and Herman Krooss. *Financial History of the United States: Fiscal, Monetary, Banking, and Tariff, Including Financial Administration and State and Local Finance.* New York: McGraw-Hill, 1963, chapters 13–16, 25, 27–28; 189–239.

Sundquist, James L. *Dynamics of the Party System: Alignment and Realignment of Political Parties in the United States.* Washington DC: Brookings Institution, 1973, chapter 8.

Sydnor, Charles S. *American Revolutionaries in the Making: Political Practices in Washington's Virginia,* New York: Free Press, 1965 (reprint of 1952 edition entitled *Gentlemen Freeholders*)

Sylla, Richard E. "Federal Policy, Banking Market Structure, and Capital Mobilization in the United States, 1863–1913." *Journal of Economic History* 29 (1969).

Taussig, Frank W. *The Tariff History of the United States.* New York: Capricorn Books, 1964 (reprint of 1931 edition; part 2, chapters 1–7).

Taylor, George R., and Irene D. Neu. *The American Railroad Network, 1861–1890.* Cambridge, MA: Harvard University Press, 1956.

Taylor, George R. *The Transportation Revolution, 1815–1860.* New York: Holt, Rinehart, Winston, 1962.

Temin, Peter. *Iron and Steel in Nineteenth-Century America: An Economic Inquiry.* Cambridge, MA: M.I.T. Press, 1964.

Temin, Peter. *Did Monetary Forces Cause the Great Depression?* New York: Norton, 1976, chapter 3.

Thach, Charles C. *The Creation of the Presidency, 1775–1789: A Study in Constitutional History.* Baltimore: Johns Hopkins University Press, 1969 (reprint of 1923 edition).

Thomas, Keith. "Work, Land, Leisure in a Pre-Industrial Society." *Past and Present* 29 (1964).

Thompson, Robert L. *Wiring a Continent: The History of the Telegraphy Industry in the United States, 1832–1866.* Princeton, NJ: Princeton University Press, 1947, chapters 13–17.

Thompson, Ross. *The Path to Mechanized Shoe Production in the United States.* Chapel Hill: University of North Carolina Press, 1989, chapters 2–9.

Tolles, Frederick B. *Meeting House and Counting House: The Quaker Merchants of Colonial Philadelphia, 1682–1763.* New York: Norton, 1963 (reprint of 1948 edition; chapters 2, 5).

Tsurumi, Yoshi. "Japanese Corporations in America: Managing Cultural Differences." In *The Multinational Enterprise in Transition: Strategies for Global Competitiveness,* edited by Phillip D. Grub, and Dara Khambata. Princeton, NJ: Darwin Press, 1993.

Tyson, Francis D. "The Negro Migrant in the North." In *Negro Migration in 1916–1917,* edited by R. H. Leavell. New York: Negro Universities Press, 1969 (reprint of 1919 report of the department of labor).

Tyson, Laura D. *Who's Bashing Whom? Trade Conflict in High-Technology Industries.* Washington, DC: Institute for International Economics, 1992, chapters 1, 3, 4.

Unger, Irwin. *The Greenback Era: A Social and Political History of American Finance, 1865–1879.* Princeton, NJ: Princeton University Press, 1964.

Updegraff, Harlan. *The Origin of the Moving School in Massachusetts.* New York: Columbia University Press, 1908.

Usher, Abbott P. "The Textile Industry, 1750–1830." In *Technology in Western Civilization,* edited by Melvin Kranzberg and Carroll W. Pursell. New York: Oxford University Press, 1967, vol. 1.

Varg, Paul A. *Foreign Policies of the Founding Fathers.* Baltimore: Penguin Books, 1970 (reprint of 1963 edition; chapters 5, 6, 9, 10).

Vickers, Daniel. "Competency and Competition: Economic Culture in Early America, part 1." *William and Mary Quarterly* 47 (1990).

Vickers, Daniel. *Farmers and Fishermen: Two Centuries of Work in Essex County, Massachusetts, 1630–1850.* Chapel Hill: University of North Carolina Press, 1994, chapter 5.

Vinovskis, Maris A. *The Origins of Public High Schools: A Reexamination of the Beverly High School Controversy.* Madison: University of Wisconsin Press, 1985, chapters 1, 2, appendices.

Walker, Francis A., ed. *A Compendium of the Ninth Census: June 1, 1870.* Washington, DC: Government Printing Office, 1872.

Walsh, Lorena S. "Land, Landlord, and Leaseholder: Estate Management and Tenant Fortunes in Southern Maryland, 1642–1820." *Agricultural History* 59 (1985).

Walsh, Lorena S. "Plantation Management in the Chesapeake, 1620–1820." *Journal of Economic History* 49 (1989).

Walters, Raymond. *Albert Gallatin: Jeffersonian Financier and Diplomat.* (New York: Macmillan, 1957, chapter 16).

Ware, Caroline F. *The Early New England Cotton Manufacture: A Study in Industrial Beginnings.* New York: Johnson Reprint, 1966 (reprint of 1931 edition).

Wareing, John. "Migration to London and Transatlantic Emigration of Indentured Servants." *Journal of Historical Geography* 7 (1981).

INDEX

About the Author

RONALD E. SEAVOY is professor emeritus of history at Bowling Green State University, Bowling Green, Ohio. Previous books by the author are *Origins of the American Business Corporation* (Greenwood, 1982); *Famine in Peasant Societies* (Greenwood, 1986); *Famine in East Africa: Food Production and Food Policies* (Greenwood, 1989); *The American Peasantry: Southern Agricultural Labor and Its Legacy, 1850–1995* (Greenwood, 1998); *Subsistence and Economic Development* (Praeger, 2000); *A New Exploration of the Canadian Arctic* (Hancock House, 2002); *Origins and Growth of the Global Economy: From the Fifteenth Century Onward* (Praeger, 2003).